A SYSTEM

JAN-PETER HARTUNG

A System of Life

Mawdūdī and the Ideologisation of Islam

HURST & COMPANY, LONDON

Hardback edition first published in the United Kingdom in 2013 by
C. Hurst & Co. (Publishers) Ltd.,
41 Great Russell Street, London, WC1B 3PL

This paperback edition, 2020

Printed in India

A Cataloguing-in-Publication data record for this book is available from the British Library.

ISBN 9781787382251

This book is printed using paper from registered sustainable and managed sources.

www.hurstpublishers.com

To the memory of Christoph Schumann (1969–2013)

CONTENTS

1

INTRODUCTION

In 1979 an apocalyptic mood spread throughout the Muslim World. After all, this year according to the Gregorian calendar coincided with the turn to the fifteenth Islamic century. As always at such times, pious Muslims were on the lookout for the signs of the hour when this world would come to an end. They were looking out for the return of the Messiah, who would, after prolonged battle, triumph over the Great Deceiver, the Antichrist, who had taken over to rule the world.

Although this apocalyptic mood rose and wore off almost cyclically, postponing the end of the world to the next turn of the century, this time it seems as if the expectations were extraordinarily high. After all, quite a number of Muslims felt that the world had indeed become ruled by the Great Deceiver, the signs of which were clearly outlined in a sound saying of the Prophet Muḥammad:

> 'The Great Deceiver has a blank eye [*mamsūḥ al-ʿayn*] and between his eyes it is written "Unbeliever".' Then he spelled it: 'k-f-r'. Every Muslim will be able to read it.[1]

Widespread unbelief, according to this *ḥadīth*, was thus one of the main characteristics of the rule of the Great Deceiver, unbelief that would spread also among the Muslims. This has been made abundantly clear in the Qur'ān, in which such a 'Muslim' would 'give nothing in charity, nor did he pray! But on the contrary, he rejected the truth and turned away! Then did he stalk to his family in full conceit!'[2] Indeed, various signs seemed to point to such a situation in 1979.

In the previous years the ruler of Iran, Muḥammad Riḍā Shāh Pahlawī (d. 1980), had increasingly oriented his rule away from the Islamic religious tradition towards the Pre-Islamic Achaemenid Persian one. His so-called 'White Revolution' (*inqilāb-i safīd*) aimed at the secularisation of law and economy, followed by a growing cultural Westernisation and the opening to Western political powers that went hand-in-hand with the brutal suppression of any opposition within Iran.[3]

Meanwhile the Egyptian President Anwar al-Sādāt, who began his reign as the 'Islamic consciousness'[4] in Nasserist Egypt, changed his foreign policy agenda owing to increasing economic and social problems inside the country. His self-portrayal as leading advocate of the Palestinians led, as it was seen by his opponents, to a betrayal of Muslim interests when al-Sādāt began to hold peace negotiations with Israel in 1977 that culminated in the US-mediated Camp David Accords in 1978 and finally in the Egyptian-Israeli Peace Treaty of 26 March 1979.

Even in the Kingdom of Saudi Arabia, based on a concordat between the ruling family Saʿūd and the *Wahhābiyya*, an extremely rigid religious scholarly movement,[5] it began to seethe. After King Fayṣal ibn ʿAbd al-ʿAzīz, a model of Islamic piety, was assassinated by his allegedly mentally disturbed nephew Fayṣal ibn Musāʿid on 25 March 1975, a young generation of scholars and religious laymen from around the Islamic universities of Riyadh, Mecca and Medina began increasingly to criticise the political and religious establishment of the kingdom for what was felt to be its deviation from the straight religious path.[6]

Finally, from the overthrow of the monarchy in Afghanistan in 1973 the political order became increasingly dominated by leftist forces, which were heavily supported by the Soviet Union.[7]

There would be even more examples from around the Muslim world that suggested a gain of power by the Great Deceiver and pointed towards the final showdown. Various personalities appeared at this point in time, who either claimed to be, or were styled, the Saviour, the Expected One or the one who will defeat the Antichrist and pave the way to Judgement Day (*yawm al-qiyāma*).[8] In the beginning, all looked very promising when, after months of mass protest, the Iranian people forced the Shah to flee the country, and the spiritual leader of the revolution, the Āyatallāh Rūḥallāh Mūsāwī K͟humaynī (d. 1409/1989), returned on 1 February 1979 to Tehran in glory.[9]

The victory of the Islamic Revolution in Iran, however, appeared to be the only success over the Great Deceiver at the turn of the fifteenth Islamic century. Elsewhere, the expectations of the predicted redeemer (*mahdī*) and his victory in the battle against the onslaught of unbelief were disappointed, indeed these expectations gave way to what Reinhard Schulze has aptly called '*anni horibiles* in the Islamic world'.[10] On 20 November 1979, the last day of the fourteenth Islamic century, some hundred armed supporters of the charismatic Juhaymān ibn Muḥammad al-ʿUtaybī (executed 1400/1980), who claimed to be the emissary of the *mahdī* Muḥammad ʿAbdallāh al-Qahṭānī (d. 1400/1979), seized the Great Mosque in Mecca.[11] After the rebels were besieged for about a fortnight, the sanctuary was finally stormed by Saudi and foreign special units and the surviving insurgents publicly executed.[12] The ruling house had been striking back and, at least for the moment, regained its control over the kingdom.

On Christmas Eve 1979 the Red Army crossed the Oxus River into Afghanistan and ended what had begun as a series of *coups d'état* with the investiture of a pro-Soviet government in Kabul.[13] Less than two years later, on 6 October 1981, the Egyptian president Anwar al-Sādāt was assassinated, because in the eyes of quite a number of Muslim activists his collaboration with Israel had him made an apostate, if not synonymous with the Great Deceiver.[14] Here, too, the joy of the assassin K͟hālid al-Islāmbūlī (executed 1402/1982) at having killed the Qurʾānic Pharaoh of the age was only short-lived. He and many of his followers were captured by the state authorities, convicted and either executed or imprisoned.[15] The Egyptian state took control again and resumed its political course.

It looked as if the end of the world had again been postponed, although the spirit of the occurrences of 1979 did not simply evaporate. Rather they brought about new and more radicalised responses, which became increasingly intertwined and culminated in the most recent events around, and since, the attacks of 11 September 2001. All those responses built somewhat on a history of Muslim religious and political thought which increasingly gained momentum in the first decades of the twentieth century. They received an enormous stimulus by the ideas of a man whose fate is also tied to the year 1979. On 22 September Sayyid Abū 'l-Aʿlá Mawdūdī, aged seventy-six, died in a hospital in Rochester, New York, while undergoing medical treatment.

This Pakistani citizen must be considered the first systematic thinker of what became known as 'Islamism': an ideology rooted in a particular understanding of Islam. As such, some of his core concepts became most influential on the further development of Islamist thought, then mainly in the Arabophone world. That Mawdūdī passed away in the ominous year of

1979 appears almost symptomatic: the time of the theoreticians seemed once and for all over, now was the chance for increasingly armed action, be it against the Soviet occupation of Afghanistan, against those who were held responsible for 'selling Saudi Arabia to the infidels', against the autocratic regime of president Ḥusnī Mubārak (b. 1928) and his National Democratic Party (*Ḥizb al-waṭanī al-dīmuqrāṭī*) in Egypt or against every other—Western and non-Western—force that obstructed the establishment of Islamic rule on earth.

However, for an understanding of the way today's Islamists think and argue it helps to gain a close understanding of the ideas of their immediate predecessors, over and above their most systematic mastermind Mawdūdī.

1) The Hermeneutical Problem and the Prism of Modernity

To understand the thinking of someone like Mawdūdī poses somewhat of a hermeneutical problem, often subsumed under the label 'insider-outsider' and closely linked to the 'Orientalism' debate that was triggered in 1978 by Edward Saïd's important book of the same name. Various ways out of this trap have been suggested and, at the same time, attempted to define the scope in which our statements about the culturally 'Other' could claim validity.[16] After all, it has to be analysed to what extent, if any, our categories are suitable for dealing with issues which are, at least at first sight, culturally clearly distinct. The problem, however, extends even further.

It has repeatedly been argued that the contemporary upsurge in any kind of religion, down to so-called religious 'fundamentalism(s)' is, as its counter project, a phenomenon of Modernity.[17] This notion of 'Modernity', in turn, has a number of implications. First, as an epochal term it claims universal validity, provided that history is seen as a monochronical process. If this is the case, then one must be able to find the markers for this epoch everywhere. This, of course, appears problematic, as Modernity has mainly been perceived as European (respectively North American) *Sonderweg*, deeply rooted in a process of increasing and all-embracing rationalisation of the lived-in world.[18] The intellectual foundations of this process can be traced back to the Renaissance and the Christian Reformation, especially to Luther's concept of man as belonging to two kingdoms, which he derived especially from his reading of the Apostle Paul's Epistles to the Romans.[19] If this is the case, then the intellectual precondition of Modernity could be subsumed in the concept of man's freedom to self-responsibly choose from a number of options to act. Indeed, the question of man's free will and, consequently, of subjectivity pervades all Enlightenment philosophies. Chosen as a central theme for the first time in the political philosophy of Thomas Hobbes (d. 1679), an intellectual thread can be followed all the way to Immanuel Kant (d. 1804) and, finally, the Idealists, especially in Germany.[20]

This subjectivity, finally, which relates to the philosophical concepts of 'freedom of choice', 'autonomy to act' and 'responsibility' for both, must be regarded as the ultimate challenge to authority. Now, it was man, and man alone, who would self-confidently generate values and norms. The validity of such man-made values and norms, in turn, would be dependent on the acknowledgement by other individuals, who, ideally, possess the same ability and capacity to bring about values and norms of their own. In short, therefore, the validity of values and norms is the result of a complex social negotiation process, in which, to apply Habermasian terminology, 'instrumental rationality' is increasingly replaced by 'communicative rationality'.[21] What all this implies is a very distinct attitude towards the past. While history is certainly appreciated not least as a reminder to act responsibly—enshrined in the historicist creed of *historia magistra vitæ*—as an authority it seems to have worn out. Now, one was looking ahead, not backwards, with 'development', initially the favourite of the romantic philosophy of nature in the late eighteenth century, and 'progress' becoming the new magic words.[22]

In contrast, a religious worldview was necessarily oriented towards a formative past, when values and norms have been ultimately established, claiming universal and (almost) eternal validity. All that man was given freedom for was to make these values and norms applicable to conditions that would change significantly in time and space. 'Development' and 'progress' are therefore hardly two concepts that would fit in here—all that is sought is stability in a contingent world. Postmodernity, the hub of which was most certainly the philosophy of Friedrich Nietzsche (d. 1900), brought exactly this anti-rationalistic appreciation of past values to the table, although, admittedly, his argument was not based on belief in numinous revelation, but rather in a new radical anthropology.[23] The anthropological turn of the late nineteenth century, however, which emphasised man's inevitable dependence on his pre-rational nature, could be focused on the past, such as in Nietzsche's thought, or towards the future, as in the theory of Karl Marx (d. 1883). In any case, it brought back a quasi-religious element that made these philosophies prone to feed into various kinds of ideologies that are 'empirically ascertainable sets of political beliefs, opinions and attitudes, consciously-held and articulated at accessible levels of coherence'.[24] As such, an ideology absorbs the quasi-religious element of these later philosophies, insofar as it is based on the assumption of an extra-human 'truth' that will necessarily prevail, either by preserving or by changing an existing social and political order. And, because a 'truth' is never negotiable, these ideologies are mutually exclusive, the same as religions are from a doctrinal point of view. What is more, ideologies almost unequivocally refer to the past for authority.

In early twentieth century British-India, where Mawdūdī developed his systematic outline, the euphoria of Modernity regarding human knowledge—now however in a positivist garb[25]—was still very much at work, while the technological developments that eventually contributed greatly to the accumulation of wealth in a so far unprecedented manner[26] seemed to perfectly justify it. Therefore, and given an increasingly globalised world,[27] any alternative outline for societal development needed to somehow come to terms with this, at least if it wanted to be regarded with any viability. For Mawdūdī, to cast Islam into an ideology appeared therefore to be a most appropriate way to relate Islam to the contemporary and heavily Western-dominated context in which he was living, while, at the same time, retaining the retrogressive method of affirming authority. This actually is what Daniel W. Brown had aptly labelled the 'Prism of Modernity':[28] the reformulation of Islam in modern terms while at the same time remaining uncompromising with regard to authority.

To be able to do so, however, and to view one's own tradition through the 'prism of Modernity', one needs to be capable of accessing the storehouses of knowledge of both 'tradition' and 'Modernity', which, in turn, requires a quite distinct personnel: after all, someone entirely absorbed in 'tradition' would most probably have serious difficulties in appreciating the thinking of 'Modernity', provided that such a person could possibly be bothered with it at all. Therefore, what it requires is an innerworldly person, someone who would creatively engage with the here-and-now, while trying to relate it to a however understood 'tradition' as the ultimate source of authority. Mawdūdī's biography is clear evidence that he was undoubtedly such a person.[29]

The 'prism of Modernity', however, is not just a one-way affair. In fact, it can be made methodologically fruitful, an aspect that Brown had not considered in his analysis. Hence, while 'tradition' may indeed be 'the stuff that is subject to change',[30] it has been questioned to what extent an 'outsider' would indeed have the chance to pinpoint and, moreover, understand it.[31] Hence, it is argued here, it is quite fortunate to have someone like

Mawdūdī, who, to use Brown's phrasing, 'rethought tradition' through the 'prism of Modernity', because from the writings of such an author one could work one's way backwards in an attempt to distil what such a thinker has considered as 'tradition', rather than to attempt to determine what 'tradition' as such might be.[32] Therefore, this approach has been widely used in the present study to analyse Mawdūdī's thought, taking seriously his claim that he was going to argue for Islam as an 'all-encompassing system of life'. Since such a systematic claim is a common feature in all modern ideologies, the 'prism of Modernity' made it possible to approach Mawdūdī and his reconceptionalisation of Islam from a Western intellectual standpoint.

2) The Book

Following Brown's reasonable suggestion 'not merely to understand the work of such individuals, but to examine the intellectual climate out of which their ideas grew and the responses their ideas have elicited',[33] the present study sets out with a discussion of the context in which Mawdūdī had developed his systematic outline. It begins with an evaluation of the formative period in Mawdūdī's biography, including a critical appraisal of the sources and, related to this, of the existing academic literature on that matter. The view is then widened to the religious and political circumstances at the time, which, as it is argued here, decisively triggered this particular response by Mawdūdī. What follows is what is called here a 'mapping of the ideological landscape' and its various constituents, which virtually constitute the 'prism of Modernity' through which Mawdūdī had viewed what he considered to be the 'tradition' and which became subsequently cast into an ideology of its own.

In the second part of the work, Mawdūdī's systematic outline is developed along the widely acknowledged lines of deductive theory building.[34] This, however, is preceded by an elaboration of Mawdūdī's critical assessment of history in general and the history of Islam in particular, leading to his own—Islamically justified—plea for a fundamental reinterpretation of Islam through the 'prism of Modernity'. Only then is Mawdūdī's whole systematic outline unravelled, first by identifying the axioms of his system and then by passing through all the deductive steps that would ultimately culminate in the concept of the 'Islamic State'. It will be shown that, such as happened with many deductive theories,[35] it was hard for Mawdūdī to maintain a logical consistency already at an early point in the development of his system. Some of these inconsistencies, however, were rooted much less in logical fallacies than in certain doctrinal issues, which could hardly be reconciled with the rest of Mawdūdī's system. Whether or not he actually was aware of these problematic points cannot be proven for sure. What will be shown, however, is that they have certainly had an impact on the practical realisation of the systematic outline, which, after all, is a vital part of any ideology.[36]

Therefore, while the third part of this study sheds light on Mawdūdī's theoretical considerations regarding the practical realisation of his systematic outline, the fourth and final part focuses on the career of Mawdūdī's thought in practice. In the first part, the adaptations and modifications towards a more radical version of his ideology in the Arab world have been analysed, focusing here mainly on Mawdūdī's true spiritual heir Sayyid Quṭb (executed 1386/1966) and various of his epigones and critics in Egypt. In the second part, however, the focus is on the historical development and changes of what was originally Mawdūdī's ideal-typical revolutionary community, the *Jamāʿat-i islāmī* (JiI), throughout South Asia. In this part it is shown that the different social and political circumstances in the various South Asian states that emerged after decolonisation caused to split apart what was once thought to be a homogeneous and unified religious-political movement-*cum*-societal model. The strategies to which each one of these eventually independent national organisations subscribed were, and are, occasionally so very different from each other that they provide implicit proof of how little Mawdūdī's systematic outline had considered variant socio-political realities and how abstract it had therefore become. Again, however, this is something it had in common with all other ideologies: even though their followers all refer to the same theoretical framework, the constraints of temporally and spatially invariant realities forced some serious amendments, which make it rather difficult to speak of one and the same ideology anymore.

Given the complexity of the matter at hand, various issues are only touched upon in the text itself, but are further discussed in the abundant notes at the end of the book, so that in many instances both should be read together.

* * *

This present study is the result of over fifteen years of critical engagement with Mawdūdī's intellectual world, on and off. What had once started as a MA dissertation in South Asian Studies at the Universität Leipzig has been moulded and re-moulded over the subsequent period. The discussions in courses, both at undergraduate and at postgraduate level, which I have taught over the years at the universities of Erfurt, Bonn and Bochum, all in Germany, have helped me considerably to rethink and systematise my initial ideas. The offer by Hurst & Co., finally, to write a book on Mawdūdī that provides a distinct approach from all of the existing academic studies, first and foremost that of Seyed Vali Reza Nasr (1996) and more recently that of Roy A. Jackson (2011), has been a great incentive to finally put my ideas down on paper. Various friends and colleagues kindly agreed to read and critically commented upon the draft in various stages of its genesis, some more than once. To everyone who, in whatever way, has contributed to the study, I wish to extend my heartfelt gratitude. This includes not least the three anonymous referees who made valuable suggestions for improvements. It should go without saying that the responsibility for every possible error or misjudgement remains entirely mine.

Some Technical Remarks

The system of transliteration, which has been adopted for all languages that use some kind of modified Arabic script, is that of the third edition of the *Encyclopedia of Islam*, because it is the one standard—and therefore authoritative—reference work that had to accommodate all the different languages in a single system and has amended some rather odd features in its preceding editions. The transliteration of all other South Asian languages, as well as of the Cyrillic script, follows the academically widely respected ALA-LC Romanisation Tables.

Only Qur'ānic quotations are given with full flectional endings, while following the common conventions to omit it for the last noun.

Book titles in the text are always given in their original language, not in English translation. While, admittedly, this may be considered rather strange by some, I have attempted to treat all the texts to which I refer in the same way by not granting some the benefit of an English translation over others. To provide English translations of the non-English titles in brackets, however, would have considerably hindered the reading flow and has therefore been ruled out.

2

THE CONTEXT

1) The Self-Staged Reformer: Mawdūdī's Formative Years

Usually, a biographical outline aims at providing the context for an understanding of a person's intellectual achievements. In Mawdūdī's case, however, it emerges that his biography was already envisioned as part of his entire project, namely to present himself in such a way that he became almost predestined for intellectual leadership. Other authors, mainly from among his immediate family and followers, have helped to perpetuate and fortify this image which has been carried on since, even in academic publications.[1] A critical distance to most of the available material is thus highly commendable.

A core text for Mawdūdī's earlier life, as well as for the illustration of his conscious self-staging, is an autobiographical article, allegedly written in 1932 and since then repeatedly reprinted. Already the story around the composition of this text clearly indicates Mawdūdī's attempt to present himself in a certain way: various editors of this text emphasise that this brief account was only written on the request of Sayyid Manẓar ʿAlī Ashhar for inclusion into his anthology *Manẓar al-kirām: Ḥaydarābād-i Dakkan ke mashāhīr kā ta<u>dh</u>kira.*[2] However, because this work had already been published by the ʿImād Press of Hyderabad in 1926, the inclusion of a text written only six years later would appear rather anachronistic. Thus, the most likely intention behind this story was to claim extraordinary prominence already at a rather young age. This is supported even further by the text itself, in which Mawdūdī presented himself as of noble descent and exceptional erudition, suggesting that it was almost destiny which directed him towards his later endeavours. After all: 'I belong to a family that has provided [Muslims] with spiritual guidance [*hidāyat wa irshād*] and lived ascetic lives for thirteen hundred years.'[3]

Apparently, Mawdūdī knew very well how to push the right buttons to prove his own eminence already by descent. Noblesse and piety were ensured by stressing the actual documented origin of his father's side of the family from the House of the Prophet (*ahl al-bayt*), as well as from Kh^{w}āja Quṭb al-Dīn Mawdūd of Chisht (d. 577/1182), a renowned early *shaykh* of the Chishtī Sufi order, the most popular Sufi order in the subcontinent from the early thirteenth century CE onwards.[4] His mother's side, however, while not of Arab descent, represented nobleness nonetheless. His maternal grandfather Mīrzā Qurbān ʿAlī Beg Khān 'Sālik' (d. 1291/1893), for example, who was demonstrably a pupil of the renowned Delhi poet Mīrzā Asadallāh Beg Khān 'Ghālib' (d. 1285/1869),[5] represented the family's affiliation with the grandees and the refined manners of the Mughal court. Such a stress on his pedigree was not just accidental—herein Mawdūdī rather followed a common pattern of establishing a hereditary claim to leadership at that time:[6] to align oneself with the traditional Muslim elite in the subcontinent, the *ashrāf*, as bearer of reformist endeavours in the aftermath of the uprising of 1857 and the subsequent imposition of direct British rule.[7] Even in following this pattern, however, Mawdūdī's stress on the genealogical aspect, especially of the paternal branch of his family and, in this context, on their religiously grounded importance, was well suited to raise Mawdūdī above other equally noble claimants to the leadership role.[8] To sustain this image even further he emphasised the importance of the awareness of tradition within the family, which he claimed was apparent not least from his having been named after the very ancestor who, at the turn to the sixteenth century, had established the family in India.[9]

Such strict adherence to a religiously grounded cultural tradition, which somehow justified a hereditary claim for communal leadership by Mawdūdī's family, would however inevitably clash with the profound societal changes which British colonial rule brought about. The predicament arising from this conflict played a major role in Mawdūdī's portrayal of his immediate male predecessors, that is to say his father Sayyid Aḥmad Ḥasan (d. 1338/1920) and his elder brother Sayyid Abū 'l-Khayr (d. 1400/1979). Claiming that his paternal grandmother was related to Sayyid Aḥmad Khān (d. 1315/1898),[10] the driving force in the establishment of a reformist

Muslim higher educational institution within the colonial framework—the *Muhammadan Anglo-Oriental College* in Aligarh—Mawdūdī argued it was just a natural step that his father had been one of the first students to enrol in Aligarh, despite the serious reservations of his grandfather, epitome of the family tradition.[11]

The dilemma of Mawdūdī's own critical appraisal of Western thought is thus already clearly reflected here. While 'at that time British education and culture were intensely disliked by the Muslims' and 'this dislike was even stronger in our family than among the common Muslims, because we were not only deeply religious but provided also religious leadership [*madhhabī pishwā'ī*]',[12] the education of Mawdūdī's father was a clear indicator for insight into the necessity that they would have to keep up with the times if they wanted to maintain a leading position within the community. In this way, already Sayyid Aḥmad Ḥasan, but even more Sayyid Abū 'l-Khayr and Mawdūdī himself, could well be classified as 'agents of change': those, namely, 'who have acted at the intersections of cultures and have formed multiple ties of identity',[13] in their case in a more reactive way in order 'to safeguard their chances in a period of rapid and profound social and political change'.[14] It is therefore not surprising that, after the Mughal court had been dissolved, Mawdūdī's status-conscious family members were on the lookout for alternative employment, which could assure the maintenance of their social standing. Thus, while Mawdūdī's grandfather Mīrzā Qurbān ʿAlī Beg Khān 'Sālik' did as his famous teacher Ghālib and others who had lost the patronage of the Mughal emperor and sought employment in the administration of the princely states of Alwar and Hyderabad,[15] his father went to the one place where, as it was claimed, the new Muslim elite of British India was forged.[16]

Aligarh's Muhammadan Anglo-Oriental College, however, was never uncontested for its adoption of a Western educational model, as well as for its openly declared unfettered loyalty to the British crown. In the early 1930s, at the time when Mawdūdī wrote his little autobiographical essay, this conflict had gained considerable momentum, which might explain why Mawdūdī stressed the incommensurateness of Aligarh's pro-Western attitude with the religious mindset that he had claimed to be prevalent in his family.[17] Interestingly, after his Sayyid Aḥmad Ḥasan's involuntary withdrawal from Aligarh at the insistence of his father, he nonetheless stuck to Westernised education: in Allahabad he successfully completed a bar examination and subsequently practised as a solicitor in a number of places until the family settled in Awrangabad, Deccan.[18] The unease which resulted from the tension between the family's aspiration as religious community leaders and the necessity to accommodate oneself with the new societal structures in order to earn one's livelihood did however not perish, but rather grew. Sayyid Aḥmad Ḥasan's turn towards ascetic mysticism is thus a clear reflection of this:

> For four years he pursued faith and mundane affairs simultaneously [*dīn wa dunyā sāth sāth*]. But then, in 1322 AH (1904 AD), when I was only one year old, the pursuit of both had become difficult for my late father. He not only gave up his legal practice [*wukālat*], but also wished the thought of worldly earnings farewell. He sold all the household goods and we left for Delhi, where we settled in an old village near the shrine [*dargāh*] of Ḥaḍrat Niẓām al-Dīn 'Maḥbūb-i ilāhī' [d. 725/1325]—God's mercy be upon him!—named ʿArab Sarāʾī. He acquired a very small piece of land and devoted all his time to religious affairs.[19]

This extreme renunciation of the world by Sayyid Aḥmad Ḥasan, which may have had an impact on his son's later critical stand towards Sufism,[20] lasted only three years. Then the evolving economic difficulties forced the family to move back to Awrangabad and Sayyid Aḥmad Ḥasan to resume his legal practice. However, as Mawdūdī hastened to add, 'He would now not take up even a small law-suit if based on lies.'[21]

The conflicting relationship between religious commitment and the necessity to pursue a worldly profession for livelihood seemingly affected the sons of Sayyid Aḥmad Ḥasan. While not much further information is available on the elder Sayyid Abū 'l-Khayr apart from him having been an editor and journalist in the first decades of the twentieth century,[22] Abū 'l-Aʿlá's own education, of which he gave a detailed account,[23] already points towards the hybridity that was later to become manifest in his writings. In this course of education he differed considerably from the way of religious education that still prevailed in *ʿulamāʾ* circles,[24] which makes one wonder about the actual degree of religious leadership held by the Mawdūdī family, at least at this point in time. Equally questionable is the level of proficiency in the religious sciences and in Arabic, which Mawdūdī was able to acquire in the several schools in which he was enrolled for varying durations in Awrangabad and Hyderabad, and later in Delhi 'with various tutors'.[25] Be that as it may, much of the later criticism which Mawdūdī received at the hands of *ʿulamāʾ* of various provenance was put down to his insufficient acquaintance with the matters as well as the elaborate methodologies of the traditional religious sciences.[26] Mawdūdī, of course, presented himself as fully accomplished in these fields, as is especially obvious from the portrayal of his extraordinary abilities in Arabic which have enabled him to translate even most complex philosophical works from Arabic into Urdu.[27] 'I remember very well that when my father saw the lucid and plain language, as well as the zest and skill of that translation [here of Qāsim Amīn's *al-Marʾa al-jadīda*] he became very happy and [my] brother was pleased, too.'[28] One wonders, however, why it was that, if Mawdūdī was really so proficient in Arabic, he required the help of *ʿulamāʾ* well trained in the language to have his very own writings translated at around the same time as he wrote his autobiographical essay.[29] It may therefore be read as his attempt to portray himself as someone who moves with great ease and proficiency inside the framework of the religious sciences.

On the other hand, Mawdūdī—here very much in the Aligarhi style—consciously stressed his studies of contemporary non-religious subjects, such as various natural sciences and history, at one of the new reformist educational institutions which, at the turn of the twentieth century, began to mushroom in the various Indo-Muslim communities.[30] While here the medium of instruction was Urdu, Mawdūdī later acquired some knowledge of the English language, first guided by a tutor, but soon, because 'the attention of a tutor was not required anymore',[31] carrying on as an autodidact. Here, too, he depicted himself as extraordinarily gifted, stating that after only two years he was able to 'study history, philosophy, political science, economics, religion and sociology in English, and even scientific topics I could understand with no difficulty'.[32]

To claim competence in the contemporary non-religious sciences, along with English as its prime medium, appears as a core element in Mawdūdī's self-promotion. After all, only one who is equally versed in the religious as well as non-religious sciences, one who has deliberately placed himself at the intersections of the indigenous and the colonial culture, could become a true 'agent of change', with enough power of judgement to pursue the best possible strategies for the advancement of one's community. Hence, when in 1917/18 the only fifteen-year-old Mawdūdī turned to writing and journalism as a means of living he depicted this not as an economic necessity, but a well-considered personal choice in accordance with his greatest talent and in view of what he wanted to achieve.[33]

At this time it was only natural that Mawdūdī, like so many adolescent boys like him, became immersed in the turbulent political events at the end of the First World War. It was the time of rising pan-Islamic sentiments among Indian Muslims, which centred on the Ottoman-held caliphate and found their expression in the establishment of countless Muslim associations in support of this cause.[34] Shortly after Mawdūdī had joined his brother in editing a daily newspaper in Bijnor in the United Provinces, they became involved in the *Anjumān-i iʿānat-i naẓr-bandān-i islām*, a Jabalpur-based local association in support of Muslim prisoners of war.[35] Its driving force, a certain Tāj al-Dīn, was also editor of *Tāj*, then an Urdu weekly that became a local speaking vessel for the emerging Caliphate Movement (*taḥrīk-i khilāfat*).[36] It was here that Mawdūdī was attracted to the religious symbolism employed by the leaders of the movement, and consequently became a sympathiser. While he most certainly made an impact here, the very role that he ascribed to himself in this context appears nonetheless rather exaggerated.[37] However, when, after the forced closure of *Tāj*,[38] the then seventeen-year-old Mawdūdī relocated to Delhi, his star began to rise: he happened to meet the two eminent scholars Muftī Kifāyatallāh Dihlawī (d. 1372/1952) and Aḥmad Saʿīd Dihlawī (d. 1378/1959), president and secretary, respectively, of the strongly Deoband-influenced *Jamʿiyyat al-ʿulamāʾ-i Hind* (JUH),[39] who commissioned him with editing the party's paper *Muslim* between 1920 and 1923, and from 1924 onwards its successor *al-Jamʿiyya*, both being published about twice a week.[40]

1.1) Writing in Turbulent Times

In the beginning, Mawdūdī's journalistic writing was little different from that of contemporary Indo-Muslim writers. During his days with *Madīna* and *Tāj* his articles consisted mainly of reports and discussions of political events in the Muslim world and of the Independence Movement in India. Remarkable are his articles on the Greco-Turkish War of 1919–22, especially on the atrocities committed by the Greeks after the occupation of Smyrna (İzmir).[41] This is remarkable insofar as similar acts of carnage were committed by the Turks on Greeks and Armenians after the recapture of the city in September 1922, but had not been addressed in Mawdūdī's articles. A conceivable reason for this might be the fact that the Greek offensive was heavily supported by Western powers, first and foremost by the British, and to fuel pro-Turkish sentiments with strongly emotive rhetoric was therefore consistent with the anti-colonial agenda of the Indian Caliphate and Non-Cooperation Movements.[42] Thus, Mawdūdī's depiction of the then current events in the Near and Middle East had a clear anticolonial, that is to say, anti-British drive.[43] In his discussions of events in India, however, communalist sentiments are already detectable, although in the beginning they were still covered by the approval of the widely accepted need for Muslim-Hindu unity in the anti-colonial struggle, and thus the emphasis was more on the maintenance of communal accord in view of the bigger enemy.[44] However, Mawdūdī was clearly aware of the religious component, which played a major part in the mass mobilisation of the Caliphate Movement.[45]

While his early journalistic writings were thus strongly dominated by anti-colonial, anti-imperialist and even anti-capitalist views, this had changed significantly by the time he took up the editorship of *al-Jamʿiyya*. By then the Caliphate Movement had largely dilapidated and given way to more fragmented and communalist responses to the colonial situation,[46] owing not least to the lack of a concrete road map for an independent India. The increased competition between the various religious communities over clientele gained momentum when, on 23 December 1926, Svāmī Śraddhānand Sarasvatī, a leader of the Hindu communalist *Ārya Samāj* and president of the extremist missionary *Bhāratīya Hindū Śuddhī Sabhā*, was assassinated by a zealous Muslim.[47] The wave of communal violence which erupted from here, fuelled by increasingly aggressive Hindu communalist propaganda, appears to have been the final reason for Mawdūdī's taking on a more outspoken Muslim stand and, thus, turning from an advocate of all Indians to an advocate of Indian Muslims alone.[48] In doing so, however, he did not, as we shall see, subscribe to the secessionist agenda of the *All India Muslim League* (AIML), led by the lawyer Muḥammad ʿAlī Jinnāḥ (d. 1367/1948) and intellectually fostered by the poet-philosopher Muḥammad Iqbāl (d. 1357/1938) whose so-called 'Two-Nation Theory' became the intellectual foundation of the state of Pakistan.

The assassination of Svāmī Śraddhānand contributed significantly to a serious change in the public perception of Islam which, in the eyes of many Muslims, was even stirred by Gandhi (Ghāndhī):[49] Islam was portrayed as an essentially violent religion, enshrined in the doctrine of *jihād* as a means to subdue all non-Muslims by force. In an attempt to counter this image, Muslim community leaders undertook various activities to correct the widespread understanding of *jihād* as a religiously legitimate war against unbelievers. These activities apparently inspired Mawdūdī to use the facilities at his hands to publicise his own views on the matter: between February and May 1927 he published in *al-Jamʿiyya* a lengthy treatise in twenty-two instalments which soon became published as his first major monograph *al-Jihād fi'l-islām*.[50] It is widely held that it was with this book that, almost overnight, Mawdūdī made his actual entry into the world of Muslim community leaders. We have, however, to ask what it was that made his treatise stand out[51] from all the various learned responses on the issue of *jihād* in the aftermath of the assassination of Svāmī Śraddhānand.

What makes Mawdūdī's discussion of *jihād* protrude from the majority of those by other Muslim community leaders is that he did not confine *jihād*, as the others had done, to defensive warfare (*mudāfʿāna jang*) only.[52] Instead, he argued for the normatively grounded permissibility, even the necessity, of offensive warfare for the sake of the 'common good' (*maṣlaḥāna jang*).[53] This was rooted in the belief in the axiomatic leadership of the righteous Muslim communities that needed to be restored after almost the entire Muslim world had been heavily shaken by the social, political and economic developments since the eighteenth century. The deteriorating religio-political situation in British India, marked by the increasingly aggressive activities of multifarious proselytisation movements from all kinds of religious backgrounds, makes Mawdūdī's emphasis on an intrinsic relationship between the self-evident authority of Muslims and offensive warfare for the sake of the 'common good' at this particular point in time perfectly explicable. Indeed, with the publication of a series of editorials, entitled *Daʿwat-i islām*, in April and May 1927, Mawdūdī himself joined in the fierce competition over clientele that raged in late colonial India. While he certainly did this when he fortified the earlier claim for axiomatic leadership of Muslims in these articles by dwelling on the examples of the Qur'ānic prophets,[54] they are remarkable for a different reason: both series of articles, *Islām kā qānūn-i jang* and *Daʿwat-i islām*, must be regarded as the earliest indications that it was during his time as editor of *Muslim* and *al-Jamʿiyya* that Mawdūdī developed a certain style and framework of reference which were to become characteristic of almost all his later writings. His argument would always remain within the confines of the authoritative texts of Islam, first and foremost the Qur'ān, as the unquestionable basis of any certainty.

However, the *Muslim* and even more the *al-Jamʿiyya* years, which came to a sudden and unexplained end in May 1928,[55] are not only important with regard to these rather stylistic developments. Closely related is the fact that many of Mawdūdī's later ideas, which would feed into his ideology as constituent parts, surfaced here in a first and yet not fully elaborate form. Thus, it is the years immediately after the decline of the Caliphate Movement that must be considered the formative period of Mawdūdī's religio-political thought proper. This is by no means surprising, given his proximity to the JUH during this time, which introduced him to a fruitful combination of high-calibre Muslim religious learning, an awareness of communal concerns and a strong political commitment. What this collaboration may also have fostered was Mawdūdī's desire for a better and more thorough religious education, which he eventually obtained, in evening classes with some Deobandi *'ulamā'* at Old Delhi's Fatḥpūrī Mosque.[56] That Mawdūdī, besides his activities for one of the major Muslim religio-political organisations in late colonial India, had obtained a Deobandī teaching permit (*ijāza*) would certainly have contributed a good deal to the increase in his self-confidence. With his Deobandī *ijāza* and his connections to leading *'ulamā'* of that school by then well respected, he was well able to pose as an *'ālim* himself. However, as will occasionally be shown throughout this book, either his erudition in religious fields was not as thorough as claimed, or, perhaps rather less likely, he deliberately deviated from the ways of traditional Indo-Muslim scholarship in pursuit of an alternative religious leadership.[57]

Of course, Mawdūdī would surely not have been drawn into the circles of politically active religious figures, and eventually become one of them himself, if the overall circumstances had not been as they were. Only the tightening colonial situation in India and beyond, coupled with dramatic and far-reaching economic, social, political and cultural changes, could evoke powerful emotional responses from among the colonised which, appropriately channelled by certain individuals and groups, would evolve into impressive anti-colonial and even revolutionary movements. The decisive influence on Mawdūdī's further career must therefore indeed be attributed to the Indian Caliphate Movement: it was the origins, course and outcomes of this movement which had drawn Mawdūdī into the field of religiously flavoured politics in the first place, but they were also responsible for him eventually turning away from the JUH and almost all other major players in India's struggle for independence. Only from his retrospective critical assessment of the Caliphate Movement was he then able to contemplate an alternative vision for an eventual independent India, a 'third way' to the then prevalent various secular or religious nationalisms.

2) The Trigger of Critique: The Caliphate Movement, 1919–1924[58]

Much has already been written about the Indian Caliphate Movement, especially with a focus on the historical events, which is why there is little need for repetition.[59] The role of the underlying emotions which, on the one hand, led to the emergence and sustenance of the movement as well as, on the other, having a decisive impact on getting Mawdūdī interested in politics, and on his subsequent criticism from which eventually his systematic thought evolved, have so far rarely been studied. Because of this importance of collective and individual emotions around the Caliphate Movement, their analysis will be the main focus here, especially since their investigation can additionally provide fresh insight into a decisive phase in the history of late colonial India.

2.1) The Insulted and Humiliated

The whole emotional response by the Indian Muslims, which had been channelled into the first major anti-colonial mass movement in the subcontinent, revolved around a perceived discrepancy between normative expectation and concrete historical realities shaped by the Western colonial presence. The normative expectation, as we have already seen, clearly shared by Mawdūdī, was rooted in the assumption of axiomatic leadership of the Muslims for humankind, enshrined in the Qur'ānic precept that 'You are the best community [*umma*] that I have brought forth among humankind; you enjoin the commendable and prevent the reprehensible [*tamurūna bi'l-ma'rūfi wa-tanhawna 'ani 'l-munkar*].'[60] Verses like this, although rather diversely discussed in the various classical Qur'ānic exegeses,[61] became increasingly the basis for an ethical maxim, which, in turn, was closely tied to Islam's eschatological dimension, as meticulously shown by Michael Cook.[62] The Muslims' claim to superior moral integrity, provided that, as the Qur'ān stipulates, they 'believe and work righteous deeds',[63] would inevitably ensure that it was they among all others who should be responsible for upholding the 'Common Good' (*maṣlaḥa*). It was especially this responsibility for the welfare of humankind that over time stipulated the moulding of the ethical maxim of enjoining the commendable and preventing the reprehensible (*amr bi'l-ma'rūf wa-nahy 'an al-munkar*) into a legal category. This theme finally gained momentum with the advent of the *Wahhābiyya* in eighteenth century Central Arabia, originating from the movement's eponym Muḥammad ibn 'Abd al-Wahhāb (d. 1209/1795), relying to a considerable extent on the earlier radical legal thought of the Damascene Ḥanbalites around Ibn Taymiyya (d. 728/1328), when the by then mainly legal concept of *amr bi'lma'rūf wa-nahy 'an al-munkar* became part of a state doctrine.[64]

These developments in the Middle East were generally known in precolonial nineteenth century India, not least through the flourishing contacts between the *'ulamā'* of the Central Arabian *Wahhābiyya* and the

Indian *Ahl-i ḥadīth* movement.[65] It is quite conceivable that this knowledge reinforced the shaping of an already prevalent image of the late Mughal period as one of political disintegration, owing to moral degeneration not only of the political elites, but of the entire Muslim community.[66] The establishment of direct British rule in the subcontinent and, related to it, the abolition of central Muslim rule was therefore to be considered only the inevitable consequence of this state of moral and political decline. The resulting feeling of humiliation,[67] reinforced by the treatment which the Indian Muslims as the former political elite received at the hand of their new overlords,[68] left mainly two choices. One was to bury one's head in the sand and accept European rule as the victory of a then superior power, an option readily taken up by many members of the former Mughal service elite. The second choice, mainly opted for by Muslim religious elites, appeared much more proactive and in line with the understanding of the basically divinely confirmed moral and, thus, political leadership of the Muslims. The colonial situation called for a thorough reassessment of the community's roots and proposals for remedies—the various learned reformist movements which evolved in the second half of the nineteenth century were the institutionalised results of these reflections.

Some of these movements, especially those which developed in North Indian Deoband and nearby Baraylī, as well as the already mentioned *Ahl-i ḥadīth*, emphasised a rather solipsistic Islamic discourse that focused on a revival of the transmitted sciences (*manqūlāt*) as well as on *fiqh*, and did not—at least initially—engage with the foundations of the changed social, economic and political circumstances in what had then become the British Raj.[69] Consequently, in line with the normatively grounded concept of *amr bi'l-maʿrūf wa-nahy ʿan al-munkar*, reform was first and foremost conceived as a reestablishment of an authentic morality, which was believed to be found among the increasingly idealised first three generations of Muslims, as epitomised in the sound Prophetic saying, 'The best among you are those of my generation, then those who follow them, and then those who follow them [*khayrukum qarnī thumma alladhīna yalūnahum thumma alladhīna yalūnahum*].'[70]

Others, first and foremost among them the founding fathers of the Muhammadan Anglo-Oriental College in Aligarh, apparently took a more intermediate position between those who for pragmatic reasons readily submitted to Western political and intellectual dominance, and those uncompromisingly upholding the normatively grounded idea of the superiority of pure Islamic knowledge which materialised in a superior morality and, thus, in the axiomatic leadership of Muslims. Contrary to the latter, the driving forces of the so-called 'Aligarh Movement' were much more ready to accept the validity of various branches of contemporary Western knowledge while not abandoning the Muslim's claim for moral and, therefore political superiority, which is why they sought theological arguments to justify these branches of contemporary Western knowledge as in full accord with the Qurʾānic revelation. It thus appears not just by accident that the movement's driving force Sayyid Aḥmad K͟hān, knighted by the British government in 1888, had spent his earlier life between the nobility of the Mughal court and the judiciary of the British East India Company. Especially experience in the latter field allowed for a more pragmatic approach to the changed circumstances, despite the strong feelings of Muslim pride and, subsequently, of humiliation in the aftermath of 1857.[71] Although it may be assumed that this latter feeling was initially mainly confined to the former Mughal ruling elites who had lost their prestigious positions, its expression in the more popular idioms of publicly-recited poetry may have helped to rouse the sentiment of loss and deprivation among the wider Muslim community: the lengthy *Musaddas* (1879) by Alṭāf Ḥusayn Pānīpatī 'Ḥālī' (d. 1333/1914), bearing the telling subtitle *On the Ebb and Tide of Islam* (*madd wa jazr-i islām*), which is said to have been publicly recited during popular Muslim religious festivals,[72] appears to be just one case in point.[73]

To overcome this crisis of self-esteem, which resulted from the discrepancy between normative expectation and a concrete historical reality, Sayyid Aḥmad K͟hān worked towards a reformed system of higher education, based on a rationalistic theology in which the authoritative sources of Islam are considered as corroboration and complement the findings of the modern empirical sciences.[74] Besides an adherence to religiously corroborated Western knowledge, Sayyid Aḥmad and his associates strongly advocated the promotion of Urdu as *lingua franca* of the Indian Muslim, which they felt to be well designed for fostering greater community cohesion.[75] Even so Sayyid Aḥmad and his camp followers faced severe criticism for their rather inner-worldly attitude. This reproach came mainly from those who insinuated that the somewhat uncritical appropriation of modern Western branches of learning by the originators of the Aligarh Movement would ultimately affirm the superiority of the West over the Muslims, and thus deprive them of their identity and, consequently, of their moral and political leadership.[76]

Such developments were by no means exclusively confined to the Indian subcontinent, but were rather apparent throughout large parts of the Muslim world which, after all, had come almost entirely under direct or indirect Western influence. The somewhat negative apprehension of the Europeans in the late eighteenth century, as we find for instance in the eyewitness account of the Napoléon-led French military expedition into Egypt by ʿAbd al-Raḥmān al-Jabārtī (d. 1240/1825), appeared still to be determined from the understanding of the Muslims' moral and even intellectual superiority, clearly rooted in the Islamic faith.[77] This attitude however considerably changed only a little while later. When al-Jabārtī reflected with some distance upon the French intermezzo in Egypt and its aftermath, he came to perceive the French in a much more positive light while, at the same time, pointing out moral decline and intellectual stagnation as the main reasons for the weakness and corruption of the Muslim societies.[78]

Jabārtī's later view was reinforced when, from the middle of the nineteenth century, the Ottoman viceroy Meḥmed ʿAlī Paşa (d. 1265/1849) had firmly established himself as virtually the independent ruler of Egypt and, in his attempts to modernise his army and administration, seen the need for a thorough exploration into European technological know-how. In his concise travelogue, the Azhar-trained Rifāʿa Rāfiʿ al-Ṭahṭāwī (d. 1290/1873), who accompanied the first of Meḥmed ʿAlī's study missions to the France of the July Monarchy, painted an image of Europeans and Muslims which clearly echoes al-Jabārtī's later assessment when al-Ṭahṭāwī expressed his hopes that 'by this work all peoples of Islam, be they Arabs or Non-Arabs, may be woken from the sleep of slackness [*nawm al-g͟hafla*]'.[79] The solution, it seemed at first, was to simply combine the determination of the Europeans, which had brought about what was considered an advancement in civilisation and the reason for the considerably Western impact on large parts of the globe within a couple of decades, with the set of values and beliefs that Islam provided. After all, 'had Islam not been supported by the might of God—Praise be Him, exalted He is!—it would be nothing in comparison to the power, the property, the wealth, the proficiency, and so on of the Franks'.[80] The answer, however, was not as easy as perhaps initially anticipated, as the constellation epitomised a serious and hardly reconcilable clash of values. On the one hand, the pragmatically inclined Egyptian rulers oriented themselves towards the political, military and economic success of the Europeans when they followed a course of hitherto unprecedented admiration of the 'Western civilisation' and of uncritical adoption of Western values to the extent that in 1878 the Khedive Ismāʿīl (d. 1312/1895) proclaimed that 'mon pays n'est plus en Afrique, nous faisons partie de l'Europe actuellement'.[81] On the other, the Egyptian *ʿulamāʾ*, upholders of the normative Islamic perspective, expressed serious disquiet at the moral foundations of the successful and apparently effective political, military and economic domination of the Europeans over Muslim societies which they considered socially rather disintegrative. While the attitude of the Egyptian *ʿulamāʾ* towards Western thought and practice returned therefore to the more critical views of the early Jabārtī,[82] the damage was already done: the overwhelming success of the Europeans in almost every field and the resulting political, military and economic domination over Muslim societies had caused increasing and widespread doubts about the further validity of Islamic morals and, consequently about the divine plan of salvation, and had thus given rise to a feeling of social anxiety.

In this context, however, it has to be acknowledged that the occurrence of such collective social anxiety at precisely this moment was by no means a phenomenon particular to the Muslim world alone. After all, the profound and rapid political, economic and social changes which the 'Age of Revolution' brought about affected many societies in a world that was moving increasingly closer together.[83] Man's growing alienation from traditional forms of 'social grouping' (*Vergemeinschaftung*)[84] had at some point led to sentiments of isolation and depression, represented in phenomena like alcoholism and a rise in what Durkheim has labelled 'anomic' suicides.[85] Leaving largely aside Durkheim's 'Theory of Fortune' (*bonheur*) as the wider framework which he had developed for the corroboration of his hypotheses,[86] his early study on suicide as a social phenomenon could nonetheless be well utilised for a better understanding of the emotional state of Muslim societies under colonial rule. The widespread feeling of dejection (*tristesse collective*) which Durkheim had diagnosed in contemporary industrial society[87] can well be stated in the Muslim context too.[88] The constant reference to a widespread moral decline that permeated the writings of Muslim scholars and intellectuals all the way to Mawdūdī and even beyond, suggests a similarity to what Durkheim identified for the Western industrial world, namely the lack of a strong 'regulative force [that] must play the same role for moral needs which the organism plays for physical needs. This means that the force can only be moral.'[89]

Now, while Durkheim ascribed this force exclusively to society, in his eyes 'the only moral power superior to the individual',[90] for Muslim thinkers, the same as for the steadfast followers of any religion, moral rules were enshrined in the texts of the divine revelation. Because of this extra-human origin these rules could, in their eyes, claim a higher degree of authority than any man-made ethics. The mere affirmation of the Qurʾānic revelation as supreme source for the generation of ethical values alone, however, did not suffice for overcoming the anxieties rooted in the aporia that was caused by the colonial situation. What was needed instead was to argue for societal advancement comparable to that of the West, although based solely on Islamic ethical principles. This, in turn, would support the claim for a much greater moral integrity and, consequently, superiority of such societal advancement over any other. Muslim scholars and intellectuals in various places at the turn to the twentieth century considered this to be about the only reasonable way to redress the 'backwardness' (*taʾakhkhur*) and 'retrogressiveness' (*rajʿiyya*) of the Muslim *umma* and to re-establish its axiomatic leadership, epitomised in the concept of *amr bi'l-maʿrūf wa-nahy ʿan al-munkar.*

In order to achieve this ultimate goal, two intermingled points needed to be addressed. First, the diverse Muslim communities all over the world had to be integrated into a single entity, in order to create what Durkheim had called a 'salutary sentiment of solidarity';[91] thus the idea of the one Muslim *umma* unified in belief (*al-umma al-wāḥida*) was re-evoked.[92] Second, to be able to do so, a smallest common denominator had to be established which would enable Muslims to overcome doctrinal differences generated over time and space and could therefore serve as an ethical reference point. Such a reference point had consequently to be looked for in a past time when the Muslim *umma* was not yet as disintegrated as it was then, hence the already mentioned time of the first few generations of Muslims, the so-called 'Pious Elders', or *salaf ṣāliḥ*, was evoked yet again. At a glimpse, such a historical recourse appears consistent with Alan Hunt's rather general suggestion that the appeal to a usually earlier period of stability or even the assumption of a pre-existing 'golden age' is a common feature of social anxiety.[93] At least in the case under investigation here, a more differentiated view would be required.

After all, the recourse to the first few generations among the Muslims was prominent in pre-colonial Muslim societies as well. However, what was called for now was not—at least not in the first place—a verbatim return to the practice of the *salaf ṣāliḥ*, a literal *imitatio Muhammadi*,[94] but much more a recourse to the ethical spirit of that generation and its application to contemporary conditions. Scholars like Muḥammad ʿAbduh (d. 1323/1905) and, to a lesser degree, his pupil and close associate Muḥammad Rashīd Riḍā (d. 1354/1935), undertook this attempt of reconciling this ethical benchmark with contemporary achievements, although only after having the latter critically scrutinised for ethical compatibility.[95] Although parallels to

Sayyid Aḥmad Khān's earlier theological thought are conspicuous especially in ʿAbduh's *Risālat al-tawḥīd* (1897),[96] the rather pithy reference to the *salaf ṣāliḥ*[97]—as Reinhard Schulze has put it, an 'ideological leading theme'[98]—seems to have appeared only with ʿAbduh and his associates. Its meaning was first and foremost symbolic, an appeal to a glorious common heritage which transgresses the spatial confines and would thus contribute towards a single and self-contained community, the *umma wāḥida.*

In British India, the evocation of a glorious Muslim past was often embedded in critical responses to Western Orientalist works on early Islamic history. Here, just as in Egypt, the reference points were no longer the great moments of Indo-Muslim history, but the formative period of Islam, including political and intellectual developments in the Middle Ages. While at a glimpse this corresponds to the developments in the Near and Middle East, especially the English works by scholars like Sayyid Aḥmad Khān and Muḥammad Shiblī Nuʿmānī (d. 1332/1914) or, a little later, the lawyer Sayyid Amīr ʿAlī (d. 1347/1928) reveal that in fact they would be classified rather as Muslim apologias, owing to what were felt to be Western attacks on basic tenets of Islam.[99] These tenets, in turn, were considered crucial symbols for creating and reinforcing the community's cohesion and reviving its self-confidence as God's 'best of all communities'.

2.2) Evoking a Collective Symbol

A significant difference in the modes of communication of all these ideas was apparent between the scholars in Egypt and the Fertile Crescent on the one hand, and Muslim South Asia on the other, which contributes to an explanation why it was in South Asia that the first major Muslim anticolonial movement took off. What is important to acknowledge in this regard is that the circle around Muḥammad ʿAbduh, commonly known as 'Salafiyya' for its reference to the *salaf ṣāliḥ* in epitomising a common history, was confined to a rather small group of religious experts. Their erudition in the religious sciences and the complex theological considerations at the foundation of their reformist agenda was perhaps the reason for the fact that, despite the evocation of a common glorious past, they did not gain mass support, nor did they necessarily aim for it. For ʿAbduh, as a leading representative of the traditional religious functionary elite, reform was a top-down affair, necessarily to be led by experts and not by laymen. Their chosen means of communication for these ideas—religious treatises and journals—were thus consequently designed only for the literate and educated. This, to an extent, went hand in hand with the movement for an Arab cultural awakening (*al-nahḍa*) of which the promotion of a high standard of Arabic language and literature was a cornerstone,[100] appearing somewhat odd in societies where about 90 per cent of the population was illiterate.[101]

In British India, the case was considerably different, despite Sayyid Aḥmad K͟hān's no less complex theological thought. This was not least so because it was neatly linked to a rather broad educational movement under direct colonial rule: because British education in their crown colony did not exactly aim at educating the masses, the initiative for this was left to the various communities themselves. While the appeal to a common history was important here as well,[102] this was directed towards raising a collective awareness first and foremost among the various and diverse Muslim communities in the subcontinent, and less towards a more abstract and normative global dimension. The core means in this was to ascribe to Urdu the status of a common language, following, in a reverse conclusion, the ideas of German Enlightenment thinkers according to which language is the chief constituent for a people and, consequently, for a 'nation'.[103] Urdu had been the most obvious choice, having increasingly transited from being the *lingua franca* of the Mughal military camps to a refined literary language at the later Mughal court,[104] thus linking the language somewhat to the last period of supreme Muslim rule in the subcontinent. Besides the more pragmatic consideration that one single language of instruction was useful in bringing about a more standardised and thus effective system of education, the promotion of Urdu was to a considerable extent also designed to unite the Indian Muslims in the light of the preference given to Hindus over Muslims by the colonial administration.[105] Advocacy of a common language and the stress on a common history went thus hand-in-hand in a process of self-assertion against other religious communities in the subcontinent as well as the colonial overlords. The outreach of this agenda did not stop at the confines of the new Muslim educational institutions. Journals and newspapers, in both Urdu and English, played an important role in the dissemination of these ideas among a wider educated audience.[106] Publicly-recited poetry, finally—and herein appears to lie the major difference to the then contemporary developments in the Near and Middle East—was one of the major tools to instill these sentiments into the wider and mostly illiterate Muslim population and helped thus to transgress the confines of an elite phenomenon.

While especially the promotion of Urdu clearly catered for the South Asian context only, in particular the evocation of a distinct Muslim history was to be reinforced by an increasing emphasis on its links with a wider Muslim *umma* and thus to help cast a wider net of Muslim solidarity in the face of the common colonial threat. In this regard the activities of versatile networkers like Muḥammad ʿAbduh's early associate Jamāl al-Dīn Asadābādī 'al-Afghānī'[107] appeared to be equally important with the stress on common Muslim institutions, places or historical events. In this context belong, among others, the somewhat glorified reminiscences of Muslim Spain and Jerusalem that had been successfully wrested from the Christian occupiers in the late twelfth century CE, or the two major sanctuaries of Mecca and Medina (*al-ḥaramayn al-sharīfayn*). Of the re-evoked institutions, the 'caliphate' gained the most prominent role as a collective symbol that was utilised for political mobilisation in one of the earliest anti-colonial Muslim mass movements in the subcontinent.

While the actual caliphate may indeed have lost its importance to a large extent with the sack of Baghdad by the Mongols in 1258 CE and finally the deposition of the so-called 'Shadow-Caliph' of Cairo by the Ottomans in 1517,[108] the idea of a supreme religio-political leader of all Muslims in the succession to the Prophet Muḥammad still possessed an enormous sentimental value.[109] Although in reality increasingly devalued to just one form of respectful title for any Muslim ruler, the concept still played an important role in Islamic political theory.[110] From the eighteenth century onwards, however, the Ottoman sultans increasingly employed the title of 'caliph' to secure loyalties in an increasingly disintegrating empire after the defeat in the Russo-Turkish War of 1768–74 and the resulting Treaty of Küçük Kaynarca.[111] This appealed to personalities as far apart as Sayyid Aḥmad Khān and Jamāl al-Dīn al-Afghānī alike, although apparently for different reasons.[112] While for the latter support for the Ottoman Sultan ʿAbdülḥamīd II (r. 1876–1909) as 'caliph' was rather a pragmatic measure than an affirmation of the Ottomans' claim,[113] the Indian scholar and his associates appear to have been more affectionate towards the sultan as the embodiment of a classical Islamic institution, at least as long as this attachment did not create conflict over their eventually declared loyalty towards the British.[114]

The reasons for the general uncritical and positive attitude of Indo-Muslim intellectuals towards the Ottoman Turks at the turn of the twentieth century remain rather unclear. One is tempted to assume that this was the result of a romantic idealisation of the Ottoman Empire, owing to the geographical distance which did not cause the same critical engagement with Ottoman imperialism as took place, for example, in directly affected regions such as Egypt and the Fertile Crescent.[115] On the other hand, Sayyid Aḥmad K͟hān's associate Muḥammad Shiblī Nuʿmānī had travelled the Ottoman Middle East in 1892 and had already gained a first-hand impression of the desolate state of the Ottoman Empire. It is therefore rather surprising that after his three-month stay at the Sublime Porte and the following travels to Ottoman Syria and Egypt, including an encounter with Muḥammad ʿAbduh, Shiblī was still full of praise for the achievements of the *tanẓīmāt* reforms and apparently little aware that the authority of the Ottoman sultan had been heavily undermined by the ever-growing Arab nationalist movements.[116] Although initially accepting the caliphal aspiration of the Ottoman sultan, Muḥammad ʿAbduh and Rashīd Riḍā withdrew their loyalty the moment it became clear that ʿAbdülḥamīd II was not willing to act in this capacity according to their normative expectations, namely as guarantor of Muslim unity in the wake of Western colonial dominance.[117] On the other hand, what might certainly have supported the perception of the Ottoman ruler by the Indian Muslims was the religious self-promotion of the sultan and his rule in an attempt to give his disintegrating empire some more cohesion.[118] The sultan did not stop there. He was actively—and successfully—craving recognition as supreme religious benefactor by the Indian Muslims when, in 1880, he had Nuṣrat ʿAlī K͟hān, an Indian living at the Porte, commissioned with editing the Turkish-Urdu bilingual journal *Payk-i islām*, which had been financed by the Imperial treasury until strong diplomatic protest by the British stopped its further publication.[119]

As stated above, Shiblī and other Indo-Muslim intellectuals upheld an admiration for the Ottoman Empire as the last Muslim state which maintained, although with huge difficulties, its independence from direct European interference at the threshold of the First World War.[120] The events on the Western frontier of the Ottoman Empire, closely observed by the Indians, fuelled their perception that the entire Muslim world was being threatened by European powers, as epitomised in a short poem by Shiblī in which he lamented the loss of the Balkan territories as a loss not only for the 'Sick Man of Europe' (*turkī kā marīḍ-i jān*) alone, but for the entire Muslim *umma*.[221]

In his observations Shiblī was joined by the luminous Abū 'l-Kalām 'Āzād',[222] a young and ambitious *ʿālim*-turned-prolific writer and journal editor who, between 1912 and 1916 in his Calcutta-based journal *al-Hilāl*, fervently propagated support for the Ottomans, utilising religious as well as patriotic sentiments for this end when he stated that 'we must always remember that the Ottoman Caliph is the guardian of the two Holy Places, and that the degradation [*tanazzul*] of Turkey is a degradation of Islam, a degradation which jeopardises not only Islam, but the honour and dignity [*ʿizzat wa iqtidār*] of the whole of Asia'.[223] Āzād must, besides Muḥammad ʿAlī 'Jawhar' (d. 1349/1931), be regarded as one of the most influential driving forces in the movement for the preservation of the caliphate held by the Ottoman sultan, which commenced right after the First Word War among Indian Muslims, initially attempting to mitigate the apparently disastrous outcome of the war for the Ottoman Turks after the Armistice of Mudros on 30 October 1918.[224]

In the beginning the commitment to the Ottoman cause was confined to a rather small number of Muslim activists from various backgrounds. Its nucleus consisted of the *Anjumān-i Khuddām-i Kaʿba*, established in May 1913 under the aegis of ʿAbd al-Bārī Farangī Maḥallī (d. 1344/1926) in an attempt to rally support in all Muslim communities under non-Muslim rule for the protection of the highly venerated religious places in the Hijaz and elsewhere in the weak Ottoman Empire.[125] All of its members vowed to put their commitment to this religio-political cause above any possible loyalty towards the British crown, which might well be considered an important indicator of the increasing confluence of pan-Islamic and anti-colonial sentiments among Indo-Muslim intellectual elites of that period.

The strategic use of various propagandistic means, coupled with the movement for mass education, helped a great deal to sensitise a wider Muslim population to the general state of the Muslim world and the need to preserve and secure central Islamic institutions of highly symbolic value for the religious self-identification of Muslims from the threat posed by non-Muslim powers. In the beginning, journals like Āzād's *al-Hilāl*, Muḥammad ʿAlī's English weekly *Comrade*, launched in January 1911, and the Urdu daily *Hamdard* established two years later, as well as Ẓafar ʿAlī Khān's (d. 1375/1956) Lahore-based daily *Zamīndār* established in 1908, played an important role in reaching out to the literate among the Muslims and arouse strong pan-Islamic and anti-colonial sentiments.[126] The common man, however, had to be approached rather by the spoken word; hence public and semipublic gatherings of various sizes were frequently held in which emotive rhetoric played an important role.

A popular means to wake the masses from the slumber of political indifference was once again publicly-recited poetry, now largely freed from the confines of technicalities and, as Ḥālī and others had intended, more related to social and political issues at hand. It was first and foremost in such congregations and by means of poetry recitals and emotive stumping speeches that, first, the feeling of deprivation and humiliation was ignited among the wider Indo-Muslim population,[127] and, second, these emotions were channelled into collective action.[128] A good example for this immediate nexus is Muḥammad Iqbāl's public recital of his poem *Jawāb-i shikwa* before a large congregation in Lahore's Bādshāhī mosque in November 1912, in which God responds with strong words to the Muslims lamenting their current situation (*Shikwa*, 1911):[129]

[Your] hands are stunned, your heart well used to heresy [*ilḥād*];
the community [*ummatī*] a reason for the Messenger's disgrace [*bāʿith-i ruswāʾī*]!
The idol-breakers are gone, left are only idolaters! [...]
This nation's good is one, [its] woe one, too;
for all the Prophet's one, one the religion, the belief one, too;
the blessed precinct [*ḥaram-i pāk*] is one, and one is God, one the Qurʾān is, too;
what great a thing it was that Muslims were one, too!
Yet, still, here you've split into sects [*firqa-bandī*] and separated do you live. [...]
From Christians you have got [your] manners, from Hindus your culture [*tamaddun*],
these are the Muslims, whose sight even shames the Jews! [...]
A Muslim you are? Is this supposed to be the Muslim's way [*andāz-i musalmānī*]? [...]
You live disgraced, having strayed from the path of the Qurʾān![130]

Iqbāl's emotive recital, clearly contrasting Indo-Muslim regionalism with the Hijaz-centred pan-Islamic ideal,[131] fell on fertile ground. In a guilt-driven wave of pan-Islamic solidarity his audience donated generously for their Turkish brethren wounded in the First Balkan War.

The successful appeal to emotions by way of utilising collective symbols, in order to receive an active response, appears to have been a common strategy.[132] What is important in this regard are two things. First, the use of emotive symbols contributed strongly to constituting an 'emotional community', to employ a rather differently defined—term coined by the medievalist Barbara H. Rosenwein.[133] This way, the Indian Muslims who, at least according to the views of their intellectual elites, lacked even the least community cohesion,[134] were moulded into a—somewhat imagined—single community which was part of an—equally imagined—much larger entity, that is, the global Muslim *umma*. Second, the use of such symbols suggests a common understanding of these symbols without the need to make it explicit. This, however, appears to be a major hermeneutical fallacy, as acknowledged by leading theorists of meaning, from Ernst Cassirer (d. 1945) to Donald Davidson (d. 2003), who conceded that there would always remain a certain quantum of uncertainty in the field of symbolic interaction.

This very fuzziness of meaning that underlies symbols could be and, in the context of the Indian Caliphate Movement, was indeed deliberately utilised, in two somewhat interdependent directions. First, although the joint appeal to the caliphate suggested a unity within the leadership of the movement, in fact it was used as a field for contest over communal leadership in a time when the *ʿulamāʾ* in general did not enjoy this position any longer in an unrestrained fashion. We find therefore numerous representatives of different and competing factions among the *ʿulamāʾ* contesting over communal leadership with a newly emerging strata of religious laymen.[135] Second, while the 'caliphate'-symbol appeared well designed to evoke pan-Islamic sentiments among the masses and to suggest a global 'emotional community' of Muslims, it could also serve a perhaps less distinctly religious nationalist agenda which, as we shall see, was to become one of Mawdūdī's main objections against the Caliphate Movement, although only in retrospect. At the forefront of this more nationalistic orientation stood, once more, Abū 'l-Kalām Āzād, arguably the leading ideologue of the movement.

2.3 A Covenant for Independence

What seems to have predestined Āzād's role as chief ideologue of the Caliphate Movement was, first, his institutional independence from Aligarh, Deoband and the like, while, second, combining thorough religious knowledge acquired in the Hijaz with a quite realistic understanding of contemporary social and political developments in India and beyond. As a 'wanderer between two worlds' he was therefore able to utilise an erudite religious language and a pragmatic political one alike, thus successfully combining traditional and contemporary idioms while using modern means of communication. In this he stood out from *ʿulamāʾ* like ʿAbd al-Bārī Farangī Maḥallī and 'Shaykh al-Hind' Maḥmūd al-Ḥasan Deobandī (d. 1339/1921),[136] but also from intellectuals like Muḥammad ʿAlī 'Jawhar', who became a 'Mawlānā' only *honoris causa*;[137] he would thus rather be comparable with free-floating intellectuals like Muḥammad Iqbāl.[138]

Āzād's being a 'wanderer between two worlds' might indeed explain a certain consistency in his intellectual biography, as Ian H. Douglas has tried to show.[139] On the other hand, from its outlook it is not really surprising that, before Douglas, many authors saw Āzād's intellectual life as clearly divided into an earlier and more religiously conscious phase and a later nationalistic one. However, if one agrees with Douglas' convincing line of argument and perceives Āzād's intellectual development as consistent in itself, then one would almost be compelled to assume that Āzād had—more or less deliberately—employed highly emotive religious language to see through an even less religious agenda, namely the independence (*svarāj*) of India from colonial rule. 'Caliphate' served him here increasingly as *leitmotif*, the epitome of non-colonial rule. In order to attain the ultimate goal of India's independence, however, it looked as if there was no other reasonable way than to ally with the non-Muslim forces of the Indian National Congress (INC). While he was by no means alone in holding this view, it was first and foremost Āzād who strove to provide also a religious justification for this kind of collaboration, demonstrating that joint action with non-Muslims for the sake of a greater good would not at all infringe the provisions of Islam.

In his presidential address to the All-India Khilāfat Conference on 25 October 1921 in Agra, he utilised the Qur'ān as well as the *sīra* of the Prophet to argue for the permissibility of Muslim-Hindu unity and non-co-operation with the British, whenever the circumstances demanded it. According to him, the Qur'ānic verses 60: 8–16 divides non-Muslims into two categories, which reflect on whether and how Muslims should interact with them. Classical *tafāsīr* apply the two verses clearly to the relationship between the early Muslims after their exodus to Medina and those who remained in Mecca, and state even the possibility that the first verse had been abrogated after the Muslim conquest of Mecca.[140] Now, Āzād, on the other hand, applied these verses to the Indian context, concluding that Hindus, whom he considered by and large not hostile towards the Muslims, could be met amicably, while the British were equated with 'those who fight you because of [your] religion, and drive you out of your homes, and support (others) in driving you out'[141] and must therefore not be turned to.[142]

While the Qur'ānic verse 60:8 had not much more to offer than that one should treat all those non-Muslims kindly and justly who show no hostility towards Muslims, Āzād needed some reinforcement to legitimise joint Muslim-Hindu action. For this purpose, he evoked the so-called 'Constitution of Medina' (*ṣaḥīfat al-Madīna*), a document of disputed authenticity,[143] which had been incorporated into the standard biography of the Prophet by Muḥammad ibn Isḥāq (d. 151/768) in the preserved redaction of ʿAbd al-Malik ibn Hishām (d. 183/833).[144] The reason why Āzād appealed to this text is the use of the term '*umma*' in it, here explicitly including the numerous Jewish tribes of Yathrib, stating that 'to the Jews who follow us belong support and equality [*al-naṣr wa'l-uswa*]. Neither shall they face injustice nor shall their enemies be aided.'[145] Āzād was correct when he stressed that the *umma wāḥida* evoked by the Prophet was then not yet confined to one single religious community, but rather was what he himself called 'a *nation*',[146] based on mutual loyalty (*al-birr*). His passionate plea for Muslim-Hindu unity, however, justified with the argument that only because of this covenant was the Medinese *umma* able to overcome its Meccan enemies, appears to be a rather convenient reduction when one considers the ill fate of the Jewish tribes after each of the three major battles between the Muslims and the Meccans.[147] Regardless of this deliberate omission, however, under no circumstance could Āzād stretch the interpretation of the sources to the extent that, in opposition to what he saw as a force of absolute political and cultural oppression, unity with the Hindus 'is a religious act [*madhhabī 'amal*] for Muslims'.[148] Hence, one is compelled to conclude that at least here Āzād had transgressed the confines of traditional Muslim scholarship and joined hands with the innovative religious laymen to which Mawdūdī also belonged.

Āzād's fervour for India's independence under the cover of Islam surely bore the desired fruits for a certain amount of time: after all, the Caliphate Movement had indeed become the first Indian mass movement for independence, including many non-Muslim activists, too. On the other hand, his clear regional emphasis had to lead inevitably to severe conflict with the other leaders of the movement to whom the preservation of the Ottoman-held caliphate, as a genuine Islamic religio-political institution, was too dear a matter to have it subordinated under anything else, however important. Hence, right from its beginnings, the rather fragile Muslim-Hindu covenant could not withstand the conflict between the various interest groups within one single religious community and was thus doomed to decline. Two aspects played a major role in this process of disintegration.

First, the Independence Movement appeared to have no uniform vision of the concrete arrangement of Indian society once independence was attained. For Gāndhī, whose 1917 petition was one of the main triggers for the movement, discussion of the future prospects should be postponed until *svarāj* was actually achieved.[149] It appears, however, that this rather reasonable position was not really shared even by Gāndhī's own comrades-in-arms: The fear of an over-representation of the interests of Hindus due to their numerical strength fuelled communalist sentiments among the Muslim leaders and, thus, in the various Muslim communities. Second, and closely related to the rise of those fears, it was felt that the interests of the Muslim minority could only be safeguarded in independent India if they remained part of a larger political structure, the Muslim ecumene under the overall political and religious leadership of the caliph. The very moment, however, when, on 3 March 1924, the institution was officially abolished by the Grand National Assembly of Turkey (*Türkiye Büyük Millet Meclisi*) under the presidency of Muṣṭafá Kemal Paşa 'Atatürk' (d. 1938) who had so far enjoyed the support of the leaders of the Indian Caliphate Movement,[150] such a vision became increasingly unrealistic. The hopes of all those Muslims who got engaged in the movement for religious reasons had thus been ultimately destroyed.

2.4) The Disappointed and Deceived

To those many sympathisers and activists of the Caliphate Movement, who, to a considerable extent, were attracted by its religious symbolism, belonged Mawdūdī:

> Because of the evil shadows [*a*<u>*th*</u>*arāt*] that surrounded us we disliked Western culture [*farangiyyat*] and Western domination [*farangī tasalluṭ*] right from the beginning and, naturally, we were prepared to support any movement that strove for freeing India from this domination, [especially] as it appealed to religious sentiments [*ma*<u>*dh*</u>*habī ju*<u>*dh*</u>*bāt*], too.[151]

Even from among the leaders of the movement not everybody was prepared to subordinate the explicit Muslim agenda, which located the movement within a wider pan-Islamic context, to the nationalist one, as Āzād did.[152] The growing distance and eventual break between Āzād and Muḥammad ʿAlī 'Jawhar' in the late 1920s, for example, owed clearly to the fact that the latter saw Muslim interests obviously endangered by the Congress-led political agenda, epitomised in the famous 'Nehru Report' of early 1928.[153] These Muslim interests, on the other hand, were by no means conceived uniformly—especially not after the abolition of the Ottoman Caliphate in 1924 deprived the Indian Muslims of a highly integrative symbol—and thus gave rise to a variety of schemes, advocated by various religious and political movements. While ʿAbd al-Bārī Farangī Maḥallī and Muḥammad ʿAlī maintained their support for a constituted caliphate and supported the former Sharīf of Mecca, Sayyid Ḥusayn ibn ʿAlī al-Hāshimī (d. 1350/1931), and the leader of the Central Arabian Āl Saʿūd, ʿAbd al-ʿAzīz ibn Saʿūd (d. 1373/1953), respectively,[154] others developed various nationalist visions for British India, be they secular or communalistic.[155]

For Mawdūdī, all this was a clear indication that pan-Islamic political mobilisation had fallen apart. This could not be hidden by the fact that some leaders of the Caliphate Movement kept up appearances for the Indo-Muslim masses by continuing their rhetoric of supporting the caliphate even after the institution had officially been abolished under Atatürk in 1924. Even the frantic attempts to find a new caliph, whether by reinstalling the Ottoman sultan or the promotion of some Arab prince, and thereby saving the institution, appeared to Mawdūdī to be a futile endeavour: for him, the caliphate had thus decayed to only a chimera.

Deeply disappointed with the movement he began to critically reassess it. Hindu-Muslim unity, which he had initially welcomed for pragmatic reasons, was based on the assumption that the political leadership in an independent India would ultimately lie with the Muslims. After all, this was suggested by men like Āzād whose earlier passionate writings had suggested that the collaboration of the Caliphate Committee and the Gāndhī-inspired Congress was only a temporary and targeted one—it was ultimately the Muslims who were to 'enjoin the commendable and prevent the reprehensible' (*amr bi'l-maʿrūf wa-nahy ʿan al-munkar*), as promised in the Qurʾān.[156] Now this authoritatively grounded claim had—almost undetected—given way to the adoption of the Western model of democracy, as the political representation of a majority vote. To Mawdūdī, who did not seem to have realised the shift in Āzād's conception of righteous leadership from the political one of the actual caliph to an ethical one of the entire *umma*, this could only mean that:

> [f]or the Hindu nation [*qawm*] this was most beneficent because they were in the majority. They understood very well that when the entire population of India would form one nation and a democratic system would be established, too, then they would enjoy the full benefit. In the end, the contribution of the Muslims would be inferior to theirs [*unke mā-taḥt*] and rather become that of their handy servants.[157]

The equilibrium of power, essential precondition for any kind of political entente, had thus clearly been shifted to the disadvantage of the Muslims. Indeed, the 'Nehru Report' of 1928 and its outright support by Hindu communalist leaders, among them Bālakṛṣṇa Śivarām Muṃje (d. 1948)—since 1927 president of the *Hindū Mahāsabhā* and one of the founding fathers of the militant *Rāṣṭrīya Svayaṃsevak Saṃgh* (RSS)[158]—and Svāmī Śraddhānand Sarasvatī reinforced such a perception. For Mawdūdī it was obvious who was to be held responsible for the betrayal of the Muslims. Although he did not explicitly name them, he clearly put the blame on the Muslim partisans of the Congress, like Āzād, Dr Mukhtār Aḥmad Anṣārī (d. 1355/1936) and others.[159]

While Mawdūdī, editor of the JUH paper *al-Jamʿiyya* from the time of the collapse of the movement onwards, clearly dissociated himself from the Congress, he also disapproved of other Muslim community leaders and their respective claims to be sole representatives of Muslim interests. If the only two available political visions among Muslim leaders in late colonial India required bowing either to the secular democracy of the Congress or to various kinds of religiously charged nationalisms, then Mawdūdī felt that he had to come up with an alternative solution of his own. His scheme, however, would have to be based on a solid theoretical foundation to be able to claim superiority over all other paths. Mawdūdī's writings from that period, culminating in 1927 in his highly acclaimed series of articles on the issue of *jihād*, in which embryonic forms of core concepts of his later systematic outline are already visible,[160] bore a clear testimony to that.

In this regard, especially the already mentioned chapter on offensive warfare for the common good (*maṣlaḥāna jang*) deserves consideration, because it revealed a fundamental presupposition for all of Mawdūdī's later thinking. In this chapter, Mawdūdī revived the understanding of the axiomatic leadership of Muslims as enshrined in the Qurʾānic precept of 'enjoining the commendable and preventing the reprehensible'. In his approach, however, he differed considerably from the above mentioned earlier thinkers who were all concerned with the reconciliation of the normative expectation to be 'the best community that I have brought forth among humankind'[161] and the socio-political realities in Muslim communities in the colonial age. While reformers in late nineteenth century Egypt and India attempted this with a much revised system of education, later activists, like Abū 'l-Kalām Āzād, were even prepared for a temporary alliance with non-Muslims to achieve this goal.[162] For Mawdūdī, on the contrary, the divinely ensured position of the Muslim community did not allow for such a conciliatory view. Instead, with reference to the Qurʾānic verse 22:41,[163] to enjoin the commendable and prevent the reprehensible meant to him first and foremost to publicly enforce the religious obligations as prescribed.[164] To achieve this, Muslims would necessarily need to act on each and every one who did not comply with these—*qua* revelation—superior obligations that, in the last consequence, entailed also physical force against those acting against the obligations.

This proactive role which Mawdūdī assigned exclusively to the righteous Muslim community and which he backed up with a reference to the Qurʾānic revelation was becoming the backbone of his proposed alternative[165] to the main proposals for the post-colonial development of the Muslim communities after the collapse of the Caliphate Movement. In this, he clearly proved himself to be a child of his time. From the mid-nineteenth century in Europe societal alternatives were proposed to the two dominant models, that is, bourgeois democracy and monarchy by the grace of God. Very soon, these new ideas, cast in revolutionary ideologies, found their way into the colonies of Western imperialist powers and served widely as models in the struggle for liberation from colonial rule and inspirations in the debate on the future development of an eventually independent subcontinent, appropriated by either secularist or communalist nationalists.[166] As ideologies, each one of these new ideas claimed superiority over all others, rooted in the claim that each one was based on sound and transcendent, hence unquestionable, theoretical foundations. As the nature of these foundations by definition precludes any reasonable debate and possible compromise, either these ways would have to be imposed on everyone, or, as Mawdūdī had suggested from a very early point onwards, the various communities in a decolonised India would have to develop in distinct ways: 'each party rejoicing in that which is with itself.'[167]

The admission of an irreconcilable rift between various communities in the subcontinent, clearly expressed by the adherence to or, at least, appropriation of key elements of contemporary Western political ideologies, represented therefore no real alternatives for Mawdūdī. His own thinking, which ultimately culminated in his systematic outline of an Islamic polity, was—in places—nonetheless clearly affected by them, if by explicit dissociation only. For a proper understanding of Mawdūdī's outline it is therefore vital to screen the ideological landscape in late colonial India before finally embarking on unfolding his system step-by-step.

3) Mapping the Ideological Landscape

In a time where the world moved increasingly together, decisively promoted by Western colonialism, various models for societal development that had originated in the West also became increasingly globalised. Indeed, already the very idea of 'societal development' contains a fairly ideological dimension, deeply rooted in the profound changes that took place in almost all European societies from the seventeenth century. The Age of Enlightenment, aptly characterised by Immanuel Kant in his famous essay *Beantwortung der Frage: Was ist Aufklärung?* (1784) as 'man's emergence from his self-imposed immaturity',[168] supported the process of secularisation and caused, therefore, a turn from the absolutistic to a democratic notion of state. Although the 'Copernican Turn',[169] reversing the fixation on divine revelation into focusing on man's mundane affairs, could do away with institutionalised religion, it had to replace it with convictions, which were not rooted any more in divine revelation, but rather in the empirical. The shifted focus to this world, in turn, brought about a new criterion of truth that had a decisive impact on the emergence of various political ideologies which all shared the claim for sole validity.

By definition each of these ideologies had to call for universal applicability, on the grounds that there had usually been at least some awareness of local specifics which, in turn, had a clear impact on the possibilities of adapting those ideologies to various regional contexts. Intellectual elites in colonies like India, while actively striving for independence from the Western powers, did nonetheless—consciously or not—subscribe to the originally Western idea of 'societal development'. In doing so they engaged intensely with the prevalent political ideologies, over and above Communism and Fascism, in their endeavour to shape a future society after decolonisation. In order to better understand the impact of these ideologies on the Indian discourse on 'development' in which Mawdūdī actively took part, a thorough anatomy of at least the two most dominant ones—Communism and Fascism—is imperative.

3.1) 'Scientificness'—Criterion of Truth for a Whole Epoch

The core assumption in the following discussion of political ideologies is that their rise was decisively fostered by the complex interplay of a mechanisation and industrialisation of *Lebenswelt*, revolutionary new insight in the natural sciences and philosophical conceptions in the aftermath of Kant's critical thought.[170] The latter had stirred up considerably almost everything that was so far considered a certainty, and led to the emergence of various world views (*Weltanschauungen*), following up Kant's statements on the 'kingdom of freedom', or on the 'kingdom of necessity' and the 'thing in itself'.[171] So, it was the German idealist philosopher Johann Gottlieb Fichte (d. 1814) who explicitly recognised this fact when he stated that 'what philosophy one chooses depends on what sort of person one is'.[172] Indeed, while the idealists followed Kant's plea for a new metaphysics to substantiate ethical principles, and became the last representatives of the 'old', i.e. systematic philosophy, the neo-Kantians attempted to purge the Kantian philosophy from everything metaphysical and pre-critical in their attempt to solve the problem of the 'thing-in-itself'.[173] The empiricism of the neo-Kantians found its mighty pendant on the British Isles in utilitarianism, setting out from pre-Kantian Scottish sensualistic epistemology and moral philosophy, revolving around the works of Jeremy Bentham (d. 1832) and even more John Stuart Mill (d. 1873), 'a philosophical patriarch for the [late nineteenth] century'.[174]

It had been especially those who might be subsumed under the label 'empiricists'[175] whose thoughts corresponded well to the socio-economic developments in Europe of the 'Industrial Revolution(s)'. Science of whatever provenance could indeed contribute significantly to these changes and it produced utilisable knowledge of the 'thing-in-itself' that, precisely because it could be utilised, was considered firm.[176] It is important here to acknowledge that the sciences from around 1830 differed considerably from traditional understanding. The differentiation into numerous areas of empirical knowledge caused the emergence of new scientific disciplines with distinct theoretical claims, although new areas of research emerged soon from the cross-pollination of these young and emancipating sciences. All was in motion, and so consequently was the underlying paradigm of the new scientific knowledge. Knowledge was not systemic, i.e. self-contained and thus finite any more, it became procedural and, thus, infinite.[177] The processual character of the new knowledge was reflected in philosophies and scientific theories, one of the most influential amongst which had perhaps been Jean-Baptiste de Lamarck's (d. 1829) and Charles R. Darwin's (d. 1882) theories of evolutionary biology, epitomised in the latter's *On the Origin of Species* from 1859 and, even more, *The Descent of Man* from 1871.[178] Parts of Darwin's theory clearly diverged from current ideas of political economy, especially those of Thomas R. Malthus (d. 1834)—specific expressions he used indicated also a close familiarity with certain aspects of the political philosophy of Thomas Hobbes (d. 1679).[179] Such divergences in biologistic and political thought helped a great deal to root Darwinian thought firmly in the field of human society.

The new scientific insights, especially in the young aspiring biology, had in turn a considerable impact on the further development of yet another philosophical current that emerged from a critical analysis of Kant's works and in opposition to the rationality-centeredness of idealism: life-philosophy.[180] Proceeding from the works of Arthur Schopenhauer (d. 1860) this was to become the most influential philosophy of the epoch that closed dramatically with the end of the Second World War.[181] 'Life' represented a fundamental category: 'It stands for the dynamic, procedural, organic, something that bears up against all opposition—against the static, abstract, mechanical, dead.'[182] In the works of authors like Nietzsche, Oswald Spengler (d. 1936) and Henri Bergson (d. 1941) the dualism of life and spirit, the latter being antithetical to life and representing the seat of rationality, took the shape of an epic battle that life was eventually to win, very much inspired by the common teleological interpretation of the Darwinian notion of the 'survival of the fittest'.[183]

Somewhat in contrast, the brief revival of idealism in British academic philosophy, mainly at Oxford, was driven more by the social conscience of its protagonists, but nonetheless also responded to the prevalent circumstances. Thus, although it originated in a reception of Kant's and Hegel's philosophy, 'their Hegelianism was redrawn and transmuted by other, notably Aristotelian, influences, and by the weight of an indigenous empiricism'.[184] By doing so, idealists like Thomas Hill Green (d. 1882), Francis Herbert Bradley (d. 1924) and Bernard Bosanquet (d. 1923) were—consciously or not—attempting to overcome the fact that by then 'between two philosophers there existed not even a communicative context, because the one was not able to relate meaning to what the other was saying'.[185] The reception of Hegel's philosophy in Britain was shrunken to little more than his concept of history,[186] which in turn made it easier to link the conception of 'development' in Romanticist and idealist thought to the biologistic understanding represented by Darwinism and utilitarian philosophy. David George Ritchie (d. 1903), a student of Green at Oxford, was central in this regard,[187] but also Bosanquet showed quite some willingness to apply a Darwinist notion to his ethical ideas.[188]

For this move towards empiricism Bosanquet was fervently criticised by the Cambridge philosopher John McTaggart Ellis McTaggart (d. 1925), whose own maverick understanding of Hegelian thought appears to have notably been influenced by Bergsonian life-philosophy.[189] Considering Darwinian and, thus, Darwinist evolutionism as too wooden and static, Bergson introduced the 'vital impetus' (*élan vital*), an animated life force designed to drive humankind to a higher consciousness, and thus smoothened the still rather stiff Darwinist model of development in stages into a dynamic flow.[190] Bergsonian intuitionism found its way to Muslim India, arguably by the mediation of McTaggart who, between 1905 and 1908, had been a teacher of Muḥammad Iqbāl.[191] The impact of the Bergsonian idealism of McTaggart can be found in Iqbāl's poetry as well as in his central *Reconstruction of Religious Thought in Islam*, based on six lectures delivered at Madras, Hyderabad and Aligarh in 1928–9;[192] it is moreover clearly detectable also in Iqbāl's later argument for a separate nation of Indian Muslims.[193]

More dominant and influential on the development of political ideologies, however, was not intuitionist critiques of empiricism and the natural sciences by Bergson and his life-philosophical and idealist epigones,[194] but the firm belief in the veracity of scientific knowledge, coupled with Lamarckist and, moreover, Darwinist evolutionism. For this, on the one hand, the ethical life-philosophy of Nietzsche and the historical one of Spengler appear to have been of exceptional importance.[195] On the other, the concept of 'development' of Romanticist and idealist philosophies became objectified through the lenses of Lamarckism and Darwinism in the historicist philosophy of the Young Hegelian Karl Marx and his associates, notably among them Friedrich Engels (d. 1895).[196] Human society, so they argued, passes through various phases of increasingly complex economic dependencies until the alienation of the productive forces from the means and fruits of production will reach its climax and ultimately result in a revolution, leading eventually to the reconciliation of the productive forces and means of production. It looks therefore as if it was indeed Darwinism, consciously or not, that became the dominant matrix for all political ideologies, rooted to a large extent in trust in the veracity of the Darwinian theory as a scientific one.

'Science'—More than just one Intellectual Lineage among Others in the Indian Debate on Development

The European discourse on 'Scientificness' at the turn of the twentieth century obviously had repercussions on the debates in the colonies. Here, as well as there, 'science' epitomised development, progress and modernity, in short, the sound basis on which any society should rest. Thus, 'science' appears indeed to be not just one intellectual lineage among other equally important ones, but rather as the 'meta-lineage' that impacted all others.[197] 'Science' made the development of the *Lebenswelt* predictable—hence 'planning' became the order of the day.[198] As a matter of fact, it was the emphasis on science and technology that was considered the driving force in vaulting India into modernity, which formed the precondition for planned national development either along the Socialist or the Fascist model. As a worldview it formed a diametrically opposed vision to Gāndhī's influential romanticism, which put the village community at the centre of an essentialised image of the Indian society in the past and future.[199]

Advocacy of either Gandhism or Scienticism had been widely utilised to discredit political opponents within the Indian independence movement. Javāharlāl Nehrū (d. 1964), the later first prime minister independent India and important reference point for diverse political groups within the discourse on India's future, used his almost unconditional advocacy of science, and thus of societal planning, to dissociate himself from Gandhism.[200] Nehrū had his plea for science embedded in a rather sketchy philosophy that perceived it as a vehicle of progress from 'culture' to 'civilisation', thus wittingly or unwittingly employing the dichotomy of Oswald Spengler's seminal work *Der Untergang des Abendlandes* from 1918 and 1922, which was almost instantly translated into English and which Nehrū had apparently known.[201]

Others, like the Bengali chemist Prafulla Chandra Roy (d. 1944), combined their scientism with an Occidentalist attitude, arguing that the modern sciences in the West owed their existence by and large to an indigenous Indian heritage alone, which had only to be revitalised. Besides, Roy, who was linked to the Bengali Hindu-reformist movement *Brahmo Samāj*, is a good example of the potential turning of an ardent advocacy of science into an advocacy of a political ideology: Roy had been an outspoken admirer of Benito Mussolini (executed 1945) and the Italian fascist movement.[202] A strong scienticist mindset is visible also in Muḥammad ʿInāyatallāh 'al-Mashriqī' (d. 1383/1963), the most prominent and explicit camp-follower of European Fascism among Indian Muslims, who studied, among other things, mathematics and engineering at Lahore and Cambridge.[203] Mashriqī's emphasis on body-politics and, linked to it, on hygiene[204] resembled to an astonishing extent the 1938 Resolution of the Congress' National Planning Commission for a eugenic programme that aimed at the restoration of the physical and psychic health of the Indian population.[205]

At the opposing end of those who integrated their scienticism into political thought stood personalities like the technocrat Akśaya Kumār Śāha (d. unknown), member of the Nehrū-headed Congress' National Planning Commission, who spent about a decade in the Soviet Union and enthusiastically followed Stalin's understanding of societal progress by way of scientific and technological advance alone.[206]

3.2) Competing Ideologies

Since man and his mundane affairs had become a point of reference for the establishment and justification of values, all 'knowledge' had to fulfil the criterion of scientificness in order to merit this label. The increasing emergence of political ideologies that one witnesses from the nineteenth century onwards follows consistently from this axiomatic claim.[207] These ideologies sought to enmesh what Michael Freeden called 'political thought-patterns' in political practice and, being mainly group manifestations,[208] they all did—and, in fact, had to—claim universal validity. Consequently, the exclusiveness of the claim that they, and only they, were able to advance society on a defined scientific basis prevented the possibility of peaceful co-existence and was thus the reason behind the fierce competition between ideologies that evolved next to each other.

It is therefore somewhat surprising that, despite their claims of universal validity, in reality most political ideologies—at least initially—did not reach beyond the confines of single nations. Indeed, 'development', the concept at the core of almost all political ideologies, was first of all understood in the context of nation-building and was thus confined in its scope of application. Hence, it appears that there was a clear contradiction between the claims of universal validity of ideologies and their confinement to a national framework. Realising that political philosophers in the Age of Enlightenment understood the 'nation' as the necessary nucleus of a universal society, however, can dissolve this contradiction.[209] Thus 'nationalism', an ideology that focuses on establishing a locally confined precondition for the universal triumph of whatever ideology, had to equally claim universal validity. Where there is no nation, so the argument runs, there cannot be a way for man's ultimate self-realisation as a social being. It becomes thus understandable why almost all Western political ideologies which found their way into colonial India had necessarily to be seen against the backdrop of an Indian nation-building and had to be appropriated accordingly. In the light of this, 'nationalism' must therefore be considered the very paramount political ideology which assembled all other ideologies, prominently amongst them Communism and Fascism, under its aegis.

a) Communism

Although socialist and communist ideas underwent significant changes over time and in different regional contexts, they can nonetheless all be traced back to the single root of Marx' dialectical materialism. Setting out from the idea of development in Romantic and idealist philosophies, and following also the Hegelian idea of a dialectic of alienation and reconciliation, Marx turned the Hegelian system upside down by stressing the decisive impact of political and economic conditions on man. Rather than Hegel's 'world spirit' (*Weltgeist*) that permeates history, it is now man's multifarious dependencies from the material world that determines his development. Although these dependencies cannot be overcome, the resulting political and economic conditions can and—this is the Hegelian legacy in Marx—in fact will necessarily be.[210]

Marx's investigation into the history of humankind, reduced to a study of the history of labour and its impact on the development of society, showed that any development was only possible by an intense struggle between those who possess the means of production and those who do not.[211] The bourgeois and capitalist society which Marx himself experienced during his time was considered, largely because of the replacement of manual labour by machines, as the society in which the alienation of the labourer from various historical circumstances, over and above the fruits of his labour, had reached its climax. In such a society it had therefore to be the proletarians who, because they 'have nothing to lose but their chains',[212] have to free themselves from all the economic and political dependencies. It was they who were to (re-)establish a society according to nature in which man is devoid of social and economic constraint and, thus, truly equal.[213]

When, in his later years, Marx turned increasingly to analysing the entwining of political and economic developments, he played a significant part in mobilising for an organised attempt to bring about the historically inevitable abolition of the class barriers. It was this organisational aspect as well as the claim for universalistic validity of the Marxian theory that had an important impact on the history of the organisation in a party as the vanguard in what was perceived as 'revolutionary world process': at the forefront of this development stood Vladimir Ilyich Lenin (d. 1924) who had been decisively responsible for forging the still pretty much philosophical Marxian theory into a political ideology. The victory of the Bolsheviks in the Russian Civil War, following the October Revolution of 1917, was considered proof of the fact that the historical development which Marx had described—on the basis of his English and Central European experience—took place at more or less the same time all over the world,[214] and sealed the vastly increased role of the Bolshevik Party as 'vanguard of the proletarian'[215] in the universal revolution. From here it was only a short step to the proclamation of the Third International (Comintern) in 1919, which aimed at committing all existing communist parties, wherever they were, to Leninism, the new variety of the Communist ideology.[216] This was the framework under which the first South Asians came into direct contact with communist ideas.

The Impact of the 'Communist Ideology' on Late Colonial South Asia

The earliest history of the emergence of Communist ideas in South Asia runs along two lines. While at the core of one stood the Bengali Narendra Nāth Bhaṭṭāchārya, better known as Mānabendra Nāth Rāy (d. 1954), who was the driving force behind the establishment of the Communist Party of India (CPI) in Tashkent in October 1920,[217] the other is closely linked to the migration of Indian Muslims to Afghanistan and the Ottoman Empire in the aftermath of the First World War and during the Indian Caliphate Movement.[218] In the early 1920s both lines joined briefly, but soon fell apart again on the ground of personal and ideological differences of their leading protagonists.

Growing from anti-British sentiments and starting with politically motivated dacoity,[219] the conversion of Mānabendra Nāth Rāy to Communism owed, according to his own memoirs, to a large extent his acquaintance with the Comintern agent Mikhail M. Borodin (d. 1951) during his exile in Mexico in late 1918,[220] while, interestingly, his biographer Samaren Roy attributes this also to a growing taste for Western thought and lifestyle.[221] Be that as it may, it was Borodin who persuaded Rāy to accompany him to Europe and on to Soviet Russia where he disembarked by the end of 1919. For the Bolsheviks, Rāy became an important asset in their attempt to overcome the embarrassment of the low international attendance at the First Congress of the Comintern in March 1919 in Moscow. Rāy himself provided for this when, still on his way to Russia, he wrote his first programmatic pamphlet, entitled *An Indian Communist Manifesto*, in which he basically applied Leninist revolutionary rhetoric to the Indian colonial situation.[222] Rāy stayed—as 'Moscow's Indian' and tireless worker for the Comintern—until 1928 in Soviet Russia, when his dangerous ideological closeness to the circle around Lev D. Trotsky (Trotskij assassinated 1940) and Nikolai I. Bukharin (executed 1938) caused him to flee the political purges of the CPSU (*čistki*) under Josif V. Stalin (d. 1954).[223] Interestingly, Rāy's bulky memoirs, finished shortly before his death in 1954, break off right before these incidents and thus did not leave any trace of blemish on Stalin.

Parallel to Rāy's ideological development, the other line in the emergence of Communist thought in late colonial India owed its origin to the attempts to expatriate Indian Muslims in Afghanistan and the Ottoman Empire to gain the widest possible support of politically still sovereign Muslim governments and even Britain's non-Muslim enemies during the First World War for, as they saw it, a *jihād* against the British in India. Therefore, soon after the October Revolution and the Treaty of Brest-Litovsk between the Bolsheviks and the Central Powers, various delegations travelled to Moscow to elicit whether support could be expected from the newly established regime in Russia. The first important one of South Asians took place in early December 1918 by the two brothers Muḥammad ʿAbd al-Jabbār (d. unknown) and ʿAbd al-Sattār Khayrī (d. unknown) from Delhi, who had both studied in Beirut until the outbreak of the First World War and were now based in Istanbul.[224] ʿAbd al-Jabbār especially had already earlier developed affinities to Leftism, given that he attended the International Socialist Congresses in Stuttgart in 1907 and, after the disintegration of the Second (Socialist) International, in Stockholm in 1917.[225] While in Soviet Russia, the Khayrī brothers delivered a long speech to the All Russian Central Executive Committee (*Vserossijskij zentral'nyj ispolnitel'nyj komitet*) in which they assured the Bolshevik leadership on behalf of the Indian Muslims that India was on the eve of a similar proletarian revolution like the one a year earlier in Russia.[226]

Only one year later, in March 1919, the Afghan ruler Amānallāh Khān (d. 1379/1960), who soon after his accession to the throne had declared war against Britain, dispatched a delegation of *muhājirūn* to Moscow to establish permanent relations with the Bolsheviks.[227] The delegation was led by Mawlānā Muḥammad Barakatallāh (d. 1346/1927) and included, among others, ʿAbd al-Rabb Peshawarī (d. unknown). Peshawarī and his associates soon dissociated themselves from Barakatallāh, because the anti-British sentiments of the former had apparently been rooted more in pan-Islamic than in Communist ideals.[228] In February 1920 ʿAbd al-Rabb and his companions established the Indian Revolutionary Association (*Inqilābīyūn-i Hind*; InRA) in Tashkent,[229] the first Indian Communist association that gained open recognition by the Bolshevik leader:

> I am glad to hear that the principles of self-determination and the liberation of oppressed nations from exploitation by foreign and native capitalists, proclaimed by the Workers' and Peasants' Republic, have met with such a ready response among progressive Indians, who are waging a heroic fight for freedom. The working masses of Russia are following with unflagging attention the awakening of the Indian workers and peasants. The organisation and discipline of the working people and their perseverance and solidarity with the working people of the world are an earnest of ultimate success. We welcome the close alliance of Moslem and non-Moslem elements. We sincerely want to see this alliance extended to all the toilers of the East. Only when the Indian, Chinese, Korean, Japanese, Persian, and Turkish workers and peasants join hands and march together in the common cause of liberation—only then will decisive victory over the exploiters be ensured. Long live a free Asia![230]

Given the unstable political situation in Russia—and especially in Muslim Central Asia—at that point in time it is not surprising that the propaganda machinery of the Bolsheviks exploited their link with ʿAbd al-Rabb's organisation to the widest possible extent and styled themselves, corresponding to the aims of the young Comintern, patron of all Communist organisations worldwide.[231]

In his unconditional admiration of the Bolsheviks, ʿAbd al-Rabb met with Mānabendra Nāth Rāy who, in turn, was the most important mediator between the Bosheviks and their Indian sympathisers, and was highly instrumental in winning over a considerable contingent of the second wave of *muhājirūn* to the Communist cause.[232] Soon, however, ʿAbd al-Rabb and Rāy fell out with each other, mainly because the former regarded the pan-Islamic ideals as still valid, even within a Communist framework.[233] Rāy, on the other hand, followed verbatim Lenin's urge for 'the need to combat Pan-Islamism and similar trends, which strive to combine the liberation movement against European and American imperialism with an attempt to strengthen the positions of the khans, landowners, mullahs, etc.'.[234]

On the other hand, it was the very same document, Lenin's so-called 'Colonial Theses', proclaimed before the Second Congress of the Comintern in July/August 1920, that caused Rāy to publicly challenge Lenin. While only a few years earlier Lenin had claimed that for only scarcely industrialised Tsarist Russia the conditions for a proletarian revolution were nonetheless given, he later basically returned to pristine Marxism by stressing that the various colonised 'Eastern' people had yet to overcome medieval feudalism by a bourgeois-democratic revolution which, in turn, would be inevitable for providing the necessary conditions for a proletarian revolution.[235] Rāy countered Lenin and developed in the following years a theoretical framework that allowed for a proletarian revolution in colonial India, thus arguing for a reinterpretation of the Communist ideology in the light of variant regional circumstances.[236] This way, the Rāyist variety of Communism provided the theoretical tools to, on the one hand, conceive the proletarian revolution within a national framework, thus anticipating Stalin's suspension of the primacy of the proletarian world revolution over the national development of socialism by utilising a deliberately distorted reading of Trotsky's 'law of uneven development',[237] while on the other hand, Rāy also upheld the Trotskyite core theory of the 'permanent revolution'[238] which provided him with a theoretical framework for the possibility of a proletarian revolution in colonial India.

The integration of the Communist ideology, be it whole or in parts, into the Indian nationalist discourse opened up possibilities for further appropriation, increasingly also by a less radical spectrum within the movement for India's independence. Inspired much more by classical Marxian theory than by Marxism-Leninism, in 1934 the left wing within the INC organised itself as the Congress Socialist Party (CSP). Although they followed the Comintern's rather awkward vilification of social democracy as 'social fascism', they were nonetheless nearer to socialist movements especially in Britain, such as the Fabian Society and the Independent Labour Party (ILP), than to Communism of the Soviet variety.[239] A main catalyst in this had once more been Nehrū who, in 1929, proclaimed for the first time publicly before the INC in Lahore:

> I must frankly confess that I am a socialist and a republican and am no believer in kings and princes, or in the order which produces the modern kings of industry, who have greater power over the lives and fortunes of men than even kings of old, and whose methods are as predatory as those of the old feudal aristocracy.[240]

Beyond such confessions, however, Nehrū remained conveniently vague with regard to his understanding of socialism. Although this brought him criticism by the orthodox Communists around the CPI,[241] for whom he did not take a clear and radical enough position, it was vital to make his own particular vision of shaping a future Indian nation more widely acceptable by diverse factions within Indian society.[242] Indeed, in his assessment of the failure of Gāndhī's non-cooperation movement, Nehrū strongly opposed the claim of all prevailing ideologies, prominently amongst them Communism, to exclusively represent the truth.[243] Such a position had of course to be opposed by the leadership of the CPI which, in the process of the disruption of the anti-colonial movement, had explicit recourse to the universal dimension of the Communist ideology while firmly rejecting Nehruvian nationalism.[244] In addition, the CPI clearly tried to benefit from the various crises within the independence movement—notably among them the collapse of the Caliphate Movement—by offering to assume the leadership on the grounds that its ideology was neither in need of religious symbolism nor confined to a particular people or community.[245]

Now, although the Communist ideology was not entirely homogeneous, all its varieties had nonetheless a clear foundation in the Marxian theory and an equally clear understanding of the relation of theory and practice. This, in turn, could not as easily have been said for Fascism, the second and competing Western ideology that found its appropriation in the late colonial Indian thought.

b) Fascism

Given the variety of origins of what might be subsumed under the generic term 'Fascism' and even the wide variety of manifestations throughout Europe and beyond, the appropriateness of such a generic concept has been, and still is, hotly debated in Fascism Studies since at least the late 1970s. While 'nominalists' like Ernst Nolte and, more recently, Ze'ev Sternhell and Roger Eatwell were searching for an ideal type that would represent the 'Fascist minimum',[246] they were seriously challenged by 'empirists' like Gilbert Allardyce. To the latter, the various 'Fascisms' that had developed in inter-war Europe were too disparate in origin, mindset and practice to support the creation of a generic definition of 'Fascism'.[247] From an empirical perspective, it looks indeed as if the various and already, in themselves, highly fragmented movements in France, Italy, Germany, Spain, Hungary, Romania and elsewhere differed too strongly from each other on crucial issues.[248] Moreover, there have been strong arguments against the intellectualisation of the various kinds of 'Fascism' because this would be rather 'incommensurable with the spirit and spontaneity of fascist action'.[249] Indeed, the relationship between theory and practice in Fascisms appears much less clear than in Communist ideologies,[250] a fact that contributed considerably to some scholars' reluctance to see 'Fascism' as a distinct ideology, or at least to attribute a single ideological basis to the various movements across Europe.

The search for a 'Fascist minimum' is nonetheless useful, at least for the present work which, after all, is not concerned with the empirical distinctions between the numerous European movements and their internal factions. 'Fascism' appears to have not been received in India and elsewhere in the colonial world first and foremost as a coherent ideal-typical construct, but as a contemporary political and social phenomenon that was understood rather as the realisation of certain ideas prevalent in Europe of the interwar period. To an outsider like Mawdūdī, the question was less whether a somewhat elaborated theory preceded a practice that found its culmination in the reigns of Fascism in Italy and National Socialism in Germany. Probably caught up in the understanding derived from Marxism, an ideological framework appeared in his eyes, like in those of a number of other intellectuals of that period, as a necessary condition for a successful revolution in the true sense of the word.[251] For the majority of political activists in the 'middle-class milieu',[252] it might well hold true that the ideational impact of an elaborate 'Fascist ideology' was much less important than to make use of Fascist symbols, metaphors and practices in their own 'self-expressionist modes of action'.[253] Mawdūdī's theoretical approach however let it appear all the more useful to look a little deeper into what had been understood as 'Fascist ideology' among numerous South Asian intellectuals at this time.

Intellectual Components of a 'Fascist Ideology'

The wide and diverse academic literature on various Fascisms suggests nonetheless a number of common intellectual currents that were absorbed into what was to become the Fascist mindset. This should not suggest, however, that the reception of these ideas took place by careful and well-reflected readings of original philosophical and other academic works. Many of these ideas became widespread by featuring in the large number of popular magazines, which began increasingly to flourish from the mid-nineteenth century onwards[254] and where, in synopses, only certain selected ideas, which were sometimes taken out of their context, were highlighted. The impact of such ideas was reinforced by the so-called '*fin de siècle* pessimism'[255] and even more during the inter-war period, characterised by an intensified lack of confidence in the prevailing strategies for coping with the contingencies of life, which provided further impetus to the belief in a growing despising of Christianity, and, instead, in Nietzsche's call for a 'trans-valuation of all values' (*Umwerthung aller Werthe*).[256] Popular magazines became major speaking outlets for alternative belief systems, many of them rooted in scientism, social and cultural Darwinism, and a new mysticism. Magazines like *Der Volkserzieher* (1897–1936) of the elementary school teacher Wilhelm Schwaner (d. 1944), for example, promoted increasingly national-liberalist and racial-nationalist ideas of a societal reformation in inter-war Germany,[257] while the various magazines of the Deutscher Monistenbund (1906–33), founded by the influential zoologist Ernst H.P.A. Haeckel (d. 1919),[258] propagated Social Darwinism and societal progress through science.[259]

Scienticism as advocated by Haeckel is especially important, as it represents one of the three major intellectual currents which, mostly mediated by popular print media, seemingly contributed to the Fascist mindset: the other two, although to a differing degree, being a certain reading of idealism and life-philosophy.

German idealism was apparently an important reference point for an intellectualised National Socialism. It was the Kantian heritage that began to form a part of the racial theory of Houston Steward Chamberlain (d. 1927), a theory that the Nazi ideologue Alfred Rosenberg (executed 1946) aimed at continuing and completing. It was especially the issue of freedom and determination that both writers picked up from Kant and his epigones, and cast into their racial theory.[260] Meanwhile, Hegelian thought was absorbed and linked with ideas of life-philosophy and scientism in Edwardian Britain, from where it began to impact Indo-Muslim thought.[261] Certain borrowings can also be recognised in the early writings of the French conservative nationalist Charles Maurras (d. 1952), founder of the right-wing Action Française.[262] Interestingly, idealism in its most radical form, namely the philosophy of Fichte and his epistemological arguments for 'fact-act' (*Thathandlung*) as man's only certainty,[263] appears not to have played any significant role in the Fascist mindset. This is surprising to the extent that it could have served as a substantiation of spontaneous action that all Fascist movements have had in common, at least in their formative period. This place, however, had instead been taken by life-philosophy.

It was thus the vitalist ideas of Nietzsche that Nolte and others claim have had a considerable impact on the thought of Mussolini.[264] In Germany, the instrumentalisation of Nietzsche's philosophy by the National Socialists was even more thorough, owing to the efforts of the philosopher's own sister Elisabeth Förster-Nietzsche (d. 1935) who had been instrumental in collating fragments from Nietzsche's estate and publishing them as the independent monograph *Der Wille zur Macht* (1901, expanded edition 1906), and the Nazi philosopher Alfred Baeumler (d. 1968), whose reading of Nietzsche became an authoritative one in the Third Reich.[265] Numerous points in Nietzsche's work, and overall life philosophy, provided for their incorporation into Fascist ideology to such an extent that this particular philosophical current was for a long time, not least thanks to the influential judgement of the Marxist George Lukács (d. 1971) in *Die Zerstörung der Vernunft* from 1954, defamed as the official philosophy of Nazism.[266]

Attractive links refer almost exclusively to the cultural-critical topoi of life-philosophy in all its varieties which would culminate in Nietzsche's demand for a 'trans-valuation of all values'. It sets out from the dichotomy between a pre-rational will, or instinct, and rationality, which reflects upon a dichotomy between a natural culture and a rationally disciplined, hence somewhat artificial culture. In this latter dichotomy lies the anthropology of life-philosophy, namely that men are not, as claimed by the rationalist Enlightenment philosophers, essentially equal. Man is a predator instead, a 'blonde beast', who naturally follows his own will—depending on the degree of following one's own will, again, men fall between those with strong wills and those with weak wills, between those who have a master morality and those with a slave morality. To follow one's own will, however, means struggle. War becomes thus the highest form of life. Only by a constant struggle will man's soul be able to arrive at ever-higher levels of being. It is the act as such, not the reflexion upon it, that reconciles man with life (*Erleben*).[267]

These elements of life-philosophy, be it of the Nietzschean, Bergsonian or Spenglerian variety, could well be utilised to justify Fascism in theory as well as in practice. Nolte has convincingly shown how the idea of 'eternal war' was prevalent in various fascisms,[268] although the enemy might have been different in each case. Nietzsche's idea of master and slave moralities was biologistically turned and then integrated into the racial doctrine of National Socialism.[269] The spontaneity and immediacy of fascist action in Italy corresponded well with Bergsonian intuitionism—Mussolini himself conceded an influence of the French philosopher on him.[270] Life-philosophical historicism *à la* Spengler, which was quite apparently influenced by Nietzschean thought, helped to justify the antagonism between two poles, here abstractly put as 'culture' and 'civilisation', by situating it within a wider temporal framework, and to justify political and cultural imperialism as well as racism and the leader principle.[271]

To come full circle, scienticism, the third important intellectual current that influenced the emergence of Fascist ideology, was closely related to biologism which, in turn, impacted some interpretations of life-philosophy. Scienticism refers on the one hand to the teleological claim of progress, on the other it has served to considerably substantiate the doctrinal racial theory that, according to Nolte, formed the core of the Nazi ideology.[272] One could argue that already Darwin's treatment of the 'races of man',[273] building on—among others—Ernst Haeckel's *Natürliche Schöpfungsgeschichte* from 1868, constituted a scientific proto-racism which was quite distinct from the metaphysical treatment of the racial issue by the Chamberlains and Rosenbergs.[274] Hitler, who, as the Führer, must be assumed to have held the sole monopoly of definition in the Third Reich,[275] appeared more in favour of the populist racialisms of Arthur de Gobineau (d. 1882) and Georges Vacher de Lapouge (d. 1936) which combined biologistic arguments with a rather trivialised cultural and social Darwinism.[276] After all, it must never be forgotten that scientificness was considered the decisive criterion of truth in that period and that therefore all doctrine had to meet this criterion to claim any validity.

Related to this almost unconditional trust in the advancement by science was the euphoria in the belief that man could master nature, a thought that originated in the rapid and profound scientific and technological advances during the Industrial Revolution(s) but was taken to the extreme by various Fascisms. The improvements in the means of warfare, culminating in the invention and production of the first ballistic missile (the so-called V-2 rocket), belong here in the same way as medical experiments on human beings in the course of euthanasia programmes.[277] Last but not least, the 'Final Solution' (*Endlösung*), the industrialised genocide of Jews during the Third Reich, was to a considerable extent rooted in a technicistic euphoria as just a variety of scientism.

There was, however, a fourth intellectual current that affected the emergence and shaping of Fascist ideology, namely Communism, which, as a competing political ideology, became Fascism's diametrically opposed counterpart. The reference to Communism has led scholars like Ernst Nolte even as far as including anti-Marxism as the central criterion of his definition of Fascism.[278] Whether or not there would be Fascism without Marxism will here be left aside. The oppositional references to Marxism or, as it is found in Nazism, to Bolshevism indeed constituted at least a central rhetorical figure within Fascism, a figure that, according to Nolte, was of systematic character.[279] The anti-bourgeois and anti-liberalist stand of Communism, on the other hand, which assigned the proletarian masses a leading role in a universalist revolutionary process, its anti-intellectualism and, finally, its idea of the necessity of a party as the vanguard in this process appeared all quite similar to elements of the Fascist mindset.[280] This somewhat schizophrenic relationship between Fascism and Communism would perhaps help to explain prevalent attempts to define Fascism by negations only:[281] namely, as an ideology that reacted to an initially related other one which, however, had already begun to be put into practice.

The Impact of the 'Fascist Ideology' on Late Colonial South Asia

As already suggested, Fascism, in a variety of its aspects, constituted yet another important role model for either economic or national development besides Socialism. Its impact was even stronger on the attempts of especially the middle class to express themselves in the British India of the early 1930s.[282] The booming national economies of the fascist regime in Italy and National Socialist Germany, as well as autoritarianist Japan, were considered valid alternatives to the Soviet planned economy in overcoming the crisis of the so-called 'Great Depression'.[283] In the search for adequate forms of political and cultural expression, Fascism appeared even more attractive to the still young Indian middle class, be they Hindus or Muslims, than for the equally juvenile working class in British India. Middle class intellectuals of both large religious groups appear to have been equally drawn towards Fascist thought and practices.

The attraction was evidently mutual. Fascist leaders in Italy and Germany were eager to establish closer relations with leading Indian intellectuals, most probably serving their own foreign-policy agenda and attempting to make anti-British allies within the British Empire. Thus, during Nehrū's stay in Switzerland in 1936, Mussolini had his respects paid to him, and despite his openly anti-fascist stand[284] he was nonetheless officially invited to Nazi Germany in the hope of the Nazi leadership that he would revise his views.[285] These sycophancies of Fascist leaders towards Nehrū were not entirely unfounded. After all, there were a number of aspects that made Nehrū appear as if—when properly persuaded—he could be won over to the Fascist 'project'. Already already in 1923, only one year after Mussolini's takeover, Nehrū referred to Fascism as the only working political system in the West besides Bolshevism.[286] While this comment was later interpreted as proof of Nehrū's early anti-fascist position,[287] it is striking that he did not consider liberalism at all, which was much more widely at work in various European countries at that time than Communism or Fascism. A way to solve this seeming puzzle is to consider this omission a deliberate one, suggesting an implicit anti-liberalism, which, in turn, might be interpreted as his rejection of the dominant political system in Britain. In this, Nehrū was quite in line with the European Communists as well as Fascists of whatever shade. Moreover, his above mentioned unconditionally positive attitude towards science and technology in the debate on the future development of India—a counterweight to Gandhism as a possible road to India's future—did to some extent fuel his use of the Spenglerian opposing terms of 'culture' and 'civilisation'. All these points, adding to Nehrū's discernible prominence within the Indian political scene at this time, made it indeed appear worthwhile for Fascist leaders to vie for Nehrū's favour.

Another prominent and influential South Asian intellectual who was courted by Fascist leaders in Europe was Muḥammad Iqbāl. Known for his Germanophilia as well as for being deeply influenced by the life-philosophical thought of Nietzsche and Bergson, he is said to have met Mussolini in 1931, during his stopover in Rome on his way back from the Second Round Table Conference in London.[288] Unlike Nehrū, Iqbāl was full of praise for the Duce, as appears from the poem in his anthology *Bāl-i jibrīl*:

An oddity [*nadrat*] of theory and practice, what thing is it? The taste of revolution;
An oddity of theory and practice, what thing is it? The youth of the nation [*millat kā shabāb*]!
From the oddity of theory and practice—the miracle of life;
From the oddity of theory and practice—a pure ruby!
Rome, the Great! Unchanged had been your heart;
What I see, oh Lord, is it in waking or in dream?
In the spring of the ancient saints—the glory of life;
The prime of life is yours, burning in the chest from the heat of desire [*sūz-i ārzū*]!
Such passion of love! Such desire [*tamannā*]! Such appearance [*nabūd*]!
In the season of the rose [*faṣl-i gul meṇ*] a flower cannot live under a cover!
From songs of longing your vast is filled;
The possession of grace [*raḥmawar*] awaited had the viol of your nature!
Grace [*fayḍ*], whose vision is it? Munificence [*karāmat*], whose is it?
His, whose care [*nigah*] is like the rays of the sun![289]

Driven less by such rather pathetic romanticism, but more by pragmatic considerations was Subhāṣ Chandra Bos (Bose), a leading Congressman and, after his marginalisation and resignation in 1939, founder of the radical left-wing All India Forward Bloc,[290] whose 'Respected Leader' (*netājī*) he remained until his unresolved disappearance in 1945. Having been one of the most outspoken opponents of Gāndhī's vision of India's future and his emphasis on non-violence (*ahiṃsā*) to achieve independence from British rule in the Congress, his advocacy of violent means, as well as his philosophical proclivities,[291] drove him to seek alternative allies in Britain's 'arch-enemies': Nazi Germany, Fascist Italy and autoritarianist Japan. In this pursuit Bose travelled repeatedly to Europe to meet high-ranking officials, including Mussolini and Hitler themselves, as well as prominently with the German foreign minister Joachim von Ribbentrop (executed 1946).[292] Is was however not Bose's 'idealist nationalism'[293] which eventually lead to his political association with Nazi Germany, but rather a pragmatic choice on the basis of the popular wisdom that the enemy of your enemy is your friend.[294]

Unlike Nehrū and Iqbāl who were supposed to be flattered by the courting of the Fascist grandees, and Bose who aligned with Fascism out of pragmatic considerations, other Indian middle class intellectuals were much more willing to absorb at least vital elements of the Fascist ideology and to creatively integrate it into their own ideological outlines. The major proponent of this tendency among Indian Muslims was certainly the already above mentioned 'Ināyatallāh 'al-Mashriqī' who wanted himself to be perceived as an inspiration for Hitler.[295] Moreover, his ideology shows some parallels to Mawdūdī's, which is why it deserves to be treated in a little more detail. In his writings, the most important of which were certainly his interpretation of the Qurʾān *al-Tadhkira* (1924), and the collection of editorials from the monthly *al-Iṣlāḥ*, published in 1931–32 under the title *Ishārāt*,[296] al-Mashriqī attempted to fuse elements of Fascist thought with a populist Islam and thus create something like 'Islamo-Fascism'. To this end and very much in line with a general trend in the exegesis of the Qurʾān at that time, al-Mashriqī attempted a 'scientific' approach to the text of the revelation,[297] but, unlike most of his counterparts, he extensively incorporated militant Social Darwinist ideas. These ideas, in turn, he related to political history, showing that the idea of the 'survival of the fittest' (*baqā-yi aṣlaḥ*)—derived from al-Mashriqī's biologistic reading of Qurʾānic verses like, for example, 2:30 and 24:55[298]—was corroborated by the course of world history. To him, the success story of Islam in its formative period owed to the fact that Islam, as revealed in the Qurʾān, was essentially a religion of war. Its decline was therefore consistently related to the gradual abandonment of this understanding,[299] while the Nazis must be appreciated as those whose ideas and actions appeared to be much more in line with the original Qurʾānic implications than those of the Muslims in al-Mashriqī's time.[300]

The only remedy to the weakness of the contemporary Muslims was a radical return to a strict corporeal regime that emphasised all military virtues: cleanliness, discipline and manliness.[301] The platform for the realisation of this was the paramilitary *Khāksār* movement, founded by al-Mashriqī in 1930.[302] This movement epitomised the activist aspect of Fascism that is usually attributed to the Italian variety. According to Daechsel, action became 'fetishised', thus almost an end in itself, implying that for the majority of followers the movement's attraction lay more in the 'ability to produce public spectacles, which encapsulated the fruits of their methodologies of self-purification',[303] than in an intellectual comprehension of al-Mashriqī's ideology.[304]

Counterparts to al-Mashriqī and his *Khāksār* can be found at around the same time within the Hindu middle class milieu as well. The most important one is without doubt the RSS, founded in 1925 by Dr Keśav Balīrām Heḍgevār (d. 1940). Initially set up in critical response to the more culturalistic *Ārya Samāj*, the RSS was transformed under the presidency of Vināyak Damudār 'Vīr' Savārkar (d. 1966) into an explicitly militant religious organisation that demonstrably drew inspiration from Fascist ideology.[305] The history of this transfer and relationship has so far rarely been studied,[306] but there is—especially in the writings of Savārkar—a clear indication of a highly selective reception and adaptation of Fascist elements into the RSS ideology.

The respective European model from which the various ideological components of the RSS drew was however dependent on the personal preferences of the RSS's leading thinkers. Thus, Bālakṛṣṇa Śivarām Muṃje, one of those who had unrestrainedly supported the original 'Nehru Report' of 1928, was more inspired by the Italian example. Having visited Italy in 1931 and met the Duce in person, the ontological militarism of Italian fascism, resembling a popular understanding of Heraclitus' famous dictum that 'war is the father of all things' (*pólemos pántōn mèn patēr éstí*), demonstrably had the most decisive impact on Muṃje's thought.[307] In contrast, Heḍgevār, Savārkar and finally Mādhav Sādaśiv Golvalkar (d. 1973) were much more influenced by National Socialism's racialist thought. Unlike the case of Subhāṣ Chandra Bose, whose direct dealings with Nazi grandees are well documented, there is so far little more than circumstantial evidence that the parallels in the National Socialist and RSS ideologies are due to a direct encounter. Tempting as it is to draw a direct line of reception, it appears more likely that the racialism of the RSS owes first and foremost to Social Darwinist and eugenic ideas most widespread in European and North American thought of the time.[308] There was, however, a general awareness of the events in Europe at the time, over and above Italy and Germany, where Fascism and Nazism appeared a quite successful alternative to liberal democracy.[309]

What united, however, the various advocates of a shaped and understood Fascism, were they Hindus or Muslims, and helped elements of Fascist ideology to take root in the Indian environment was, first, a fervent and total rejection of Gāndhī's politics of non-violence as a means in the Indian struggle for independence, but, second, a feeling of communal superiority. More precisely, these advocates of Fascism shared the revulsion of Gāndhī's strategy with other nationalist currents, such as the rather socialist and secularist approach of the Nehrū faction within the Congress or the leadership of the AIML, the element of communal superiority, most often clad in a racialist garb, was distinctive to the camp-followers of Fascism. This may explain why other religiously grounded political visions, prominently among them Mawdūdī's top-down model of an Islamic polity, had to devote much more effort to positioning themselves towards these rather separatist forms of nationalism, based on an assumed natural distinction in various nations within one and the same territory.

In the following chapters, therefore, Mawdūdī's model shall be reconstructed step by step, not least so as to be able to better appreciate its eventual impact, or at least the impact of individual elements, on the development of contemporary Muslim political thought in South Asia and beyond. Taking seriously his aspiration of systematisation in unfolding his outline, this will be pursued in three successive steps. The first, comprising of the first chapter in section C, consists in Mawdūdī's own endeavour to situate his outline in an idealized historical context. This approach was meant to relate his project to a succession of more or less successful attempts to religious reformation, going all the way back to the early days of Islam. Hereby, Mawdūdī was able to position himself at the culmination point of an Islamic history of revivalism; at the same time he would have wanted to take the wind out of the sails of any possible critic of the rather unorthodox way in which he developed his outline. In the second step, the discussion of which takes up the following four chapters of section C, this outline is unfolded as an Islamic 'Theory of Practice' that Mawdūdī had claimed was developed in a deductive manner. Chapter D, finally, constitutes the third step and will investigate into how Mawdūdī envisioned this theory to be put into practice.

3

FORGING A SYSTEM

1) The Location of the System

A prerequisite for the reconstruction of Mawdūdī's attempt to provide an alternative ideological outline is a closer understanding of the wider spatial and temporal framework in which his system had been situated. His rather schematic conception of history, albeit not presented in a systematic and comprehensive manner before 1940, was well designed to serve exactly such a framework. The lateness of this systematic development of this particular conception might be explicable by the fact that, on the one hand, it resulted from Mawdūdī's longer-term analysis of the current situation of Muslims in general, and in British India in particular, sparked off by his retrospective critical assessment of the Indian Caliphate Movement of the early 1920s; while on the other, this conception appears to have not least been a result of Mawdūdī's critical analysis of other prevalent ideologies and their respective conceptions of history, epitomised in the popular concept of societal 'development'.

While Mawdūdī by no means dismissed the idea of 'development' or 'advancement', his claim to provide an ideology on a basis entirely different from those of all other prevalent ideologies made it almost necessary for him to also derive the cornerstones for his conception of 'development' from within his normative Islamic framework of reference. In this regard, Mawdūdī utilised the Qur'ānic epochal term 'jāhiliyya' and linked it to the concept of 'renewal' as it is found among the authoritative statements of the Prophet. Mawdūdī radically reinterpreted both conceptual terms in a highly creative, although—as we will see—rather problematic manner, to fit them into his ideological outline. In order to better comprehend the extent of these reinterpretations, first a cursory glance at the classical usages of both terms seems appropriate.

1.1) History between Ignorance and Islam

a) The Natural State—The Concept of 'jāhiliyya' in Classical Times[1]

Referring to a period of ignorance, heathendom and polytheism (*shirk*) before man came to know about the conclusive revelation of God's fundamental oneness and His commandments, the concept of 'jāhiliyya' was understood as the antonym of 'Islam' already in the earlier periods of Islamic history.[2] Thus, history was perceived as two-parted, which corresponded with the history of salvation as outlined in a number of Qur'ānic verses where the term *jāhiliyya* is used in this regard.[3] Both periods, *jāhiliyya* and Islam, are connected by the time of the prophetic mission of Muḥammad (*nubuwwa*).

Nonetheless, in Islamic historiography the epoch of *jāhiliyya* was not seen as monolithic, but rather internally stratified. The dichotomous periodisation had to comply with the Islamic narrative that the Qur'ānic revelation was just a repetition of all earlier divine revelations to man. Thus, mainly with a recourse to the Qur'ānic verse 33:33, where the term 'first/old *jāhiliyya*' (*al-jāhiliyya al-ūlá*) appears, the period of *jāhiliyya* became commonly divided into an earlier phase which comprises the period between the prophets Adam and Noah, or from Noah to Henoch (Idrīs), and a later one that covers the time between Jesus and Muḥammad.[4] Although it was in the Islamic context that the term *jāhiliyya* received its distinct meaning, the term had already been in use in pre-Islamic Arabia.

In view of the early Arabic meaning of *jāhil*, it was Ignaz Goldziher who understood *jāhiliyya* as a time of savageness, but not as a weakness of character or ignorance. Instead, the term is used as an antonym of *ḥalīm* (mild, docile) and refers to a wild and impetuous character, which, according to the values prevalent in pre-Islamic Arabian tribal society, was not necessarily considered a bad quality. Muḥammad will certainly have known of this early Arabic meaning—the profound changes that his mission brought to the social fabric of the Arabian peninsula supported the creation of a dichotomy between the past and the present, each one defined rather as a particular but antagonistic state (*ḥāl*) of societal development. According to Shepard, the term *jāhiliyya* as used in the Qurʾān refers then in the first place to the moral principles of those who were opposed to the Prophet and the young proto-*umma*.[5] As such, *jāhiliyya* relates to attributes which were seen as diametrically opposed to the ethical concepts of Islam, namely those that put an emphasis on tribal belonging and, resulting from it, tribal pride which, in turn, was seen as responsible for tribal feuding and blood vengeance, but also the worship of tribal deities.[6] By contrast, Islam proposed an unconditional equality of man by birth, derived from them being all creatures of the One God and, therefore, being obliged to follow His revealed Law only. Obedience to this divinely decreed law was of extraordinary importance to guarantee social cohesion in a community which was—at least ideally—not any longer based on descent (*nasab*). Adherence to the new faith constituted from now on the criterion for social belonging, religious virtue (*sābiqa*) the only valid criterion for any vertical social mobility. In this constellation, the originally rather value-free if not positively connoted term 'jāhil' and its derivatives underwent thus a semantic shift already in the early days of the Muslim community, and became an antithetical term to 'Islam'.[7] Thus the developments support Koselleck's proposition that what he calls 'asymmetrical counterterms' is always formed and utilised by conflicting groups in situations where the space is too confined to allow for avoiding conflict by evading each other.[8] While initially the term may have indeed been understood rather as designation of a certain period in time, from the time of the Qurʾānic revelation onward it became increasingly charged also with qualitative meanings. This way, it developed increasingly into an 'asymmetrical counterterm' to 'Islam', both designations now epitomising a particular constitutionality of a given society.

Although the 'asymmetrical counterterms' were morphed into the dichotomous conception of history divided into a time of *jāhiliyya* and a time of Islam, their function as epochal terms had seemingly never really been abandoned and it was thus left to the preferences of the respective writers to highlight either aspect of the terms. This was made easier because while the advent of Islam caused the most dramatic changes to the ethical and religious mindset of the traditional Arab tribal society, some of the old ways seemed to have survived even among those who had embraced the new religion from an early stage, as the authoritative texts of Islam testify. Thus, the renowned medieval jurist, Ashʿarite theologian and

Qurʾānic commentator ʿAbdallāh ibn ʿUmar al-Bayḍāwī (d. 685/1286), for example, apparently acknowledged the temporal aspect of 'jāhiliyya' in his interpretation of the mentioned verse 33:33. On the other hand, when he suggested a differentiation between the 'old *jāhiliyya*' and a later one (*al-jāhiliyya al-ukhrá*), the latter being considered a relapse into heathendom *after* the prophetic mission of Muḥammad,[9] Bayḍāwī clearly acknowledged the meaning of the term as a description of a certain state, as a '*jāhiliyya* of iniquity [*fusūq*] against Islam'.[10] According to this, 'Islam' and 'jāhiliyya' may indeed exist at the same time, yet the terms refer to different cultural levels associated with succeeding periods.[11]

The understanding of *jāhiliyya* as a moral state that persists among Muslims had been perpetuated through the ages especially by certain conservative religious circles, over and above Ḥanbalī scholars like Ibn Taymiyya in the thirteenth and Muḥammad ibn ʿAbd al-Wahhāb in the eighteenth century.[12] It was especially the latter who characterised the Muslims of his time as living in a state of *jāhiliyya*, because they had adopted beliefs and practices which, according to Ibn ʿAbd al-Wahhāb and his followers, were not supported by the authoritative texts of Islam. This general thrust appears to have continued well into the nineteenth and early twentieth centuries, as is evident in the writings of scholars like Muḥammad ʿAbduh and Rashīd Riḍā. In their incomplete Qurʾānic commentary, as well as the journal *al Manār* between 1897 and 1935, mouthpiece of the Salafiyya movement, considerable space was devoted to a reassessment of the relationship between *jāhiliyya* and Islam. Now, however, secular tendencies in the wake of Western colonialism were added to the markers of the state of *jāhiliyya*.[13] From here, it had only been a short step to Mawdūdī's own reformulation of this epochal-*cum*-state descriptive term.

b) A Spectre is Haunting the Muslim World—Mawdūdī's Reinterpretation of the Concept of 'jāhiliyya'

Although Mawdūdī's conception of *jāhiliyya* can be seen as rooted in the outlined tradition, he differs from the majority of his predecessors insofar as he understood this term now exclusively in a typological manner and not any more, even remotely, as an epochal designation. Stripped bare of every historical connotation, Mawdūdī was able to approach the meanings of 'jāhiliyya' and 'Islam' by a recourse to temporally invariant philosophical core questions, known to us since Greek antiquity, but asked even more vividly in Kant's *Kritik der reinen Vernunft*: What can I know? What ought

I to do? What may I hope?[14]—questions that may be subsumed in the over-arching one, asked later in his *Anthropologie in pragmatischer Absicht*, namely: What is man?[15]

According to Mawdūdī, there are various possible answers to these essential questions. They would have, however, to be scrutinised one by one with regard to their compatibility with the asked questions and their respective potential to answer them, including their characteristics and consequences, and finally to be classed within the narrow dichotomy of 'jāhiliyya' and 'Islam'. Thus, while at first glance this suggests a rather inductive approach, Mawdūdī's preconceptions, derived from his distinct reading of the authoritative texts, prove that this was not really the case: the cases which Mawdūdī had selected for discussion and on which he had certainly spent a lot of ink would all meet his distinct definition of 'jāhiliyya':

> The meaning of 'jāhiliyya' in Islam comprises every course of action [*har ṭarz-i ʿamal*] which runs counter to the Islamic culture, Islamic morals and conduct, or Islamic mentality; and 'jāhiliyyat-i ūlá' means all those evils [*burāʾiyāṇ*] in which the people of Arabia and every other people the whole was involved in.[16]

What is clear from this definition is that for Mawdūdī 'jāhiliyya' came indeed to mean exclusively 'ignorance' towards God, His Prophet and the revelation, or, for the pre-Islamic period, 'lawlessness'.[17] In a keynote address on the matter, delivered in February 1941 to the Council of Islamic Studies at the Islāmiyya College of Peshawar, Mawdūdī linked his definition of 'jāhiliyya' to various possible answers to the above philosophical core questions, each one of which would qualify for a distinct form of 'jāhiliyya'. The first one of these would be 'sheer ignorance' (*jāhiliyyat-i khāliṣa*), characterised by solely 'relying on one's own senses [*apne ḥawās par iʿtimād kar le*] [...], and forming an opinion on all matters on this basis alone'.[18] The second form of *jāhiliyya* which Mawdūdī distinguished appears to be somewhat related to the first one, since 'a result is derived from the contemplation over sensations, together with imagination [*wahm*] and analogical reasoning [*qiyās*]'.[19] Under this second form of *jāhiliyya* Mawdūdī subsumed polytheism, as well as monasticism and finally every pan- and panentheist tendency, epitomised in the ʿAṭṭārian credo 'All is He (*hama ūst*)'.[20] Both forms of *jāhiliyya*, in their respective manifestations, stand naturally in stark contrast to 'Islam', where 'as solution to all these issues one accepts what the prophets, who claim to have direct knowledge of the Truth [*ḥaqīqat*], offer'.[21]

'Sheer ignorance', according to Mawdūdī, indicates a state in which there is no transcendent sovereignty that could serve as source of knowledge and guidance. In this state, man would be little more than an animal species, whose birth and existence are purely accidental and have no higher meaning; and what goes for man, goes, more or less, for the whole universe. Because of the absence of any transcendent law, which would help regulate man's life, he becomes his own and autonomous master, free from any responsibility and accountability to anyone else. The only benchmark for his actions is the increase in his individual benefits and the satisfaction of his needs.[22]

To allow under these conditions, nonetheless, for social coexistence, man has to set up rules and regulations by himself. By doing so, he styles himself the ultimate authority to regulate his own and his fellow men's conduct. Consequently, misconduct in this world is only judged and sanctioned by thisworldly courts, because each and every act and its consequences are confined to this world; an otherworldly trial is not considered in this conception.[23]

According to Mawdūdī, a particular model of society resulted from this exclusively this-worldly and individualistic attitude. Within this model, those people who are best able to see their respective individual interests through would then fill the leading positions. Consequently, the weak and powerless would have to obey—society would be ruled, as Mawdūdī explicitly stated, according to the Machiavellian principle of immoralism in ruthless pursuit of one's own interest in the field of politics.[24] Because of the fact that such a society aims solely at the maximisation of individual benefits, it leads consequently to feudalistic and capitalist societies. Strangely, though, Mawdūdī had even Communism counted among those societies based solely on the pursuit of individual interests, largely perhaps because 'sometimes even the proletarians [*mazdūr*] will erect their dictatorship by disruption'.[25] All these models of society, he concluded, do not contribute to social justice (*ʿadl*) and a responsible attitude towards the world:

> The basic conduct of every individual in this society rests on the conviction [*taṣawwur*] that the world and all its wealth is a fully laden table [*khʷān-i yaghmā*] and man is free to lay his hand on it at will [*ḥasb-i manshāʾ*] and whenever possible.[26]

The philosophical core question regarding the meaning of life, however, cannot sufficiently be answered by the approach of 'sheer ignorance'. Judging from its consequences, Mawdūdī concluded that this approach does not at all correspond with reality.[27]

A similar result Mawdūdī conceded to approaches that attempt to answer the philosophical core questions by a combination of contemplation over sensations, imagination and analogical reasoning, which all fall under the second form of *jāhiliyya*. As the first of these approaches, Mawdūdī considered polytheism (*shirk*), which he saw as each and every this-worldly phenomenon related to some transcendent beings responsible for these phenomena, so that the fortune or misfortune of man depends entirely on the pleasure or disapproval of these beings. Polytheism, so Mawdūdī wrote, is the idea of a supreme deity (*allāh*) and numerous subordinated ones. This, in turn, would inevitably lead to a division of power and sovereignty.[28] By means of conjecturing about sensual data and attempts at analogous reasoning, man tries to identify the transcendent beings which would be based entirely on these particular and rather uncertain data. Of interest here is that Mawdūdī attributed this approach towards the world, and to answering the philosophical core questions, also to all those people who are blessed with a divine revelation but have nonetheless soon resorted to their old ways. Here we find a clear echo of the earlier authoritatively grounded view that a considerable number of Muslims had relapsed into heathendom already at around the time of death of the Prophet Muḥammad.[29] Like especially the Ḥanbalite scholars among them, Mawdūdī branded popular customs among Muslims closely associated with Sufism, as well as Shiite Islam, as polytheistic.[30]

This fact is quite important, as it reflects clearly the South Asian situation and can to some extent be considered as Mawdūdī's contribution to the heated debate over the permissibility of certain elements in Sufi practices in the subcontinent and beyond that arose in the early nineteenth century and are continued to some extent until today.[31] These elements, which are also widespread in mainstream Shiite Islam, include the pious visitations of graves of deceased Muslim dignitaries, including the prophets and their family members, and the related practice of pleading for intercession (*tawassul*). Mawdūdī however took the legal and theological argument of his precursors even further by scrutinising the social and political consequences of that issue, and he concluded that these practices would inevitably lead to similar results to what he had labelled 'sheer ignorance', namely the dominance of man over man.

Here too, however, Mawdūdī went beyond the traditional argument, and, in subsuming various ideologies originating from Western thought under 'polytheism', he appeared rather close to more contemporary thinkers like Muḥammad 'Abduh and Rashīd Riḍā. The way Mawdūdī arrived at this conclusion is of the utmost importance, as it enabled him to develop his particular understanding of *jāhiliyya* only by a high degree of abstraction from the Islamic authoritative framework. This abstraction, along with the otherwise much despised analogous reasoning, made it thus possible for Mawdūdī to perceive *shirk* also expressed in political and economic phenomena like 'nationalism', 'racism', 'imperialism', 'capitalism' and 'class struggle',[32] in short, every social and political expression based on the inequality of man.

Although, so far, Mawdūdī's argument revolved around man's self-imposed sovereignty over this earth, flight from this world is not considered an appropriate solution. Asceticism or monasticism (*rahbāniyyat*), the renunciation of everything worldly and the negation of all physical needs as the only way to liberate the soul and find deliverance from any worldly suffering, is for Mawdūdī, who might have had the example of his own father's brief but intense foray into ascetic Sufism in mind,[33] just another form of 'ignorance'. Because the individual is alienated from society, individualism is once more promoted which, in its final consequence, will again create only opportunities for the suppression of man by man.[34]

That Mawdūdī referred here once again to Sufism is especially remarkable, because his criticism was usually not directed towards elements within the Islamic religious tradition, but rather—consistently with his goal to develop an alternative ideology—towards the other ideologies prevalent in the early twentieth century. That he did nevertheless vigorously attack especially Sufism could however well be explained in relation to his wider agenda in which there was only little room for a rather inward oriented piety.[35] It was not least over this question that he was soon clashing with leading representatives from among the *'ulamā'*, first and foremost those who were closely associated with the *Tablīghī Jamā'at* (TJ).[36] Indeed, 'Sufism' appears to have served as an ideological combat term for Mawdūdī, symbolising what Ahmed Mukarram has aptly labelled a 'guidance'-oriented theological as well as an action-theoretical paradigm, which is almost diametrically opposed to Mawdūdī's own 'governance'-oriented position.[37] It is therefore hardly surprising that the third subspecies of the second form of *jāhiliyya* that Mawdūdī discussed, namely the pan- and panentheistic approach to answer the philosophical core questions, was once more closely related to Sufi thought. Although, according to Mawdūdī, this approach assumes that nothing exists out of and by itself, but all is really a creation by the One God, it implies nonetheless that 'all existing things [*tamām mawjūdāt*] are the outer manifestations of the one being [*ek hī wujūd kā ẓuhūr-i khārijī*], only this being exists, everything else does not'.[38] This belief, so Mawdūdī argued, completely disempowers man and reduces him to a puppet of his Creator. Consequently man loses his initiative and becomes passive and ignorant, and follows freely his own personal desires alone, without responsibly calculating the consequences of his actions.[39]

From this analysis, Mawdūdī concluded that neither approach was suited to answer the philosophical core questions on the meaning of life in a satisfying way. All the approaches discussed thus far, so he said, are based on ignorance (*jāhiliyya*) and not on knowledge (*ʿilm*), hence their social and political consequences. Confronted with an unfamiliar and incomprehensible world, Mawdūdī conceded, man might have originally existed in a state of ignorance and disorientation and therefore accepted as real only what he could absorb with his senses.[40] In the wake of the negative effects that result, however, man would eventually have to resort to the only possible alternative, namely to accept the message of the prophets of God—first and foremost among them Muḥammad—as the only valid explanations of reality. This concept, labelled the 'Islamic Path' (*islāmī ṭarīqa*), is, according to Mawdūdī, a scientific one, which provides answers to all questions of life in a reality-compatible and consistent manner:

> Whenever you are confronted with such a situation [*ṣurat-i ḥāl*] your first endeavour is to search for a person who claims to know a solution. Then, on the basis of circumstantial evidence [*qarāʾin se*], you seek to satisfy yourself regarding whether or not such a person is trustworthy [*qābil-i iʿtimād*]. Then you go ahead under this guidance. When it is proven by experience [*tajriba se thābit ho jātā he*] that the information he provided has not led to any negative result whilst you acted on it, then you are convinced that this person possessed the requisite knowledge and that this information [*maʿlūmāt*] supplied by him [...] was sound [*ṣaḥīḥ*]. This is a scientific way, and if there is not any other scientific way, then this must be the only correct one for formulating one's viewpoint [*rāʾy*].[41]

Clearly, the way in which Mawdūdī depicted the discovery of 'Islam' as the only way to provide satisfying answers to all of man's urgent questions and, moreover, a guideline to act in a contingent world reminds one strongly of an experimental design. This, along with the fact that Mawdūdī tried to sell his solution—'Islam'—as a scientifically verified insight, is clear proof that Mawdūdī moved well within the confines of the—Western-dominated—contemporary discourse on science as the only acceptable means to generate truths. It also shows that, even though his alternative outline would consistently have to be based on an essentially different framework of reference from all other competing ideologies, Mawdūdī appeared to be much a child of his time, rather than being able to escape the globally shared trust in societal advancement by the insights of science alone. That his claim for scientificness was, in fact, more an appeal to common sense than anything else, may remain open to conjecture.

Because 'Islam', as envisioned by Mawdūdī, is an all-embracing path, it can—by definition—never coexist with *jāhiliyya*. This fact is quite significant, as it explains why in some sermons delivered to Punjabi villagers during the formative phase of the later JiI in the late 1930s or early 1940s[42] Mawdūdī constrained his conception of 'jāhiliyya' even further when he moved it close to the antagonistic concept of unbelief (*kufr*): 'Unbelief means refusal to obey God; Islam means [...] refusal to accept any path, law [*qānūn*] or order which stands against the guidance sent down from God.'[43] The differences in Mawdūdī's varying portrayals of the dichotomy of 'jāhiliyya' and 'Islam' is quite enlightening, as it reveals already here one of the core dilemmas in Mawdūdī's entire systematic outline. While, on the one hand, he allowed for the trial-and-error-approach of the experimental sciences, consistent with the basic premise of man's ability to make deliberate choices, on the other he dogmatically demanded the unconditional acceptance of what he considered to be ultimately true. This irresolvable dilemma that, as we shall see in the following chapters, pervades his entire systematic outline appeared every now and then on the surface. It has, however, been summed up well in the following passage:

> One way to reach a decision in every eventuality has been laid down in the Book of God and in the Sunna of His Messenger other ways are prompted by the desires of your lower self [*nafs kī kh*ʷ*āhishāt*], by the ways of your ancestors, or by man-made laws. If one discharges the way that God has laid down and decides for some other way, then he basically chooses the path of unbelief. If one had chosen this manner for every aspect of his life then he is a complete unbeliever [*kāfir*].[44]

The looming equation here of *jāhiliyya* with unbelief might be seen as perhaps one of the most consequential potentialities in Mawdūdī's ideology, a potential that was later realised mainly in the course of its selective reception especially in the Arabic-speaking world.[45] Moreover, the *de facto* equation of *jāhiliyya* with *kufr*—the latter being a term that, unlike the former, is inseparably linked to legal effect[46]—is a clear indication that, on the one hand, 'Islam' for Mawdūdī was not just one of a number of possible choices, nor was it only the best of all choices, but it was the only choice to be considered legitimate. One the other hand, it is once more proof of Mawdūdī's exclusively typological understanding of *jāhiliyya*: as the antithesis of Islam, characterised only by man's non-compliance with the revealed law (*sharīʿa*), it can well exist synchronous to Islam, which explains why classical exegetes like al-Bayḍāwī stressed the fact that 'traces of ignorance' (*amruʾ jāhiliyya*) had survived within the Muslim community.[47]

There might however be a favourable explanation for why Mawdūdī—despite fully acknowledging the fact that God had endowed man not only with the ability to act but also with reason (*ʿaql*) and free will (*ikh̲tiyār*) in order to distinguish between good and evil—had quite soon adopted this rather dogmatic and uncompromising position: after all, there seemed to be a considerable impact of Nietzschean 'ethical life-philosophy'[48] on the rather traditional Islamic anthropology, an impact that had been made quite acceptable in South Asian Muslim circles not least through the intellectual activities of Muḥammad Iqbāl. This second anthropological provision, hardly justifiable by a recourse to the authoritative texts of Islam, stipulates that man is essentially a selfish, fallible and weak creature that loves to take the line of the least resistance and strives mainly for personal gain, a fact that is even repeatedly addressed in the authoritative texts of Islam.[49] Man's lower drives need therefore to be rationally disciplined, in order to make social co-operation possible in the first place. The conflicting relationship between man's drives and his rationality had been a, if not *the*, central element in Nietzsche's philosophical thought for which he was applying the beautiful metaphors of the Dionysian and the Apollonian, epitomising the two principles of free-spirited and arty pleasure and its disciplining reason.[50] Mawdūdī, who must certainly have got a whiff of that Nietzschean spirit that was around at the time, acknowledged the necessity of disciplining man in his pursuit of personal pleasure and benefit by a rational principle.

In diametrical opposition to Nietzsche, however, to whom man's liberation from the yoke of rationality was the ultimate goal of man's every endeavour, for Mawdūdī, who was here much more in line with Nietzsche's idealist opponents, the rational principle was the epitome of a guide which would help man in making his decisions for the morally better and, only by this way, to get a truly satisfying answer to the philosophical core questions. Now, the only guides who, in Mawdūdī's eyes, were fully able to do so were the prophets of God, and they would therefore take up an exceptional position in his conception of 'Islam' as the counter-term to 'jāhiliyya'.[51] As prophets they were not only in the privileged position to communicate God's commandments to man, but also to authoritatively explain them. Despite this, man was still tempted by the wide range of choices and all sorts of things around him, which is why he was in urgent need of the occasional reminder. This, according to Mawdūdī, was the reason for God to send prophets to man in different times and different places who would convey His message and urge man to abide by it. However, the continuous existence of *jāhilī* thoughts and practices, even after the Prophet Muḥammad, was proof enough for Mawdūdī that man had not changed much since God had sent Adam as the first prophet of Islam. But how could man be chastened after God had declared Muḥammad to be the 'seal of the prophets' (*khatam al-nabiyīn*)?[52]

1.2) Cyclical Renewal

To overcome this rather substantial dilemma, Mawdūdī resorted again to the authoritative texts of Islam and utilised the quite common concept of periodic religious renewal (*tajdīd al-dīn*). Like we have already seen with others of these authoritatively grounded concepts, Mawdūdī also reinterpreted this concept against the backdrop of contemporary thought, which was not necessarily Islamic. To understand the extent and the course of his reinterpretation of the *tajdīd*-concept, here, again, a discussion of how it had been understood and used in the past, and certain problems related to the concept, is in place.

a) Where There is no Prophet—The Paradigm of Renewal in Islamic History

According to Muslim understanding, all divine revelation to man came to an end when the Prophet Muḥammad, allegedly in connection with his Farewell Pilgrimage to Mecca in 632 CE, passed Qur'ānic verse 5: 3 on to his followers: 'This day I have perfected your religion for you, completed My favour upon you, and have chosen for you Islam as your religion.'[53] On the other hand, and perhaps not unrelated to the understanding of a persistent *jāhiliyya*, Muḥammad himself appeared to have been quite conscious of the danger of the disintegration of his community after his death because of the various temptations that would lead man astray and, thus, cause the *umma* to fall apart.[54] This decay of the community and of religiosity was even predicted in the eschatological seventy-fifth chapter of the Qur'ān where God anticipates that: 'Nay, but ye love the fleeting life and leave alone the Hereafter. [...] So he gave nothing in charity, nor did he pray! But on the contrary, he rejected Truth and turned away!'[55]

Given such pessimistic scenarios, it seemed reasonable to search for a device which could save the *umma* from what appeared to be its inevitable downfall, thus a mechanism for restoring the original religiosity within the community of believers in the absence of yet another prophet-to-come. Indeed, such a contrivance had developed from authoritative sayings of the Prophet, although not before the tenth century CE. In the canonical *ḥadīth*-collection of Abū Dāwūd, a popular Prophetic saying predicts a periodical restoration of the original religiosity:

Sulaymān ibn Dāwūd al-Mahrī handed down to us, that Ibn Wahb had narrated from Saʿīd ibn Abī Ayyūb, who was told by Sharāḥīl ibn Yazīd al-Muʿāfirī, he by Abū ʿAlqāma, and he from Abū Hurayra who came to know that the Messenger of God—Peace be upon him and prayer—says: 'Indeed, at the head of each century God sends this community someone who restores their religion [*inna 'llāha yabʿathu li-hādhihi al-ummati ʿalá ras kull miʾa sana man yujaddidu lahā dīnahā*].'[56]

While this appears to propose exactly the remedy for the dilemma in which the Muslim *umma* was trapped, there are nonetheless a number of problems with this *ḥadīth*. One is that it only appears in this one particular canonical collection, a fact which suggests that its veracity was not unanimously trusted, even though some sayings attributed to Ibn Ḥanbal predict someone who 'makes sound [*yuṣaḥḥiḥu*] their religion', or who 'teaches them the [right] ways [*sunan*] and removes the lie from the Messenger of God'.[57] The second and perhaps more severe problem is closely related to the former and concerns the reliability of Abū Hurayra (d. ca. 58/678): although considered one of the chief transmitters of Prophetic *aḥādīth*,[58] his trustworthiness in this capacity has been seriously doubted from quite an early time[59] which, of course, has considerably fostered suspicions over the veracity of this *ḥadīth*.[60] Moreover, Abū Hurayra's Southern Arabian descent has frequently served as explanation for his acquaintance with Jewish traditions and sources which, in turn, has contributed to the theory that the concept of *tajdīd* was actually derived from Jewish thought.[61] Whether or not this is the case is outside the scope of the present work. Besides continuous doubts about the veracity of this *ḥadīth* for the given reasons and its alleged roots in the Jewish religious tradition, there are a few more important observations which will help to place it better within the wider Islamic mindscape.

The first point relates to the early Mālikite traditionist ʿAbdallāh ibn Wahb (d. 197/813) who stands almost at the end of the chain of transmitters (*isnād*) of this particular Prophetic saying, and who is credited with having mainly specialised in collecting eschatological traditions.[62] This suggests that the idea of *tajdīd* was originally linked to Islamic eschatology, a possibility that is supported by the fact that Abū Dāwūd classed it at the beginning of the *Kitāb al-malāḥim*—the *Book of the Final Battles*—in his collection of *ḥadīth*.[63] The eschatological dimension of the *ḥadīth* had become quite prevalent by the late medieval period, as the example of the Egyptian Shāfiʿite jurist and polymath Jalāl al-Dīn al-Suyūṭī (d. 911/1505) testifies. That it was especially al-Suyūṭī who stressed that particular dimension was not accidental, as the scholar lived at the turn of the second Islamic millennium which somewhat resembled the apocalyptic expectations very much prevalent during the formative period of Islam.[64] While scholars have recently voiced their doubts that the concept of *tajdīd* had been linked to apocalyptic thought much before the tenth century CE,[65] it is a fact that—given especially the year of his death—the widely acknowledged first 'Renewer of the Age' (*mujaddid*), the eighth Umayyad Caliph ʿUmar ibn ʿAbd al-ʿAzīz (d. 101/720), was often associated with apocalyptic thought in the formative phase of Islam. Indeed, in some early non-canonical *ḥadīth*-collections he was even considered to be the 'Rightly Guided One' (*al-mahdī*), or as being identical with Jesus returning at the End of Times.[66] While this confluence of the *mujaddid* with the *mahdī* would be revived much later on, it first needs to be understood how and why the *tajdīd*-concept suddenly gained prominence from the late tenth century CE onwards.

For this it seems helpful to acknowledge that, at the turn of the twelfth century CE, Abū Ḥāmid al-Ghazālī deliberately used the *tajdīd* concept as a strategy to legitimise his revivalist claims. At the end of his *Munqidh min al-ḍalāl* he gives a paraphrase of the *ḥadīth*, although here it reads, 'God—Praise be to Him!—had indeed promised the vivification of His religion [*bi-iḥyāʾ dīnihi*] at the head of each century.'[67] From the context in which this paraphrase occurs, as well as from his avoiding the verb '*yujaddidu*', it becomes quite obvious that al-Ghazālī did not want the figure of religious revival to be understood in an eschatological sense, but rather to legitimise his revivalist project by at least implicitly assigning it the rank of the centennial religious renewal, thus disguising it almost with the appearance of a divine assignment.[68] As such it continued to be interpreted over the centuries, as the remarks by Murtaḍá al-Zabīdī (d. 1205/1791) in the introduction to his expansive commentary on al-Ghazālī's *magnum opus*, the *Iḥyāʾ ʿulūm al-dīn*, provide vivid proof.[69]

From the deliberate use of the concept of cyclical renewal and/or revival by al-Ghazālī a few points appear remarkable. Departing from the fact that someone was usually awarded the honorific 'Renewer of the Age' 'by the opinion, based on plausibility, of their contemporaries',[70] the notion could be employed for a variety of ends. Thus, Landau-Tasseron convincingly argues that the use of the title of *mujaddid* was for quite a long time very much confined to Egypt and the Shāfiʿites, thus linking the concept to the rise and spread of Shāfiʿism and, come to that, of Ashʿarism.[71] The widespread acceptance of al-Ghazālī as the *mujaddid* of the fifth Islamic century may serve just as a vivid illustration. For Landau-Tasseron, the concept of *tajdīd* did in fact serve mainly as a legitimisation for al-Shāfiʿī's contributions to the development of Islamic thought in order to skirt the possible allegation of bringing in 'unlawful innovation' (*bidʿa*). *Tajdīd* was thus used rather as a cover-up—the lines of *mujaddidūn* were constructed retrospectively, in order to comply with the content of the *ḥadīth*.[72] If this holds true then the widespread existence of lists of *mujaddidūn* throughout long periods of Muslim history and the Muslim world within a particular current of Islamic thought could well be explained as a means to establish legitimacy of rule and thought, the same as a pedigree (*shajara*) of teachers and pupils, or a spiritual lineage (*silsila*) in Sufism. The metahistorical dimension, expressed in the relation of *tajdīd* to eschatological thought proper, had considerably shrunk, if it was not entirely lost, at least until a few centuries later.

The increasing shift of the *tajdīd*-concept from a meta- to a more concrete historical level indicates yet another important development that is already suggested by al-Ghazālī's use of the authoritatively grounded idea of cyclical religious renewal and/or revival, namely the beginning of a growing merger of various and initially distinct concepts, such as *tajdīd*, *iṣlāḥ*, *iḥya'* or *iqāmat al-dīn*, that all aimed somehow at a restoration of Islam. Ghazālī's understanding of his own project as a contribution to the periodic 'revivification' (*iḥyāʾ*) of the religion, corresponding with his above paraphrase of the *mujaddid-ḥadīth*, suggests that the concept of periodic religious renewal had become used increasingly to explain the eventual occurrence of social, political and intellectual crises within the Muslim community, and as the way to overcome these. For such an inner-worldly understanding of decline and restoration a variety of terms were used which, however, mostly lack the element of periodicity that is found in the concept of *tajdīd*: 'Reform' (*iṣlāḥ*) and 'Establishment of the Religion' (*iqāmat al-dīn*) are just two examples of concepts used.[73]

The frequent recourse to the concept of *tajdīd*, instead of *iṣlāḥ* or *iḥyāʾ*, by religio-political reformers and reform movements throughout the centuries requires nonetheless an explanation.[74] Although the eschatological dimension remained certainly a decisive factor, the sidelining of the metahistorical level suggests that we are now confronted with a rather socio-critical, thus clearly innerworldly, phenomenon which David Cook has conveniently labelled 'moral apocalyptic'. While the criticism of a prevailing situation and the call for change had been embedded in the narrative of the 'Portents of the Hour', thus emphasising the severity of the situation as well as the inevitability of change, the eschatological reference was only rhetorical, the actual frame of reference in fact was the here-and-now.[75]

In India, this shifted meaning of the *tajdīd*-concept rose to prominence, at the latest, at the turn of the second Islamic millennium with the Naqshbandī Sufi Aḥmad Fārūqī Sirhindī (d. 1034/1624), a staunch critic of the religious policies of the Mughal rulers Akbar and Jahāngīr, who became during his lifetime known as 'Renewer of the Second Millennium' (*mujaddid-i alf-i thānī*).[76] That the self-confident Sirhindī did not explicitly refuse this epithet provided a new impetus for the entire issue, which requires an explanation. After all, the original Shāfiʿite-Ashʿarite nexus of *tajdīd* hardly applied in the predominantly Ḥanafite-Māturīdite subcontinent, nor was there much need for Sirhindī to safeguard himself from the possible allegation of bringing about religious innovation by utilising the *tajdīd*-concept. Indeed, the principal motivation behind his implicit claim to be not only the 'Renewer of the Century' but the 'Renewer of the Millennium' (*mujaddid-i alf*),[77] and by this deliberately deviating from the stipulations of the *mujaddid ḥadīth* that does not refer to the millennium at all, appears rather to have been to legitimise his claim to religio-political leadership against the monopoly held by the Mughal ruler. The fact that according to the authoritative texts a *mujaddid* is always divinely sent (*yabʿathu*), as suggested almost at the same time by the Egyptian al-Suyūṭī,[78] certainly provided Sirhindī's claim to leadership with an advantage. Only such God-given leadership, or *imāma*, one may argue, can guarantee the strict adherence of the community to the *sharīʿa*, which, in turn, is vital for the chances of each and every believer for salvation in the Hereafter.[79] From here, it was only a short step to the reactivation of the initially eschatological nexus between the 'Renewer of the Age' and the 'Rightly-Guided One', that is to say, the *mujaddid* and the *mahdī*.

A vivid example of the instrumentalisation of this link for the sake of justifying a claim to religio-political leadership is the so-called *jihād* Movement of the reformist Sufi-scholar ʿUthmān ibn Fūdī (d. 1232/1817) in the Sudanic Belt (*bilād al-sūdān*) at the turn of the thirteenth Islamic century.[80] Relying heavily on the thought of the sixteenth century North African Mālikite jurist Muḥammad ʿAbd al-Karīm al-Maghīlī al-Tilimsānī (d. ca.

909/1503–4) and, thus, indirectly on that of al-Suyūṭī,[81] Ibn Fūdī employed the latter's modification of the *mujaddid-ḥadīth*, according to which 'at the head of each century God sends a *scholar* to the people [*yursal allāh ʿāliman li'l-nās*] to renew for them their religion'.[82] This variant reading of the *mujaddid-ḥadīth*, along with the time of Ibn Fūdī's appearance, corresponded well with apocalyptic promises widespread in Hausaland,[83] which is why it is easily conceivable that Ibn Fūdī was even seen as the 'Rightly Guided One' (*al-mahdī*), although he seemed smart enough not to put forward this claim himself. On the other hand, Ibn Fūdī is said to have employed the accepted Prophetic saying about twelve rightly guided successors of the Prophet before the Hour and,[84] by conveniently omitting the important part that 'All of them will be from the Quraysh',[85] he styled himself explicitly the last righteous leader before the advent of the *mahdī*. Although he, like Sirhindī or, come to that, also al-Ghazālī, nowhere explicitly claimed to be the *mujaddid* of the thirteenth century,[86] for a considerable time he did not reject the use of this epithet by his followers during his lifetime.[87]

Of crucial importance is that, after the successful *jihād* of the Fulānī from 1804 and the unification of the Muslim states in the Caliphate of Sokoto under Ibn Fūdī as 'Commander of the Faithful' (*amīr al-mu'minīn*), a tradition of *tajdīd* in West Africa had been created that could serve the legitimisation of every religious reformist agenda, ranging from the vivification of religious knowledge to attempts to Islamise the prevalent social and political order.[88] This is a significant development, which found its pendants also in other parts of the Muslim world. In the Indian subcontinent, for example, a tradition of *tajdīd* had been devised which ran almost exclusively along the lines of Sirhindī's Sufi lineage of the Naqshbandiyya-Mujaddidiyya. Most instrumental in fortifying this tradition was the celebrated Shāh Walīyallāh Dihlawī (d. 1176/1762)[89] who, by implicitly claiming the title himself,[90] helped a great deal to detach the *tajdīd* paradigm from its confinement to the 'head of each century'. Shāh Walīyallāh was indeed styled the major point of reference for all the diverse Muslim reformist currents in the colonial period, ranging from the Deobandīs to Muḥammad Iqbāl.[91] By then, the earlier devised Indian tradition of *tajdīd* had also been retrieved from the confines of the Naqshbandiyya-Mujaddidiyya, and this is how it had finally come down to Mawdūdī. Devoid of its initial eschatological dimension, as well as its limitation to only certain points in time and particular groups, Mawdūdī was able to make it subject to fresh systematic deliberation in the course of his attempt to recast Islam into an ideology.

b) The Upward Spiral—Mawdūdī's Reinterpretation of the Renewal Paradigm

It appears only consistent with his other time- and development-related considerations that, instead of eulogising those who were traditionally credited with the epithet of the 'Renewer of the Age', Mawdūdī reinterpreted also the *tajdīd* paradigm in a rather typological way. This is quite remarkable because the quasi-historical account of alleged renewers that he provided in his programmatic work on the matter, *Tajdīd wa iḥyāʾ-i dīn*, first published in 1940, appears at first to resemble the traditional lists of *mujaddidūn* which, after all, was still the most common way of dealing with this topic in Muslim learned circles.[92] On closer examination, however, it appears that instead of highlighting their achievements in the restoration of Islam, Mawdūdī rather referred to the deficiencies in their respective renewal. In view of his radical typological distinction of 'Islam' and 'Ignorance' this appears quite plausible: after all, the possibility of a synchronous existence of both, Islam and *jāhiliyya*, needed to be systematically justified.

For Mawdūdī, therefore, the 'onslaught of the *jāhiliyya*'[93] set in shortly after the demise of the Prophet, during the 'Rightly-Guided' Caliphate of ʿUt͟hmān ibn ʿAffān (assassinated 55/656), when the lands of Islam had vastly expanded and the administrative tasks of the head of the Muslim *umma* had therefore increased. Although Mawdūdī could have associated some of ʿUt͟hmān's political decisions in favour of his clansmen of the Banū Umayya to the theme of the *jāhiliyya* regaining power, he did rather attribute this development to the fact that ʿUt͟hmān 'was not a bearer of all the qualities that were given to his glorious forerunners'.[94] This is remarkable to some extent, because the creeping nepotism during ʿUt͟hmān's reign[95] could have served well as an indication of the ingress of a somehow autonomously acting *jāhiliyya* that consequently led to the rise of social and economic unbalance. This, after all, was seen by Mawdūdī as symptomatic of a state of *jāhiliyya*. That he was nonetheless rather gentle in his assessment of ʿUt͟hmān's personality might have been due partly to his respect towards a renowned companion of the Prophet. Decisive must have been rather systematic reasons, as *jāhiliyya* resulted for Mawdūdī from a particular worldview, not in the first place from clearly distinct *jāhilī* actions. This is why, although ʿUt͟hmān's abilities to govern were indeed somewhat played down, the roots of the incipient *jāhiliyya* needed nonetheless to be located outside ʿUt͟hmān's actual rule. It is most likely for this systematic reason, along with the more pragmatic one of avoiding being accused of diminishing the role of a widely acknowledged early companion of the Prophet, that Mawdūdī remained conveniently woolly when pointing out those to be held responsible:

During the time of his [i.e. ʿUthmān's] caliphate the *jāhiliyya* had found the opportunity to penetrate the Islamic social system [*islāmī niẓām-i ijtimāʿī*]. The honourable ʿUthmān—May God be pleased with him!—working tirelessly in attempting to halt the path of danger [*khaṭare kā rāsta*], but it did not stop. After him, the honourable ʿAlī—May God be pleased with him!—proceeded and tried the utmost to protect the political might of Islam from the sway of *jāhiliyya*. Although he, too, sacrificed himself, the counter-revolution [*inqilāb-i maʿkūs*] could not be stopped. Finally, the era of the caliphate along the Prophetic patter [*manhāj-i nubuwwa*] came to its close; tyranny [*mulk-i ʿaḍūḍ*] took its place.[96]

The tyranny, which took over from the time of ʿUthmān's caliphate, was, in Mawdūdī's eyes, not that of an overtly non-Islamic government which could then be legitimately fought. The tragedy was rather that those tyrannical governments considered themselves still Islamic, although in reality they were dominated by the different forms of *jāhiliyya*, were it 'sheer ignorance', 'polytheism', 'monasticism', or 'pan- and panentheism'. The development of monarchic rule from the debris of the caliphate, as well as the impact of non-Islamic ideas and practices of newly converted Muslims—sometimes even actively supported by the 'worldly oriented scholars [*dunyā-parast ʿulamāʾ*]'[97]—were to him all indications of Islam's decline. Now, as we have already seen, such a rather pessimistic image of Islam was not unusual at this time,[98] but no one had painted such a radically black picture of almost the entire Islamic history as Mawdūdī has done.

According to him, none of the depicted renewers of the age were able to truly overcome the onslaught of *jāhiliyya* in their respective times and places. Indeed, if one follows Mawdūdī's argument, the renewal of Islam in each century spiralled downward in degree, as the *jāhiliyya* grew stronger, smarter and more varied, until it has reached its present stage. Consequently, the 'Renewers of the Age' would have needed to be more capable each century to meet all these challenges. Mawdūdī's verdict on everyone he discussed, stretching from al-Ghazālī via Ibn Taymiyya and Aḥmad Sirhindī to Shāh Walīyallāh Dihlawī and, interestingly, Sayyid Aḥmad Barelwī,[99] appears quite harsh: all of them—so Mawdūdī said—have ultimately failed, partly because they misjudged the situation, and partly because they lacked appropriate support.[100] It is remarkable how strongly Mawdūdī's pessimistic view of Islamic history reminds one of

Nietzsche's understanding of the triumph of the Apollonian rationality over the Dionysian artistic drive and, thus, the constitution of what Nietzsche had called the 'theoretical man'.[101] Therefore, as already suggested above, Nietzsche would have rather called for a return to the *jāhiliyya* as the Dionysian, the primordial culture which is closest to what he called 'life', namely, the will to power.[102] To do so, Nietzsche, after all still a creature of the Enlightenment, needed man to be freed from all rationally comprehensible values, a fact that determined not least his rejection of religion which is so vividly expressed in his provocative statement 'God is dead! [*Gott ist todt!*]'.[103]

However, as already touched upon, regardless of the various parallels between Nietzsche's and Mawdūdī's respective views on history, they differed greatly in their respective judgement on the role and place of religion and rationality. For Mawdūdī, man needed the domestication of his drives by some regulating principle, the most supreme of which was religion, of which, in turn, Islam was the highest possible manifestation. Seemingly influenced by Iqbāl,[104] Mawdūdī did not perceive religion and life as antagonistic, but rather as almost synonymous; *jāhiliyya*, on the contrary, would mark man's alienation from the very essence of Islam. Rationality was part of man's nature according to creation, its use had thus been divinely sanctioned, at least as long as it was always and exclusively made in the service of religion.[105] Thus, as long as everything brought forth by man could be justified from a religious point of view, then Mawdūdī saw no hindrance in man's intellectual and technological progression. However, for most of Islamic history this has not been the case. On the contrary, the caliphate, the unique religio-political institution of Islam, which was to safeguard the 'Common Good' as the principle goal of the *sharīʿa*,[106] had degenerated into monarchies[107] and thus promoted the detachment of every aspect of life from Islam.

Hence, it was the task of the *mujaddidūn* to readjust what had become corrupt in a time when prophecy had ceased, but, according to Mawdūdī, none of them had really been able to roll back the increasing alienation of man from Islam and, therefore, to stop the new advance of the *jāhiliyya*. Thus, in a theory structurally resembling Nietzsche's view of history as an eternal struggle of two opposed principles in which every attempt of the Dionysian to return to the surface is checked by a new and improved counterattack of the Apollonian, Islam is time and again overcome by various forms of *jāhiliyya*. The *mujaddidūn* had so far only been able to renew Islam partly at the most[108] and bring it back to only an already degenerated level. History according to Mawdūdī could therefore be perceived as a downward spiral, starting from Islam at its pristine and most perfect state during the lifetime of the Prophet and the first two 'Rightly-Guided' Caliphs, and ending in Mawdūdī's present time, when almost all Muslim countries were under the rule of non-Muslim Western colonial powers.

According to Mawdūdī, the present situation was bad indeed, but not hopeless. There was still an opportunity to turn the spiral upward, to once and for all overcome the *jāhiliyya* in its countless forms and to bring about the final triumph of Islam. For this, however, a person was needed who was better able than all preceding *mujaddidūn* to critically assess the present situation in its entirety and to bring about an all-comprehensive renewal of Islam that would help its establishment all over the world. This one Mawdūdī called the 'Ideal Renewer' (*mujaddid-i kāmil*), an expression which reminds one strongly of the mystical conception of the 'Ideal Man' (*al-insān al-kāmil*) of Ibn ʿArabī (d. 638/1240) and, later, Iqbāl's 'Believing Man' (*mard-i muʾmin*).[109] The similarities between Mawdūdī's and Iqbāl's concepts are striking indeed: a courageous and active *primus inter pares*, who, in the case of Iqbāl, will be the self-fulfilled man while, in the case of Mawdūdī, he will 'establish a caliphate after the Prophetic pattern [*manhāj al-nubuwwa par*], the advent of which had been announced'.[110] This prediction was backed up by Mawdūdī with a somewhat faulty quote from a sound Prophetic *ḥadīth*, according to which God, after having established the religion by His mercy and by way of prophethood (*inna awwal dīnakum nubuwwa wa-raḥma*), will bring forth a caliphate after the prophetic pattern (*thumma takūnu khilāfa ʿalá manhāj al-nubuwwa*) at a later stage. Eventually, this caliphate will be substituted by kingship and arrogance (*mulk wa-jabariyya*), which in turn will be replaced by tyranny (*mulkan ʿaḍūḍan*). This will last until God terminates it and reinstalls the caliphate after the prophetic pattern.[111]

The implications of this *ḥadīth* for Mawdūdī's understanding of history and the place and role of his 'Perfect Renewer' must not be underestimated. First of all, his rather positivist reading of this Prophetic tradition led him to assume a five-stages circular model of history. Four stages—from the divine revelation via a sequence in succession of the Prophet to kingship and tyranny—would spiral downwards in a decline of the political order, while the fifth, in turn, would spiral upwards, back again to the second stage, that is, the caliphate in succession of the Prophet. To enhance the relevance of Mawdūdī's own systematic outline it was important to perceive the actual situation as already at the close of the fourth level:

It [i.e. the mentioned *ḥadīth*] refers to five stages of history, three of which have already passed and the fourth one is passing right now. As to the fifth stage, which had been predicted, all the signs [*qarāʾin*] are suggesting that the history of man is fast heading towards it. All man-made 'Isms' have been tried out and did, by and large, not work. Now, after becoming exhausted, there is no other remedy left for man than to return to Islam.[112]

The pseudo-apocalyptic mood that Mawdūdī had created here was supportive of one of his most controversial moves, namely to identify his *mujaddid-i kāmil* with the eschatological figure of the *mahdī*. Although playing with this term of an already established meaning, Mawdūdī, somewhat resembling Ibn Fūdī about a century and a half earlier, clearly detached it from its eschatological context and took it into the existing world. There was no talk at all about the *mahdī*'s appearance at the end of time and the final battles, which immediately precede Judgement Day. Explicitly disregarding those accepted *aḥādīth* which foretell the circumstances of the advent of the *mahdī* and his identity,[113] Mawdūdī constructed the image of a most able and contemporary worldly leader who would fulfil the prophecy of the re-establishment of the caliphate along the lines of prophethood:[114]

In my opinion the coming one will be the most modern leader of his age, who possesses deep analytical insight [*mujtahidāna baṣīrat*] in all the modern sciences of the time and understands well all the important issues of life. He will establish his prestige by his rational and intuitive statesmanship [*ʿaqlī wa dhihnī riyāsat*], political prudence [*siyāsī tadabbur*] and confidence in his skills of warfare [*jangī mahārat ke iʿtibār*] and prove himself as the most modern of all the moderns [*tamām jadīdoṇ se baṛhkar jadīd thābit hogā*]. [...]

In my understanding the *mahdī* will, like any other revolutionary leader [*inqilābī līdʾar*] in this world, have to exert intense efforts and overcome dilemmas on his way. On the sole fundaments of Islam he will establish a new 'School of Thought' [*madhhab-i fikr*], change the mentalities, and initiate a strong movement, which will be cultural [*tahdhībī*] and political in one. [The adherents of] Ignorance will try to crush him with all their powers, but in the end he will check the ignorant might, overcome it, and establish a strong Islamic state which will on one hand enforce the full spirit of Islam, and on the other bring the scientific progress to its highest top. As it has been ordained in the *ḥadīth*: 'His government will please those who belong to the heavens and those who belong to the earth, the heavens will open and shower their blessings and the earth will throw out all its treasures.'[115]

What Mawdūdī did here resembles quite strikingly the shift from a *historia sacra*, or history of salvation, to a *historia profana*, or political history, that occurred in eighteenth century Western historical thought.[116] That is, pointed, Enlightenment thought. Eschatology is brought into this world, the end of history, which was conjured in Francis Fukuyama's controversial book of the same title from 1992, does not mean the end of the world. Similar to various social and political utopias, Mawdūdī aimed at establishing an Islamicate possibility of salvation in this world.

That Mawdūdī had never explicitly denounced the widespread allegation that he wanted himself to be seen as the 'Rightly-Guided' saviour does not diminish the importance which the concept of the *mahdī* played in his idea of history. To bring this highly meaning-laden concept into play may however have had not only theoretical reasons. After all, his demand for a worldly reformer who would fully comprehend the prevalent situation and effectively counter the multifarious manifestations of *jāhiliyya* by a most timely alternative plan seemed somewhat to match with his own project to recoin Islam into an ideology, a consistent and self-referential 'system of life'. We will now have to see whether he did indeed manage to deliver on his ambitious aspiration.

2) The Foundation of the System

Consistent with his goal of casting Islam into an ideological system, Mawdūdī was following the by then long since cross-culturally acknowledged rules of logical deduction. He had to find a small number of axioms from which, in a series of deductive steps, he would then unfold his elaborate and yet self-contained system. Indeed, Mawdūdī apparently had accepted this challenge when he stated that:

> Islam [...] is a well arranged system, the basis of which had been determined as a number of firm principles [*chand maḍbūṭ uṣūloṇ par*]. From its corner stones to the least little detail, every thing is in a logical relation [*manṭiqī rabṭ*] to its fundamental principles.[117]

In order to meet this challenge Mawdūdī had to search for axioms which would be firm enough to bear the weight of the entire ideological building erected on them. The only possible place where they could be found was, according to Mawdūdī, the most authoritative document of Islam, that is, God's conclusive revelation to man in the Qur'ān—his quest for these axioms had thus been inseparably linked to his argument for the ultimate authority of the Qur'ān.

2.1) The Understanding of the Qur'ān

Indeed, Mawdūdī's search for and justification of the axiomatic terms, or, as he called them, 'principles', had to be preceded by a systematic vindication of the pre-eminent position of the Qur'ān—a tendency already conceivable during his time as editor of *Muslim* and *al-Jamʿiyya*[118]—and, even more, of the possibility for man to independently approach it and comprehend its meaning. To do so, Mawdūdī had first to dabble as a theologian and to discuss God as the source of the revelation as well as the relationship between God and man. Following quite consistently from his pessimistic view of Islamic history, Mawdūdī rejected, although nowhere explicitly, the validity of any earlier exegetical effort. He blamed the semantic shifts that occurred over time in the Arabic language for an increasing miscomprehension of the text of the revelation, of the 'true meaning' (*aṣlī maʿnī*) of the Qur'ānic key concepts.[119] Once this 'true meaning' had been lost or forgotten, all the efforts of the exegetes were essentially doomed to fail. Therefore, what was needed was a fresh and radically different approach to the text, a particular and so far unprecedented reading of the Qur'ān, which could recover the 'true meaning' of the Qur'ānic key concepts. This, in fact, was exactly what Mawdūdī attempted in a great number of his writings, especially in his six-volume Qur'ānic commentary *Tafhīm al-qur'ān* which he began in 1942 and composed with interruptions over the next three decades.[120]

That Mawdūdī undertook the immense effort to compile a commentary of the whole Qur'ān, which aimed—as the title clearly states—at understanding (*tafhīm*) rather than explaining (*tafsīr*),[121] is significant. After all, apart from Ibn Taymiyya to whom we owe the voluminous *Tafsīr al kabīr*, none of the grandees whom he had earlier discussed as commonly accepted 'Renewers of the Age' had presented the world with an exegesis of the entire Qur'ānic text.[122] From their various writings, however one may assume that they consciously aimed at explicating the Qur'ānic message in their own respective time, as is shown by the following statement of Shāh Walīyallāh Dihlawī, which suggests that a timely interpretation of the Qur'ān had been a major constituent of *tajdīd*:

> You, whether of high or low [rank] [*chi khawāṣṣ wa chiʿawāmm*], do not overstrain your own intellect with its [i.e. the Qur'ān's] memorization, but rather with listening to it, as We have laid it on Gabriel's tongue. Hence, this is still Our responsibility: For the explanation of the Qur'ān [*tawḍīḥ al-qur'ān*] We will decree in every age a body [of persons] that will succeed in explaining what is unclear in the Qur'ān [*gharīb-i qur'ān*], elucidate the words [*bayān*] and the reasons for sending them down, so that the true import [*ṣadq-i ḥukm*] of these words may be known and the significance may be manifest to you.[123]

Despite such statements, which assured the possibility of an appropriate interpretation in every age by way of divine guidance, Mawdūdī remained and—for the sake of cohesion of his entire systematic outline—had necessarily to remain sceptical. After all, if timely exegesis of the Qur'ān was indeed an essential part of the revivalist efforts of the *mujaddidūn*, then, consistently with Mawdūdī's earlier negative portrayal of the past renewers, their efforts in the field of exegesis had to be deficient, too. Therefore, he stated that all he could see was at the best only a selective exegesis of the Qur'ān, which was not best suited to enhance a proper understanding of Islam in its respective time and space. To counterbalance this and to substantiate his own claims for a radical reassessment of Islam in his time, Mawdūdī had to offer an approach to the Qur'ān in its entirety, although we shall see that his comments by no means discuss the entire text in due width and depth. His Qur'ānic commentary provides nonetheless a key to the understanding of his entire system of thought. Here, Mawdūdī introduced most visibly a hermeneutical approach that permeated his entire interpretation of Islam. As with his conception of history, Mawdūdī's methodology to access the Qur'ānic text fitted well into the general intellectual landscape of the first decades of the twentieth century. Although Mawdūdī's hermeneutics are far away from the rather complex philosophical ideas of Wilhelm Dilthey (d. 1911), Martin Heidegger (d. 1976) or, later, Hans-Georg Gadamer (d. 2002), his approach to the Qur'ānic text appears nonetheless nurtured by the same spring, namely the role of 'time' in the relationship between author, text and reader, and its impact on conveying 'meaning'.[124]

Mawdūdī's solution for overcoming the hermeneutical dilemma rooted in 'time' consisted of two steps. The first one simply eliminated 'time' as a decisive factor in the process of understanding, on the basis of the axiomatic assumption of an element of timelessness in the Qur'ānic revelation. Herein lies the conjecture that the Qur'ān includes an essential core (*dhāt*) which man is able to understand, regardless of his place in time and space. This eternal message, however, was embedded in multifarious time- and space-bound accidents (*aʿrāḍ*) which man must acknowledge as such, in order to comprehend the Qur'ānic message with some prospect for success. In this light, the reproach that Mawdūdī had laid at the door of all previous *mujaddidūn* would be that their interpretations had solely been confined to the accidents without identifying the essence of the Qur'ān, which is why, as a logical consequence, even their understanding of the accidentals had to be, and, in fact, had been distorted.

The fundamental precondition for any of man's attempts to understand timeless essence as well as time-bound accidents of the Qur'ān, however, is rooted in the Qur'ānic anthropology, ultimately amounting to the fundamental issue of man's freedom of choice which, as already pointed out, was to become the Achilles' heel of Mawdūdī's systematic outline. Given the extraordinary importance that this anthropological issue already had for identifying the axioms on which Mawdūdī's entire system was eventually to rest, one would at least at this point expect a thorough and well-structured explication. The fact that this was never the case, and that Mawdūdī's thoughts here appeared rather scattered throughout his conceptual writings, points clearly towards the already mentioned fact that he had been somewhat trapped in the anthropological dilemma between man's freedom of choice and his absolute dependence from God. That Mawdūdī was not able to eventually overcome this had a considerable impact on the systematics of his entire outline, as we shall see every now and again.

a) Yes, We Can Do It!—Man, Rationality and Divine Revelation

What transpires from everything said so far is that Mawdūdī considered it perfectly possible for man to understand at least the essence of the Qur'ān in a direct and unmediated way. This ability was not limited to a particular group of specially equipped people. Shāh Walīyallāh's above given view was that this aptitude was entirely dependent on God bestowing His grace upon selected individuals, but Mawdūdī would have categorically rejected this as entirely baseless and, thus, unjustified. In contrast, his own epistemological optimism appeared to him much better to justify as it corresponded more closely to the Qur'ānic conception of man. In the course of creation God bestowed man with reason and, subsequently, with free will which, in turn, ensured that the essential meaning of the Qur'ānic revelation was always accessible by man:

> The Lord of the World, who is the Creator of the whole universe, King and Sovereign [*farmān-rawā*], had spawned man for this part of his fathomless kingdom, which is called 'earth'. He had given him with the ability to know, to think and to understand [*jānne awr sochne awr samajhne kī qūwateṇ*], the faculty to distinguish between good and evil [*bhalā'ī awr barā'ī kī tamyīz*], and bestowed him with choice and volition [*intikhāb awr irāda kī āzādī*] and with the capacity to exercise his potentials. In short, He gave him a kind of autonomy [*khūd-ikhtiyārī*] and made him His vice-regent on earth.[125]

Strikingly, Mawdūdī could apparently not have been bothered to back up the crucial anthropological trait inherent in this frequently reused passage[126] with any reference, be it from the Qur'ān itself or other places. This is indeed remarkable, as he could have done so even from the text of the Qur'ān itself, where man is repeatedly called upon to use his rationality to comprehend the revealed message (*a-fa-lā ta'qilūna*).[127] This is what a proper theologian would traditionally have done. After all, the issue of man's free will and rationality was right from the beginning at the core of theological thought and hot debate.[128] Hence, one is tempted to consider Mawdūdī's way of dealing with the issue as a major lapse, which, if avoided, would have left him much less prone to the massive criticism by the *'ulamā'*. Yet again, Mawdūdī proved to have been a true child of his time when he realised man's, albeit limited, autonomy not by a recourse to the Qur'ānic text itself, but rather by logically deducing it from his own empirical observations which corresponded once more with his black-and-white view of history. If, as history had shown, it was possible for man to adhere to any other way of life than Islam, then man has to have indeed some freedom of choice. True enough, in the introduction to his Qur'ānic commentary he conceded that man was equally free to choose Islam or any other path, an insight which would later enter his systematic outline as the concept of *dīn*.[129]

Such an anthropological argument for man's ability to correctly understand the Qur'ānic text served as justification for an unmediated reading, almost similar to the argument that someone like Luther invoked in support for a direct and individual study of the Bible.[130] This resemblance between Mawdūdī's and an Evangelical approach to Scripture—just by the way—may not be just accidental, given the legacy of increasing Muslim-Christian learned encounters due to the massive presence of especially Presbyterian missionaries in the subcontinent since the early nineteenth century.[131] In consequence of the hermeneutical presupposition of man's essential potential for an unmediated approach to the text of the Qur'ān, all human authoritative claims were dismissed, which in turn is why Mawdūdī had no need to refer to any other preceding Qur'ānic commentary, in order to more or less guide him towards a closer understanding of the Qur'ān itself. Indeed, for the sake of consistency of his systematic approach it appeared even vital to not rely on any authority other than his own intellectual capacity, which God Himself had justified as absolutely sufficient in the Qur'ān. Such optimism about the general possibility of acquiring true knowledge, very much in line with the philosophical *zeitgeist*, caused a number of considerable problems. The first one is of a systematic kind. If each and every human being possesses the same ability to understand the essence of the Qur'ān and, consequently, to derive from it maxims to act, then the need for a *mujaddid* would be obsolete and, thus, core elements in Mawdūdī's conception of history would be at jeopardy. The second problem was that with this fundamental anthropological determinant he implicitly rejected the monopoly of definition that was traditionally held be the classically trained *ʿulamāʾ*. For most of them, there was understandably no way to condone this approach. Hence, they strongly reproved Mawdūdī for commenting on the Qurʾān exclusively on the basis of his own reasoned opinion (*tafsīr biʾl-ray*) while at the same time deliberately blanking out the established methodology in this field of learning.[132]

Related to this criticism of the way in which Mawdūdī approached the Qurʾān is yet another point. Although Mawdūdī's reading of the Qurʾān may not be considered the first fundamentalist one in history, it is nonetheless considered to be one of the constitutive texts to a newly emerging sub-genre of Qurʾānic exegesis. To label it 'political commentary' (*tafsīr siyāsī*), as has frequently been done in polemical writings by the mainly learned opponents of Mawdūdī and those in his fairway,[133] does however not do it full justice. Although Mawdūdī's way of exegesis shrinks the many possible dimensions of the Qurʾān which were always considered in classical *tafāsīr* to a sociopolitical one alone,[134] it goes nonetheless beyond mere politics when it addresses, for example, ethical issues, such as individual perfection by orienting oneself to God's commandments and the Prophetic examples. Judging from this and from the fact that also his concept of history blanks out to a large extent the important eschatological dimensions, one may perhaps best consider Mawdūdī's approach to the Qurʾān first and foremost as this-worldly (*dunyāwī*).

Such being the case, one might be tempted to see Mawdūdī having performed a kind of 'Copernican Turn', something that, in consequence, would almost credit him with the aura of an Enlightenment thinker, a distinction which he would most probably have liked a lot. Such a comparison, however, appears to be a little too far-fetched. Unlike Kant, for example, Mawdūdī did not show any rigour at all as far as the issue of God and religion was concerned. Although he, like the Enlightenment thinkers, put man and his earthly life into the spotlight,[135] he did certainly not go beyond belief and maintained the religious view of God and institutionalised religion as a 'regulative',[136] that is to say, something man has necessarily to refer to in order to justify values.

Thus, in consequence and quite contrary to Kant and those in his wake, Mawdūdī, trapped in the confines of positive religion, assigned the Qurʾān and its originator a higher degree of reality and, thus, binding nature with man and the world that surrounds him. Herein lies an important factor that shaped Mawdūdī's distinct approach to the text of the revelation in which he also differed from many other contemporary readings of the Qur'ān which all share what Rotraud Wielandt has appropriately called the 'awareness of the cultural distance between the world in which the Qur'ānic message was primarily communicated and the modern world'.[137] Yet, Mawdūdī's perception of the Qur'ān as being of higher reality than the changing world around him had a considerable impact on his practical approach to his already mentioned solution for overcoming the hermeneutical dilemma.

First of all, he had to disentangle what he himself had named 'the local colour [*maqāmī rang*]' of the early messages, and the 'statements [*bayān*] they contain which are of universal benefit [*'ālamgīr ṣadāqateṇ*]'.[138] These 'universally beneficent contents', so Mawdūdī stated, are eternal and unchangeable; they constitute thus the above-mentioned essential (*dhātī*) message of the Qur'ān. Only the linguistic codes used to transport the eternal message vary in time and space—and here he argued almost as contemporary linguists such as the Egyptian Naṣr Ḥāmid Abū Zayd (d. 1431/2010) would have done.[139] The ultimate task of everyone seriously engaged in Qur'ānic exegesis would therefore be to filter out these eternal contents of the Qur'ānic text, in order to gain a thorough understanding of God's final revelation to man. The fundamental error of all previous exegetes, and consequently the reason why man might well dismiss them, was that they had attempted to rather apply the Qur'ān to variable issues in a changing world, thus assigning the world too much of a reality. In the eyes of Mawdūdī and others who followed him here, his freshly attained understanding of the nature of the Qur'ānic message and the subsequent approach to the text went far beyond even the classical explication of, for example, grammar and prosody, which they considered rather redundant.

Interestingly, while on the one hand he assigned the world a clearly inferior position and therefore rebutting more or less all previous classical exegetes, the eternal issues which Mawdūdī distilled from the Qur'ānic text and which, at the same time, set the limits of man's scope for interpretation were exclusively very mundane ones, revolving around:

> organising all those who respond to this mission and guidance [brought to man by the prophets] into one such community [*umma*] in which, on the one hand, one rests his own system of life [*zindagī kā niẓām*] on the divine guidance, and which, on the other hand, strives for the reformation of the world [*dunyā kī iṣlāḥ*].[140]

Consequently, in one of his presumably earlier treatises on the issue, *Qur'ān kī siyāsī ta'līmāt*, Mawdūdī drew in a nutshell, from a range of only thematically assorted Qurʾānic verses, all the sociopolitical concepts that were to play key roles within his system design[141] and which were echoed in his later contribution to a widely recognised edited volume on Muslim philosophy by Muḥammad Miyāṇ Sharīf (d. 1385/1965).[142] Likewise, in his treatises on economics, Mawdūdī derived all economic principles that mattered to him from his selective and even frequently decontextualised reading of Qurʾānic verses, as will be discussed in greater detail in the appropriate place.[143] We shall also see later on that it is not least this confinement of the Qurʾānic message to mundane matters only that provided many of Mawdūdī's adversaries with ammunition against him.

At this point, however, yet another issue deserves to be highlighted which sheds further light on Mawdūdī's particular approach to the text of the Qurʾānic revelation. Indicative in this regard is his statement that the Qurʾān would provide only:

> [general] principles and universalia [*uṣūl awr kulliyāt*], the basic purpose of which it is not only to provide clear [*waḍāḥat ke sāth*] intellectual and moral foundations, but also to properly consolidate them by intellectual argument [*ʿaqlī istidlāl*] and emotional appeal.[144]

What Mawdūdī indicated in this passage was that the text in itself is not perceived as a coherent narrative[145]—a fact that most exegetes would probably agree to—but rather as a vast reservoir of scattered meaning, presented in 'various ways and each time in different words'.[146] Unlike the classical *mufassirūn*, however, Mawdūdī took this widely accepted fact as occasion to utilise the Qurʾān primarily as a supplier of terms and concepts of such a generality that they could serve as axioms for his conception of Islam as a self-contained and self-sufficient system. Those terms and concepts were not necessarily found in a contextualised reading of the Qurʾān, as suggested by the classical *mufassirūn* as well as by those whom Mawdūdī considered somewhat defective *mujaddidūn* in their respective references to the Qurʾān. To identify these terms and concepts and to acknowledge their respective importance, the entire Qurʾān had to be thoroughly combed through and the scattered evidence gathered, in order to finally give the text a new internal systematic meaning. However, the doctrine of God's oneness (*tawḥīd*) as Mawdūdī's point of departure for the formulation of the first two axiomatic terms on which his entire system was ultimately to rest upon indicates that, however innovative his approach to the Qurʾān was, Mawdūdī did nonetheless remain within the confines of those core themes of the Qurʾānic message which classical exegesis had established.

2.2) Four Basic Qurʾānic Terms

a) God Active—God Passive

To begin with, although Mawdūdī's first two terms refer to the Qurʾānic concept of God, the fundamental doctrine of *tawḥīd* seems to have played only an implicit role. In his argument on the nature of God, which, as we will see, falls into two complementary aspects, the Qurʾānic chapter 112 (*al-Iḵẖlāṣ*), encapsulating this core tenet of Muslim faith, had no distinguished role at all to play. In addition, his commentary on this chapter in *Tafhīm al-qurʾān* remained surprisingly conventional and does not hint at an extraordinary importance of the doctrine of *tawḥīd* for the elaboration of Mawdūdī's system of thought.[147] This is indeed somewhat startling even if we credit the fact that his elaboration on *sūrat al-iḵẖlāṣ* might have been written rather late, because one would nonetheless assume that Mawdūdī had set out from his exegesis of this central Qurʾānic reference to God's oneness and developed his system in logically consistent steps from there. It appears, however, quite the other way round. The impact of his earlier writings, first and foremost the highly controversial *Qurʾān kī chār bunyādī iṣṭilāḥeṉ* from 1941, on Mawdūdī's reading on *sūrat al-iḵẖlāṣ* is quite obvious. Although not in line with the chronological order of his writings, it is nonetheless deemed useful for maintaining a systematic elaboration of Mawdūdī's outline of Islam to start from his commentary on that particular Qurʾānic chapter.

Especially significant is his interpretation of the first verse 'Say: He is God, One! [*qul: huwa 'llāhu aḥad*]'. The meaning of *al-aḥad*, as discussed by Mawdūdī, could refer to God's indivisibility or 'internal oneness', or to His peerlessness (*yagāna*) or 'external oneness', depending on one's understanding of the grammatical structure of the sentence.[148] This twofold meaning was already novel, as the purport of *al-aḥad* had traditionally been explained as unequivocally synonymous with *al-wāḥid*.[149] Mawdūdī however decided to understand *al-aḥad* not as a postpositional attribute, but rather as predicate in the nominal clause 'God is one', explaining that this implies that all the qualities which God possesses are unique and possessed by no one but Him alone.[150]

From here and without putting too fine a point on it, Mawdūdī continued by referring to those two terms that he had earlier identified as the first two of his axiomatic Qurʾānic terms on which his entire system would eventually rest: master or lord (*rabb*), and deity (*ilāh*), or that what is worshipped (*maʿbūd*).[151] *Tawḥīd* is not further problematised or credited with even the meanest discussion here, beyond the rather elegant statement that this is 'the first fundamental doctrine [*ʿaqīda*] of Islam'.[152] Although there is relatively little further direct reference to the doctrine of *tawḥīd*,[153] it nonetheless pervades Mawdūdī's entire systematic outline of Islam. In *Qurʾān kī c̲h̲ār bunyādī iṣṭilāḥeṇ* he stated that he who does not comprehend the meaning of Mawdūdī's four axiomatic terms—the first two of which were *rabb* and *ilāh*—will not be able to understand the true meaning of *tawḥīd*.[154] It is therefore that we need to have a closer look at *rabb* and *ilāh* as two complementary aspects within a conception of God, which Mawdūdī had derived from his particular reading of the Qurʾān.

Following the logical path of deductive theory building, it appears quite consistent to first build up a system on a single major axiom, i.e. the oneness of God, which is then subsequently diffused into various derivatives. Thus, in a next step Mawdūdī needed to argue for aspects of God which can be derived from His oneness, but must nonetheless never dilute this fundamental doctrine by suggesting either an atomistic multiplicity in God, or an inherent interdependence of these multiple parts, as this would again somewhat contradict the feature of God being self-sufficient and everlasting (*ṣamad*). To convincingly circumvent these dangers one would necessarily have to delve rather deeply into the various theological arguments that had originated already in the formative period of Islam. That Mawdūdī, for whatever reason, did not take this very road left his own explications to appear rather shallow and made his ideas once more prone to all kinds of learned criticism.

The two aspects of God, represented by his first two axiomatic terms *rabb* and *ilāh*, were thus introduced by Mawdūdī without a proper rational argument other than that they belonged to four terms which appeared frequently throughout the Qurʾānic text, and that, if these terms were not properly comprehended, 'the entire Qurʾān will be without any meaning [*be-maʿnī*]'.[155] Although this can hardly be considered a proper justification for his choice of these four terms, it appears nonetheless consistent within Mawdūdī's systematic outline: God as 'master' or 'lord' (*rabb*) stresses His capacity as creator and law-giver. The word *rabb* was first explained in five lexicological meanings, which, according to Mawdūdī, were all to be found in the Qurʾān.[156] In a next step, he lined up at length numerous Qurʾānic verses to prove the various notions (*tak̲h̲ayyulāt*) of *rabb* in pre-Islamic times, 'which to refute [*tardīd*] the Qurʾān came [down]'.[157] Finally, Mawdūdī boiled down the various meanings of the term that occur in the Qurʾān to the one that he claimed the Qurʾān actually wanted to radiate:

From the consecutive reading of all these verses it is clearly understood that the Qur'ān uses 'Lordship' [*rubūbiyyat*] as exactly synonymous with sovereignty [*ḥākimiyyat awr sulṭānī*], and the concept of 'rabb' that it presents to us means that He is the supreme ruler [*sulṭān-i muṭlaq*] of the universe and its sole master [*mālik wa ḥākim*].[158]

Rabb, as it were, represents the active side of God, which is responsible for the existence of the universe and its arrangement in an utterly working way (*mukammal niẓām*).[159] Although Mawdūdī did nowhere say so explicitly in this regard, it is this very aspect of the Divine that caused His repeated revelation to humankind and, in the course of this, the decree of a code of belief and practice that corresponds with the perfectly designed mechanisms that make God's creation work. Although highly speculative, one may assume that Mawdūdī had deliberately avoided using the term '*sharīʿa*'—'Islamic normativeness'[160]—and wilfully decided for applying 'system' or 'arrangement' (*niẓām*) instead. This could eventually be read as his attempt to show that obedience to the *sharīʿa* would be perfectly in line with all those rules and regulations that govern nature. Obedience to the *sharīʿa*, so to speak, is to obey the law of nature, or, in other words, the *sharīʿa* is the only way to lead a life in accordance with nature. If this assumption was in any way viable, it would well support Mawdūdī's earlier stated claim that Islam is the only world-view in accordance with nature.[161]

Logically corresponding to God's active aspect and obedience to His law is a rather passive and receptive aspect that Mawdūdī had found in the term *ilāh*, or deity. In explicating what he believed was the proper Qur'ānic meaning of this term, Mawdūdī proceeded in an way analogous to his portrayal of *rabb*. After a discussion of its lexicological meaning and the use of *ilāh* in pre-Islamic times as it appears in the Qur'ān,[162] Mawdūdī concluded that the primary meaning of this term would be 'an object of unconditional service and adoration' (*ʿibāda* or *parastish*). As such, it is synonymous with *maʿbūd*, the object of veneration.[163] While this synonymy as such is hardly disputable, it is nonetheless important to understand why Mawdūdī brought the term *maʿbūd* into play at all. After all, the semantics of the term *ilāh* itself do not explicitly cover man's position in relation to it, but the term *maʿbūd* clearly does, and gives thus a new emphasis to the semantics of *rabb* as well:

A person who in a supernatural sense regards someone his helper, remover of difficulties, fulfiller of desires, one who answers his invocations [*duʿāʾeṇ*] and bestower of gains and losses does so because this being [*hastī*] enjoys in his eyes a kind of authority [*nawʿiyyat kā iqtidār*] over the arrangement of the universe. [...] Hence, the basic spirit of Godhood is authority [*pas ulūhiyyat kī aṣl rūḥ iqtidār he*].[164]

There are a number of systematic reasons why the importance of this strategic steering from *ilāh* towards God's active aspect as *rabb*, backed up also by classical Arabic dictionaries,[165] must not be underestimated. Mawdūdī had to avoid even remotely suggesting that God is somewhat of a conglomeration of separate aspects or natures. Therefore, and consistently with the doctrine of *tawḥīd*, *rabb* and *ilāh* owe themselves to one and the same reason, that is God's unlimited power (*iqtidār*), epitomised in the sixty-ninth of His ninety-nine Beautiful Names, the 'Powerful' (*al-qādir*). The second systematic reason for the confluence of *ilāh* and *rabb*, perhaps more tersely expressed in the confluence of *maʿbūd* and *rabb*, is that the authority with which God created the universe, and which Mawdūdī considered the essence of *rabb*, is the reason why man's service and adoration must be exclusively directed towards God as *ilāh*, or *maʿbūd*.[166] Consequently, it is in the Qurʾānic concept of *ʿibāda*—dependence (*bandagī*), submission (*iṭāʿat*) and devotion (*parastish*)[167]—that the creative and law-giving aspect of God finds its human equivalent, and Mawdūdī his third axiomatic term. His three Qurʾānic core concepts *rabb*, *ilāh* and *ʿibāda* link God and man to each other and establish a kind of reciprocal, although asymmetrical, exchange relationship. What is more important, however, is that already these three axiomatic terms form a hermetically closed and self-referential framework which later came to be only multiplied in the course of the elaboration of Mawdūdī's systematic outline; hence a close understanding of the intrinsic relationship of these three terms is indispensable.

As *rabb*, the one indivisible (*aḥad*) and peerless (*wāḥid*) God created the universe and man therein, and endowed His creation with rules and regulations for its frictionless functioning. While for the larger part of creation these rules and regulations take on the form of laws of nature, the case of man is somewhat different. Man stands out from all creation because he was given rationality and, resulting from it, free will.[168] Hence he has a certain scope to either act according to, or against nature. Because human rationality finds its primary expression in complex systems of structured verbal communication[169] God uses human language as a means to periodically warn man of the possible consequences of his eventual deviance from the laws of nature, and repeats His rules and regulations in a way customised for man, that is, the *sharīʿa*. This way, man is reminded of his dependence from his creator, as well as his assigned place and role within creation. With His ultimate call, the Qurʾān, God established, on the basis of His authority, that man, like the rest of creation, is entirely dependent on His mercy and that He, therefore, is the only being justly entitled to worship (*ilāh* or *maʿbūd*). The only adequate response to God's final appeal to man and His revitalisation of the *sharīʿa* by way of the Qurʾānic revelation would be that man delivers himself entirely to God and makes Him the sole object of his worship:

> It appears clear that the entire mission [*daʿwat*] of the Qurʾān is only [to point out] that dependence [*bandagī*], submission [*iṭāʿat*] and worship [*parastish*] is [solely] to God. However, to restrict the meaning of *ʿibādat* [...] to just a single one means to restrict the mission of the Qurʾān. The logical consequence of this is that those who understand the Qurʾānic message in such a restricted way will affect their belief [*īmān*] and their devotion [*pay-rawī*] will be defective.[170]

Although Mawdūdī's conception of *ʿibāda* remained so far rather abstract, he was nonetheless already heavily criticised for the fact that he portrayed the relationship between God and man exclusively in this very hierarchical way—as relationship between master and slave, of one who issues orders and the other who cannot but comply. What the majority of his critics, among them of course those *ʿulamāʾ* from around the TJ, objected to was that Mawdūdī had conveniently ignored the role of man's unconditional love, or enrapture (*maḥabba*, or *ʿishq*) as a complementary aspect of *ʿibāda*.[171] Again, Mawdūdī's deliberate disregard of the emotive level of the relationship between God and man, which suggested a more egalitarian relationship as lovers, may be linked to his particular bipolar view of Islamic history. Strongly linked to the Sufi idea of man's approximation of the divine,[172] this appears as a thought that Mawdūdī had strongly associated with the monastic form of *jāhiliyya*.[173] For him, the relationship between God and man had to have a strong societal relevance, and therefore the more intimate relationship between lover and beloved appeared largely unsuitable as the basis for his idea of Islam as a 'system of life'.

In this way, Mawdūdī's tacit disapproval of *maḥabba* as an integral part of *ʿibāda* goes once again hand in hand with his rather negative judgement of those personalities who were widely acknowledged as 'Renewers of the Age'. A considerable number of them had had a strong Sufi background and therefore considered *maḥabba* an essential part of their understanding of *ʿibāda*.[174] Even Ibn Taymiyya, the 'Renewer of the Seventh Islamic Century' who is known for his staunch traditionalist stand and whose affinities to Sufism are still not entirely clear, considered 'love' (*ḥubb*), besides 'submission' (*dhull*), an integral part of *ʿibāda*.[175] For Mawdūdī, such an individualistic approach to *ʿibāda*, following—to use Weberian terminology—an 'ethics of ultimate ends' (*Gesinnungsethik*),[176] would nothing but weaken the role of Islam as a socio-political force. It is in this question that we encounter a clash of two paradigms that, in its consequence, refers to two almost diametrically opposed views of what became Mawdūdī's fourth and final axiomatic term that he had derived from the Qur'ān: *dīn*.[177]

b) You have the Choice!—Mawdūdī's Concept of 'Dīn'

The Qur'ānic term 'dīn' constitutes the glue which ties Mawdūdī's other three fundamental Qur'ānic terms together. It justifies *ʿibāda* out of the acknowledgement of God's ultimate authority as *rabb* and *ilāh*.[178] As it brackets the divine and human dimension, it has therefore to be a comprehensive term (*jāmiʿ iṣṭilāḥ*), somehow recalling the Hegelian 'whole'. Interestingly, Mawdūdī's statement that 'the word "state" [*ist'et*], as used in the present time, approximates to it, up to a certain extent'[179] reinforces this reminiscence of Hegelian thought even further,[180] all the more since Mawdūdī conceded that *dīn* is even more comprehensive than the modern philosophico-political understanding of 'state'.

Dīn reflects the perspective of man. Although created and purposefully put in this world by God, man is generally free to accept any authority other than God, and to submit to this authority instead. To follow these alternative authorities would, according to Mawdūdī, mean to follow their respective *dīn*:

> [*Dīn*] is understood as law [*qānūn*], code [*ḍābiṭa*] path [*sharīʿa, ṭarīqa*], or the system of thought and action to which man commits his life. [...] If the authority [*iqtidār*] is that of some monarch [*pādishāh*], then man follows the monarch's *dīn*, if the authority is that of Paṇḍits and priest, then man follows their very *dīn*, and if the authority is that of a family, a clan or the masses [*jumhūr-i qawm*], then man follows their *dīn*. Thus, whose decree is acknowledged as the supreme decree and whose verdict as the ultimate dictum, and one whose path man travels, the *dīn* of whom he follows.[181]

So far, Mawdūdī's notion of *dīn* was still consistent with his earlier concession of free will and freedom of choice to man. As in all ideologies, however, this 'freedom' was conditional and, thus, clearly distinct from 'arbitrariness', which was not the case with the philosophical antecedents of political ideologies. The early Fichte, for example, after all perhaps the most radical theorist of 'freedom' as the fundamental anthropological determinant, considered 'arbitrariness' the most pristine, because unconditional form of freedom,[182] a thought that was later to be found even more pointedly in Nietzsche's life-philosophy. Ideologues, in contrast, although they tend to acknowledge the existence of a free will, refer to restrictive circumstances, for the first time epitomised in Friedrich Engels' popular phrase that 'freedom is the insight into necessity'.[183] 'Necessity' is always perceived as something objective, something outside man's power of disposition from which he cannot escape. What 'history' has been for Communism, or 'providence' for Fascism, was for Mawdūdī the firm belief in God as creator and master over all of creation that drastically reduced man's freedom of choice to the 'insight into necessity'.[184] Therefore, although Mawdūdī conceded a hypothetical possibility of submitting oneself to an authority other than God, within his own system he did not allow for any choice when it came to the acknowledgement of authority. To recognise any authority other than God would then consequently mean to embrace an entirely different 'system of life'.

Consistent with the hermetic and self-referential nature of a system, and something that Mawdūdī's systematic outline of Islam shared with any other ideology, the 'objective' justification for submission to the authority of God alone came from within the system itself. For this, Mawdūdī utilised Qur'ānic verses such as 3:85: 'And whosoever seeks a *dīn* other than Islam, never will it be accepted from him [...] [*wa-man yabtaghi ghayra al-islāmi dīnan fa-lan yuqbala minhu*].'[185] This implicit concession of the existence of '*dīn*s of ignorance' (*adyān jāhiliyya*) parallel to Islam corresponds clearly to Mawdūdī's earlier outlined reinterpretation of the classical concept of *jāhiliyya* and his subsequent dichotomous differentiation of 'Islam' and 'jāhiliyya'. The point which Mawdūdī tried to ultimately prove with his inbuilt references to the Qur'ān was that all sets of rules and regulations incorporated in any such *dīn* would be diametrically opposed to Islam and therefore against nature. In consequence, to cling to a *dīn* other than Islam will advance man's alienation from nature and, thus, ultimately lead to the doom of humankind. In close correspondence with the general intellectual drift in the 'Age of Ideologies', it was therefore imperative for Mawdūdī to overcome the traditional occupation with metaphysics and epistemology and replace it with a theory that aimed—in Marx's words—not at an interpretation of the world, but at changing it.[186] Such an aspiration would, of course, lead to a contention which is not any longer based on rational argument and consensus, but on intransigent conflict. Mawdūdī must have been well aware of this when, again arguing with a Qur'ānic passage (8:39) as objective proof of the validity of his ideology, he stated that:

> the followers of the *dīn* of Islam have been ordered to fight on earth, and not to pause until the infestation [*fitna*], i.e. [all] the prevalent systems which are based on

a revolt against the divine foundation, have been wiped out again and the only way of obedience and submission [*niẓām-i iṭāʿat wa bandagī*] is exclusively for God.[187]

Man, it emerges from here, has indeed a choice. What sort of *dīn* one chooses depends on what sort of person one is, just to paraphrase Fichte's famous dictum.[188] Once this choice is made, however, man has divested a large amount of his freedom as he puts himself under the restrictions of objective necessities. *Dīn*, for Mawdūdī, is 'a complete system of life [*niẓām-i zindagī*], including all of its faith-related, intellectual, moral and practical aspects'.[189] These aspects, one could argue almost in an idealist manner, include a spirit that remains a constant within an unstable and changing world, although Mawdūdī himself nowhere explicitly referred to *dīn* as a kind of Hegelian 'spirit' which pervades the entire history of the Abrahamic religions. In fact, his understanding of the term appears not entirely unequivocal, which makes is difficult to finally grasp its actual meaning. In his controversial *Risāla-yi dīniyyāt* from 1932, for example, he specified (the Islamic) *dīn* as unconditional belief in and submission to God, as 'something that the teachings of all the Prophets had in common',[190] and something that, unlike the *sharīʿa*, had remained unchanged.

Sharīʿa, in turn, he had defined in the same place as the 'ways of worship, foundations of social life, rules of mutual transactions and relationships, the definition of what is allowed and what forbidden, what permissible and what not'.[191] According to Mawdūdī, each Prophet had brought a new *sharīʿa* that had abrogated the previous one.[192] This clearly is not consistent with the Islamic tradition, which holds that all the revelations and, thus, their inherent 'Islamic normativeness' (*sharīʿa*) are all descending from the single *umm al-kitāb*, the celestial matrix of any divine revelations. Consistently, therefore, the *sharīʿa* must also be one and the same.[193] Mawdūdī, on the contrary, might have had rather effective legislation in mind when speaking of *sharīʿa*, which becomes clear from the fact that he considered external regulations (*aḥkām*) and positive laws (*qawānīn*) to be part of the *sharīʿa*, while they were traditionally regarded as its derivatives.

However, if *sharīʿa* is really understood as a body of applicable rules, then Mawdūdī's concept of *dīn* as something total and unalterable that refers to the general nature of the relationship between God and man makes some sense within the attempt to (re)construct his ideology as system. That Mawdūdī used the terms 'law' (*qānūn*) and 'path' (*sharīʿa*) in his other, above given definition of *dīn* can, however, hardly be seen as anything else but a terminological inconsistency on his behalf which puts the original systematic of his thought somewhat in danger. The importance of this flaw must not be underestimated, because a terminological inconsistency already at this early stage within a systematic outline will have an irreparable effect on all the stages that follow.

Regardless of this weak spot, the importance of the concept of 'dīn' for Mawdūdī's entire systematic outline cannot be overestimated. While here it was used almost synonymously with 'ideology' or 'system', as the demarcation line between 'Islam' and 'jāhiliyya', it was later going to also play a significant role as a force of cohesion for Mawdūdī's envisioned ideal Islam community, that is, the Islamic state. Beyond these two critical purposes that the concept of 'dīn' has to serve in Mawdūdī's system design, it held yet at least one other importance. 'Dīn' was to be for Mawdūdī the tool to overcome the repeatedly mentioned dilemma of man's divinely decreed freedom of choice and his determination by God's revealed law, ultimately enshrined in the Qur'ānic revelation. While, in places, Mawdūdī conceded man an almost unlimited freedom of choice and had thus shrunk even *dīn* on the basis of the Qur'ānic revelation as one choice among other equally valid ones, he introduced the concept of 'nature' to distinguish between commendable and reprehensible *adyān*. Therefore, and quite consistent with his ideological mindset that rested on the fundamental dichotomy of 'us' and 'them', Mawdūdī distinguished between appropriate and wrong choices, styling in the process the Islamic *dīn* the only sound, because natural one. However, while the concept of 'dīn' may have helped Mawdūdī to at least attempt a way out of the dilemma of man's freedom of choice and concurrent determination by God, we shall see that it was still not a sufficient tool to prevent Mawdūdī becoming increasingly entrapped in contradictions, the more his system became complex. Mawdūdī seemed to have been quite aware of that, although, because of the fundamental position that the axiom of man's freedom occupies in his intellectual edifice, all his occasional attempts to resolve these inconsistencies were thus doomed to fail.

3) The Core of the System

If one looks for a lowest common denominator in Mawdūdī's four axiomatic terms from which the next deductive step in the elaboration of the system could be taken, one would have to grant this to power, or authority (*iqtidār*). Mawdūdī's interpretation of two aspects of God, an active one as lord (*rabb*) and a passive one as deity (*ilāh* or *maʿbūd*), establishes although it is hierarchically structured, an exchange relationship between man and the divine that, in the eyes of Mawdūdī, refers exclusively to man's inner-worldly activities.[194] In contrast to the much maligned Sufi who perceives this relationship as much more personal, intimate and egalitarian, in Mawdūdī's outline there is little space for individualistic approaches. The creative and law-giving aspect of God finds its mundane counterpart in man's unconditional and total submission to Him (*ʿibāda* or *iṭāʿat*), so that the plurality of humankind is herein condensed to the generic concept 'man'.[195] Herein we encounter yet another feature of ideologies in general—one may think in this regard of derivatives like 'proletariat' in communist, or 'racial corpus' (*Volkskörper*) in National Socialist ideologies.

The condensing to a generic concept and, thus, the exclusion of any non-discursive and individualistic approach to the divine had far-reaching consequences for Mawdūdī's system. As man is considered not in his multifarious individuality but rather as a single agent, there can only be one kind of response to God. This response, in turn, is reflected in Mawdūdī's quest for the firm fundament of a durable and, at the same time, fully functional human society. Within this human society, however—and here Mawdūdī's fundamental dilemma comes once again into play—there is a certain range of choice and individuality which we have already most vividly witnessed with regard to *dīn*, the spirit which permeates all aspects of human life but might vary according to the all-encompassing worldview that one chooses to accept as true. Yet, there is no room to negotiate over the transcendent principle that underlies a certain *dīn*. Neither can man arrange terms with history, nor with destiny, leaving out God. Though almost certainly not intentionally, Mawdūdī seems to have implicitly taken over the Kantian notion of a 'kingdom of nature', or 'kingdom of necessity', and a 'kingdom of ends'.[196] This distinction, however, this 'Doctrine of the Two Kingdoms',[197] is of crucial importance for the further unfolding of Mawdūdī's systematic outline. It is a necessary conception for arguing against any kind of absolute determinism on earth, and, instead, for the justification of freedom of choice, thus establishing an almost Protestant work ethic.[198] Again, because of the earlier mentioned massive public presence of Protestant missionaries in India especially since the mid-nineteenth century,[199] Mawdūdī had most certainly been fairly familiar with the core tenets of their thought, and a subconscious influence can therefore safely be assumed.

A key concept within Mawdūdī's idea of two—although interrelated—spheres, or 'kingdoms', which finally rooted his outline clearly in the realm of the political, is a particular understanding of 'sovereignty' (*ḥākimiyya*).

In this regard it must have played well into Mawdūdī's hands that, traditionally, the term or, coming to that, any of the derivatives of the Arabic verbal root *ḥ-k-m*, was considered semantically not congruent when applied to God and man respectively.[200] In a first step, he narrowed the diverse meaning of *ḥākimiyya* down to 'sovereignty'[201] and used thus a term that was first introduced into political thought by the French political philosopher Jean Bodin (d. 1596).[201] Therefore, while looking at Mawdūdī's considerations one needs to always bear in mind the meaning that the term 'sovereignty' has in Western political theory. In a second step, however, Mawdūdī established his own 'Doctrine of the Two Kingdoms' which enabled him to produce a coequality between 'sovereignty' which applies to God and another one applies to man. The difference between these two concepts of 'sovereignty', however, lies in the spatial scope of the power of control. Thus it makes sense to differentiate between 'absolute' and 'relative' sovereignty and to first discuss them separately.

3.1) Absolute Sovereignty—The Reign of God

Consistent with the requirement of self-referentiality of a system, Mawdūdī's understanding of God's absolute sovereignty corresponded with his notion of *rabb*, when he stated that:

> Based on this conception of creation [*kāʾināt ke isī taṣawwur*] the Qurʾān states that the true sovereign [*farmān-rawā awr ḥākim*] of man is He who is also the sovereign over creation. He alone is in reality also the sovereignty over the human transactions [*muʿāmalāt*]; apart from Him no human or non-human power exists independently and is authorised to make decisions. [...] Man, too, is in the necessary realms of his life [*zindagī ke g͟hayr-ik͟htiyārī ḥiṣṣe meṇ*] subjected to His sovereignty and power of disposition, just as everything, from the single atom to the universal arrangements is subjected to it.[203]

From this justification of God's sovereignty, derived from the fact that the One who brought about creation is necessarily also its Supreme Lord, it appears that Mawdūdī used the terms 'Lord' and 'Sovereign' synonymously, as he stated explicitly in his discussion of the Qurʾānic term *rabb*.[204] On the other hand, he might have been aware of the terminological problems that might arise if *rubūbiyya* and *ḥākimiyya* were used fully interchangeably. He therefore introduced a modification that related both concepts better to each other and, thus, lifted their congruency. While *rubūbiyya* became now, in the words of the German neo-Kantian philosopher Ernst Cassirer (d. 1945), a 'substance' to describe a feature of God's being, *ḥākimiyya* was made its corresponding 'function', describing an essential activity of God.

For Mawdūdī, the prime function of the Creator, after calling the universe into being, was to issue rules and regulations for its functioning so that sovereignty thus became largely identical with legislative force, which is why Mawdūdī spoke of God's sovereignty as 'legal sovereignty' (*qānūnī ḥākimiyya*).[205] This legal sovereignty, however, remains not unchallenged, as—consistent with his earlier thoughts on *dīn*—Mawdūdī conceded the possibility of competing legislations. With this, he was well in line with the classical Islamic tradition, as he referred to al-Ṭabarī's exegesis of the Qurʾānic verse 16:36 who wrote:

> And it says God the Most High: 'Oh, ye people, We had send a messenger to every community that precedes you, just as We have send to you, for that you serve God alone, do not associate any partner to Him, bring Him obedience and are sincerely loyal to Him. 'And eschew the idol [*wa-ujtanibū al-ṭāghūt*].' And He says: 'And keep away from Satan and beware of deviating and avoiding the path of God, for that ye may not get lost.'[206]

That man's general ability potentially follows any legislation other than God's is fully consistent with Mawdūdī's emphasis on man's free will and, consequently, his ability to choose from a variety of options. However, as emerges already from al-Ṭabarī's statement, not all possible and existing legislations are considered equal. Man therefore needs guidance to find his way through the jungle of available legislations, many of them man-made. This, in Mawdūdī's eyes, is exactly why the prophets were indispensable. God sends His prophets as guides for humankind towards His 'supreme legislation' (*bālātar qānūn-sāzī*).[207] Although man possesses the ability to decide for any other and, from Mawdūdī's point of view, inferior legislation, such a choice would have to be considered a clear deviation from the natural way which aims at harmony between Creator and creation. It would therefore lead to 'unbelief, error, injustice and sinfulness [*kufr wa ḍalālat awr ẓulm wa fisq*]',[208] in other words, to conditions which Mawdūdī had earlier attributed to the *jāhiliyya*. The submission to God's supreme legislation in turn is devotion; the acknowledgement of God's 'legal sovereignty' corresponds with His being as *ilāh* or *maʿbūd*, terms that in this context have also become essential attributes of God.

What results from here is a rather complicated matter. After all, so far not every legal implication of the Qurʾān is unequivocal, and not all legal rulings from the Sunna of the Prophet are easily applicable to any spatial and temporal context. In the past therefore, the division of powers along

Montesquieuian lines had not yet been entirely clear and became thus subject to contestation. While the supreme legislative was indeed with God, it was the Muslim jurist who derived, in the words of Baber Johansen, 'probable, but fallible interpretation of infallible texts'.[209] Since these interpretations of the *fuqahā'* resulted quite frequently in positive law, the jurists assumed some legislative power, too. Positive law however had to be enforced. This was not within the scope of the *fuqahā'* but remained with the ruler as the executive force. The relationship between ruler and jurist, or *'ālim* in general, had thus mostly been one of conflict over the monopoly of interpretation and means of reinforcement. Courtly patronage was a common tool to bend the *'ulamā'*—trustees of the religious knowledge—to the will of the ruler, privileges were meant to help the scholars to find interpretations of the authoritative texts that would support and, this way, legitimise the political decisions of the ruler.[210]

For Mawdūdī, such a constellation appeared rather unsatisfactory as it left far too much room for the abuse of power by way of decisions on the edge of legitimacy within a religious framework. Consequently, the subordinated legislative force needed to be wrested from the various kinds of *'ulamā'*, over and above the jurists, who traditionally held this position and who had been blamed many a time for the frequent abuse of their position for their own personal benefit.[211] Mawdūdī's conception of Islam as a 'system of life', as well as his understanding of 'man' in a generic way, were both therefore systematic tools to prevent the *'ulamā'* from claiming an exceptional role for themselves. If, according to his anthropological understanding, all human beings were endowed with the same reason and called upon by God to use it for a better comprehension of the text of the revelation, then the interpretations of the *'ulamā'* were potentially as fallible as those of any other man. The historically grown social and political prestige of the *'ulamā'* could therefore not serve as a justification of any elevated position within society—for Mawdūdī's systemic elaboration, setting out from a metaphysical rather than an empirical perspective, they had first to be levelled into humankind.

3.2) Relative Sovereignty—Man as God's Deputy on Earth

While the absolute sovereignty of God was beyond any dispute for Mawdūdī, as appears from the fact that his reading of the relevant Qur'ānic verses seems not to have caused any room for uncertainty, he spent considerably more ink on the elaboration of man's relative sovereignty. This, however, is easily explained by the fact that Mawdūdī's primary aim was to work out the conditions for the possibility of a durable, while fully functional, human society. Hence, he remained largely within the realm of political theory rather than holding forth about theology and metaphysics. Consequently, his concern with, and most likely also his comprehension of, metaphysical issues went only as far as he required them for deduction of the constituents of his political theory. In this, his ideology appeared once again formally in line with others. Although Communism needed to routinely refer to a *de facto* metaphysical concept of 'history' in the understanding of historical materialism, as Fascism referred to 'providence' and 'destiny',[212] the prime concern for both had always been the elaboration of the actual social and political practice which, however, resulted necessarily and irreversibly from the external, objective and therefore unswayable principle, be it 'history' or 'providence'.

For Mawdūdī to establish the absolute sovereignty of God was thus a necessary precondition to define the realm of man, the 'kingdom of ends' within the Islamic *dīn* as a frame of reference. Similar to the Kantian understanding of man's 'kingdom of freedom' and 'kingdom of ends' within a wider and, at the most, only partly cognisable 'kingdom of nature', Mawdūdī embedded the realm of man within the sphere of divine government. Within his own realm, man was to have rights, although limited, which in turn must result in man possessing a certain amount of sovereignty himself.

Interestingly, in his writings Mawdūdī never used the term 'ḥākimiyya' with regard to man. This might be for systematic reasons, which, however, can only be postulated. First, for the sake of clarity and consistency of his outline, Mawdūdī was to avoid further terminological doublings. Second and perhaps more important still, the concept that Mawdūdī utilised for his ends relates man's sovereignty clearly to the absolute sovereignty of God.[213] Man possesses no authority, no rights of disposal, not even free will *per se*, but only by the grace of God—hence the term 'ḥākimiyya' was reserved exclusively for God:

> Even in the free realms of man's life [*zindagī ke ikhtiyārī ḥiṣṣe meṇ*] His sovereignty is not inoperative, but, by means of his revealed books, the last of which is the Qur'ān, He calls to consciously and voluntarily [*shuʿūr wa irāda ke sāth*] acknowledge His sovereignty and to decide to subordinate to it.[214]

In Mawdūdī's thought, man's sovereignty is clearly distinct from what he critically and, partly, even polemically branded as the 'people's sovereignty' ('*umūmī ḥākimiyya*) of Western democracies. For him, man's sovereignty has to be perceived as an efflux of God's absolute sovereignty for it is given to him on certain conditions, but can be taken away from him at any time, in case he fails to meet these conditions.[215] The term that Mawdūdī called into play for designating man's relative sovereignty, as clearly distinct from God's *ḥākimiyya*, was 'deputyship', *khilāfa*.

a) *Khilāfat Allāh—Khilāfat Rasūl Allāh*

The term *khilāfa*, of course, is historically encumbered. Initially it denoted the successors to the Prophet Muḥammad in the political and religious leadership of the young Muslim *umma*, the *khilāfat rasūl allāh*.[216] As such, the term is and of course cannot be of Qur'ānic usage. What is more important is that the successors to the Prophet were not appointed by God, but by the decisions of leading representatives of the *umma*.[217]

For Mawdūdī, however, whose growing lack of confidence in the history of the Muslims after the death of the Prophet we have discussed at length, decisions made by men can never have sufficient authoritative force. Moreover, he needed, as shown, to link the concept of *khilāfa* to the *ḥākimiyya* of God. Therefore, he had again to resort to the text of the Qur'ānic revelation where the term and other derivatives of the verbal root *kh-l-f* appear a number of times. Consequently, in his explanation of the most popular Qur'ānic verse on the matter (2:30): 'I will appoint a *khalīfa* on earth [*innī jā'ilun fi'l-arḍi khalīfatan*]', he set off with a first and most general definition of the term *khalīfa*:

> *Khalīfa* is one who, in a certain dominion [*milk*], exercises the powers [*ikhtiyārāt*] conferred upon him in the capacity of a deputy [*nā'ib kī ḥaythiyyat*]. A *khalīfa* is no Master [*mālik*] [by himself], but basically the Master's deputy. His powers are not essentially [*dhātī*] his own, but were bestowed to him by [his] Master. In reality, he cannot act on his own intent, but his works are entirely done on the Master's purport.[218]

His recourse to the Qur'ān enabled Mawdūdī, first, to dissociate his own particular notion of *khilāfa* from the historical caliphate in the succession to the Prophet Muḥammad, and, second, by introducing the concept of *khilāfa* to establish a relationship between God and man on the question of authority and sovereignty. The notion of *khilāfa* he was referring to was theological rather than historical, it was the concept of *khilāfat allāh*, that is, the believing man's trusteeship of God on earth, in opposition to *khilāfat rasūl allāh*, which is the historical Caliphate in the succession to

Muḥammad. The distinction between the two was nothing new. Already the North African polymath Ibn Khaldūn (d. 808/1406), to whom we owe an important political theory and who gained renewed popularity in Indo-Muslim thought of the early twentieth century,[219] highlighted the differences between what he called 'caliphate *in concreto*' (*khilāfat bi-aṭlāq*) and 'caliphate *in abstracto*' (*al-khilāfa al-ʿāmma*).[220] This way, although only at a first glimpse, it appears that Mawdūdī was in good company.

However, consistent with his intention to develop an empirically grounded general theory of the history of human society, Ibn Khaldūn's emphasis was clearly on the 'caliphate *in concreto*', or *khilāfat rasūl allāh*. Not so Mawdūdī. For him, the historical caliphate was only relevant as far as it had been embedded into his understanding of Islamic history as a history of religious decline.[221] To Mawdūdī, it indicated the beginning of a change in the understanding of sovereignty and, thus, of an increasing detachment of man's mundane affairs from his initial trusteeship of God.[222] Not least because of this historical development, the *khilāfat rasūl allāh* was only of little use for someone who, unlike Ibn Khaldūn, intended do forge a rather *pre*scriptive political theory. Therefore, Mawdūdī could not but focus almost entirely on the *khilāfat allāh*.

Even with this confinement of *khilāfa* to *khilāfat allāh*, however, Mawdūdī developed a particular reading which, although not entirely inconsistent with the classical exegetical tradition, is clearly the result of a constriction of the variety of interpretations to a single one that has emphatically been adopted from the late nineteenth century onwards. As demonstrated by Saudi Arabian scholar Jaʿfar Shaykh Idrīs, the medieval traditions of various provenance, ranging from al-Ṭabarī (d. 310/923) to Ibn Kathīr (774/1373), did not, like Mawdūdī, hold an unequivocal view on the matter, although they all agreed largely with the fact that the verb *khalafa* includes a temporal dimension and, thus, *khalīfa* was first and foremost to be understood as 'successor' (*li-annahu khalafa alladhī kāna qabluhu*).[223] Although arguing from a distinct traditionalist point of view, Idrīs seems right to assign the shift towards an understanding of *khilāfa* as man's trusteeship on earth to an increasingly anthropocentric perspective. Whether or not it is useful to pin the beginning of this on the mystical philosopher Ibn ʿArabī[224] will be left undecided here. Of importance, however, is certainly the renewed emphasis on man's rationality in the thinking of the scholars of the so-called 'Salafiyya' movement in North Africa and the *Bilād al-Shām* at the turn of the twentieth century which clearly took place under the direct influence of Western post-Enlightenment thought.[225] It was especially

Muḥammad ʿAbduh and Muḥammad Rashīd Riḍā who, in their unfinished *Tafsīr al-manār*, confined the meaning of *khilāfa* in their exegesis of verses like the above mentioned 2:30 to man's trusteeship on earth.[226]

Important here is their argument that 'man'—here, too, as a generic term—was endowed with reason and, thus, granted 'unlimited capacities [*al-qūwa ghayr-maḥdūd al-istiʿdād*], unlimited desires, unlimited knowledge and unlimited action'.[227] Because of this, ʿAbduh and Riḍā concluded that God gave man:

> [...] domination over the earth [*mulkahu al-arḍ*] and made all His worlds subservient to him, and also did He give him laws and legislation [*aḥkāman wa-sharāʾiʿan*] which put a limit on his actions and on his conduct so that no individuals or groups may infringe upon each other's rights.[228]

Mawdūdī basically followed the same line,[229] although in an increasingly politicised way. While for the Salafiyya scholars man's trusteeship was epitomised rather in the Biblical '[...] and fill the earth and subdue it [...]',[230] Mawdūdī understood *khilāfa* indeed exclusively as a political term, that is, solely as a tool to legitimise political rule. Crucial to his politically confined understanding was Mawdūdī's interpretation of the Qurʾānic verse 24:55 which can be seen as at the core of his argument:

> God has promised those of you who believe and work righteous deeds [*amanū minkum wa-ʿamilū al-ṣāliḥāt*] to make them *khulafāʾ* on earth [*la-yastakhlifannahum fi'l-arḍ*], just as He has made those who lived before them to *khulafāʾ*.

It is this verse which, according to Mawdūdī, 'sheds an extraordinarily clear light on the Islamic theory of state [*riyāsat*]'.[231] In this, his argument was developed in a twofold way. First, he suggested that the personal suffix *-hum*, which God had used in His address to man, refers clearly to a collective that He will establish as *khalīfa* on earth. Unlike verses such as 2:30, in verse 24:55 a qualifying criterion is provided that singles out a particular group of humankind: those, namely, 'who believe and work righteous deeds'. According to Mawdūdī, it is clear that the people God has chosen as representative of His absolute sovereignty on earth can only be the 'community of believers' (*ahl-i īmān kī jamāʿat*).[232] In a rather lengthy interpretation of this Qurʾānic verse in his commentary *Tafhīm al-qurʾān*, Mawdūdī argued that, by abrogation of all previous divine revelations, the only possible candidate would be the Muslims.[233] A Muslim, on the other hand, is not Muslim by birth—a view that Mawdūdī shared with many other revivalist thinkers—but has only to become one by belief and action alone.

Second, 'belief' and 'righteous deeds', and thus *khilāfa*, applies only to a polity (*ḥukūma*) that aims at 'erecting Islam on a strong basis',[234] that is, one which does not allow for the slightest *shirk* to prevail. To be able to do so, *khilāfa* had to form a crucial part of Mawdūdī's theory of governance and was consequently rendered as 'vice-regency'.[235] To distinguish it from the historical caliphate in the succession to Muḥammad, Mawdūdī introduced the notion of 'people's viceregency' (*ʿumūmī khilāfat*). Setting out from the popular Prophetic *ḥadīth*: 'You all are a shepherd and responsible for the flock [*kullukum rāʿin wa-kullukum masʾūlun ʿan raʿiyyatihi*]',[236] he concluded that 'one *khalīfa* is in no respect lower than another *khalīfa*'.[237] This fact, which served to support Mawdūdī's understanding of the Islamic polity as an essentially democratic one, is backed up with a number of further common Prophetic sayings which indicate the idea of a society that is not stratified by birth, social status or economic wealth, but by religious merit (*sābiqa*) only.[238] Consequently, by creating a congruence between individual and collective interest, individualism is dismissed.[239]

Here, at least, one is strongly reminded of the conception of 'sovereignty' (*souveraineté*) and 'general will' (*volonté générale*) in the political philosophy of Jean Jacques Rousseau (d. 1778), which was later adapted in practice during the Jacobin phase of the French Revolution.[240] Although Mawdūdī tried hard to dissociate himself from any kind of Western conceptions, over and above those which had led to the establishment of political orders during Mawdūdī's own time,[241] parallels and, thus, possible influences are hard to ignore.[242] Like Rousseau, Mawdūdī endeavoured to reconcile the conflict between individual and society in bringing about a congruence of man's self-determination and social order. This is done by harmonising, in Rousseau's thought, 'subjective rationality' and 'objective nature', the latter, in Mawdūdī's words, being identical with God.[243] Such a totalitarian understanding of democracy would, of course, only be practicable if men were indeed equally preconditioned and, thus, the generic term 'man' was corresponding with reality. Here we face a grave category error because the necessary separation of prescriptive and descriptive levels becomes blurred. We will see later on that, because of this, Mawdūdī's conception of democracy bears dangers similar to those of Rousseau when it came to its practical implementation.[244]

Rousseau's conception, however, was entirely rooted in the anthropological conception of the eighteenth century Enlightenment and was therefore confined to the realm of man only.[245] In contrast, Mawdūdī's idea of man's relative sovereignty as an outflow of God's absolute sovereignty could not be well equated with democracy as it was widely understood during Mawdūdī's time. In order to distinguish his envisioned political system and, at the same time, to further dissociate himself from Western concepts of democracy, Mawdūdī coined the neologism 'theo-democracy' (*ilāhī jumhūrī ḥukūmat*).[246] According to this idea, while it formally corresponds to any modern political theory after Charles de Montesquieu (d. 1755)—Mawdūdī's conception provides for a division of powers into legislative (*qānūn-sāzī*), judiciary (*ʿadālat kā shuʿba*) and executive (*intiẓāmī shuʿba*)—the legislative power would entirely rest with God, while the other two powers would then fall into man's resort. Although one may argue that this is quite a simplification of classical Islamic political theory,[247] it is consistent with Mawdūdī's emphasis on man's rationality that grants him a 'kingdom of ends'.

Of interest in this context is the relationship between the legislative and the judiciary, because it suggests that God has issued clear and, thus, applicable legal ordinances which man needs only to enforce on earth. This, however, stands in some contrast to Mawdūdī's constant emphasis on man's rationality and the necessity to use it for the interpretation of the authoritative texts. Indeed, he conceded that the *sharīʿa* contains unclear ordinances, which have to be clarified, first, by independent rational effort (*ijtihād*) by each Muslim capable of it, and second, by the consensus (*ijmāʿ*) of the entire Muslim community.[248]

Here, Mawdūdī admitted for the first time that, despite the normative prejudgement of man's equal ability to understand the authoritative texts of Islam, empirically humans possess different capabilities. When he did so, Mawdūdī—certainly involuntarily—provided once again clear evidence for the fact that, in order to make his systematic outline work even in theory, he would occasionally have to allow for inconsistencies. In this case and without any further explanation or even acknowledgement, Mawdūdī diluted his generic term 'man' which had so far served his ends quite well. Now that the term apparently had reached the limits of its usefulness for his outline, Mawdūdī shifted his focus from an abstract normative level to a more empirical one. Now, somewhat in accord with this shift in his anthropology, he had recourse to the historical caliphates in the succession to the Prophet and, in analysing the 'democratic spirit' (*rūḥ-i jumhūriyyat*) of the early, especially Medinese, Caliphates, conceded to the *khilāfāt-i rāshidīn* an almost paradigmatic role: the caliph, elected by way of counselling, was and remained just *primus inter pares*, an idea which proved influential on Mawdūdī's thinking, as we shall see below. As such, the caliph was criticisable by and accountable to the community, a fact that Mawdūdī illustrated by various examples he drew from classical *ḥadīth*- and *ṭabaqāt*-works as well as classical historiography.[249] Moreover, in a subsequent chapter of his most comprehensive work on the matter, *Khilāfat wa mulūkiyyat*, published as late as 1966, he even tried to back up his image of the democratically-oriented 'Rightly-Guided' Caliphates by referring to the classical Ḥanafite legal position on the issue in the famous *Kitāb al-kharāj* of Abū Yūsuf Yaʿqūb ibn Ibrāhīm al-Kūfī (d. 182/798).[250]

What is important to understand here is that Mawdūdī's recourse to the 'Rightly-Guided' Caliphates as the 'touchstone [*miʿyār*] for the execution of the religious, political, ethical and social system of Islam'[251] suited perfectly well his later argument for the leadership of some selected individuals within a fundamentally egalitarian polity. In defining the actual state-to-be, however, Mawdūdī hardly got any more concrete, a fact that would inevitably lead to serious discrepancies between this and his attempt to realise the Islamic State as the ultimate goal. Thus, it appears that Mawdūdī devoted so much attention to the discussion of his understanding of leadership chiefly in order to dissociate his concept from what he saw as thinking diametrically opposed to the democratic spirit of the 'Rightly-Guided' Caliphates. To this end, Mawdūdī finally introduced the term 'kingship' (*mulūkiyya*) into the debate.

b) Caliphate versus Kingship

Already in medieval Islamic political thought, we find a fundamental differentiation between kingship and caliphate, something that, at a first sight, seems almost coextensively applied by Mawdūdī. Revealing in this regard is yet again the classification in Ibn Khaldūn's *Muqaddima*:

> Natural kingship [*al-mulk al-ṭabīʿī*] means to cause the general public [*al-kāfa*] to act as required by purpose and desire [*al-gharaḍ wa'l-shahwa*]. Political [kingship] means to cause the general public as required by rational insight [*al-naẓr al-ʿaqlī*] into the means to furthering their worldly ends [*al-maṣāliḥ al-dunyawiyya*] and avoiding anything that is harmful in that respect. The caliphate means to cause the general public to act as required by religious insight [*al-naẓr al-sharʿī*] into their ends in the other world as well as in this world. These have bearings upon [the ends in the other world], since all worldly conditions are to be considered in the light of their ends in the other world. Thus, it [i.e. the caliphate] in reality is a substitute [*khilāfa*] for the Lord of the Path [*ṣāḥib al-sharʿ*, i.e. Muḥammad] inasmuch as it serves, like him, to protect the religion [*ḥirāsat al-dīn*] and to exercise rule in the world [*siyāsat al-dunyā*].[252]

We have, of course, to bear in mind that, because his aim was more to explain reality then to develop any metaphysical outline, when speaking of 'caliphate' Ibn Khaldūn had rather the historical so-called 'Rightly-Guided' Caliphs in mind. His classification of government into 'caliphate' and 'kingship' (*mulūkiyya*) could nonetheless still be well utilised by Mawdūdī, although for this he had to return to his earlier generic notion of 'man' as a generic term. Thus, while thinkers like Ibn Khaldūn held a quite empirical view of man, i.e. to accept the wide variety of individuals within humanity, Mawdūdī was operating with a single individual in whom the deputyship of God's Messenger and man's deputyship of God on earth would ultimately fall. The important lesson Mawdūdī could have learned from Ibn Khaldūn's classification was that kingship is confined to worldly ends alone, an orientation towards an externally given, so that an objective regulation that includes an explicit eschatological dimension is no necessity at all. On this point, Ibn Khaldūn and Mawdūdī could well have agreed.

Unlike Ibn Khaldūn, however, for whom 'kingship' formed 'an institution that is [only] natural to man [*manṣib ṭabīʿī li'l-insān*]',[253] Mawdūdī considered it rather the opposite: as kingship is not ordained by God, and it is exclusively God's commandments that Mawdūdī saw as according to nature, it follows logically that kingship cannot be something natural. Therefore, and consistent with his standard way of developing his points on the basis of a recourse to the Qurʾān, his argument on this point, although not systematically formulated, ran as follows. Because in the Qurʾān the term *mālik* is frequently used as an epithet for God—a view that was prominently held by renowned classical exegetes, too[254]—man considering himself *mālik* would move him close to assuming divinity.[255] This, in turn, had to be regarded a clear violation of man's expected subordination to God and his acknowledgement of God's absolute sovereignty:

> If someone begins either to see himself as the Master [*mālik*] or to use the powers that were conferred upon him in whatever manner he pleased [*man-māne ṭarīqe se*], or if he, instead of the True Master, acknowledges someone else as master, follows his aims and executes his rules [*aḥkām*], then these would be considered as acts of treachery and revolt [*ghaddārī awr baghāwat ke afʿāl*].[256]

It is thus very likely that, within his outline, Mawdūdī established in the concept of 'kingship' yet another 'asymmetrical counter-term', which we introduced earlier as such a distinctive feature of ideologies.[257] As such, 'kingship' should not be seen as an empirical term, even though Mawdūdī himself made it appear in extensive *Khilāfat wa mulūkiyyat* as if indeed it was. Here, he devoted a lot of time and space to pointing out how 'kingship', from the establishment of the Umayyad dynasty by Muʿāwiya ibn Abī Sufyān (d. 60/680) onwards, had destroyed what he imagined as the original Islamic social, political and economic order.[258]

There are, however, a few reasons that support a consideration of Mawdūdī's understanding of 'kingship' in a topological rather than an empirical manner. A clue is provided by the conclusion of his treatment of the transformation of the historical caliphates into monarchies. Here, Mawdūdī emphasised that it was especially the 'democratic spirit' of Islam that was still maintained during the 'Rightly-Guided' Caliphates[259] and considerably declined from the time of the so-called First *fitna* of 656–61 CE onwards. The 'democratic spirit', in turn, constitutes the essence of *khilāfa*, which is sanctioned by the Qurʾān and which needs therefore to be considered as the antonym to 'kingship' as a social and political order based on inequality that evolves from the different preconditions of individual human beings. In this regard one is tempted to even draw a parallel with Communist political and economic thought. 'Kingship' would then represent the particular interests of the class of exploiters, whereas 'khilāfa' represented the general interest that, in Communist ideology, is identical with the interest of the working class.[260] 'Khilāfa', thus, would be the only true guarantor of social justice and contributes to the Common Good (*maṣlaḥa*), while 'kingship' is diametrically opposed to it.[261] Moreover, the progression from righteous caliphal to unjust monarchical rule served once again as proof for Mawdūdī's model of Islamic history as one of religious and political decline, epitomised in the already mentioned Prophetic *ḥadīth* according to which the 'caliphate after the prophetic pattern' became gradually replaced by an increasingly tyrannical kingship.[262] As on almost every other level of Mawdūdī's deductive system, however, this relationship could also be read the other way around. His bipolar understanding of history in 'Islam' and various degrees of *jāhiliyya* would then constitute the backdrop against which the dichotomy of 'caliphate' and 'kingship' is interpreted.

To keep the predominance of this historicist matrix in his entire systematic outline in mind is helpful for understanding in that, when speaking of 'kingship', Mawdūdī, after all very much a child of his time as well as his Indian environment, really had the monarchies of the past and present in mind. Against this backdrop 'kingship' was considered a topos under which Mawdūdī subsumed all those social and political formations which stood counter to his conception of Islam as a radically egalitarian and, thus, democratic social and political order. The role of this term within Mawdūdī's ideological outline must therefore not be underestimated.

Ultimately, it represented the culmination of Mawdūdī's critical treatment of all prevailing political ideologies, subsumed under the catch phrase 'nationalism' (*qawmiyya*) which had been the focus of his criticism right from the beginning. This is quite understandable if one recalls that during the years in which Mawdūdī developed the core of his ideological outline, nationalist movements of various *couleurs* had become the major pillars of the Indian struggle for independence. Moreover, as seen above,[263] the various nationalist conceptions prevalent in India in the two decades before its independence from British colonial rule drew a lot of their inspiration from various political ideologies predominant in Europe at that time. It is therefore that within his critical analysis of 'nationalism' one finds Mawdūdī's most explicit discussion of Western political ideologies.

Nationalism—The Kingship of the Modern Age

Mawdūdī's critical discussion of 'nationalism' is embedded in his examination of the Indian independence movement in the aftermath of the Caliphate Movement of the early 1920s, very much centred on the INC and its leading figures. While this meant first and foremost Javāharlāl Nehrū, Mawdūdī increasingly included later on also those from among the Muslim leadership who supported the cause of the INC, prominent among them the two Deobandī *ʿulamāʾ* Husayn Ahmad Madanī (d. 1377/1957), then president of Mawdūdī's former employer, the *Jamʿiyyat al-ʿulamāʾ-i Hind*,[264] and ʿUbaydallāh Sindhī (d. 1363/1944).[265] In 1938, at the peak of the movement, Mawdūdī had his views, which he had presented in various earlier articles, collectively published in three subsequent volumes as *Musalmān awr mawjūda siyāsī kashmakash*. Although a small disclaimer in later editions states that this book owes very much to the particular circumstances of that time,[266] Mawdūdī's later writings on the matter show that his basic argument remained largely unchanged. The point of departure for what he called the 'Theory of Nationalism' was Nehrū's autobiography, published for the first time only two years before Mawdūdī's *Musalmān awr mawjūda siyāsī kashmakash*, where the future first prime minister of independent India had his ideas on an Indian nation elaborated.

These ideas set out from the eighteenth century European understanding of a nation as a people tied to a distinct territory, sharing the same cultural and, thus, historical narrative.[267] In such a conception, evolved during the

European Enlightenment, religious identity occupies at the most a subordinated role, one had first of all to identify with everything that can be derived from inhabiting a determined territory. Nehrū had this understanding of a nation, coupled with elements from Marxian theory stratifying the Indian nation along the lines of economic classes.[268] In Mawdūdī's understanding, this appeared to be rather inconsistent, because while the idea of a 'nation' suggested an equality between all its members, the idea of 'class' clearly referred to internal differences. If the dominant class interest is that of a majority, then, so Mawdūdī argued, the 'class' concept would play into the hands of the Hindu religious majority.[269] Although it is true that in reality the Hindus were also economically privileged—a fact that Nehrū himself frankly acknowledged[270]—from a theoretical point of view Mawdūdī wrongly implied that Nehrū had considered 'economic class' and 'religion' as equivalent. In fact, since Nehrū's nationalistic framework was essentially secular, 'religion' played indeed a subordinated role in the constitution of an Indian nation.[271]

Since for Mawdūdī 'religion' held an equal position as 'nation' for Nehrū, it was consistent for the former to emphasise the contradictoriness of conceptions such as 'Muslim nationalism' or 'Muslim socialism'—to him they were to be considered equally absurd as 'Communist fascism' or the like.[272] In doing so, Mawdūdī not only rejected the Nehruvian idea of a secular Indian nation, but repudiated no less fervently the nationalism of Jinnāḥ's AIML which revolved largely around Iqbāl's idea of a Indo-Muslim nation, entitled to an independent national territory.[273]

The Islamic state that Mawdūdī had in mind did not, like the 'Pakistan' of the AIML, result from the communalism prevalent in British India at that time and the ensuing political and economic resentments of Indian Muslims.[274] His state, based on the absolute and undisputable veracity of God's supreme sovereignty and the limited sovereignty of the believing man as crown of His creation, was necessarily a universal one. With regard to this universalism, Mawdūdī acknowledged that his political ideas shared some particularities with Marxist ideology when he referred to the example of the Second International (1889–1916), where the joint cause of proletarian internationalism transcended national boundaries.[275] However, when he concluded that 'the same way as the communists establish their own particular theory, the Muslims [will] establish their own theory, too',[276] Mawdūdī involuntarily revealed that his systematic thoughts owed very much to his desire to dissociate himself from other prevalent political ideologies in the subcontinent, the communalism-inspired particularism of the

AIML as well as the socialism-inspired universalism of the Nehrū faction within the INC. Besides the AIML and INC, however, it would have been only consistent also to dissociate himself explicitly from the 'Islamo-Fascism' of al-Mashriqī's *Khāksār* which apparently was even closer to Mawdūdī as it, like him, argued from a normative rather than from an empirical level. It is therefore somewhat surprising that the *Khāksār* have apparently not been considered a major competitor,[277] which is why Mawdūdī's refutation was concentrated more on the nationalisms of the AIML and INC.

The crucial problem that Mawdūdī saw in these two representations of nationalism in late colonial India was that both would aim at only a section of humankind, confined by either religious creed or by territorial belonging.[278] Such exclusivism stands in stark contrast to the Qurʾān-based idea of equality of all men and would thus indeed lead to an unsound kind of competition between them, resulting in feelings of pride and superiority (*iftikhār*), which, in their most extreme consequence, lead to the aggrandisement of one's own people (*qawmī istiʿalāʾ wa istikbār*) and finally to imperialist attitudes (*qayṣariyyat*).[279] Mawdūdī's second objection against the two forms of Indian nationalism appears somewhat odd in the light of his earlier argument for the collective *khilāfa* in an almost Rousseauian guise, because he reproached all the Nehrūs and Jinnāḥs to demand a complete extinction of individuality for the sake of the collective, as the individual is forced to become entirely identical with the whole, a thought that clearly echoes Enlightenment and idealist political philosophies.[280] To back up his argument, Mawdūdī quoted at length, although conveniently omitting what did not serve his purpose, from then popular American academic works on the evolution of contemporary Western political thought.[281] To deliberately use these kind of works fulfilled a twofold purpose for Mawdūdī. First, by drawing from Western academic works he attempted to provide his argument with greater credibility. Second, the common understanding that the origins of Western political thought date back to Hellenic times helped Mawdūdī a great deal to treat 'nationalism' and, thus, the cradle of social inequality as the sole creature of European political philosophy. Hence, Aristotle's distinction between citizens (*polítes*) and barbarians (*bárbaroi*) is consequently presented as Mawdūdī's crown witness.[282]

This rather negative portrayal of Aristotle, whose massive impact on the development of Muslim philosophical thought was conveniently ignored by Mawdūdī, is significant. After all it was he whose political thought is much more based on empirical observation than that of his teacher Plato. This fixation on earthly matters, in turn, which by Mawdūdī's time had undergone a metamorphosis into empiricism,[283] could be blamed as being responsible for man's increasing desire to exploit the earth to as large an extent as possible.[284] This pessimistic outlook was not Mawdūdī's alone, but was shared even with earlier Western socio-critical thinkers like Rousseau,[285] although to conclude from this the emergence of the nation was solely Mawdūdī's doing. In his eyes, because of man's preoccupation with mundane affairs, nations would thus only be interest-led associations, their single objective being to better exploit the resources of the world in a situation of fierce competition. If this was indeed the case, then even a supposed 'Muslim nation' or 'Hindu nation' in India would be stripped bare of any true religious element—'religion' declines thus to only a symbolic, but otherwise hollow shell in order to unite a certain number of people in their pursuit of exploiting the world. For Mawdūdī, linking his own terminology with Ibn Khaldūn's purposefully coined concept of 'ʿaṣabiyya', the social cohesive force could thus only be an *ʿaṣabiyyat-i jāhiliyya*, lacking any true spirituality but being determined instead by worldly desire alone.[286] However, while even for a keen observer of his empirical surroundings like Ibn Khaldūn 'religion' played a major role in strengthening the social glue within a tribal nomadic society (*ʿaṣabiyya*),[287] in a nationalist line of argument 'religion' would be considered rather counterproductive, even if its emotional value was widely acknowledged and therefore employed for strategic reasons.[288]

To prove his point, Mawdūdī referred to the recent example of the young Turkish Republic and the thought of its leading theoretician Mehmet Ziya 'Gökalp' (d. 1924), embodiment of his number one adversary since the collapse of the Indian Caliphate Movement of the early 1920s.[289] Although Gökalp's thoughts appeared to be not much different from Nehrū's later concept of an Indian nation, defined by a common 'culture' that provided the vehicle for progressing towards a single 'civilisation'—the ideological nucleus of Nehrū's Indian nation[290]—they were nonetheless of special significance for Mawdūdī. After all, the Republic of Turkey emerged from the Ottoman Empire which, especially by Muslims abroad, was considered an Islamic state, not least because of the nominal Caliphate that the Ottoman sultan claimed since 1517.[291] Keeping in mind Mawdūdī's active involvement in the Indian Caliphate Movement, his retrospective criticism which we have earlier identified as the prime trigger for his own religio-political considerations,[292] he regarded Turkish nationalism and its leading ideologues as the gravediggers of a central Islamic political institution and, therefore, of Islam in general.

While, on a more abstract level, 'kingship' had been established as a topological counter-term to 'caliphate', corresponding to Mawdūdī's earlier and equally topological dichotomy of 'jāhiliyya' and 'Islam', 'nationalism' became for him the concrete contemporary manifestation of 'kingship'. Because of this and the correlation between 'kingship' and 'jāhiliyya', Mawdūdī had to construe 'Islam' consequently as the incorporation of all values that are diametrically opposed to those of 'nationalism', thus, as an ideology that is characterised by a spirit of equality of all men regardless of their birth, of universal mutuality between them and of man's responsibility for his handling with the earthly resources.[293] Of course, such an image of 'Islam' does not at all correspond to the historical reality of Muslim societies, in which gender inequality and slavery were the normal order of the day.[294] As has already occurred in other places, however, Mawdūdī's highly idealised understanding of 'Islam' was indeed not intended to comply with the various manifestations of Islam as they were really practised throughout the Muslim world. As his analysis of Muslim history in the course of his reinterpretation of the concept of *jāhiliyya* has shown, scarcely any of the historical Muslim societies after the 'Rightly-Guided' Caliphates fulfilled Mawdūdī's narrow criteria of 'Islam'. The allegedly Islamic rule of later times was thus similar to 'kingship' and, as just another expression of *jāhiliyya*, not so very different from contemporary nationalism.

The nationalist threat seems however to have been so overwhelmingly strong that Mawdūdī was prompted to go even one layer beneath his analysis of nationalism as a political phenomenon or ideology proper. Apparently, he was well aware that the originally Western ideology of nationalism and its subsequent manifestation in various nationalist movements were deeply rooted in modern Western ethical concepts.[295] Any examination of Mawdūdī's critical evaluation of 'nationalism' would therefore be incomplete without acknowledging his early treatises on ethics, all written in 1923–2 while he was still editor of *al-Jamʿiyya*.[296]

Given the tremendous impact of British thought on the intellectual constitution of colonial India, it is not surprising that the majority of authors whose views Mawdūdī discussed were either utilitarians or British idealists. Even earlier authors, starting with Plato and Aristotle, but prominently also Hegel, appear to be perceived largely through the prism of British moral philosophies at the turn of the twentieth century.[297] In fact, Mawdūdī's discussion of social ethics, first published as a series of disconnected articles in the monthly magazines *Humāyūn* (Lahore) and *Ṣirāṭ al-mustaqīm* (Hyderabad)[298] and only much later collated as *Akhlāqiyyāt-i ijtimāʿiyya awr uskā falsafa*, appears to be his most explicit and thorough treatment of Western thought. This is even reinforced by the fact that, at first sight, this work appears rather descriptive and misses the explicit contrasting of *jāhilī* and Islamic viewpoints that became typical for almost all of Mawdūdī's later writings. However, when put into the wider framework and especially when linked to his critical look at nationalism, it becomes clear that his investigation into Western ethics had to fulfil only one single purpose, namely to reveal the roots of the much despised nationalism even further.

As the premise for all social ethics, Mawdūdī established the relationship between individualism and collectivism, which he put more pointedly in Spencerian terms as the relationship between 'egoism' (*anāniyyat*) and 'altruism' (*ikhwāniyyat* [sic]). As the two diametrically opposed positions in assessing this relationship, he consequently presented the positions of Herbert Spencer, epitome of the positivist point of view, and Hegel as representative of the idealist one.[299] Without making it explicit, one may assume that all the following considerations were reflected against the backdrop of the tension between these two poles. Mawdūdī's clear dismissal of Spencer's ultra-liberalist advocacy of individuality over the collective, however, indicates the direction in which Mawdūdī's own thoughts would be moving. For him, there is no real alternative to collectivism, although the answer that he was later going to give also differed considerably from the idealist position.

Historically, Mawdūdī set out from the comparison of the Platonic and the Aristotelian understanding of the relationship between ethics and politics. Outlining the ethical considerations in Plato's *Politeía*, Mawdūdī stressed the fact that a state could only be good as long as the eternal ideas of the virtues (*maḥāsin*) are realised.[300] The initial spark for a Western *Sonderweg*, however, was clearly given by Aristotle who derived ethical values not from non-spatial and atemporal ideas (*parádeigma*) of the pure heaven (*en katharōi ouranōi*)[301] but from man's earthly activities: 'happiness' (*eudaimonía*) is therefore acquired by human practice and, given the fact that man is by nature a 'political animal',[302] the state is the primary means for the realisation of happiness.[303] This worldly attitude that increasingly constituted humankind as creator of its own norms and values was somewhat challenged by Stoic and early Christian fatalistic ethics. Their overemphasis on a teleologically pre-arranged world, however, epitomised in the concepts of 'fate' (*heimarméne*; *fatum*) and 'providence' (*prónoia*; *providentia*), confines man to appropriation (*oikeíosis*) only, and thus leaves no space for autonomy.[304]

At first one may assume that an approach that deduces ethical norms from a divine source was more to the liking of Mawdūdī. The Stoic and early Christian understanding of God as an entirely distant and unapproachable being that neither really communicates with man nor leaves him real space to act did not meet Mawdūdī's own conception of God and His relation with man. Here, we are somehow reminded of his strong repudiation of monasticism and pantheism in his discussion of the various forms of *jāhiliyya*.[305] It is therefore not surprising that, although misinterpreting Stoic ethics as being led by the maxim 'The whole world is ours' (*sārā jahān hamārā*),[306] Mawdūdī dismissed it clearly by stating that 'their entire conception of ethics appeared meaningless and impracticable [*be-maʿnī awr nā-qābil-i ʿamal*]'.[307] He therefore continued to discuss the issues pertaining to ethics only with regard to its social relevance, thus focusing on social ethics as opposed to individual ethics. For this, he basically presented the arguments of the two mentioned diametrical poles which dominated the debate on the matter in Britain at that time, namely positivism, including utilitarianism, and idealism.

Although one might be tempted to read Mawdūdī's discussion of various viewpoints regarding the origins of man's social consciousness as a matter-of-fact treatment of the issue, one should always bear in mind that Mawdūdī had to disagree with almost all the propositions that he presented. Be it an ethics that revolves around a hedonistic pursuit of happiness,[308] or an ethics in which an individual brings himself in congruency with the whole,[309] Mawdūdī's main point of criticism was most certainly the anthropocentrism of Western ethical thought.

His further exposition run very much along the lines of early Enlightenment philosophers, namely the assumption of a natural state of humankind which is characterised by a life not yet regulated by self-imposed rules for co-existence. The anthropological basis for this, of course, has to be man's freedom of thought and act (*āzādī yā ḥurriyat-i fikr wa ʿamal*)—this, in turn, after acknowledging man's individual sovereignty (*malikiyyat*) and reflecting upon the interest in survival, leads eventually to the conclusion of a social contract (*muʿāhada*).[310] It is highly illuminating that Mawdūdī created here an intellectual genealogy from Plato, via Aristotle, to the contractual theories of Thomas Hobbes (d. 1679) and Rousseau, without much differentiation in their respective views, because this supports once more our suspicion that he pursued a particular aim with his exposition of Western social ethics.[311] Indeed—although Mawdūdī drew this conclusion only in a later writing from 1941[312]—from such a purpose-built association of a given number of people it would only be a short step to the self-perception of such a group as 'nation' and the ideological consolidation of the purpose of their association as 'nationalism'. Interestingly, his discussion of how a hierarchically arranged set of ethical maxims is derived from the philosophical anthropology that builds on the premise of man's autonomy and freedom of choice appears, however, to a certain extent similar to Mawdūdī's own understanding of man's freedom of choice as discussed above.[313]

Mawdūdī's discussion of the derivation of ethical maxims is, however, not only significant because of this similarity with his own understanding of man as a free being, but also reveals how he creatively absorbed Western philosophical and political thought. Although he departed from what might be read as a paraphrase of Kant's categorical imperative (*c̲h̲āhī'e yā na c̲h̲āhī'e* [sic]), and derived from here a set of interdependent ethical values such as life (*ḥayāt*), freedom (*āzādī*), autonomy (*malikiyyat*) as a natural disposition (*sīrat*), law (*ā'īn wa qawānīn*), sincerity (*ṣadāqat*) and, finally, communal betterment (*taraqqī*),[314] his understanding remained short of a crucial point of transcendental and idealist philosophies. Although Kant and his idealist epigones produced ethical values indeed from man's self-reflection, they nonetheless never dismissed the necessity of the idea of a transcendent being, i.e. God, as the ultimate justification of these ethical values.[315] Since all over Mawdūdī's treatment of the origin of ethical values in Western thought the transcendent is never mentioned, it appears safe to assume that his understanding of these ideas was indeed mediated by their either positive or negative appropriation in British thought at the turn of the twentieth century.[316] The idea of God as man's ultimate point of reference appears much less pronounced by the British idealists than by their German predecessors,[317] indeed, for the utilitarians such an idea of God would even run counter to their fundamental ethical principle of hedonism. For them God—and by this they referred exclusively to the God of the Bible—was relevant only insofar as His revealed commandments corresponded, as John Stuart Mill aptly put it in his programmatic essay *Utilitarianism*, to 'the requirements of utility to a supreme degree'.[318]

It has, however, to be acknowledged that even though Mawdūdī's understanding of the development of social ethics in Western thought, all the way from Greek antiquity, was derived from and subsequently presented mainly through the prism of British idealism and utilitarianism, even then it appeared rather superficial.[319] However, if this treatment by him is seen within the wider framework of the systematic outline of Islam that he was beginning to develop a few years later, then one may come to a more lenient judgement. Overall, although grossly simplified, the picture that Mawdūdī provided is not incorrect and appears moreover sufficient to enable Mawdūdī to conclude with a plea to acknowledge the 'true religion' (*sachcha madhhab*) as the only means to achieve the ultimate level of moral integrity.[320] From here one can spin the thread to the assumption that the anthropocentric view which had dominated Western thought at least since the Enlightenment is not suited to serve as a foundation for a set of firm universal social ethics, but would rather confine it to a restricted number of people who, in a deliberate act of externalisation, subscribe to a moral and, consequently, political standard. The fact that these standards can vary according to different agreements concluded by different groups of people would, in turn, be responsible for the parallel existence of various polities based on different sets of values. The crux is now, as one could spin the thread even further, that in order to justify their authority, these values need to be regarded as if they were universally valid. At this place, finally, it becomes fully evident that Mawdūdī's elaboration on social ethics pursued indeed a particular aim, as here it comes full circle with Mawdūdī's criticism of nationalism.

Values which were created and set as absolute by man himself, he would argue, would inevitably lead to conflict between 'us', those who submit to these values, and 'them', those who do not. The claim of superiority of one's own values over those of others, well exemplified during Mawdūdī's lifetime by Communism and Fascism at work,[321] does not lead, either in the eyes of Mawdūdī or in those of the idealist philosophers he was referring to, to an ethical betterment of humankind as a whole. The only remedy, thus Mawdūdī argued consistently, would be to accept the facticity of an entirely transcendent creator who has set man in this world, supplemented with a mission and a set of rules and values to act upon. To submit to this creator, finally, implies acknowledging one's subordinated position, the mission and the set of rules. In Mawdūdī's parlance, it means recognising God as lord (*rabb*), that is, as absolute sovereign (*ḥākim*) over all of creation, and as object of veneration (*ilāh*). It means furthermore to accepting and following the set of rules incorporated in the Qurʾānic revelation, and it means that as long as man fully submits to God and obeys His rules, man is His trustee on earth (*khalīfat allāh*). Important in order to make this all work is to remember that man—and here Mawdūdī overlapped again, at least to some extent, with the Western political philosophers he was so eager to dissociate himself from—possesses some degree of autonomy and freedom of choice which he may employ for the emendation of humankind by submitting to God, or which he would also be able to use also for the satisfaction of his personal desires, regardless of anyone else. For Mawdūdī, however, as well as for Western thinkers from Aristotle to Hobbes and beyond, the latter would mean to act against man's nature as *zōon politikón*, and would cause him to fall back to the state of 'war [...] of every man against every man',[322] or, as Mawdūdī saw it, a war of every nation against every nation. For Mawdūdī, therefore, the task stood to develop an alternative societal framework in which man's *khilāfa* could practically be realised. It would then however be this very framework which, consistent with Mawdūdī's earlier concession, based on the fundamental premise of man's freedom of choice, that there are other possible *adyān* besides the Islamic one, is the one that Mawdūdī would eventually enter into competition with other ideologies.

4) The System at Work

Since in Mawdūdī's understanding of the Qur'ānic message Islam was essentially oriented towards the realisation of an adequate worldly order,[323] it is only consistent that the societal framework for the actual realisation of man's *khilāfa* cannot be anything but a political structure, the 'Islamic state' (*ḥukūmat-i islāmī*). However, in dissociation from nationalism, rooted in territorial and linguistic commonalities,[324] Mawdūdī's conception of state had to differ considerably. To some extent it resembled—willingly or unwillingly—the idealist-Hegelian one, which did not revolve around a defined territory as *conditio sine qua non* for a state, but lay rather in the objectivation of the idea of morality that, in turn, applies first of all to the individual.[325] After all, morality, with Kant, is the deliberate subordination of each and every one under the categorical imperative to 'act only according to that maxim whereby you can at the same time will that it should become a universal law';[326] hence individuality and universality fall ultimately into one. What the 'moral law' (*Sittengesetz*) was for the idealist philosophers in the wake of Kant, was for Mawdūdī the *dīn*: a stable and all-embracing 'system of thought and action to which man commits his life'.[327]

Since for Mawdūdī *dīn* is an ideological concept, that is all-pervasive and irrefutable by rational means, its acceptance, as outlined above,[328] becomes a matter of conviction. As such, Mawdūdī's *dīn* resembled to some extent the idealist's self-deduced 'moral law' as the precondition for all action. In the same way as man has the free choice to accept or not accept the idealist's 'moral law', he would have a choice when it comes to the Islamic *dīn*. Accordingly, the decision as to what kind of polity man will be living in is subject to his own responsible choice.

Where Mawdūdī however clearly differed from the idealist-Hegelian conception of the state as the 'ethical idea' was that Hegel clearly recognised the historicity of communities. His state was therefore to be realised only within these respective spatial confines—as much as he may have wished for an universal ethical polity, he did not dare to impose the values he held dear on others and by this to severely reduce their own respective freedom of choice. In the aftermath of Hegel, however, this significantly changed. Leading Young Hegelians, prominently among them Marx and Engels, have turned Hegel's idea upside down and argued that, although man possesses free choice *in potentia, in actu* it is however limited by his dependency on the material world which, in turn, shapes his social world. Consequently, man can only create morality within the confines of the acknowledgment of his dependence on non-man-made factors. Because the transformation of Hegelian thought by Marx and Engels discharged into an outline of an ideology, it appears not surprising that Mawdūdī's views on this matter appeared to be of structural similarity. As already outlined above,[329] for him the choice was only for or against the Islamic *dīn*. Once the decision had been made in favour of it, then morality cannot be derived by subjective reflection, but only from what is divinely ordained. An 'ethical' or, as Mawdūdī himself labelled it, 'ideological state' (*jamāʿatī awr maslakī ist'et*) founded on this premise has, like the societal vision of Communism, necessarily to claim universal validity, a similarity which Mawdūdī himself was not afraid to even openly acknowledge.[330] Since Mawdūdī's state would be—in a Hegelian paraphrase—the 'actuality of the (Islamic) *dīn*', and the *dīn*, in turn, depended on acknowledgement only, Mawdūdī's state could not be spatially confined:

> Islam does not recognise any geographical, colour or linguistic bars. It puts forward its constitution [*dastūr*], purpose [*maqṣad*] and reformist programme [*iṣlāḥī progrām*] before all men. Whoever embraces Islam, no matter what race [*nasl*], people [*mulk*] or nation [*qawm*] he may belong to, can join the community that will be established to run the Islamic state.[331]

The task of the ideological state would *idealiter* be an ethical one, namely to provide the organisational framework for enabling its citizens to lead the

'Islamic Way of Life'. On the other hand, Mawdūdī was well aware of the significant differences of what this would mean in concrete terms. Therefore, if he did not want the Islamic state to be understood as a mere conglomeration of people, the only common denominator of whom would be their however designed commitment to Islam, the polity must necessarily have a certain administrative structure. Its necessary administrative super structure (*Überbau*) would first and foremost perform a supervisory function and ensure the maintenance of an uniform ethical standard and, whenever necessary, enforce it by legal means.[332] This, at first glance, seems, of course, to contradict Mawdūdī's collectivist and egalitarian conception of the *khilāfat allāh*: does not his fundamental anthropological understanding rule out any kind of societal stratification by definition? A closer look into Mawdūdī's writings reveals that he tried to develop arguments which were meant to resolve this contradiction and allow for leadership in an egalitarian setting.

4.1) The Leviathan and his Limbs

Mawdūdī's understanding of early Islamic history, that is, the times of the Prophet and of the Medinese Caliphs, coupled with his conception of the *khilāfat allāh* which, in turn, constituted the foundation of his idea of the Islamic way of governance as a 'theo-democracy', had yet to find its pendant in practice. After all, his aim was not confined to providing only an abstract theoretical framework, but rather a well-grounded structure, which could possibly be applied to the social and political reality. Although there is no solid textual evidence, it can nonetheless be assumed that Mawdūdī considered grassroots democracy as an impracticable solution for his envisioned Islamic state. After all, an equal participation of each and every member of the polity in the making of any political decision could only work in a consistent and spatially very much confined political entity.[333] This, however, as already stated, inevitably clashed with Mawdūdī's ethical or ideological state which, by definition, could not be territorially restricted but had to assume a global and thus decentralised dimension instead. Besides, the concept of grassroots democracy was too deeply rooted in Western political thought and had barely had a substantial equivalent in Islamic history,[334] which might be added as just another reason for being dismissed by Mawdūdī.

For him, therefore *khilāfat allāh* could only mean that every citizen of the state was equally preconditioned and had thus the same basic potential to take part in political decision-making processes. The only practicable way for this, however, was to develop mechanisms for the selection of a limited number of representatives who, in turn, would be the ones to arrive at actual political decisions. Because this resembled clearly a Western representative democracy and would thus clash with Mawdūdī's aversion against the foundations of any Western political system, he required a solid Islamic basis for the selection process. Such a basis Mawdūdī claimed to have found in the classical Islamic institution of mutual consultation (*shūrá*) 'without [which] the pursuit of societal works would not only follow the ways of the *jāhiliyya*, but would openly reject a rule [*ḍābiṭa*] which God has prescribed'.[335] This institution, rooted in pre-Islamic Arab customary law,[336] has, owing not least to the efforts of Mawdūdī, enjoyed an enormous revival in contemporary times. It has been brought forward mainly by Muslim apologists as occidentalist arguments for the 'essentially' democratic spirit of the Islamic concept of governance to respond to the politically momentous Western-orientalist conception of 'oriental despotism', somewhat frequently applied to Islam.[337] This perception, however, appears as a somewhat deliberate distortion of the historical practice.

Its most democratic shape in the Islamic context involved the practice of mutual consultation, perhaps in the Qur'ānic chapter of the very name, when it was declared a virtue of the believers, even though it was not indicated how exactly *shūrá* should actually be practised.[338] As such, the Qur'ānic injunction appears somewhat as a democratisation of the pre-Islamic tribal institution of a 'Council of Nobles/Elders' (*mala*) which acted as a supervisory body to prevent the abuse of power by single individuals, even if of all people it was Quṣayy ibn Kilāb (*c.* fourth century CE), 'unifier' (*mujammi'*) of the tribal union of the Quraysh and therefore ancestor of the Prophet Muḥammad, who was the first to claim for himself what Dostal calls 'sacral chieftainship'.[339] However, since in pre-Islamic tribal Arabia access to decision-making processes was not open to everyone, but confined only to those male members of the tribe who were of the appropriate age, the pre-Islamic custom of *shūrá* could barely be considered egalitarian or, come to that, proto-democratic.

The consultative practice of the Medinese Caliphs appears to have diverted considerably from the Qur'ānic injunction and dissolved into combination with pre-Islamic tribal practice. When, for the settlement of his succession, the dying second Caliph 'Umar ibn al-Khaṭṭāb ordered the appointment of a *shūrá* consisting of five, six or seven selected virtuous Muslims, he deliberately wanted to exclude the very powerful *ṭulaqā'*, that is, those who had converted to Islam only after the successful Muslim conquest of Mecca in 630 CE.[340] Building on this example, *shūrá* soon became institutionalised as an electoral tool under the Umayyads,[341] leading to the belief that the elected one enjoyed the approval of the entire Muslim community when, in fact, he had been nominated with caliphal blessing. This rather deviant use of the Qur'ānic principle of mutual consultation, already from a very early point in Muslim history, needs to be kept in mind in order to understand the motives behind Mawdūdī's particular employment of the concept of *shūrá*.

a) *Primus inter pares*—The Principle of Leadership

Apart from stressing its obligation for every Muslim,[342] with the introduction of the principle of *shūrá* into his ideology Mawdūdī pursued a rather profane goal: *shūrá*, in its first and more general form, was—like it was since the late Medinese Caliphate—an electoral tool, aimed at a transfer of power by a set group of people to one from amongst their midst who was to serve as the head of the entire community:

> The use of the term 'caliph' [in reference to him] does not imply that only he alone is the Caliph, but that the *khilāfa* of the common Muslims had been concentrated in his venerable personality [*us kī dhāt-i girāmī meṇ murakkaz ho ga'ī he*].[343]

As such, the *shūrá* appears almost as the Hobbesian process, in which the members of a polity alienate their natural rights—here their *khilāfat allāh*—in a voluntary act for the sake of a greater good.[344] Unlike Hobbes, however, according to whose mechanistic and additive understanding the singular will of the sovereign results from the transfer of the sum of all singular wills within the polity, Mawdūdī's model appears rather dynamistic. Here, the intensity of the *khilāfat allāh* is greatest in the elected representative.

Even so, what both Hobbes and Mawdūdī have in common is that the leader of the community emerges himself from that very community[345] and is selected because he was considered—in Hobbes—the most likely person to guarantee the protection of his subjects, or—in Mawdūdī—'the most honoured of you in the sight of God [*akramakum 'inda allāh*]' who is 'the most righteous of you [*atqākum*]'.[346] Also, after the conferral of 'all their power and strength upon one man'[347] for both Hobbes and Mawdūdī, the election cannot be reversed unless Hobbes' sovereign has been proven unable to provide his subjects with the necessary protection,[348] or unless Mawdūdī's leader has deviated from the path of righteousness.[349]

After he was elected he will exercise full authority in every respect [*siyāh wa sapīd ke ikhtiyārāt*]. He will be completely relied upon and, as long as he follows the laws of God and the Messenger, he will enjoy full obedience [*uskī kāmil iṭāʿat kī jāʾegī*].[350]

Mawdūdī's understanding of the powers of such an elected person is reflected in the title of 'commander' (*amīr*) which he chose for the designation of this bearer of the concentrated *khilāfat allāh*. After all, the relationship between command and absolute obedience is justified by the Qurʾānic dictum 'Oh ye who believe! Obey God, and obey the Messenger, and those invested with command among you [*wa-ulī 'l-amr minkum*]',[351] as well as by Islamic tradition. Classical Islamic historiography referred to this term with regard to the election of Abū Bakr al-Ṣiddīq (d. 13/634) as successor of the Prophet in the political and religious leadership of the young Muslim *umma*.[352] Ibn Khaldūn referred to its use within the Abbasid nomenclature, saying that '[the *amīr*] had power over the other ranks and exercised control over everything, either as [the ruler's] delegate or through being usurping control [*immā niyāba aw istibdād*]'.[353]

The *amīr*'s function as the true ruler's deputy was quite consistent with Mawdūdī's systematic outline. Since man as such cannot be the supreme ruler, as this position is reserved for God alone, he is inevitably confined to the rank of a deputy, provided that he 'believes and works righteous deeds'. From among all the *khulafāʾ allāh* the most pious person is selected in an act of transferring the powers of every single *khilāfat allāh* to him and, thus, making him 'caliph of the caliphs' (*khalīfat al-khulafāʾ*). As such, the *amīr* stands out in the crowd as the prime representative of man's deputyship of God on earth. Less democratic than Mawdūdī wanted us to believe, his concept of *imāra* resembled much more the Principate of the Roman Empire at the turn of the common era, when especially the first emperor Gaius Julius Octavius 'Augustus' (d. 14 CE) tried hard to achieve a balance between the preservation of the republican facade and the enforcement and legitimisation of their own claims to power.[354] This impression is reinforced even further by the fact that Mawdūdī introduced a consultative council, the *Majlis-i shūrá*, 'trusted by the common Muslims [and ...] elected by the votes of [the common] Muslims',[355] to which the *amīr* must resort for counselling—here *shūrá* assumed a second and more concrete meaning within Mawdūdī's general outline. The powers of Mawdūdī's *Majlis-i shūrá* were however only *in potentia*; *in actu* the *amīr* would not be obliged to bow even to the majority vote within the council, but—and here there is clearly a potential for autocratic decisions:

according to Islam it is possible that the opinion of a single person will be sounder [*bar ḥaqq*] than the unanimous opinion of the entire council. If this is the case, then there would be no reason why the truth should be given up only because its supporters are in the minority and error is accepted only because it has the support of the majority. Therefore, the *amīr* has the right [*ḥaqq*] to agree with the majority or with the minority. The *amīr* would even have the right to assert his opinion against the entire council.[356]

The monopoly of definition conceded to the *amīr* appears once again almost similar to the relationship between emperor and the senate of imperial Rome. While the emperor was considered the first or most noble among the senators (*princeps/ordo senatorius*), he enjoyed nonetheless almost unlimited autonomy in his decisions, even though they had to be formally approved by the senate.[357] In this way, and whether or not it was really intended that way, the senate appeared only as a handy tool to publicise and justify the emperor's decisions and give it thus the illusion of a truly democratic body.

While we possess sufficient historical evidence with regard to imperial Rome, the question of how the selection process of *amīr* and *Majlis-i shūrá* was to be carried out in practice remained rather vague, at least in Mawdūdī's earlier writings. This was only to change with the establishment of the JiI in 1941, the vehicle for the practical realisation of Mawdūdī's ideological outline, as we shall see in detail below.[358] In the founding phase of the JiI, the *amīr* and *Majlis-i shūrá* were, according to Nasr, initially elected by a simple majority vote of only a very small supreme body.[359] Only later, in the revised statutes of the JiI of 1956, was it suggested that the election would have to take place during the General Assembly (*arkān kā ijtimāʿ-i ʿāmm*), which usually congregated about every five years.[360] From this it appears as if in the very beginning Mawdūdī was not much concerned with the elaboration of the actual mechanisms for running the Islamic state. As in other ideologies, too, Mawdūdī's thought revolved first and foremost around rather abstract principles, which would need considerable revision once attempts were made to put them into actual practice. Consequently, most of his understanding of the electoral process appears only in a negative form, namely by his rejection of candidature (*umīdwārī*), campaigning and party formation as elements in the democratic process in the West, or, as Mawdūdī has put it, 'the cursed way of the satanic democracy'.[361] The categorical exclusion of standard methods to determine a representation of majority interests, and the lack of any alternative proposals leave room for speculation.

After all, how and by whom should suitable candidates for the office of *amīr* and for the *Majlis-i shūrá* be determined? An obvious suspicion—and here again a parallel to the practice in ancient imperial Rome suggests itself—would be that according to his ideas, first, aspirants to any of these offices are not found among those whom Mawdūdī frequently labelled the 'common Muslims' (*ʿāmm musalmān*) and, second, that the members of the *Majlis-i shūrá* owe their appointment to the subtle intervention of the *amīr* while he in return is confirmed by the council members.[362] Evidence from the internal politics that took place during the founding phase of the JiI confirm these suggestions.[363]

Equally vague as the election procedure Mawdūdī kept the actual tasks of the *amīr*. In a short undated speech on the occasion of one of his re-elections as *amīr* of the JiI, Mawdūdī assumed that the prime task of the *amīr* would remain as outlined in classical Islamic legal and political theory, namely to administer the 'common good' (*maṣlaḥa*).[364] Whatever the 'common good' may be in each and every case,[365] according to Mawdūdī the *amīr* will be able to intuitively recognise it, because his relationship to the other members of the community is one of deep-felt affection and compassion.[366] To refer in this regard to the practice of the 'Rightly-Guided' Caliphs[367] makes good sense, because the orientation of all political decisions on the *maṣlaḥa* dates back at least to the Caliphate of ʿUmar ibn al-K̲h̲aṭṭāb. In determining the 'common good' counselling especially with legal experts was inevitable and had therefore been made a criterion for 'just rule'.[368] Again, however, counselling might just serve as superficial legitimisation of rule with majority appeal, while the actual impact of the counsellors' advice on decisions remains just as disputable as the eventual servility of the council towards the ruler. Such possible divergence between Mawdūdī's normative expectation and a concrete sociopolitical practice may again explain why Mawdūdī remained rather unspecific when it came to the elaboration of part of his ideological outline for its practical implementation. This applies not only to the concrete tasks of the *amīr*, but also to those of the *Majlis-i shūrá*, after all Mawdūdī's Islamic substitute for a parliament.

b) The Separation of Powers

In Mawdūdī's conception of the Islamic state there is little mention of any other office or committee than those of the *amīr* and the *Majlis-i shūrá*, which would assume governmental responsibilities. Considering the *amīr* as the 'first among the senators', he sees all the political powers of the Islamic state as remaining in the hands of this council. This, in turn, implies that in Mawdūdī's Islamic state the separation of powers into legislative, executive and judicial ones—common sense in all modern political theory and practice[369]—is at the most provided only functionally, but not personally.[370]

Because of this, the *Majlis-i shūrá* would have to consist of men who were capable of dealing with all the affairs of the state in an appropriate manner and were thus able to advise the *amīr*. Mawdūdī's earlier writings are again not elaborate enough to derive sufficiently detailed information on this—here, the general focus was much more on the Islamicity of the practice of *shūrá*. In later publications, however, and most probably in recognition of the urgent need to go more into detail in order to better prepare for the practical realisation of his ideas, Mawdūdī suggested the council to be composed largely of traditionally educated Muslim scholars (*ʿulamāʾ*), but also of graduates from modern education institutions and people in technical professions.[371] This way he felt that everyday considerations and decisions would be made within a solid religious legal framework, a framework that determined the first of the three powers, namely the legislative.

Legislative power is, of course, significantly restricted by the fact that true legislation can only be from God alone. Since Mawdūdī made unquestioning obedience to God and His *sharīʿa* a core criterion for being a Muslim, the *Majlis-i shūrá* within his conception of an Islamic state was therefore not entitled to create law. It would however be able to derive positive, and thus applicable, law (*qānūn*) from its timely interpretation of the sources of the *sharīʿa*.[372] An absolute precondition for this, in turn, would evidently be the qualification of the *ahl al-shūrá* for independent reasoning (*ijtihād*),[373] a demand quite consistent with classical political theory.[374] Although frequently mentioned in various of his earlier writings, Mawdūdī's ideas of *ijtihād* appear rather amateurish which may be explained by the fact that he lacked proper and thorough training in *fiqh*, hence his rather simplistic understanding of the scope and practice of *ijtihād*—quite distinct from its detailed discussion in the *fiqh*-literature[375]—as

> the comprehension of the fundamental principles of religion [*dīn kā uṣūl-i kulliya*], the judging of states of contemporary culture [*tamaddun*] and its trends [*irtiqāʾ*] from a sound Islamic point of view and the determination of the changes in the legal principles [*uṣūl-i sharʿ*] to be effected in the traditional cultural patterns in the spirit of the *sharīʿa*, with a view to fully attaining its ultimate ends [*maqāṣid*] and to finally enable Islam to assume the world leadership under the reformed [*ṣaḥīḥ*] conditions.[376]

As authority on the issue of *ijtihād*, Mawdūdī referred to Shāh Walīyallāh Dihlawī, the study of whose works he strongly recommended in order to grasp the principles of this method of legal norm derivation.[377] The passages which Mawdūdī quoted from Walīyallāh's *Muṣaffá*, a Persian commentary on Mālik ibn Anas' *al-Muwaṭṭa*, in which the celebrated Delhi scholar stressed that '*ijtihād* is in every age a collective obligation [*ijtihād dar har ʿaṣr farḍ bi'l-kifāya ast*]',[378] do not reveal any further indication as to how *ijtihād* should eventually be practised. For this, we may safely conclude, Mawdūdī depended indeed on sufficiently qualified religious legal scholars within the *Majlis al-shūrá*. Consequently, the *amīr*, as first counsellor among equals, would then have to be the one with the best qualification to practise *ijtihād*.[379]

The definition of the executive power (*intiẓāmī shuʿba*) remained just as weak as that of the legislative one in Mawdūdī's earlier theoretical writings on the Islamic state. One may, however, assume that it is the state's organisational superstructure, consisting of *amīr* and *Majlis-i shūrá*, which will exert its duty to enforce the rulings of the judicative power according to the Qurʾānic precept to enjoin the commendable and prevent the reprehensible (*amr bi'l-maʿrūf wa-nahy ʿan al-munkar*).[380] According to Mawdūdī, this ethical-cum-legal injunction, considered to be an individual duty of every Muslim (*farḍ ʿayn*),[381] is indeed the primary rationale of Islamic governance,[383] which might be explained from the fact that the government of Mawdūdī's Islamic state is ideally to be considered just the first among equals within the polity. Thus, while, in general, every Muslim has the same rights and duties and, in an ideological or ethical state, is supposed to assume public responsibility, the executive—presumably identical with the legislative—holds the power of definition of what is meant by 'commendable' (*maʿrūf*) and 'reprehensible' (*munkar*). While Mawdūdī remained once again vague with regard to the actual executive arrangements, one could devine nonetheless a fair idea of what was meant by it from how these issues were dealt with in the JiI especially during the early years under Mawdūdī's leadership.[383]

Finally, the judicative power (*ʿadālat kā shuʿba*) Mawdūdī discussed only with regard to the proposition that the *amīr* and the members of the leading political bodies do not enjoy any special legal status.[384] This, of course, appears to have been rather wishful thinking and would be practicable only if one considers the judiciary of the state as being put in charge by others than those who hold the executive power. There is, however, no indication in Mawdūdī's writings that the judiciary would be appointed by the entire community, although he stressed that the judge (*qāḍī*) 'does not sit on the seat of justice in the capacity of a representative [*nā'ib*] of the *amīr* or caliph, but as a representative of God, Almighty'.[385] This proves once again that Mawdūdī was initially not very much concerned with establishing concrete provisions for the judicative power in the Islamic state. In my opinion, this did not even change later on, because neither Mawdūdī himself nor the JiI ever come close to taking over the responsibility for running a state, and this, in turn, could conveniently postpone any further and more concrete elaborations on the division of powers for the time being.[386]

While his thoughts on the concrete internal structure of the envisioned Islamic state remained thus rather rudimentary, cultural and economic issues were treated at length in Mawdūdī's political writings. Especially at the time of Partition and the early Pakistan years, a vivid interest in questions concerning economics is apparent. Although at first glance somewhat contradictory, this can perhaps again best be explained by the fact that Mawdūdī's outline of Islam as an all-encompassing 'system of life' was first and foremost an Islamic reaction to other political ideologies prevalent at the time, while its actual implementation was of rather secondary importance, at least during the 1930s and most of the 1940s.

4.2) An Islamic Contribution to the Critique of Political Economy

Mawdūdī's interest in economics was by no means only accidental. After all, it was especially economics that had been fundamentally linked to those conceptions of statehood which reflected on the colonial practice in the Indian subcontinent. At least since the seventeenth century political philosophy of Thomas Hobbes the understanding of the state as the best means to peacefully secure man's individual self-preservation dominated British political thought. Instrumental governance, in turn, was closely linked to the economic success of each individual member of a polity.[387] Setting out from this point it was not least Adam Smith (d. 1790) who, in his influential *Inquiry into the Nature and Causes of the Wealth of Nations* (1776), paved the way for the very British liberalism that served as a justification of colonialism and was thus very much at work in British India.[388] It is thus only consistent that Mawdūdī's critical discussion of political economy also referred explicitly to aspects of Smith's moral philosophy among those of the utilitarians who provided—although to a varying extent—the theoretical tools for British imperialism.[389]

This, by implication, means that, according to Mawdūdī, imperialism had to be understood only as a political consequence of a capitalist understanding of economics, which, in turn, resulted from a certain anthropologically grounded ethics. Therefore, if Mawdūdī really wanted to thoroughly criticise a political system as *jāhilī*, he had to extend his analysis beyond the mere political and to investigate the nature of the underlying economic system and, digging even deeper, ethics. It was thus only consequently that Mawdūdī devoted considerable time first and foremost to a review of capitalism (*niẓām-i sarmāyadārī*). In a second, although equally logical step he engaged in an investigation into alternative current economic models which, especially in view of the Great Depression of the 1930s, had proven themselves equally, if not more successful. Even further, the alternative economic models provided by Communism and Fascism were both united in a criticism of the prevalent liberal market economy and its consequences for the political system. Given the fact that both ideologies were of considerable appeal for indigenous Indian elites[390] Mawdūdī had to treat both as major competitors to his own criticism of capitalism and the political institutions that resulted in it.

In this regard an interesting observation can be made which, again, hints at Mawdūdī's difficulties in maintaining a systematic ideology while, at the same time, rejecting all alternative ideologies. To be able to successfully undertake the criticism of ideology, namely, one would have to seriously challenge the premises on which an ideology is based. Mawdūdī's comparatively expansive discussion of economics, however, strongly suggests that he got trapped in the same anthropological understanding as Liberalism and Communism. Man's happiness lies by and large in his economic conditions and politics is therefore to be considered only as a means of securing the economic prosperity of a given community.[391] What can be concluded from this acknowledgement of economics as a fundamental anthropological determinant by Mawdūdī are two main things: first of all, it has to be assumed that Mawdūdī's rejection of all other prevailing ideologies could not be rooted in a critique of their respective political economies, but must necessarily be based on something beyond the realm of economics and even to some extent beyond economic ethics; second, however, it adds to the proof of Mawdūdī having very much been a child of his time, which is why his entire systematic outline has necessarily to be reconstructed against the backdrop of this period.

This second point became quite obvious in Mawdūdī's discussion of 'capitalism' which followed—although it was never explicitly acknowledged—very much in the wake of Marxian historicism, as he had begun by tracing the roots of capitalism in feudalism (*niẓām-i jāgīrdārī*), investigating the religious justification of an estate-based society, its decentralised political structure and its little developed division of labour.[392] Although in an overtly simplified outline, Mawdūdī continued by discussing the emergence of an urban proto-bourgeoisie during the Renaissance period and from there the advent of what he called 'medieval liberalism' (*dawr-i mutawassaṭ kā libaralizm*). Fostered by Machiavellian thought, man increasingly began to understand the world around him as a repository of resources to be exploited to one's personal benefit.[393] When stressing the fact that the emancipating 'bourgeois class' (*būrzhuwā ṭabaqa*) was only replacing the feudal landed gentry in exploiting a 'class of commoners' (*ṭabaqa-yi ʿawāmm al-nās*), Mawdūdī's references to Marxian and Marxist class rhetoric appeared most obvious.[394] Finally—and still following the Marxian historicist narrative—it was the Industrial Revolution (*ṣinʿatī inqilāb*) which caused the emergence of the capitalist mode of production proper, coupled with the political economic thought of classical liberalism. Consequently, Mawdūdī discussed at quite some length principles such as the acknowledgment of private property (*shakhṣī milkiyyat*), free enterprise and competition, all of them rooted in an understanding of Economic and, resulting from it, Social Darwinism, and the resulting plea for a state politics of non-intervention (*riyāsat kī ʿadam-i mudākhalat*) in private economic enterprise.[395] Such an economic system, Mawdūdī thus concluded, demands a particular form of political government, namely that of a parliamentary democracy.

It is clear from this line of argument that every alternative outline of a free market economy will have to set out from different premises, or at least from a fundamental reinterpretation of the premises of classical liberalism. Although far from Rousseau's conclusive argument for an ethical concept of governance, these alternative models were still based on the Genevan's core conviction that social and political inequality among men on the grounds of economic disparity is not a preferable state.[396] Consequently, a political system designed only to safeguard such inequality is to be categorically rejected and in its place a state has to be installed that guarantees an equal distribution of wealth among the members of a given society. This, in turn can only work if the sanctity of private property, especially of the means of production, is irreversibly lifted and property is redefined in collective terms.

Among these alternative ideologies, Communism was the most radical advocate of the abandonment of private property and the collective administration of the means of production and the fruits of reproduction. Building up critically on earlier romantic ideas of a non-profit oriented just polity, such as Rousseau's,[397] it was finally Marx and Engels whose 'Critique of Political Economy' provided the theoretical framework for the elaboration of an actual communist economy in Soviet Russia. While Mawdūdī apparently harboured quite some sympathies for the fundamental Communist idea of overcoming the increasing alienation of the productive forces from the product of their labour by a designed social revolution,[398] he remained clearly critical towards various premises of Marxian theory and even more its attempt to apply it in practice in Soviet Russia.

Thus, although employing the term 'class' (*ṭabaqa*) himself, it appears that Mawdūdī shared neither the Marxian universalist notion that 'all hitherto existing history of society is the history of class struggle',[399] nor the fundamental Marxian understanding of labour as the most basic human disposition.[400] Because Mawdūdī held a much more lenient position towards the private property of the means of production, he was emphatically critical towards the historical necessity of 'expropriation of the immediate producers, i.e., the dissolution of private property based on the labour of its owner'[401] and the transition into collective property.[402] However, Mawdūdī's main criticism was not directed at Marxian theory but first and foremost at the reality of Soviet political economy. This was not surprising, as after all it was the economic progress in the Soviet Union in the 1920s and 1930s that received increased interest from Indian intellectuals.[403]

The secret of the Soviet economic success as opposed to a declining liberal capitalist market economy during the Great Depression appeared predominantly to be rooted in the governmental administration of economic affairs on the basis of collective property. While a planned economy was already suggested by Marx for the 'first phase of communist society',[404] it was Lenin who outlined the necessity 'to bring social production and the distribution of products at once under the *control* of the Soviets of Workers' Deputies'[405] already before the October Revolution, and he made it even more concrete during the civil war, employing the terms 'centralisation' and 'plan'.[406] Although Mawdūdī did not bother to discuss the imposition of the Soviet planned economy as the complicated historical process that it was,[407] his critical assessment of it and its wider societal implications appears nonetheless largely correct.

His criticism, epitomised by the actual Soviet practice and consequences of the expropriation especially of landed estates and forced collectivisation, revolved by and large around the universal claim of the Communist ideology for truth that resulted, as he said, in despotic practices.[408] Citing from Lenin's *Zadači sojusov molodeži* (2 October 1920), Mawdūdī established the Communist premise of a distinct ethics which 'is entirely subordinated to the interests of the proletariat's class struggle'[409] and which therefore seems to justify also violent means. The role of the Communist Party as the standardbearer of the 'dictatorship of the proletariat' (*mazdūroṇ kī d'ikt'et'arship*) appeared problematic in two ways. First, it assumed the party's ability to determine the collective needs of the hour and the most appropriate way to satisfy them.[410] Second, according to Mawdūdī, these claims led to an extreme accumulation of political power as the party directives were to be enforced by dictatorial means, represented by the so-called 'administrative-command system' that included an unmitigated planned economy.[411] In Mawdūdī's eyes this was a highly questionable way to overcome the economic, social and political injustice caused by liberalist capitalism, especially from a different ethical point of view. Consequently, he turned then to an investigation of the second economic alternative to capitalism in his time, namely Fascism.

Mawdūdī's assessment of Fascist and National Socialist critiques of political economy and their own respective solutions was, like his assessment of Communism, rather simplistic and levelled significant differences between the developments in different countries and even within the many Fascist movements. Regardless, his understanding of various implications of this particular approach, which he considered sound and useful (*ṣaḥīḥ awr mufīd*), is nonetheless rather correct and also his main points of criticism appear still quite valid.

Setting out from a class model like Communism,[412] the Fascist solution for overcoming class struggle over resources and, thus, social and political influence, was quite distinct.[413] Receiving an enormous boost, if not its initial spark, from the difficult economic situation of the interwar period, there was first certainly a strong anti-capitalist element in Fascist thought, evident from Mussolini's early Marxist leanings,[414] as well as from the leftist wing in the early *National Socialist German Worker's Party* (NSDAP), led by the brothers Otto (d. 1974) and Gregor Strasser (assassinated 1934).[415] These anti-capitalist tendencies were however rather short-lived. While the Strasser brothers were soon marginalised by the more conservative wing in the party led by Hitler himself, at least with the *Carta del Lavoro* of 1927 Mussolini made it ultimately clear that he was not any longer inclined to follow the Communists' key demand to abolish private property of the means of production.[416] Conceding economics an importance only as subordinated to politics[417] as for instance Hitler did in his 1927 pamphlet *Der*

Weg zum Wiederaufstieg, the main feature of Fascist political economy of whatever provenance became the direct state intervention into a capitalist process of production:[418] whether the economy was actually restructured, as in Italy, as a network of self-governing corporations (*corporazioni*), or whether, as in the Third Reich, the strategically rather useful 'corporation' (*Stand*) remained *de facto* only a more or less empty phrase.[419] State intervention in what had earlier been a free market economy appears indeed to be the smallest common denominator in all Fascist societies.

Of extraordinary importance for a closer understanding of Mawdūdī's points of critique of the Fascist conception of economy is a comprehension of its underlying premises, which revolved first and foremost around the role that the Fascist state played. Whether or not the respective Fascist ideologies were based on a doctrinal racial theory, all of them stressed the universal superiority of one particular community over all others, and did thus not profess to aim at commutative justice. After all, the Fascist ideology was rooted in an adaptation and elaboration of the classical theories of Social and Cultural Darwinism, but unlike in classical liberalist thought, it was not any longer the single individual that prevails against others economically and, as a result, also socially and politically, but the collective instead. What makes scholars like Roger Eatwell consider Fascism a 'third way' alongside liberalism-*cum*-capitalism and Communism is its obvious borrowings from both. While there was no objection to private ownership of the means of production, Fascist leaders and economists did not share the liberalist belief in individualism and, thus, the conviction that the state must not interfere in any economic enterprise. Like the Communists, they strongly advocated the supremacy of the state in defining the needs of the community, directing every individual enterprise towards the fulfilment of these needs and, consequently, guarding the subordination of all individual interests under the communal one, which was, in turn, to be defined and supervised by the state.[420]

Mawdūdī managed quite some appreciation for the Fascist critique of the Communist understanding of economic class as the societal unit with the strongest adhesive force, and its categorical rejection of private property, its critique of the classical liberalist understanding of the state and its alternative employment policy.[421] Nonetheless, although seemingly acknowledging Fascism as a 'third way' alternative to Communism and Liberalism, from Mawdūdī's criticism it becomes clear that in reality he did not see much difference from the Bolshevist experience, as he made clear in a speech at Aligarh Muslim University in October 1941.[422] Interestingly,

Mawdūdī was not much bothered by the fatal consequences of Fascist economies, especially the German one that, after all, had led to a war of aggression and to what Baker calls a 'genocidal slave and permanent war economy'.[423] Mawdūdī's two main objections referred to, first, the national chauvinism of Fascist regimes which he had already strongly criticised in his treatise on nationalism,[424] but, second, first and foremost the state intervention in all areas of life which, in the economic field, became manifest in a centrally planned national economy (*markazī manṣūbabandī niẓām-i maʿāshī*). Indeed, just as in Soviet Russia, a planned economy required the subordination of every individual interest under the state regime; 'this way the people [*qawm*], government [*riyāsat*], state [*ḥukūmat*] and ruling party [*ḥukmarān pārt'ī*] have been merged into one single item'.[425] As a result of this politics of identification, even constructive criticism and a deviant personal opinion were not possible anymore. To safeguard this total identification of the individual with the collective for the sake of a greater good, the political system had inevitably to become highly oppressive.[426] Mawdūdī's final point of critique referred—acknowledging Fascism's initial anti-capitalist leanings—to the fact that the Fascist reforms of the capitalist economic turned out to be only cosmetic (*andarūnī iṣlāḥāt*).

* * *

Mawdūdī's critical assessment of the Communist and Fascist answers to the economic question prominently on the grounds of their emphasis on planning had very concrete reasons, but their dismissal owed almost exclusively to systematic ones. Given the fact that societal planning, above all in the economic field, was a core issue in the debates within the wider independence movement in late British India, Mawdūdī, too, had to position himself. While there appeared to be an overall agreement that, especially in view of the Great Depression of the 1930s, classical liberalism had ultimately worn itself out, the economic growth in the Soviet Union, Fascist Italy or National Socialist Germany at the very same time had caused an increased interest in planned economy.[427] From this point it appeared quite natural that Mawdūdī, too, began to analyse the potential of Communism and Fascism with regard to his efforts to cast an ideology of his own. As a result of these analyses, however, although some sympathies for the anti-capitalist impetus of Communism and Fascism can hardly be denied, he had to dismiss a state-planned economy mainly, if not solely, for systematic reasons. Since his entire outline was based on the firm conviction of man's inextricable dependence from divine guidance, man—even with the best of intentions—could never become an utterly reliable source for determining his own needs, as well as appropriate action to fulfil these needs in the best possible way.[328] By implication, therefore, maxims to act had necessarily to be derived on some superior and transcendent source, that is, God.

In his resulting endeavour to provide yet another alternative answer to the liberalist economy apart from Communism and Fascism, Mawdūdī resorted, willingly or unwillingly, to that camp of Western political theory which perceived governance less instrumental than ethical. In these theories it was not the state that helped its subjects to lead a prosperous life, but it was each and every individual who, as a citizen, put him- or herself in the service of the common good. In this camp of Western political theory belongs Rousseau's conception of a state which unites all individual wills (*volontés particulières*) in a general will (*volonté générale*) that 'is always for the common good (*bien commun*)',[329] as well as Hegel's state as 'the actuality of the ethical Idea'.[430] In the political thought of the British idealists around Bradley and Bosanquet, finally, these ideas were received and developed further and thus introduced to the discussion on political economy in late and post-Victorian Britain and, eventually, in the British Raj.[431] The discussion of economic issues among the British idealists, however, was limited mainly to polemics against all those among their ideological opponents who assigned the main driving force in the society to economy and were thus constricting the totality of social practice to only one—although admittedly important—field.[432] Because, so they argued especially against their materialist adversaries of every colour, an economy was based first and foremost on exchange relationships between two or more parties, and as these relationships have, for the sake of mutual dependability, necessarily to be put on a legal basis, it can only be law and, consequently, ethics that must necessarily dominate all practical areas.[433] Ethics, in turn, would have to be based on responsibility against oneself and anyone else in the sense of Kant's categorical imperative.

As shown earlier, 'ethics of conviction' have been given an important place in the foundation of Mawdūdī's systematic outline. It is therefore also ethics that played a decisive role in his economic thought. Ethical maxims, in turn, should never be derived from concrete and changing societal conditions, but only from a stable and transcendent source. In this, however, Mawdūdī's own 'Critique of Political Economy' appeared to be much more in line with those who were criticised by Marx, Engels and those in their wake, namely the idealists who, after all, had generally been much closer to Mawdūdī's thinking.[434]

Mawdūdī's economic ethics, just like any other human value, were once more derived from the fundamental relationship between God as creator and man as part of creation. As always backed with plenty of Qur'ānic references,[435] Mawdūdī's economic understanding was rooted in the belief that since God had created the natural resources He had also determined the handling of these resources through natural laws and directives to man (*sharīʿa*). Thus, God emphatically permits man to use the earth, but responsibly, that is only within the confines of His laws.[436] Here once again applies Mawdūdī's notion of God's unlimited sovereignty. It is solely His prerogative to set the limit for what is permitted and what not—the terms Mawdūdī used here with reference to some Qur'ānic commentaries were confined only to the extreme opposites *ḥalāl* and *ḥarām*, thus dissolving the rather elaborate scale of moral evaluation of human acts and relationships as it was developed in classical Islamic law.[437] Within this radically revised ethical framework God clearly permits private property, but only as long as man does not use it to gain profit of secondary order, that is, by lending mobile or immobile property for interest (*ribā*).[438] The permissibility of private property and the prohibition of usury by divine verdict epitomise Mawdūdī's criticism of capitalism as well as Communism:

> We will have to remember that we cannot choose a free [*be-qayd*] economy like that of the capitalist system and we cannot establish collective control [*ijtimāʿī kant'rol*] over the entire economy like the communist system. We will have to establish a free system of economics within certain limits [*ek pāband-i ḥudūd-i āzād-i maʿīshat kā niẓām*]. [...] It would be devoid of the wrong methods, which produce unnatural class distinctions [*ghayr fiṭrī ṭabaqāt*] and between those classes which nature itself produces it would bring about cooperation [*taʿāwun*] instead of conflict [*nizāʿ*]. [...] On wealth acquired in ways permitted by Islam, individuals will have all those rights of ownership and use [*tamām ḥuqūq-i taslīm*] that Islam has permitted.[439]

From Mawdūdī's points of criticism of capitalism as well as Communism it appears that his alternative draft lined much more up with elements in Fascist economic political thought, as for example with the National Socialist idea of the 'despotism of financial credits' (*Despotie des Leihkapitals*) which was to be broken.[440] The issue of the prevention of interest-based profit, however, suggests once more a certain inconsistency in Mawdūdī's argument which is certainly rooted in the hardly reconcilable conflict between his Western-inspired anthropology and his dogmatic adherence to the Qur'ānic precepts at the same time. If one takes it seriously that man, because of his nature, is permitted to acquire and possess private property at his free disposal, than he might well be entitled to sell his property for money which he may again invest at his wish. On the other hand, Mawdūdī stressed with reference to various Qur'ānic passages that 'all that is in the heavens and the earth belongs to God [*illāhi mā fi'l-samawāti wa-mā fi'l-arḍ*]',[441] which implies that man cannot possess anything and thus, has no discretionary power whatsoever.[442] It might however be possible to attempt resolution of this dilemma by taking into consideration the special relationship between God and man. As part of creation man is entirely dependent on God. Consequently, God alone bestows every possibility of discretional power upon man and one may therefore assume that God can also take it away at any time. On the lines of the hierarchical relationship between God and man, which in political terms is expressed as a relationship between an absolute sovereign (*ḥākim-i muṭlaq*) and His deputy (*khalīfa*), in economic terms one may consider man as custodian of God's earthly possessions. If this holds true, then man has been left no choice but to administer what had been entrusted to him according to the rules and regulations that have been passed onto him with his trusteeship. Within this framework of rules and regulations, in turn, man can indeed enjoy a certain autonomy.

While on this ground one might assume that all men were treated as equal with regard to their material possessions also, and that Mawdūdī's alternative ideological outline would therefore provide for the removal of economic inequality, this was not the case. Quite to the contrary, economic inequality to Mawdūdī was also God given, and he justified this view with further Qur'ānic references among which the verse 6:165 appears especially significant:

It is He who had made you deputies on earth [*khalā'ifa 'l-arḍ*]: He had raised some above others by ranks [*darājāt*], so that He may test you in what He had given you.[443]

That Mawdūdī applied the differences between men, which are stated in this verse, to economic imbalance, can serve as a good illustration for his particular approach to the Qur'ānic text: while traditional exegetes would never dare to squeeze a verse into the confines of an actual socio-political practice,[444] it is perhaps one of the most vivid features of the contemporary *tafsīr dunyāwī* that, setting out from empirical observation, an agreement between reality and the Qur'ānic text is established. This, of course, granted exegetes like Mawdūdī much more flexibility and allowed them room for interpreting and reinterpreting one and the same passage, always in view of their respective ends at hand.[445] In this actual case, Mawdūdī used a traditionally much wider interpreted Qur'ānic verse to explain and justify the fact of economic disparity, setting out from a premise diametrically opposed to Enlightenment thinkers like Rousseau, namely that it is inequality which is natural and that every attempt to establish equality would therefore be against nature, or the divine arrangements of creation. What is derived from this premise is vital, because it reflects on the ethical dimension. Despite his natural a disposition, man's task is nonetheless to ensure as great as possible degree of social (and economic) justice (*ʿadala-yi ijtimāʿiyya*).[446] This can, of course, only be achieved by orienting oneself to an externally given catalogue of do's and don'ts. In Mawdūdī's view it is therefore the Qur'ānic duty of almsgiving (*zakāt*) that would assure economic justice.[447]

This, finally, is the very moment when for Mawdūdī the Islamic state has to come into play, as the controlling agency to ensure a basic level of material security for every member of the society. The necessity of such an institution arose from the fact that Mawdūdī—as Hobbes did—perceived humankind by nature as selfish and greedy and, left to itself, unable to act ethically.[448] The state appears therefore first and foremost as a moral institution, although with legal powers. With regard to economics it does not, like the Fascist state, aim at utilising individual economic entrepreneurship for collective ends, but to supervise the legitimacy of the means to acquire wealth according to the prevailing understanding of the revealed injunctions.[449] Only in cases where these rules have been broken will the state impose sanctions that, however, are in the first place not intended to deter, but rather to re-adjust the economy within the divinely ordained limits of permissibility. Consequently, punitive measures would therefore be mainly of the economic kind as well—any unlawfully or unethically acquired wealth would be apportioned among needy community members.[450]

All in all, as far as economics are concerned the Islamic state as envisioned by Mawdūdī had two major functions. On the one hand it acted as a supervisory authority which oversaw that the economic activities of each and every member of the community remained within the confines of what God had made permissible, while on the other it functioned as stakeholder of the economically less fortunate, the incapable and under-aged.[451] In this group, however, belong also those who are exempted from full participation in the society by what Mawdūdī considered divine decree.

4.3) At the Fringes of Democracy: Cracks in the System

Mawdūdī's particular understanding of economics, here especially economic disparity as man's natural disposition, posed a serious challenge to his egalitarian claim, epitomised in the concept of man as *khalīfat allāh* which, in turn, formed the basis for Mawdūdī's vision of a 'theo-democratic' form of governance. Other than the theorists of Communism, who assumed that collective possession of the means of production would inevitably lead to the levelling of social differences, Mawdūdī, who had rejected the materialistic premises of the Communist solution, concluded from his Qur'ān-based belief in God-given economic inequality that social stratification is also natural and therefore inevitable. On the one hand, the relationship between the economic and the social was hereby not seen as a causal, but rather a mutual one. Economic difference was thus not first and foremost down to individual success in an open market situation where everybody proceeds from equal prerequisites, but to a considerable part also to the social position which was assigned to each individual by nature, or God. Hence, some sections of the community are by definition socially underprivileged. Their social status, on the other hand—and here Mawdūdī's initial egalitarianism was seriously crumbling—reflects on their economic and also political disadvantage. The example *par excellence* in Mawdūdī's outline for such less favourable treatment by nature is women.

Other groups within Mawdūdī's envisioned polity suffer economic and political disadvantages not because of the social status assigned to them by nature, but because of their legal status. This appears even more problematic because it appears to reduce Mawdūdī's above outlined anthropology, according to which all men are equal by nature, almost to absurdity. On the other hand, Mawdūdī could again counter with reference to the Qur'ān that the *khilāfat allāh* was explicitly confined to 'those who believe and work righteous deeds'.[452] As the Qur'ānic text goes on it becomes clear that this verse refers only to those who 'will worship Me and not associate anything else with Me [*amnan yaʿbudūnanī lā yushrikūna bī shay'an*]',[453] that is, in the common understanding, the Muslims only.[454] In Mawdūdī's polity all non-Muslims are therefore excluded from God's trusteeship on earth *qua* Qur'ānic dictum and are thus legally very much restricted in their possibilities for political decision making.

Mawdūdī's particular views on women and non-Muslims made them the two major groups which somehow fall through the cracks of Mawdūdī's conception of the Islamic state as a 'theo-democracy' and therefore put the validity of his entire system to the test from a theoretical angle.[455]

a) 'And Remain in your Houses':[456] The Place of Women

Mawdūdī's discussion of the role and place of women within his conception of the Islamic state and his fervent plea for gender segregation, first and foremost elaborated in his book *Parda* (1939), is once again closely linked to his criticism of Western social ethics and his attempt to provide an alternative societal model to the various ones that were discussed among intellectual elites in late colonial India.[457] To some extent this was quite consistent, given that the beginning of women's movements in the Muslim world was closely related to the discourse on modernisation to which the discussion of Muslim nationalism belonged also;—those debates in turn were decisively shaped by Western influences. That Mawdūdī put these influences exclusively down to European colonialism shows his selective and rather narrow understanding of historical developments.[458] Overall, however, the pattern of his criticism, although phrased here in a much more polemical manner, appeared to be the same as in other of his works.

The root of all evil was to be found in man's dissociation from values set by an extra-human agent and his unjustified reliance on his own intellectual abilities to create new values, a development that was much fostered by the Enlightenment movement and the political developments in its wake.[459] In the eyes of Mawdūdī, although he considered the insurgence against an unjust and somewhat outdated social and political order perfectly justified, he was critical that these developments gave way to:

> an extreme notion of personal freedom that aimed at bestowing full freedom and total liberty [*ḥurriyyat-i tāmma awr ibāḥat-i muṭlaqa*] to the individual [*fard*] as against society widely acceptable. It was pleaded that the individual should have the right to do anything that he liked according to his fully autonomous choice [*pūrī khūd-mukhtārī ke sāth apnī marḍī ke muṭābiq*], and the freedom to refrain from anything that he disliked. Society had no right to restrict his personal freedom.[460]

Although Mawdūdī was certainly right as far as the emphasis on freedom for a reformulation of social ethics is concerned, his understanding of the ethical implications however appeared somewhat distorted when he boiled them down to a changed understanding of gender relations. Man and women, he argued, were not anymore equal only in moral and more general terms, but increasingly in every respect. Fostered by the development of capitalism, this would inevitably lead to the economic independence of women and, finally, to a 'free intermingling of the two sexes'.[461] To prove his point, Mawdūdī painted a grim picture of the moral state of Europe since the late eighteenth century, for which he dwelt on a number of Western sources to enhance the veracity of his portrayal. His selection of authors and sources is significant in this respect, because it can not only explain how Mawdūdī came to such a rather distorted understanding of Western morality, but it also illustrates once again the selective and in most places not very profound utilisation of Western references in Mawdūdī's works in general.

The most extensive of Mawdūdī's three case studies is France, although almost exclusively based on the 1925 English translation of *D'Indiscipline des mœrs* (1921) of the staunchly Catholic sociologist Paul Bureau (d. 1923).[462] Bureau belonged to a circle of Catholic social scientists around the journals *La réforme sociale* and, from 1886 onwards, *La science sociale*, which aimed at further developing the highly normative roadmap of the social theorist Frédéric Le Play (d. 1888) for a conservative moral reform of contemporary society.[463] At the core of their reformist thought stood, as was to be expected, a revival of the particularistic family. Obviously, prevalent social practices in rapidly changing early industrial societies were diametrically opposed to the understanding of the family as upholder of traditional, or religious social values and, thus, as a nucleus for a stable society. Bureau's clearly interest-led exposure of what he felt was a highly corrupt moral state of France and its historical genesis therefore played very much into the hands of Mawdūdī. The fact that Bureau's work had been translated into English only shortly after its first publication by the conservative Victorian physician Mary Anne Scharlieb (d. 1930), who repeatedly accompanied her husband to India and worked there as a doctor,[464] might explain the prominence that Bureau's book gained in English-reading circles in British India.

The reason for the receptivity of such ideas in educated Indo-Muslim circles could well be found in a confluence of a restrictive Victorian sexual morality prevalent in the colonial discourse in India and the indigenous criticism of lax sexual morals among the 'Urdu middle-class',[465] here however blamed on the negative influences that the Western consumer society had on indigenous elites.[466]

Mawdūdī's discussion of the moral state of the United States and, although only briefly, of the United Kingdom, was based on sources which equally reflect on, or at least fuel, Victorian sexual morality. The driving force behind the juvenile court in Denver, Ben Barr Lindsey (d. 1943), although holding vastly different values, provided with his *Revolt of Modern Youth* (1925) an image of the impact of the modern consumer society on children.[467] Likewise, Mawdūdī referred to *The Laws of Sex* (1921) of the leader of the suffragist movement in Maryland, Edith Houghton Hooker (d. 1948), whose gloomy picture of prevalent sexual morals in the US were strongly reminiscent of the one that Paul Bureau had provided for France.[468] Edith Belle Lowry's (d. 1945) *Herself: Talks with Women Concerning Themselves* (1911) served Mawdūdī as yet another supporting argument for the moral state of young people in the US by a staunch Victorian moralist.[469] The reference to the controversial Protestant physical culturist Bernarr [*sic*] Macfadden (d. 1955),[470] in turn, shows perhaps more clearly than others that Mawdūdī's sources, besides reflecting a Victorian criticism of sexual morality and its social implications, were almost exclusively popular ones. This assessment extends also to his references for the British context: here it was first and foremost George Ryley Scott (d. 1943), author of the popular bestseller *A History of Prostitution* (1936), who provided Mawdūdī with a picture of a morally declined United Kingdom,[471] which was well supplemented by the *Guide to Modern Wickedness* (1939) of the popular philosopher and radio broadcaster Cyril E.M. Joad (d. 1953).[472]

The grim picture of the moral state in developed industrial societies in the West, which Mawdūdī had drawn as a combination of the continuous pursuit of material greed and sensual desires, reflected upon the East—here again Mawdūdī had his view confined only to colonial India—and was shown as causing an almost similar decline of moral values among the educated middle class.[473] Then, acknowledging once more man's ability to choose a life according to nature, that is Islam, or against nature, that is *jāhiliyya*, Mawdūdī raised the—purely rhetorical—question:

> Are you prepared to embrace the consequences of the Western lifestyle [*maghribī muʿāsharat ke un natāʾij ko*] which have already appeared in Europe and America, as the natural and inevitable consequences [*ṭabiʿī awr yaqīnī natāʾij*] of this way of life?[474]

Given his selection of reference works, it is hardly surprising that Mawdūdī's answer revolved, like that of Paul Bureau, Edith H. Hooker and others, around the family as the nucleus of a stable and natural society. Although this may at first glance be reminiscent of the Aristotelian notion of the household (*oíkos*) as the smallest social unit,[475] Mawdūdī—after all, highly critical of Aristotelian social and political thought—did not attribute the origins of the family to economic reasons, but rather to the need to curb the animal-like sexual urge for the sake of evolutionary advancement.[476] In arguing this way, Mawdūdī proved himself once more a child of his time, as pretty much the same arguments were used by political economists and social Darwinists in the wake of Thomas Malthus and Herbert Spencer.[477]

What is significant for the continuation of Mawdūdī's argument and what distinguished him from the named social Darwinists is his belief in the prevalence of religion already at the transitional stage from animal to man.[478] Although Mawdūdī offered no explanation of how he thought this might be possible one may assume that he presupposed the existence of religion from the creation of the world. Consistent with this line of argument is also his postulation of the prevalence of divinely ordained rules and regulations (*sharī'a*) which aim at the establishment of a 'pure civilisation' (*madaniyyat-i ṣāliha*) and which man is generally able to obey or disobey. Yet again, Mawdūdī pointed to man's choice to live according to or against nature. To lead a life according to nature, however, means to accept man's animal character and physical differences, epitomised in the two sexes.[479] Their existence, according to the Qur'ān part of creation,[480] is interpreted by Mawdūdī as follows:

> The relation of the pairs [*zawjiyyat*] basically implies that one part should be active [*fi'l*], the other part receptive and passive [*qabūl wa infi'āl*], the one prompt to influence [*ta'thīr*], the other to be influenced [*ta'aththur*], one part fastening [*'āqidiyyat*] and the other to be fastened [*mun'aqidiyyat*]. [...] This very relation is prevalent in all arrangements [*tarkībāt*] and by these arrangements runs everything in the created world.[481]

With regard to the relation between men and women Mawdūdī referred to the famous Qur'ānic verse 2:223—'Your women are farms for you [*nisā'ukum ḥarthun lakum*]'[482]—which for him made it a clear 'biological fact [*ḥayātī ḥaqīqat*]'[483] who was to be the active and who the passive and receptive part.

Interestingly, to back up his argument of a dominant and a dominated gender based on the different biological disposition of men and women Mawdūdī did not rely on the Qur'ān alone, but additionally deployed the opinions of Western medics as well. In this, he did even not refrain from referring to the Soviet endocrinologist Anton Vital'evič Nemilov (b. 1878) and his widely read popular scientific book *Biologičeskaja tragedija ženščiny* (1925) which had been translated into English in 1932.[484] In this book the author agreed with Mawdūdī by conceding man a greater mental creativity than women, because the latter are trapped in hormonal changes which make them emotionally as well as physically unstable.[485] The major problems in gender relations, Nemilov concluded, would result in the discrepancy between the reality of important biological differences between man and women and the normatively grounded claim for social, economic and political gender equality.[486]

The impressive array of other authorities to which Mawdūdī referred seemed to confirm Nemilov's findings and add thus more weight to them. As a byproduct, they were obviously intended to lead Mawdūdī's readers to believe in his erudition in Western academic literature.[487] Both impressions however can easily be destroyed. A closer look reveals that almost all further references are to be found in Nemilov's book.[488] This, in turn, provides evidence for the fact that Nemilov himself had selected these authors to back up his own arguments. What perhaps weighs even more heavily is that not all of them were beyond dispute,[489] for others appeared even predominantly in contexts which Mawdūdī had earlier harshly criticised and which, had he been aware of them, he would have most certainly avoided.[490]

Be that as it may, all of Mawdūdī's Qur'ānic and Western scientific references were aimed at supporting his understanding that 'within the family arrangement [*khāndān ke naẓm meṇ*] the nature of the male would be that of a custodian [*qawwām*]'.[491] The word choice is significant here,[492] as it ascribed the male a role within the family that echoed the command structure between God as supreme commander and man as His immediately subordinated deputy. In that role it must of course be the male who defines the rules which the female has to obey. Consequently, 'her freedom of choice [*khūd-ikhtiyārī*] is restricted as compared to that of an adult male'.[493] These restrictions, in turn, all under the pretext of safeguarding public morality within the Islamic community, affect the social and economic mobility of women.[494] Mawdūdī did not even—at least nowhere explicitly—concede them the role as primary teachers of the children, a role that even conservative and more solipsistic movements like the TJ have emphatically stressed.[495] In Mawdūdī's 'neopatriarchal'[496] understanding of gender relations there was little room for stressing female virtues. Women were, by and large, supposed to 'remain in their houses'[497] and as such they were, almost as in the Aristotelian conception,[498] not considered to contribute significantly to the political decision-making in Mawdūdī's Islamic state. The fact, however, that for the exclusion of women from public affairs no unequivocal systematic reason can be found, as well as Mawdūdī's expansive discussion of the role of women in Western societies, suggests that his outline of gender relations within this polity owed first and foremost to what he perceived as moral decline, triggered by the impact of Western sets of values on Muslim societies at the turn of the twentieth century.

b) 'Being Brought Low':[499] The Place of Non-Muslims

The second group that was excluded from active participation in the political decision-making within Mawdūdī's envisioned polity was, as stated above, the non-Muslims. His consideration of this issue is equally problematic from a systematic point of view as the gender issue. Mawdūdī's treatment of the religious minority issue stood in considerable conflict with his earlier outlined pessimistic view of Islamic history and, resulting from it, his assessment of personal and textual authority. Without any further explanation, Mawdūdī used almost exclusively medieval and early modern Ḥanafī *fiqh* works, alongside the Qur'ānic commentary *Fatḥ al-qadīr* of the eighteenth century Yemenite scholar Muḥammad ibn ʿAlī al-Shawkānī (d. 1250/1834) and even Aḥmad ibn Yaḥyá Baladhūrī's (d. 297/892) expansive annals *Futūḥ al-buldān*.[500] All these works, one could argue, have been composed during what Mawdūdī had considered elsewhere a period of religious and subsequent political decline, which is why his reference to them appeared somewhat problematic with regard to the maintenance of his systematic claim.

On the other hand, Mawdūdī had been left rather little choice. The necessity to find formal solutions concerning non-Muslims occurred most pressing not before the expansion of the early Muslim caliphates.[501] Thus, although based on scattered Qur'ānic injunction and Prophetic traditions, clear rulings appear first in the course of the development of Islamic *fiqh*. This, however, may not be the only reason for Mawdūdī's deviance from his hermeneutical principles to base his deductions only on extra-human sources. There might even be a systematic justification for this, rooted in the idealistic nature of Mawdūdī's conception of a state. Since his state was not to be a territorially defined nation state, but rather a trans-territorial 'ideological' one[502] or, in Hegelian terms, 'the actuality of the ethical idea',[503] Mawdūdī's prime concern had to be the preservation of its ideological purity. In the light of this conception his explications on the legal status of religious minorities would become redundant since only Muslims would qualify as citizens and, non-Muslims would, by definition, remain entirely outside the state. What Mawdūdī was actually concerned with instead was how to deal with apostates, or citizens of the Islamic state who had renounced its underlying ideology,[504] a problem that was triggered in Mawdūdī's thinking as early as the mid-1920s, owing largely to the impact of the *śuddhī* movement of the *Ārya Samāj* on the Muslim communities in late colonial India.[505]

The Islamic law of apostasy, however, has developed parallel to the elaboration of minority law in *fiqh*.[506] Therefore, although not necessarily required, it was technically not wrong to embed the discussion of the issue of apostasy into a historical survey of Islamic minority law. To determine the position of, and the way to deal with, an apostate, Mawdūdī set out from the classical legal typology of non-Muslims—those with whom Muslims have a contract of protection (*muʿāhadūn*), those who have been overcome in battle (*maftūḥūn*) and all others within a Muslim polity.[507] The first two groups, originally confined only to the People of the Book, that is Jews and Christians, became wards (*ahl al-dhimma*): they were granted the right of residence and to more or less freely practise their respective religion, and protection of their life and property in exchange for payment of a *per capita* tax (*jizya*).[508]

What appears significant is Mawdūdī's interpretation of the Qurʾānic term 'those who have been brought low' (*al-ṣāghirūn*) when he stressed that 'the sound position of wards [*dhimmiyoṇ ke ṣaḥīḥ pozīshan*] under Islamic rule is to be content to remain of low rank [*ṣāghirūn*]. As wards they cannot attempt to become of high rank [*kābirūn*].'[509] Even though Mawdūdī was apparently not too much bothered with the issue of non-Muslims, this very interpretation contains an implicit stimulus to convert to Islam for everyone who wanted to improve his or her social status and become thus a full-fledged member of the Islamic state with every right to take active part in the political decision-making process. Unlike the above outlined understanding of biological difference and its multifarious practical consequences, this appears again in line with Mawdūdī's anthropology. After all, man was, according to Mawdūdī, bestowed with sufficient freedom of choice, which is why, as a logical consequence, no one would need to remain a non-Muslim forever. Interestingly, however, nowhere in Mawdūdī's writings has this been spelt out, and it may thus be interpreted as a deliberate consideration in a time when religious competition in the subcontinent was extraordinarily strong,[510] and may, in turn, serve as a further indication that his prime concern was the state of religiosity of the nominal Muslims rather than to make converts.[511] In this Mawdūdī appears to have been more in line with the mindset of the TJ.[512]

There remained however a major difference between Mawdūdī and the TJ in their respective understanding of how to deal with those nominal Muslims whose beliefs and practices appeared not at all in conformity with the basic tenets of Islam. While the 'guidance-oriented' grassroots approach of the TJ was considered merely an offer to deviant Muslims to return to the 'Straight Path' and thus increase their chances of salvation in the Hereafter, Mawdūdī's 'governance-oriented' approach,[513] aiming at the preservation of the state-supportive ideology, could not allow for any leniency. Therefore, for the Muslims living in the Islamic state of Mawdūdī, the sword of Damocles of the accusation of apostasy (*irtidād*) hung constantly over their heads.

Apostasy (*ridda*) is generally considered a grave offence and entails therefore severe penal consequences. While the Qurʾān does not provide clear and unequivocal guidance for how to deal with *ridda*, all the canonical schools of Sunnite *fiqh* agreed from an early point in time as death as the only appropriate penalty, building upon the sound Prophetic *ḥadīth*: 'Whoever changes his religion, kill him [*man baddala dīnahu fa-aqtūluhu*]'.[514] Two points however arise which clearly show that the early Muslim jurists were quite aware of the sensitivity of the matter. The first one refers to the problem of how the offence of apostasy could be defined in legal terms: what, in other words, would be objective criteria to prove completely unambiguously that a believer had deliberately fallen away from Islam? The second point is closely related. Given the insight that apostasy is most difficult to prove beyond doubt, the question arose whether an accused should always be given the opportunity to repent (*istitāba*). Already on this point the authoritative texts, here first and foremost the Prophetic *aḥādīth*, were not unequivocal any more,[515] which is why one finds to some extent considerably different viewpoints on this matter in the various Sunnite *madhāhib al-fiqh*.[516]

Over time the originally rather pluralistic legal understanding of apostasy has increasingly become narrow. At the helm of this process were yet again Ḥanbalī scholars, prominently among them Ibn Taymiyya and the Central Arabian scholars of the *Wahhābiyya*.[517] It was then first and foremost Muḥammad ibn ʿAbd al-Wahhāb, the latter movement's eponym, who, in his *Rasāʾil*, worked towards a congruency of orthopraxy and orthodoxy,[518] a congruency that was to pursue a remarkable career especially in Islamist circles. Someone was only to be considered a Muslim if his or her belief found an adequate representation in his or her acts. Mawdūdī himself followed this very understanding when he stressed that:

> 'Islam is first of all the name of knowledge [*ʿilm*] and, after knowledge, the name of action [*ʿamal*]',[519] that 'after you have acquired knowledge it is a necessity to also act upon it',[520] and that 'a Muslim is distinct from an unbeliever [*kāfir*] only by two things: one is knowledge, the other action [upon it]'.[521]

For authors in the wake of such a narrowed understanding of orthodoxy, prominently among them Mawdūdī, the emphasis had been clearly shifted from the eschatological dimension, leaving the ultimate judgement over individual belief to God alone, to a more this-worldly and community-oriented dimension. For a state that is based on an ideology rather than on territorial confines, keeping its ideological foundations clean must consequently be its main concern. Hence, certain parallels can be drawn with other ideological states that have existed earlier or at the time when Mawdūdī forged his own systematic outline of an Islamic state. While the 'Terreur' during the French Revolution (1793–94), led by the Jacobins around Maximilien de Robespierre (executed 1794), was justified with reference to the enlightened virtue-state (*état de la vertu*),[522] the ruthless persecution of alleged and actual dissidents in Stalin's Soviet Union in the 1930s (*čistki*) was equally carried out under the pretext of preventing the disintegration of the Communist Party as the necessary vanguard in working towards the classless society.[523] Given the immense threat that possible dissidents pose for the subversion of the very foundations of an ideological state—be it Robespierre's virtue-state, Lenin's Communist state or Mawdūdī's Islamic state—drastic measures were needed to eradicate any possible source of danger straight away. Penance was in this regard a luxury that could, if at all, only be afforded in those rare cases where the greater good was at stake, which might well explain why in Mawdūdī's major treatment of the issue of apostasy, originally published in *Tarjumān al qur'ān* between October 1942 and June 1943, the question of *istitāba* played next to no role. Although he acknowledged that the various *aḥādīth*, as well as the statements of early authorities in all four canonical schools of Sunnite *fiqh*, and historical accounts relating to the practices of the 'Rightly-Guided' Caliphs, which Mawdūdī lined up to prove his point, refer frequently to this issue,[524] he nonetheless disregarded them, succinctly stating that granting the opportunity to repent would have rather been a discretionary provision, while the only thing with legal force was the death penalty for an apostate.[525]

Since Mawdūdī shared the view that a person's belief becomes manifest in his or her acts, and since it would be these activities that had an effect on this person's social environment, his main concern was to prevent the public dissemination of every belief which stood contrary to Islam. On this point, again, the irrelevance of the question of religious minority rights for Mawdūdī with regard to his ideological state becomes visible. Traditionally, at least according to Ḥanafī *fiqh*, the *ahl al-dhimma* would be allowed to practise their religious rituals even publicly—although they were usually confined to their neighbourhoods—and to have their own places of worship.[526] In a trans-territorial polity such as the one envisioned by Mawdūdī, however, this would necessarily amount to the propagation (*tablīgh*) of religions and worldviews other than Islam, which would then seriously endanger the ideological foundations of the state. It is therefore consistent that, in his treatise on the law of apostasy, Mawdūdī made clear that:

> we do also not tolerate the propagation [*daʿwat*] of any religion that is opposed to Islam. To grant other religions and ways [*madhāhib wa masālik*] the right to propagate [*tablīgh kā 'ḥaqq'*] and then to declare the Muslims' change to another religion a criminal offence [*jurm*] [are affirmations which] contradict each other. The second law [*qānūn*] automatically negates the first issue [*chīz*].[527]

Consequently, to allow *ahl al-dhimma* to follow their respective religions publicly would, in Mawdūdī's conception of the Islamic state, clearly contradict his understanding of the law of apostasy. Therefore, the *ahl al-dhimma* following a *dīn* other than Islam—which, according to Mawdūdī, they do only out of capriciousness,—can by definition not be members of his Islamic state:

> We want to block entrance into our society [*jamāʿat*] of those people who are afflicted with the disease of capriciousness [*talawwun kā marḍ*] and keep on playing with theories for their own amusement, and who lack totally the stability of belief and character [*ray awr sīrat*] which the construction of a system of life [*niẓām-i zindagī kī taʿmīr*] requires.[528]

As a result of this most explicit statement, Mawdūdī's views on the place and role of minorities in the Islamic state might be summarised as follows: theoretically and in accordance with classical legal rulings, followers of other religions, as long as they are recognised as *dhimmī*, may take residence under Muslim rule and are permitted to maintain their religious identity. They will, however have to pay a '*per capita* protection tax' (*jizya*) as a sign that they have been 'brought low' and, consequently, will not enjoy any right to active political participation.[529] In Mawdūdī's eyes, however, the admission of non-Muslims to a Muslim polity, which is not territorially defined but by the adherence of its citizens to a single ideology, bears the danger of granting them *de facto* more rights then they were entitled to according to Islamic law.[530] Besides, they would seriously undermine the ideological foundation of the state. It appears therefore prudent to completely exclude followers of other religions, be they *ahl al-kitāb* or others, *a priori* from the Islamic state—the essential accession criterion would only be their voluntary conversion to Islam which, however, is an irreversible decision:

'No compulsion is there in religion [*lā ikrāha fi'l-dīn*]'[531] means that we do not compel anyone to come into our religion. And this is truly our practice. However, we initially warn whoever would come and go back that this door is not open to come and go. Therefore anyone who comes should decide before coming that there is no going back. Otherwise he should kindly not come.[532]

This, finally, is the crunch point of Mawdūdī's conception. Once one has decided to become a member of the Islamic state he must never be allowed to leave it alive. The state, in turn, is responsible for keeping its foundations clean, so that to impose and execute the death penalty for an apostate would be the only reasonable measure.[533] 'Apostasy', finally, is understood as failing loyalty in a twofold way: first, loyalty to God and, second, loyalty to the community of believers which, in Mawdūdī's understanding, constitutes the Islamic state, the latter being the reason why 'apostasy' becomes thus identical with 'high treason'.

Interestingly, in the same way as in his discussion of the issue of women, here, too Mawdūdī did not use his Islamic conception to dissociate himself from Western values and practices, but tried rather to utilise them for his own ends. While the parallels to other ideological states have already been mentioned above, Mawdūdī himself referred explicitly to 'those democratic states the history and theoretical foundations [*naẓariyyāt*] of which have been a lesson in democracy for the modern world and which today have the honour of holding high the banner of the democratic system',[534] namely the examples of Britain, the United States and Switzerland,[535] to prove that even a democratic state exerts its '[inherent (*dhātī*)] right to use force [*jabr awr qawt*] to protect its own existence and order [*apne wujūd awr apne niẓām*]'.[536] This comparison, however, is somewhat flawed. While Mawdūdī was quite clear on distinguishing a historical legal normativeness from historical legal practices in the Muslim context, he conflated the normative premises of democracy with historical practices without acknowledging any conflict. Although the modern understanding of democracy is rooted in the understanding of man's freedom of choice and thus the contractual and absolutely voluntary nature of any political association,[537] the historical practice in all three of Mawdūdī's case studies[538] has shown that also in outspoken democracies considerable numbers of people were forced against their will to remain within the association and to bow to the vote of either the majority or those who have the political means to subdue others.

As in the case of women, Mawdūdī's understanding concerning religious minorities, including those whom he considered apostates from Islam, dealt a considerable blow to his initial egalitarianism, rooted in his anthropology and manifest in his conception of a 'theo-democratic' political system. While non-Muslims by birth, ultimately subsumed under the label 'unbelievers' (*kāfirūn/kuffār*), have, by definition, no place in Mawdūdī's Islamic state, the state ultimately exerts an enormous control over the righteousness of its Muslim subjects and threatens them constantly with their physical elimination in case they do not meet the expected standard of belief as expressed in their actions. While Mawdūdī remained by and large vague as to what this standard would be in detail,[539] the potential to despotic solutions in the name of a greater good, as witnessed in other ideological states, is clearly visible and reduces Mawdūdī's idea of a democratic system of governance almost to absurdity.

Whether or not this rather sobering outlook corresponds with the realities in South Asia and beyond will therefore necessarily be discussed in greater detail in the second chapter of section E. It will become clear that Mawdūdī's systematic outline, as had been developed so far, was confronted with serious challenges at various times and different places that put its claim for universal validity seriously to the test, and resulted soon in either significant modifications or even tacit amendments.

First, however, yet another conceptual step needs to be considered that serves as a link between the theoretical outline and its practical realisation. This nexus was meant to be provided by Mawdūdī's concept of the 'Islamic Revolution', coupled with his idea of a societal vanguard as its bearer. Both conceptions will therefore be discussed next, before we can turn to an investigation into the fate of Mawdūdī's ideas in various actual sociopolitical contexts.

4

MAKING A SYSTEM HAPPEN

1) 'An Idea which has Found its Bayonets':[1] The Concept of 'Revolution'

Consistent with the anti-colonial component of Mawdūdī's project, a change in governance, coupled with the necessary change of the economic system which politics aims to secure, has to be so far-reaching that it can best be described as a 'revolution'. The possibility to apply this term to societal contexts, however, was the result of a profound semantic shift which occurred in sixteenth century Europe. From a term that originally denoted the circular motion of the stars and the planets, it became then consciously applied also to long-term and, even more, sudden political upheaval which would necessarily discharge into social change:[2] 'Every revolution dissolves the *old order of society*; to that extent it is *social*. Every revolution brings down the *old ruling power*; to that extent it is political.'[3] To perceive the dissolution of an old order as something desirable was even in early modern Europe a revolutionary development in itself but the absence in Muslim societies of such decisive economic change as the Industrial Revolution brought to Europe prior to nineteenth century colonialism, seems a major reason why Muslim political thinkers maintained a negative attitude towards political revolution for considerably longer. To introduce a theoretical concept of 'revolution' with positive connotations is therefore, besides the reinterpretation of the concept of *jāhiliyya*, perhaps the most significant contribution of Mawdūdī to the Islamist discourse and beyond.

1.1) Taking Fate into One's Own Hands: The Trans-Valuation of Political Change

Historically, systematic considerations of societal upheaval oscillated mainly between two poles which date back to Greek antiquity and were appropriated by medieval Muslim thinkers. While for Plato a forced change of the constitution of a polity (*metabolē perì tàs politeías*) by a section of society was seen as a great evil even if the constitution of that society appeared deficient,[4] his pupil Aristotle appeared to be less idealistic when he considered revolution (*metabolē*) and civil strife (*stásis*), although not desirable, under certain circumstances nonetheless justifiable.[5] From these two apparently insurmountable positions two distinct traditions evolved that, as we shall hypothesise here, were somewhat reconciled in Mawdūdī's concept of 'revolution'.

Initially both medieval Christian and Muslim thinkers clearly advocated the Platonic approach, although the term 'revolution' was not explicitly used in the context of constitutional history and law.[6] For Muslims the desire for community cohesion appeared even stronger in the light of the traumatic communal experience of the so-called 'infestations' (*fitan*) between 656 and 661 CE, which, after all, led to an irreconcilable split in the early Muslim *umma*.[7] Political stability was thus desirable at any price and this theme runs through the history of Muslim political thought all the way into the twentieth century.[8] This perception did not even change when pro-modernist Muslim thinkers, like the Egyptian ʿAbd al-Raḥmān al-Jabartī, engaged with the French Revolution of 1789–99. What was perceived as a 'key event with model character at the threshold of our [!] Modernity'[9] by Westerners, was considered a 'deviation' (*k͟hurūj*) by Jabartī,[10] and an 'insurgence' (*fitna*) by others.[11] This perception only began to change with the mid-nineteenth century anti-European uprisings in India (1857–58) and Egypt (1881–82), as well as the Mahdī movement in Sudan (1881–99). All three events have equally been perceived as 'revolution' (*t͟hawra*),[12] although not yet necessarily with a positive connotation in mind. The revolt led by the high-ranking Egyptian officer Aḥmad ʿUrābī Pāshā (d. 1329/1911), however, was already the result of a 'structural transformation of the public sphere' in late Ottoman Egypt and, although aiming at independence from Western influences, was nonetheless consequently driven by the spirit of the French Revolution and the constitutionalist idea of political self-determination.[13] From the perspective of the nominally ruling Ottoman sultan, however, the revolt could publicly only be declared a 'rebellion' (*ʿiṣyān*),[14] a fact that vividly illustrates the tension between the traditional Muslim desire for political stability and the aspirations of new functional groups in Muslim countries. Constitutionalist movements elsewhere in the Muslim world, on the other hand, have initially not been perceived as revolutions, as the Persian Constitutional Movement (*mashrūṭiyyat*) of 1905–11 illustrates. Here, too, the 'revolutionary spirit' owed a considerable amount to structural changes in the late Qājār society and the emergence of an increasingly powerful middle class.[15]

The phase shift from the Platonic model with its emphasis on political stability to a more Aristotelian one where, in order to secure each and everyone's felicity (*eudaimonía*), the forced substitution of a state's constitution was permissible under certain circumstances could, however, hardly have been achieved from within the Sunnite Islamic tradition,[16] but indeed owed more to an increased interaction with Europe and the structural transformations which resulted from it. In Europe, in turn, the orientation towards the Aristotelian model was closely related to proto-Enlightenment thought which emerged most vividly and perhaps for the first time in the political philosophies of Thomas Hobbes and John Locke at on the eve of the so-called 'Glorious Revolution' of 1688.[17] While, however, this event rather aimed at the restoration of the condition prior to the Civil War of 1642–9 and could thus at best be considered a conservative revolution, it introduced nonetheless a positive connotation to the concept of 'revolution' which, in political terms, acceded to paradigmatic status with the French Revolution of 1789–99.[18] Indeed, near contemporaries such as the historian François-Auguste Mignet (d. 1884) conceded to Montesquieu, Voltaire (along with the other *Encyclopédistes*) and Rousseau, the same three social theorists whom Mawdūdī mentioned in this regard, the role as intellectual pioneers of the revolution.[19] Especially one distinct reading of Rousseau's political philosophy was utilised by a particular political orientation which dominated the second—the Jacobin—phase of the revolution.[20]

While an increasingly irreconcilable tension between the interests of the absolute monarchy and an increasingly strong bourgeoisie became the societal premise for the revolution, the fundamental theoretical premise, which was clearly reflected in the societal one, was the idea of man's freedom of will and, therefore, of choice. It was this very theorem that enabled the French Enlightenment philosophers to rationally question everything based on a different premise, be it in theory or also in practice. What resulted from here was a new understanding of the role of the state, namely to ensure the preservation of everyone's individual freedom and equality before the law.[21] The French Revolution may thus be understood as a radical attempt to put this philosophical premise into practice by making it a cornerstone of republican France.[22] While, for philosophers like Rousseau, a humanist education was the key for raising man's awareness of his own freedom of will and choice, radical political forces of the French Revolution had this enlightened idea dogmatically narrowed down and instrumentalised for their own political ends:[23] the revolutionary government of the Jacobins, considerably influenced by Robespierre and those loyal to him, set out from the premise of already enlightened citizens who, following from the postulation of natural equality, would not develop any personal interest or aspiration. Citizens and sovereign thus become one, everything else was consequently considered as against the law of man's natural equality.[24]

Above anything else, it was the tension that arose between the ideological postulation of man's equality, theoretical precondition for the enlightened subject, and the actual social and political situation that caused the regime of the Jacobins to decay to a dictatorship, their infamous 'Terreur'.[25] It was the bloody outcome of the French Revolution and, not least, the later Napoleonic attempts to export the revolution by force, that, more than anything else, shaped its reception throughout Europe and fostered the refinement of its theoretical framework, resulting in the emergence of two opposing factions. The first one built up on Fichte's unreserved positive assessment of even the Jacobin phase of the French Revolution, considering it the best possible means under the given circumstances to ensure the self-realisation of man's primary anthropological determinant, namely 'freedom of will and choice'.[26] Coupled with Hegelian 'historism' (*Historismus*) and the idea of man's alienation from his actual nature, 'revolution' became the essence of all societal development in Marxian political theory, epitomised in the famous sentence at the beginning of the *Manifest der Kommunistischen Partei*: 'The history of all hitherto existing society is the history of class struggles.'[27]

'Revolution' in the wake of Marx became thus historically inevitable, departing from the understanding that, first, the state was the result of the economic developments and the irreconcilable class differences rooted herein,[28] and, second, that, before the state 'dies out of itself',[29] these class differences could only be overcome by violent means.[30] Consequently, the 'proletarian revolution' cannot but be a global one which will continue until the state as such has been cancelled out and is replaced by the 'dictatorship of the proletariat' or, following Trotsky, by 'democratic dictatorship'.[31] This universalist claim, symbolised in the *International Workingmen's*

Association (IWA; 1864) and the subsequent *Second* (1889), *Third* (1919) and *Fourth International* (1938), held a considerable attraction for people under colonial rule, as anti-colonial struggle could well be integrated into the framework of the 'proletarian revolution'.[32] It was not least because of this that the concept of 'revolution' gained a positive connotation among Muslim intellectuals under colonial rule, also, although not necessarily in terms of the French Revolution or the Marxist understanding of the 'proletarian revolution', but more in terms of fighting against foreign control and presence, thus reinterpreting the Enlightenment concept of *liberté* in terms of national self-determination (*al-ḥurriyya al-qawmiyya*).[33]

The theme of self-determination, coupled with the corresponding anthropology, was very much at the centre of the revolutions of 1830–48 throughout Europe, all of which built upon the paradigm of the French Revolution of 1789.[34] Indeed, even the factional divisions from that time have since been reinvoked in every revolution, as Lenin's explicit references to the major parties of the French revolutions and their equation with the Menshevik and Bolshevik factions within the *Russian Social Democratic Labour Party* (*Rossijskaja Sozial-Demokratičeskaja Rabočaja Partija*) vividly illustrates.[35] Thus, the Jacobin legacy continued to live in Communist movements throughout the world, building up on Robespierre's justification of drastic measures in view of a greater good.[36]

Against this understanding of revolution as an inevitable historical necessity—upheld primarily by Communist movements—stood a second faction in the further development of the theoretical framework on 'revolution' which was rather made by scepticism not about revolution as such, but about the course it took in France. Partly influenced by the criticism expressed by Edmund Burke (d. 1797), although without necessarily drawing the same traditionalist conclusions, it was Hegel who introduced the element of 'responsibility' into the philosophical debate on freedom, based on the acknowledgement of a common tradition.[37] Although the principle of 'responsibility' appears to have certainly played a role in the European revolutions of 1848–49, mainly sustained by libertarian currents and initially conceived as the evolutionary transition to a bourgeois and civil society, it was conveniently ignored by all those anti-liberal forces which, while stressing 'freedom' as a fundamental anthropological determinant, apparently accepted the Hegelian confinement to the adherents of a common tradition. Like in Marxist interpretations, 'freedom' became reduced to the essential constituent of a single people, thus—using Engels' famous dictum—to 'the insight into the necessity of an *inner* nature'.[38] In Fascist

Italy, finally, both interpretations, the Fichtean and the Hegelian, were initially blended to coin a distinctly new understanding of 'revolution'.

In his official *Storia della rivoluzione fascista* (1937) the lawyer Roberto Farinacci (d. 1945), between 1925 and 1926 secretary of the *Partito Nazionale Fascista* (PNF) and therefore second in command in Mussolini's Italy, depicted the rise of Fascism in Italy as a proletarian revolution, which was heavily influenced by the events in Russia in 1917 and after.[39] Employing a strong Marxist class rhetoric, Farinacci's understanding of the Fascist insurgence as 'revolution' appeared to be much different from the later developments in Germany, which had rather been considered the culmination of the so-called 'Conservative Revolution'.[40] Dismissing the Russian Revolution as a national insurgence,[41] Farinacci was not only able to justify the national confines of the Fascist insurgence, he even depicted Fascism as a *total* revolution, because it did not aim only at overcoming the class antagonisms, but at an all-embracing revision of a society which, for him, had become synonymous with 'nation' as well as 'state'.[42] Farinacci's 'revolution' suggested thus a clear break with the past and the creation of an entirely new society on the debris of the old order, based on an altogether new set of values.

The National Socialists, too, perceived their rise to power as a revolution.[43] Unlike that of their Italian counterparts, however, their doctrinal stand against Communism prevented them right from the beginning from any possible appropriation of the Marxist notion of freedom as an 'insight into the necessity of a outer nature' and, consequently, did not build up on the proletarian revolutions of the early twentieth century. Because the Nazis did not acknowledge the materialistic constraint on freedom, they were able to perceive their insurgence as a much more consequent and, thus, far more radical revolution. The revolution of the Nazis, intellectually based on particular Right Hegelian readings of especially Hegel's *Rechtsphilosophie*,[44] was essentially a conservative one, explicitly opposed to liberalism and parliamentary democracy, as well as Marxist internationalism.[45] Revolution, for the lawyer Edgar Julius Jung (killed 1934), one of the main proponents of the Conservative Revolutionary movement, was necessarily oriented towards national self-determination and against 'the doctrinal cosmopolitanism of the German left, [...], the proletarian internationalism [, which] was only the continuation of the degenerated cosmopolitanism that emerged from the intellectual decadence of the German middle class'.[46] While the Italian example was generally appreciated by the masterminds of the Conservative Revolution, nonetheless they never grew tired of emphasising the national differences in the pre-revolutionary situations and warned—in true Hegelian manner—against an adoption of the Italian model, as well as against a possible Fascist International.[47] What united the various Fascist movements nonetheless, and coincided somehow even with the Communist understanding, was that they all considered the role and the character of the party as a revolutionary vanguard.[48]

Both the economy-based determinism of the Communists and the more culture-based determinism of the Fascists found respective equivalents within the Indian independence movement, which, in turn, reflected upon various notions of nationalism. While Indian Communists like Mānabendra Nāth Rāy explicitly advocated Soviet-inspired 'Jacobinism',[49] leading members of the INC, first and foremost Nehru, were, although clearly inspired by the Soviet example,[50] more inclined to choose moderate means for the revolutionary liberation struggle. On the other hand all those factions within the wider Indian independence movement which were driven by strong communalist leanings were much closer to Fascist conceptions of 'revolution'. Here belong Jinnāḥ's AIML with its demand for a separate national territory for Indian Muslims, and Mashrīqī's paramilitary *Kh̲āksār*, as well as the Hindu-nationalist wing of the INC, led by Bāl Gaṁgadhar Tilak (d. 1920) and Aurobindo Ghoṣ (d. 1950), and paramilitary Hindu-outfits such as the RSS.[51]

1.2) The Process of the Islamic Revolution

While Mawdūdī's entire project can clearly be located within the anti-colonial struggle for self-determination, his opposition to any form of at least conventional nationalism could be identified as a decisive reason why his approach to fundamental societal change cannot be filed under one of the two above outlined options. His approach to 'revolution' was thus rather—consciously or subconsciously—in line with more conservative, and perhaps considerate, reactions to the French Revolution of 1789–99 that were espoused by men like Edmund Burke and Hegel, but without going as far as Fascist theorists of 'revolution'.[52] On the other hand, at least as far as the totalitarianism of his envisioned societal change is concerned, he appeared nonetheless susceptible to the impact of those concepts of 'revolution' which were advocated by the camp-followers of either Communism or Fascism. Although there is no explicit textual evidence in Mawdūdī's writings, the fact that both ideologies were gratefully received and popularised by Indian intellectual elites of the late colonial period makes such an influence on Mawdūdī's thinking highly probable.

First and foremost, however, as in all the theoretical considerations of the possibility as well as the legitimacy of forced societal change, Mawdūdī's understanding of 'revolution', too, is once again related to the anthropological core issue of man's freedom of choice and action.[53] Rather than radical theorists of freedom, like Fichte in his reflections on the French Revolution, Mawdūdī appeared much more in line with their critics. While the former would subordinate everything to man's preservation of his freedom and, therefore, go even as far as to establish capriciousness as man's ultimate anthropological determinant, which, in turn, would inevitably lead to an understanding of 'revolution' as a legitimate attempt to reconcile man's estrangement from his nature,[54] the moderate, or conservative faction was much more reluctant, as its protagonists had been clearly aware of eventual ethical problems which such a radical understanding may promote. Hegel's emphasis on man's liability for the results of his free choice and the historical determination of the range of options to choose from[55] was clearly responsible for the fact that, although initially welcomed, the French Revolution was, in view of its course, seen as rather problematic.[56] For thinkers like Hegel and his true epigones, a revolution was first of all a process of intellectual reflection in which 'the spirit' becomes 'certain of itself' and, thus, man develops a moral worldview.[57] 'For it is a false principle that the fetters which blind Right and Freedom can be broken without emancipation of conscience—that there can be a Revolution without a Reformation.'[58]

Mawdūdī would have fully agreed with this. For him, too, 'revolution' could not be understood as a violent break with history, which would mean the abolition of the entire foundation of human existence, that is to say God's absolute sovereignty and man's mere trusteeship on earth. Societal change could therefore only be justified as a result of a collective consciousness, which had to be created in a lengthy process:

> After all, reform [*iṣlāḥ*] can only set out from the point that, firstly, the longing for one's own free will [*kh͟ūd-mukh͟tārī*] is abandoned from man's mind, and, secondly, that it is realised that the world in which we are living is not just a kingdom without a king. Quite the opposite, it has indeed a king [*pādishāh*] whose reign [*salṭanat*] does not need [man's] recognition, nor can it be destroyed by it, or can there be no arguing about the transgression of the limits of his dominion.[59]

While this is generally in line with the Hegelian view on societal change, there are nonetheless fundamental differences which ultimately led Mawdūdī to reject Hegel's ultimate insight into the irreversibility of the historical process, based on his acceptance of freedom as man's primary anthropological determinant and epitomised in the famous epigram 'what is rational is real, and what is real is rational'.[60] As outlined above, Mawdūdī understood history not as a one-dimensional and directed process, but, although he maintained the teleological element, rather as an upward spiral through time, oscillating between conditions of societal perfection (*islām*) and man-made conditions of deficiency (*jāhiliyya*).[61] While, like Hegel, Mawdūdī depended inevitably on a concept of 'freedom of choice' for the elaboration of his systematic outline, the *telos* in his conception of history had nonetheless to differ considerably from that of Hegel. For the latter, history aimed ultimately at the creation of 'self-awareness', which 'is none other than the progress of the consciousness of freedom; a progress whose development according to the necessity of its nature'.[62] Individual freedom, according to Hegel, is somewhat curtailed by man's historical placing in society—here the Kantian categorical imperative comes into effect and contributes to the development of the 'Ethical State', that is, the realisation of freedom in an institution. Regardless of all possible commonalities between the two concepts of history which reflect upon the understanding of forced societal change, the absence of any reference to man's dependence on God and His guidance through revelation led to a fierce rejection of Hegel's understanding by Mawdūdī:

> If you just think about what dangerous kind of philosophy this really is, this concept of the History of Human Civilisation [*tahdhīb-i insānī kī tārīkh kā yah taṣawwur*] which rose in the mind of this character, how could you then expect even a few of the values of those periods of civilisation [*adwār-i tahdhīb*] to survive in which Abraham, Moses and Muḥammad—God's Blessing be upon all of them!—lived? How could someone ever fall back on the age of Prophethood and the Caliphate of the Rightly-Guided ones for guidance and orientation? In a manner of speaking, this is such an elaborate and systematic intellectual assault that it cuts out even the root of religious thought as soon as it hits someone's mind.[63]

Mawdūdī's appreciation of a glorious past, the values of which need to be restored, appears, at least at first glance, much more in line with the Nietzschean critique of the one-dimensionality of historism, measured by the work of man's rationality through the history of the world.[64] While, as elaborated above, Mawdūdī seems to have followed the Hegelian line of thought as far as conceding man the possibility to decide for a *dīn* other than Islam, he argued, again almost like Nietzsche, that any *dīn-i jāhilī* would be artificial and, consequently lead man away from his natural determination. However, in another turn towards the Hegelian position, societal development for Mawdūdī culminated in the creation of 'self-awareness', but this 'self-awareness' would be, unlike for Hegel and his epigones, no reflexive affirmation of one's individual freedom and the reflection of this insight in society, but rather the knowledge of man's determination through creation and, resulting from this insight, the exertion of responsibility against the Creator and the rest of creation. The 'Ethical State' of Mawdūdī would therefore mean the realisation of these dependencies, epitomised in the *dīn-i islāmī*.

It is obvious that such a rather intellectual process differs considerably from all previous notions of 'revolution' in the Muslim context. Here it means no sudden societal upheaval, which would result in the destruction of all prevalent structures and values in a society and the creation of some altogether new ones. For Mawdūdī, as well as for Hegel, such changes need first to be intellectually appropriated, in order to prevent a dictatorship like that of the Jacobins in France and the Bolsheviks in Soviet Russia.[65] This appropriation, in turn, clearly lacks the eruptive spontaneity of the political revolutions in the wake of the French one of 1789–99. This may explain why, as Nasr has rightly pointed out,[66] Mawdūdī apparently did not have a clear-cut concept of 'revolution'.

On the other hand, we need to acknowledge that for the designation of the aspired change Mawdūdī used nonetheless the term 'revolution'. Could we perhaps insinuate that he had not been entirely aware of the implications, which would doubtlessly arise from the use of this term? Despite his occasional flaw, this would nonetheless fail to do Mawdūdī the justice he deserves. In an attempt to retrieve Mawdūdī's honour, therefore, one may argue that 'revolution' in his understanding does not refer to the actual process, but rather to the comprehensiveness of the desired societal change, namely the fundamental re-valuation of the prevalent mainly Western-inspired values and structures. It would therefore certainly be legitimate to characterise the process with regard to its eventual result as revolution (*inqilāb*), while the process itself would perhaps be more appropriately described as reform (*iṣlāḥ*).[67] Such a confluence of 'revolution' and 'reform' appears moreover fully consistent with Mawdūdī's theoretical premise of cyclical renewal (*tajdīd*), because according to this no entirely fresh start would ever be possible, but only the attempt at a regressive reconciliation of normative expectation and actual societal practice. Since, according to Mawdūdī, this practice had deviated from the norm to such an extent that the renewal had to embrace and decisively reform every part of society, the label 'revolution' in a very original understanding of the term appears after all perfectly justified.[68] Prime target in Mawdūdī's conception of forced societal change, be it labelled 'reform', 'renewal', or 'revolution', are all those institutionalised values which were historically not rooted in the Islamic normative framework, first and foremost, of course, any form of 'nationalism'. In an organism, as which Mawdūdī wanted his state to be understood,[69] anything which is not a natural part of it is prone to be rejected as artificial tampering:

To think of giving to a people a constitution *a priori* is a whim, overlooking precisely that element which renders a constitution something more than a product of thought. Every people, therefore, has the constitution which suits it and belongs to it.[70]

Once again, it seems, Mawdūdī's viewpoint appeared as an interesting synthesis of elements in Hegelian and Nietzschean thought, because in the interpretation of Hegel's above statement Nietzsche would have claimed that a people's constitution needed not just to be the historically solidified product of this people's rational choices through the ages, but to correspond to man's nature. Mawdūdī would therefore not have agreed with Hegel's idea of a constitution being the result of an evolutionary process of man's deliberate choices, because, as is clear from Mawdūdī's understanding of history, man had over time deviated from the natural path, that is, the path outlined in the Qur'ān. A 'revolution' was therefore inevitably needed to restore the natural order of things where all artificially created contradictions were removed and humankind had been readjusted and became, once again, 'a community justly balanced [*ummatan wasaṭan*]', as epitomised in the Qur'ānic verse 2:143, for 'that ye might be witnesses over the people, and the Messenger a witness over yourselves'.[71] In his interpretation of this verse, Mawdūdī stated:

The purpose of creating 'a community justly balanced' according to this Qur'ānic verse is [...] that in the Hereafter, when humankind will be accounted for, the Messenger, as representative, bears testimony for the fact that he had instructed us to sound beliefs, virtuous acts and a system of justice [*fikr-i ṣaḥīḥ awr ʿamal-i ṣāliḥ awr niẓām-i ʿadl*] and has shown how to put all this into practice accordingly. Following the Messenger's example, you will be called to bear witness for the common people [*ʿāmm insāne*] and to testify that you have had spared no effort in passing on to them what the Messenger had passed onto you. Thus, the position to testify before God, which has been conferred to a person or group in this world, amounts actually to their leadership [*imāmat awr pīshwāʾī*].[72]

The justly balanced, or natural community would, as occurs from Mawdūdī's exegetical statement, again become the promised 'best community that God had brought forth among humankind'. Consequently, it would end the political and economic leadership of the West that Mawdūdī faced and resume the leadership in the world as the community that 'enjoins the commendable and prevents the reprehensible' (*amr bi'l-maʿrūf wa-nahy ʿan al-munkar*).[73] This leadership, although promised, does however not come by itself, but has rather to be earned, which is where Mawdūdī's 'revolution' would be situated. In proposing the way forward for the way such a most comprehensive change was to be achieved under the prevailing conditions, Mawdūdī was yet again much closer to the French and German Enlightenment philosophers than he would have wanted to openly admit. Echoing them,[74] Mawdūdī stressed the importance of education as the key to the creation of Muslim 'self-awareness' which, in turn, would eventually overturn man's alienation and reconcile him with his true nature. Hence, it is 'knowledge [*ʿilm*] alone [which] grants man the viceregency [of God] on earth'.[75]

The proposed aim of education, to foster the intellectual and moral reformation of Muslims, was not new. Indeed, here Mawdūdī joined a long line of multifaceted efforts, which in South Asia gained momentum after the Sepoy Uprising of 1857–58 and the subsequent incorporation of the Subcontinent into the British Empire.[76] Mawdūdī did not embark on a thorough analysis of the various movements which emerged in the second half of the nineteenth century and which differed over sometimes rather marginal doctrinal and ritualistic issues. For him, they could all be grouped into two camps, a traditionalist one and a modernist one.[77] While he found useful elements in both of them, Mawdūdī was nonetheless quite outspoken in his criticism, as he saw neither of them able to bring about the desired reformation which would eventually become manifest in Mawdūdī's 'Ethical State', the *ḥukūmat-i islāmī.* The traditionalists, typified by the Deoband movement, albeit very versed in religious matters, lacked a proper connection to the social and political practice:

> There are people who are very familiar with the religion, believe in it and even act accordingly, but the aim of their life is not its establishment [*magar us ko qāʾim karne kī saʿī wa juhd un kā waẓīfa-yi zindagī nahīṇ hotā*]; with piety and deeds [*nīkī wa ʿamal ke sāth*] they are rather engaged in their own worldly affairs. Doubtlessly, they are righteous people and, as soon as the Islamic System of Life has been erected, they will also be good citizens. But where the System of Ignorance [*niẓām-i jāhiliyyat*] prevails entirely and the task would therefore be to remove it and to establish the System of Islam instead, the mere existence of such pious people cannot achieve the least.[78]

The other strand, epitomised by the Aligarh Muslim University, seemed more likely to produce active members of the society by their efforts to combine Islamic education with modern applied sciences. Mawdūdī appeared therefore quite in accord with Sayyid Aḥmad Khān's rationale for the establishment of a reformist educational institution for Indian Muslims after the establishment of direct British colonial rule over the subcontinent, that is to say to offer them 'a modern education in order to secure their economic and political stand and to ensure that they are not deprived by other people under the new administrative order'.[79] The way this goal was pursued in Aligarh, however, appeared to Mawdūdī not appropriate at all:

> If this university produces graduates similar to those being produced by other state universities, if this university also produces facsimile Englishmen [*waysī ṣāḥib log*], Indian nationalism [*hindī waṭan-parast*] or even socialist heresies [*ishtirākī malāḥida hī*], what was the need, then, to establish a separate university for Muslims at the cost of hundreds of thousands of rupees? [...]
>
> Its students are indistinguishable from those of another state university. They are completely devoid of Islamic character [*kerekt'ar*], Islamic spirit [*ispirit*] and Islamic conduct [*ṭarz-i 'amal*]; Islamic thinking [*tafakkur*] and Islamic outlook [*dhihniyyat*] are altogether lacking in them.

Moreover, quoting the experiences of a young Aligarh graduate, he continued:

> In Aligarh, I encountered the final stage in the evolution of foreign infestation and westernisation [*khārijī fitna awr tafarnīj*] of the Islamic world, that is Communism. At first, I did not consider westernisation [*maghribiyyat*] a potential threat, but my experience at Aligarh revealed the truth to me. A considerable number of people in this centre of Islamic India [i.e. Aligarh] have turned apostates [*murtadd*] and have become eloquent preachers of Communism. [...] It [i.e. Communism], being a world movement, has come to serve as justification of their moral weakness, heresy and loose thinking.[80]

According to Mawdūdī, the major fallacy of its founding fathers lay in that they assumed a compatibility of Islamic and Western contents of education, which, in fact, were incompatible (*munafī*)—hence the entire Aligarh project was doomed from its inception.[81] Departing from the understanding of an axiomatic leadership of Islam, Western and Islamic contents must never be treated as equal or complementary, but would rather have to be perceived in a hierarchical order. Thus, what Mawdūdī was calling for was basically an Islamization of contemporary Western knowledge. This had to go hand in hand with a radical—say revolutionary—revision of the Islamic sciences. Consistent with Mawdūdī's direct and unmediated approach to the text of the Qur'ān, as outlined above, he openly called for a rigorous purge of the Islamic sciences from the ballast of the Muslim exegetic tradition.[82]

Given Mawdūdī's critical stand towards the existing educational strategies among Indian Muslims, be they 'traditionalist' or 'modernist', the question remained: what exactly should the educational system look like in order to fit Mawdūdī's objective? After all, it had to promote the creation of a Muslim 'self-awareness', considered to be the necessary precondition for effective societal change. This Muslim 'self-awareness', in turn, was perceived as the reconciliation of an estranged humankind with its nature as divinely created beings. In the late 1930s, Mawdūdī claimed to have been asked by the *Council for the Reform of the Syllabus and the Religious Sciences* of Aligarh Muslim University (*Majlisi iṣlāḥ-i niṣāb wa dīniyyāt*) to submit a proposal for a revised curriculum. Not lacking in self-confidence, Mawdūdī declared that this proposal of his, although directed to his commissioners, would apply to all Muslim educational institutions in India, traditionalist and modernist alike.[83] Be that as it may, this proposal appears to be the most concrete explanation of Mawdūdī's own ideas of an Islamic education, which caters for his ultimate goal of societal change into a *ḥukūmat-i islāmī*, and this is why it definitely deserves a closer look.

The rationale (*takh̲ayyul*) behind his educational model was clearly stated: 'If you want to revive Islamic culture and, instead of lagging behind the time, to lead on, then you will have to re-establish the broken bond between the two.'[84] How Islam is best brought up-to-date Mawdūdī elaborated in the following text, based on establishing his own approach to the textual basis of Islam as the only valid one. This includes the purge of the traditional contents of religious education from 'dull material [*kh̲ushq kalāmī tafṣīlāt*]',[85] that is, mainly those materials which dominated the curricula in traditional religious education. The yardstick should only be rationality (*ʿaql*) and 'common sense' (*fiṭrī wajdān*) but the study of traditional Islamic subjects such as dogmatics (*ʿaqīda*), ethics (*akh̲lāq*) or Islamic History should be confined to the Qurʾān and the example of the Prophet and the Companions alone.[86] According to Mawdūdī is was not necessary to study all the subjects in depth, nor was it required to acknowledge the Islamic exegetical tradition or, come to that, to differentiate between Sunnite and Shiite views.[87] The aim would thus not be, as in traditional religious education, to acquire in-depth knowledge of particular fields, but rather to gain a general and largely unmediated religious understanding of various issues, clearly aiming first and foremost at the creation of Islamic sentiments among students which could in turn be utilised for the establishment of Mawdūdī's envisioned Islamic state.

Herein, Mawdūdī clearly followed a utilitarian and by no means idealist understanding of education. In the wake of the much despised Jeremy Bentham and John Stuart Mill, knowledge, in order to be considered valid, had to be functional and, thus, proven useful for some practical end.[88] The educationalists of the eighteenth century, many of whom can be considered idealists, and their nineteenth and early twentieth century' epigones, on the contrary had a much broader understanding of education, based on their ideal of the comprehensively educated individual personality for whom no possible content of knowledge was considered redundant.[89] Mawdūdī, instead, obviously followed the goal-oriented constriction of knowledge and methodology, and therefore the customisation of the educational system that appears to feature in all political ideologies of whatever provenance. A basic but nonetheless firm knowledge of what he considered core issues to generate a Muslim 'self-awareness' appeared to be all that was needed to undertake the task to reconcile the 'Islamic culture' with the present time. Only on the basis of such a developed sound and solid 'self-awareness', one is compelled to conclude, would Muslims be able to confidently face non-Islamic fields of learning. After all:

> Western sciences and arts as such are beneficial and Islam is not hostile towards them. On the contrary, I say that, insofar as the respect for knowledge [*ḥaqāʾiq ʿilmiyya*] is concerned Islam is friendly towards it as well as it is friendly towards Islam. Hostility is not between knowledge and Islam, but between Westernisation and Islam.[90]

What Mawdūdī wanted to be understood as 'Westernisation', in turn, has already been repeatedly outlined above. While Islam is based on firm truths (*ḥaqāʾiq*), Western knowledge is mainly not. Mawdūdī called it 'hypothetical' (*mafrūḍī*), based rather on impressions (*wajdāniyyāt*) than anything else, which inevitably leads to the distortion of the established truths.[91] Consequently, to make the knowledge that it produces entirely compatible with and appropriate for Muslims, the West would have to ultimately abandon its claim to universal truth.

Mawdūdī's plans for a revision of Muslim education in the subcontinent did not remain abstract theoretical considerations. In order to realise them, he called for a critical scrutiny of the existing literature for both Islamic as well as non-Islamic subjects. At first glance, there is nothing to object to in that demand, but, as one might already suspect, Mawdūdī had ulterior motives for this which, once again, put him well in line with all those others who attempted to enforce an ideology in practice. The objective of Mawdūdī's demand for a scrutiny of all existing textbooks was first and foremost to select only those works which seemed in line with his own educational programme, to amend and modify others and to present them in a more contemporary idiom, whether in Urdu, Arabic or English,[92] and to simply discharge the rest of them. Formalities were at the most of secondary importance, as is proven especially by Mawdūdī's indifference toward the actual language of instruction. All that counted for him was the content, the validity of which had to be measured by its effect, namely whether it could contribute to generating a Muslim 'self-awareness' which could then be utilised for the project of a revolutionary reconstruction of the entire society as *ḥukūmat-i islāmī.*

Consistent with his demand for a broad reformist educational movement as the precondition for the revolutionary transformation of the present society, Mawdūdī introduced, in his 1941 key treatise *Islāmī ḥukūmat kis ṭaraḥ qā'im hotī he?*, a further and more dynamic definition of 'Islam':

> In principle, 'Islam' is the name of a movement [*taḥrīk*] that, on the [acceptance of the] concept of the sovereignty of the One God, strives to erect the entire building of human existence.[93]

With a view on Mawdūdī's whole conceptual writings, his two definitions do not appear neither mutually exclusive, nor did the second definition necessarily suggest an amendment of the first one which laid the stress more on the systematic character of his conception, but appeared therefore much more static than his second definition. In the light of Mawdūdī's particular understanding of the *ḥukūmat-i islāmī,* somehow resembling an idealistic reading of Rousseau's political philosophy which perceives the individual and collective will as necessarily congruentit is possible in a way to see the revolutionary movement which sets out for the realisation of the *ḥukūma* and the *ḥukūma* as ultimate result of this effort as identical. Besides, Mawdūdī emphasised that the Islamic polity will be continuously developing, which, in turn, demands a perpetuation of the revolutionary effort, although borne by an increasingly large group of people.

Initially, however, and here he followed once more in the wake of the Enlightenment thinkers, Mawdūdī acknowledged that his Islamic revolution, beginning with the education of the Muslim masses and advancing from there, would have to be sustained by a rather small number of individuals. The development of such a numerically small but powerful vanguard as the precondition for a successful Islamic revolution appeared very much in line with Mawdūdī's perception of other, non-Muslim, revolutionary movements, beginning with the French Revolution of 1789–99. It also corresponded well with his organicist understanding of society. What remains therefore for us to discuss is Mawdūdī's particular views on this vanguard as the nucleus of the Islamic revolution and, consequently, the Islamic state.

2) The Society of Enlightenment: *Jamāʿat-i islāmī*

Organicist models of society were not a feature particular to Mawdūdī, or to the Muslim context alone. They were rather widespread in the early twentieth century, especially in racial-nationalistic circles throughout Europe and beyond, but there were pre-modern antecedents in Western as well as in Islamic thought.[94] As in Mawdūdī's thought, they were also closely linked to the understanding of 'revolution' not as a one-time successfully completed act, but rather as a process which would gradually take possession of the entire polity, although this does not exclude the eventual violent revolutionary eruption. Frequent references to the 'organicist nation' (*la nation organique*) or 'integralist nationalism' (*nationalisme intégral*) in the political thought of the *Action Française* founder Charles Maurras, or to the 'racial corpus' (*Volkskörper*) in National Socialist parlance provide clear evidence for it[95]—they were clear expressions of the impact that biology, first and foremost in the guise of Darwinism, had on the general thinking of that time.[96]

What belongs almost inevitably to this kind of organicist conception of society is a rhetoric of illness and physical as well as mental weakness, of decline and dysfunction.[97] Radical societal change, or revolution, is thus portrayed as an absolute inevitability for the recovery of the entire collective corpus. Although he rarely employed biologistic terminology Mawdūdī, as we have seen, shared this kind of rhetoric on almost every major point. After all, his picture of the Muslim *umma* was one of a community in nearly constant decline, whether caused by the degeneration of their own political and religious leaders or by external forces and so, in consequence, he called for a radical reversion to its original religious constitution as the only possible cure.

Important, however, is that those who advocated societal chance in such organicistically, or integralistically envisioned polities needed to determine the very organ responsible for triggering this change, which, over time, would adjust all the other organs of the collective corpus in order to guarantee its trouble-free operation. The image of a dysfunctional body provided just that. Some parts of the body are more affected by the disease than others, some are even almost beyond cure, while others remain more resistant to the onslaught of the original causative agent and its secondary derivatives. Again, this is something Mawdūdī held in common with almost all other political ideologies of the day. Be it 'imperialist parasitism',[98] the Jew as 'the eternal parasite, a scrounger who spreads out like a harmful bacillus'[99] or characteristics of the *jāhiliyya*, the 'germs [of which] prove more dangerous [...] than the germs of bubonic plague and cholera',[100] they all use a medical terminology that corresponded to the image of the society as an infected body. In every context, however, there are parts within all these infected societies that seem immune, or at least more resistant to the afflicting disease.[101] It would therefore inevitably be this very part that would have to bring about diagnosis as well as cure. All these ideas, however, could only develop on the ground prepared by the Enlightenment movement which, with its stress on individual freedom of choice and autonomous will, had ultimately laid down that a remedy for the ailment of a community is rarely sought somewhere outside that community.[102]

2.1) The Good, the Better and the Best among Humankind

At this point, however, we are confronted with a serious problem which had already troubled the Enlightenment philosophers, although even they were not able to come forward with a satisfying solution. Already Kant had acknowledged that 'it is difficult for each separate individual to work his way out of the immaturity which has become almost second nature to him',[103] but, on the other hand, he remained not too pessimistic when he conceded that:

> [t]here is more chance for an entire public enlightening itself. This is indeed almost inevitable, if only the public concerned is left in freedom. For there will always be a few who think for themselves, even among those appointed as guardians of the common mass. Such guardians, once they have themselves thrown off the yoke of immaturity, will disseminate the spirit of the rational respect for personal value and for the duty of all men to think for themselves.[104]

Although Mawdūdī followed Kant's suit when he acknowledged that 'the number of those who try for reform and reconstruction [*iṣlāḥ wa ta'mīr*] is infinitesimal [*āt'e meṇ namak ke barābar he*]'[105] he was nonetheless firmly convinced that they were definitely out there.

For getting the prospective reformers into action, however, two preconditions needed to be fulfilled, one of which Mawdūdī apparently had already taken for granted, as he had not bothered to mention it: the existence of a public sphere which enabled people of all kinds of background to negotiate collective values. What for Kant and his contemporaries was certainly a most exciting fundamental social and political development, which made their philosophical outlines only possible,[106] appeared to be not much of an issue about one and a half centuries later. The second precondition for activating the vanguard of the Islamic revolution was that it would need to already incorporate the moral values which it was then to impart to its fellow Muslims.

The emergence of a new economic and social class which increasingly aspired for political participation challenged the established order—based on social estates and revolving around divine kingship—in its foundations.[107] Their aspiration resulted in the emergence of ideally domination-free spaces in which 'events and occasions [... are] open to all, in contrast to closed or exclusive affairs',[108] that is to say, in which opinions—again ideally—were freely exchanged, regardless of the social status of the participants. These spaces could be, and were in fact, physical ones: as salons, lodges, coffee-houses and theatres they provided the spatial framework for the second and perhaps more important dimension of the 'public sphere', namely the appropriation of events and ideas, disseminated beforehand by the emerging print media, in open debates and discussions.[109] Of course, even then various social and economic groups were, at least initially, excluded, as the basic precondition for any meaningful participation in these debates would be education, which, in turn, was largely dependent on some economic security.[110] It was therefore only the '«bourgeois» [who was] the real carrier of the public, which from the outset was a reading public'.[111] Both aspects of the 'public sphere', the spatial as well as the intellectual, made the Societies of Enlightenment eventually hotbeds of revolution.

By the time that Mawdūdī began to develop his systematic thought, such a profound societal transformation was already in full progress outside Europe also. As a journalist for various Urdu newspapers and journals, he was himself a representative of the flourishing mass media scene in vernacular languages which had emerged in the Indian subcontinent about a century ago.[112] With the end of the Mughal court and, thus, of courtly patronage of the literati, many people found new employment in the British colonial administration and began to increasingly orient themselves away from the 'Indo-Persian aristocratic culture' towards the 'world of norms and standards of the British bourgeoisie'.[113] These 'agents of chance',[114] be they Indian or British, established countless literary societies and debating clubs, many of them devoted to a refinement of morals (*tahdhīb al-akhlāq*) by public discourse.[115] While these associations were, much like those in seventeenth and eighteenth century' Europe, confined mainly to the literate and economically more prosperous, the gatherings for poetic recitals (*mushāʿira*) were, at least theoretically, also open to the illiterate. Poetry became therefore, as has been illustrated above in the example of the Caliphate movement in the early 1920s,[116] a major tool for a wider dissemination of ideas beyond the print media, and for the inclusion of wider parts of the society into the debates over common values.

While Mawdūdī certainly benefited from all these developments, he maintained the more elitist self-image of the Enlightenment philosophers as the educators of the people: to guide them towards the acknowledgement of 'their capability to make a right choice'.[117] Indeed, in Mawdūdī's eyes the Islamic revolution, portrayed above, would initially have to be carried out by those very same people who, as he mentioned, 'try for reform and reconstruction'.[118] Besides their determination to bring about revolutionary change to the entire society,[119] they needed to qualify as the vanguard by their unquestionable moral integrity.

To this matter, Mawdūdī devoted a lot of space. The role of morality for his entire systematic outline has already been discussed at length.[120] What is important here is that the vanguard of the Islamic revolution is required to already possess, or at least to cultivate, all those moral qualities which would constitute the ethical foundation of the *ḥukūmat i islāmī*, only that it was not to enjoy the benefit of a polity that provided the ideal conditions for development of these qualities. In a speech delivered on 21 April 1945 to dedicated Islamic workers at Pat'hānkot' in Northeastern Punjab, Mawdūdī elaborated in great detail on his understanding of the various stages which would eventually lead to moral perfection—in Mawdūdī's eyes an inevitable precondition for engaging in pursuit of the Islamic revolution.[121] In arguing his case, he referred—without explicitly stating it—to the almost paradigmatic early battles of Badr, Uḥud and Aḥzab between the then Medina-based Muslims and the infidel Meccans. It was never a matter of number, but—and this is the common religious interpretation of these events throughout the ages—only of the morality of the Muslims that decided their victory or defeat.[122] Hence:

> [i]f in this world there was a organised group [*munaẓẓam grūh*] which, alongside basic morals [*bunyādī akhlāqiyāt*], had internalised the vigour of Islamic morals, and made use of the material resources, too, it would be unthinkable and even against nature that another group could maintain leadership [*imāmat wa qiyādat*] in the world.[123]

The core of Mawdūdī's concept of refined Islamic morality, repeated almost mantra-like, rested on an inseparable connection of theory, or doctrine, and practice (*fikr wa ʿamal kī waḥdat*). Its various elements, which he presented as hierarchically arranged, are interesting indeed, as they correspond—again without Mawdūdī giving any further reference—to a well-known sound Prophetic *ḥadīth* which had been appropriated almost one-to-one in Sufi conceptions of the development of piety.[124] Faith (*īmān*), submission (*islām*), godliness (*taqwá*) and benevolence (*iḥsān*) are the four stages which, for Mawdūdī, represented the four degrees in the development of an Islamic morality that, in the end, would bring about the much desired bond of theory and practice.[125] Only those who have comprehended the necessity of this kind of moral development, eventually reflected in outward signs like appearance or actions, would qualify as members of the admittedly rather small vanguard which would inevitably bring about the desired fundamental change in leadership of the world (*inqilāb-i imāmat*) and, thus, profound societal change.[126]

In a next step, Mawdūdī proposed four further principles to which the entire group of activists must subscribe, as 'every reasonable person knows very well that no change of the society [*ijtimāʿī niẓām*] could be achieved by the attempts of a single person only' and, thus, 'it is necessary for those kind of people who in fact are willing to do something to do it as a group [*jamāʿat*]'.[127] While he did not expand on this any further, we shall see that systematic reasons for this urge to form an elitist collective, the stem cell of the envisioned sound society, can well be found.

One example of such a group of high Islamic morality, which perhaps contributed to further shaping his understanding of this, Mawdūdī encountered in early 1939 when he observed the grassroots movement TJ at work in the Mewāt district, a little south of Delhi, and happened to meet its founder and first *amīr* Muḥammad Ilyās Kāndhalawī (d. 1363/1944).[128] What apparently impressed him during his visit, to the extent that he mentioned it repeatedly in various articles in *Tarjumān al-qurʾān* and other journals, was the profound societal change that the activities of the movement brought about in the previously rather heterodox Mewāt region.[129] Mawdūdī felt this confirmed his so far only theoretical understanding that a degenerated society could indeed be thoroughly reformed from within by a small group of devoted and morally upright activists.

This understanding, however, was not particular to Mawdūdī alone. As stated, the idea of a small principled elite within an, at best, deficient polity was quite common to almost all other political ideologies at the time.

Where they differed, however, was on whether in the course of the transformation of the society the elite needed to gradually dissolve into the wider population, or whether it should remain a small and exclusive elite, thus as an everlasting vanguard. On this question, Mawdūdī parted company with the TJ,[130] as the latter clearly aimed at a continuous increase in their numbers by absorbing everybody who had reformed according to the standard set by the group.[131] For Mawdūdī, however, who held a firm belief in a political elite, the more exclusivist models of organisation which were closely tied to the then widespread political ideologies of Communism and Fascism must have been much more appealing.

Initially, though, the theorists of Communism, then rather philosophical and not yet pragmatically inclined, placed much emphasis on the collective of an entire class which will have to bring about the proletarian revolution,[132] a conception that appeared somewhat much more in line with the views held by the masterminds of the TJ. This crucial Marxian idea, however, underwent a drastic metamorphosis in the organisational thoughts of Lenin and his epigones. While the early Lenin envisioned 'an organisation that will consist of professional revolutionaries and be led by the real political leaders of the entire people',[133] this still rather amorphous idea gained further shape soon after the October Revolution in 1917. While the Bolshevik party was allowed to grow into a mass organisation, Lenin called for its internal stratification, identifying the Politburo of the Central Committee as the core.[134] The Politburo became a numerically strongly confined body of professional party workers grouped around the secretary-general. Its members were, ideally, considered to be those most loyal to the secretary-general as well as the party's ideology, hence the very best of Communists. While theoretically the main decision-making body was the Party Congress, in reality those powers lay with the Politburo alone.[135] However, even within the emerging oligarchy of the Central Committee and its innermost circle, the Politburo, members would have to constantly prove themselves as the best within the party by steadily affirming their extraordinary loyalty to party leader and ideology.[136] Especially under Lenin's successor Stalin, leader and ideology became increasingly synonymous and party unity was staged by rituals of declaring loyalty.[137] Whoever failed to prove this loyalty was consequently seen as a dissenter and ruthlessly persecuted.

When the political left in British India transitioned from mere dacoity in the underground of the big cities[138] to a more public organisation in the wake of the Bolshevik revolution of 1917, it clearly adopted the Leninist concept of the party as 'vanguard of the working class', or, in this case, of the Indian independence movement.[139] On the other hand, and perhaps under the impression of the growing internal stratification, or 'nomenklaturisation', of the Bolshevik party especially after the death of Lenin in 1924, leaders like Mānabendra Nāth Rāy (Roy) still envisioned the CPI as a revolutionary mass party.[140] Until the mid-1930s, the party remained rather badly organised,[141] its organisational pattern remained rather close to Lenin's ideas and did not follow Stalin's establishment of the *nomenklatura*. While this could be read as a reflection of the growing dissociation of individual CPI leaders like Rāy from Stalin there may have been one more obvious reason. Unlike the Bolsheviks, the CPI was not yet in a position of power and, thus, not in need of an apparatus of professional bureaucrats to run the state—at this stage the only semi-legal CPI had to subscribe more to strategies of infiltration of various other organisations.

Therefore, one is inclined to conclude that the elitist conception of political leadership entered the Indian mindset less by a conscious adaptation of the later Bolshevik model, than by an engagement with the Fascist ideology, first and foremost with National Socialism which had been equipped with a rather elaborate worldview prior to its seizure of power.[142] This worldview was developed and adhered to by a small elitist group, the nucleus of the *National Socialist German Workers' Party* (NSDAP), founded in February 1920, and later to provide leadership of the *German Reich*.[143] In a way similar to Bolshevism since Stalin and many, if not all, other fascisms,[144] the centrality of the leader made personal closeness to him the main criterion for inclusion into this elitist inner circle of the movement. Like the Central Committee of the Bolshevik party and its various subsections, first and foremost the Politburo, the National Socialist establishment, too, became internally stratified into groups which were even more elitist than others. A first expression of this elitism might have been the fact that, following mass joining of the party after the seizure of power in 1933, the leadership imposed a hold on membership applications.[145] It seems thus that at this point if the party was to maintain its semblance as vanguard of the 'national revolution', this could only be done by keeping membership restricted to those who had themselves proven worthy. Yet, within the party the *Schutzstaffel* (SS), grown from Hitler's personal guard unit, considered itself the best of the best, 'nothing else but the most perfect organisational manifestation of Hitler's doctrine'.[146]

What makes the SS exceptionally interesting for our case and where it clearly differed from the Communist elitist organisational model was the self-image of the SS as the progressively developing paradigm of the society *after the completion* of the 'national revolution'. Here we are strongly reminded of Mawdūdī's two complementary definitions of 'Islam', as outlined above.[147] To comply with their self-image as true embodiment of the National Socialist doctrine, the SS organisation had to restrict its membership even more than the party did—the main criterion for the selection was identification with the racial ideology at the core of National Socialism, conformity to the Aryan ideal.[148] The exclusivity of the membership was epitomised in the self-image of a 'National Socialist soldierly order of Nordic defined men and [...] a sworn community of their kin [*Sippe*]'.[149] As such, they would always—even after the completion of the 'national revolution'—play the role of a yardstick for the proper National Socialist man, woman and family.[150] The idea of the 'order', reminiscent of the much-detested Christian monastic fraternities, also suggested moral superiority of its members.[151] Indeed, they perceived themselves as the genuine revolutionaries, as those whose cultural department *Ahnenerbe* claimed the monopoly for the radical and scientifically grounded 're-valuation of all values' and their implementation into wider society.[152] Their efforts to revive the 'original Germanic spirituality' were meant to reconcile the estranged German with his true nature, after all a vital precondition for establishing the National Socialist state proper.

It appears certainly provocative and, at first sight, even highly inappropriate to relate the organisation of the National Socialist movement, especially the SS as its most chauvinistic and felonious manifestation, to Mawdūdī's organisational conception. The structural parallels, however, are conspicuous, as we have already hinted at a few times. This might not even be surprising because the militant Hindu Communalist RSS, as well as Ināyatallāh Khān al-Mashriqī's *Khāksār* movement, both of which Mawdūdī was demonstrably familiar with,[153] drew much of its inspiration not only in doctrinal, but also in organisational matters from its German paragon.[154] The *Khāksār*, too, it seems, would have had to monitor its membership, because it needed a considerable audience for its public self-staging which was reminiscent of the NSDAP *Reichsparteitage* at Nuremberg. However, while al-Mashriqī followed the model of the Nazi *Sturmabteilung* (SA) and SS almost verbatim, including even the body cult of the latter,[155] Mawdūdī, on the contrary, appeared, as has repeatedly been outlined above, rather critical towards Fascist ideology for various and mainly systematic reasons. His appreciation of al-Mashriqī and the *Khāksār* can thus only be related to the movement's aim of establishing an

Islamic state, by which it stood out from the various other Muslim political movements at the close of the colonial period, but Mawdūdī disapproved almost instantly of the *Khāksār*'s violent means of achieving this goal. Having said that, the parallels between the National Socialist movement and Mawdūdī's organisational conceptions do need to be confined to structural matters only and may rather be attributed to the general *zeitgeist* which caused organicist concepts of society and related elitist and concentric models of socio-political reformist movements to spread far beyond European borders.

The envisioned collective, or community (*jamāʿat*), which Mawdūdī considered a necessity for any successful revivalist work and which would be characterised by various lofty moral criteria,[156] was conceptualised as tripartite. It would consist, first, of a rather small and semi-exclusive core group of devoted activists who were considered the 'pillars' (*arkān*) of the collective and who were grouped around the *amīr* as the central point of reference.[157] They, again, would be enclosed by a larger circle which was to consist of permanently affiliated 'workers' (*kārkun*) who, in turn, were finally to be embraced by a rather large following of only loosely associated 'sympathisers' (*muttafiqūn*).[158] Right from the beginning, Mawdūdī was adamant in keeping the numbers of *arkān* and *kārkun* rather limited.[159] Their revolutionary activities would be transmitted to the wider society by the host of *muttafiqūn* and would thus eventually transform or 'heal' the entire social and political body from within.

Hence, although they all belonged to the same envisioned community—the 'best one which God had brought forth among humankind'[160]—they differed from each other in their degree of commitment, which in turn resulted from their respective extent to which they had realised the necessary Islamic morality. According to Mawdūdī, the 'best community' will thus still be internally stratified. Followed by the *kārkun*, the *arkān* are on the very top of the scale, while the vast majority, the *muttafiqūn*, although somehow still part of that virtuous community and thus considered better than the rest of the society, are the lowest among the three. In the beginning, however, it was only the first two and, yet clearly defined groups which together formed the nucleus of the *Jamāʿat-i islāmī* (JiI), Mawdūdī's 'Society of Enlightenment' and, at the same time, empirical litmus test for his so far only theory-confined systematic outline.

2.2) Community as Society—The Ethical State

Little of Mawdūdī's writings on the Islamic movement from around the late 1930s offers a clear idea of the concrete organisational principles, which, in turn, allows for speculation that the JiI was initially not only to become the tool in pursuit of the Islamic revolution, although over time the emphasis had clearly shifted there. To set up a group of activists deeply committed to the cause of the revolutionary transformation of the entire society also opened for Mawdūdī the opportunity of organising the group along the lines of the society-to-be. Consequently, the JiI would then represent the model for the *ḥukūmat-i islāmī*, the Islamic state—they were to be identical in structure as well as in the modes of operation.

It appears vital to understand the ideas which underlie such a multilayered conception of *jamāʿat*, even more so as it is again a clear reflection of a general mode of thinking at that time and will thus help us to further enhance our understanding of Mawdūdī's thoughts within the overall intellectual climate of the age. In their origin, these underlying ideas have again developed within the area of tension between the two major moral philosophical currents in the late and post-Victorian era, that is to say idealism and utilitarianism.[161] Mawdūdī's conception of *jamāʿat* which stretched from a small elitist group to the entire society had apparently been rooted—at least to some extent and most likely rather unwittingly—in a combination of the two idealist conceptions of development, or, better perhaps, in an emanation out of a single entity[162] and of the logical identity of part and whole, the latter an idea fully fleshed out by Hegel. Although constituted by its parts, he argued, the whole is always more than a mere aggregation of them as it is furthermore characterised—and this is the crux of Hegelian dialectics—by the complicated and often conflicting relations of its parts among themselves as well as to the whole.[163]

This idea, however, was stripped of the complex dialectics and was then appropriated by classical utilitarianism.[164] For Mill, for example, the whole was indeed just an aggregation of its parts,[165] an approach that helped him to eventually justify the basic principle of utilitarian ethics,[166] according to which the pursuit of happiness by an individual contributes to universal happiness as the ultimate value.[167] While, admittedly, this rather atomistic understanding of the relationship of part and whole by the utilitarians appeared diametrically opposed to the holistic conception of the Hegelian idealists—something that would eventually have an enormous impact on their respective understanding of the role of the state for the individual—

both outlines appear not quite as different in their consequences regarding human agency. After all, the adherents of both philosophical currents were equally concerned with the question of how individually binding ethical values are generated in a given society.[168] This concurrence appears to have helped the development of an 'organicism' in which the initially utilitarian notion of society as a the notion of 'natural organism' became redefined by the later idealists as a 'moral organism'.[169] In this way, the earlier antagonistic views of utilitarians and idealists on the relationship of individual and society, or state,[170]—practical expression of the part-whole-relation—have been merged somewhat. Only then had 'organicism' become fit to finally start its career in various and even conflicting political ideologies.

Whether Communism or Fascism, let alone Mawdūdī's Islamism, the ideologies all all agreed on the fact that only a part of the society was capable of bringing about profound social change and, thus, promote the eventual ultimate realisation of humanity in a time of increasing 'dehumanisation'.[171] In Hegelian terms, this means the reconciliation of man with his true essence, that is, freedom:[172] in Mawdūdī's terms with man's nature, that is, his createdness and the resulting dependence on his Creator. However, while in Hegel this reconciliation could only be achieved by an almost simultaneous moral self-perfecting of each single member of a society, his revolutionary posterity considered certain parts of the society better capable than others of bringing about the desired result.[173] Even so, it was believed that the elitism of such a single group did not develop simultaneously among its members, but needed intellectual impulses and organisational directions by single extraordinary individuals, or leaders.

While the main task of these leaders would be to provide an ideological framework as the overarching set of rules for the core group, organisational patterns needed to be developed, too, within which the members of the groups would be able to align themselves to the ideological principles. It seems as if 'the preferred spatial incarnation of [a movement's cultural or] political goals'[174] for all kinds of religious and/or political movements at that time, whether in the West or in colonies such as British India, was indeed the spiritual and/or military camp.[175] Given that these camps were tied closely into the educational aspirations of the self-styled proponents of 'Enlightenment' in the colonies, it appears plausible to trace their origins to the emerging youth movements at the turn to the twentieth century, first and foremost the *Boy Scouts* in Edwardian England and the *Wandervögel* in Wilhelmian Germany, which both later developed multifarious ramifications. However, if the idea of the camp, as appropriated by the various religio-political movements in late British India, was indeed rooted in these earlier youth movements, then it makes sense to emphatically include it in the three notions of 'spaces of self-expression', that is, 'spatial practice', 'representation of space' and 'representational space', which Daechsel proposed.[176] However, he applies these notions primarily to militantly inclined Indian middle class organisations and their respective camps, as was the case with uniformed movements such as the *Khāksār* or the Hindu RSS.[177] As our case at hand suggests, considerable attention should also be paid to the educational or character-forming component that was playing a considerable role in various other partly also middle class movements and camps.

It is with the camps that the sociological distinction between 'community', or rather social grouping, and 'society',[178] and their interrelationship gained momentum. Be it the *Boy Scouts* or the *Wandervögel*—blueprints for the 'political camp-culture' in the colonies—both aimed at a moral purge and restitution of the 'old and unspoiled' values within an initially rather confined section of the young population, hence creating a vanguard in counteracting the multifarious dangers that the industrialised world was facing. Many of these movements focused not only on moral education alone, but combined it also with physical, including hygiene, education.[179] As such, their ultimate goal was to create a community of exemplary morals and physical strength which was to reach out into the wider society and, thus, eventually cause its gradual transformation.

In the interwar period, however, derivatives of these initially moralist movements became increasingly politicised as camps were thus no longer restricted to the youth movements alone, but served increasingly as ideological cadre training units for various socio-political movements.[180] It was only then that the idea of the camp community, now more clearly adhering to the leadership principle, as nucleus of a revolutionary movement for the transformation of the present society received a considerable boost.[181] It seems as if Mawdūdī, like so many others at that time,[182] was considerably inspired by these developments and in consequence his initial organisational efforts resulted in the establishment of the proto-JiI as a camp community.

In the Muslim context, however, camps apparently assume a wider but distinct symbolic dimension, too. As a place of contemplation and withdrawal from the morally questionable majority society, they link the present to the historical practice of the *hijra*, paradigmatically performed by the Prophet Muḥammad and his Meccan companions.[183] As such, a departure from an infidel society is, as it were, a testimony of faith, and draws a clear line between 'them' and 'us', thus between unbelief and righteousness.[184]

While *hijra* had become a crucial element in classical legal and political thought on the rights and duties of believers under various forms of political rule,[185] it gained an emphatically practical relevance in early twentieth century British India. Dwelling on the rather pragmatic Islamic legal position that Muslims may still be permitted to live under non-Muslim rule as long as they are not hindered in the performance of their religious duties—a position most prominently held by Shāh Walīyallāh Dihlawī's son Shāh ʿAbd al-ʿAzīz (d. 1239/1824)[186]—it was during the Caliphate movement that Muslim leaders called for collective exodus. In this regard ʿAbd al-Bārī Farangī Maḥallī and Abū 'l-Kalām Āzād both issued legal opinions (*fatāwá*) in May and July 1920, respectively.[187] Especially to the latter, *hijra* to Afghanistan as the nearest possible country under Muslim rule became considered to be yet another handy strategy in the anti-colonial struggle of Indian Muslims, and to appeal to it even as a believer's individual religious obligation (*farḍ ʿayn*) appears as yet another emotive ace up Āzād's sleeve.[188] Even though the rather short-lived *hijra* of summer 1920 was overall a disaster, the idea of *hijra*—cutting oneself off from social relations for the sake of religion[189]—afterwards became rooted in the minds of Muslim religious activists throughout the Muslim world, so also in Mawdūdī's:

> For a person who believes in God's *dīn* it can only be permitted to live within a System of Unbelief [*niẓām-i kufr*] under the following conditions: The first is that he is striving for the victory of Islam on this territory and to replace the System of Unbelief with Islam, as had been done by the prophets—Peace be upon them!—and their initial followers. The second is that he really lacks any means [*rāh*] to emigrate and that he is therefore forced to stay there, but with dislike and disgust. To remain in the Abode of Unbelief on others than these two conditions is an established sin [*mustaqil maʿṣiyyat*]. For this sin, there will be no excuse, not even the weighty one that on this earth there is no such an Abode of Islam to which one could emigrate. Even if an Abode of Islam did really not exist, had God not made mountains and forests, where man could eat the leaves from the trees and drink the milk of the goats and where he could escape from obeying the rule of unbelief [*aḥkām-i kufr*]?[190]

As can be seen here, on this point Mawdūdī went even as far as demanding that, whenever emigration to another country was—for whatever reason—not an option, then one must establish domination-free spaces within one's own country. The establishment of such spaces, however, was again not Mawdūdī's own invention, but had historical precedence, although it was not usually in the manner of Mawdūdī's suggested outdoor romanticism. The most widespread practice in this regard had been the establishment of a pious and charitable endowment, a *waqf* (pl. *awqāf*). While, ideally, such institutions grow out of private immovable property which is determined for an explicitly pious purpose and thus made inalienable, in reality this has frequently been used as private asset protection especially in periods of political instability.[191] In the days immediately before the coming of the Rāj, many landowning Muslim families had resorted to this artifice in order to avoid possible expropriation by the colonial administration.[192] While in the first decades of British rule over India there was much uncertainty over the fate of the *awqāf* due to conflicts with British property and tax laws, with the adoption of the *Mussalman Wakf* [sic] *Validating Act* of 1913, propelled largely by Muḥammad ʿAlī Jinnāḥ, the British finally withdrew from their interference in the creation and administration of any kind of *awqāf* and granted these powers entirely to the religious community.[193]

After the collapse of the Caliphate movement and, in its aftermath, the increased competition between all kinds of organisations which advocated the particular interests of various religious and economic groups during the Indian struggle for independence, *awqāf* emerged as a handy tool in evading the grasp of the British. In combination with the idea of the camp, they could well be, and, in fact, have been utilised as domination-free spaces to coordinate the activities of different Muslim groups. Thus, it is not really surprising that, after his relocation to Hyderabad in the Deccan in 1930, Mawdūdī, too, flirted with the idea of establishing a *waqf* for his own ends.[194] For a brief moment, following the disappointing collapse of the Caliphate Movement, Muslim-governed Hyderabad seemed to him a good starting point for his revivalist endeavours, although he was certainly aware of the complex and ambivalent relationship between the ruling Niẓām ʿUt͟hmān ʿAlī Khān ʿĀṣaf Jāh VII' (d. 1386/1967) and the British, a fact that is corroborated by various of his early writings on the matter.[195] Why, in the end, Mawdūdī's plans did not commence is difficult to evaluate on the basis of the sources available.[196] Whatever the other reasons, one may have been that Mawdūdī got into contact with the retired revenue officer and committed Muslim Leaguer C͟hawdhurī Niyāz ʿAlī who was planning to turn his own sixty acre estate in Jamālpūr, a hamlet (*bastī*) in Northeast Punjabi Pat'hānkot', into a *waqf*.[197] While almost no further information on Niyāz ʿAlī is available, it is quite probable that the AIML had constituted an important link between him and Muḥammad Iqbāl, who by then had proposed his so-called 'Two-Nation Theory'[198] which became the founding principle of the AIML-led 'Pakistan Movement' (*taḥrīk-i Pākistān*). Iqbāl had consequently been approached by Niyāz ʿAlī for counsel on how the intended *waqf* might best be used in the interest of the Indian Muslims.

Iqbāl is said to have suggested the establishment of a model reformist educational institution on Niyāz ʿAlī's endowment. His son Jāwīd (b. 1343/1924) stated in the voluminous biography of his father that already in July 1936 Iqbāl had unsuccessfully sought intellectual as well as logistical assistance from the then Shaykh al-Azhar, Muḥammad ibn Muṣṭafá al-Marāghī (d. 1364/1945), who was a pupil of Muḥammad ʿAbduh and shared his teacher's reformist proclivities.[199] It was then that Mawdūdī's name came into the picture as one of the possible candidates for the administrator (*sarbarāhī* or *mutawallin*) of Niyāz ʿAlī's *waqf*.[200] The increasing communal tension in the Hyderabad state and the many contenders who courted the ruling monarch in the hope of exerting decisive influence over him[201] did not provide favourable conditions for Mawdūdī's initial plans to start his revivalist work there. This might have been at least one major reason for offering himself to Niyāz ʿAlī as administrator of the latter's *waqf* and his increasing openness to relocate to the Punjab. While his eventual appointment came rather out of the failure to find another suitable candidate, Mawdūdī's hagiographers spent a lot of time in establishing him as the most obvious choice by moving him closer to Iqbāl than he actually was.[202] Indeed, given the prominent position which Iqbāl held among Indian Muslims, it seems as if his blessing of Mawdūdī's appointment was well designed to enhance the latter's own standing within the community.

In reality, however, Mawdūdī could have barely be bothered about Iqbāl's vision for the *waqf* at Pat′hānkot′. While on the surface he apparently agreed to Iqbāl's suggestion to establish a model educational institution with a defined curriculum to train a new Muslim elite for India, in reality he did what overseers of *awqāf* have frequently done throughout history, namely to utilise it for one's own ends.[203] Iqbāl's death only one month after Mawdūdī's arrival at Pat′hānkot′ would therefore not have been entirely unwelcome, as it must certainly have relieved Mawdūdī of the pressure of justifying his activities to Iqbāl. On the other hand, he and his associates could well have portrayed the later JiI as having originally being the brainchild of Iqbāl. In the years to come, this appeared most helpful when the organisation began to establish itself in Pakistan, even though Mawdūdī had been one of the most outspoken critics of Iqbāl's 'Two-Nation-Theory' as the ideological foundation of the new territorial national state for the Indian Muslims.

To whom the enterprise at Pat′hānkot′ owed its name 'Idāra-yi dār al-islām' is not clear. It is however a fact that this name linked nicely to the *hijra* theme as well as to the 'camp' idea outlined above, and, although it is quite likely that the man behind the name was Iqbāl rather than Mawdūdī,[204] it fitted thus perfectly well into Mawdūdī's organisational ideas. Indeed, in his editorial in the July 1938 issue of *Tarjumān al-qur'ān*, the journal which Mawdūdī had been editing since September 1932, he stated:

> This is not a territorial *dār al-islām*, but [rather] a conceptual [*maqṣadī*] one, meaning that the objective of this enterprise [*idāra*] or movement is to make India once again abode of Islam and preparing Muslim youths [*naw-jawānān-i islām*] for this objective through knowledge, conduct and sports. For this reason alone this name had been suggested, for it makes its aim entirely clear. It does not however imply that the *dār al-islām* had in fact already been realised, but rather that we are determined to bring about its establishment, just as some grouping [*jamā'at*], by calling itself 'Svarāj Party', 'Home Rule League' or 'National Congress', implies that self-governance is already in place, home-rule effectively established, or the nation has become a fact. [...]
>
> This, then, is the reason why this very place, in which the enterprise is set up, was given the name 'dār al-islām'. Just as a building called 'Svarāj Bhavan' does not imply that self-governance had been realised in there, but rather that it is the centre of a movement for self-governance, to call the centre of a movement for [the establishment of] the abode of Islam precisely 'dār al-islām' cannot mean anything other than that it is the nerve centre of this movement [*is taḥrīk kā markaz-i 'aṣabī*]: From this very nucleus the abode of Islam will emerge into being.[205]

Indeed, as occurs already from this quote, Mawdūdī devoted at around this very time quite some thought to the originally territorial concept of 'Abode of Islam' (*dār al-islām*) which suggests that he really wanted to appropriate it into his own conceptual framework. While, from the outset, this was a highly complex and controversially discussed legal issue, necessary in determining the public applicability of the *sharī'a*,[206] for Mawdūdī it appeared to be also more of an ethical scheme.[207] As such, its counterterm was not 'Abode of War' (*dār al-ḥarb*), which would be defined by varying legal norms, but it had rather to correspond to Mawdūdī's own ethical dichotomy of 'Islam' and 'unbelief' (*kufr*), or 'ignorance' (*jāhiliyya*), hence the ensuing opposite for him had to be 'Abode of Unbelief' (*dār al-kufr*).[208] As he considered '*dār al-islām*' characterised by the permeation of 'Islam' in every sphere of public as well as private life, be they ideational or material,[209] there is good reason to equate it with the idea of Mawdūdī's ethical 'Islamic state'. Moreover, as the state was not, in the first place, conceived, in the narrow sense, as a political set-up of people and institutions which are entrusted with the exertion of general binding allocative, regulative and coordinating functions, or even in the slightly broader Weberian sense,[210] but rather more philosophically as the social manifestation of a collective will, 'state' and 'society' would necessarily fall into one, the same as 'community' and 'society' earlier on.

Applied to the enterprise at Pat'hānkot' and corresponding with Mawdūdī's organicist view of society in general, this would mean that the *Idāra-yi dār al-islām* was indeed envisioned as a model for his entire ideological framework, that is, the Islamic state, or society. Hence, territory always played a subordinate role at most, while the emphasis was clearly on absorbing more and more parts of the social body into the core community of believers. While, at first glance, the main objective of the *Idāra-yi dār al-islām* for Mawdūdī appeared to be, as stated by Nasr, 'an experiment at constructing an *ummah* (holy community)',[211] the issue might in fact have been a bit more complex. A careful look at the terminology used here might get us a little further. While, admittedly, Mawdūdī had occasionally employed the term 'umma', it did not appear at all in those writings which deal with his organisational ideas. Here, the term 'jamāʿa(t)' had mainly been adopted instead. While 'umma' and 'jamāʿa' had increasingly been used by Muslim as well as non-Muslim writers interchangeably for 'community', Gardet's plea for acknowledging the subtle semantic distinction becomes even more valid in the present case. '*Umma* is the community as constituting a nation on a religious-legal basis; while *djamāʿa* [*sic*] is the whole body of believers united by their common faith.'[212] While the point of reference in 'umma' is its head as the upholder of the 'common good' (*maṣlaḥa*) by means of 'good governance' (*al-siyāsa al-sharʿiyya*),[213] in 'jamāʿa' the stress is laid rather on 'the bond which fashions from a group of individuals a community of believers'.[214]

We may therefore safely conclude that what Mawdūdī tried to establish at Pat'hānkot' was first and foremost a small, elite community of equals, bound together by the all-encompassing religious principles as outlined in Mawdūdī's own programmatic writings. The rationale behind this was, at least in theory, to constantly expand this group without allowing the emergence of an internal hierarchy on the basis of stronger or lesser adherence to its foundational religious principles, until humankind in its entirety had been absorbed. Mawdūdī did not allow for the development of—in Weberian terms—an 'associative social relationship',[215] or 'society', out of his initial core community. This does not mean, however, that Mawdūdī categorically precluded any possible 'consociation' (*Vergesellschaftung*). For him, the 'community' (*jamāʿat*) on the basis of an individually felt communal spirit, did not stand in contrast to a society which Weber had defined as based on 'a rationally motivated adjustment of interests or a similarly motivated agreement, whether the basis of rational judgement be absolute values or reasons of expediency'.[216] While for Weber religion 'ascribes legitimacy to a social order by virtue of [...] *affectual*, especially emotional, *faith*',[217] for Mawdūdī this did not at all run counter to Weber's rationality-based modes of legitimisation of a social order. Mawdūdī's conception of '*dīn*' and the plural existence of it, which was rooted herein,[218] allowed room for rational choice. Based on his reading of the Qur'ān he conceded that man had the ability to decide for or against what for him was 'deduced as an absolute',[219] namely the reality of God, the world as His purposeful creation, His revelation to humankind and His plan of salvation. The lines of 'belief' and 'knowledge', in the world of positivists and utilitarians a fundamental and necessary dichotomy,[220] became blurred here once again. For Mawdūdī, yet again more in line with idealist thought, 'knowledge' was essentially based on socially shaped and therefore initially variable 'belief'. Both 'belief' and the resulting 'knowledge' are confined to the individuals or groups who adhere to it and shape their social reality accordingly.

As there is no ultimate criterion to prove the superiority of one belief over another, a social group can be enlarged only by the use of force, be it physical, economical or rhetorical, while accession to the group is, however, still dependent on individual rational choice. While, for instance, ʿInāyatallāh al-Mashriqī's *Khāksār* opted for physical confrontation,[221] Mawdūdī decided, as is apparent in his concept of 'revolution',[222] in favour of the power of speech. The small elitist core *jamāʿat* which began to establish itself at Pat'hānkot' was therefore seen as the vanguard, the best of the best, the nucleus of the universal *jamāʿat*-to-be. It was there that they would train and prepare themselves to eventually go out to seize the world.

2.3) Training the Cadres and Organising the Vanguard

In the beginning of the *Idāra-yi dār al-islām*, Mawdūdī complied with the wishes of Chawdhurī Niyāz ʿAlī and Iqbāl and began to establish an educational institution of some sort. This, however, should perhaps not be regarded as too much of a concession by Mawdūdī, as it appears so far consistent with the idea of shaping an elitist core community along the lines that Mawdūdī had himself worked out. Given that at that point in time he did not yet command a uniform group of devotees he first needed the small group of only twelve people[223] who joined the project right at the beginning to be sworn to his ideology. This appeared to have been even more necessary as the majority within this small group had been recruited from among the barely educated people in the surrounding area.[224] While, given his vision of the *Idāra-yi dār al-islām* as a place where highly trained Muslim intellectuals would come together to develop strategies for communal leadership,[225] the ailing Iqbāl must have been rather disappointed by the random recruitment to the project, although it would have certainly benefited Mawdūdī's own ends. After all, here he was supplied with enthusiastic but still mouldable people whom he could hope to bring into line. Hence, the first step was to educate them while, at the same time, train them in strategies for missionary activities (*daʿwat*).[226]

Mawdūdī also attempted to enhance the credibility of the project in the eyes of the Indian Muslim community by inviting some forty reform-minded *ʿulamāʾ* to join, a call to which only a very limited number responded positively.[227] One of these, the young Deobandī scholar Muḥammad Manẓūr Nuʿmānī from Lucknow (d. 1417/1997), introduced Mawdūdī early in 1939 to the TJ from whom Mawdūdī received further inspiration as to how to modify the activist approach of the occupants of *Idāra-yi dār al-islām*.[228] Set in an almost similar environment, Mawdūdī's small *jamāʿat* began to almost identically employ the strategy of proselytising tours (*gasht*).[229] intellectually and also physically fortified,[230] they set out to preach in village and small town mosques and thus to impart their understanding of the central message of Qurʾān and Prophetic Sunna to the predominantly rural population. The crucial difference from the TJ, which led very soon to the explicit dissociation of Nuʿmānī and other learned associates from Mawdūdī,[231] was not so much the strategy (*rāh-i ʿamal*) but the particular understanding of the Qurʾānic message and Prophetic mission. The centrality of governance (*ḥukūmat*) in Mawdūdī's exegesis[232] aimed not just at the creation of a somewhat uniform but essentially individual Islamic piety—the main objective of the TJ—but rather at the evolution of a religio-political vanguard which would bring about the Islamic revolution and, upon success, take on government responsibilities.[233] Consequently, the community at Patʻhānkotʻ had already at a very early stage to develop an internal structure which would correspond to the Islamic state-to-be.

On 12 October 1938, only a few months after Iqbāl's passing away, Mawdūdī and his fellows took the first steps in this direction. A consultative council (*majlis-i shūrá*) of five was elected from among the 'pillars' (*arkān*) of the community which, in turn, elected a 'chief' (*ṣadr*)—not yet an *amīr*—from amongst themselves. Unsurprisingly, the elected *ṣadr* was Mawdūdī himself.[234] While mutual consultation was to play an important role in Mawdūdī's conception of democracy within his envisioned Islamic state, for the numerically still very small *jamāʿat* at Pat'hānkot' *shūrá* served at first as an internal organisational principle while maintaining the illusion of parity within.[235] On the other hand, the inner stratification of the community by consensual approval ensured Mawdūdī's monopoly of definition during the continuing intellectual, moral and, although soon to a rather negligible degree, physical moulding of all the members of the *Idāra-yi dār al-islām* community. By the end of 1938 the strategic objectives of the community's missionary activities had become largely amended. Now, and once again consistent with Mawdūdī's ideology, they went beyond mere preaching against what they felt was *shirk* in the Punjabi Muslim village communities and targeted also nationalist as well as pious but politically passive Muslims.[236]

Especially the more or less explicit turn against Muslim nationalism, chiefly advocated by the AIML, led to increasing tension between Muslim Leaguer C͟hawdhurī Niyāz ʿAlī as founder (*wāqif*) of the *Idāra-yi dār al-islām* and Mawdūdī as its mere administrator, as the former felt that the increasing politicisation of the community at Pat'hānkot' violated the stipulated purpose of the *waqf*.[237] Meanwhile, the community had not only grown, but gained also considerable solidity in its worldview, so that Mawdūdī could safely risk open confrontation with Niyāz ʿAlī, and eventually, on 25 January 1939, he resigned from his position as administrator of the *waqf* and relocated to Lahore.[238] As a result the enterprise at Pat'hānkot' fell apart in two distinct institutions which both kept 'dār al-islām' in their names. First, there was C͟hawdhurī Niyāz ʿAlī's *waqf*, which had been renamed 'Dār al-islām t'rast'', and second, there remained a separate *Idāra-yi dār al-islām* under the aegis of Mawdūdī and his associates in operation.[239] Although the sources remain silent on this it is certainly safe to assume that in the following period Mawdūdī was going back and forth between Lahore and Pat'hānkot'. Whether it was indeed the experience of urban Lahore which strengthened the conviction in Mawdūdī to cast his ideas into an even firmer organisational form cannot be answered with certainty.[240] It appears more consistent with the present line of argument to attribute the foundation of the actual JiI, by a congregation of seventy-five associates on 26 August 1941 in Lahore,[241] to the fact that by then Mawdūdī's following had grown considerably, beyond Punjabi villagers, and his ideology had been sufficiently rooted in the community to give it the necessary solidity and cohesion.

5

THE RECEPTION OF A SYSTEM

1) Appropriation in Theory: Sayyid Quṭb and the Muslim Brethren in Egypt

While Mawdūdī claimed universal validity for his ideology and an equally universal applicability of the organisational model that he presented in the embryonic JiI, he still had to honour this claim in practice. In the beginning, however, the efficacy of his thought was clearly restricted, first and foremost because of the language barrier. After all, almost all of Mawdūdī's earlier writings were exclusively in Urdu, while the JiI responded clearly to the particular Indian situation at the time. Mawdūdī himself appears to have been quite aware of that fact, which is why the translation of core writings of his in various languages—be they Indian vernaculars or others—had been a matter very dear to him. At the 1945 annual convention (*ijtimāʿ-i salāna*) of the JiI at Lahore, it was agreed that, to start with, four shorter treatises should be translated into Arabic, Tamil, Hindi, Sindhi and English, first and foremost among them Mawdūdī's controversial *Qurʾān kī c̲h̲ār bunyādī iṣṭilāḥeṇ.*[1]

Instrumental in having his works translated into Arabic, despite Mawdūdī's own claim of high proficiency in that language,[2] were his early associates from the *Nadwat al-ʿulamāʾ* in Lucknow, an institution well known for its high standards in Arabic language training and its close links to Muslim intellectual circles in the Near and Middle East.[3] The driving force behind this development was Sayyid Abū 'l-Ḥasan ʿAlī Nadwī, younger brother of the then head (*nāẓim*) of the institution and very soon one of Mawdūdī's most outspoken critics, who was set to play nonetheless a crucial role in the dissemination of Mawdūdī's ideas in the Middle East. It was he who brought Mawdūdī into contact with Masʿūd ʿĀlam Nadwī (d. 1373/1954), a follower of the *Ahl-i ḥadīth* movement and experienced former editor of the *Nadwa*'s first Arabic periodical *al-Ḍiyāʾ*.[4] Masʿūd ʿĀlam, who could also pride himself with excellent contacts in the Arabian Peninsula, was consequently commissioned with the translation of programmatic writings by Mawdūdī and other JiI cadres into Arabic, a project which, in 1949, led to the establishment of the *Dār al-ʿurūba*, the JiI's marketing department for the Arabic-speaking world.[5] Most crucial, however, was that Abū 'l-Ḥasan ʿAlī Nadwī embarked on an extended tour of the Middle East in 1951, including a lengthy stay in Egypt. Despite the fact that Nadwī had broken off with Mawdūdī almost a decade earlier, it was by his doing that Mawdūdī's writings became finally introduced to members of the JiI's Egyptian counterpart, the *Society of the Muslim Brethren* (*Jamʿiyyat al-Ikhwān al-Muslimīn*; JIM), from where various of his key concepts began their triumph across the Muslim world.[6] The catalyst herein was without doubt Sayyid Quṭb, who, at the time of his meetings with Nadwī, was in the ascendant and set to become one of the JIM's leading ideologues.

The concrete course of the reception of some of Mawdūdī's core concepts by Quṭb, who would soon interweave them—in a radicalised form—into his own ideological conceptions, is not entirely clear, as we do not possess unequivocal source evidence for this. The evidence allows generally for two possible scenarios, which are not mutually exclusive, so that both could have occurred. The first emerges from the fact that, by 1951, nine crucial writings of Mawdūdī were available in Arabic in editions of a few thousand copies each, among them, besides the above mentioned *Qurʾān kī chār bunyādī iṣṭilāḥeṇ*, now also *Islām kā niẓām-i ḥayāt*, *Tajdīd wa iḥyāʾ-i dīn*, *Islām awr jāhiliyyat*, *Islām kī naẓariyya-yi siyāsī*, *Insān kā maʿāshī masʾala awr uskā islāmī ḥall*, *Islāmī ḥukūmat kis ṭaraḥ qāʾim hotī he?* and *al-Jihād fī'l-islām*.[7] All these listed titles together would already suffice to provide an Arab reader with the cornerstones of Mawdūdī's ideology, beginning with his idea of Islam as a holistic system, continuing with his dichotomous view of history and his model of renewal, his bipolar conception of God and man's relation to either aspect, God's sovereignty and the believing man's trusteeship on earth, Mawdūdī's views on economic matters, finally culminating with his concept of revolution. Besides, the report of the 1951 annual *ijtimāʿ* of the JiI in Karachi suggests that all these titles were readily available in JIM circles in Cairo and beyond.[8] It is therefore not groundless to assume that Sayyid Quṭb had already come across Mawdūdī's writings by himself and without the mediation of Nadwī.

The second scenario, which is the one that has been advocated by Damir-Geilsdorf, is that it was rather Nadwī's own Arabic writings, first and foremost his seminal *Mā-dhā khasira al-ʿālam bi-inḥiṭāṭ al-muslimīn?* (1947), had shaped Quṭb's views on various terms associated with Mawdūdī.[9] Quṭb was evidently familiar with this work and held it in high esteem, as is shown by the fact that in 1952 he contributed a short preface to its second edition.[10] While he appreciated Nadwī's use of terms that would later commonly appear in Sayyid Quṭb's ideological outline,[11] Nadwī himself readily acknowledged as having then been under the influence of the writings of his one-time companion Mawdūdī.[12] Therefore, whether Sayyid Quṭb had been directly influenced by Mawdūdī's thoughts by his own unmediated reading of the latter's writings, or indirectly by way of Nadwī's early writings, the impact of Mawdūdī's ideas on the elaboration of Sayyid Quṭb's ideological thought cannot be argued away.

These ideas and concepts feature in all of Quṭb's core writings composed after 1951, first and foremost in his Qurʾānic commentary *Fī ẓilāl al-qurʾān*, published between 1951 and his death in 1966, and his ostensibly most radical final work *Maʿālim fi'l-ṭarīq*, written during his imprisonment in 1962 and first published in 1964. Although published for the first time in 1949, which was shortly before his supposedly decisive study trip to the USA,[13] Quṭb's earliest Islamist treatise *al-ʿAdāla al-ijtimāʿiyya fi'l-islām* was constantly reworked and amended. Its final revised edition, published in 1964, contained explicit references to Mawdūdian terms and concepts, which is why this work needs to be considered here as well.[14] However, what is important to acknowledge is that these terms and concepts had not been borrowed systematically and one-on-one, but were rather appropriated selectively and, at the same time, also creatively. Such a selective reading was not accidental because to a considerable extent it was certainly the result of the current social and political situation in Egypt, which had rather been distinct from that in the Indian subcontinent at this time. Moreover, it was this particular situation that was responsible for the fact that in Quṭb's writings Mawdūdī's terms and concepts experienced a radicalisation of far-reaching consequences. It was therefore in their Quṭbian guise that they became adaptable to militant Islamist thought, and also its critics discussed them rather with Quṭb in mind.

1.1) A Radicalised Framework

It is quite interesting that Sayyid Quṭb did not aim at casting Islam into a self-contained system, at least in not the way Mawdūdī did. This is remarkable, as Quṭb followed Mawdūdī almost verbatim in perceiving Islam as a stable (*thābit*) and comprehensive (*shāmil*) system (*niẓām*) that corresponds to the divine order of the universe:[15] hence it is, as Mawdūdī has not grown tired of stressing, 'natural'. For Quṭb:

> [w]hat makes this path distinctive is that this *dīn* is an indivisible whole [*kull lā yutajaza'u*]. Its worship and social relations, its laws and moral guidance. Its devotional practices are not separated in their nature or their goals from its provisions for government and social affairs. [...] 'The profession of faith that there is no god but God' [...] means one complete programme for life [*manhajan kāmilan li'l-ḥayāt*] [...].[16]

However, that this systemic understanding had been fully elaborated only as late as 1962 suggests that here, too, Quṭb had developed this understanding under the influence of Mawdūdī's writings.[17] This assumption is underlined by the fact that, like Mawdūdī, Quṭb equated *dīn* with *niẓām*, labelling the latter the 'modern terminology [*fi'l-iṣṭilāḥāt al-ḥadītha*]'.[18] Thus he used *dīn* in the same way as Mawdūdī, namely as a comprehensive and natural—say divinely ordained--worldview that existed well alongside other equally comprehensive ones, which however did not enjoy divine approval.[19] Consistent with this systematic claim, 'Islam' as a whole comprises numerous sub-systems (*nuẓum*)[20] but these sub-systems had rarely been spelt out by Quṭb. As compared with Mawdūdī, Sayyid Quṭb had focused even more on governance, the consequence of which on other subsystems he elaborated somewhat less and only with regard to their eventual interfaces with the political.[21]

The reference to Islam as a 'total system', however, was critical for the core dichotomy in Quṭb's thought, namely that of 'Islam' and 'ignorance', or *jāhiliyya*. While for Mawdūdī these bipolar concepts were necessary for his elaboration of the Islamic system at the core of his writings, most of Quṭb's thinking seems to have revolved around the 'jāhiliyya'-concept as the opposite of 'Islam', the 'dīn' that was to be counteracted. This shift in emphasis, which eventually made Quṭb's notions much better utilisable for militant Islamists than Mawdūdī's, appears to have been the result of the concrete social and political circumstances in Egypt in the middle of the twentieth century.

The growing movement for the country's independence from its protective power Britain after the downfall of the 'Urābī-led uprising in 1879–82 had resulted in the official establishment of the Kingdom of Egypt (*al-Mamlaka al-miṣriyya*) in 1922, which, from its inception, followed a rather secularist course, a course that became enshrined in the Constitution of 1923. Consequently, the establishment of the JIM in 1928 by the school-teacher Ḥasan al-Bannā, who besides had been a prominent pupil of Rashīd Riḍā, appeared therefore to be the first substantial religious response to the societal course of the Kingdom.[22]

In the 1930s the young Sayyid Quṭb, then a writer and literary critic not yet affected by the JIM, began to slowly turn away from his initially modernist inclinations and to engage increasingly critically with the Arab nationalist and secularist writers of that period, prominent among them the poet ʿAbbās Maḥmūd al-ʿAqqād (d. 1964) and also the Nobel laureate Ṭāhā Ḥusayn (d. 1973), whose *Mustaqbal al-thaqāfa fī Miṣr* (1938) somewhat epitomised the spirit of that period.[23] The JIM during this time attempted to counteract these secularist tendencies by repeatedly appealing to the success Egyptian monarchs to adjust their government to the requirements of Islam.[24] At the same time, the organisation was accused repeatedly of subversive and sectarian activities, while internally there was considerable dissent over the course of action pursued in an autocratic manner by al-Bannā.[25]

Growing economic difficulties and social tension, coupled with a not too subtle exertion of political influence on the Egyptian king by the British in the course of the Second World War, caused disillusion with the constitutional monarchy to run rampant and provoked numerous social and political groups and movements, among them the JIM, to increasingly oppose the once very much venerated Fārūq I.[26] In consequence, the JIM received its first boost of radicalisation, and Ḥasan al-Bannā swore his followers to what he saw was their fate in the near future:

> I would like to admit frankly to you that your mission [*daʿwatukum*] is yet unknown to many people; as soon as they know it and realise its purpose they will meet it with the severest opposition and the cruellest enmity. You will then be obliged to face countless hardships and obstructions. [...] All the governments will obstruct you and each one of them will try to restrict your activities and block your path.
>
> All the usurpers [*al-ghāṣibūn*] will exert every effort to restrain you and to extinguish the light of your mission. They will win the help of weak governments, weak morals and of the hands stretched out, towards them for begging and towards you for evil and hostility [*bi'l-isāʾa wa-ʿudwān*]. [...] This will lead you to the stage of trial [*dawr al-tajriba wa'l-imtiḥān*], wherein you will be imprisoned, detained and banished; your property will be confiscated, your special activities stopped and

your homes searched. Indeed, your period of trial may last long. [...] However, God has promised that He will grant victory to all the *mujāhidīn* and reward to all those who work righteous deeds. [...] Are you resolved, my brethren, to be the defenders of God [*anṣār allāh*]?[27]

Clearly, such prospects were much more severe than those faced by Mawdūdī and the JiI in their founding phase and can well explain a drive towards a more radical worldview. This perspective is well expressed in *al-ʿAdāla al-ijtimāʿiyya fī'l-islām*, widely considered to be Sayyid Quṭb's first Islamist work, in which for the first time he expressed his conviction that there was no alternative to an Islamic social and political order for the solution of all the prevailing evils in society.[28] While this demand was certainly not new to the JIM,[29] Quṭb was the first who offered a much more concrete idea of what such an order should look like and with its impressively forceful language, it was no surprise that this work became extremely popular within JIM circles right from the start.[30] When he returned from his sojourn in the USA, however, Quṭb, who came soon to replace the assassinated Ḥasan al-Bannā as leading ideologue of the JIM, shifted the emphasis in his writings clearly towards criticism of Western culture. After all, it was the influence of this culture on the Muslim mind that Quṭb held almost exclusively responsible for all the social and political maladies throughout the Muslim world. Consequently, in the early 1950s he openly called for violent resistance against the 'white man' (*al-rajul al-abyaḍ*):

The white man treats us with contempt, while we tell our children in the school of his civilisation, his loftier principles and exalted example. In the souls [*nufūs*] of our children we saw sentiments of admiration and respect for the master [*al-sayyid*] who tramples all over our dignity and enslaves us. Let us strive to sow the seeds of repugnance, of hatred and revenge into the souls of our children. Let us teach them from early childhood on that the white man is the enemy of mankind and that it should crush him by the first occasion. And let us make sure that the Western colonialism [*al-istiʿmār al-gharbī*] trembles when it sees us sowing these seeds.[31]

The similarity of Quṭb's terminology to that in Frantz Fanon's (d. 1961) anti-imperialist and anti-racist writings, here especially *Peau noire, masques blancs* (1952) that almost instantly became a classic, suggests that by the early 1950s Quṭb's orientation was still not entirely Islamist, but first and foremost anti-colonial. On this point, he agreed again with Mawdūdī, of whose works he would have heard. Quṭb's refutation of all the societal models that originated in the West was, therefore, the same as Mawdūdī's, based on an elaborate critique, although much weaker, of materialism as the common basis of Liberalism and Communism, the two political master ideologies that remained after Fascism had largely burned out and lost its attraction for non-Westerners:[32]

> Man has made various advances in his pursuit to utilise the resources of the universe [*al-quwá al-kawniyya*]. His achievements in the fields of industry and medicine are extraordinary when compared with the past, and new triumphs still wait on this way. But what is the impact [*athar*] of all this on his life, what on his soul? Has he found happiness? Has he found tranquillity [*al-ṭuma'nīna*]? Has he found peace? Not at all! What he has found instead is misery, worry and fear, neurological and psychiatric diseases, widespread deviance [*shudhūdh*] and crime. Moreover, it has not caused any advance whatsoever in the formulation of a [sound] concept regarding the human existence and the objectives of human life. When today's civilised man compares this with its Islamic concept, then this very civilisation appears to shrink into insignificance [*qazāma*].[33]

While statements like this suggest that Quṭb had sternly rejected any possible impact of Western thought right from the beginning, even if only for the sake of the advance of Islam, this was certainly not the case. Whereas later he criticised even thinkers like Muḥammad ʿAbduh, Rashīd Riḍā and Muḥammad Iqbāl for their attempts to utilise certain Western ideas,[34] in the early 1950s he seemed, unlike Mawdūdī, not yet even opposed to nationalism (*qawmiyya*). Admittedly, however, Quṭb never considered nationalism an end it itself, but rather, like Ḥasan al-Bannā before him, a useful 'step on the path' towards a fully Islamic society.[35] This initially pro-nationalist attitude owed clearly to the different conditions in late colonial India and post-Second World War Egypt. It changed, however, very soon after the *coup d'état* of the so-called 'Free Officers Movement' around Gamal Abdel Nasser (Jamāl ʿAbd al-Nāṣir; d. 1390/1970), who became president, euphemistically known as the 'July Revolution' of 1952. While the JIM under its second 'General Guide' (*al-murshid al-ʿāmm*) Ḥasan Ismāʿīl al-Huḍaybī (d. 1393/1973) strongly supported the overthrow of the monarchy and was therefore rewarded with its legitimacy when all other political parties were banned, it soon fell into disgrace and, only one year after Quṭb had officially joined around 1953, was subsequently dissolved and its leading members prosecuted.[36] From this moment until his execution by hanging on 29 August 1966, Quṭb spent a total of eleven years and almost four months in various Egyptian prisons.

The experience of illegality, persecution, lengthy spells of imprisonment and severe torture—regardless of the age and gender of the detainees[37]—was, in sad fulfilment of Ḥasan al-Bannā's earlier prediction, a situation much more serious than that in the Indian subcontinent. Although Mawdūdī and the various emerging national branches of the JiI also faced persecution at various points in time,[38] the suffering was little in comparison to the hardship that the members and sympathisers of the JIM had to endure. It was therefore not surprising that many of them, prominently also Sayyid Quṭb, developed a considerably radicalised view and, in the end, agreed to violence as the only means left. This, finally, is the context in which Quṭb wrote his most efficacious works, like *Maʿālim fi'l-ṭarīq*, or radically reworked earlier works, like *al-ʿAdāla al-ijtimāʿiyya fi'l-islām*, and this is then also the context in which, finally, core concepts of Mawdūdī's ideology underwent a major transformation.

a) Jāhiliyya *and* Islām

The most important term which Quṭb is likely to have inherited from Mawdūdī, and which, in its radicalised form, was soon to take a prominent place in the thinking of especially violence-prone Islamists in the aftermath of Quṭb, is without doubt the concept of 'jāhiliyya', which is inseparable from 'Islam' as its 'asymmetrical counterterm'. Compared with other dual concepts, however, we do not have solid textual evidence that Quṭb had indeed adopted these terms from Mawdūdī. Therefore, Damir-Geilsdorf might be correct to assume that Quṭb's attention to the concept of *jāhiliyya* was drawn rather from Abū 'l-Ḥasan ʿAlī Nadwī's Arabic *Mā-dhā khasira al-ʿālam bi-inḥiṭāṭ al-muslimīn?* Indeed, in his preface to the second edition from 1952, Quṭb happily acknowledged that:

> the author consistently used the term 'jāhiliyya' whenever he speaks of the depravity of mankind after the Muslims ceased in its leadership. It is a term that points exactly to the author's understanding of the true difference between the spirit of 'Islam' and the materialistic spirit [*al-rūḥ al-māddī*], which dominated the world before Islam, and which dominates it [also] today, after Islam had forsaken [its] leadership. This is the true nature of 'jāhiliyya'.[39]

To complicate matters even further, the notion of 'jāhiliyya' as asymmetrical counterterm to 'Islam', even if still rather vague, appears to have been somewhat present in the mind of Muslim intellectuals in Egypt even before Quṭb's encounter with Nadwī.[40] This point had already been stressed, if only in an embryonic form, in an article by William E. Shepard, but is most vigorously emphasised by Sayed Khatab.[41] Although the latter outlined the presence of the concept of 'jāhiliyya' in the Arabic literature of the late 1920s and 1930s, and attempted to show that Quṭb had developed a however rudimentary understanding of *jāhiliyya* already during that early period,[42] the clear topological meaning that the term had assumed around 1960 seems still to be down chiefly to Mawdūdī's so far unprecedented systematic considerations.

It shall nonetheless be conceded here that, although not fully spelt out, a certain understanding of temporal and spatial invariance of characteristics that Quṭb would later attribute to the *jāhiliyya* had indeed already existed in his thought as early as 1939, when he first published his first major religious treatise on Qur'ānic aesthetics, *al-Taṣwīr al-fannī fi'l-qur'ān.*[43] In conclusion to his attempt to develop a typology of the various human characters (*namādhij insāniyya*) that appear in the Qur'ān, and which include hypocrites (*munāfiqūn*) and 'those who reject the truth (*al-ḥaqq*)', Quṭb stated that:

> These types [*namādhij*], which we have established this way, are dispersed without a particular order, and they are dispersed in the folds of society at all times and places. The Qur'ānic language has portrayed them most clearly and the eye cannot be fooled, considering that this mankind remains the same throughout all times.[44]

Quṭb's reference to the temporally and spatially invariant existence of unbelief and hypocrisy might indeed be considered the fertile humus on which a typological concept of *jāhiliyya* could soon be cultivated. For the time being, however, Quṭb's primary concern seems to have been more to prove the universal applicability of the Qur'ānic text, which, after all, had only a few years earlier been considerably challenged by Amīn al-Khūlī (d. 1399/1969), then Professor of Arabic Literature at the Cairo University, in his writings at around the same time.[45]

Also in the first couple of editions of *al-'Adāla* said there was no explicit reference to 'jāhiliyya' as a particular state of a society.[46] However, some ideas in this work contributed to his eventual receptivity of Mawdūdī's concept. In order to understand these ideas, one needs to realise the impact that especially the Communist ideology has had on Egypt after the end of the Second World War and, subsequently, the effective collapse of Fascism as yet another role model for societal development in Asia and Africa. Indeed, Communism was reported to have received an enormous boost from the Soviet Union overcoming the Nazi occupation, which gave hope of ending the still ongoing British presence in Egypt that the established political parties responded ineffectively to, and because of the increasingly severe social and economic tension in Egyptian society.[47] Consequently, in the late 1930s and the 1940s Egypt saw the emergence of a number of Communist organisations and movements, which—in a way almost similar to the situation in British India in the 1920s and 1930s—had a great impact on the public discourse on societal development.[48] Their core themes of 'social justice', 'freedom' and 'democracy',[49] however, were not owned by the Communists alone. The JIM, for example, was also engaging in the discussion on these themes,[50] and this was apparently the context in which Sayyid Quṭb presented his *ʿAdāla.*

As Mawdūdī was working himself out on the competing ideologies around him, Sayyid Quṭb, too, did his utmost to make unequivocally clear that, although there might admittedly be certain semantic parallels in his arguments to those of Communism, he did not consider the latter an alternative to the Islamic development of Egypt and beyond.[51] Like Mawdūdī, although nowhere near as systematic, Quṭb expanded his critique of the two prevailing dominant ideological alternatives, namely Liberalism, or Capitalism, and Communism. However, while Liberalism had seriously been considered a viable model for societal development in late colonial India, and Mawdūdī had therefore had to engage with it quite extensively, for Quṭb this necessity seems to have not been that urgent.[52] More pressing appeared to be the dissociation from Communism as an ideology equally committed to social justice and economic balance as Islam. In Quṭb's thinking, all three competing ideologies—Liberalism, or Capitalism, Communism and Islamism—constituted clear-cut and self-containing 'blocs' (*kutlāt*) or 'camps' (*muʿaskarāt*),[53] hybrid forms of which would by definition not be possible. Thus, while in *al-ʿAdāla* and his treatises composed almost immediately after his return from the USA Quṭb moved evidently more and more towards his later dichotomous thinking, this became fully-fledged only after 1952, most likely under the strong influence of Mawdūdī's writings.

In February 1952, which was almost exactly one year after his meeting with Abū 'l-Ḥasan ʿAlī Nadwī,[54] Sayyid Quṭb published the first instalment of his Qur'ānic commentary *Fī ẓilāl al-qur'ān* in *al-Muslimūn*, the official monthly journal of the JIM.[55] While the release of the entire thirty-part work was stretched over a period of seven years, mainly because from 1954 Quṭb spent most of his time in jail,[56] his exegesis of the verse 5:50, the first one in which the term 'jāhiliyya' appears, was released some time in 1953, the year Quṭb formally joined the JIM. Here, it appears, Quṭb used the term 'jāhiliyya' for the first time unequivocally as a designation for a particular state and, in the same way as Mawdūdī, as an antonym to 'Islam':

> The meaning of *jāhiliyya* in this text is defined the same way as God had lined out and defined it in His Qur'ān. It means the rule [*ḥukm*] of people over people,

because this signifies the submission [*ʿubūdiyya*] of people to people, the refutation of submission to God alone and the rejection of His godhead [*ulūhiyyat allāh*], while acknowledging instead the godhead of some human being, and that submission is therefore due to them instead of God.

As such, the term *jāhiliyya*, as it is used here, does not refer to the state [*fitra*] at a particular period of time, but to a certain condition [*waḍʿ min al-awḍāʿ*]. This condition existed yesterday, it exists today and it may exist tomorrow. Whenever it exists, though, it must be described as *jāhiliyya*, which stands in contrast to Islam, and is incompatible with it.[57]

In his interpretation of the verse 33:33, after all *the* crucial Qurʾānic verse with regard to 'jāhiliyya',[58] which was published almost immediately before his first imprisonment in January 1954, we can see how Quṭb's earlier thought from *al-Taṣwīr al-fannī* had now become merged into the concept of 'jāhiliyya':

Jāhiliyya is not the particular state of a certain period of time [*fitra muʿayyana min al-zamān*], but a particular social condition and the essence of a particular philosophy of life [*dhāt taṣawwurāt muʿayyana li'l-ḥayāt*]. Therefore, it is well possible to encounter such a condition, to encounter such jāhiliyya thinking at any time and in any place, which clearly proves the persistence of the *jāhiliyya*.

On this scale, we can say that today we live in a state of blind *jāhiliyya*, which reflects vulgar tastes and unrefined concepts [*ḥaywāniyyat al-taṣawwur*], pulling mankind down to a low level [of civilisation]. And when we have been taken down, then there will be neither purity in, nor integrity and blessing for a society that leads such a life. Only a society that adopts the means of purification [*wasāʾil al-taṭahhur wa'l-naẓāfa*] that God had set for man's path attains purity from sin and the liberation from the 'First *jahiliyya*'. The first to practice this [path] were the members of the household of the Prophet—God's peace and prayer be upon him!—and attained such purity and radiance.[59]

As is seen from the two comments on 5:50 and 33:33, respectively, by the end of 1953 the core concepts of Quṭb's entire thought, prominently among them 'jāhiliyya' and its asymmetrical counterterm 'Islam', and the multifarious interrelations of all these concepts, had already been well established. What is more important, still, is that already in the fifth, eighth and ninth parts, all written in the early 1950s, Mawdūdī explicitly quoted at length from the Arabic translations of *Parda*, *Taḥrīk-i islāmī kī akhlāqī bunyādeṇ* and *al-Jihād fi sabīl allāh*,[60] which clearly proves that by then at the latest Quṭb was familiar with various of his writings.

Now, while it is disputed whether in the revisions he undertook on *Fī ẓilāl al-qurʾān* during the last years of his life Quṭb shifted the emphasis from a more aesthetic appreciation of the Qurʾān to a stress on its activist aspects—including, among others, the further elaboration of 'jāhiliyya'[61]—it appears that in his later writings, especially in his most popular and influential *Maʿālim fi'l-ṭarīq*, he was adding just an edge. Owing most certainly to Quṭb's experiences during his long spells of imprisonment, *Maʿālim* emerged as a passionate political pamphlet rather than a considerate and systematic religious treatise. This fact had a considerable impact on the way in which the dichotomy of 'jāhiliyya' and 'Islam' was portrayed here.[62]

While earlier Quṭb was still speaking in a somewhat differentiating manner of various co-existing ideological blocs, by 1962, when the first parts of *Maʿālim* were smuggled out of prison,[63] this view had largely been dissolved in favour of a clearly bipolar worldview:

> Islam acknowledges only two kinds of societies [*mujtamaʿāt*]: The Islamic society and the *jāhilī* society. The 'Islamic society' is that, which follows Islam in doctrine and worship, in the code of conduct [*sharīʿa*] and in organisation, in morals and manners [*khuluqan wa-sulūkan*]. The 'jāhilī society' is that society, which does neither follow Islam, nor its doctrine, or its concepts, its values and standards [*taṣawwurātahu wa-qayyimahu wa-mawāzīnahu*], its organisation and code of conduct, as well as its morals and manners.[64]

More than in all his former writings, in *Maʿālim* Quṭb was concerned with this dichotomy, which would eventually facilitate a rather simplistic, though highly appealing, self-righteousness and mentality of 'you are either with us or against us'.[65] Such righteousness, this claim to be about the only one in a position to save mankind from its inevitable doom, is, of course, highly elitist. Quṭb seems to have been fully aware of that fact and, although unlike Mawdūdī he had not developed a consistent theory of revolution and leadership, he evidently had a notion of a morally superior vanguard (*al-ṭalīʿa*) as the main carrier of the desired societal change.[66] The notion that this change is ultimately inescapable and, moreover, almost imminent, is strongly reminiscent of Marxist rhetoric. The conditions for change are right when the irreconcilable social and economic antagonisms have become exacerbated to such an extent that they can only be overcome by force. Indeed, for Quṭb the dominance of the *jāhiliyya* could hardly be any greater:

> If we look at the foundation of today's way of living, it becomes clear that the world is entirely steeped in 'jāhiliyya', from which emerge the living conditions and their regulations [*muqawwimāt al-ḥayāt wa-anẓimatuhā*]. This can neither be diminished by all the enormous material comforts [*al-taysīrāt al-māddiyya al-hāʾila*], nor by the excellent material innovations [*al-ibdāʿ al-māddī al-fāʾiq*]![67]

What substantiates these parallels with Communist ideology even more and suggests that, despite Quṭb's repeated rejection of Communism as a reasonable alternative for societal development,[68] he had been considerably influenced by it, was his characterisation of the *jāhiliyya* as 'one man's domination over another [*ḥākimiyya al-bashar li'l-bashar*]'.[69] This might be considered a clear reference to the Marxian theory of domination and the resulting explanation of all kinds of artificial inequalities in a society, but, moreover, it is reminiscent of Mawdūdī's characterisation of the various forms of *jāhiliyya*, the smallest common denominator of which had been exactly that.[70] In order to overcome all inequalities, epitomised in the all-pervasive *jāhiliyya*, the political superstructure needs to be fundamentally changed.[71] How this was to happen, however, Quṭb explained in a manner that was open to various interpretations by posterity, as we shall see further below.

What emerges from Quṭb's discussion of 'jāhiliyya' is that he rarely gave a more concrete definition of what 'jāhiliyya' would actually be. In this, he was certainly not as systematic as Mawdūdī who, in contrast, attempted some formally positive description when he differentiated between various kinds of 'jāhiliyya'.[72] In the end, however, Quṭb's definition by negation—'jāhiliyya' as the absence of 'Islam'—leads somehow to the same result. In order to understand what is meant by 'jāhiliyya', one needs therefore to understand what is meant by 'Islam'. Quṭb's definition of 'Islam', in turn, was extremely condensed and revolved around yet another of Mawdūdī's central dichotomies, although again in a somewhat radicalised form: God's absolute and unlimited sovereignty (*ḥākimiyya*) and man's servitude (*ʿubūdiyya*).

b) Ḥākimiyya *and* ʿUbūdiyya

As in Quṭb's treatment of 'jāhiliyya', his analysis of the relationship between God and man, and the resulting fundamental differences in their powers of disposal, had also become increasingly radical towards the end of his life. However, the concept of God's unlimited sovereignty (*ḥākimiyya muṭlaqa*) over the entire universe, including the world of man as just one part of it, appears to be one that resembled Mawdūdī's notion as the strongest of all similar concepts. Although its nucleus can be traced back to Quṭb's 1951 treatise *al-Salām al-ʿālamī wa'l-islām*,[73] that is, before his definite acquaintance with Mawdūdī's writings, the first thorough treatment it received, if not before one of the later revisions of *al-ʿAdāla*, then perhaps already under the influence of the latter.[74] Consequently, in *Maʿālim* Quṭb explicitly referred to Mawdūdī's notion of God's authority (*rubūbiyya*), on which the latter had stressed in *Qur'ān kī c̲h̲ār bunyādī iṣṭilāḥeṇ* that:

[t]he Qur'ān proves with very strong arguments [*ṭāqatwar istidlāl*] that the universe is a whole and self-contained system [*mukammal niẓām*]. Therefore, there cannot be the slightest doubt that any act of providence, to whatever degree, could depend on any other being than the one in whose hands rest the supreme authority [*iqtidār-i aʿlá*]. [...] Evidently, the core of this system is that providence of every kind is peculiar to God, who has brought this system into existence.[75]

Quṭb followed suit, when he stated that man:

is not capable to change God's practice regarding the universal laws [*sunnat allāh f'l-qawānīn al-kawniyya*], which govern the universe and its derivatives. Therefore, he should turn his life voluntarily towards Islam and implement God's *sharīʿa*—His sovereignty—into every aspect of life. [This way,] there may be harmony [*tansīq*] between the voluntary [*irādī*] and the natural [*fiṭrī*] aspects of his life, and harmony between the whole of his existence and its parts, and the universal existence.[76]

From the implicit acknowledgement of man's free will and, resulting from it, his ability to act autonomously, in turn, Quṭb was confronted with a similar anthropological dilemma as Mawdūdī had been a few decades earlier.

God's sovereignty and supreme authority are unquestionable as whoever questions them would derive 'little else but defective understanding, conflicting ideas and precipitated theories',[77] as Quṭb quoted in his *Khaṣā'iṣ al-taṣawwur al-islāmī wa-muqawwimātuhu*, written between 1950 and 1961, from Abū 'l-Ḥasan ʿAlī Nadwī's *Mā-dhā khasira al-ʿālam bi-inḥiṭāṭ al-muslimīn*. Instead man, purposefully created, is compelled to accept things as they are and to do what he is ordered by divine decree, in order to fulfil his assigned role within the whole of creation. Hence man's task can only be one of 'servitude' (*ʿubūdiyya*). 'Servitude', in turn, was a comprehensive concept for Quṭb, and in this he followed a conservative and action-oriented tradition that can be traced all the way back to at least Ibn Taymiyya. For the medieval traditionalist, the sole pronouncement of the Islamic creed was equally insufficient as a criterion for Muslimness as the mere fact that one was born to Muslim parents. What was required was to prove one's faith in actions, hence the striving for, and the obedience to, the *sharīʿa* that played the role of a benchmark.[78] Later thinkers followed suit, and so did Mawdūdī when he repeatedly declared that Islam consisted of a conformance of proper thought, or belief (*fikr*), and adequate action (*ʿamal*). Quṭb stood in this very tradition when, in his 1960 *Hādhā al-dīn*, he stressed that the acknowledgement of God's ultimate sovereignty would imply the acknowledgement of His *sharīʿa* and, consequently, striving for its implementation in every aspect of life:

We are strictly compelled to strive for realising this [divinely ordained] programme [*manhaj*], in order to claim for us the attribute 'Islamic'. The first pillar of Islam, namely, is that we profess that there is no deity but God and that Muḥammad is God's Messenger. The profession that there is no deity but God means, firstly, to adjudge God—Exalted He is!—[His] divinity [*al-ulūhiyya*] and to not associate Him in any of the related attributes [*fī khāṣiyya wāḥida min khaṣāʾiṣihā*] anyone from His creation. The first attribute of divinity is the veridicality of absolute sovereignty [*ḥaqq al-ḥākimiyya al-muṭlaqa*], from which results the prerogative [*ḥaqq*] to issue laws to the servants of God [*ʿibād*], to prescribe them their ways of life [*manāhij ḥayātihim*] and the value [*al-qiyam*] on which this life is based upon.[79]

All this stressing of man's need to comply with what is ordered by God clearly shows some unease with the fact that man was given free will and, by this, the capacity to decide whether to obey or disobey God's commandments.[80] Mawdūdī had tried to reconcile this in his notion of 'khilāfa', as the embodiment and justification of man's limited sovereignty on earth.[81] In Quṭb's thinking, however, the idea of man's trusteeship on earth had right from the beginning not been extraordinarily strong, and had over time become marginalised even further, while his notion of man's servitude gained much more momentum. This shift in emphasis is quite apparent if one compares, for example, his exegesis of the Qur'ānic verse 2:30, which belonged to his earliest ones that had been published in early 1952 in the JIM periodical *al-Muslimūn*, and his exegesis of 24:55, published two years' later in anticipation of his first imprisonment. For the first verse, which had traditionally been interpreted as God's investment of powers in His first apostle Ādam, Quṭb still seemed to have followed the then widespread understanding that Ādam, as the first of its kind, represented the whole of humanity, and God had therefore granted man as such discretionary powers over the earth:

And it was His supreme volition to hand over the reins of this earth to this new creature [*al-kāʾin al-jadīd fiʾl-wujūd*] and to give it a free hand, so that it may use, develop and transform all the forces and resources of this earth for the display of the wish [*mashīʾa*] of the Creator, and—God willing!—to carry out the mighty mission with which it had been assigned by God.[82]

The image of the 'free hand', which suggests a certain freedom to act, became considerably played down by the time Quṭb published his commentary on 24:55, after all the crucial verse for Mawdūdī's justification of man's collective trusteeship on earth. While the latter put the stress clearly on the term 'He makes them trustees [*yastakhlifannahum*]',[83] for Quṭb the emphasis was more on the phrase 'those of you who believe and work righteous deeds [*amanū minkum wa-ʿamilū al-ṣāliḥāt*]',[84] that is to say, on the prerequisites for man's *khilāfa*.[85] Hence, he went on to elaborate on faith (*īmān*) as a 'complete way of life [*manhaj ḥayāt kāmil*]',[86] that is an all-encompassing and practicable code, rooted in unconditional submission, *ʿubūdiyya*. While, in his earlier exegesis of 2:30, he conceded man the ability to commit corruption and shed blood, regardless of him being God's appointed trustee on earth, he suspected that there might even be some virtue in such deviant conduct, as:

> behind such apparent partial evil lies a greater and wider good [*khayr*], a good for perpetual development [*al-namuw al-dāʾim*] and progress [*al-raqqī al-dāʾim*], and a good for the changes and a good for the ceaseless endeavour and pursuit.[87]

Only some two years later, however, Quṭb emphatically stressed that 'those of them [i.e. people] who spread corruption and injustice [*al-baghī wa'l-jawr*], and decay to the stages of animals are not appointed as trustees on earth'.[88] Clearly, by then Quṭb had already developed a more radical and bipolar view of 'us' and 'them'. While he did not deny man his autonomy to act, which, after all, had been bestowed upon man by God, he did not consider those who failed to meet the expectations of God and the community of believers to belong to those who had been entrusted by God with His trusteeship because they 'believe and work righteous deeds'. In this, he was much more pithy than Mawdūdī had ever been, although the latter would have certainly agreed with the consequences that Quṭb drew from verse 24:55. His more pointed position correlated quite well with his equally bipolar view of 'jāhiliyya' and 'Islam', but opened the doors wide open for a more radical appraisal of 'them'. As they are not part of the collective *khilāfa*, they would stand completely outside the Muslim community and, consequently, would enjoy no rights within the Islamic legal framework.

At first sight, this does not pose a major problem, as those who stand outside the *khilāfa* will create their own distinct framework of reference, including a legal one. The matter, however, happens to be more complicated, because Quṭb, the same as Mawdūdī before him, considered only the Islamic framework to correspond with the natural order of things; in his own words: 'There is unity or harmony between the laws [*al-nawāmīs*] that govern the world and those that govern the entire universe.'[89] This, in turn, would indeed imply that, from his perspective, no one could ever stand outside the Islamic legal framework. Early Islamic jurisprudence had very soon developed a practice that applies to this problem: *takfīr*, or the practice of accusing someone of unbelief, with all of its legal consequences. In *Maʿālim*, finally, but also already in *Hādhā al-dīn* and most explicitly in the posthumously published *Muqawwimāt al-taṣawwur al-islāmī*, these thoughts have gained considerable momentum. To stand outside Islam was now considered to be an attack on Islam, which would require appropriate action.[90] Such action, however, would not have to be directed solely against those who claim authority for themselves—here Quṭb was implicitly referring to basically all present governments—but also everyone who would—actively or passively—support them. The required response had been laid down in the authoritative texts of Islam and subsequently in the classical Islamic legal literature. These illegitimate claimants of authority, all considered 'false gods' (*ṭawāghīt*), and their 'helpers' (*anṣār*) have to be declared infidels (*kuffār*) and subsequently to be punished, in its ultimate consequence, with their death.[91] To act as defender of God's *ḥākimiyya* was considered an essential part of man's *'ubūdiyya*, and would therefore—as had been declared already centuries earlier by Ibn Taymiyya and, in his wake, by Muḥammad ibn 'Abd al-Wahhāb—become a definite criterion of faith.[92] Thus, the 'partisans of God' (*ḥizb allāh*) have to distinguish themselves from their opponents—the 'partisans of Satan' (*ḥizb shayṭān*)—by embarking on *jihād* on the Path of God, even for the physical elimination of the enemy:

> There had a single justification been established for killing [*qitāl*]—whenever the killing cannot be avoided—which is that it is considered to be *jihād* on the Path of God. This, by definition, sets the objective of the believer apart from the objective of an unbeliever: 'Those who believe fight on the Path of God [*yuqātilūna fī sabīl allāh*], and those who do not believe [*kafarū*] fight on the Path of the false god [*al-ṭaghut*]. So fight against the friends of Satan, for feeble indeed is the cunning of Satan.'[93]

It occurs thus that the concept of *jihād* against the unbelievers, the latter being epitomised in the term *ṭāghūt*, became the final brick in the edifice of Sayyid Quṭb's ideas. As in the outline of Mawdūdī, *jihād* would be the way to eventually realise the ideal society, built upon the unconditional acknowledgement of God's absolute sovereignty and man's confinement to equally unconditional obedience.

c) Jihād fī sabīl allāh

Mawdūdī's *al-Jihād fi'l-islām* was among the very first of his books to be translated into Arabic and, coupled with the fact that its title is quite catchy, it promised a comprehensive insight into the Islamist perspective on the matter. It is therefore not surprising that Sayyid Quṭb in his most expansive treatment of the issue of *jihād*, included in his exegesis of the eighth *sūra* of the Qur'ān, relied heavily on Mawdūdī's earlier expositions. It is here that Quṭb decided on the most extensive quote from one of Mawdūdī's writings, which suggests an extraordinary closeness between the two at this point. Moreover, Quṭb's rather long introductory remarks for his exegesis of this *sūra*, published in its initial version shortly before his first imprisonment in 1954, had been included almost verbatim as a separate chapter in *Maʿālim*, although interestingly without the lengthy quote from Mawdūdī's Iqbāl Day lecture, delivered on 13 April 1939 in Lahore and later published as *al-Jihād fī sabīl allāh*.[94]

By then, Mawdūdī's view on the matter of *jihād* had become much more pointed than in his earlier work *al-Jihād fi'l-islām* from 1927. In the lectures that he delivered to Punjabi villagers right after the establishment of the 'Idāra-yi dār al-islām' at Pat'hānkot', collectively published as *Khuṭbāt*, he had already developed a view almost similar to Quṭb's. With recourse to the Qur'ānic verses 58:14–19 and 58:21, he stated that:

> [f]rom these verses it will occur most clearly that, if there was any other *dīn* established besides the *dīn* of God, and if any Muslim had suffered under these conditions, then the true believer [*mu'min-i ṣādiq*] can be identified according to whether or not, after having destroyed the invalid *dīn* [*dīn-i bāṭil*], he strives for to establish the true *dīn* [*dīn-i ḥaqq*].[95]

Indeed, for Mawdūdī, too, *jihād* became a religious duty, and as such it joined the usually five so-called 'pillars of faith' (*arkān*) as the sixth and, besides the Islamic creed, most important one:

> If you truly consider this *dīn* to be the truth [*ḥaqq*], then there will be other way for you but to strain every nerve for the establishment of this *dīn* on earth; you will either succeed in establishing it, or you will give up your life [*jān*] it its attempt. This is the very touchstone, by which [alone] the sincerity of your belief [*īmān wa iʿtiqād kī ṣadāqat*] can be measured. If your belief is pure, then you will not be able to rest comfortably under any other *dīn*, not to speak of you serving it, enjoying to be eating the bread earned by this service, or finding comfort and easy sleep. [...] But, if you live quietly under any other than the *dīn* of God and acquiesce this situation, then you are not really a believer, no matter how assiduously you offer your prayers, how many hours you spend in contemplation, how well you may comment on Qur'ān and Ḥadīth, or how much you season the philosophy of Islam.[96]

In pretty much the same spirit Mawdūdī delivered his 1939 Iqbāl Day lecture in Lahore, which Sayyid Quṭb had widely quoted in *Fī ẓilāl al-qur'ān*,[97] and wherein Mawdūdī stated, with recourse to the Qur'ānic verse 3:110, that the task of the 'partisans of God' (*ḥizb allāh*) was not only to spread the word of God from the pulpit but 'to crush oppression, dissent, mischief, immorality, transgression and unlawful profiting in this world *by force* [*bi-zawr*], to end the providence of the 'lords besides God', and to establish virtue [*nekī*] instead of vice [*badī*]'.[98] What can clearly be deduced from here is that Mawdūdī had increasingly shifted towards the endorsement of armed action in pursuit of the ultimate goal, the establishment of the *ḥukūmat-i islāmī*.

That Quṭb had quoted him in his Qur'ānic commentary, however, seems to have been of little more use than being only a back-up. After all, Mawdūdī's elaborations here, although passionately presented, were not very systematic in character and, although he hinted at the commendable nature of armed *jihād*, Mawdūdī did not develop a consistent argument to substantiate this view. Quṭb, on the other hand, because the justification of armed *jihād* was at the core of his conception of the matter, referred rather to the peculiar evaluation of the validity of the various Qur'ānic verses on the subject by Ibn Taymiyya's most famous pupil Ibn Qayyim al-Jawziyya (d. 751/1350). Based on the chapter on 'The Measures that he [i.e. the Prophet] had ordered regarding [the Treatment of] the Unbelievers and Hypocrites, from the Time of the Mission until the Moment of [his] Death' in Ibn Qayyim's *Zād al-maʿād fī hadī khayr al-ʿibād*, Quṭb developed a taxonomy which ascribed to many verses on the issue of *jihād* an only temporary validity, while considering others—mainly those that refer to offensive *jihād* as religious duty—to be absolute, that is, spatially and temporally invariantly valid.[99]

Quṭb's taxonomy, based on Ibn Qayyim's classification of four phases in the course of the revelation, revolved around the fourth and final one, which, without explicitly employing the classical exegetical tool of abrogation (*naskh*),[100] suggested that what had been revealed in the ninth *sūra* of the Qur'ān would stay as a conclusive provision (*ḥukm nihā'iyya*) and diminish all other statements on the matter to provisions valid only for one particular phase in the course of revelation (*aḥkām marḥaliyya*).[101] The conclusive provision, according to Quṭb's understanding of Ibn Qayyim, was to act, if necessary by force of arms, against the unbelievers, hypocrites and even 'the enemies [of Islam] from among the "People of the Book" [*ahl al-kitāb*], until they pay the per-capita-tax [*jizya*] or embrace Islam',[102] in short, against everyone who stands against the realisation of God's ultimate sovereignty and, subsequently, man's assigned place as God's faithful servant. Once again, perhaps under the impact of the then prevalent Socialist thought, Quṭb described his concept of *jihād* as theologically liberation, when he stressed that the *jihād* he had in mind was aiming at 'the defence of man against all those elements [*ʿawāmil*] which limit his freedom [*ḥurriyatahu*]'.[103] 'Freedom', on the other hand, meant the universal emancipation from 'servitude to the servants of God',[104] from 'all rule [*sulṭān*] that is not the rule of God'.[105]

From here it is not difficult to establish an intrinsic link between Quṭb's concept of *jihād* and Mawdūdī's concept of 'revolution'.[106] In fact, in Quṭb's notion of *jihād* both concepts appear to have been merged. Consequently, in his exegesis of the eighth *sūra*, Quṭb quoted Mawdūdī on the equation of *jihād* and 'revolution':

> In reality 'Islam' is a revolutionary worldview and programme [*inqilābī naẓariyya wa maslak/fikra inqilābiyya wa-manhāj inqilābī*], which seeks to alter the social order of the whole world and rebuild it in conformity with its own tenets and ideals. 'Muslims' are that International Revolutionary Party [*bayn al-aqwāmī inqilābī jamāʿat/al-ḥizb al-inqilābī al-ʿālamī*] organised by Islam to carry into effect its revolutionary programme. And 'Jihād' refers to that revolutionary struggle [*inqilābī jadd wa juhd/al-kifāḥ al-inqilābī*] and utmost exertion which the Islamic Party brings into play to achieve this objective.[107]

While here Quṭb stuck to Mawdūdī's term 'inqilāb', a little later, in his discussion of verse 8:39, where God commands the believers to 'fight them [i.e. the unbelievers] until there is no more infestation [*fitna*] and the *dīn* is all God's', he used the more common Arabic equivalent 'thawra' when stressing that Islam 'signifies a *total revolution* against the sovereignty of a human being, whatever its forms and shapes, systems and situations'.[108] For Quṭb, perhaps even more than for Mawdūdī, a 'revolution' is aimed at the removal of social and economic inequality and deprivation among men, the roots of which one may trace to human nature.[109] Because every man-made social order and its underlying ethico-philosophical foundation are inevitably based on stratification of a diverse kind—even if only a division of labour—it becomes prone to injustice. This idea, as stressed above, was at the core of Mawdūdī's somewhat detailed discussion of the various manifestations of *jāhiliyya*,[110] and, although not as systematically outlined, it had been the same in Quṭb's conception. Consequently, only an Islamic society, in which the *sharīʿa* had thoroughly been implemented and man had therefore no real legislative powers, would be able to fundamentally solve the problem of social and economic injustice, as Quṭb had concluded already in *al-ʿAdāla*.[111] Hence, a total revolution was urgently needed for the sake of mankind.

In pursuit of this revolution—or *jihād* in the Path of God, as Quṭb had called it in an attempt to dissociate his idea of 'revolution' from its Western conception[112] no means should be precluded straight away. Although violence was certainly not the preferred way for him, he was clear that sometimes the circumstances would leave little choice but to take to arms when aspiring to a higher end.[113] Once more, such a mentality of 'the end justifies the means' is something all political ideologies have in common, and thus Quṭb as well as Mawdūdī held their Communist and, in the case of the latter, also Fascist adversaries much closer than they would have liked to admit. However, both were ideologues rather than military strategists, which explains why Quṭb remained still rather woolly when discussing the armed *jihād* (*al-jihād bi'l-sayf*). In his exegesis of the Qur'ānic verse 9:123: 'Oh ye who believe! Fight the unbelievers who are near you, and let them find you rigorous',[114] he devoted quite some time to arguing that this was to be a permanent and universally valid directive (*ḥukm nihā'iyya*) which justified offensive *jihād* against all unbelievers within reach, for the sake of spreading Islam.[115] Compared with this, the term 'harshness' (*ghilẓa*) was merely explained as 'applying only against those who fight [*yuḥāribū*] and having to remain within the limits of general manners [*ḥudūd al-ādāb al-ʿāmma*] of this *dīn*',[116] that is, within the moral and legal framework of Islam. Although Quṭb stated that the touchstone would always have to be human dignity (*al-riʿāya li-karāmat al-insān*), which extends even to the fighting enemy, let alone civilians,[117] he did not give even a remote definition of what he wanted to be understood as an enemy combatant. For those who came after him, this has therefore become one of the main points in which Quṭb's ideological outline, influenced to a considerable degree by the earlier thoughts of Mawdudi, became further radicalised.

1.2) After Quṭb

While, at first glance, Quṭb's ideological outline appeared to be much less cohesive and systematic than Mawdūdī's, this was not really the case. It was actually quite the opposite, as Quṭb had succeeded in presenting his ideas in a much more tightly-knit manner, thus hiding the various deductive steps in the process of the evolution of Mawdūdī's system behind a very emotive presentation. Therefore, it is safe to assume that all the various elements of Mawdūdī's outline were present in Quṭb's, too. The way, however, in which he had developed and presented various core concepts—here first and foremost 'jāhiliyya' and 'jihād'—[118] along with the worsening situation in Egypt and the Near and Middle East, placed them at the centre of a heated debate on the strategic development of the JIM-led Islamist movement in the region.

On this debate, in turn, the JIM would eventually split into a more moderate faction led by the then *murshid al-ʿāmm* Ḥasan al-Huḍaybī and a more radical one around the followers of Quṭb, the so-called 'Quṭbists' (*al-quṭbiyūn*), led not least his younger brother Muḥammad Quṭb Ibrāhīm (b. 1337/1919).[119] This latter faction gave way eventually to a complete dissociation from the JIM and the establishment of more radical outfits, culminating in the *Tanẓīm jamāʿat al-jihād*, which came to be led, among others, by the two physicians Sayyid Imām al-Sharīf (a.k.a. ʿAbd al-Qādir ibn ʿAbd al-ʿAzīz, a.k.a. Dr Faḍl; b. 1369/1950) and Ayman al-Ẓawāhirī (b. 1370/1951). Indeed, in his *Fursān taḥta rāyat al-nabī*, first published in December 2001 in ten instalments in the international Arabic daily *al-Sharq al-Awsaṭ* and widely considered a manifesto of *al-Qāʿida*, al-Ẓawāhirī emphasised the importance of Quṭb for the constitution of the militant Islamist movement in Egypt and beyond:

> Under the shadow of Nasser's regime the Islamic movement received a decisive blow with the execution of Sayyid Quṭb and his comrades—God's mercy be upon them!—and the arrest of thousands of brethren of the Islamic movement. But, while on the surface it was apparently calm, hidden beneath it seethed an engagement with the ideas of Sayyid Quṭb and his mission, and the beginning of the formation of the nucleus [*nawāt*] of the contemporary Jihād Movement in Egypt [*al-ḥaraka al-jihādiyya al-muʿāṣira fī Miṣr*]. Thus emerged the very nucleus that the writer of these lines had joined.[120]

The moderate faction, too, emerged in an—although rather critical—engagement with Quṭb's ideas, and, at least in one case, even explicitly with those of Mawdūdī. Its viewpoint was epitomised in the seminal *Duʿāt, lā quḍāt*, written around 1969 and first published in 1977. This work, widely attributed to Ḥasan al-Huḍaybī,[121] is widely regarded as a very considered and rather sophisticated Islamist response to the emergence of the increasingly militant groups referred to by al-Ẓawāhirī. Moreover, it has since become the creed of the JIM.[122] For the radicals in the wake of Quṭb, however, who in addition belonged already to a different generation, the JIM had soon lost its appeal anyway, as it was not any longer considered a vital tool in the struggle for a just Islamic social and political order.

a) The Times are Ripe for Change: The Radical Response

In the earlier 1970s, the radical heirs to Quṭbian thought were less concerned with modifying and advancing his ideology of *jihād*, but rather with considerations regarding strategy. The cornerstone for these was a differentiation of a 'period of weakness' (*marḥalat al-istiḍʿāf*) and a 'period of implementation' (*marḥalat al-tafīdh*) of the righteous community, which was rooted in Quṭb's interpretation of Ibn Qayyim's thoughts on the validity of the various Qur'ānic revelations regarding *jihād*.[123] After the ruthless persecution of the JIM that culminated in the execution of Sayyid Quṭb and two other Muslim Brethren, the advocates of a thoroughly Islamic society found themselves certainly in a 'state of weakness', as conceded by al-Ẓawāhirī in the above quote. Therefore, although radical Islamist groups mushroomed throughout Egypt from at least the late 1960s, the restrictive measures by the government authorities forced them to develop mainly underground and rather informally.[124] This, however, appeared quite consistent with Quṭb, who would have argued that this weakness within an overwhelmingly *jāhilī* environment would not yet allow for offensive action. Therefore, passive resistance and thorough preparation for the *jihād* was to be the order of the day. Not unlike Mawdūdī, Quṭb called on the righteous Muslims to withdraw themselves from the *jāhilī* society and to form themselves into the very vanguard that, after having gathered enough strength, would eventually lead the way.

It is inevitable that the theoretical basis of Islam (i.e. the doctrine) materialises right from the start in an organic and active group [*tajammuʿ ʿuḍwī ḥarakī*]. It is equally unavoidable that such an organic and active group separates itself from the *jāhilī* society, becoming independent and distinct from the active and organic *jāhilī* society that aims at the invalidation [*ilghāʾ*] of Islam. Pivot of this new group is the new leadership [*al-qiyāda al-jadīda*], epitomised in the Prophet—God's prayer upon him and peace!—and, after him, in all the Islamic leadership that strove for bringing the people back to God's sole divinity, his lordship, guardianship, sovereignty, might and His laws [*ulūhiyyat allāh waḥdahu wa-rubūbiyyatihi wa-qawwāmatihi wa-ḥākimiyyatihi wa-sulṭānihi wa-sharīʿatihi*]. Everyone who bears witness that 'There is no deity but God and Muḥammad is God's Messenger' should withdraw his loyalty [*walāʾ*] from the prevalent *jāhilī* society, which he has forsaken, and from the leadership of this group, in whatever form it may appear, be it in the guise of religious leadership by seers, priests, magicians or astrologers, or in the form of political, social or economic leadership, as it was the case of the Quraysh. He will have to restrict his loyalty to the new organic and active Islamic group and to Muslim leadership [alone].[125]

While it is difficult to disentangle the finer points of the respective strategies of the various radical Islamist groups in the wake of Sayyid Quṭb, the first one that became publicly known for having put this agenda into practice was a group called *Jamāʿat al-muslimīn*, centred around the engineer Shukrī Aḥmad Muṣṭafá (executed 1399/1979). During his imprisonment in 1965 for his activities on behalf of the JIM, Muṣṭafá ass in an increasingly radicalised cell of inmates which, after his release in 1971, dissociated itself clearly from the JIM. At the core of the worldview of this group was an exaggerated version of Quṭb's above plea. Shukrī Aḥmad Muṣṭafá's followers withdrew themselves, in reminiscence of the Prophet's exodus from Mecca, from the Egyptian 'jāhilī' society by ceasing their interaction with the majority society to the greatest possible extent. Interestingly, however, in the few accessible primary documents[126] the term 'jāhiliyya' nowhere appear.[127] It was substituted by the terms 'associationism' (*shirk*) and 'unbelief' (*kufr*), which rattled around already in Quṭb's later writings, although he had hardly elaborated on the very serious legal consequences inhere inheres especially in the latter term. For the worldview of Shukrī Muṣṭafá and his followers, the substitution of 'jāhiliyya' with 'kufr' was only consistent with their strategy. In a state of weakness, a withdrawal from the majority society was the logical consequence of the earlier condemnation of the entire Egyptian society for unbelief,[128] a practice that caused the group to become more widely known as *Jamāʿat al-takfīr wa'l-hijra*. The appropriate punishment of the apostates, however, was not suspended, but rather only postponed until the righteous community, that is *Jamāʿat al-takfīr wa'l-hijra*, would have assumed sufficient strength to pursue an offensive *jihād* and, after its successful completion, would enforce the due punishment.

When, on 4 July 1977, members of the group abducted and executed the then Egyptian Minister for Pious Endowments (*wazīr al-awqāf al-miṣrī*), the Azhar-trained *ʿālim* Muḥammad Ḥusayn al-Dhahabī, on the accusation of unbelief, it seemed as if they considered themselves strong enough to emerge from their retreat and follow the Prophetic example to 'fight the people until they [all] testify that there is not deity but God and that I am God's Messenger'.[129] However, when the group was subsequently caught by the government authorities and its leaders tried and executed, Shukrī Muṣṭafá conceded in court that, despite generally welcoming the killing of al-Dhahabī, the moment chosen for it was perhaps premature and the community still in the 'phase of weakness'.[130] While one may argue that, because of this, the *Jamāʿat al-takfīr wa'l-hijra* was doomed to fail, the abduction and subsequent killing of al-Dhahabī—untimely or not—caused the radical Islamist discourse to gain momentum. The issue of *takfīr* began to increasingly revolve around the question of to what extent the political establishment—first of all, the heads of state—was to be held responsible for the continued existence of the *jāhiliyya* within the whole society. Was not the shepherd, according to the sound Prophetic saying, the shepherd fully responsible for his flock,[131] and has not the whole might of the righteous champions on the Path of God therefore to be directed first and foremost against these functionaries? The theological and legal concept underlying this is known as *takfīr al-ḥākim*, broadly conceived already in Ibn Taymiyya's discussion of the apostasy of the Mongol Īlkhānids, in the epistles of Muḥammad ibn ʿAbd al-Wahhāb and, although nowhere explicitly, also in Quṭb's concept of *jihād*.[132] Quṭb's steady emphasis on the ruler as 'ṭāghūt'—a Qur'ānic term that denotes any idol that leads astray from the submission to God and, in its singular form, has also been used as a synonym of Satan[133]—suggests seeing in him the root of all evil. Consequently, his and his associates' instant removal would have to be placed at the core of any successful *jihād*.

The first of the radical groups in Egypt that had explicitly been acting on that was a group that called itself *Shabāb Muḥammad*, but because of its activity, became later known rather as *Munaẓẓamat al-fanniyya al-ʿaskariyya*. Headed by Ṣāliḥ Sirriyya (executed 1394/1974), a Jordanian of Palestinian descent and a former member of the now globally acting *Ḥizb al-taḥrīr al-islāmī*,[134] the group launched an unsuccessful armed attack on the Military Academy in Heliopolis in April 1974, considered to be the first step in a *coup de'force* to overthrow the government and install a truly Islamic regime.[135] Sirriyya had been in contact with Zaynab al-Ghazālī and also, if only loosely, with Ayman al-Ẓawāhirī,[136] and, in this way, had certainly become acquainted with the thought of Sayyid Quṭb. Merged with elements of the *Ḥizb al-taḥrīr* ideology, which stressed the necessity of overthrowing the top level of government for a successful Islamisation of the entire society,[137] Sirriyya confined his *takfīr* mainly to the head of state, while arguing that the belief, or unbelief, of the common citizens would depend on whether or not they submitted to the power of the ruler.[138] Unlike Shukrī Muṣṭafá, Sirriyya frequently used the Quṭbian notion of the 'society of ignorance' (*mujtamaʿ jāhiliyya*), which, following an idea already embryonic in Quṭb, he conflated with the 'unbelieving' or 'associationist society' (*mujtamaʿ kāfiriyya* or *mushrikāna*). In mapping the *jāhiliyya* within the society, Sirriyya also lashed out at all competing political ideologies, first and foremost Communism (*al-shujūʿiyya*) and Socialism (*al-ishtirākiyya*), the latter having been very much on the agenda of various Arab countries at that time—as 'Baʿthism', in Syria and Iraq, and as 'Nasserism' in Egypt. Sirriyya also resembled Mawdūdī in his outspoken rejection of nationalism as the 'kingship of the modern age', when he stated:

The moment that the people embrace the foundations of patriotism and nationalism [*mabādiʾ al-waṭaniyya wa'l-qawmiyya*] they begin to live in an unbelieving and ignorant culture [*al-turāth al-jāhilī al-kāfir*] and acknowledge it. When the patriots of Egypt evoke the Pharaonic culture and are proud of it, and elevate it over Islam, then this is unbelief. And the nationalists evoke the pre-Islamic Arabic culture [*turāth al-jāhiliyya al-ʿarabiyya*] and are proud of it. He, who among them even name his son 'Lahab', is proclaimed 'Abū Lahab'—God shall curse him!—by the people.[139]

For all sincere Muslims it would therefore be a matter close to their hearts to immediately remove the heads of state by force and replace them with a religious ruler. In order to stress this point, Sirriyya quoted an altered Prophetic *ḥadīth*, in which he predicted that 'he who dies and has neither raided [*lam yaghzū*], nor thought about raiding will die the death of the *jāhiliyya*'.[140] Given the gravity of the situation, Muslims could not wait any longer for the 'phase of weakness' to pass and they would have to act immediately. And, although Sirriyya and his *Shabāb Muḥammad* failed with their attack on the Military Academy in Heliopolis, they had succeeded in creating the initial spark for an increasingly violent realisation of Quṭb's and, thus, implicitly, Mawdūdī's ideologies.

Former members of the *Shabāb* began to merge into other radical Islamist groups, which began increasingly to rise among mainly male Muslim students on the university campuses throughout Egypt.[141] From these groups, all using the generic name 'Islamic Society' (*jamāʿa islāmiyya*), two more distinct organisations eventually emerged, with common ideological as well as personal overlap,[142] but, at least in the beginning, with a clear geographical reference. The first one, the *Tanẓīm al-jihād al-islāmī*, originated from, and flourished mainly in, Cairo and the Lower Egyptian university towns. The second was the *Jamāʿa islāmiyya*, developed initially as the umbrella of the numerous *jamāʿāt* on various campuses in the country, and soon dominated by the more violent discourse of the groups in the Upper Egyptian university towns of al-Minyā and Asyūṭ. There it embarked on seeking open confrontation with the government of Muḥammad Anwar al-Sādāt, yet another member of the 'Free Officers Movement' of the late 1940s and early 1950s.[143] Both groups, the *Jihād al-islāmī* and the *Jamāʿa islāmiyya*, soon began to employ the services of the blind Azhar-trained scholar ʿUmar ʿAbd al-Raḥmān (b. 1357/1938) to such an extent that the radical *ʿālim* soon became to be publicly considered *spiritus rector* of the *Jamāʿa islāmiyya*.[144]

Shortly after his imprisonment for having delivered a fierce anti-Nasser sermon in 1971, ʿUmar ʿAbd al-Raḥmān excelled in a radical elaboration of the 'Qurʾānic Position Towards its Adversaries'—*Mawqif al-qurʾān min khuṣūmihi*—which was basically a rather lengthy justification of armed offensive *jihād*, based on an interpretation of *sūrat* al-Tawba. While little new can be learned from this work, it is nonetheless important to acknowledge that in it, ʿUmar ʿAbd al-Raḥmān kept the Mawdūdian and Quṭbian terminology and methodology very much alive. For instance, he frequently used the term 'jāhiliyya' to denote the state of the absence of Islam, spoke of Islam as a self-contained system or referred to Quṭb's taxonomy regarding the validity of various Qurʾānic statements on the issue of *jihād*. Clearer than Quṭb, however, the blind Azharite stressed the divine sanctification, the decree on killing unbelievers, including the so-called 'People of the Book', that is, Jews and Christians.[145] Finally, ʿUmar ʿAbd al-Raḥmān did as Sayyid Quṭb had done before him and quoted Mawdūdī's Iqbāl Day speech on the issue of *jihād* almost in its entirety,[146] thus proving just how relevant the South Asian ideologue had remained for current Islamist movements and organisations. To emphasise this importance, ʿUmar ʿAbd al-Raḥmān found quite eulogising words for Mawdūdī, stating that his 1939 explication on *jihād* was 'a valuable and comprehensive inquiry [*al-mabḥath al-mujmal al-qayyim*]' into a 'most significant and profound issue for the establishment of the Islamic movement',[147] which is it was worth quoting extensively.

While ʿUmar ʿAbd al-Raḥmān, not least perhaps because of his standing as *ʿālim* as well as his disability, had confined himself to the '*jihād* with the pen and tongue', those in his orbit linked these thoughts to violent action. In the aftermath of Sādāt's US-mediated peace treaty with Israel in March 1979, which followed the Camp David Accords one year before, and the president's subsequent purges of the Islamist opposition, activists from the various radical outfits in Egypt triggered an insurgency in 1981, culminating in what became known as the 'Autumn of Fury'. Spurred by the success of the Islamic Revolution in Iran in early 1979[148] and fuelled by *jihādī* and also sectarian rhetoric, the electrical engineer Muḥammad ʿAbd al-Salām Faraj (executed 1402/1982) dismissed the Quṭbian distinction of a 'period of weakness' and a 'period of enforcement' and argued for immediate armed action.[149] For him:

> [t]he implementation of the decrees of God [*aḥkām allāh*] is an obligation [*farḍ*] for the Muslims. Consequently, establishing the Islamic State [*al-dawla al-islāmiyya*] is an obligation for them, because if the necessary [*al-wājib*] cannot be accomplished other than by this, then this becomes a necessity itself. Likewise, if the state cannot be established other then by fighting [*qātil*], then fighting is a necessity for us. Besides, the Muslims have unanimously agreed upon the necessity [*farīḍa*][150] for

the establishment of the *khilāfa*, the declaration of which depends on the existence of the centrepiece, which is the Islamic State. And, because 'Whosoever dies without having a *bayʿa* on his neck, he will die the death of the *jāhiliyya*', the re-establishment [*iʿāda*] of the *khilāfa* has to be the aspiration of every Muslim, in order not to come under the consequence of the *ḥadīth*, as *bayʿa* here means the *bayʿa* of *khilāfa*.[151]

Apart from the *khilāfa*, which is clearly meant here in its historical form as *khilāfat rasūl allāh*, Faraj resembled nonetheless numerous elements of Mawdūdī's ideological outline, although without explicitly referring to him and even to Quṭb. A viable conclusion from this might be that by then the chief tenets of Mawdūdī's thought had already been so deeply ingrained into the mindset of radical Islamists beyond the Indian subcontinent that it had become almost common knowledge, and hence the need to refer to the originator of these ideas had become somewhat redundant. With his *Farīḍa ghāʾiba*, the text from which the above quote has been drawn, Faraj himself became a point of reference for radical Islamists, thus in a sense abrogating the chain of references all the way back to Mawdūdī and even Quṭb.[152] Faraj's text, which introduced recourse to Ibn Taymiyya's *fatāwá* against the Mongols into the debate,[153] was widely considered the theoretical justification for the public assassination of president Anwar al-Sādāt during a military parade in Cairo on 6 October 1981 by a group of men around the Minyā-born military cadet Khālid al-Islāmbūlī.[154] Both men, Faraj and Islāmbūlī, had been in close contact with Karam Muḥammad Zuhdī (b. 1369/1950), initially a high-ranking cadre of al-Minyā's *al-Jamāʿa al-islāmiyya*,[155] about whom we shall hear a little more in the following chapter, but who, for the moment, may serve only as an indication of the complex interpersonal network of radical Islamists and Islamist outfits in Egypt of the 1970s and beyond.

With Faraj, however, the ideological torch had finally passed on to the key figures of the *Tanẓīm al-jihād al-islāmī* and from there to transnationally acting organisations such as *al-Qāʿida*. For its ideologues-*cum*-field-experienced activists, like al-Ẓawāhirī and even more Sayyid Imām al-Sharīf, Mawdūdī's categories had not played any role significant enough to feature prominently in their writings, even though Mawdūdī is openly acknowledged as an important mastermind of Islamism.[156] However, for them, too, the crucial terms and concepts of Mawdūdī might have already been regarded as common sense and, thus, would not have merited a proper discussion. As common sense, however, a much-radicalised version of Mawdūdī's ideas had eventually returned to South Asia, where it fell on the understanding ears of those irregulars who, in the borderland between Pakistan and Afghanistan, readied themselves for the decisive battle against the worldwide-dominating *jāhiliyya*, and for the establishment of the Islamic State.

b) Trying for Readjustment: The Moderate Response

Huḍaybī, descendant of a noble family and a judge by profession, became the *murshid al-ʿāmm* of the JIM in 1951, that is, before the so-called 'July Revolution' of the Free Officers around Nasser.[157] Like most of the leading figures of the JIM, he was instantly arrested when the organisation fell from Nasser's grace, and, in December 1954, he was among the first Muslim Brethren to be sentenced to death by hanging, a judgement that was soon after commuted to a severe prison sentence.[158] This, along with his temporary resignation from office in October 1952 in protest at the decision by the Consultative Assembly (*al-hay'a al-tasīsiyya*) of the JIM to register as a political party, which to him represented clearly a departure from al-Bannā's original idea of the organisation,[159] certainly increased his credibility among the Muslim Brethren as the true continuator of the founder's legacy. Such an enhanced authority was apparently needed for 'some discussion of the various views that have surfaced from time to time, and for which, however, there is no evidence for [their] correctness [*al-ḥaqq*]' and 'a clarifying response referring to the mighty book of God and the Path [*sunna*] of His Messenger—prayer and peace be upon him!—to provide evidence of the truth in a clear manner'.[160]

Clearly, al-Huḍaybī felt that the 'prison years'—Krämer uses the historically heavily loaded label 'infestation' (*miḥna*)[161]—had contributed considerably to the disintegration of the JIM and the subsequent rise of various ideological views, which were certainly not in line any more with the original principles proposed by al-Bannā. As its *murshid ʿāmm*, it remained his responsibility to bring the organisation back on track and provide it with a timely authoritative ideological foundation. As the overwhelming majority of the radicalised outlines revolved around the 'ideological triad of jāhiliyya–takfīr–jihād',[162] which had been triggered by Sayyid Quṭb and become solidified in the writings of those in his wake, al-Huḍaybī consequently targeted these very concepts and tried to argue that their radicalised understanding appeared to be somewhat unjustified.[163] Interestingly, however, he elaborated his critique with reference not to the writings of Quṭb and his Egyptian epigones, but instead to Mawdūdī. This had occasionally been attempted as an explanation,[164] but, from a systematic point of view, all these explanations appeared somewhat unsatisfactory. After all, why would al-Huḍaybī remain silent on those who apparently had undermined the original ideology of the JIM and resort rather to an explicit critique of the works of someone from South Asia, if not for the fundamental influence that Mawdūdī's concepts had on the genesis of a radical Islamist ideology in Egypt? Therefore, to focus on Mawdūdī appears quite consistent in order to get to the very root of what al-Huḍaybī considered as misinterpretations.

Consequently, while at the core of al-Huḍaybī's criticism of Mawdūdī's concepts stood 'jāhiliyya' and 'ḥākimiyya', the two concepts prominently popularised by Sayyid Quṭb, he seems to have been well aware of the fact that especially 'ḥākimiyyat allāh' resulted from Mawdūdī's axiomatic definitions of the twofold aspect of God, that is 'rabb'—His law-giving aspect that demands unconditional obedience—and 'ilāh', the divine aspect that receives and acknowledges this unconditional obedience. Therefore, al-Huḍaybī quoted at length from the Arabic translation of Mawdūdī's expositions on these two terms in his *Qur'ān kī c͟hār bunyādī iṣṭilāḥeṇ*,[165] which, just on the sidelines, proved once more the efficacy of Mawdūdī's thought on the further developments of the Islamist ideology. Both terms, al-Huḍaybī made clear, must not be reduced to only one single meaning, but have rather distinct denotations in each and every instance that they are used in the Qur'ān.[166] Against Mawdūdī's claim that the respective original meaning of the four axiomatic Qur'ānic terms had got lost over time and needed therefore to be uncovered again, al-Huḍaybī countered with recourse to numerous Qur'ānic verses that, given the dogma of the universality and timelessness of the Qur'ānic message, a sincere believer would be able to understand the true meaning of these terms in every place and at any time simply by closely reading the Qur'ān.[167]

Without going too deep into detail, al-Huḍaybī's critical discussion of 'jāhiliyya' and 'ḥākimiyya'—after all the core of his refutation of the Quṭbist understanding—deserves nonetheless some remarks.[168] The latter concept, emanating in Mawdūdī's thought from his axiomatic Qur'ānic terms, could be easily dismissed by al-Huḍaybī on the basis that the term as such does not appear in the Qur'ān and is thus the result of a rather speculative and hardly sustainable deduction from the active aspect of God's essence as 'rabb'.[169] The discussion of 'jāhiliyya', in contrast, had to take up much more space, because this term is evidently mentioned in the Qur'ān. The implicit criticism of Mawdūdī's notion and of those in his wake is pretty much reflected in al-Huḍaybī's stressing of the timelessness of the Qur'ānic message which can well be understood, and subsequently be followed, at any time and any place. Hence, 'jāhiliyya' cannot, as in Mawdūdī's and his epigones' writings, denote a general and an historical mode, which overshadows the entire world and is thus to be held responsible for the fact that the true meaning of Qur'ānic key terms and concepts has over time become forgotten. Rather, it refers—as 'jahl'—to an individual attitude, to 'ignorance' in the proper sense of the word, as, since the revelation of the Qur'ān, man has the ability as well as the chance to accept the universal truths of Islam. He who does not accept it is therefore indeed deliberately ignorant of the Qur'ānic message.[170] Even here, however, al-Huḍaybī took quite a humble position, when he conceded the possibilities of individual misjudgements (*khaṭa*) due to man's erroneous nature and even of coercion (*ikrāh*) that could drive a person to outwardly forsake his or her religious beliefs.[171] Both individual error and coercion by an external force would then count as mitigating circumstances and, consequently, do not automatically make a believer into an unbeliever.

All these rather moderate counter-arguments to the worldview of the 'Quṭbists' had a decisive impact on the issue of the 'Islamic State' and the necessity of its establishment. After all, for Mawdūdī and those in his trail it was only the Islamic State that could guarantee the comprehensive implementation of the *sharīʿa*, which, in turn, would alone enable Muslims to lead an Islamic way of life. Backing up his view on governance with numerous references to classical works on Islamic jurisprudence, theology and political theory,[172] al-Huḍaybī argued in favour of the re-establishment of the historical Islamic Caliphate, that is, of a religious and political authority which would oversee the Islamicity of the *umma* along the lines of *al-amr bi'l-maʿrūf wa'l-nahy ʿan al-munkar*. Hence, the Islamic State (*al-ḥukūma al-islāmiyya*) and the rightfully appointed leader (*al-imām al-ḥaqq*) would necessarily fall into one,[173] an idea that clearly expressed al-Huḍaybī's doubts about the ability of each and every ordinary believer to correctly interpret the authoritative texts of Islam and to act accordingly—an ability clearly conceded by Mawdūdī and Quṭb. What is evident from al-Huḍaybī's discussion is that he had clearly been aware of the dangers inherent in such an epistemological optimism. Consequently, the authority of the adequately trained *ʿulamā'*,[174] under the supervision of the *imām al-ḥaqq*, whoever he may be in reality, over the interpretation of the authoritative texts of Islam had to be restored, in order to avoid possible distortions in the understanding of the divine message by the ordinary believer and the practical consequences that would arise from this. Whenever the leader does not fulfil his duty, the community should show patience (*ṣabr*)—a virtue strongly emphasised in the Qur'ān[175]—instead of resorting to impetuous active and possibly violent resistance.[176]

The influence of al-Huḍaybī's moderate Islamism, theoretically elaborated in *Duʿāt, lā quḍāt*, eventually had repercussions also beyond the JIM, which—as a consequence of al-Huḍaybī's legacy—had meanwhile begun to increasingly flirt with the idea of entering into the parliamentary process.[177] Since the late 1990s, some course correction along very similar lines also took place within the radical Islamist milieu in Egypt. Here, too, Quṭbian notions of militant resistance against the so far 'unbelieving' political establishment, including the inevitable collateral damage, were considerably criticised and were subsequently eschewed. However, this process was fuelled less by motives similar to those of al-Huḍaybī, than by the pragmatic insight that the ability to act had become increasingly limited, owing to the rather effective and ruthless counter-strategies by the government authorities, which led to lengthy prison sentences for thousands of militants, and even to frequent executions. Therefore, in March 1997 the imprisoned leadership of the *Jamāʿa islāmiyya*, prominent among them the above mentioned Karam Muḥammad Zuhdī, called upon their brethren to quit their violence, a call that was not obeyed then, as the fatal attack on Western tourists in Upper Egyptian Luxor by activists of the *Jamāʿa islāmiyya* in November 1997 vividly demonstrated. In October 1998, however, ʿUmar ʿAbd al-Raḥmān, who had meanwhile been imprisoned for life at the US federal penitentiary in Butner, NC, for his involvement in the 1993 World Trade Center bombing, issued a statement that called for a change of strategy: the cadres of the *Jamāʿa islāmiyya* should shift their activities from militancy to propagating Islam through writing and preaching,[178] thus pretty much following the lines of al-Huḍaybī. Only five months later the Constitutive Council of the *Jamāʿa islāmiyya*—most of its members in jail—endorsed this appeal and the organisation finally submitted and put down its weapons.[179]

This, of course, was first and foremost only a call for a truce, not a change of principles. An ideological change took place only in January 2002, when six imprisoned leaders of the *Jamāʿa islāmiyya*, one of them being again Karam Zuhdī, released a four-volume revision of their former core doctrine, revolving around the Quṭbian 'ideological triad' of *jāhiliyya*, *takfīr* and *jihād*. At the centre of their argument, however, was a stress on the 'Common Good' (*maṣlaḥa*) as the ultimate touchstone for every activity, which, at times, would demand even coming to terms with a government whose

Islamicity is in doubt.[180] Thus, what the revision entailed was a rejection of the 'the-end-justifies-the-means' attitude that political ideologies all have in common, and a plea for a much more considered assessment of the compatibility of chosen means with the welfare of the entire polity. To consider the whole society would however only work if the practice of *takfīr*, central for all the radical organisations in the wake of Quṭb, had been checked and the authority over it, in its ultimate consequence, conveyed back to the properly trained religious jurists, the *fuqahā*ʾ.[181] In the light of all this, the view on '*jihād* at all costs' had also been thoroughly revised. What is most important in this regard is that, with recourse to five examples from early Muslim history and considering its impact on the 'Common Good', the revisionists declared it at least highly questionable to wage *jihād* against an existing political authority.[182] With this, they clearly went against the arguments of Zuhdī's former companion ʿAbd al-Salām Faraj, who had elevated armed *jihād* to an individual duty (*farḍ ʿayn*) for each and every Muslim,[183] and thus to a fundamental criterion of faith. Interestingly, though, to support the revised viewpoint of the *Jamāʿa islāmiyya* leadership, the six revisionists relied heavily on the works of Ibn Taymiyya, proving in this way that the medieval traditionalist had been a quite complex and erudite thinker, who must not be reduced only to his *fatāwá* on the Mongols.

Overall, the revision had severe systematic consequences. By pleading for a more differentiated view and a healthy degree of modesty when forming an opinion in religious matters, the revisionists of the *Jamāʿa islāmiyya* had virtually stripped the Islamist ideology bare. Although they still remained outspoken against any other political ideology[184] and had also not abjured their goal to establish an Islamic State, even this latter concept had become somewhat hollowed out. Although the revision did certainly re-legitimate the state and ascribe it the monopoly over selected religious duties, such as the call for *jihād*, there seems nonetheless a certain shift in the emphasis towards the society as a whole for the realisation of its comprehensive Islamisation. In this, a certain parallel can be detected with various national branches of Mawdūdī's JiI, which had developed since the partition of India in 1947.

2) Modification in Practice: The *Jamāʿat-i islāmī* beyond Mawdūdī

On the eve of Partition, on 26 April 1947, Mawdūdī delivered a historic address to the annual convention (*ijtimāʿ*) of the JiI in southern Madras. In this speech, he acknowledged the inevitability of the fact that the British

Raj would very soon give way to two distinct Indian nation states, which, in the end, would also tear the members of the JiI somewhat apart.[185] After Mawdūdī had outlined his understanding of the future scenario especially for those Muslims who would remain in India, he uttered his doubts that this new state would indeed treat all of its citizens equally, and suggested a number of hypothetical alternative ways for Muslims to situate themselves in post-independent South Asia, and he swore them to uphold the aim of the movement, namely to keep steadfastly working for bringing about the Islamic revolution.[186] To this end, Mawdūdī proposed a refined four-point action plan, which he considered equally applicable to the future India as well as Pakistan. He stated that 'it is obvious to us that both, India and Pakistan, will be running along Western-made political patterns, and the results, which these patterns have brought about in the West, will also be borne here.'[187]

Consequently, Mawdūdī asked his followers to, first, continue their missionary work among Muslims, including in the task the correction of the deeply ingrained prejudice that Indian Hindus and Muslims would constitute two distinct and completely incompatible nations. The eventual success of these missionary efforts among Muslims, so Mawdūdī hoped, would then also trigger among the non-Muslims the desire for societal change along Mawdūdī's lines and, thus, eventually embrace the entire Indian population. In this way, Muslims would also realise that the models of the reform-oriented educationalists, first and foremost among them the Aligarh movement, had ultimately failed and that only the reformist model of the JiI could bring about the desired better society. Here, extraordinary responsibility would lie on the shoulders of the literati who, in their widely circulated writings, would substantially criticise the various public institution of the prevalent society and propose the model of the JiI instead. Finally it would be the task of the JiI's workers (*kārkun*) to produce the ideological literature of the movement in all the various vernacular languages and, by distributing it and by delivering public speeches, just as Mawdūdī himself had done in the late 1930s in rural Punjab, would pave the way for the eventual success of the Islamic revolution.[188] All in all, regardless of the looming division of the JiI in the course of partition of what had once been the British Raj, Mawdūdī, still acting as the ideologue that he was, did not at all retreat from the universalism of how the Islamic revolution was to be pursued. Soon, however, he was overtaken by the actual developments in the various new polities, and, while in his Madras speech migration to Pakistan appeared not to be the first among all options, he personally seems to have soon given in and joined the massive flow of migrants into the first Muslim nation state ever, and settled down in Lahore. Meanwhile, the distinct ideological, political and social realities in Pakistan and India began to impact the JiI in both states and caused it to reshape.

2.1) The Predicament of Religious Nationalism: The *Jamāʿat-i islāmī* of Pakistan

To establish the JiI's headquarters in Lahore was a decision of far-reaching consequences. Being set now in a political environment that claimed the representation of common interests based on religious identity, Mawdūdī and his followers demanded a true commitment of the leadership around Jinnāḥ by seeing religious principles duly enshrined in the Pakistani Constitution. Right from its first session on 10 and 11 August 1947, however, the Constituent Assembly made it plain that the state-to-be would treat all of its citizens, regardless of their respective religious belonging, equal, or, as Jinnāḥ put it: 'In course of time Hindus would cease to be Hindus and Muslims would cease to be Muslims, not in the religious sense, because that is the personal faith of each individual, but in the political sense as citizens of the State.'[189] For Mawdūdī and his followers, in turn, this was a clear indication that the religious component in 'Pakistan' was only a rhetorical means to a very profane end. Consequently, it became a main objective for the JiI to strongly oppose these rather secular tendencies, and to ensure that the Constitution, which would eventually take effect, was truly based on Islamic principles.[190]

Soon it became clear that this agenda was somewhat different from the one to be followed by the JiI in India, which is why already in April 1948 the two branches in Pakistan and India parted ways[191] and Mawdūdī took charge as *amīr* of the Pakistani side.[192] He and his followers now concentrated all their effort on promoting an Islamic constitution for Pakistan. The Pakistani government, under considerable pressure from various groups inside as well as by its conflict with India over Kashmir, from the outside, acted restrictively. In October 1948 Mawdūdī and other eminent members of the JiI-P were arrested for subversion, their various journals closed down and their funds frozen.[193] While in jail, Mawdūdī saw the necessity of forging a strategic alliance with the *ʿulamāʾ* whom he had earlier despised for systematic reasons.[194] Unsurprisingly, the historiography of the JiI-P attributes to this pragmatic accord the Constituent Assembly's adoption on 12 March 1949 of the so-called 'Objectives Resolution', which, in its first paragraph, echoed Mawdūdī's earlier notions of God's *ḥākimiyya* and the believers' *khilāfa* on earth.[195]

This development, from a full and uncompromising rejection of the Pakistani government and its various bodies to advocacy of constitutionalism, formed the first stage in the transition of the JiI-P from the 'Society of Enlightenment' to a major political party in the parliamentary landscape of Pakistan. At this stage, however, its leadership still perceived the organisation more as a rather small and exclusive group of the highest moral integrity, as the 'best which God had brought forth among humankind' who therefore would 'enjoin the commendable and prevent the reprehensible (*amr bi'l-ma'rūf wa-nahy 'an al-munkar*)'.[196] Consequently, when the first Provincial Assembly elections for Punjab were announced to be held in early March 1951, the JiI-P had already moved away from its initial call upon Muslims to boycott any election unless it was based on an Islamic constitution. However, although it was not any longer opposed to participation in elections, the JiI-P did not nominate candidates of its own, but saw its role—in keeping with the Qur'ānic injunction to 'enjoin the commendable and prevent the reprehensible'—as rather confined to the moral assessment of the nominees.[197]

In this light can also be seen its massive participation in the anti-Aḥmadiyya agitation of 1953–54. The open declaration of his affiliation with the controversial Aḥmadiyya by the first Pakistani foreign minister Muḥammad Ẓafarallāh Khān (d. 1405/1985) gave a certain substance to the suspicion that the Pakistani government was deeply infiltrated by apostates, which, in turn, was considered once more proof of the actual impiety of the Pakistani state.[198] Mawdūdī himself, not long released from jail, was for a long time rather reluctant to join hands with those from among his compatriots who demanded direct action to be taken. Although he made his position towards the Aḥmadiyya clear already in summer 1952,[199] it was not before his *Qādiyānī mas'ala*, the comprehensive reckoning with them, was published in March 1953, that he was catapulted to the head of the movement. In this work, Mawdūdī accused the Aḥmadīs, against whom 'all the Muslims are unanimous in their verdict of *kufr*',[200] of subversive political ambitions, which would eventually culminate in the establishment of an Aḥmadiyya state within Pakistan. Employing once more his biologistic language when comparing the Aḥmadīs with 'a cancer [*saraṭān*] [that is] eating up and gradually consuming the vitals of the Muslim society [*muslim mu'āshare kā jism*]',[201] Mawdūdī called for them to be removed by force of the from Pakistani society, that is to be publicly declared apostates and, as the ultimate consequence, to be subject to the death penalty as the only adequate sentence. As the situation was further exacerbated, the government imposed martial law and Mawdūdī was once again detained for stirring sectarian strife in Pakistan, this time even sentenced to death, a verdict that, on government intervention, was later reduced to a lengthy spell in prison.[202]

However, the most decisive event, which brought about the most profound transformation of the JiI-P, took place immediately after Mawdūdī's early release from jail in May 1955 and what Nasr calls the 'Māchhī Got'h-Affair'.[203] The fast-growing political aspirations of the JiI-P since Partition had led to the development of an increasingly professional stratum of party administrators that worked in the JiI-P's headquarters in Lahore. Bureaucratisation, in turn, always increases the potential for abuse of power by office holders,[204] and the JiI-P was, despite its lofty goals, certainly not immune to this. Thus, during the 1954 annual congregation (*ijtimāʿ*), the report of which was conveniently left out of the published proceedings of these gatherings, a high-ranking member of the JiI-P publicly accused another leading member of severe corruption.[205] The following investigation (*jāʾiza*), ordered by Mawdūdī himself, revealed that this was by no means an isolated incident, but that the abuse of power permeated the whole bureaucracy of the organisation, including even its *amīr* Mawdūdī.

Consequently, at the end of these tedious investigations in November 1956 the *Majlis-i shūrá* released an evocative four-point resolution, in which the JiI-P was accused of having seriously deviated from its original course, enshrined in the four-point action plan adopted during the 1951 *ijtimāʿ*, where the emphasis was laid on moral, and not political, reformation.[206] Moreover, the resolution criticised the canonical status that some of Mawdūdī's writings had meanwhile acquired in the eyes of numerous members of the JiI-P, a fact that had led them to neglect that, according to the JiI-P's statute,[207] the only binding decisions were those derived by the *Majlis-i shūrá* in mutual consultation and solely on the basis of Qurʾān and Prophetic Sunna.[208] In general, the four-point resolution was a serious criticism by the somewhat *ʿulamāʾ*-dominated *Majlis-i shūrá* of the transformation of the JiI-P into a political party and, related to that, also of Mawdūdī's increasingly autocratic style of leadership, which greatly facilitated the sacrifice of once dearly held religious principles for the sake of rather short-lived political influence.[209] Mawdūdī, whose spells in jail had gained him enormous popularity, saw his own position threatened by the resolution of the *Majlis-i shūrá*, so in return he accused its members of unworthy motives and demanded their resignation.[210] Once again, after the first major factional dispute within the JiI in 1942, as a result of which a considerable number of mainly *ʿulamāʾ* left the organisation,[211] its leadership seriously fell apart into two factions, one grouped around Mawdūdī and the other around his long-term foe Amīn Aḥsan Iṣlāḥī (d. 1418/1997). Almost re-enacting the events around the fatal *shūrá* meeting of October 1942 in Delhi, the argument between the two factions within the JiI resulted in the temporary resignation of Mawdūdī from the office of *amīr*, and eventually Iṣlāḥī's ultimate break with the JiI-P.[212] In the end, the *Majlis-i shūrá* summoned all the members of the JiI-P for an *ijtimāʿ* to Southern Punjabi Māchhī Got'h where the dispute should be resolved once and for all. The outcome of the meeting was quite devastating. Mawdūdī was not willing to make any concessions and, as a result, Iṣlāḥī and some sixty-five other members, many of them *ʿulamāʾ*, left the JiI-P for good.[213] Mawdūdī, in turn, although already well known for his indulgence in long speeches, rose now even above himself when he delivered a six-hour[214] speech that finally sealed the departure of the JiI-P from a rather confined community of high moral integrity to become a political party proper.

The text of this speech of Mawdūdī's, a little later published as *Taḥrīk-i islāmī kā āʾinda lāʾiḥa-yi ʿamal*, is somewhat crucial, because it suggests, first, that Mawdūdī's later thought remained indeed rather consistent with his earlier ideas, and, second, that the fundamental point of contention between Mawdūdī and Iṣlāḥī regarding the aims and strategies of the JiI-P were much more the result of a serious misunderstanding. The crux of this misunderstanding appears to have been seated in Mawdūdī's deliberately woolly choice of conceptual terms, which left a wide range of possible interpretation by different individuals. At the centre of the dispute was his concept of 'establishment of religion' (*iqāmat-i dīn*) that was written into the statutes of the JiI-P of 1952 as the organisation's ultimate objective (*naṣb al-ʿayn*). While Mawdūdī stressed that in the commentary on this article the notion of *iqāmat-i dīn* corresponded clearly with the text of the first statutes of 1941, namely 'to establish the divine government on earth and to obtain heavenly pleasures in the Hereafter [*dunyā meṇ ḥukūmat-i ilāhiyya kā qiyām, awr ākhirat meṇ riḍā-yi ilāhī kā ḥuṣūl*]',[215] he had rarely outlined in detail how this lofty objective was to be achieved. For Iṣlāḥī, on the other hand, the 1951 four-point action plan, after all adopted with Mawdūdī's approval, clearly represented a hierarchy of efforts, beginning with the most important, namely the individual purification, whereas the transformation of the political system played the least weighty role. For

Mawdūdī, in contrast, the four points represented various phases in the revolutionary process, beginning with individual betterment, which was the precondition for forming a community of virtuous men, as they had done between 1936 and 1939 in Pat'hānkot', followed by the community reaching out into the wider society and culminating in the transformation of the political system:[216]

The ultimate goal of all our endeavour is a revolution in leadership [*inqilāb-i imāmat*], which we strive to achieve in this world to its utmost degree. This means that, after the leadership of the sinners and impostors [*fussāq wa fujjār kī imāmat wa qiyādat*] has been ended, a system of virtuous leadership [*imāmat-i ṣāliḥa kā niẓām*] will be established. We consider this very effort the [only] means to attain the heavenly pleasures.[217]

In these two perspectives on the four-point plan of 1951, we seem to witness the recurrence of the events from the founding phase of the JiI, when leading *ʿulamāʾ* like Muḥammad Manẓūr Nuʿmānī and Abū 'l-Ḥasan ʿAlī Nadwī had resigned for similar reasons. Thus, Mukarram's analytical dichotomy of 'governance'-versus 'guidance'-orientation could surely also be applied to the argument between Iṣlāḥī and Mawdūdī, although, unlike Nuʿmānī and Nadwī, Iṣlāḥī did not go as far as submitting to the Sufism-inspired 'guidance'-orientation of the TJ.[218]

Mawdūdī, however, took not the least responsibility for any of the misunderstandings that had led to these and similar developments.[219] Quoting at length from a wide array of his own earlier writings and, thus, reducing the criticism of the *Majlis-i shūrá* regarding the importance of his writings for the decision-making processes within the JiI-P to absurdity, he set out to prove that he had never changed, withheld or even obscured the political objectives of his ideology, which had then become the JiI's ideology. Similar to the importance that Communism and Fascism attributed to the leading role of the party,[220] Mawdūdī stressed the role that, as vanguard of the Islamic revolution, the JiI-P would have to play for the welfare of the masses, which, in turn, were in urgent need of proper guidance. However, to ensure this guidance, the vanguard would need to bring about the framework conditions necessary for the religious reformation of each and everyone.[221] The only appropriate way to achieve this goal under the present conditions—and herein, although he had clearly changed his earlier views, Mawdūdī differed greatly from the Communist and Fascist models—would be to actively participate in the public elections and to use the parliamentary way to step-by-step establish the Islamic system of life. To justify this considerable change of policy, Mawdūdī declared any non-constitutional way to change the government in a constitutional democracy as not permitted by the *sharīʿa*.[222] Such an acknowledgement of the present political structures, along with the pronounced ultimate goal of the JiI-P, left few alternatives to accommodating its strategies and effectively becoming a proper political party. Consequently, the religious *daʿwa*, which dominated the JiI's activities since its inception, was to be continued, but would now assume the form of canvassing. In contrast to his stance back in 1951, when the JiI-P participated only indirectly (*bi'l-wāsiṭa*) in the Punjab provincial elections, Mawdūdī now called explicitly for their direct (*bi-lā wāsiṭa*) participation, as it would clearly befit a political party in a parliamentary system.[223]

Although it is clear that from now on that pragmatism was dominating the course of the JiI-P, one may not want to go to the extreme and consider these developments the 'end of ideology', as Nasr has done.[224] The constant recourse to the catchwords and core themes of the JiI's ideology in all of Mawdūdī's later writings and speeches, such as his invocation of the ongoing battle between 'Islam' and 'jāhiliyya' (*is waqt islām awr jāhiliyya kā maʿraka*),[225] the necessity of acknowledging God's supreme sovereignty (*allāh kī ḥākimiyyat ko taslīm karnā*) or the reference to the 'Islamic state' (*ḥukūmat-i islāmī*), the 'Islamic system of life' (*islāmī niẓām-i zindagī*) and the ultimate goal of the 'establishment of religion' (*iqāmat-i dīn*),[226] suggest that the ideology was still very much prevalent.

The continuing adherence to this ideology, if only by reference to various catchwords, also reflected the structural transformation of the JiI-P in the aftermath of the 'Māchhī Got'h Affair', when it developed various features quite similar to those of other political parties with an uncompromising ideology. First, in a way recalling the Bolshevik Party under Stalin or the various Fascist parties, Mawdūdī's position in the JiI-P became almost ritually elevated, his word sacrosanct and his writings canonical. Hence ideology and leader were increasingly set as one, a synonymy that did not diminish with Mawdūdī's death in 1979. Related to the indefeasibility of the leader was that almost unconditional loyalty to the leader became paramount. Anyone who dared to waver was considered a serious threat to the healthy organism which Mawdūdī depicted the JiI-P to be, and would consequently have to be removed. This practice, again, found precedent in the Stalinist purges between 1936 and 1938 and purges of the *Partito Nazionale Fascista* during Farinacci's term as Party Secretary in 1925 and in the Nazis' 'Night of the Long Knives' in 1934. Finally, the bureaucratisation of the JiI-P continued to be consistently pursued, and as a result the party developed tightly organised and centrally administered structures.[227]

From then on, the JiI-P actively took part in the parliamentary process in Pakistan, more often in opposition to the government but sometimes, as for example during the eleven years' reign of General Zia ul-Haq (Muḥammad Ḍiyā' al-Ḥaqq; d. 1409/1988), as its close ally.[228] At times, they formed strategic alliances with other opposition parties, such as, between 1988 and 1990, with the *Pakistan Muslim League* (PML) faction of Muḥammad Nawāz Sharīf (b. 1949) and the *Jamʿiyyat-i ʿulamā-yi islām* (JUI) in the *Islāmī Jumhūrī Ittiḥād*, or, since 2002, with the two major factions of the JUI, the *Jamʿiyyat-i ʿulamā-yi Pākistān* and even the Shiite *Taḥrīk-i jaʿfariyya-yi Pākistān* in the religious *Muttaḥida-yi majlis-i ʿamal*.[229]

2.2) The Predicament of Secularism: The *Jamāʿat-i islāmī* of India

At the annual convention of the JiI in April 1948 in Allahabad in north India, Mawdūdī—then still the *amīr* of the JiI on both sides of the border—gave his consent to the establishment of an autonomous JiI of India,[230] stating that '[a]fter the partition of the people the situation had now become such that it seems impossible to maintain the organisation [*naẓm*] of the Jamāʿat'.[231] In August of the same year the eleven members of the Central *Majlis-i shūrá* for India assembled for the first time in Malīḥābād near Lucknow under the presidency of Abū 'l-Layth Iṣlāḥī Nadwī (d. 1412/1992).[232] He, who had been appointed *amīr* on Mawdūdī's suggestion, had, unlike the latter, undergone a full traditional education at the *Nadwat al-ʿulamā'* in Lucknow,[233] and it was perhaps for this reason that he eventually developed a different perspective on things. This, however, was not a straightforward development as in the beginning, Nadwī stuck firmly to the path outlined by Mawdūdī. During the inaugural session of the *ijtimāʿ* in April 1948 in Allahabad, he rebuked the proposal by a senior member for drastic changes in the Indian branch of the organisation, stating that '[we] are not prepared to depart from our path and method [*apnā maslak awr ṭarīq-i kār*]', nor 'are we at liberty to change [our] aims and principles [*maqāṣid awr uṣūl*]'.[234]

The JiI-H under Nadwī's leadership maintained this view for over a decade. Given the specifics of the original Indian Constitution of 1950 as an emphatically secular one,[235] it was thus 'secularism', which for Mawdūdī was a major point of contestation that, remained the organisation's enemy number one. Consequently, the Constitution was not to be acknowledged, and neither was any institution that emerged from the new Indian national identity. This explains why the leadership of the JiI-H called strongly upon

Muslims to boycott the first National Elections under the new Constitution in 1951–52.[236] Instead, they aimed at subverting the secular system by appealing to the Hindu majority to use their numerical advantage for the establishment of a religious state based on their respective *dīn*, or 'system of life'. 'We would prefer that to the secular [*lā-dīnī*] systems of Europe. If, in this system, Muslims like us will be punished with the death, then we would even be willing to accept that.'[237] The rationale behind this was that to Nadwī and his compatriots it appeared easier to compete with an alternative religious ideology than with a secular one. Herein, however, they had already moved away from Mawdūdī's unspoiled thought, in which a stratification of the various *jāhilī* world views into more or less preferable ones was not specified.

At any rate, before such a fundamental societal change in India could happen, the JiI-H itself took a most drastic turn when, in 1962, a rather reluctant Nadwī called upon Indian Muslims to partake in the upcoming third parliamentary elections.[238] This development, however, was not a sudden one. Already two years earlier, when Nadwī still maintained the original universal aspiration of the JiI-H against the advocacy of particular interests by the Indian political parties,[239] the *Majlis-i shūrá* had discussed the amendment of various articles in the statute (*dastūr*) of the organisation, which under the current circumstances had been regarded as not appropriate any more.[240] One year later it passed two remarkable resolutions, in which its members considered it advisable to co-operate (*taʿāwun karnā*) with the government and the various communities, and in which they revised their views on 'secularism', re-defining it and declaring it conducive to their own Islamic agenda.[241] Such resolutions and the subsequent amendments of the statute of the JiI-H paved the way for it to eventually become an ardent advocate of democracy and its secularist foundations, and, in this way, considerably depart from the line determined by Mawdūdī.

The road to the eventual firm entrenchment of this new attitude towards 'secularism' was however not straightforward. In 1972, Nadwī presumably became victim of a palace coup within the higher echelons of the JiI-H and was subsequently replaced as *amīr* by his long-time companion and secretary general (*qayyim*) since 1948, Muḥammad Yūsuf ibn Tafaḍḍul Ḥusayn (d. 1411/1991),[242] before, in 1982, Nadwī was re-elected. In the nine years of Muḥammad Yūsuf's interim leadership, the JiI-H backtracked somewhat on its more dogmatic original ideology. This might, to an extent, have had something to do with the *amīr*'s international activities, first and foremost in the Mecca-based and strongly Wahhābiyya-influenced *Muslim World League* (*Rābiṭat al-ʿālam al-islāmī*).[243] This was perhaps indicated by the fact that he was usually seen wearing the *ghutra*, the all-white Saudi Arabian variation of the traditional Arabian headdress, Wahhābī-style without the typical rope circlet (*aqāl*). On the other hand, a possible explanation of the renewed emphasis on the original and rather uncompromising stance of the JiI-H under Muḥammad Yūsuf is that, unlike his predecessor Abū 'l-Layth Iṣlāḥī Nadwī, the new *amīr* had been a product of the colonial educational and administrative system,[244] a stain from which he might have felt he urgently needed to cleanse himself. Overall, however, he seems not have sat too firmly in the saddle of the *amīr*. Whatever the dynamics between him and the other members of the *Majlis-i shūrá* may actually have been, the core strategy document for the following four years, issued in April 1972, suggested that Muḥammad Yūsuf's staunch opposition to any change of policy was still countered by considerable pragmatism. Therefore, 'although the *Jamāʿat-i islāmī Hind* does so far not participate in the elections, it may do so at the appropriate time in future on the basis of its own principles [*apne uṣūloṇ ke taḥt*]'.[245]

The political developments in India in the mid-1970s accelerated this process. With the JiI-H banned and many of its leading members imprisoned during Indirā Gāndhī's emergency rule between 1975 and 1977,[246] the provisional (*hangamī*) *Majlis-i shūrá* came somewhat under the influence of *zugzwang*. It was however not until after the Emergency that, on the basis of a poll conducted among all JiI-H members, the *Majlis-i shūrá*, although still rather reluctant, passed a resolution that conditionally allowed members of the JiI-H to vote in various elections.[247] Consequently, the relevant article in the statute was changed and the four-year plan of April 1972 modified, now securely anchoring the possibility of taking part in the elections 'on the basis of [the JiI-H's] own principles'.[248] Indirā Gāndhī's emergency rule arguably proved to have been far too much of a threat to the very existence of the JiI-H to allow for the luxury of dogmatically clinging on to some idealistic principles, even if a change meant overruling its *amīr*.

On the other hand, the internal conflict between the explicitly stated objective, namely the 'establishment of religion [*iqāmat-i dīn*], which, to be precise, means establishing the whole religion of Islam [*pūre dīn-i islām ko qāʾim karnā*] [...], the perfect and best system of life',[249] and the increasing concessions to the actual political and social situation was in a way epitomised by the considerable influence that Mawdūdī still exerted over the JiI-H. Although this may not have gone as far as Agwani wants us to believe,[250] Mawdūdī remained the ultimate decision making authority, especially with regard to possible modifications of the doctrine.[251] With Mawdūdī's demise in 1979, however, and Abū 'l-Layth Iṣlāḥī Nadwī resuming the office of *amīr* in 1982, the JiI-H became more autonomous on doctrinal issues.

The next four-year strategic plan, passed in April 1986, emphatically stressed voting by JiI-H members in the elections as the major means to pursue the still unchanged objective, that is the 'establishment of religion'.[252] By then, the majority among the leadership of the JiI-H had realised that the maintenance of democracy and pluralism was—at least for the time being—the most appropriate framework to secure the public consideration of Muslim interests. In the course of increasing communalisation of Indian politics, epitomised in the destruction of the historic Bābarī Mosque in Ayodhyā in north India in 1992 by Hindu militants, and the government of the Hindu right-wing *Bhāratīya Janatā Party* (BJP) between 1998 and 2002, the JiI-H transformed, thus, into the most ardent defenders of democracy.[253]

2.3) *Khilāfa* at Work: The *Jamāʿat-i islāmī* of Bangladesh[254]

On 1 October 2001 the JiI could celebrate its biggest political success since its inception in 1942: As part of the *Bangladesh Nationalist Party* (*Baṃglādeś Jātīẏatābādī Dal*; BJD), led by the former president's widow Khāledā Ziẏā (Khālida Ḍiyā'; b. 1945), they won seventeen seats in the general elections and were subsequently entrusted with two ministries in Ziẏā's government.[255] Interestingly, it was neither of the so-far discussed big national branches of the JiI that managed to achieve this result, but the rather young *Bāṃglādeś Jāmāẏāte Islāmī* (JiI-B), which, at the time of Partition, consisted of exactly one single member.[256]

Indeed, there is little indication that religio-political movements like the JiI has had much impact on the Muslims in Bengal. The common argument made by scholars of Islam in Bengal that this was because of the deeply rooted affinity of Bengali Muslims to popular religious practices,[257] something that had tempted authors like Asim Roy to speak in a somewhat essentialising way of a 'syncretistic Islam',[258] appears somewhat unconvincing, given the prominence of Sufi traditions and the occasional overlaps with Hindu popular religiosity all over the Indian subcontinent. The slight impact that organisations like the JiI made in Bengal may have rather to do with the extraordinary relevance of the Bengali language for the identity of the Bengali Muslims, to whom the Urdu-based tradition of Mawdūdī and his followers must have appeared rather alien. In adapting to this fact, Mawdūdī presented himself during an *ijtimāʿ* in Dacca in as late as 1956 as an advocate of Bengali as an official language of Pakistan equal to Urdu, and publicly acknowledged the cultural and economic discrimination of Bengalis at the hands of the Pakistani government.[259]

However, Mawdūdī's sympathy for the concerns of the Bengalis, even for those few of the Bengal cell of the JiI-P was feigned. It appears as if he, too, regarded the Bengalis with prejudicial suspicion and had repeatedly dispatched activists from West Pakistan to organise the Bengali cell.[260] Although in 1956 the first Bengalis were appointed (!) to the offices of *amīr* and secretary general (*qayyim*), respectively, with Abdur Rahīm (ʿAbd al-Raḥīm; b. unknown) from southern Bariśāl in 1951 and Golām Āzam (Ghulām Āʿẓam; b. 1341/1922),[261] it was still felt by the centre that they would need to be guided by members from West Pakistan.[262] Such a patronising attitude proved to be a misapprehension of the specific Bengali situation, clearly indicated by the very slow growth of the JiI-P in East Pakistan.[263] Even after the *Majlis-i shūrá* dispatched a delegation of six of its members to East Pakistan,[264] the leadership of the JiI-P still underestimated the traditional loyalty of the Bengali Muslims to the AIML—after all, that party had been founded in 1906 in Dacca mainly on the initiative of the Nawwāb of Dacca Khʷāja Salīmallāh Bahādur (d. 1333/1915). This loyalty only gradually faltered with the disdainful attitude of the ML leaders towards West Pakistan and it was not before the mid-1960s that the JiI-P came to be considered as a religio-political alternative.[265]

Much of the Bengalis' reluctance to embrace the JiI had certainly to do with the organisation's uncompromising stand towards Bengali nationalism, and the report of the annual *ijtimāʿ* of the JiI-P in Karachi in late November 1955 reveals as much.[266] This attitude even hardened when, in February 1966, the left-wing nationalist *Awami League* (*Āoẏāmī Līg*; AL) of Mujibur Rahmān (Mujīb al-Raḥmān; killed 1975) adopted its legendary Six Point Programme, a proposal for the transformation of Pakistan into a federation, and the *de facto* roadmap for provincial autonomy of East Pakistan.[267] Although somewhat ambivalent between its critical stand towards the secularist Second Martial Law regime of Muḥammad Ayyūb Khān (d. 1394/1974) on the one hand[268] and Bengali nationalism on the other, by 1969 the East Pakistani unit of the JiI-P had decided to fully side with the Pakistani government for the sake of national integration, although not refraining from its demand for levelling out the economic disparities between East and West Pakistan.[269] In terms of ideology, it entirely followed the lines of the centre of the JiI-P, as can be seen from the list of essential readings for cadres in English and Bengali.[270] Things however changed considerably when the Pakistan's military-bureaucratic leaders ordered the military crackdown in East Pakistan in March 1971, following their non-acceptance of the AL's landslide victory in the national elections of October 1970 and the understandable fury of the Bengali masses over what they saw as the West Pakistanis' mockery of democracy.[271] Now, the East Pakistani unit of the JiI-P began to free itself from being a mere stooge of the JiI-P's centre, although, like a child eager to prove itself to its parents, with a zealotry the results of which adhere to the JiI-B today.

Subscribing to the government's conspiracy theory and accusing Mujibur Rahmān and his followers of apostasy, Golām Āzam, then secretary general (*qayyim*) of the East Pakistani unit, assured the West Pakistani commander-in-chief of the JiI's full support in whatever was needed to restore Pakistan's national integrity.[272] Recruiting mainly from its student wing, the *Islāmī Chātra Saṁgha* (ICS),[273] the JiI began to openly form various paramilitary forces, such as the *al-Badr* and *al-Shams* brigades, and joined other militant outfits such as the *Rāzākār* (*Riḍākār*), all of which had been legitimately created under the *Pakistan Army Act* of 1952.[274] The high command over these irregular forces was allegedly entrusted to Matiur Rahmān Nizāmī (Muṭīʿ al-Raḥmān Niẓāmī, b. 1362/1943),[275] a leading ICS activist from the University of Dhaka who was later to become Āzam's successor as *amīr* of the JiI-B and eventually, in 2001, Minister for Agriculture in Khāledā Ziyā's BJD government. All the paramilitary forces became subsequently involved in heinous atrocities not only against the *Mukti Bāhinī*, the armed wing of the Bengali nationalists, but increasingly also against civilians, among them mainly intellectuals and members of religious and ethnic minorities.[276] For this reason, the leading cadres of the East Pakistani JiI-P and of the paramilitary forces had little option left than to undertake what they euphemistically called their 'collective exodus' (*sāṁgaṭhānik hijrat*) to West Pakistan after the surrender of the Pakistani army on 16 December 1971.[277] They were subsequently accused of having committed serious war crimes, and the first Home Minister of Bangladesh, Abul Hasnat Muhāmmad Qamaruzzamān (Abū 'l-Ḥasanat Muḥammad Qamr al-Zamān; assassinated 1975), declared immediately after independence that none of them would stay untried. By April 1973 the collation of evidence was completed and 115 persons had been identified who would have to face trial, a considerable number of them having been members or associates of the JiI-P.[278] However, with the accused in exile and Pakistan not about to extradite them, these tribunals were first put on hold and, owing to the political developments in the following time, eventually suspended.

Meanwhile, the expatriates fervently joined the campaign for the non-recognition (*nā-manẓūr*) of Bangladesh by Pakistan, which was mainly carried on by the JiI-P's radical-activist student wing, the *Islāmī Jamāʿat-i Ṭalaba* (IJT),[279] and which continued even after, in 1973, the Pakistani government of Zulfikar Ali Bhutto (D̲h̲ū 'l-Fiqār ʿAlī Bhut't'o; executed 1979) had decided to officially recognise the sovereignty of Bangladesh. The increasing impact of the IJT on the agenda of the JiI-P is of quite some importance, as it marks the advent of a new generation within the leadership of the JiI-P, indicated by Mawdūdī's resignation from the office of *amīr* after having suffered a mild heart attack in February 1972, and the transfer of responsibilities to Miyāṇ Ṭufayl Muḥammad (d. 1430/2009), a founding member of the JiI in 1942.[280] The activists from East Pakistan, first and foremost those from around the ICS, were decisively involved in this generation shift. The time in which they were merely Mawdūdī's parrots had incontrovertibly passed, and now they acted with considerable self-confidence, reflected not least in their almost cocky responses to the accusation of war crimes during the War of 1971.

Already during the war, especially Golām Āzam and the later first official *amīr* of the JiI-B, Ābbās Alī Khān (ʿAbbās ʿAlī K̲h̲ān; d. 1420/1999), were not shy in publicly justifying the various atrocities committed by the Pakistani army and the various paramilitary outfits, and even later announcing that they had done nothing wrong.[281] This more offensive position, however, soon gave way to a more defensive one, in which the JiI-B leadership sternly denied its involvement in any war crimes and blamed an AL-led 'smear campaign' (*apapracāra*), aimed at defaming the JiI-B as a political opposition.[282] In return, however, they lashed out against the AL and its allies during the war and accused them of having committed cruel acts of retribution against alleged dissidents themselves.[283] In whitewashing their dubious activities, however, the JiI-B cadres could rely on support from abroad. As late as May 1973, Mawdūdī and an aged Muḥammad Amīn al-Ḥusaynī (d. 1394/1974), former Grand *muftī* of Jerusalem and after the Second World War a core figure in the establishment of an 'Islamist International',[284] extended their moral support, praising the '*mujāhidūn*' of *al-Badr* and *al-Shams* as upright patriots. In a joint communiqué they stated that, 'If such young men in East and West Pakistan would enthusiastically work and serve their country, then—God willing—Pakistan would be saved from this accidental infestation [*ʿāraḍī āzmāʾish se*], which troubles it at present.'[285]

Given the offensive apologetics of the East Pakistani JiI-P leadership regarding their involvement in what are commonly seen as severe human rights violations, it is not surprising that a potential for violence remained within the organisation and its affiliates, most prominently within the ICŚ. The frequently atrocious activities of their numerous cadres, directed mainly against political adversaries, were largely responsible for the situation in which 'violence has [...] become endemic in Bangladeshi student politics'.[286] On the other hand, after the JiI—now as JiI-B—became officially legitimate again in May 1979, the militants of the ICŚ came to be utilised by the JiI-B for the intimidation of the political opposition during each of its election campaigns.[287] Moreover, the rather ambivalent stand of various Bangladeshi governments towards the Islamicity of the Bengali state—first and foremost the two successive military dictatorships of Ziẏāur Rahmān (Ḍiyāʾ al-Raḥmān; assassinated 1981) and Husein Muhāmmad Erśād (Ḥusayn Muḥammad Irshād; b. 1930) between 1975 and 1990, as well as the BJD governments under Khāledā Ziẏā between 1991 and 1996 and 2001 and 2006—facilitated links between the ICŚ and various *jihādī* outfits in Bangladesh, such as *Hizbut Tauhīd* (*Ḥizb al-Tawḥīd*), *Jāmātulmujāhidīn Bāṃlādeś* (*Jamāʿat al-Mujāhidīn Bangladesh*) and *Śahādate Hikma* (*Shahādat-i Ḥikma*).[288]

Prior to these developments, however, the JiI needed to re-emerge from the underground, where it managed to still be alive and active after 1971. Instrumental in this were Ziẏāur Rahmān's attempts to religiously legitimise the military regime after his *coup d'état* in 1975.[289] This course facilitated the return of Golām Āzam in 1978, although, since the AL had deprived him of his citizenship, on a Pakistani passport, a fact which was to lead to serious arguments with the authorities. Āzam's 'return' to Bangladesh, ostensibly to help the young state to maintain its Islamicity and to protect it from Indian interference, and his subsequent, although only informal, election to the office of *amīr*[290] led eventually to a split in the JiI. This rift resulted initially from a contestation of leadership by its earlier *amīr* Abdur Rahīm, who was repatriated to Bangladesh four years prior to Āzam, and a subsequent argument over the most appropriate strategy to Islamise the society.[291] Eventually, a disgruntled Abdur Rahīm left the JiI and, in 1979, founded the Islamist *Islāmī Aikkya Joṭ* (IAJ), while the Āzam-led faction established the JiI-B as a new and independent organisation.[292]

Its political programme for the next few years revolved mainly around the substantiation of its legitimacy, epitomised by the demand for the restoration of Golām Āzam's citizenship, which to a considerable extent determined the JiI-B's attitude towards the successive Bangladeshi governments.[293] Only in April 1993, during Khāledā Ziẏā's first term as prime minister and after a failed attempt by the *Ekāttarer Ghātak Dālāl Nirmul Kamiṭi* in 1992 to bring him to trial for his activities during the 1971 War,[294] was Golām Āzam finally granted Bangladeshi citizenship. This, however, was preceded by a long tug of war between the government and the emerging civil society over his status that eventually ended with his official pardon.[295]

With this, the long and intricate process of the JiI's official rehabilitation in Bangladesh came to an end. Within Bangladeshi society, however, the rift between the AL-led nationalists, who were not going to forget the role that the JiI-B establishment had played in 1971, and Islamistically inclined groups remained as it was. Hence, national politics oscillated between these two poles and, at one time, favoured Mujibur Rahmān's daughter Śekh Hāsinā Uẏājed (Shaykha Ḥasīna Wājid; b. 1947) and her AL, while, at another, it preferred the BJD-dominated alliances led by Khāledā Ziẏā. The fate of the JiI-B rested with the latter—hence it suffered a serious setback in the 1996 parliamentary elections, while returning to power in 2001, now under its new *amīr* Matiur Rahmān Nizāmī.[296]

Ideologically, however, there was little movement within the JiI-B. Its statute of 2008 shows little difference from that of the JiI-P in terms of objectives and strategies.[297] Mawdūdī's ideological writings maintained canonical status and especially his *Tafhīm al-qur'ān* appears to serve JiI-B activists as central to their understanding of the Qur'ānic revelation and its societal implications.[298] Obviously, too much of the organisation's time and resources were consumed by its involvement in *Realpolitik* to enable it to process the challenges of reality into modifications of the ideology. The pragmatic departure from Mawdūdī's rather uncompromising views on the role of women from the late 1930s owed mainly to the increasing competition for the votes of especially economically deprived women among the various political parties in Bangladesh in the late 1990s,[299] might well be seen in this light. As interesting as the attempts by leading male JiI-B cadres to theoretically substantiate the careful empowerment of women might be, they posed no dramatic challenges to the JiI's overall ideology. Rather they only smoothed the somewhat misogynic edges of Mawdūdī's earlier expositions by emphasising the importance of women within the Muslim community,[300] and thus generated sympathies among non-JiI-B women for their cause, without actually discussing their role in, and possibilities of contributing to, the eventual Islamic state.[301] The fact that so far all the JiI-B parliamentarians, as well as the party's officials, had always exclusively been men, suggests that women are still deprived of their participation in the *khilāfat allāh*, a fact that is unlikely to be changed once the Islamic state had been realised.

2.4) *Khilāfa* at War: The *Jamāʿat-i islāmī* in Kashmir and Sri Lanka

When, in mid-August 1947, India and Pakistan parted ways, one of the areas that remained with an undecided status was the Princely State of Jammu and Kashmir, for the last century under the rule of the Ḍogrā Hindu *rājas* of Jammu.[302] The problem over its future arose in the first place from the state's particular religious composition. While the Kashmir valley and the tribal areas in the northwest were almost exclusively inhabited by Muslims, the southern region of Jammu and the eastern region of Ladakh were predominantly Hindu and Buddhist, respectively. Consequently, in the fierce competition over the accession of the various areas in British India to either India or Pakistan prior to Partition, Nehrū—himself a Kashmiri—and Jinnāḥ, as the driving forces behind both options, worked hard to get a majority of community leaders on their respective sides and, thus, to justify their vision of the political future of the princely state.[303] Communal tension since the early 1930s, considerably fuelled by the last Ḍogrā *mahārāja* Hari Siṃgh (d. 1961), added its share to the situation on the eve of Partition.[304] It was in this climate that the idea of a distinct Kashmiri culture, 'kashmīriyyat', was evoked prominently by Shaykh Muḥammad ʿAbdallāh (d. 1402/1982) and his *All-Jammu and Kashmir Muslim Conference* (AJKMC), founded in August 1932, to suggest independence from India as well as Pakistan as the most viable political alternative.[305]

Among Kashmiri Muslims, the divide appears to have run—and, to an extent, still runs today—between the advocates of a more culturalist and those of a more universalist viewpoint. Among the latter were the representatives of the various nineteenth-and early twentieth-century Muslim reformist movements in the valley, first and foremost the *Ahl-i ḥadīth*,[306] the *Majlis-i aḥrār-i islām*[307] and not least also the JiI, which, although very small, was nonetheless formally present in the region from 1942 under the leadership of the local secondary school teacher Saʿd al-Dīn Tarabālī (b. unknown).[308] In April 1945, Tarabālī and three of his associates met

Mawdūdī during the first All-Indian *ijtimāʿ* at the *Idāra-yi dār al-islām* in Pat'hānkot', where they were heartily accepted into the ranks of the *arkān*.[309] Before Partition, however, when the 'Kashmir problem' crystallised, Mawdūdī apparently had neither a specific interest in, nor distinct directives for, the region. Even after Partition, when the political status of Kashmir remained undecided and Pakistan unofficially supported an invasion by mainly Pashtun tribals, the region was relevant to Mawdūdī only in terms of his views on the Islamicity of Pakistan. Consistent with classical Islamic law, Mawdūdī made publicly clear that it would have been the duty of an Islamic ruler to *officially* declare an offensive *jihād* (*jihād al-ṭalab wa'l-ibtidāʾ*), but the covert operation that actually occurred had, in his eyes, to be regarded as illegitimate.[310] When Pakistan finally went openly to war with India over Kashmir in late October 1947, Mawdūdī very much welcomed it, while tacitly embracing the few members of the JiI from those parts of Kashmir annexed by Pakistan during this First Indo-Pakistani War into the fold of the JiI-P.

Meanwhile, the Srinagar-based cell of the JiI came under the supervision of the JiI-H, although here, too, it does not seem from the official literature that the Kashmir issue was a major concern for its leadership. However, the quite different framework of political conditions in Kashmir, mainly its still undecided political status, the massive presence of Indian forces and the communal tensions to a degree that was then unparalleled in the rest of India, caused the *Majlis-i shūrá* of the JiI-H in spring 1953 to allow its Kashmiri cell (*ḥalqa*) to form its own independent organisation, at least for the time being.[311] By comparison, its pendant in the Pakistan-held part of Kashmir, the *Jamāʿat-i islāmī Āzād Jammūṇ wa Kashmīr* (JiI-AJ&K), remained for most of the time subordinate to the JiI-P, despite the fact that the state—then separated from the socalled 'Northern Areas'—was granted constitutional autonomy status in 1970.[312] Only in 1983 was it allowed a statute of its own, which, although on the whole it repeats the statute of the JiI-P verbatim, contains an addition to the commentary on article 4 (objectives) that states that:

> [t]he second objective [*maqṣad*] of the JiI-AJ&K is the [successful] conclusion of the liberation movement for Kashmir. For this, and in the light of the geographical setting, as well as the ideological affinities [*naẓarīyātī taʿalluq*], the predominant Muslim majority of the state [*riyāsat*] shall accede the whole state to the Islamic Republic of Pakistan.[313]

This pro-Pakistani attitude of the JiI-AJ&K, which ran somewhat contrary to Mawdūdī's earlier critical views on the ideological foundation of the state, was far from being unprecedented. Indeed, the JiI had been at the forefront of those who had advocated Kashmir's accession to Pakistan even before Partition. Material to elucidate this serious early deviation from the JiI's ideology is scarce, but it may perhaps be explained as a reaction to the culturalistic agenda put forth successfully by Shaykh ʿAbdallāh's and his *Jammu and Kashmir National Conference* (JKNC), in which the AJKMC had been transformed in June 1938, and its open leanings towards Nehrū-advocated secularism.[314]

When the autonomous JiI-J&K was established in 1953, the situation had gained momentum. The Indo-Pakistani War of 1947–48 had brought the 'Kashmir issue' onto the international stage and resulted in the adoption of Resolution 47 by the Security Council of the United Nations that ordered a plebiscite over the political future of Kashmir held at an unspecified point in time and under the auspices of the UN. Nehrū had relented by having the Indian Constitution modified to such an extent that in 1952 Shaykh ʿAbdallāh's JKNC had openly declared its sympathies for a state that acknowledged Kashmir's special status pending the plebiscite.[315] Very soon, however, it became clear that New Delhi considered Article 370, which granted Kashmir its special status within the Indian Union, to be only a means to the subtle incorporation of the state. Consequently, the following decades saw a constant tug of war between the respective Indian and Kashmiri aspirations, resulting in an oscillation between repressive measures by the Indian authorities and a series of accords between the INC and JKNC.[316] The one conducted between Shaykh ʿAbdallāh's son Fārūq ʿAbdallāh (b. 1356/1937) and Rājīv Gāndhī (assassinated 1991) in 1986 was the prelude to the very straw that finally broke the camel's back. The secular electoral alliance of the two parties forced any political alternative to be religiously biased.

The meanwhile numerically grown JiI-J&K, which had so far concentrated its efforts mainly in the field of education and which so far had only meagre success in its parliamentary participation,[317] sensed that its time had come after all. Together with various other small Muslim religio-political parties and movements, it formed the *Muslim Muttaḥida Maḥādh* (MMM) which stood in the 1987 State Assembly elections.[318] When it one only four seats, suspicion spread almost immediately that the elections had been massively rigged. Following the mass protests, all four MMM members of the State Assembly publicly resigned in August 1989[319] and the representative of the JiI-J&K, Sayyid ʿAlī Shāh Gīlānī (b. 1348/1929), at that time its *amīr* and widely considered to be the JiI-J&K's chief ideologue—which was why he had repeatedly been imprisoned since the early 1960s by the Indian authorities—considered publicly for the first time the possibility of a defensive *jihād*.[320]

However, before these thoughts could actually be put into practice, another group got there first. On 31 July 1988 the *Jammu and Kashmir Liberation Front* (JKLF), which, with its co-founding figure Maqbūl Bhat' (executed 1404/1984), already had a martyr to show, successfully inaugurated the militant insurgency with two bomb blasts in central Srinagar.[321] While the JiI-J&K joined the insurrection against what was seen as Indian occupation with its own militant outfit *Ḥizb al-mujāhidīn* (ḤM) in 1991, it had actually to fight on two fronts. While the first was clearly against Indian hegemony, the second was directed against all those forces in the liberation movement that upheld the banner of 'kashmīriyyat' and advocated political independence from either India or Pakistan. The efforts of Gīlānī, who had once again been detained in 1990 under the Public Safety Act, were thus directed first and foremost towards dismantling this culturalistic ideology and, in a second step, to justify the JiI-J&K's fervent advocacy of accession to Pakistan.

For the first task, Gīlānī argued within the standard universalistic framework of the JiI. He affirmed the JiI's universal quest for the 'establishment of religion' (*iqāmat-i dīn*) that emanated from the idea of the unity of humankind as creation of the One God.[322] If this idea holds true, then there can be only one single truth, which needs to be unearthed by its most fervent advocate, the JiI. Consequently, the JiI:

> is not a communalist, patriotic [*waṭan-parast*], nationalist, selfish or particularistic [*mafād-parast*] organisation, but rather an organisation of universal nature [*'ālamgīr ḥaythiyyat kī tanẓīm*], which transgresses all those established boundaries and extends its invitation to all servants of God, the One and Peerless.[323]

This universalistic notion of the JiI-J&K's agenda, however, became somewhat obscured by Gīlānī's unconditional acknowledgement of the Two-Nation Theory, which goodwill may be read exclusively as an echo of Mawdūdī dichotomy of 'Islam' and 'jāhiliyya',[324] but which, especially in the light of Gīlānī's advocacy of Pakistan, also tastes like an appropriation of the AIML's notion into the ideological framework of the JiI-J&K. Without explicitly referring to Hindus, Gīlānī's relating of this discourse to the actual precarious situation of Muslims in Kashmir, and his emphasis that by fair means Kashmir would have become a part of Pakistan by right in 1947, suggest that he was not entirely opposed to the culturalistic nationalism of Iqbāl and Jinnāḥ. Unlike them, however, Gīlānī followed Mawdūdī suit in seeing the real threat to a distinct Muslim identity in 'secularism' and 'communism'. It was, he thought, the adherence of Muslims to these two irreligious political ideologies that would weaken them in their struggle against the Indian occupation.[325] With this line of argument, Gīlānī implicitly lashed out against the likes of the JKNC and JKLF, the advocates of 'kashmīriyyat' as the local version of secularism and, subsequently, of Kashmiri independence based upon this ideological construct.

The agitation against the romantic notion of a tolerant and acculturalistic Sufi version of Islam, mainly associated with the so-called Rishīs,[326] was by no means a novelty in the activities of the JiI-J&K. Already its first *amīr*, Saʿd al-Dīn Tarabālī, argued strongly against the widespread popular customs in the valley, which were associated with *shirk*, and referred to the sober variety of Sufism brought there in the fourteenth century CE by Mīr Sayyid ʿAlī ibn Shihāb al-Dīn Hamadānī (d. 786/1385) of the Kubrāwī Sufi order.[327] Gīlānī, too, adhered to the notion that it is possible for Sufism not to conflict with the observance of the *sharīʿa*.[328]

One of the requirements of the *sharīʿa*, which he evoked in light of the situation in Kashmir in the early 1990s, where 'the Islamic places of worship [*shaʿāʾir-i islām*] are disgraced and the religious values are trampled upon',[329] was the collective duty (*farḍ*) for armed *jihād*. Consequently, he argued, those Muslims who did not follow the call shall receive divine punishment (*ʿadhāb-i ilāhī*).[330] There is an implicit threat in this, as the *jihād* Gīlānī called for while he was imprisoned in an Indian jail was not only directed against the oppression by the Indian government, but also against what was seen as deviation from proper and scripture-based Islam, that is to say, against all those Muslim groups in the Valley that shared neither the JiI-J&K's vision of Islam nor its political agenda.

Highly instrumental in this endeavour was the ḤM as the armed wing of the JiI-J&K,[331] founded in April 1990 by schoolteacher 'Master' Muḥammad Aḥsan D'ār (b. 1379/1960) and led by the JiI-J&K-member Sayyid Muḥammad Yūsuf Shāh, better know by his *nom de guerre* 'Sayyid Ṣalāḥ al-Dīn' (b. 1365/1946). Their first major attack was the assassination of the *Mīr Wāʿiẓ-i Kashmīr* Muḥammad Fārūq, holder of the hereditary highest religious office in the Valley, on 21 May 1990, on the allegation that he had negotiated with the enemy.[332] More than the JKLF, for instance, the ḤM could utilise the over four decades-old organisational network of the JiI-P and JiI-AJ&K, which eventually helped it to marginalise the JKLF as the leader of the insurgency. Logistics were provided on the Pakistani side of the border, the Pakistani Inter-Service Intelligence (ISI) acting as the conduit and linking

Pakistan's involvement in the Afghan resistance to the Soviet military invasion since 1980 to the support of those militant groups in Kashmir who aimed at the accession to Pakistan.[333] Also helpful in this context was that since 1987 the JiI-P was led by Qāḍī Ḥusayn Aḥmad (b. 1357/1938), a Pashtun from Pakistan's then North-West Frontier Province, who had good personal links to the Pakistani tribal areas and into Afghanistan.[334] The ideological justification for the ḤM's advocacy of Pakistan, however, was provided once more by Gīlānī.

Pakistan, he stated, was an ideological state (*naẓariyātī mamlakat*), indicated by the attribute 'Islamic' in its official designation, and as such quite in keeping with the JiI's understanding of statehood. The best proof for this, so he argued, was the 'Objectives Resolution' of 1949, which by then had found its way into the Pakistani Constitution and which, to Gīlānī, indicated that 'the state of Pakistan had [indeed] returned with determination towards the spirit of the Islamic system [*ruḥ-i islāmī niẓām kī ṭaraf*]'.[335] Because the Muslims of Kashmir were part of the global Muslim ecumene, it would run 'counter to the social and even wider definition [*ijtimāʿī awr wasīʿtar mafād*] of "Islamic community" [*millat-i islāmiyya*], whose sole societal foundation is the Islamic creed [*kalima-yi ṭayyiba*]', to strive for its separation, 'least so when they share ideological, cultural and communal relations with some Muslim state, as well as a common border'.[336] Besides, he continued his argument, Pakistan had spent massive material and spiritual resources in its support of its Kashmiri brethren for over forty years—an argument that may sympathetically be read as yet more proof of the Islamicity of Pakistan, but could also be interpreted as a hint that the Kashmiris would somewhat owe their brethren from across the border.[337] Taking together these and other arguments by Gīlānī, there would be no other acceptable way than Kashmir's accession to Pakistan, which is why, in January 1993, Gīlānī assured the then Prime Minister of Pakistan Muḥammad Nawāz Sharīf in a lengthy letter of the unfettered loyalty of the JiI-J&K and ḤM, stressing that they would both work, with their respective means, for Kashmīr's accession to Pakistan.[338]

The Pakistani authorities responded positively to such a commitment and extended special logistic and ideological support to the ḤM and JiI-J&K. With such substantial aid the ḤM was soon able to oust the JKLF from its leading position among the various militant outfits active in the Kashmir Valley. Unfortunately, however, with the ḤM establishing itself at the helm of the pro-Pakistan militants in the Kashmir Valley, training its cadres in various camps in Pakistan, Afghanistan and Azad Kashmir,[339] we are entering a grey area, which can only be slightly illuminated by textual studies alone. Neither can it be clearly established whether and, if so, to what extent the JiI-P or the JiI-J&K had an impact on the command structure of the ḤM—which resembled the organisation of the JiI[340]—nor from where and how the ḤM recruited its cadre,[341] and with which other militant organisations it collaborated in the Valley and beyond. However, the albeit scarce evidence that exists on links with the Afghan *Ḥizb-i islāmī* of Gulbuddīn Ḥikmatyār (b. 1366/1947) and the *Ittiḥād al-islāmī* of ʿAbd al-Rabb-i Rasūl Sayyāf (b. 1365/1946)[342] suggests that the JiI-backed militants of Kashmir had soon become part of a transnational network of militant Islamist groups and individuals. Moreover, it casts some light on the shadier areas, in which the JiI-P was active beyond its open involvement in party politics and the parliamentary process in Pakistan.

The official position that, on the contrary, the JiI-H had taken on what it referred to only as the 'Kashmir problem' (*masʾala-yi Kashmīr*) shows how far the two largest national branches of the JiI had grown apart since 1948. In the official resolutions issued by the *Majlis-i shūrá* under its *amīr* Muḥammad Sirāj al-Ḥasan since May 1990 it expressed its great concern about the serious situation in the Kashmir Valley, but, unlike its counterparts in Pakistan and in Kashmir itself, it did not support the militant insurgency as the only remaining alternative. Instead, it regretted the spiral of violence—explicitly referring to the assassination of the *Mīr Wāʿiẓ-i Kashmīr* Muḥammad Fārūq—urging the Kashmiris to show patience and endurance (*ṣabr wa taḥmīl*), while appealing to the Indian government to end its repressive and arbitrary politics towards Kashmiri civilians, and to restore human rights and democracy in the Valley by calling for fresh and fair elections. At the same time, however, they also implicitly called upon the Pakistani government for non-interference and acceptance of the right of the Kashmiris to self-determination.[343]

* * *

Meanwhile, the situation in Sri Lanka, despite being rocked by civil war between 1983 and 2009, differed considerably from the one in Kashmir as well as from Pakistan and Bangladesh.[344] After all, Muslims in the island state constituted a significant but nonetheless small minority of about 8 per cent of the total population, settled mainly in harbour towns along the eastern and western coast, including the capital Colombo, and in and around Kandy (*Kaṇṭi*) in today's Central Province.[345] Unlike the majority of Muslims on the South Asian mainland, those in Sri Lanka, commonly labelled 'Moors', originate mainly from Arab Ḥaḍrāmī merchants who settled on the island from the eighth century CE onwards. Moreover, in terms of cultural proximity they appear to be closer to the Malay archipelago than to Northern India, a fact that is underlined by the adherence to the Shāfiʿite school of *fiqh* instead of the Ḥanafiyya.[346] This said, the Sri Lankan Muslims belong to a distinct cultural and also linguistic environment that proved in the past to be a rather serious barrier to the influx of ideas from the north, and it is therefore rather surprising that the JiI found its way here in 1947. It was a certain Jeylānī Cāypu (Jīlānī Ṣāḥib; d. 1401/1980) from Kāyalpaṭṭinam in Tamilnadu in south India who is said to have by then established personal contact with Mawdūdī.[347] Indeed, the reports of the annual gathering of the JiI in 1947 stated that two Tamil-speaking workers (*kārkun*) were in charge of the translation of some of Mawdūdī's works into Tamil. It is, however, somewhat revealing that the selection of texts for translation included prominently the *Khuṭbāt*, Mawdūdī's collected speeches to Punjabi villagers on Islamic basics.[348] It suggests that, with something almost similar to the attitude towards East Pakistan-*cum*-Bangladesh, the Urdu-centric leadership of the JiI felt the need to instruct the South Indian Muslims even on the essentials of their religion.

Jeylānī Cāypu is said to have moved to Sri Lanka, where he worked as the JiI representative until, in 1954, he officially established the Sri Lankan branch of the JiI (JiI-SL).[349] His relocation to Sri Lanka was not really exceptional for, after all, the common descent from Arab merchants with Shāfiʿite affiliations had helped the extremely status-conscious Marakkāyar Muslims of southern Tamilnadu to maintain close links with their brethren and sisters in Sri Lanka and even beyond throughout the centuries.[350] By the time of Jeylānī Cāypu's arrival on the island the tension between the major linguistic and religious groups in Sri Lanka, the roots of which were to be found in the increasingly ethno-centric anti-colonial movement, had considerably heightened. Even the introduction of universal suffrage by the British colonial administration could not prevent the political advocates of the Tamil speakers feeling somewhat uneasy with their eventual proportional representation in the various political institutions. When, following independence in 1948, Sri Lanka's first prime minister, the Sinhalese community leader Ḍon Stēpan (Don Stephen) Sēnānāyakā (d. 1952), had the country finally converted into a majoritarian state by denying the mainly Tamil-speaking subjects of Indian origin the right to claim Sri Lankan citizenship, he gave way to the rise of Tamil ethno-nationalism that was eventually to turn into a civil war.[351]

While this ethnic conflict was gaining momentum, the Sri Lankan Muslims, the vast majority of whom were Tamil-speakers, were forced to assert themselves, thereby creating the roots of what Dennis McGilvray appropriately labels 'Moorish political identity'. Unlike the Sinhalese and the non-Muslim Tamils, the 'Moors' based their identity clearly on religion and had thus been able to transgress the linguistic confines by including also a small number of Sinhalese and Malay Muslims.[352] Moreover, their religion-based ethnicity, which made them the third largest ethnic group in Sri Lanka—shown in the inclusion of a green band in the national flag—gave them the opportunity to politically ally themselves with either linguistic group. On the other hand, however, this also created the strong potential to estrange them from their fellow Tamil-speakers and, thus, placed them between the lines of Sinhala and Tamil ethno-nationalists, the latter increasingly represented by the *Liberation Tigers of Tamil Eelam* (*Tamiḻīḻa Viṭutalaip Pulikaḷ*; LTTE), officially founded in 1976.

The catalyst for the development of such a predominantly religion-based ethnicity were the activities of the Egyptian Aḥmad ʿUrābī Pāshā, leader of the 1881–82 anti-colonial uprising in Egypt—the so-called 'ʿUrābī Revolution'—who, after its failure had been exiled in 1883 by the British administration of Egypt to what was then called Ceylon. During his nineteen years of exile ʿUrābī gave a considerable impetus to the reformation of Muslim education and was instrumental in reminding the Sri Lankan 'Moors' of their extra-territorial roots.[353] The JiI-SL actively participated in this process of cultural self-assurance of the Sri Lankan Muslims by applying various universalistic categories of Mawdūdī's ideology and, in this way, helped to broaden the gap between them and their fellow Tamil-speakers even further. In the beginning, the JiI-SL activists devoted much of its energy to 'correcting' the prevalent understanding of Islam, mainly in study circles and by producing and distributing various periodicals: in the 1950s, Jeylānī Cāypu edited the Tamil journal *Aruḷ Jōti*, which, in March 1970, was replaced by *Alhasaṇāt* and its Sinhalese pendant *Prabōḍaya*.[354] The fact that the JiI-SL also tried to reach the literate Sinhalese population indicated its opposition to a language-based ethnicity, very much in correspondence with Mawdūdī's rejection of any kind of nationalism that was based, among other things, on a common language.[355] Such an openness to both of the major conflicting ethnonationalist parties, which was by no means exclusive to the JiI-SL, made the Sri Lankan Muslims most vulnerable to all kinds of threats especially from the largest ethnic minority in the island state, that is the non-Muslim Tamil speakers. With the outbreak of the

LTTE-led Tamil insurgency in 1983, which soon morphed into a civil war, Muslims came under severe threat from their fellow Tamil speakers.

Surprisingly, while a section of the Muslim intelligentsia reacted to the heightened tension by establishing the *Sri Lanka Muslim Congress* (SLMC) in 1981 under the leadership of the influential lawyer Mūkammatu Ucaiṇ Mūkammatu Aṣrap (Muḥammad Ḥusayn Muḥammad Ashraf; d. 1421/2000),[356] the JiI-SL apparently did not contribute to the Sri Lankan Muslims' quest for political representation. There might however be systematic reasons for this. Other than nationalistically inclined Muslim intellectuals like Aṣrap, the JiI-SL leadership felt that Muslims had a much better chance to overcome their precarious situation if they became unified on doctrinal grounds. As they were weakened as a community by serious factionalism, rooted in economic disparities between East Coast and West Coast 'Moors', adherence to various local popular religious beliefs and practices, as well as deeply ingrained clientelism, the LTTE had an easy job with cleansing the territories under its control from the Muslim population, as happened on the Jaffna peninsula in Northern Sri Lanka in June 1990.[357] Even under war conditions, the JiI-SL saw therefore its prime task in the field of education and community relief.[358] Here, they were always competing with other more recent reformist movements in Sri Lanka, such as the *Taplīk Jamāt* (TJ), active there since 1953, and the strongly Saudi Arabia-influenced and -supported *Tavhīt Jamāt* (*Jamāʿat al-Tawḥīd*), already established in 1947.[359]

Instrumental in countering the latter, which had a considerable impact on the university campuses, was, and is, the JiI-SL's student wing, the *Ṣrīlaṅkā Islāmiya Māṇavar Iyakkar* (*Sri Lanka Islamic Student Movement*), established in Colombo in 1980. In lobbying among the wider Muslim population, however, the charitable activities of the JiI-SL were, and are, crucial. After the disastrous tsunami tidal wave in December 2004, for example, which affected first and foremost the strongly Muslim-populated Eastern Province, the JiI-SL was one of the first non-governmental organisations in the island state to engage in relief and rehabilitation programmes.[360] In spring 2009, almost immediately after the military defeat of the LTTE by government forces,[361] the JiI-SL was one of the first Muslim organisations in Sri Lanka that not only demanded government action for the resettlement of those Muslims who had been expelled from the Northern Province by the LTTE in 1990, but also recognised the need for civil initiatives.[362]

To form a counterweight to the government's course of continuing ethnic polarisation, the JiI-SL gave itself a decidedly integrative profile, which was somewhat reminiscent of the JiI-H's staunch advocacy of secularism. Indeed, it seemed as if the JiI-SL, like its larger sister organisation in India, accepted that given the minority status of Muslims in Sri Lanka and, in addition, the complex ethnopolitical situation in the island state, no idealistic religious-political agenda could reasonably be pursued. Therefore, apart from its study circles, set mainly in the urban middle-class milieu and aiming at the preservation of a distinct cultural identity, and the various internal congregations—called 'camp' (*muʿaskar*) here rather than 'gathering' (*ijtimāʿ*)—the JiI-SL, strongly resembling the JiI-H on this point, apparently kept its ideological orientation rather in the background. Such a similarity, in turn, coupled with the claim for the universal validity of Mawdūdī's ideology, and the potential for transregional co-operation of its advocates rooted herein, would suggest close co-operation at least between these two national organisations. Surprisingly, however, this appears not to be the case. The JiI-SL appeared to have, at least for most of the time, hardly been on the radar of its larger sister organisations, whether in India, in Pakistan or elsewhere.

The JiI-P appears to have not even acknowledged the existence of the JiI in Sri Lanka, at least as far as appears from the published reports of the annual *ijtimāʿāt.*[363] The interest of the JiI-H meanwhile for a long time did not stretch beyond the Indian borders—its Tamil members were incorporated into the Madras cell that also included Mysore in predominantly Kannaḍa-speaking Karnataka.[364] Even after the outbreak of civil war in Sri Lanka and the militant activities of the LTTE spilling over into India, culminating in the assassination of Prime Minister Rājīv Gāndhī during an election campaign in Madras in May 1991, the resolutions issued by the *Majlis-i shūrá* of the JiI-H in this regard suggested only a general concern over developments in the island state, but none in particular over the situation of the Sri Lankan Muslims or the JiI-SL.[365]

Such an indifference towards the JiI-SL by its larger sister organisations up north demands some explanation, which, given the almost complete absence of any academic research into the JiI-SL, can, of course, only be hypothetical and tentative. At first sight, one is tempted to assume that the language barrier between all the various national branches of the JiI was too high to be overcome, an argument, however, which is easily invalidated by the fact that the JiI-B operates in a very distinct language as well. It seems much more as if the indifference towards the Sri Lankan branch of the JiI was nothing extraordinary as all national branches followed very specific agendas, resulting from the socio-political particularities in the respective countries. Mawdūdī's original ideology, enshrined in his early writings, became increasingly less of a point of reference beyond the mere symbolic. In this way, the rather abstract notion of 'establishment of the religion' (*iqāmat-i dīn*), the ultimate objective of all the various national branches of the JiI and, thus, their somewhat smallest common denominator—was filled with considerably different meanings, which somehow forestalled a transnational discussion of aims and strategies. The indifference of the other national branches towards the JiI-SL may therefore be seen in this very light. The JiI-SL itself appeared to be equally little concerned with its sister organisations and focused its entire attention on the Sri Lankan situation. This appears to have changed only recently, when the JiI-SL utilised the network of Islamist organisations in their humanitarian activities in the aftermath of the 2004 tsunami. Its current *amīr*, Raṣīt Hajjul Akpar (Rashīd Ḥajj al-Akbar; b. 1380/1960), met with various representatives of the JiI branches of Pakistan and elsewhere and secured their mainly material and financial support of the JiI-SL's relief work.[366] It might well be that it is not least because of this efficient transnational network that the JiI-SL stands out from other Sri Lankan NGOs while, at the same time, it may also be an expression of the continuous competition with other Muslim revivalist groups and movements in Sri Lanka, first and foremost with the TJ. While its piety-oriented and Sufism-inspired understanding of Islam had gained the TJ a much larger following in Sri Lanka than the JiI, its reluctance to activate its resources—the TJ is after all one of the best-organised Muslim religious grassroots movements—[367] for humanitarian aid[368] had most certainly worked to the advantage of the JiI.

6

CONCLUSION

September 2011 marked a full decade since the fatal attacks of *al-Qāʿida* activists on the World Trade Center in New York and the Pentagon in Washington, DC brought Islamism to the forefront of public awareness around the globe. Suddenly, even people who had hardly been touched by anything Islam-related would by now have heard of Sayyid Quṭb, whom the massive and ongoing media coverage usually portrays as the intellectual force behind militant Islamists around the globe. Mawdūdī, on the other hand, receives almost no mention, and where he does receive some, he appears only as a somewhat remote progenitor of Islamism, whose scope of impact is mainly confined to the Indian subcontinent. This, as the present study has shown, hardly does credit to the impact that Mawdūdī has actually had on the development of Islamist thought in general. His influence was clearly discernible when, in as late as August 2003, Ayman al-Ẓawāhirī, in his *Iʿzāz rāyat al-islām*, declared that:

> the *jāhiliyya* is not a historical condition, but rather a condition [*ḥāla*] that occurs whenever its constituents [*muqawwimātuhā*] appear in the open or below the surface [*fī waḍʿ aw niẓām*]. In its core [*fī ṣamīmihā*] it is the orientation in rule and legislation towards the interests [*ahwāʾ*] of man, not towards the path of God [*manhaj allāh*] and His *sharīʿa* for one's life. And these interests can be the interests of an individual, the interest of a class, the interest of a community, or the interests of a perfect generation [*jīl kāmil*] among the people ... What they all have in common is that they do not orient themselves towards God's *sharīʿa* [but towards] interests.[1]

This passage clearly showed that concepts coined by Mawdūdī and gratefully embraced by thinkers like Sayyid Quṭb were still very efficacious, even without an explicit recourse to its originator. This holds not only true for the radical and militant Islamists, but for the moderates, too. For instance, the widely respected, now Qatar-based Egyptian *ʿālim* Yūsuf al-Qaraḍāwī (b. 1338/1921), a formerly radical Muslim Brother and now one of the figureheads of the so-called 'Moderation Movement' (*ḥarakat al-wasaṭiyya*),[2] used the Mawdūdian concept of 'jāhiliyya' frequently and apparently without any pain, in his writings from as recently as 2007.[3] That today Mawdūdī, and, in cases also Sayyid Quṭb, does not need to be mentioned anymore by those who freely employ their terms and concepts is not really exceptional. Concepts that initially have a clearly defined place within particular philosophical outlines, including those of an ideological character, become quite commonly detached from their original frameworks while they are absorbed into the common language and appropriated by other ideologies. Thus, for example, we find frequent mention of the 'invisible hand', initially a core idea in Adam Smith's political economy, or of the 'survival of the fittest', a phrase coined by Herbert Spencer that became similarly crucial in Darwin's theory of biological evolution, without any reference to either its originators or the initial framework into which these terms belong.[4] Meanwhile, the originally Marxist concept of 'exploitation' has made it into the vocabulary of feminism and antiracism.[5] We may therefore well assume that some of Mawdūdī's concepts, prominently among them 'jāhiliyya' and 'ḥākimiyya', have over time become common knowledge, which is why it is not deemed necessary either to mention him as the one who introduced these particular notions, or to recall the place and functions that these concepts held within his entire outline.

In those cases where he is nonetheless referred to, reference is overwhelmingly to various single concepts, detached from their actual location within Mawdūdī's systematic framework. A reason for this may be found in the strained relationship of theory and practice, and reflects indeed an inherent problem of any theory-building. A theory, and this certainly includes political ideologies too, is usually put to the test in practice, and it is then that an almost indefinite number of marginal, or 'initial' conditions come into play that need to be accommodated in the course of refinement of this theory.[6] This process of continuous revision of a theory, especially one that claims universal validity, bears admittedly the dangers of eroding the systematics of the theory and shrinking the scope of its application to such an extent that little but hollow phrases will remain.

This, however, need not necessarily be a negative thing. Because of their high level of abstraction, these concepts could then be filled with various meaning while at the same time offering the chance to claim adherence to the universalistic principles of the initial ideology. This is what happened to the big categories of Marxism-*cum*-Communism, such as 'class struggle', 'means of production', 'productive forces' and so on, and this is what happened also to core categories of Mawdūdī's Islamist ideology. The appropriation of these categories by Sayyid Quṭb provides clear evidence for this. While Quṭb did certainly not adopt Mawdūdī's whole systematic outline, including the various patterns of argument, he nonetheless took over various of Mawdūdī's core ideas. These ideas, in turn, were sharpened in the social and political reality of Egypt in the 1950s and early 1960s and, in this way, became prone to an increasing restriction to the triad of *jāhiliyya*, *takfīr* and *jihād* by Muslim radicals in the wake of Quṭb. Even then, Mawdūdī was still occasionally referred to, whether by the blind scholar ʿUmar ʿAbd al-Raḥmān or by theorists-*cum*-warriors like Sayyid Imām al-Sharīf.[7]

Anyway, because the emphases of today's militant Islamists had significantly shifted from those of Mawdūdī in the 1930s and early 1940s, these references could only be little more than just symbolic. A quite similar development can be observed in South Asia in the various attempts to put Mawdūdī's ideology into practice. Here, at any rate, the reason would rather have to be sought in the fact that his systematic outline was far too abstract to be possibly put into practice. Hence, even in Pakistan under the direct aegis of Mawdūdī, the ideology had to be considerably amended to make it practically viable, which became especially obvious in Muslim minority societies such as those in the Indian Republic or Sri Lanka, where the reference to Mawdūdī had indeed become almost entirely symbolic.

Such a fate, however, Mawdūdī seems to share with the masterminds of other ideologies. Just as the founding fathers of Communism—Marx, Engels, Lenin, Stalin, Máo Zédōng—was elevated in the 'really existing socialisms' of the Eastern bloc to such an extent that they remained otherwise empty shells, Mawdūdī was morphed into a mere icon, venerated for his important theoretical groundwork, but with only limited relevance for the actual realities of the JiI throughout the subcontinent.

This must not, however, lead us to diminish Mawdūdī's importance for the development of contemporary Muslim thought of whichever brand. His typological turn of the originally epochal term 'jāhiliyya' has become widely accepted by today's Muslims across the board, many of them perhaps not even aware of its origins and the important role that it had to play in Mawdūdī's systematic framework. Similarly, the understanding of Islam as an all-encompassing and self-sufficient system of life, which had not been clearly expressed prior to Mawdūdī, has made it into the subconscious of very many Muslims of various and even diametrically opposed traditions. In governance-oriented circles his emphasis on God's unlimited sovereignty (*ḥākimiyya*), in the late 1960s still heavily disputed by Ḥasan al-Huḍaybī and the like, has become increasingly appreciated as a core doctrine for Islamists around the globe.[8]

Now, while most of Mawdūdī's concepts have arguably survived rather in radical Islamism, it is certainly remarkable that his idea of democracy, rooted in his interpretation of *khilāfa* as God's bestowal of the believing man with limited sovereignty on earth, has found its correspondence in more moderate Islamist circles. The early Muslim Brother ʿAbd al-Qādir ʿAwda (d. 1374/1954), for example, argued very much along the same lines as Mawdūdī.[9] That Mawdūdī's ideas would feed even into opposing views within the Islamist spectrum is clear proof of the enormous richness of his ideological outline. Its systematics were most definitely the result of Mawdūdī's involvement with competing ideologies, very much benefited by the historical context in which he drew up most of his theoretical writings. In this, he clearly differed considerably from his epigones in the Arabic speaking world. For the early theorists of the JIM, for example, a thorough analysis of the philosophical foundations of Western political ideologies, after the Second World War mainly liberalism and Communism, had to be relegated to a back seat in favour of discussion of an Islamic alternative of societal development within the Islamic framework of reference.[10] Mawdūdī, however, appears to have been much more committed to contesting the quite successful Western political ideologies, which meant also investigating their respective philosophical foundations. After all, he argued:

> [t]he French Revolution [of 1789–99] had required the particular moral and intellectual foundations provided by leaders like Rousseau, Voltaire and Montesquieu. The Russian Revolution [of 1917] could only transpire because of the ideas of Marx, the leadership of Lenin and Trotskij, and by means of the many thousands of socialist activists [*ishtirākī kārkunoṇ hī kī bi-dawlat*], the life of whom had already been shaped by socialism. The National Socialism of Germany, in turn, could [only] take root in the very moral, psychological and cultural humus that was prepared by the conceptions [*naẓariyyāt*] of Hegel, Fichte, Goethe, Nietzsche and many other thinkers, and by the leadership of Hitler. In exactly the same manner the Islamic Revolution can only be brought about when a mass movement [*ʿumūmī taḥrīk*] is raised

on the basis of the Qur'ānic theories and concepts and the example and practice of Muḥammad that, with powerful effort, shall result in changing the entire intellectual, moral, psychological and cultural foundations of social life [*ijtimāʿī zindagī*]. It passes my understanding how any movement of a nationalistic kind, with its background of an imperfect educational system like the one prevalent among us, which is based on utilitarian morals and pragmatism [*ifādī akhlāqiyyat awr maṣlaḥat-parastī*], could ever bring about an Islamic Revolution![11]

Such an implicit acknowledgment of the need to investigate the intellectual roots of all other prevalent political ideologies in order to present a competitive counterdraft also had, as has been argued in the present study, a decisive impact on Mawdūdī's aim to project Islam in a similarly systematic way. Therefore, while Gudrun Krämer appears to be perfectly right when she states that such a creative process will appear as 'bricolage', her conclusion that this would not result in a 'coherent whole' seems a bit too harsh.[12] Although, as has been shown on occasion, Mawdūdī's outline included the odd fallacy, based much less on a possible inability to draw logically consistent conclusions than on the incompatibility of Mawdūdī's deductive methodology with the revealed contents as his benchmark, the building that he had set out to erect is perhaps as consistent as it gets. Moreover, that Mawdūdī's rather formalistic methodology, after all imperative for every modern attempt at theory-building, has not been followed up by posterity, even by those who have been and still are relying on his conceptions, may also be interpreted in his favour. After he had exerted so much effort to re-conceptualise Islam through the 'prism of Modernity', those who came after Mawdūdī have perhaps considered his groundwork sufficient enough for them to not reinvent the wheel, but to rather continue where Mawdūdī himself had stopped.

NOTES

1. INTRODUCTION

1. Muslim (1424/2004), 1435 (*Kitāb al-fitan wa-ashrāṭ al-sāʿa, bāb dhikr al-dajjāl wa-ṣifatihi wa-mā maʿahu*, Ḥadīth 5, no. 8259).
2. Qurʾān 75 (al-Qiyāma): 31–3.
3. See Arjomand (1988), pp. 71–4.
4. Schulze (2000), p. 199.
5. See Peskes (1993), pp. 242–9; for the early *Wahhābiyya* in general see Steinberg (2002).
6. See Hegghammer/Lacroix (2007), pp. 105f.
7. See Schulze (2000), pp. 229–33.
8. The references in the canonical *ḥadīth*-literature are manifold. See, for example, Abū Dāwūd (1983), IV: 106–9 (*Kitāb al-mahdī*, Aḥādīth 1–12, nos. 4279–90); Ibn Māja (1373/1954), II: 1366–8 (*Kitāb al-fitan, bāb khurūj al-mahdī*, Aḥādīth 1–7, nos. 4082–8); al-Tirmidhī (1938–58), IV: 505 (*Kitāb al-fitan, bāb mā jāʾ fīʾl-mahdī*, Aḥādīth 1f, nos. 2230f).
9. See Arjomand (1988), pp. 134–46. For Khumaynī's religious justification of his political agenda see Khumaynī (s.t.).
10. Schulze (2000), p. 225.
11. For the thoughts of Juhaymān al-ʿUtaybī, see the edition of his epistles by Aḥmad ([3]2004), esp. pp. 185–223. Mark also the parallels between al-ʿUtaybī's *Awthaq ʿará al-īmān*, which resembles to a large extent the work of the same name by Sulaymān ibn ʿAbdallāh Āl al-Shaykh (executed 1206/1818), the grandson of Muḥammad ibn ʿAbd al-Wahhāb. See Āl al-Shaykh (s.t.).
12. See Hegghammer/Lacroix (2007), pp. 112f.
13. See Schulze (2000), pp. 229–32.
14. See ʿAbd al-Raḥmān (s.t.), pp. 93 and 123. For a theoretical justification of Sādāt's assassination see Faraj (1981). Also, see below, Chapter E.1.2.a.
15. See Aḥmad (1988), pp. 104–21 and 161–4.
16. See, for example, McCutcheon (1999), pp. 1–10; Hartung (2002), pp. 143–7.
17. See, for example, Büttner (1996); Riesebrodt (2001); Ruthven (2004).
18. See Weber ([9]1988), pp. 1–16; Habermas ([5]1996), p. 9
19. See Luther (1995), I: pp. 239–63 (*Von der Freiheit eines Christenmenschen*; 1520).
20. See Habermas ([5]1996), pp. 26–33.
21. See idem ([11]1994), p. 71.

22. See Koselleck (1989), for example, pp. 25–34, 59–65 and 78; Habermas ([5]1996), pp. 22–6.
23. See ibid., pp. 104–29.
24. Freeden (1996), p. 7.
25. See Habermas ([11]1994), pp. 88–115.
26. See Hobsbawm (1975), pp. 43–63 and 294–305; idem (1992), pp. 207–17 and 285–97.
27. See idem (1975), pp. 64–87.
28. See Brown (1996), pp. 1–5. Brown, however, has used the term 'Modernity' with a small initial, which, to my understanding, refers less to a philosophical framework than more generally to the *zeitgeist* of a particular historical epoch, the beginning of which is usually attributed to the fundamental changes of the 1780s, brought about by what Eric Hobsbawm has labelled the 'dual revolution', that is, the Industrial Revolution and the French Revolution of 1789. See Hobsbawm (1992), p. 11. I have however decided to consider Modernity as the philosophical framework proposed by Jürgen Habermas ([5]1996), which conveniently also includes those reactions that have frequently been categorised as 'Postmodernity', hence my use of 'Modernity' with a capital initial.
29. His biography has comprehensively been discussed by Nasr (1996), pp. 9–46, and more recently, although not entirely flawlessly, by Jackson (2011), pp. 9–80. Therefore, in the present work only those parts of Mawdūdī's life have been investigated that actually triggered off his revivalist thought.
30. Brown (1996), p. 2.
31. See McCutcheon (1999), pp. 5f and 260–73 (Donald Wiebe: *Does Understanding Religion Require Religious Understanding?*).
32. See, for example, Hartung (2001), pp. 108–11; idem (2002), pp. 143 and 147f.
33. Brown (1996), p. 5.
34. See Popper (1935), pp. 4–6, 12–16 and especially 26–51; Stark/Bainbridge (1987), pp. 13–15.
35. See, for example, the various critiques on the attempt at a deductive general theory of religion by Rodney Stark and William S. Bainbridge (ibid., passim), e.g. Wallis/Bruce (1984), pp. 14–21.
36. See Freeden (1996), p. 5.

2. THE CONTEXT

1. A prominent case in point for this would be Nasr (1996), pp. 9–26, who, in his detailed study on Mawdūdī, has unfortunately not exercised enough source criticism when discussing Mawdūdī's biography.
2. See Būht'a ([3]1989), p. 23; Mawdūdī ([2]1990), p. 8.
3. Ibid.
4. See ibid., pp. 8–10. For Mawdūdī's paternal pedigree, see ibid., pp. 30–32. Mawdūdī gave 537/1142 (p. 9) and 527/1133 (p. 32) as Khʷāja Mawdūd's year of demise. The academic secondary literature, however, appears to agree on 577/1182.
5. See ibid., pp. 9f; also ʿAbd ([3]1988), p. 47. Ghālib's own letters corroborate this. See Ghālib (1951), pp. 119f (two rather intimate letters to Sālik, dated 1864), also pp. 75f, 80 and 90 (here, Sālik is favourably mentioned in letters to ʿAlāʾ al-Dīn Aḥmad Khān 'ʿAlāʾī' [d. 1301/1884]); also Ḥālī (1971), p. 116.
6. See, for example, Hartung (2004b), pp. 199–201.
7. See Wright Jr. (1999), pp. 654f; Jalal (2001), pp. 46, 58, 92f et passim.
8. Compare, for example, the emphasis of Abū 'l-Kalām 'Āzād' (d. 1377/1958), the later first Minister of Education of independent India and leading member of its Constituent Assembly, on his descent from prominent scholars and Sufis around Aḥmad Fārūqī Sirhindī (d. 1034/1624) in the late sixteenth century, and Shāh ʿAbd al-ʿAzīz Dihlawī (d. 1239/1824) in

the late eighteenth. See Douglas (1988), pp. 30–37. It seems that Āzād tried to compensate this way for his 'inferior' paternal pedigree.

9. See Mawdūdī ([2]1990), pp. 9, 15 and 31.
10. See ibid., p. 11. I was unable to find any corroborating evidence for this.
11. See ibid., p. 12.
12. Ibid., pp. 11f.
13. Reetz (1997), p. 9 (transl. JPH).
14. Ibid., p. 11 (transl. JPH).
15. See Samiuddin (2007), II: p. 535.
16. See, for example, Lelyveld (1978), pp. 102f, 120–4 and 217–20; Jalal (2001), pp. 61–8.
17. See Mawdūdī ([2]1990), p. 12.
18. See ibid., pp. 12f. The seventeenth Niẓām of Hyderabad, Mīr ʿUthmān ʿAlī Khān 'Āṣaf Jāh VII' (d. 1386/1967), happened to be one of the main sponsors of Aligarh's *Muhammadan Anglo-Oriental College* and he ensured the employment of its graduates in the administration of his state. See Pernau (1999), p. 2747. It appears very likely that Sayyid Aḥmad Ḥasan, too, benefited from this very arrangement.
19. Ibid., p. 14.
20. See below, Chapter C.1.1.b; also Nasr (1996), pp. 122–5.
21. Mawdūdī ([2]1990), p. 14.
22. See ibid., p. 20.
23. See ibid., pp. 16–20 and 23; Būhtʹa ([3]1989), pp. 20–22 (*Merā bachpan*; n.d.).
24. See, for example, Hartung (2009), pp. 235–41.
25. Mawdūdī ([2]1990), p. 23.
26. See Zakariyyā ([6]1983); Nuʿmānī (1998), pp. 79–144; Nadwī ([2]1400/1980).
27. See Mawdūdī ([2]1990), pp. 26f; ʿAbd ([3]1988), pp. 68f. There is, however, no proof that Mawdūdī had indeed translated either the important *al-Marʾa al-jadīda* (1901) by the influential Egyptian reformer Qāsim Amīn (d. 1326/1908), or substantial parts of the most challenging *al-Ḥikma al-mutaʿāliya fi'l-asfār al-ʿaqliyya al-arbaʿa* (completed around 1628) of Mullā Ṣadr al-Dīn al-Shīrāzī (d. 1045/1635). Interestingly enough, Mawdūdī precautionally pointed out that, 'God knows where the pages of this translation might be today.' (ibid., p. 27). Unfortunately, Nasr follows entirely Mawdūdī's self-portrayal and, for reasons not entirely clear, suggests even a considerable influence of Mullā Ṣadrā's philosophy on Mawdūdī's thought. See Nasr (1996), pp. 24f.
28. Mawdūdī ([2]1990), p. 28.
29. See Hartung (2004b), p. 299.
30. See Mawdūdī ([2]1990), pp. 17f.
31. Ibid., p. 21.
32. Ibid. Later hagiographies, like the one by Chawdharī ʿAbd al-Raḥmān 'ʿAbd', went even as far as crediting Mawdūdī with the translation of two books from English into Urdu as early as 1920. See ʿAbd ([3]1988), p. 65.
33. See Mawdūdī ([2]1990), pp. 20 and 28.
34. See, for example, Qureshi (1999), p. 29; also below, Chapter B.2.
35. Mawdūdī ([2]1990), p. 20. The scope of the political impact of that association would eventually need to be assessed by a close scrutiny of the relevant security files of the British colonial administration, kept in various Indian archives.
36. See below, Chapter B.2.4.
37. See Mawdūdī ([2]1990), pp. 21–3; also ʿAbd ([3]1988), pp. 64f.
38. See Minault (1982), p. 124.
39. For Kifāyatallāh, see Riḍwī (1992–3), II: pp. 79–81; Qureshi (1999), p. 470. For Aḥmad Saʿīd not sufficient biographical information could be found. On their political role in the

Caliphate Movement, see Minault (1982), pp. 60f, 79–82, 103, 171 et passim; Qureshi (1999), pp. 131f et passim.

40. See Mawdūdī (²1990), pp. 23f; also ʿAbd (³1988), pp. 65f.
41. See Būht'a (³1989), pp. 92–104 and 129f. Most of the articles reprinted here are undated, but have been grouped in the section of writings published between 1920 and 1924. Mawdūdī's commitment to support the Turks in their conflict with Greece fitted well into wider pro-Turkish activities in India, as exemplified by the creation of the *Smyrna Relief Fund* in support of Turkish victims of this conflict. See Minault (1982), pp. 137f et passim.
42. This is corroborated by the fact that even the British government in London was very much aware of the eager exploitation of the Greek massacre of Turks in Smyrna (İzmir) by 'Moslem propagandists' to further anti-British and pan-Islamic sentiments (BL I.O. L/P&S/11/185 [P 1370/1920]). Also, see Özcan (1997), p. 193.
43. See, for example, his articles 'Mamālik-i islāmiyya kā mustaqbal awr Briṭāniyya-yi ʿuẓmá', 'Briṭāniyya awr Turkī' and 'Miṣr kī andarūnī āzādī kā iʿlān awr ek lamḥa-yi ʿibrat wa baṣīrat', in Būht'a (³1989), pp. 130–34 and 145–9.
44. See, for example, Mawdūdī's critical discussion of the impact of the 1922 Bardoli resolution by the Congress in which Gāndhī was able to prevail against the demand for mass civil disobedience and, thus, contributed largely to the disintegration of the Caliphate Movement, in ibid., pp. 115–26. On the resolution, see Minault (1982), pp. 183–5; Qureshi (1999), pp. 313–16.
45. See Būht'a (³1989), pp. 127f (*Musalmānoṇ kī rāh-i ʿamal awr ʿulamāʾ-i kirām kā farḍ*; n.d.); also in greater detail below, Chapter B.2.
46. On emergence and development of communalism in colonial India, see, for example, Hartung (2004b), pp. 143–55.
47. Svāmī Śraddhānand, although known for his strong reservations towards Muslims, initially took part in the leadership of the transcommunal movement for independence. See Minault (1982), pp. 70, 77f and 83. In the course of reappearing communalism, however, he initiated the so-called movement for 'purification' (*śuddhī*), an aggressive proselytisation movement that targeted non-*Ārya Samāj* movements as well as Muslim groups (see ibid., pp. 193f; Fischer-Tiné [1995]).
48. See Mawdūdī, 'Swāmī Shraddhānand kā dardnāk qatl', *al-Jamʿiyya*, 4:46 (23 Jumādá al-ākhira 1345/29 December 1926), pp. 2f; idem, 'Swāmī Shraddhānand ke qatl kā muqaddima', *al-Jamʿiyya*, 5:4 (13 Rajab 1345/18 January 1927), pp. 4 and 68; 5:5 (17 Rajab 1345/22 January 1927), pp. 4 and 6f; 5:8 (28 Rajab 1345/2 February 1927), p. 4; 5:10 (7 Shaʿbān 1345/10 February 1927), pp. 4 and 9.
49. See, for example, ʿAbd (³1988), pp. 70f; Brown (2011), p. 62. There was, however, a combination of factors which occurred at around that time that may have had an impact on Gāndhī's disappointment in the Indian Muslims. In 1920, for instance, after serious disagreement over Gāndhī's politics of non-violence, Jinnāḥ had resigned from his membership of the INC and became president of the increasingly separatist AIML. Beyond his disappointment, however, I could not find clear textual evidence that Gāndhī indeed took a more communalistic stand from the end of the 1920s.
50. See Mawdūdī, 'Islām kā qānūn-i jang', *al-Jamʿiyya*, 5:8 (28 Rajab 1345/2 February 1927), pp. 2f; 5:29 (29 Shawwāl 1345/2 May 1927), pp. 2f; also idem (1995), pp. 17–19.
51. See, e.g., Aḥmad Saʿīd Dihlawī, 'Mawlānā Aḥmad Saʿīd ṣāḥib kā maktūb ed'it'er-i bīdār ke nām', *al-Jamʿiyya*, 6:16 (5 Rabīʿ al-awwal 1346/2 September 1927), pp. 3f; Hartung (2004b), p. 297.
52. See Mawdūdī (1995), pp. 53–82.
53. See ibid., pp. 86–149.

54. See Mawdūdī, 'Daʿwat-i islām', *al-Jamʿiyya*, 5:24 (11 Shawwāl 1345/14 April 1927)—5:34 (19 Dhī 'l-qaʿda 1345/22 May 1927).
55. The last issue of *al-Jamʿiyya* under the editorship of Mawdūdī appeared on 14 May 1928 (no. 7:32). From the following issue onwards it was edited by an Abū 'l-Bayān Uways.
56. See Nasr (1996), p. 18. Once more, Nasr's argument is based entirely on Mawdūdī's somewhat pompous autobiographical essay (Mawdūdī [²1990], p. 23) and hagiographical material (ʿAbd [³1988], p. 65) and still awaits, therefore, proper corroboration.
57. See Hartung (2001), pp. 191f.
58. This Chapter owes decisively to the input I have received as visiting researcher at the Centre for the History of Emotions at the Max Planck Institute for Human Development, Berlin, during April 2010. I am especially grateful to Margrit Pernau and Ute Frevert who have generously invited me to their institution.
59. See, for example, Minault (1982); Qureshi (1999).
60. Qurʾān 3 (Āl ʿImrān): 110. Also, see ibid., 3 (Āl ʿImrān): 104, 114; 9 (al-Tawba): 71 and 112; 22 (al-Ḥajj): 41.
61. Compare, for example, al-Ṭabarī (1322/2001) V: pp. 661f, 671–7 and 699f, XI: p. 556, XII: pp. 15–7, XVI: pp. 587f; al-Bayḍāwī (1330h), II: pp. 35f and 38, III: pp. 74 and 82, IV: p. 56; Ibn Kathīr (1407/1987), I: pp. 399–405 (here especially on the first part of 3:110), II: p. 383, III: p. 237; even al-Ālūsī (s.t.), IV: pp. 21f, 27f and 34, X: p. 135, XI: pp. 31f, XVII: pp. 164f. Also, see Cook (2000), pp. 17–31.
62. See ibid.
63. Qurʾān 24 (al-Nūr): 55.
64. See Ibn Taymiyya (1403/1983); idem (³1408/1988), pp. 65–7; Ibn Ghannām (²1405/1985), for example, pp. 371–3 and 405–7 (although nowhere explicitly referring to the Qurʾānic precept); Cook (2000), pp. 145–502; Steinberg (2002), pp. 341 and 397–403.
65. See Hartung (2004b), pp. 224f and 342; Riexinger (2004), pp. 523–37; Preckel (2005), pp. 231–41.
66. Prominently Dihlawī (1396/1976), I: p. 256: 'If an unbeliever happens to be the ruler [*agar kāfirī bādshāhī bāshid*] or there are those in command [*taḥkīm*] under whom cases are decided not according to the *sharīʿa* but at the point of the sword, and whose activities are confined to collecting revenue, but who is by no means striving for the establishment of the religion [*iqāmat-i dīn*] by waging *jihād*, establishing penal law [*iqāmat-i ḥudūd*] and enacts its rulings, then he cannot be a caliph. This, however, is most dominant in our present time.' Also, see idem (1986), I: pp. 29, 37–43 and 290–96, II: pp. 370–72.
67. It was the French political scientist and popular writer Dominique Moïsi who, although on a rather speculative basis, had recently argued for a relationship between feelings of historical decline and humiliation. See Moïsi (2010), pp. 107–11.
68. See, for example, Khān (²1971), pp. 117–22 and 137–42.
69. See, for example, Metcalf (1982), pp. 100–4 et passim; Preckel (2005), pp. 331–412.
70. al-Bukhārī (1425–6/2005), pp. 637f (*Kitāb al-shahādāt, bāb lā yashhad ʿalá shihādat jawr idhā ushhida*, Ḥadīth 3, no. 2652); also, with slight differences, Muslim (1424/2004), pp. 1255f (*Kitāb faḍāʾil al-ṣaḥāba, bāb faḍl al-ṣaḥāba—rāḍī allāhu ʿanhum—thumma alladhīna yalūnahum*, Aḥādīth pp. 3f, 6f, 9 and 11, nos. 6364f, 6367f, 6370 and 6372).
71. See Khān (1872), pp. 45–53; Troll (1978), pp. 29 and 61–5.
72. See Ḥālī (1889), p. 8.
73. Ḥālī himself was one of the main driving forces towards a reform of the classical Indo-Persian poetical rules, away from the rather solipsistic 'games with words' of the poets, and from the confines of the court and exclusive poetic gatherings (*mushāʿirāt*), towards a more 'natural poetry', using a simple, object-related and highly emotive language which reaches out into the wider society. See Pritchett (1994), pp. 134f, 157–60, 164–6 and 179–

83. A comprehensive study on the audiences of poetic recitals especially after 1857, which would provide more solid insight into the ever-widening circle of the addressees, remains yet to be written. For initial thoughts on the issue, see ibid., pp. 70f; Rahman (1983), especially pp. 81f.

74. For the still most comprehensive analysis of Sayyid Aḥmad Khān's approach to Qur'ān and Prophetic Sunna, see Troll (1978), pp. 144–222.

75. See Lelyveld (1978), pp. 125f; Minault (1982), pp. 8 and 10. These developments, however, did not appear out of the blue, but were rather preceded by the so-called *Delhi College* where, for more than three decades before the uprising of 1857, Muslim and British scholars attempted a convergence of 'Oriental' and Western knowledge. Already by then, Urdu was selected as a means of reaching a wider audience, although then not necessarily aiming exclusively at Muslims. See idem (1999), pp. 126–34; Pernau (2006), pp. 7–32; idem (2008), pp. 109–17.

76. One of the most staunch critics of Sayyid Aḥmad Khān was the native Iranian Jamāl al-Dīn Asadābādī 'al-Afghānī' (d. 1314/1897), who, in his *Ḥaqīqat-i madhhab-i naycharī wa bayān-i ḥāl-i naycharīyān* (1881) and a later article in *al-ʿUrwa al-wuthqá* (see al-Afghānī/ʿAbduh [²1421h], pp. 444–9 [*al-Dahrīyūn fi'l-Hind*; 1884]; Keddie [1968], pp. 130–80), explicitly accused Sayyid Aḥmad Khān of having dangerously deviated far from even the basic Islamic tenets, and all only in order to please the British. See also Hildebrandt (2002), pp. 220–24.

77. See, for example, al-Jabārtī (1975), pp. 43–7 [10–7 Arabic text], where the author meticulously lists the linguistic mistakes in the Arabic proclamation by the French forces, and idem (1389/1969), pp. 31–5.

78. See idem (1975), pp. 23–5; idem (1998), III: pp. 140, 148–50, 170f, 299–305, 314 and 561–3.

79. al-Ṭahṭāwī (2002), p. 24.

80. Ibid., p. 29.

81. Cited in Schölch (1972), p. 391.

82. Similar developments took place in the Iran of Nāṣir al-Dīn Shāh Qājār (assassinated 1313/1896) and his successor Muẓaffar al-Dīn (d. 1324/1907) and finally gave way to a total rejection of the government's policies by the Shiite *ʿulamāʾ* in Iran and Iraq. This repudiation received its first major climax in the so-called 'Tobacco Protest' of 1890, following the Shāh's granting of a concession of the monopoly on tobacco products to a British entrepreneur in exchange for substantial financial aid. See Lambton (1965); Moaddel (1992); for attempts to instrumentalise the 'Tobacco Protest' for fuelling pan-Islamic sentiments, see Keddie (1972), pp. 335–72.

83. See Hobsbawm (1992), pp. 207–22; idem (1975), pp. 48–68.

84. For this complex processual term, see Weber (⁵1972), pp. 21–3 and 212–381.

85. See Durkheim (1897), pp. 264–90. Durkheim's subsequent and lengthy application of the anomic suicide type to divorced men (pp. 290–311) however followed rather the then dominant biologistic arguments and appears thus rather disconcerting for the contemporary reader.

86. See Flam (2002), pp. 70–75.

87. See Durkheim (1897), pp. 418–20 and 423f.

88. See, for example, Riḍā, '«wa-Mā kāna rabbuka li-yuhlika al-qurá bi-ẓulmin wa-ahluhā muṣliḥūn»', *al-Manār*, 1:31 (2 Jumādá al-ākhira 1316/18 October 1898), pp. 585–92 (the verse that constitutes the title is Qur'ān 11 [Hud]: 117); idem, 'al-ʿĀlam al-islāmī wa'l-istiʿmār al-ūrūbī', *al-Manār*, 14:5 (29 Jumādá al-ūlá 1329/28 May 1911), pp. 347–52, and 14:6 (30 Jumādá al-ākhira 1329/27 June 1911), pp. 432–40. I am grateful to Umar Ryad (Leiden), a proven expert on Rashīd Riḍā, for drawing my attention to these articles.

89. Durkheim (1897), p. 275 (transl. John A. Spaulding and George Simpson).

90. Ibid.
91. Ibid., p. 429.
92. This idea is rooted in the Qur'ānic revelation: 'And verily, this community of yours is a single community [*ummatan wāḥidatan*], and I am your Lord. Therefore, fear me [alone]!' (23 [al-Mu'minūn]: 52). For the invocation of this unity by appealing to a common cultural history, see, for example al-Afghānī/ʿAbduh ([2]1421h), pp. 131–7 (*al-Waḥda al-islāmiyya*).
93. See Hunt (1999), p. 512. Hunt's remarks here are based on conclusions drawn by the Birmingham sociologist Stuart Hall (b. 1932) and his associates in their 1978 study *Policing the Crisis: Mugging, the State, and Law and Order*, a work that focuses on a particular situation in England of the 1970s. To apply these conclusion one on one to other situations seems at best premature.
94. The reference to the *salaf ṣāliḥ* by the Central Arabian Wahhābiyya or the South Asian *Ahl-i ḥadīth* appears to have been much more literal than that of the Sayyid Aḥmad Khān or Muḥammad ʿAbduh and their respective associates.
95. See Riḍā (1420/1999), IV: pp. 34f (on 3 [Āl ʿImrān]: 104, where the study of psychology [*ʿilm al-nafs*], sociology [*ʿilm al-ijtimāʿ*] and political science [*ʿilm al-siyāsa*] was, among others, included in a curriculum that aimed at producing a new Muslim intellectual vanguard; also Cook (2000), pp. 508–11; Hildebrandt (2002), pp. 235 and 244f.
96. For a concise exposition and discussion of ʿAbduh's theology, see ibid., pp. 237–58. Also, see Riḍā (1420/1999), IX: pp. 440–46 (on 7 [al-Aʿrāf]: 199), X: pp. 464–6 (on 9 [al-Tawba]: 67).
97. For ʿAbduh and his associates, the *salaf ṣāliḥ* were not confined to the first three generations of Muslims, but included also medieval luminaries. See ʿAbduh ([8]1373h), p. 138.
98. Schulze (1990), p. 47 (transl. JPH).
99. See, for example, Troll (1978), pp. 112–43.
100. See, for example, Glaß (2009).
101. See Rugh (1984), pp. 256–8. At the turn of the twentieth century, the rate of illiteracy in Egypt was 90 per cent, around 1947 it was still 70 per cent, overall 65 per cent for males and 84 per cent for females.
102. One would want to think in this regard of the mentioned numerous historiographical works of Sayyid Aḥmad Khān, Shiblī Nuʿmānī, or Sayyid Amīr ʿAlī. See, for example, Troll (1978), pp. 364–6; Hartung (2004b), pp. 75–81.
103. See, for example, Kant (1974), XII: pp. 658–60 (*Anthropologie*); Fichte (1845–6), VII: pp. 314–27 (*Reden an die deutsche Nation*; 1808); also Anderson (1991), pp. 67–82 et passim.
104. See Lelyveld (1993), pp. 60 and 63–7.
105. See, for example, Ḥālī (1958), p. 142.
106. See Stark (2003); Daechsel (2006a), pp. 14 et passim; Pernau (2008), pp. 263–70.
107. For his life and works see the studies by Keddie (1968), pp. 3–97; idem (1972); and by A. Albert Kudsi-Zadeh.
108. See, for example, Nallino (1917), pp. 15f.
109. See Hassan (2008), pp. 28–75.
110. See Hartung (2011), pp. 304 and 318 n.
111. See Nallino (1917), pp. 16–18; Kramer (1986), pp. 6–9; Bezikoğlu (2001), p. 76. The appellation 'Supreme Caliph of Islam' (*ḫilāfet-i kübra-yı islāmiye*), as well as the claims of religious suzerainty that came with it, was later enshrined in the Ottoman Constitution of 1876. While Halil İnalcık points out that the caliphate has been a significant pillar of Ottoman imperial ideology since the conquest of the Hijaz in 1517, it gained considerable momentum during the reign of ʿAbdülḥamīd in the late nineteenth century. See Deringil (1998), pp. 46f.

112. See Keddie (1968), p. 19; idem (1972), pp. 99 and 130; Minault (1978), pp. 5f.
113. See al-Afghānī/ʿAbduh ([2]1421h), pp. 120f (*al-Qaḍāʾ wa'l-qadr*), pp. 333f (*Furṣa sāniḥa*), pp. 344f (*Masʾala al-miṣriyya al-duwaliyya*). Kramer (1986), pp. 7f, is not entirely correct when he states that al-Afghānī's appeals in various articles in *al-ʿUrwa al-wuthqá* aimed at fuelling Muslim sentiments in support of the 'Ottoman caliphate'. Nowhere in these articles have the terms 'caliphate' and 'caliph' been used in relation to the Ottoman sultan. This apparently happened only a generation later, as Rashīd Riḍā's well-known book *al-Khilāfa aw al-imāma al-ʿuẓmá* (Cairo: Maṭbaʿat al-manār 1341/1923) testifies for. The book had originally been published in six instalments in *al-Manār* between December 1922 and May 1923. See especially part six (24:4 [29 Shaʿbān 1341/16 April 1923], pp. 360–73).
114. See Khān ([2]1916), pp. 7–9; Douglas (1988), pp. 148.
115. See, for example, Keddie (1968), p. 54; idem (1972), pp. 151f; also, although on a rather hypothetical basis, Douglas (1988), p. 195.
116. See Nuʿmānī (1999), pp. 36, 105–13 and 194f. While initially denying the Ottoman sultan the rightful caliphate, which was to be held only by a member of the Quraysh, by the time of the Balkan Wars Shiblī openly supported the Ottoman caliphate. See Qureshi (1999), pp. 57f.
117. See Riḍā, 'al-Iṣlāḥ al-dīnī al-muqtaraḥ ʿalá maqām al-khilāfa al-islāmiyya', *al-Manār*, 1:39 (3 Shaʿbān 1316/17 December 1898), pp. 764–71, here pp. 765f; also Keddie (1968), pp. 30f; Kramer (1986), pp. 27–35.
118. See Deringil (1998), pp. 44–92 and 169f.
119. See ibid., p. 149; Özcan (1997), pp. 117–19; Qureshi (1999), p. 42.
120. See Minault (1978), pp. 43f.
121. See Minault (1978), pp. 43f; also Daechsel (2006a), p. 136.
122. Already from the fifth issue of his Calcutta-based journal *al-Hilāl* (i.e. from 11 August 1912 onwards), Āzād reported continuously and in quite some detail on the developments in the Ottoman Empire under the heading 'Ottoman Affairs' (*shuʾūn i ʿuthmāniyya*).
123. Āzād, 'Ek ʿaẓīm al-shān ijtimāʿ', *al-Hilāl*, 2:7 (12 Rabīʿ al-awwal 1331/19 February 1913), p. 5. His later and more rational argument for the Indian Muslims' support for the Ottoman-held caliphate was that the caliph was to be obeyed by all Muslims under non-Muslim rule who had even the duty to fight a defensive (*difāʿī*) *jihād* for its preservation. See idem (1963), pp. 143–69 and 219–25; Hardy (1971), pp. 23 and 30f. Interestingly, Āzād's treatise on the 'caliphate question', entitled *Masʾala-yi khilāfat wa jazīrat-i ʿarab*, emanating from his presidential address to the Khilāfat Conference of Bengal in Calcutta on 28 February 1920, was translated into Arabic and serialised in nine parts as 'al-Khilāfa al-islāmiyya' in *al-Manār* between 28 January and 18 December 1922. I am grateful to Muhammad Qasim Zaman (Princeton, NJ) for drawing my attention to this fact.
124. See Nehru ([14]2001), p. 40; Douglas (1988), p. 174.
125. See Minault (1978), pp. 35–8; Douglas (1988), p. 115; Ṣiddīqī (1998), pp. 162–7; Qureshi (1999), pp. 60f; Robinson (2001), pp. 153–5.
126. For Āzād, see ibid., p. 99; for Muḥammad ʿAlī, see Hasan (1992), p. 81. Also, Qureshi (1999), p. 64.
127. See Minault (1974), pp. 459f; Qureshi (1999), pp. 31f. For plenty of examples and a discussion of Muḥammad ʿAlī's political poetry, see Ṣiddīqī (1998), pp. 207–69.
128. For the necessity of generating strong emotions for social movements see, for example, Pettenkofer (2006), pp. 2646.
129. Here, Iqbāl used the well-known metaphorical language of love poetry to evoke emotions such as 'pain' (*dard*), 'constraint' (*majbūr*), 'anxiety' (*be-tāb*), 'powerlessness' (*muḍṭar*), along with a strong longing to overcome these states. See Iqbāl ([2]1926), pp. 177–87. Inter-

estingly, we have an almost identically named earlier poem by Ḥālī where the language appears even more emotive than in Iqbāl's later one. See Ḥālī (s.t.); also Jalal (2001), p. 65.

130. Ibid., pp. 222, 224 and 226f. For the mentioned recital in Lahore, see Qureshi (1999), p. 58.
131. Especially verses like 'Although the jar is Persian, Hijazi is my wine; although the song is Indian, Hijazi is my tune' (Iqbāl [²1926], p. 187) from *Shikwa* aimed certainly at evoking such pan-Islamic sentiments. 'Hijaz', of course, represents here the cradle of Islam; hence 'Hijazi' stands for the original Islamic religiosity and its institutions.
132. See White (1990), pp. 47f and 63f; Pettenkofer (2006), pp. 261f.
133. See Rosenwein (2006), 24–7. Also, see idem (2002), pp. 842–5; Plamper (2010), pp. 252f. Rosenwein's rather shallow definition of the concept as 'precisely the same as social communities' (Rosenwein [2002], p. 842; Plamper [2010], p. 252), however, appears not much different from Max Weber's much earlier conception of 'community' (see Weber [⁵1972], pp. 21f) which did not need to refer to emotions at all. To mark a reasonable difference, I think that the role of rational criteria, such as 'a common stake, interests, values, and goals' (Rosenwein [2006], p. 24) which, according to Rosenwein, reflect on a community's understanding and management of emotions (cf. Bourdieu [1979], pp. 189–248, 433–5 et passim), needs to be played down relative to the role of emotions for the constitution of a community.
134. See Minault (1982), pp. 3f.
135. This is perhaps most vividly illustrated by the shift in influence on the Caliphate Movement from ʿAbd al-Bārī Farangī Maḥallī—after all one of its initiators—to Abū 'l-Kalām Āzād, but also by the later rift between Āzād and Muḥammad ʿAlī. See Hasan (1992), pp. 87–90; Robinson (2001), pp. 156f.
136. For Maḥmūd al-Ḥasan's biography, see Riḍwī (1991–2), II: pp. 33–6; Metcalf (1982), passim. On his role within the Caliphate Movement, see Minault (1982), pp. 27–32, 103f and 121f; Qureshi (1999), pp. 471 et passim. For his rather ambivalent stand towards Āzād, see Douglas (1988), pp. 100, 139 and 171.
137. See Robinson (2001), p. 156 n.23.
138. See, for example, Shaikh (1992).
139. See Douglas (1988), p. 155.
140. See, for example, al-Ṭabarī (1322/2001), XXII: p. 571; al-Bayḍawī (1330h), V: p. 129.
141. Qurʾān 60 (al-Mumtaḥina): 9.
142. See Āzād (1959), pp. 36f.
143. See Serjeant (1978), who states that the 'Constitution' consists of eight distinct treaties, issued by the Prophet over a period of seven or even more years.
144. See Ibn Hishām (²1375/1955), I: pp. 501–4.
145. Ibid., II: p. 503.
146. Āzād (1959), p. 39 [italics JPH] Āzād used here the English term 'Nation' (*neshan*) as well as the rather complex Urdu term *qawm*. Also, see Serjeant (1978), pp. 4f.
147. See Ibn Hishām (²1375/1955), II: pp. 190–203, 233–52 and 273–6; al-Ṭabarī (²1426/2005), I: pp. 382–4, II: pp. 406–8 and 416–20.
148. Āzād (1959), p. 42.
149. See Būht'a (³1989), pp. 111–13 (*Hamārā naṣb al-ʿayn*; ca. 1922); Qureshi (1999), p. 345.
150. See ibid., pp. 173, 247, 288f, 297, 315, 326f and 338–41. In the early 1920s, Arab intellectuals and community leaders, too, gave similar support to Atatürk whom they saw as the saviour of the Ottoman Caliphate from the grip of the Entente powers. See, for example, Riḍā, 'Ẓafar al-turk bi'l-yunān', *al-Manār*, 23 (29 Rabīʿ al-awwal 1341/19 November 1922), pp. 713–19; also, see Kramer (1986), pp. 73–9; Hassan (2008), pp. 68 and 79.
151. Mawdūdī (²1990), p. 20; also Būht'a (³1989), pp. 127f (*Musalmānoṇ kī rāh-i ʿamal awr ʿulamāʾ-i kirām kā farḍ*; n.d.).

152. The Deobandī *ʿulamāʾ* under 'Shaykh al-Hind' Maḥmūd al-Ḥasan had already in 1920 been explicitly critical towards what they felt was a sacrifice of religion for short-term political aims. See Qureshi (1999), p. 274.
153. See Hasan (1992), pp. 89f. On the Nehru Report, see Nehru ([14]2001), pp. 172f; Hasan (1987), pp. 166–74; Zachariah (2004), pp. 61f.
154. See Minault (1982), pp. 206f; Kramer (1986), pp. 106–22.
155. See Mawdūdī ([2]1997), pp. 6f.
156. See Āzād 'Maqālāt: al-Amr bi'l-maʿrūf wa'l-nahy ʿan al-munkar', *al-Hilāl*, 1:5 (11 August 1912), pp. 4–6, 1:6 (18 August 1912), pp. 2–8, 1:7 (20 August 1912), pp. 8–12; also Douglas (1988), pp. 140f.
157. See ibid., p. 8.
158. See Hasan (1987), p. 175; also Mawdūdī, 'D'akt'ar Mūnje awr ittiḥād kānfrins', *al-Jamʿiyya*, 6:28 (25 Rabīʿ al-thānī 1346/22 October 1927), 2, and 6:29 (29 Rabīʿ al-thānī 1346/26 October 1927), p. 2.
159. See Hasan (1987), p. 2, pp. 183–209; also Mawdūdī, 'D'akt'ar Anṣārī kā bayān', *al-Jamʿiyya*, 6:14 (27 Ṣafar 1346/26 August 1927), p. 2, and 6:15 (1 Rabīʿ al-awwal 1346/29 August 1927), p. 2.
160. Compare, for instance, Mawdūdī (1995), p. 27, with Chapter C.2.2.b below.
161. Qurʾān 3 (Āl ʿImrān): 110.
162. See Douglas (1988), pp. 127–9.
163. '[They are] those who, if We establish them on earth, establish regular prayer and give regular charity [*alladhīna in makkannāhum fi'l-arḍi aqāmū al-ṣalāta wa-ātawū al-zakāt*], enjoin the commendable and prevent the reprehensible.'
164. See Mawdūdī (1995), pp. 91–4.
165. See ʿAbd ([3]1988), pp. 78–80.
166. See Zachariah (2005), p. 4.
167. Qurʾān 30 (al-Rūm): 32 [*kullu ḥizbi bi-mā ladayhim fariḥūn*]. Cited in Mawdūdī (1995), p. [illegible].
168. Kant (1974), XI: p. 53 (A 481).
169. On this term see ibid., III: p. 25 (B XVIf [*Kritik der reinen Vernunft: Zweite Auflage*; 1787]).
170. See Stegmüller ([4]1969–75), I: pp. xxviii-xxxii; Hobsbawm (1992), pp. 285–305.
171. See, for example, Kant (1974), III: p. 27 (B XXI [*KdrV*]) et passim; VII: pp. 66f (BA 74–6 [*Kritik der praktischen Vernunft*; 1788]); Stegmüller ([4]1969–75), I: p. xxxix.
172. Fichte (1845–6), I: p. 434 (*Erste Einleitung in die Wissenschaftslehre*; 1797).
173. See Liebmann (1865); pp. 70–110; Cohen ([6]1898), p. xxvi.
174. Den Otter (1996), pp. 14f.
175. See Schnädelbach (1983), pp. 108–14.
176. The basis for this trust in scientific knowledge was already laid out in Kant's critical philosophy, where he assigned 'physics'—in his days synonymous with Galilean-Newtonian mechanics—the status of a 'paradigmatic science'. See Kant (1974), III: pp. 21f (B X [*KdrV*]); Schnädelbach (1983), p. 98.
177. See Stegmüller ([4]1969–75), I: pp. xxx-xxxv; Schnädelbach (1983), pp. 108–14; Hobsbawm (1992), pp. 289–97 and 336–57.
178. See ibid., pp. 80 and 99; Crook (1994), pp. 6–28 et passim; den Otter (1996), p. 52.
179. Darwin's explicit references in his own writings to theorists of Social Darwinism like Herbert Spencer (d. 1903) and Thomas Henry Huxley (d. 1895), and political economists like Malthus is a clear indication of the divergence of biological and social theories at this time. See Darwin (1871), I: pp. 101f, 132, 191 and 318f. Also, see Crook (1993), pp. 13–20; Schweber (1980); Young (1985), pp. 612–22.
180. See Schnädelbach (1983), pp. 128 and 180f. The difficulty of translating the German term

'*Lebensphilosophie*' into English has been highlighted by Eric Matthews to whom we owe the English translation of Schnädelbach's important book (Cambridge et al.: CUP 1984). Matthews, although acknowledging the awkwardness of the translation as 'life-philosophy', has nonetheless argued his case by pointing out possible misleading associations of 'philosophy of life'. This is why it is deemed reasonable to follow Matthews' translation.

181. See Schnädelbach (1983), pp. 172 and 180.
182. Ibid., p. 174 (transl. JPH: Matthew's translation of this passage seems rather verbose and thus not sufficiently succinct, which is why I have decided against using his translation rather than my own).
183. Paul Crook made clear that Darwin himself had denied any *telos* in the evolutionary process. See Crook (1994), p. 8.
184. Den Otter (1996), p. 8.
185. Stegmüller ([4]1969–75), I: p. xlii (transl. JPH).
186. See den Otter (1996), pp. 27f. Because of this only partial and rather topological reception of Hegelian thought, the notion of idealism in the British context was clearly distinct from German idealism of the late eighteenth century. A major consequence of this was that the systemic demand of the latter was suspended by the British epigones.
187. See Crook (1994), pp. 115f; den Otter (1996), pp. 92–8; Boucher (1997), pp. 68–93.
188. See Halliday (1971), pp. 394 and 400f; Nicholson (1990), pp. 181–97 (here a careful analysis of the commonalities and differences in Spencer and Green); den Otter (1996), pp. 98–101; Boucher (1997), pp. 50–67. Darwin himself, although holding firm to the eudaemonist principle of the utilitarians, departed from Kantian ethics in his discussion of the genealogy of man, thus offering a link for the idealists. See Darwin (1871), I: pp. 70f and 97–104.
189. Parallels are quite obvious in McTaggart's seminal work *The Unreality of Time* of 1908, which appears quite similar to Bergson's concept of *durée* (only approximated in English as 'duration'), first elaborated in his doctoral dissertation *Essai sur les données immédiates de la conscience* from 1889. See Kolakowski (1985), pp. 12–23; compare Rochelle (1996), pp. xxviii-xxx.
190. See Kolakowski (1985), pp. 53–9 and 68–71; Crook (1994), pp. 69f.
191. See Schimmel (1963), pp. 37 and 321. The influence of McTaggart on Iqbāl has so far rarely been studied (I am only aware of Javed Majeed's article from the early 1990s). However, because this could hardly have been achieved within the scope of the present work, most of my statements about this are based on circumstantial evidence rather than on a systematic study. Iqbāl's most explicit analysis of McTaggart's philosophy appears to be his brief memorial article 'McTaggart's Philosophy' from 1932. See Iqbāl (1973), pp. 140–51; also Schimmel (1963), pp. 283 and 322. Bausani (1954), pp. 182f, considers Bergson proper to have been the major Western philosophical influence on Iqbāl.
192. See Iqbāl (1934), pp. 44–55 and 92f; Bausani (1954), p. 182; Majeed (1993), pp. 209f and 218f; Hartung (forthcoming). Majeed argues that the influence of McTaggart's and, come to that, of Bradley's metaphysics is also strongly visible in Iqbāl's poetry, which served as a major vehicle for his philosophical thought. See Majeed (1993), pp. 211–17 et passim. This, however, would be quite consistent with the stylistic changes that life-philosophy introduced: Nietzsche, for example, made extensive use of the literary genre of the aphorism as a means of transporting his ideas, in conscious distinction from the logic-based prose of rationalist philosophies.
193. See his famous presidential address to the 21st Annual Session of the AIML in Allahabad, 29 December 1930, in idem (1973), pp. 3–15; cf. McTaggart (1996), pp. 69–96.
194. See Kolakowski (1985), pp. 1–11; Crook (1994), p. 68.

195. See ibid., pp. 8, 13 and 68f. Interestingly, Aschheim (1992) does not, at least not explicitly, link Nietzschean life philosophy to the then prevalence of Darwinism.
196. See Marx/Engels (1956–90), XXX: pp. 248f (*Marx to Engels*, 18 July 1862); Crook (1994), pp. 13, 74 and 208 n. 19.
197. This would explain why 'science' had 'longer lineages, in fact, than "socialism"' (Zachariah [2005], p. 235). On the other hand, I would argue against Zachariah that 'science' had no lineages of its own (see ibid.), but was the lineage that impacted all others.
198. See Hobsbawm (1992), pp. 32–9 and 64–9.
199. See Zachariah (2005), p. 240.
200. See ibid., pp. 238–40. On Nehrū's growing discontent with Gāndhī, especially after the latter's retreat from active Congress politics in 1934, see Nehru (^{14}2001), pp. 504–36; Zachariah (2004), pp. 54 and 79.
201. See Nehru (^{14}2001), p. 350; Zachariah (2005), p. 238. Cf. Spengler (^{42}1922–^{47}3), I: pp. 42–9. It has however to be emphasised that Nehrū perceived the relation of 'culture' and 'civilisation' in a way diametrically opposed to Spengler: while Nehrū saw the advance of a culture into a civilisation as positive, Spengler saw herein a decline.
202. See Zachariah (2005), pp. 241f.
203. See K̲hān (1416/1995), pp. 22f; Daechsel (2006b), pp. 448f.
204. See idem (2006a), pp. 81–90 and 104f.
205. See Zachariah (2005), p. 248.
206. See Zachariah (2004), pp. 192f; idem (2005), pp. 253f. The core theses of Śāha are to be found in his *India on Planning: Planning for Liquidation of Unemployment and Illiteracy* from 1948.
207. It has been argued that to speak of 'political ideology' is tautological. See Freeden (1996), p. 9. If, however, as it is argued here, scienticism is understood as an ideology, too, and, moreover, as the epistemological basis of every social and political utopia, then the alleged tautology in 'political ideology' is clearly dissolved.
208. See ibid., p. 5.
209. See, for example, Kant (1974), XII: pp. 658f (A 297f [*Anthropologie in pragmatischer Absicht*; 1798]); Fichte (1845–6), VII: pp. 274–7 (*Reden an die deutsche Nation*; 1808); Hegel (^{3}1996), VII: pp. 338f (*Grundlinien der Philosophie des Rechts*; 1821); XII: p. 527 (*Vorlesungen über die Philosophie der Geschichte*; 1822–30). These noble and lofty ends of the Enlightenment philosophers have, however, to be perceived within the framework of the various societal mechanisms, which are described by Anderson (1991), pp. 37–46 and 67–82.
210. See Marx/Engels (1956–90), XL: pp. 510–22 and 568–87 (*Ökonomisch-Philosophische Manuskripte*; 1844).
211. This is pithily expressed in the famous sentence of the *Manifest der Kommunistischen Partei* from 1848: 'The history of all hitherto existing society is the history of class struggles.' Ibid., IV: p. 460 (transl. Samuel Moore).
212. Ibid., IV: p. 493.
213. See ibid.
214. Cf. Lenin (1962–70), I: p. 299 (*Čto takoe "druz'ja naroda" i kak oni vojujut protiv social-demokratov?*; 1894): '[...] the exploitation of the working people in Russia *is everywhere capitalist in nature*, if we leave out of account the moribund remnants of serf economy; [...]' (italics in the original).
215. Ibid., XXV: p. 404 (*Gosudarstvo i revoljucija*; 1917).
216. See ibid., XXIX: pp. 305–13 (*Tretij Internacional i ego mesto v istorii*; 1919). The idea that 'Leninism', as the paradigm for communist party organisation, should be confined only to the Russian local context and was even here only valid during Lenin's lifetime (see Joshi/Josh [1992], I: p. 12) cannot be accepted on the grounds of the canonical status that

Lenin's political thought enjoyed throughout, and even beyond, the Eastern bloc past the Stalin era.

217. See Adhikari (1971–82), I: pp. 215–33; Joshi/Josh (1992), I: pp. 47, 61 et passim; Roy (1997), pp. 58f.
218. See Ansari (1990), pp. 15–32; Reetz (1995), pp. 72f. Also, see below, Chapter D.2.2.
219. See Roy (1964), pp. 3–13; Adhikari (1971–82), I: pp. 140f; Roy (1997), pp. 2–13; also Ray (1985).
220. See Roy (1964), pp. 182–212; Roy (1997), pp. 22–30.
221. See ibid., p. 23.
222. See ibid., pp. 39–42; for a reproduction of the text see Adhikari (1971–82), I: pp. 151–5.
223. See Roy (1997), pp. 83–6.
224. See Ansari (1990), pp. 24 and 249f; Adhikari (1971–82), I: pp. 93–5.
225. For a positive appraisal of the 1907 congress see Lenin (1962–70), XIII: pp. 75–93 (*Meždunarodnyj socialističeskij kongress v Štuttgarte*; 1907). On the fringes of the 1917 congress, the Khayrī brothers signed the declaration of the non-European participants in which, among others, the decolonisation of India was demanded. See the text of the declaration in the *Bulletin du Parti national égyptien*, November 1917, pp. 41–6.
226. See Adhikari (1971–82), I: pp. 97–102.
227. See ibid., I: pp. 118–28; Ansari (1990), pp. 24–6; Reetz (1995), pp. 24–33 and 72f.
228. See ibid., pp. 25f; Qureshi (1999), p. 212.
229. See Ansari (1990), pp. 26f.
230. Lenin (1962–70), XXXI: p. 138 (*Indijskoj revoljucionnoj associacii*; 1920).
231. See the response of the InRA to Lenin's address as published in the official organ of the Bolshevik Party: 'The Indian revolutionaries express their deep gratitude and their admiration of the great struggle carried on by Soviet Russia for the liberation of all oppressed classes and peoples, and especially for the liberation of India. Great thanks to Soviet Russia for her having heard the cries of agony from the 315,000,000 people suffering under the yoke of imperialism. The mass meeting accepts with joy the hand of friendship and help extended to oppressed India.' *Pravda* no. 108, 20 May 1920.
232. See Ansari (1990), pp. 30–36.
233. See Roy (1964), pp. 464f; Roy (1997), p. 58.
234. Lenin (1962–70), XXXI: p. 149 (*Doklad komissii po nacional'nomu i kolonial'nomu voprosam*; 1920).
235. See Joshi/Josh (1992), I: pp. 42–4. This position of Lenin echoes clearly what Marx had stressed in his articles on the British rule in India: 'The bourgeois period of history has to create the material basis of the new world [...] When a great social revolution shall have mastered the results of the bourgeois epoch, the market of the world and the modern powers of production, and subjected them to the common control of the most advanced peoples, then only will human progress cease to resemble that hideous, pagan idol, who would not drink the nectar but from the skulls of the slain.' Marx/Engels (1956–90), IX: p. 226 (*The Future Results of British Rule in India*; 1853). Also, with regard to early twentieth century India, see Zachariah (2005), p. 84.
236. See Adhikari (1971–82), I: pp. 178–88 (Rāy: *Roy's Supplementary Colonial Theses*; 1920) and 363–410 (Rāy: *India in a Transition*; 1922); Joshi/Josh (1992), I: pp. 44–9.
237. The 'law' was first conceptualised in Trotsky's *Itogi i perspektivy* (1906) and emphasised the mutual independence of national social and economic developments while, at the same time, acknowledging the interdependence of these unevenly developing countries within a larger 'world society'. See Trotsky (1962), pp. 169–77. Trotsky himself had evidently been aware of Stalin's abuse of his theory when, in his *Permanentnaja revoljucija* (1930), he accused Stalin of 'making a fetish of the law of uneven development [and]

proclaim[ing] it a sufficient basis for national socialism, not as a type common to all countries, but exceptional, Messianic, purely Russian'. (Ibid., p. 25).

238. See ibid., pp. 115–36 and 239–47.
239. See Zachariah (2005), pp. 226–9; for the Muslim context see Ansari (1990), pp. 114–18.
240. Zaidi (1976–85), IX: p. 611.
241. See Nehru ([14]2001), p. 591; Joshi/Josh (1992), I: pp. 176–81; II: pp. 82–8 and 142–7.
242. See Ansari (1990), p. 82.
243. See his presidential address at the UP Political Conference, 13 October 1928, in Adhikari (1971–82), II: p. 187; also see Joshi/Josh (1992), II: pp. 81f.
244. See Adhikari (1971–82), II: pp. 465–72 (*Communism and Nationalism*; 1925).
245. See ibid., II: pp. 209–16 (*Manifesto on the Hindu-Moslem Unity and Swaraj*; 1923) and 267–72 (Rāy: *The Abolition of the Khilafat*; 1924); Ansari (1990), pp. 67–71.
246. See Nolte (1963), pp. 47–58; Sternhell (1989), pp. 12–50; Eatwell (1996).
247. See Allardyce (1979); also the comments of Stanley Payne and Ernst Nolte and Allardyce's response following immediately after Allardyce's article. See ibid., pp. 389–98. Here, whenever the term is capitalised it shall denote a somewhat ideal-typical ideology, while in all other cases it refers only to the Italian case.
248. The absence of a doctrinal racial theory in the Italian case, while such a theory was of immense importance to National Socialism, may just serve here as a case in point. See ibid., pp. 381f; Gentile (1975), pp. 209–18; Sternhell (1989), pp. 12f; Eatwell (1996), pp. 307f.
249. Allardyce (1979), p. 378. This would be confirmed by the fact that Alfred Rosenberg's bulky and best-selling *Der Mythus des 20. Jahrhunderts* from 1930, the 'alleged fundamental book of the National Socialist worldview' (Nolte [1963], p. 61 [transl. JPH]), was considered 'too intellectual' by Hitler and, thus, was of rather limited importance for National Socialism at work. See ibid., p. 404; Eatwell (1996), p. 311.
250. For example, see Nolte (1963), pp. 128–30 and 445–50.
251. See, e.g., Mawdūdī (1972a), pp. 15–19; Daechsel (2006b), pp. 450f.
252. See idem (2006a), pp. 12–15.
253. Ibid., p. 16. Also, see ibid., pp. 35–59 et passim.
254. See Zimmermann (2006), pp. 21–8; Panesar (2006), pp. 26–8.
255. Crook (1994), p. 67.
256. See Nietzsche ([2]1988), V: p. 126 (*Jenseits von Gut und Böse* [*JGB*]; 1886), VI: pp. 51f and 154 (*Götzen-Dämmerung*; 1889). A vivid expression of the pessimistic *zeitgeist* of the interwar period is Spengler ([42]1922–[47]3).
257. See Panesar (2006), pp. 42–98.
258. Haeckel is considered a major proponent of scientific evolutionism in general who was even praised by Darwin himself as one of his forerunners. See Darwin (1871), I: p. 4, also pp. 126, 142, 202 and 323. Haeckel's so-called 'recapitulation' theory in particular contributed a great deal to the development of a scientifically justified racism and the legitimisation of eugenics as part of the idea of 'racial hygiene'. See Schnädelbach (1983), p. 124.
259. See Panesar (2006), pp. 106–14 and 123–47; Crook (1994), p. 30.
260. See Chamberlain (1916), p. 30; Rosenberg (1930), pp. 128 and 138n.
261. See Iqbāl (1934), pp. 49–55, 67f, 92f and 105; idem (1343sh), pp. 262f, 265 and 267f (*Payām-i mashriq*); Schimmel (1963), pp. 321f and 330.
262. Especially Maurras' ideas of state and sovereignty, and of nature is reminiscent of a particular and decontextualised understanding of Hegel's *Grundlinien der Philosophie des Rechts*. See Nolte (1963), pp. 145–7 and 183f.
263. See Fichte (1845–6), I: pp. 91 and 95f (*Grundlage der gesammten* [sic] *Wissenschaftslehre* [*GGWL*]; 1794).
264. See Nolte (1960), pp. 303–15; (1963), pp. 218 and 221; Gentile (1975), pp. 4, 7f and 55; idem

(1996), pp. 14 and 70; Aschheim (1992), p. 133; Sternhell (1989), pp. 270 and 281f. Sternhell, however, sees no direct impact of Nietzsche and Bergson on Mussolini, but only through the mediation of the French political philosopher Georges Eugène Sorel (d. 1922), Sternhell's principal witness for the 'antimaterialistic revision of Marxism'. See ibid., pp. 53–125 and 314.

265. See Aschheim (1992), pp. 45–50, 233f and 239f.
266. See Schnädelbach (1983), pp. 173f, 179 and 189; Sternhell (1989), p. 335; Aschheim (1992), pp. 276–80.
267. The term is only inadequately rendered by 'experience'. '*Erleben*' implies an instinctive and, thus, not rationally calculated act of self-vitalisation (*Er-Leben*).
268. See Nolte (1963), pp. 154–7, 308–12 and 494f; Yack (1986), pp. 356–64; Aschheim (1992), pp. 252 and 265; Crook (1994), pp. 69 and 160.
269. See Aschheim (1992), pp. 247–51; Spengler ([42]1922–[47]3), I: pp. 42–53, II: pp. 132–224. For a contemporary example, see Rosenberg (1930), pp. 27–140 et passim.
270. See Nolte (1963), pp. 308 and 572 n.37; Gentile (1975), p. 55; also cf. Schnädelbach (1983), p. 185.
271. See ibid., pp. 188–91; Aschheim (1992), pp. 157 and 196–8. Interesting to note, in his *Jahre der Entscheidung* from 1933 Spengler explicitly dissociated himself from Hitler and National Socialism, which deems him too plebeian, while at the same time he praised Mussolini as the incorporation of a new Caesarean imperialism.
272. See Nolte (1963), pp. 345–55.
273. See Darwin (1871), I: pp. 214–50. Darwin's *Descent of Man* was almost instantly translated into German (1871) by the zoologist Julius Victor Carus (d. 1903) and found thus its way into the German debate on anthropogenesis.
274. Even then, Rosenberg conceded that 'racial history is natural history', adding 'and mystic of the soul as well'. Rosenberg (1930), p. 29 (transl. JPH).
275. See Nolte (1963), p. 54.
276. See Hitler (1930), pp. 168f, 276–8 and 317–24; Nolte (1963), pp. 346–51.
277. The National Socialist programme of euthanasia was part of the 'racial hygiene', the roots of which could again be found in Lamarckian and Darwinist thought. The meaningfulness of eugenics was a widespread conviction among biologists and Social Darwinists from the 1890s onwards and gained momentum during the First World War when it had finally been coupled with life-philosophical thought. See Aschheim (1992), pp. 92 and 161f; Crook (1994), pp. 71, 83–91, 119–24 and 159–75. Halliday (1971), pp. 398–402, goes even as far as to define Social Darwinism as synonymous with eugenics.
278. See Nolte (1963), p. 51. Sternhell (1989), p. 14, does however not agree with Nolte's perception of Fascism as a response to Marxism, but sees it rather as its specific anti-materialistic and anti-rationalistic revision.
279. See Nolte (1963), pp. 529 and 541–5.
280. See idem (1960); Sternhell (1989), pp. 266–9.
281. See Eatwell (1996), pp. 304 and 308–10.
282. See Zachariah (2005), pp. 6f, 43, 92 and 181.
283. See Rothermund (1996), pp. 87–97.
284. See Nehru ([14]2001), p. 600; Zachariah (2004), pp. 87 and 105; idem (2005), pp. 233f; Framke (2007), pp. 11–23.
285. See Zachariah (2004), p. 78; idem (2005), pp. 233f.
286. See Nehrū in Framke (2007), p. 11.
287. See Nehru ([14]2001), pp. 400, 445, 498 and 591; Framke (2007), pp. 11f. This seems to have been the generally held view within Marxist-leaning academic circles, as is Framke's ref-

erence to Diethelm Weidemann, between 1975 and 1988 director of the Department of Asian Studies at Humboldt University in East Berlin.

288. See Schimmel (1963), p. 52. Fabei (2002), pp. 40f, basically relying on an earlier article by Claudio Mutti ('Fascismo e Islam', *Storia del XX secolo* 3 [1997], pp. 43–9), does however not confirm this audience, although he provides indication for Iqbāl's positive perception of Italian Fascism.
289. Iqbāl (1935), pp. 202f. With Italy's invasion of Ethiopia in October 1935, however, Iqbāl's admiration for the Duce cooled considerably, as proven by a later poem of the same title in his anthology *Ḍarb-i kalīm* (1937). See idem (1999), pp. 149f.
290. See Bose (1998), pp. 1–7 and 10–13.
291. In his 'Personal Testament', written during detainment in 1940, Bose praised Hegelian idealism, Bergsonian life-philosophy and Spencerian Social Darwinism as among the most useful philosophies of his time. See ibid., pp. 140–43; Daechsel (2006a), p. 37. It is however interesting to note that, despite this, Bose held the view that 'Naziism [*sic*] has no philosophy, so far as I am aware of' (Bose [1998], p. 140).
292. See Sareen (1996), pp. 1–46, documents in ibid., pp. 87f, 163–7, 265–70, 299–303 and 406f; Zöllner (2000), pp. 28–33.
293. Daechsel (2006a), p. 37.
294. See Sareen (1996), p. 18; Zöllner (2000), pp. 48–53; Zachariah (2004), p. 110; Daechsel (2006a), p. 40.
295. See al-Mashriqī (1416/1995), pp. 267f. In his editorial 'Harr Hit'lar kī mashhūr sawāniḥ-i ʿumrī «Māʾī st'ragal», yaʿnī «Merī kashmakash» kā urdū meṇ tarjama awr khulāṣa', *al-Iṣlāḥ*, 2:20 (7 Ṣafar 1354/31 May 1935), al-Mashriqī even claimed to have met Hitler in as early as 1926; later on he translated the abridged English version of *Mein Kampf* by Edgar Dugdale (d. 1964) into Urdu. See ibid; Baljon (1961), pp. 11f; Daechsel (2006a), p. 48; idem (2006b), p. 452.
296. See Khān (1416/1995), pp. 27–30; Baljon (1954), p. 188; Daechsel (2006b), p. 450. Only the first volume of *al-Tadhkira* was published during the author's lifetime, the second one was published posthumously in 1964.
297. See al-Mashriqī (1976), pp. 42–70; Daechsel (2006b), pp. 453–62. A major protagonist of the so-called *tafsīr ʿilmī* subgenre of Qurʾānic exegesis is considered to be the Egyptian Ṭanṭāwī Jawharī (d. 1359/1940), whose *al-Jawāhir fī tafsīr al-qurʾān al-karīm* was first published between 1923 and 1935, thus at around the same time as Mashriqī's *al-Tadhkira*. See Baljon (1961), pp. 5f, 50, 52, 59, 65f, 92f and 105. The jurist and author Sayyid Amīr ʿAlī (d. 1347/1928) was yet another example from India of an attempt at a scientific interpretation of Qurʾānic contents. See Ali (1928).
298. See al-Mashriqī (1976), pp. 70–89; Daechsel (2006b), p. 454. Compare Mawdūdī's interpretation of the named verses below, Chapter C.3.2.a.
299. See al-Mashriqī (1416/1995), pp. 42–157.
300. See Daechsel (2006b), p. 461.
301. See al-Mashriqī (1416/1995), pp. 237–42; Baljon (1954), pp. 189–98; idem (1961), pp. 76f and 91f; Daechsel (2006a), pp. 51, 85–91 and 115f; idem (2006b), p. 456.
302. To form such paramilitary organisations appears to have been common among the political movements of this time. See idem (2006a), p. 39; also below, Chapter D.2.2.
303. Idem (2006b), p. 468.
304. See ibid., p. 451; idem (2006a), pp. 116–18.
305. On the origins of the RSS and its religious environment, see Hartung (2004b), pp. 149–55; Daechsel (2006a), pp. 416; Delfs (2008), pp. 87f et passim.
306. On this, however, we eagerly await the publication of the PhD dissertation of Maria

Framke (Jacobs University Bremen) on the *Perception and Impact of European Fascism in India, 1922–1945* (submitted 2011).

307. See Delfs (2008), pp. 78–84.
308. See ibid., pp. 57–9, 105–14, 120f et passim.
309. This emerges, for instance, from Golvalkar's *We, or Our Nationhood Defined*, first published in 1939 and reprinted in ibid., pp. 172–226. For explicit references to either German theorists or historical events in and around Germany in the 1930s, see ibid., pp. 193, 200, 202f and 204.

3. FORGING A SYSTEM

1. This section owes considerably to the input I have received from Justyna Nedza (Bochum), for which I am most grateful.
2. See Doumato (1995), p. 352; also al-Ṭabarī (1322/2001), VIII: p. 503 (on 5 [al-Mā'ida]: 50, here even explicitly naming the Jews), XIX: pp. 99f (on 33 [al-Aḥzāb]: 33).
3. See Qur'ān 3 (Āl 'Imrān): 154; 5 (al-Mā'ida): 50; 33 (al-Aḥzāb): 33; 48 (al-Fatḥ): 26.
4. See al-Ṭabarī (1322/2001), XIX: pp. 97–9; Goldziher (1961), p. 220.
5. See Shepard (2001), p. 38; also Goldziher (1961), p. 225.
6. See Ibn Hishām ([2]1375/1955), I: p. 336: 'We were an ignorant people [*qawman ahl jāhiliyya*], worshipping idols, eating carrion, committing shameful deeds [*al-fawāḥish*], we disrespected the ties of kinship [*al-arḥām*] and violated the duty of faithfulness [*al-jiwār*]; and strong among us devour the weaker ones.'
7. This seems to have happened in a way similar to the establishment of the asymmetrical counterterms 'Hellenes' (*éllines*) and 'Barbarians' (*bárbaroin*) in Greek antiquity. See ibid., pp. 218–29.
8. See Koselleck (1989), pp. 246f.
9. See al-Bayḍāwī (1330h), IV: pp. 162f. This interpretation was supported by Bayḍāwī's reference to two sound Prophetic sayings, according to which there were still 'traces of the *jāhiliyya*' in one of his companions. See, for example, al-Bukhārī (1425–6/2005), p. 27 (*Kitāb al-īmān, bāb al-ma'āṣī min amr al-jāhiliyya wa-lā yukaffaru ṣāḥibuhā bi-irtikābihā ilá bi'l-shirk li-qawl al-nabī: innaka amru' fīka jāhiliyya*, Hadīth 1, no. 30); Muslim (1424/2004), pp. 827f (*Kitāb al-'īmān, bāb iṭ'ām al-mamlūk mimā yakul wa-ilbāsihi mimā yalbasu wa-lā yukalifuhu mā yaghlibuhu*, Aḥādīth 1–3, nos. 4204–6). Also see Kister (1990), p. 3.
10. al-Bayḍāwī (1330h), IV: p. 163.
11. See, for example, Koselleck (1989), p. 223.
12. See Ibn Taymiyya (1413/1993), pp. 79–91 et passim; Peskes (1993), p. 45.
13. See Riḍā (1420/1999), VI: pp. 422f (on 5 [al-Mā'ida]: 50); idem, 'Sukhāfa bi-shā'ir al-salām fi'l-jāhiliyya wa'l-islām', *al-Manār*, 5:13 (01 Rajab 1320/03 October 1902), 517–20; 'Man ḥarrama al-khamr 'alá nafsihi fi'l-jāhiliyya', *al-Manār*, 9:12 (29 Dhī 'l-ḥijja 1324/13 February 1907), pp. 942–5.
14. See Kant (1974), IV: p. 677 (B 833).
15. See ibid., XII: p. 428 (BA 27); compare Mawdūdī (1990b), p. 119: 'Who am I? What am I? Am I responsible or irresponsible? Am I independent [*khūd-mukhtār*] or subordinated [to someone]? If I am subordinated, then to whom, and if I am accountable, then to whom? Has my earthly life an end [*ma'ād*] or not, and if it has, what is it?'
16. Idem (1949–72), IV: p. 91.
17. For this widespread meaning of 'jāhiliyya', see Bosworth (1965), p. 381; Shepard (2001), p. 37.
18. Mawdūdī (1990b), p. 122.
19. Ibid., pp. 122f.

20. On this famous religious conviction of the Sufi poet Farīd al-Dīn al-ʿAṭṭār of Nishapur (killed 627/1230), see Schimmel (1975), pp. 147f and 274–86.
21. Mawdūdī (1990b), p. 123.
22. See ibid., pp. 123–5.
23. See Mawdūdī ([7]1994), pp. 15f; also Nedza (2008), p. 69.
24. See Mawdūdī ([7]1994), p. 17; compare Machiavelli (1979), pp. 47–9.
25. Mawdūdī (1990b), p. 128.
26. Ibid., p. 129.
27. See ibid., pp. 130f: *wah amr-i wāqiʿa ke muṭābiq nahīṇ he.*
28. See Mawdūdī ([7]1994), pp. 18f.
29. A case in point is the so-called '*ridda*-wars' under the first 'Rightly-Guided' Caliph Abū Bakr (d. 13/634) against those nomadic and sedentary tribes in the Arabian peninsula who had renounced Islam, especially immediately after the death of the Prophet. See, for example, al-Ṭabarī ([2]1426/2005), II: pp. 530–59.
30. See Mawdūdī ([7]1994), p. 19.
31. This debate owed to a considerable extent to the activities of the so-called *Ṭarīqa-yi muḥammadiyya* around Sayyid Aḥmad Barelwī and Shāh Ismāʿīl Dihlawī (both killed 1246/1831). Their views on the matter, heavily resembling Wahhābī positions, have been enshrined in their *Ṣirāṭ al-mustaqīm* and *Taqwiyyat al-īmān*. See, for example, Hartung (2004b), pp. 108–17; idem (2008); Riexinger (2004), pp. 238–68.
32. See Mawdūdī ([7]1994), p. 22.
33. See above, Chapter B.1.
34. See Mawdūdī ([7]1994), pp. 23–5.
35. Besides Sufism, Mawdūdī named 'Neo-Platonism, Yoga, [...] Christian monasticism, Buddhism, and so on' (ibid., p. 23) as examples of monasticism.
36. See, for example, Zakariyyā ([6]1983); Nuʿmānī (1989); Nadwī (1400/1980); idem ([2]1400/1980); idem ([4]1418/1997). For two analyses, see Mukarram (1992), pp. 182–306; Hartung (2004b), pp. 133–42. For the TJ and its impact on Mawdūdī, see below, Chapter D.2.1 and D.2.2.
37. For this terminology, see Mukarram (1992), pp. 9–11 et passim.
38. Mawdūdī (1990b), p. 137.
39. See ibid., pp. 138f.
40. See ibid., p. 140.
41. Ibid.
42. See Mawdūdī (1972b), pp. 22; also below, Chapter D.2.3.
43. Mawdūdī (1972b), p. 81.
44. Ibid., p. 82.
45. See Nedza (2008), pp. 74–97. The appropriation of various elements of Mawdūdī's ideology by leading thinkers of the Egyptian Muslim Brotherhood is discussed in some detail below, Chapter E.1.
46. For a good discussion of the theological and legal implications of *kufr* and, resulting from it, the practice of accusing someone of unbelief (*takfīr*) in classical Sunnite Islam, see ibid., pp. 23–43. For a discussion of Mawdūdī's understanding of the legal implications resulting from the practice of *takfīr*, see below, Chapter C.4.3.b.
47. See al-Bayḍāwī (1330h), IV: pp. 162f.
48. For this apt term, see Schnädelbach (1983), p. 192.
49. See below, notes pp. 53f.
50. See Nietzsche ([2]1988), I: pp. 82 and 149–56 (*Die Geburt der Tragödie aus dem Geiste der Musik*; 1872).
51. See Mawdūdī ([7]1994), pp. 30–33.
52. See Qur'ān 33 (al-Aḥzāb): 40; also al-Bukhārī (1425–6/2005), p. 867 (*Kitāb al-manāqib, bāb*

khātam al-nabīyīn, Ḥadīth 1, no. 3534); Muslim (1424/2004), p. 1146 (*Kitāb al-faḍāʾil, bāb dhikr kawnihi ṣallá allāh ʿalayhi wa-salam khātam al-nabīyīn*, Aḥādīth 1–6, nos. 5853–8). Mawdūdī refers to the Qurʾānic passage as well as to the cited *aḥādīth* in a response to a question by a reader of *Tarjumān al-qurʾān*, dated 16 April 1950 and written from Multan's New Central Jail where Mawdūdī served a term for his uncompromising stand in the constitutional debate in Pakistan. See Mawdūdī (1995–6), I: pp. 23–5 (*Khatam-i nubuwwat*; 1950).

53. Qurʾān 5 (al-Māʾida): 3. This verse, according to the classical Muslim tradition, was revealed to the Prophet at Ghadīr Khumm, after his final pilgrimage (*ḥujjat al-wadāʿ*) in Dhī ʾl-ḥijja 10 AH on his way back to Medina. See, for example, al-Ṭabarī (1322/2001), VIII: pp. 80f. It is, however, not discussed in the *Sīra* of Ibn Hishām (²1375/1955), II: p. 601f.
54. See, for example, the sound Prophetic saying: 'And my community will split into seventy-three sects [*firaq*] and all of them will go to hell except one: This is [my] community [*hiya al-jamāʿa*].' Ibn Māja (1373/1954), II: p. 1322 (*Kitāb al-fitan, bāb iftirāq al-umam*, Ḥadīth 3, no. 3993); al-Tirmidhī (1938–58), V: pp. 25f (*Kitāb al-imān, bāb mā jāʾ iftirāq hādhihi ʾl-umma*, Aḥādīth 1f, nos. 2640f); Abū Dāwūd (1983), IV: pp. 197f (*Kitāb al-sunna, bāb sharḥ al-sunna*, Ḥadīth 1, no. 4596); Ibn Ḥanbal (1413/1993), II: p. 438 (Ḥadīth no. 8370). For an extensive discussion of this presumably apocryphal *ḥadīth*, see van Ess (2011), I: pp. 7–64.
55. Qurʾān 75 (al-Qiyāma): 20f and 31f.
56. Abū Dāwūd (1983), IV: p. 109 (*Awwal kitāb al-malāḥim, bāb mā yudhkar fī qarn al-miʾa*, Ḥadīth 1, no. 4291). Extensively on this *ḥādīth*, see Corrado (2011), pp. 8–14.
57. See, for instance, Ibn al-Jawzī (1417/1996), p. 57.
58. See, for example, al-Baṣrī (1418/1997), II: pp. 276–8.
59. See, for instance, the account of the discussion by religious dignitaries and Caliph Hārūn al-Rashīd over the reliability of the traditions transmitted by Abū Hurayra, in al-Khaṭīb al-Baghdādī (1931), XI: p. 201. Also, see Lazarus-Yafeh (1986), p. 100; Badry (1998), p. 90.
60. See al-Ṣaʿīdī (1416/1996), p. 8. On the other hand, the traditionist al-Ḥakīm al-Naysābūrī (d. 405/1014) apparently did not agree with the sceptics, as in his *Mustadrak ʿalá ʾl-ṣaḥīḥayn* he classified this *ḥadīth* as 'sound' (*ṣaḥīḥ*). See Algar (2001), p. 292.
61. See Lazarus-Yafeh (1986), pp. 100–3.
62. See Landau-Tasseron (1989), p. 81.
63. Friedmann (1971), p. 14; idem (1989), pp. 95–7; Landau-Tasseron (1989), pp. 80–82; Algar (2001), pp. 292f. This would be supported even more if one recalls that apocalyptic thought in Islam owes a great deal to Christian and, especially, Jewish influences (see Cook [1997], pp. 37f; idem [2002], passim; Furnish [2005], pp. 8–11) with which Abū Hurayra was supposedly quite familiar.
64. See Landau-Tasseron (1989), p. 81. Here, she refers especially to al-Suyūṭī's *Tanbiʾa bi-man yabʿathu allāh ʿalá ras kull miʾa* (MS Leiden, Or. 474) where he refers to another *ḥadīth* that predicts a calamity (*fitna* or *miḥna*) at the head of each century, which will be restored by the Renewer of this Age. Apocalyptic thought, however, is prevalent in numerous of al-Suyūṭī's writings, for example in his *Kashf ʿan mujāwaza hādhihi al-umma al-alfa*.
65. See prominently Lazarus-Yafeh (1986), pp. 99 and 101. The works of David Cook on early Muslim apocalyptic writings appear to corroborate the insignificance of *tajdīd* during the first few Islamic centuries.
66. See Ibn al-Jawzī (1417/1996), p. 57; Cook (2002), pp. 37 and 139f; Landau-Tasseron (1989), p. 113.
67. al-Ghazālī (²1969), p. 49.
68. See ibid.; Landau-Tasseron (1989), p. 86; Algar (2001), p. 297 n. 20.
69. See al-Zabīdī (1414/1994), I: pp. 26f.

70. Badr al-Dīn al-Ahdal (d. 855/1451), *al-Risāla al-marḍiyya fī nuṣrat madhhab al-ashʿariyya*, cited in Landau-Tasseron (1989), p. 91.
71. See ibid., pp. 94–107. Also, although it is rather implicit, but mainly relying on the authority of the Shāfiʿite jurist Abū 'l-ʿAbbās ibn Surayj (d. 306/918), see al-Zabīdī (1414/1994), I: p. 26. On the close-knit relationship of Shāfiʿite *fiqh* and Ashʿarite *kalām*, see Halm (1974), pp. 32–40; Johansen (1999), p. 8.
72. See Landau-Tasseron (1989), pp. 107–113. For criticism, compare Algar (2001), p. 298 n. 22.
73. In the light of this, Landau-Tasseron's criticism of John Obert Voll's remarks on *tajdīd* as 'a call for reform' (Landau-Tasseron [1989], p. 79; also see Voll [1983], p. 33), based on the assumption of a deviant *umma*, might be a bit too harsh. Here, it seems, Voll's rather historical argument was countered from a normative level, laying stress on the consecutive (*mutawātir*) Prophetic *ḥadīth* according to which 'my community will never agree upon error' (al-Tirmidhī [1938–58], IV: p. 466f [*Kitāb al-fitan, bāb mā jāʾ fī luzūm al-jamāʿa*, Ḥadīth 3, no. 2167]; Ibn Māja [1373/1954], II: p. 1303 [*Kitāb al-fitan, bāb al-suwād al-aʿẓm*, Ḥadīth 1, no. 3950]).
74. For discussion of a selection of these movements, see Levtzion (1986).
75. See Cook (1997), pp. 38f.
76. See Friedmann (1971), pp. 14–21; Haar (1992), pp. 145–53; Alvi (1994), pp. 2–6. Johan G.J. ter Haar however emphasises that Sirhindī only implicitly considered himself a *mujaddid*, but called himself rather '*qayyūm*', i.e. 'he who supports [Creation]'. See Haar (1992), p. 157. There is a lot of speculation about whether it was indeed Sirhindī's former fellow student, the renowned philosopher ʿAbd al-Ḥakīm Siyālkotʾī (d. 1067/1656), who first assigned this epithet to Sirhindī. See ʿAlī (1897), p. 110; Jelumī (1324/1906), p. 415; Friedmann (1971), pp. 14 n. 7 and 103; Alvi (1994), pp. 3 and 5. As all these authors base their argument on hagiographical material, the veracity of this statement is to be doubted, at least for the time being.
77. See Friedmann (1971), pp. 18–20; Algar (2001), p. 298.
78. See ibid., p. 297
79. See Crone (2004), pp. 21–3.
80. See Ibn Fūdī (1985), p. 7 (Arabic text), p. 74 (translation). Clarke (1980), p. 327, wrongly attributes the reference to the *mujaddid* to Ibn Fūdī's *Tanbīh al-ikhwān ʿalá aḥwāl arḍ al-Sūdān*. Compare the translation of this text by Palmer (1914–15).
81. On al-Maghīlī, see Cuoq (1975), pp. 433–6; Rebstock (1978).
82. Ibn Fūdī (1985), p. 7 (Arabic text), p. 74 (translation). For the same passage in al-Maghīlī's letter to the Sultan of Songhai, Askia Muḥammad Turé (d. 934/1528), see Quoq (1975), p. 405: 'C'est pourquoi on rapporte qu'au début de chaque siècle Dieu envoie aux hommes *un savant* pour renouveler leur religion.' (author's emphasis).
83. See Ibn Fūdī (1985), pp. 78f.
84. See Algar (2001), p. 298.
85. This sentence is, in variations, part of the relevant *aḥādīth* in most of the canonical Sunni collection of *ḥadīth*. See al-Bukhārī (1425–6/2005), p. 1791 (*Kitāb al-aḥkām, bāb al-umarāʾ min Quraysh*, Ḥadīth 2, no. 7140); Muslim (1424/2004), p. 926 (*Kitāb al-imāra, bāb «al-nās tabaʿ li-Quraysh» waʾl-khilāfa fī Quraysh*, esp. Ḥadīth 11, no. 4604); Abū Dāwūd (1983), IV: p. 106 (*Kitāb al-mahdī*, Ḥadīth 1, no. 4279); al-Tirmidhī (1938–58), IV: pp. 503f (*Kitāb al-fitan, bāb mā jāʾ an al-khulafāʾ min Quraysh ilá an taqūma al-saʿa*, Ḥadīth 1, no. 2227). Given the importance of the Prophet's tribe for the leadership of the *umma* in this saying, it is quite understandable that it had been incorporated in major Shiite collections of *ḥadīth*. See, for example, al-Kulaynī (1426/2005), III: p. 2052 (*Rawḍat min al-kāfī, bāb ḥadīth islām ʿAlī—ʿalayhi al-salām*, Ḥadīth 6, no. 15281); compare also Ibn Abī Ṭalib (1410/1990), p. 141 (sermon no. 141).

86. This is contrary to Algar (2001), p. 298, who states that Ibn Fūdī was 'proclaiming himself to be both the last *mujaddid* and the last of the twelve caliphs'.
87. See Ballū (1951), pp. 185–9. This source, however, appears problematic as Muḥammad Bello (d. 1253/1837) was the son and successor of his father and might have employed the notion of *mujaddid* for his own legimatory purposes.
88. See Loimeier (1993), pp. 26–32. Revealing is the major work *al-ʿAqīda al-ṣaḥīḥa* of the late Supreme Judge of Nigeria's Kaduna State, Abubakar Gummi (d. 1413/1992), in which he basically echoes Ibn Fūdī's arguments from his *magnum opus*, *Iḥyāʾ al-sunna wa-ikhmād al-bidʿa*, and nowhere uses the word *tajdīd* or any of its derivatives. See Jūmī (1392/1972).
89. See Friedmann (1971), pp. 105f, who refers to Shāh Walīyallāh's *Risālat-i shawāhid al-tajdīd*. Interestingly, elsewhere (Dihlawī [1396/1976], I: p. 271) Shāh Walīyallāh did not mention Sirhindī in his discussion of *mujaddidūn* of various Islamic centuries. On Walīyallāh himself and his place in Indo-Muslim history, see, for instance, Metcalf (1982), pp. 35–43 et passim; Hartung (2004b), pp. 58–62; Riexinger (2004), pp. 71–81.
90. See Algar (2001), pp. 300f. Indeed, posterity agreed, largely regarding him as a *mujaddid* even beyond the subcontinent. See, for example, al-Ṣaʿīdī (1416/1996), pp. 334f, where, interestingly, Shāh Walīyallāh is only marginally referred to as a follower of the Naqshbandiyya, but rather as a reviver of the religious sciences in the wake of Ibn Taymiyya.
91. For the Deobandī reference to Shāh Walīyallāh, see prominently Riḍwī (1992–3), I: pp. 12–16 and 86–102; for Iqbāl, mainly by official Pakistani scholarship, see Halepota (1974a) and (1974b).
92. See Mawdūdī ([7]1994), pp. 52–120. Almost all the persons discussed here appear also in the work of al-Ṣaʿīdī (1416/1996): the 'Rightly-Guided' Caliphs (pp. 20–38), the Umayyad Caliph ʿUmar ibn ʿAbd al-ʿAzīz (pp. 46–50), two of the founders of the four canonical schools of Sunni religious law (pp. 72–6 and 102f), Abū Ḥāmid al-Ghazālī (pp. 138–40), Ibn Taymiyya (pp. 199–202) and Shāh Walīyallāh Dihlawī (pp. 334f). Interestingly, Aḥmad Sirhindī is nowhere mentioned in Ṣaʿīdī's work.
93. Mawdūdī ([7]1994), p. 34.
94. Ibid. In a footnote to this sentence, Mawdūdī referred to a legal opinion (*fatwá*) by 'some of the noble jurisconsults [*baʿḍ muftīyān-i kirām*]' in which he was accused of hereby derogating Caliph ʿUthmān. He defended himself by stating that this was a purely academic question over which contesting views should be permitted. This is noteworthy, as Mawdūdī used here an exit strategy that he himself had denied many of his adversaries, but on the other hand it indicates once more that, as an 'agent of change', Mawdūdī had moved in different and sometimes even diametrically opposed arenas.
95. See al-Ṭabarī ([2]1426/2005), II: pp. 813–17; extensively also Madelung (1997), pp. 78–140.
96. Mawdūdī ([7]1994), p. 34. For the expression 'caliphate along the Prophetic pattern', see Ibn Ḥanbal (1413/1993), IV: pp. 371f (Ḥadīth 18366), and below in this Chapter.
97. Ibid., p. 37.
98. See above, Chapter B.2.1; also Hartung (2004b), pp. 409–12 and 417 n. 495.
99. To consider Sayyid Aḥmad Barelwī a *mujaddid* is not too common even in South Asia. That Mawdūdī did so nonetheless might have owed predominantly to the impact the hagiographical work on Sayyid Aḥmad by his former companion Sayyid Abū 'l-Ḥasan ʿAlī Nadwī has had on Mawdūdī. See Nadwī ([7]1406/1986), II: pp. 525f. On Nadwī's relation to Sayyid Aḥmad, see Hartung (2004b), pp. 216–22.
100. See Mawdūdī ([7]1994), pp. 109–19.
101. See Nietzsche ([2]1988), I: pp. 83–111 (*Geburt der Tragödie*). For a preliminary attempt to understand Mawdūdī's concept of history through the prism of Nietzschean thought, see Hartung (1999), pp. 48–52.
102. See Nietzsche ([2]1988), V: p. 208 (*JGB*).

103. Ibid., III: 481; IV: pp. 8 and 111 (*Also sprach Zarathustra*; 1883–85). In the widespread popular understanding of this statement as an 'atheist creed', there was rooted also Mawdūdī's rejection of life-philosophy. See Mawdūdī (1990f), pp. 447–9.
104. See Iqbāl (1934), pp. 103f.
105. On the issue of rationality, free will and choice see more detailed below, Chapter C.2.1.a.
106. See Hartung (2011), pp. 297f.
107. See Mawdūdī ([7]1994), p. 36; idem (1997), pp. 96–144.
108. See idem ([7]1994), p. 46 and especially p. 52, where he speaks of 'partial renewal [*juzawī tajdīd*]'.
109. See Iqbāl (1343sh), pp. 5–54; Zwanzig (2008), pp. 75–96.
110. Mawdūdī ([7]1994), p. 50. Posterity, especially from around the JiI, has indeed attempted to establish a synonymy between Mawdūdī's and Iqbāl's concepts. See, for example, Gīlānī (1992), pp. 84–90.
111. Ibn Ḥanbal (1413/1993), IV: pp. 371f (Ḥadīth 18,366). In an extensive footnote Mawdūdī wrongly states that this *ḥadīth* would be found in the collections of Muslim, Tirmidhī and Ibn Māja and in al-Ḥakīm al-Naysābūrī's *Mustadrak*. A variant reading however is only found in al-Dārimī (1398/1978), II: p. 113 (*Kitāb al-ashraba, bāb mā qayyala yakūnu al-khamr*, Ḥadīth 6). Moreover, Mawdūdī claimed to quote from the *Muwāfaqāt fī uṣūl al-sharīʿa* of the Mālikite jurist Abū Isḥaq al-Shāṭibī of Granada (d. 790/1388); however, only a paraphrase of this *ḥadīth* is given. See al-Shāṭibī (s.t.), I: p. 97.
112. Mawdūdī ([7]1994), p. 48 n.1.
113. See Abū Dāwūd (1983), IV: pp. 106f (*Kitāb al-mahdī*, Ḥadīth 4, no. 4282); Ibn Māja (1373/1954), II: pp. 1367f (*Kitāb al-fitan, bāb khurūj al-mahdī*, Aḥādīth 4f, nos. 4085f); al-Tirmidhī (1938–58), IV: p. 505 (*Kitāb al-fitan, bāb mā jā' fi'l-mahdī*, Ḥadīth 2, no. 2231). Also, see Furnish (2005), pp. 11–17. On Mawdūdī's explicit disregard of the eschatological connotation of the *mahdī* as stated in the *aḥādīth*, see Mawdūdī ([7]1994), pp. 150f and 157f; idem (1995–96), I: p. 48 (*Mas'ala-yi mahdī*; 1946).
114. See idem ([7]1994), pp. 50 and 152.
115. Ibid., pp. 50f. Interestingly, Mawdūdī's recourse to the *ḥadīth* appears, moreover in a passage that deliberately does not correspond at all with the injunctions in all those accepted Prophetic traditions that deal with the figure of the *mahdī*.
116. See Koselleck (1989), pp. 17–66.
117. Mawdūdī (1972a), p. 5.
118. See above, Chapter B.1.1.
119. See Mawdūdī ([7]1996), p. 8.
120. Although logically coherent with his critical understanding of Islamic history, it is nonetheless remarkable that Mawdūdī, whose own proficiency in Arabic was at the most mediocre (see above, Chapter B.1), felt confident enough to dismiss all the classical Arabic *tafsīr* works and presumed himself more able to deduce the 'true meaning' from the Qur'ān than some native-speaker trained in the science of Qur'ānic exegesis.
121. See Hamza/Rizvi/Mayer (2008), p. 51.
122. Interestingly, although commonly included in the lists of *mujaddidūn*, the Egyptian polymath Jalāl al-Dīn al-Suyūṭī is not discussed by Mawdūdī. Having written a substantial part of the most popular and concise *Tafsīr al-jalālayn*, he might have served as yet another counterproof to Mawdūdī's claim that early *mujaddidūn* had not contributed significantly to the field of Qur'ānic exegesis. Whether this was the reason why Mawdūdī conveniently omitted the discussion of al-Suyūṭī as renewer of the tenth Islamic century must remain a matter of speculation.
123. Dihlawī (1396/1976), I: p. 51.
124. Clearly inspired by the ideas of Bergson, the issue of time has been discussed at length

in Iqbāl's lectures on *The Reconstruction of Religious Thought in Islam* and elsewhere, and the general debate on that matter in the early twentieth century had at least by this channel become well known in Indo-Muslim intellectual circles of that time. See Iqbāl (1934), pp. 44f, 49–51 et passim.

125. Mawdūdī (1949–72), I: pp. 16f. On the issue of man's vice-regency on earth see below, Chapter C.3.2.
126. See, for example, Mawdūdī (1982), p. 9.
127. See Qur'ān 2 (al-Baqara): 44 and 76; 3 (Āl ʿImrān): 65; 6 (al-Anʿām): 32; 10 (Yūnus): 16; 11 (Hūd): 51; 12 (Yūsuf): 109; 21 (al-Anbiyā'): 10 and 67; 23 (al-Mu'minūn): 80; 28 (al-Qaṣaṣ): 60; 36 (Yā-Sīn): 68; 37 (al-Ṣāffāt): 138.
128. See, for example, van Ess (1991–7), IV: pp. 482–512.
129. See Mawdūdī (1949–72), I: p. 17. For the discussion of Mawdūdī's understanding of *dīn*, see below, Chapter C.2.2.b.
130. Compare Luther (1995), II: pp. 197–224 (*Ein kleiner Unterricht, was man in den Evangelien suchen und erwarten soll*; 1522).
131. See Powell (1993), where the relationship is analysed mainly by the encounters in learned disputations (*munāẓarāt*). However, the impact that Christian missionary activities in the subcontinent may have had on the approach to the Qur'ān among Indian Muslims remains, to my best knowledge, yet to be thoroughly investigated.
132. See, for example, Zakariyyā ([6]1983), pp. 30–57; Nadwī ([4]1418/1997), pp. 76–8 et passim. On the other hand, Mawdūdī's supporters followed him in this approach to the Qur'ān almost verbatim. See, for example, Siddiqi (1979), p. 31.
133. See, for example, Nadwī ([2]1400/1980), p. 21: 'He had introduced a new type [*namūna*] in the exegesis of Islam and the Qur'ān that has gained some political shade [*siyāsī rang*].' In the Arabic translation of this work, published after Mawdūdī's demise, Nadwī appeared even less lenient and used the phrase 'political exegesis' right in its title. See al-Nadwī ([2]1400/1980). Nadwī's deliberate use of this label was derived from a fundamentally different understanding of Islam (on this understanding, see Hartung [2004b], pp. 117–23 and 132–42). The use of the term 'political' as a polemical one was and is widespread among those who hold a similar view of Islam, which is mainly rooted in an adherence to a sober Sufism. I am grateful to Andreas Christmann (Braunschweig) for drawing my attention also to the Syrian scholar and Sufi Muḥammad Saʿīd Ramaḍān al-Būṭī (b. 1348/1929) who, like Nadwī, used the attribute 'political' as a polemical term in a pejorative sense.
134. See Nasr (1996), p. 61.
135. See, for instance, Mawdūdī (1949–72), I: pp. 19f.
136. See Kant (1974), IV: pp. 582–605 (B 697–732 [*KdrV*]), especially p. 602 (B 727).
137. Wielandt (2002), p. 137.
138. Mawdūdī (1949–72), I: p. 21. Also, see ibid., I: p. 35.
139. For Abū Zayd and his philological-hermeneutical approach to the Qur'ān, based on the earlier thought of Amīn al-Khūlī and most widely elaborated in his seminal *Mafhūm al-naṣṣ* from 1990, see Wielandt (2002), pp. 131–7; Thielmann (2003), especially pp. 94–113; more recently also Hildebrandt (2008).
140. Mawdūdī (1949–72), I: p. 19.
141. See idem (1997), pp. 13–55.
142. See idem (1963), pp. 191–8. The said volume was edited on behalf of the *Pakistan Philosophical Congress* which at the time was presided over by Muḥammad Miyāṇ Sharīf, a true epigone of Muḥammad Iqbāl. That Mawdūdī was invited to contribute is remarkable, but may be seen as an indication of the struggle of the philosophers in the young Pakistani state to define themselves in dissociation from the Indian sister organisation. See Hartung

(forthcoming). Interestingly, however, this article suggests that Mawdūdī has used a number of classical Arabic commentaries which however do not really fit into a single pattern. They range from the Muʿtazilite *al-Kashshāf ʿan ḥaqāʾiq al-tanzīl wa-ʿuyūn al-aqāwīl* of Abū 'l-Qāsim al-Zamakhsharī (d. 538/1144), Ibn ʿArabī's Sufic interpretation *Aḥkām al-qurʾān* and Bayḍāwī's Ashʿarite inspired *Anwār al-tanzīl wa-asrār al-tawīl*, to the *Tafsīr al-qurʾān al-ʿaẓīm* of Abū 'l-Fidāʾ ibn Kathīr (d. 774/1373). See Mawdūdī (1963), for example, pp. 179, 181, 184, 189 et passim. In the light of his systematic rejection of any earlier exegetical effort these references appear somewhat strange. One possible explanation may be that in such an internationally acclaimed volume Mawdūdī wanted to appear as someone well acquainted with the classical Islamic literature on the matter.

143. See below, Chapter C.4.2. It is striking that in later expositions on economic issues from the 1950s and 1960s, in which he attempted to answer more concrete questions, Mawdūdī had argued more with the Prophetic example, as well as what could be named as 'common sense'. See, for example, idem (1995–6), I: pp. 240–72, II: pp. 297–330, IV: pp. 133–59.
144. Idem (1949–72), I: p. 37.
145. See ibid., I: pp. 13–5.
146. Ibid., I: p. 14.
147. See ibid., VI: pp. 530–43. Interestingly, Mawdūdī's commentary on this particular *sūra* was not included in Hamza, Rizvi and Mayer's topological anthology of Qurʾānic commentaries, despite containing a section on *tawḥīd*. See Hamza/Rizvi/Mayer (2008), pp. 491–575.
148. See Mawdūdī (1949–72), VI: pp. 536f. On the terms 'internal' and 'external oneness', see Hamza/Rizvi/Mayer (2008), p. 492.
149. See, for example, al-Ṭabarī (1322/2001), XXIV: p. 730; Ibn Kathīr (1407/1987), IV: p. 609. Both, *al-aḥad* and *al-wāḥid*, belong to the so-called ninety-nine 'Beautiful Names' of God (*al-asmāʾ al-ḥusná*).
150. See Mawdūdī (1949–72), VI: p. 537.
151. See ibid.
152. Ibid, VI: p. 533.
153. For example in his *Risāla-yi dīniyyāt*, first published in 1932, Mawdūdī seemed to have consciously circumvented the use of the term *tawḥīd* when actually discussing God's oneness. See idem (1970), pp. 82–90. A little further on in the same treatise, however, he employed the term nonetheless, although without any introduction or additional elucidation. See ibid., pp. 91 and 98.
154. See idem (⁷1996), p. 7.
155. Ibid.
156. See idem (1949–72), I: p. 44; idem (⁷1996), pp. 31–37. Here, Mawdūdī quoted, without giving proper references, from the rather late and comparatively concise *Muḥīṭ al-muḥīṭ* of the Lebanese Maronite scholar Buṭrus al-Bustānī (d. 1300/1883). Cf. al-Bustānī (1867–70), I: pp. 740f. This is remarkable and requires an explanation, as the *Lisān alʿarab*, for example, provides a much more detailed discussion of the term. See Ibn Manẓūr (1300–7h), I: pp. 384–93. It is conceivable that Mawdūdī, who did not shine as a philologist, was looking for a less differentiated reference point than the classical Arabic dictionaries, which would have complied also with the degree of proficiency in that language. On al-Bustānī and the nineteenth century Arabic encyclopaedias, see Glaß (2009).
157. Mawdūdī (⁷1996), p. 37.
158. Ibid., p. 79.
159. See ibid., p. 80.
160. For this highly useful translation of *sharīʿa*, see Johansen (1999), p. 39.
161. See Mawdūdī (1990b), pp. 149–53.

162. See idem ([7]1996), pp. 11–19. Again, compare al-Bustānī (1867–70), I: p. 35, whereas the *Lisān al-ʿarab* would have provided a more differentiated discussion of this term. See Ibn Manẓūr (1300–7h), XVII: pp. 358–63.
163. See Mawdūdī (1970), p. 81; idem ([7]1996), p. 11. This corresponds to the meaning of *ilāh* in the *Lisān al-ʿarab*. See Ibn Manẓūr (1300–7h), XVII: pp. 358 and 360.
164. Mawdūdī ([7]1996), p. 19.
165. See Ibn Manẓūr (1300–7h), XVII: p. 359. Mawdūdī however does not refer to the *Lisān al-ʿarab*.
166. See Mawdūdī ([7]1996), p. 79.
167. See ibid., pp. 81f and 98. Compare al-Bustānī (1867–70), II: pp. 1325–7.
168. See Mawdūdī (1949–72), I: pp. 16f; and above.
169. This is perhaps best illustrated by the fact that the phrase 'zōon lógon échōn' which Aristotle had used in his *Politiká*, and which is commonly rendered as 'political animal', can be translated as both: 'an animal possessing speech' or 'an animal possessing rationality'. See Aristotle (1984), II: p. 1987 (1253a).
170. See Mawdūdī ([7]1996), p. 98.
171. See Zakariyyā ([6]1983), pp. 33–45; Nadwī ([2]1400/1980), pp. 68–74 and 84–93.
172. See Schimmel (1975), pp. 94f and 130–48.
173. See above, Chapter C1.
174. See, for example, al-Ghazālī (1377/1957), IV: pp. 286–92; Friedmann (1971), pp. 18f.
175. See Ibn Taymiyya (1396/1976), pp. 44 et passim. For Ibn Taymiyya's alleged affinities to Sufism, see Makdisi (1974).
176. See Weber ([5]1972), pp. 267f and 355–59.
177. For these two conflicting paradigms, see Hartung (2004b), pp. 123–33.
178. See Mawdūdī ([7]1996), p. 109.
179. Ibid., p. 108.
180. See Hegel ([3]1996), XII: pp. 56f (*Rechtsphilosophie*).
181. Mawdūdī ([7]1996), p. 107.
182. See Fichte (1845–6), VI: pp. 80–89 et passim (*Beitrag zur Berichtigung der Urtheile des Publicums über die französische Revolution*; 1793).
183. Marx/Engels (1956–90), XX: p. 106 (*Herrn Eugen Dührings Umwälzung der Wissenschaft*, better known and henceforth referred to as '*Anti-Dühring*'; 1877–78). For Hegel's earlier understanding of the relation between freedom and necessity, to which Engels explicitly referred in this context, see Hegel ([3]1996), VI: pp. 1064f (*Wissenschaft der Logik II*; 1816); VIII: p. 271 (*Encyclopädie der philosophischen Wissenschaften im Grundrisse I*; 3rd edn. 1830); IX: p. 781 (*Encyclopädie II*).
184. See Mawdūdī ([7]1996), p. 80.
185. See ibid., p. 110. Here, however, Mawdūdī's translation of this part of the verse differs slightly from his rendering in *Tafhīm al-qurʾān*. Compare idem (1949–72); I: p. 270. The verse as such had been regarded as unequivocal by Mawdūdī, as he did not feel the need to comment upon it.
186. See Marx/Engels (1956–90), III: p. 535 (*Thesen über Feuerbach*; 1845). Also, see Koselleck (1989), pp. 339–48.
187. Mawdūdī ([7]1996), p. 111.
188. See Fichte (1845–6), I: p. 434 (*Erste Einleitung WL*). Compare Mawdūdī (1972b), p. 122.
189. Idem ([7]1996), p. 110.
190. Idem (1970), p. 148.
191. Ibid.
192. See ibid; idem (1972b), pp. 123f. In the sermons delivered to Punjabi villagers in 1938, Mawdūdī even claims that the Prophet Muḥammad explicitly abrogated all previous

sharīʿāt, which implies that he who follows any of them other than Islam 'is in fact obeying not the command of the master [*āqā kā hukm*], but follows his own dictates [*dil kā kahā*]. Therefore, he is deviated from servitude and becomes, in religious terms, an unbeliever [*kāfir*].' Ibid, p. 124.

193. Interestingly, elsewhere in his *Risāla-yi dīniyyāt*, Mawdūdī characterised the *sharīʿa* as universal and eternal (*ʿālamgīrī awr dāʾimī*), but claims this quality only for the *sharīʿa* of Islam. See idem (1970), pp. 183f.
194. See Hartung (2000), pp. 84f. To see the roots of religiosity in an exchange relation between God and man is quite common in abstract theories of religion that emphasise 'purposive-rational action' (*zweckrationales Handeln*). See Weber (^{5}1972), pp. 245–59; Stark/Bainbridge (1996), pp. 55–87.
195. The anthropological quest was a constant theme in Western philosophical thought, beginning in Greek Antiquity. The credit for linking anthropology to pragmatics for the first time, however, belongs to Kant. His emphasis on 'what [the human being] as a free-acting being makes of himself, or *can*, or *should* make of himself' (Kant [1974], XII: p. 399 [BA IV (*Anthropologie*); transl. Robert B. Louden], emphases added) provided some fertile ground for a radicalised anthropology in later ideologies.
196. See ibid, VII: pp. 66–74 (BA 75–88 [*KdpV*]). Kant's idea was, of course, strongly influenced by Lutheran thought, especially the ideas Luther had laid down in his 1523 treatise *Von weltlicher Obrigkeit, wie weit man ihr Gehorsam schuldig sei*. See Luther (1995), IV: pp. 36–84.
197. Compare ibid, pp. 44–7. The term as such is not Luther's own, but was rather coined in the early twentieth century in the course of systematisation of the Lutheran theology.
198. Compare Weber (^{9}1988), p. 69.
199. See above, Chapter B.3.
200. See Khir (2006).
201. See Mawdūdī (1997), p. 15 (here the English expression 'sovereignty' is put in brackets after *ḥākimiyya*). In the *Lisān al-ʿarab*, *ḥākimiyya* is not explicitly discussed, although it can be inferred from the treatment of *ḥākim*. See Ibn Manẓūr (13007h), XV: pp. 31–3. Equally missing still is an explicit discussion in al-Bustānī (1867–70), I: pp. 430f.
202. 'La souveraineté est la puissance absolue et pérpetuelle d'une République.' (Bodin [1986], I: p. 179).
203. Mawdūdī (1997), p. 20.
204. See idem (^{7}1996), p. 79.
205. See Mawdūdī (1997), pp. 28–30.
206. al-Ṭabarī (1322/2001), XVI: pp. 216f. Mawdūdī's Urdu paraphrase of this statement provides a good example for his rather tendentious interpretations of classical texts. It reads as follows: 'Every being [*hastī*] that revolts against God and is worshipped instead of Him, either by constraining a worshipper with its force [*us ke jabr se majbūr hokar*], or [even] by wishing to do so, is an idol [*ṭāghūt*], irrespective of whether it is some man, the devil [*shayṭān*], an idol [*but*] or anything else.' (Mawdūdī [1997b], p. 25 n.1).
207. See ibid., pp. 28f; also idem (1990b), p. 140.
208. Idem (1997), p. 27.
209. Johansen (1999), p. 37.
210. See Hartung (2011), pp. 298–301. The understanding of the ruler who bent the implications of the authoritative texts for their own benefit is vividly reflected in Mawdūdī's discussion of kingship. See below in this Chapter.
211. This was a widespread and popular criticism throughout the Muslim world that gained momentum especially in the nineteenth and twentieth centuries. See, for example, Riḍā, 'Sajāyā al-ʿulamāʾ', *al-Manār*, 1:25 (19 Rabīʿ al-thānī 1316/6 September 1898), pp. 462–7;

idem, 'Taʿlīm fī madāris al-ḥukūma', *al-Manār*, 3:18 (16 Shaʿbān 1318/7 December 1900), pp. 657–60; idem, ''Ulamāʾ al-dīn', *al-Manār*, 4:11 (1 Jumādá al-ūlá 1319/16 August 1901), pp. 401–11; idem, 'Waẓāʾif ʿulamāʾ al-dīn', *al-Manār*, 4:12 (16 Jumādá al-ūlá 1319/31 August 1901), pp. 441–8; idem, 'Ḥāl al-muslimīn fi'l-ʿālamīn wa-daʿwat al-ʿulamāʾ ilá naṣīḥat alumarāʾ wa'l-salāṭīn', *al-Manār*, 9:5 (1 Jumādá al-ūlá 1324/23 June 1906), pp. 357–65; idem, ''Ulamāʾ Tūnis wa Miṣr, wa-Jāmiʿ al-Zaytūna wa'l-Azhar', *al-Manār*, 10:1 (28 Muḥarram 1325/13 March 1907), pp. 71–7.

212. See, for example, Gentile (1996), p. 143; Dube (2004), pp. 167–75.
213. See Mawdūdī (1972a), p. 37. Once, however, the term 'ḥākimiyya' appears in Mawdūdī's writings with regard to man, but, in contrast to God's sovereignty proper, only as 'limited people's sovereignty' (*maḥdūd ʿumūmī ḥākimiyya*). See ibid., p. 25.
214. Mawdūdī (1997), p. 20.
215. See ibid, p. 30.
216. For a critical discussion of the shift in the caliphal nomenclature see Crone/Hinds (1986), pp. 4–23; Madelung (1997), pp. 46 and 80f.
217. See, for example, al-Baṣrī (1418/1997), III: pp. 22f, 44–7 and 133–9; al-Ṭabarī (^{2}1426/2005), II: pp. 512f and 750–5, III: pp. 829–31. Shiite narrative will however differ on the question of the appointment of Muḥammad's cousin and son-in-law ʿAlī ibn Abī Ṭālib (assassinated 40/661) as Caliph. See, for example, the *Kitāb al-irshād* of the Shaykh al-Mufīd (d. 413/1022): al-Baghdādī (1381/1962), pp. 91–104, especially pp. 96–102.
218. Mawdūdī (1949–72), I: p. 62. Compare idem (1997), p. 31; also al-Bayḍāwī (1330h), I: pp. 134f; al-Ṭabarī (1322/2001), I: pp. 47581; Ibn Kathīr (1407/1987), I: pp. 72f.
219. For example, see Iqbāl (1934), pp. 16, 91, 134f, 118–38 and 149f; Mawdūdī (1997), pp. 98, 196f and 235; idem (1995–96), IV: pp. 219–21 (*al-Khilāfat yā ḥukūmat*; 1961).
220. See Ibn Khaldūn (1320h), p. 181.
221. One may of course argue that Ibn Khaldūn, too, focused on the question of societal rise and decline. His emphasis, however, was more on the quality of the social cohesive force (*ʿaṣabiyya*), which is only reinforced by religion. See below in this Chapter.
222. See Mawdūdī (1997), pp. 96–144; idem (1949–72), III: pp. 419f. In his commentary on the Qurʾānic verse 24 (al-Nūr): 55, Mawdūdī quoted from the sermons of ʿAlī ibn Abī Ṭālib which were collated by Muḥammad ibn Ḥusayn, known as 'al-Sharīf al-Raḍī' (d. 406/1015), as *Nahj al-balāgha*. In this passage, ʿAlī cautioned the then Caliph ʿUmar al-Khaṭṭāb (assassinated 23/644) to never put military strength over trust in God. Mawdūdī, however, has—presumably on purpose—inserted a part of the Qurʾānic verse 24:55 into his quotation which is not a part of the sermon. Compare Ibn Abī Ṭālib (1410/1990), pp. 144f (sermon no. 146).
223. See Idris (1990), pp. 100f. Also, see al-Ṭabarī (1322/2001), I: p. 477; Ibn Kathīr (1407/1987), I: pp. 73f. Mawdūdī, however, was quite aware of the various semantics, as he describes three different usages of the term, two of which amount to 'trusteeship' (*niyābat*) and only one to 'succession' (*jā-nishīnī*). See Mawdūdī (1949–72), III: p. 418.
224. See Idris (1990), p. 105.
225. On the Salafiyya movement in general, see Shinar/Ende (1995); Hourani (2003), pp. 103–92 et passim. On the issue of rationalism, see Hildebrandt (2002); idem (2007), pp. 196–8 et passim.
226. See Riḍā (1420/1999), I: pp. 209–17.
227. Ibid., I: p. 216.
228. Ibid.
229. With regard to the so-called *āyat al-istikhlāf*, i.e. 24 (al-Nūr): 55, Mawdūdī referred explicitly to what he called the 'new exegetes' in his Qurʾānic commentary and, in this way, positioned himself in a particular exegetical tradition. See Mawdūdī (1949–72), III: p. 418.

230. Genesis 1.28.
231. Mawdūdī (1972a), p. 38.
232. See idem (1997), p. 33.
233. See idem (1949–72), III: p. 417.
234. Ibid., III: p. 419.
235. See idem (1972a), p. 37. Here, Mawdūdī has given the English term even before the Urdu one.
236. See ibid., p. 38. The apparently sound *ḥadīth* is found in Muslim (1424/2004), p. 930 (*Kitāb al-imāra, bāb faḍīla al-imām al-ʿādil wa-ʿuqūba al-jāʾir wa'l-ḥathth ʿalá al-rifq bi'l-raʿiyya wa'l-nahy ʿan idkhāl al-mashaqqa ʿalayhim*, Ḥadīth 4, no. 4617); Abū Dāwūd (1983), III: p. 130 (*Kitāb al-kharāj wa'l-imāra wa'l-fayʾ, bāb mā yulazimu al-imām min ḥaqq al-raʿiyya*, Ḥadīth 1, no. 2928); al-Tirmidhī (1938–58), IV: p. 208 (*Kitāb al-jihād, bāb mā jāʾ fi'l-imām*, Ḥadīth 1, no. 1705); Ibn Ḥanbal (1413/1993), II: p. 162 (Ḥadīth 6020). The essence of the *ḥadīth* is referred to in classical legal works where the issue of caliphal responsibility is discussed. See, for instance, Abū Yūsuf (1346h), p. 15; Ibn Taymiyya ([3]1408/1988), pp. 12f.
237. Mawdūdī (1972a), p. 38.
238. See ibid., pp. 38–42. On the role of the *sābiqa*-principle for the determination of religious and political leadership in the early Muslim *umma*, see Madelung (1997), pp. 58 and 77; Noth (1998), pp. 97–100.
239. See Mawdūdī (1972a), pp. 42f.
240. See Rousseau (1967–71), II: pp. 281f (*Discours sur l'économie politique*; 1755), pp. 522–4 (*Du Contrat social ou Principes du droit politique*; 1760–62), III: pp. 242–325 (*Émile ou De l'éducation*; 1762).
241. See, e.g., Mawdūdī (1972a), pp. 26–9 and 42f; idem (1990f), pp. 442–59.
242. For an explicit reference to Rousseau's concept of *volonté générale*, see idem (1990c), pp. 188f.
243. See Vossler (1963), pp. 118f et passim.
244. For the practical adaptation of key elements of Rousseau's political philosophy during the regime of the Jacobins in the French Revolution between 1792 and 1794, see Robespierre (1912–67), IX: pp. 463–71 (*Déclaration des droits de'l homme et du citoyen*; 24 April 1793); also below, Chapter D.1.
245. See Rousseau (1967–71), III: pp. 184–216 (*Émile*); Vossler (1963), pp. 156–63 and 381f.
246. See Mawdūdī (1972a), p. 25.
247. See, for example, Hartung (2011), pp. 295–8.
248. See Mawdūdī (1972a), pp. 25f.
249. See Mawdūdī (1997), pp. 93–5. His references include the *Ṭabaqāt al-kubrá* of Ibn Saʿd (d. 230/845), the *Kitāb al-mabsūṭ* by Muḥammad ibn Aḥmad al-Sarakhsī (d. ca. 500/1106), the *Sīrat ʿUmar ibn al-Khaṭṭāb* by Abū 'l-Faraj ibn al-Jawzī (d. 597/1201), *al-Riyāḍ al-naḍira fī manāqib al-ʿashara* by Muḥibb al-Dīn al-Ṭabarī (d. 694/1295), *Kanz al-ʿummāl* by Muttaqī al-Hindī (d. 975/1567), as well as the *tafsīr* of Ibn Kathīr and al-Ṭabarī's *Taʾrīkh*.
250. See ibid., pp. 265f. Compare Abū Yūsuf (1346h), pp. 12–20. Interestingly, Mawdūdī did not distinguish here between the individual Medinese Caliphs, as he did elsewhere when he ascribed the beginning of the *jāhiliyya* in Islamic times to the caliphate of ʿUthmān ibn ʿAffān. See above, Chapter C.1.1.b.
251. Mawdūdī (1997), p. 95. See also ibid., p. 193.
252. Ibn Khaldūn (1320h), p. 180.
253. Ibid., p. 177.
254. See, for example, al-Ṭabarī (1322/2001), I: pp. 155–7, V: p. 302. Mawdūdī himself did not dwell on a closer definition of the term *mālik*. Compare Mawdūdī (1949–72), I: pp. 44 and 243.

255. See, e.g., idem (1972a), pp. 15–17.
256. Idem (1949–72), I: p. 62.
257. See Koselleck (1989), pp. 246f.
258. See Mawdūdī (1997), pp. 145–61.
259. See ibid., pp. 93–5.
260. See, for example, Marx/Engels (1956–90), VIII: pp. 196–9 (*Der achtzehnte Brumaire des Louis Bonaparte*; 1852).
261. For a historical discussion of the relationship between caliphate, kingship and *maṣlaḥa*, see Hartung (2011), especially pp. 295–301.
262. See above, Chapter C.1.2.b. For versions of the mentioned *ḥadīth*, see al-Dārimī (1398/1978), II: p. 113 (*Kitāb al-ashraba, bāb mā qayyala yakūnu al-khamr*, Ḥadīth 6); al-Shāṭibī (s.t.), I: p. 97.
263. See above, Chapter B.3.
264. On Madanī, in his time one of the leading representatives of Deobandī scholarship, see Riḍwī (1992–93), II: pp. 82–4 and 208–11; Hartung (2004b), pp. 239–43.
265. On Sindhī, another beacon of Deobandī political activity within the anti-colonial movement, see Riḍwī (1992–3), II: pp. 65–7; Hartung (2004b), pp. 245–9. Strangely though, the most outspoken Muslim advocate of the INC, Abū 'l-Kalām Āzād, nowhere received even the least mention by Mawdūdī.
266. See Mawdūdī ([6]1947–55), II: p. 4.
267. See ibid., II: pp. 40f; compare Nehru ([14]2001), pp. 431f.
268. See Mawdūdī ([6]1947–55), II: pp. 42f; compare Nehru ([14]2001), pp. 588–93 et passim.
269. See Mawdūdī ([6]1947–55), II: pp. 43–9.
270. See Nehru ([14]2001), p. 460.
271. See ibid., pp. 374–80.
272. See Mawdūdī ([4]1994), p. 109.
273. Interestingly, Nehrū, too, rejected the idea of a 'Muslim nation', although his line of argument ran quite differently from Mawdūdī's: 'The Muslim nation in India—a nation within a nation, and not even compact, but vague, spread out, indeterminate. Politically, the idea is absurd, economically it is fantastic; it is hardly worth considering.' Nehru ([14]2001), p. 469.
274. These resentments were echoed in all political movements and parties inspired by communalism and, above all, drawing on elements of European Fascist ideology. See above, Chapter B.3.2.b. It is interesting to note that resentments have also been identified as one of the constituents of a Fascist ideology. See ibid.; Nolte (1963), especially pp. 142–5 and 486–91.
275. See Mawdūdī ([4]1994), pp. 107f.
276. Ibid., p. 108.
277. The reasons for this are not yet entirely clear and must remain speculative for the time being. It could however well be that al-Mashriqī's scienticist world view, resulting less in a clear political programme but, first and foremost, in what Daechsel called a 'cult of violence and [preferably spontaneous] action' (Daechsel [2006b], p. 472), i.e. a massive presence in the public domain by the creation of public spectacles, was not considered an equally serious political ideology by Mawdūdī to engage in serious argument with.
278. See Mawdūdī ([4]1994), pp. 126f.
279. See ibid., pp. 114f.
280. See ibid., p. 114; compare, for example, Rousseau (1967–71), II: pp. 522f (*Contrat social*); Fichte (1845–6), III: pp. 202–4 (*Grundlage des Naturrechts nach Principien der Wissenschaftslehre*; 1796); Hegel ([3]1996); VII: pp. 399–404 (*Rechtsphilosophie*); Boucher (1997), pp. xxf.
281. See Mawdūdī ([4]1994), pp. 116–22; compare Coker (1934), pp. 443–8; Leighton (1937), p. 439.

282. See Mawdūdī (^{4}1994), p. 112; compare Aristotle (1984), II: pp. 1987f (1252b), II: pp. 1991f (1255a f).
283. See above, Chapter B.3.1.
284. See Mawdūdī (^{4}1994), pp. 137f.
285. See Rousseau (1967–71), II: pp. 228 and 230–34 (*Discours* [...] *sur l'inégalité parmi les hommes*; 1755).
286. See Mawdūdī (^{4}1994), p. 138.
287. See Ibn Khaldūn (1320h), pp. 143–5 and 149–52.
288. For examples of the utilisation of emotive religious symbols in political movements, see above, Chapter B.2.2.
289. See Mawdūdī (^{4}1994), pp. 132–5; compare also Hartung (2000), pp. 78–80 and 87.
290. See Berkes (1954), especially pp. 383–7.
291. For the issue of the caliphate, then nominally held by the Ottoman sultan, see above, Chapter B.2.2.
292. See above, Chapters B.1.1 and B.2.4.
293. See Mawdūdī (^{4}1994), pp. 122–5 and 127–9.
294. The widespread practice of slavery had apparently been sanctioned in the Qur'ān (see, for example, 16 [al-Naḥl]: 75, even more 24 [al-Nūr]: 32). For an overview, see Brunschvig (1960).
295. See Mawdūdī (1993a), pp. 30f.
296. See ibid., p. 7.
297. See, for instance, ibid., p. 26
298. See ibid.
299. See ibid., pp. 22–4. While Spencer's position, most probably based on *The Principles of Ethics* (1893), is only paraphrased, Hegel is quoted at length, although without giving any bibliographical references. From the text itself, it appears that Mawdūdī quoted, in a rather weak Urdu translation, from the third part of the *Grundlinien der Philosophie des Rechts*. Compare Hegel ([illegible]1990), VII: pp. [illegible]f. Whether this quote is based on S.W. Dyde's English translation from 1896 cannot be assured, although the presumption cannot be discounted, given that Mawdūdī quoted from one of the four most frequently cited Hegelian texts in Britain. See den Otter (1996), p. 27.
300. See Mawdūdī (1993a), pp. 25f and 72f. Mawdūdī referred to a *Tārīkh-i akhlāqiyyāt* of Henry Sidgwick (d. 1900), which most probably means his *Methods of Ethics* (1874), and to the *Companion to Plato's Republic for English Readers* (1895) by Bernard Bosanquet which is most probably the prism through which Mawdūdī read the *Politeía*. See ibid., p. 26; den Otter (1996), pp. 46 and 49f.
301. See Plato (1995–6), IV: pp. 290f (109 St f [*Phaídon*]).
302. See Mawdūdī (1993a), p. 24.
303. See Aristotle (1984), II: pp. 1737f (1099bf [*Politiká*]); II: pp. 2100–2 (1323a-1324b [*Ēthikà nikomácheia*]).
304. See Mawdūdī (1993a), pp. 27–30. These thoughts can be found in *De fato* of Tullius Cicero (d. 43 BCE) as well as, only in Christian guise, in the *Ethica seu scito te ipsum* of Peter Abelard (d. 1142). Compare Cicero (1853), 264–83; Abaelardus (1971).
305. See above, Chapter C.1.1.b.
306. Mawdūdī (1993a), p. 28.
307. Ibid.
308. See ibid., pp. 36f. Although Mawdūdī referred explicitly to John Stuart Mill's *Utilitarianism* from 1861, the *Science of Ethics* (1882) of Leslie Stephen (d. 1904), the early *Outlines of a Critical Theory of Ethics* (1891) by John Dewey (d. 1952) and the Gifford Lectures 1935–36 by William D. Ross (d. 1971), published as *The Foundations of Ethics* (1939), it is highly

doubtful that Mawdūdī had indeed read these works. The Urdu translations of the titles, as well as naming some 'Gifford' as the author of the latter work, suggest that Mawdūdī's knowledge of utilitarianist ethics was derived at best from longer and rather superficial features in various popular magazines available in India.

309. See ibid., pp. 38–40. Here, although without reference to any particular work, Mawdūdī referred explicitly to Hegel. His understanding of Hegel's philosophy of spirit seems to have derived rather from its appropriation by the British idealists around Green, Bosanquet and Bradley. Compare den Otter (1996), pp. 78–80.
310. See ibid., pp. 49–56.
311. Compare Plato (1995–6), I: pp. 314f (368St f [*Politeía*]); Aristotle (1984), II: p. 2056 (1295a [*Politiká*]); Hobbes (1957), pp. 84–93; Rousseau (1967–71), II: pp. 522f and 525–7 (*Contrat social*). The revival of Rousseau's contractual theory in late nineteenth century British idealist thought (see Nicholson [1990], pp. 199–205, 209 et passim; den Otter [1996], pp. 34f; Boucher [1997], pp. 21, 25, 130f, 279 and 285) and the importance of Hobbes' political philosophy for utilitarianism (see Nicholson [1990], pp. 141 and 200; Crimmins [2002]) might explain why Mawdūdī referred explicitly to these two thinkers.
312. See Mawdūdī (1994), p. 18.
313. See above, Chapter C.2.1.a.
314. See Mawdūdī (1993a), pp. 57–65.
315. See, for example, Kant (1974), III: p. 33 (B XXXI [*KdrV*]), IV: pp. 671–95 (B 825–59 [*KdrV*]); Hegel ([3]1996), II: pp. 424–33 (*Glaube und Wissen*; 1802), XVI: pp. 11–246.
316. This is corroborated first by Mawdūdī's frequent references to authors and works of either the British idealist or the utilitarian camp, even when discussing the Hellenic ethics of positive (*aretai*; *maḥāsin*) and negative virtues (*kakía*; *maʿāʾib* [*sic*]). See Mawdūdī (1993a), pp. 72–99. Here, he refers for instance to *The Elements of Ethics* (1892) by John Henry Muirhead (d. 1940), Leslie Stephen's *Social Rights and Duties* (1896), Mill's *Utilitarianism*, *Body and Mind: An Inquiry into their Connection and Mutual Influence* (1870) by Henry Maudesley (d. 1918), and *Crime and Causes* (1891) by William D. Morrison (d. 1943) (although Mawdūdī grossly misspelled his name as 'Mārlīn'). He also mentioned Bradley, H. Thomas Buckle (d. 1862), an Arthur Ford who most probably was *not* identical with the US-American spiritist, the historian Thomas Carlyle (d. 1881), and, surprisingly, John Milton (d. 1674) and his *Paradise Lost* (1667). The identity of a number of other names that Mawdūdī mentioned could not be established.
317. On Thomas H. Green's rather ambiguous understanding of the role of religion, see Nicholson (1990), pp. 266f n.57, 267 n.64 and 289 n.99. Compare Mawdūdī (1993a), pp. 117–19.
318. Mill (1963–91), X: p. 222; also quoted in van den Beld (2001), p. 384.
319. There are two possible explanations which can be derived especially from Mawdūdī's problematic quotations from various works, including Plato's *Politeía* (see, for example, Mawdūdī [1993a], p. 55), Aristotle's *Politiká* and *Ēthikà nikomácheia* (see, for example, ibid., pp. 55 and 73) and Hegel's *Vorlesungen zur Philosophie der Geschichte* and *Grundlinien der Philosophie des Rechts* (see, for example, ibid., pp. 70, 74 and 139). The first and perhaps more favourable explanation is that Mawdūdī acquired his knowledge of these texts from existing weak translations into Urdu and synopses in popular Urdu magazines. The second would attribute to Mawdūdī personal shortcomings in his ability to either comprehend or translate these admittedly highly challenging texts.
320. See ibid., pp. 139f.
321. See Mawdūdī ([4]1994), pp. 17f, 126–32 et passim.
322. Hobbes (1957), p. 83.
323. See Mawdūdī (1949–72), I: pp. 33–5.

324. See, for example, Anderson (1991), pp. 67–82 et passim.
325. See Hegel ([3]1996), VII: pp. 399–415 (*Rechtsphilosophie*).
326. Kant (1974), VII: p. 28 (BA 17 [*Grundlegung zur Metaphysik der Sitten*; 1785]).
327. Mawdūdī ([7]1996), p. 107.
328. See Chapter C.2.2.b.
329. See above, Chapter C.3.2.b.
330. See Mawdūdī (1972a), p. 36.
331. Ibid., p. 35.
332. Compare idem (1997), pp. 70–72.
333. This fact is best illustrated by recalling that grassroots democracy originated in the rather small and thus manageable ancient Greek *póleis*. Plato, for instance, assumed an ideal number of 5,040 citizens of a *pólis* (see Plato [1995–6], II: pp. 114–6 [737 Stf (*Nómoi*)]). Aristotle is even of the opinion that a spatially and numerically large *pólis* 'can rarely, if ever, be well governed [*eunomeisthai*]' (Aristotle [1984], II: pp. 2104f [1326a; *Politiká*]).
334. See, for example, the deeply-rooted reservations about grassroots democracy of the philosopher Abū Naṣr al-Fārābī (d. 339/950), epitomised in his concept of the non-virtuous city. See al-Fārābī ([6]1991), pp. 166–70.
335. Mawdūdī (1949–72), IV: p. 508. Also, see idem (1997), pp. 34f (*Qur'ān kī siyāsī taʿlīmāt*; n.d.), pp. 64f (*Islām ke uṣūl-i ḥukmarānī*; n.d., here quoting the examples of the 'Rightly-Guided' Caliphs ʿUmar ibn al-Khaṭṭāb and ʿAlī ibn Abī Ṭālib as they appear in the *Rūḥ al-maʿānī* of Abū 'l-Thanā' Maḥmūd al-Ālūsī [d. 1270/1854] and Muttaqī al-Hindī's *Kanz al-ʿummāl*). Compare al-Ālūsī (s.t.), XXV: p. 46. In the Islamic tradition, however, the obligatory character of *mushāwara* was quite disputed. See Badry (1998), pp. 91–104.
336. See Dostal (1991), p. 196; al-Baghdādī (2001), pp. 406f.
337. See Badry (1998), pp. 15–34 and 215f; Noth (1998), p. 99. For the history of the European concept of 'Oriental despotism', see Osterhammel (1998), pp. 271–99 and 304–9. Predominantly with political analysts and policy-makers, however, this notion has well persisted until today, as Samuel P. Huntington's (d. 2008) still highly influential thesis of the 'Clash of Civilizations' from 1993 provides vivid evidence.
338. Qur'ān 42 (al-Shūrá): p. 38: '[...] those who conduct their affairs by [mutual] consultation [*wa-amruhum shūrá baynahum*]'. Also, see al-Baghdādī (2001), pp. 407f.
339. Dostal (1991), p. 197; also see ibid., pp. 194–9; al-Baghdādī (2001), p. 406.
340. See Kister (1964); Badry (1998), pp. 79–81 (although without an explicit reference to the *shūrá* of ʿUmar); Crone (2001), pp. 39. For historical accounts of the *shūrá* that finally elected ʿUthmān ibn ʿAffān as the next caliph, see al-Baṣrī (1418/1997), III: pp. 44f; al-Ṭabarī ([2]1426/2005), II: pp. 750–55.
341. See Crone/Hinds (1986), pp. 63–8 and 127f; Madelung (1997), pp. 68–77.
342. See Mawdūdī (1949–72), IV: pp. 508–10.
343. Idem (1972a), pp. 43f.
344. Compare Hobbes (1957), p. 112.
345. I have deliberately chosen the masculine form, as it appears that all public offices are the prerogative of man only. For a detailed analysis of Mawdūdī's view on the gender issue, see below, Chapter C.4.3.a.
346. Qur'ān 49 (al-Ḥujurāt): p. 13, quoted in Mawdūdī (1972a), p. 44.
347. Hobbes (1957), p. 112.
348. See ibid., p. 144.
349. This, however, does not imply that Mawdūdī envisioned the head of the state to be in office for life, as suggested by Badry (1998), p. 580.
350. Mawdūdī (1972a), p. 44. Also, see Mawdūdī's speech on the occasion of his first election

as *amīr* of the JiI on 26 August 1941 in Lahore: Qayyim-i Jamāʿat-i islāmī Pākistān (1989–96), I: pp. 26f.

351. Qurʾān 4 (al-Nisāʾ): 59. On various classical interpretations of *ulū ʾl-amr* see Badry (1998), pp. 149–53.
352. See al-Baṣrī (1418/1997), III: p. 133; also al-Ṭabarī ([2]1426/2005), II: p. 510; Crone/Hinds (1986), pp. 19–22; Madelung (1997), pp. 28–56; Hartung (2011), p. 297.
353. Ibn Khaldūn (1320h), p. 226.
354. See Bleicken (1978), pp. 9–13 and 17f; Brunt (1984), pp. 427 et passim.
355. Mawdūdī (1972a), p. 45.
356. Ibid. Badry (1998), p. 235 n. 296 rightly points out that this position of Mawdūdī's is confined only to his idealtypical state construct and has later, when put into practice in the JiI, undergone considerable metamorphoses.
357. See Brunt (1984), pp. 426f and 442–4.
358. See below, Chapter D.2.b.
359. See Nasr (1994), p. 51. The author however provides no reference for this statement.
360. See Qayyim-i Jamāʿat-i islāmī Pākistān ([23]1997), pp. 24–6.
361. Mawdūdī (1972a), p. 46. The same sentiment was repeated in Mawdūdī's speech on the occasion of the 29th anniversary of the establishment of the JiI in 1970. See idem ([2]1997), pp. 38f. For other contemporary views on the matter, especially those which are explicitly opposed to Mawdūdī's uncompromising opinion, see Badry (1998), pp. 288–304.
362. Compare the practice under the Emperors Augustus and Tiberius (d. 37 CE) when members of the Senate came entirely from the Roman aristocracy and often appointed on the strong suggestion of the emperor. See, for example, Brunt (1984), pp. 423 and 442f. Mawdūdī's distinction regarding a qualified representation of the commoners reflects the classical distinction among men in *khāṣṣa* and *ʿāmma*. See, for example, Badry (1998), pp. 159f and 599.
363. During the founding session of the JiI on 26–27 August 1941 it was predominantly the members of the first *Majlis-i shūrá* who elected Mawdūdī as first *amīr* and Muḥammad Manẓūr Nuʿmānī as his deputy (*nāʾib-amīr*). See, for example, Nuʿmānī (1998), pp. 41f; Qayyim-i Jamāʿat-i islāmī Pākistān (1989–96), I: pp. 22–5; Gīlānī (1992), pp. 140f; also Nasr (1994), pp. 21f
364. See Mawdūdī ([2]1997), p. 4.
365. For a discussion of the history of the issue of *maṣlaḥa* as a benchmark for 'good governance' (*al-siyāsa al-sharīʿa*), see Hartung (2011), pp. 297f.
366. See Mawdūdī ([2]1997), pp. 4–6.
367. See Qayyim-i Jamāʿat-i islāmī Pākistān (1989–96), I: p. 25.
368. See Hartung (2011), pp. 297 et passim.
369. The division of powers was introduced in modern political theory first by John Locke (d. 1704) in his second *Treatise of Government* (1689) (see Locke [[6]1970], pp. 364–72 et passim). and was even more pronounced in Montesquieu's *De l'esprit des lois* (1748).
370. Here one has, of course, to distinguish between Mawdūdī's ideological outline and the attempts to put this into practice as authenticly as possible in the JiI from 1941 onwards. Practical restraints however have repeatedly required revisions and slight alterations and led to more practical solutions. See Nasr (1994), pp. 26–43; and below, Chapter E.2. For example, nowhere in Mawdūdī's earlier conceptual writings was the office of the 'secretary' (*qayyim*), as it was created in 1941, mentioned, let alone its theoretical justification.
371. See Mawdūdī ([2]1997), pp. 41f. In reality, however, the notion of *ʿālim* appears to have been a rather wide one.
372. For the issue of the legislative force and the role of the early Muslim *fuqahāʾ* therein, see Hartung (2011), pp. 298–302.

373. Although this had hardly been spelled out explicitly, the tasks assigned to the *Majlis-i shūrá* in the statutes of the JiI nonetheless suggest rather clearly the necessity of such a qualification. See Qayyim-i Jamāʿat-i islāmī Pākistān ([23]1997), pp. 33–5; idem (1989–96), I: pp. 58f.
374. See Badry (1998), pp. 144–6 and 148.
375. See, for example, Hallaq (1984), pp. 4–20. For the first systematic major discussion of the methodology, see al-Shāfiʿī (s.t.), pp. 476–503, especially p. 477, where *ijtihād* is explicitly equated with analogous reasoning (*qiyās*): 'These are two terms that mean the same [*hummā ismān li-maʿnan wāḥidin*]'.
376. Mawdūdī ([7]1994), p. 45. This view has apparently remained stable in Mawdūdī's thought, as he repeated it much later in an article in *Tarjumān al-qurʾān*. See idem (1995–96), III: p. 234 (*Ijtihād ke ḥudūd*; August 1962).
377. See idem ([7]1994), pp. 101f.
378. Quoted in ibid., p. 101.
379. Here, of course, we may detect yet another conflict between normative expectation and practical realisation in Mawdūdī's efforts, because of his, at best limited, ability to actually exert *ijtihād*, Mawdūdī could have never been appointed *amīr* of the JiI. Significantly, however, Mawdūdī did not stress the ability for *ijtihād* as a necessary qualification for the 'Perfect Renewer' (*mujaddid-i kāmil*), or *Imām al-mahdī*. Compare ibid., pp. 46–51.
380. See Qurʾān 3 (Āl ʿImrān): 104, 110 and 114; 9 (al-Tawba): 71 and 112; 22 (al-Ḥajj): 41; also above, Chapter B.2.1.
381. See Mawdūdī (1997), pp. 72–5 (*Uṣūl-i ḥukmarānī*). Here, Mawdūdī referred to a number of sound Prophetic *aḥādīth* to support the obligatory character of this Qurʾānic injunction: for example, Muslim (1424/2004), p. 52 (*Kitāb al-īmān, bāb bayān kawn al-nahy ʿan al-munkar min al-īmān, wa-inna 'l-īmān yazīdu wa-yanquṣu, wa-inna 'l-amr bi'l-maʿrūf wa'l-nahy ʿan al-munkar wājibān*, Aḥādīth 1 and 3, nos. 82 and 84 [The latter *ḥadīth* was neither fully nor correctly quoted by Mawdūdī!]; al-Tirmidhī (1938–58), IV: pp. 468f (*Kitāb al-fitan, bāb mā jāʾ fi'l-amr bi'l-maʿrūf wa'l-nahy ʿan al-munkar*, Aḥādīth 1f, nos. 2169f); Abū Dāwūd (1983), IV: pp. 123f (*Kitāb al-malāḥim, bāb al-amr wa'l-nahy*, Aḥādīth 5 and 9, nos. 4340 and 4344); Ibn Māja (1373/1954), II: p. 1329f (*Kitāb al-fitan, bāb al-amr bi'l-maʿrūf wa'l-nahy ʿan al-munkar*, Aḥādīth 9 and 11, nos. 4011 and 4013).
382. See Mawdūdī (1997), p. 65 (*Uṣūl-i ḥukmarānī*).
383. See Nasr (1994), pp. 26f. Unfortunately, however, I was unable to find substantial corroboration for Nasr's statement in the material consulted. Also, see below, Chapters D.2.3 and E.2.1.
384. See Mawdūdī (1972a), p. 47.
385. Ibid.
386. It has to be stressed here that, although the JiI has been part of government coalitions in Bangladesh, in Jammu and Kashmir, and in various provincial governments in Pakistan, it has so far nowhere enjoyed government majority. See below, Chapter E.2.
387. See Hobbes (1957), pp. 219–32. The emphasis on 'prosperity' and the 'contentments of life, which every man by lawful industry, without danger or hurt to the commonwealth, shall acquire to himself' (ibid., 219) appears as a consequential tapering of the Aristotelian ideal of the 'good life' (*eudaimonía*) to economics above everything else. Cf. Aristotle (1984), II: pp. 1736–8 (1099a-1100a [*Politiká*]).
388. See Smith (1893), pp. 428–502, especially pp. 436–58 (*Causes of Prosperity of New Colonies*). It has recently been stressed that the reception of Smith's ideas by nineteenth century utilitarian philosophers, like Bentham and Mill, was far from uniform. See Pitts (2003), pp. 205 and 220f.
389. See Mawdūdī (1993a), p. 69. Here, Mawdūdī referred in a rather simplistic manner to

Smith's *Theory of Moral Sentiments* from 1759, stating that in his deontology Smith had differentiated between absolute (*qaṭʿī*), collective (*ijtimāʿī*) and individual (*infrādī*) duties, only the first two of which were to be enforced by constitutional law.

390. See Rothermund (1996), pp. 87–97; Zachariah (2005), pp. 6f, 43, 92 and 181.
391. Compare Smith (1893), pp. 22f; Mill (1963–91), III: pp. 799–804 and 913–71 (*The Principles of Political Economy*; 1848); Marx/Engels (1956–90), IV: p. 482 (*Manifest der Kommunistischen Partei*; 1848); Lenin (1962–70), XXV: pp. 391–4 (*Gosudarstvo i revoljucija*; 1917). The masterminds of Fascism, however, hardly shared such an economy-centred view. Mussolini (1951–62), XXXIV: p. 119 (*La dottrina del fascismo*; 1932), for example, made clear that '[il fascimo] non crede possibile la «felicità» sulla terra, come fu nel desiderio della letteratura economicistica del '700, e quindi respinge tutte le concezioni teleologiche per cui a un certo periodo della storia ci sarebbe una sistemazione definitiva del genere umano.' Compare also Hitler (1930), pp. 164 and 680; Rosenberg (1930), pp. 28, 39, 194 and 202.
392. See Mawdūdī (1969), pp. 8–11.
393. See ibid., p. 14; compare Machiavelli (1979), p. 67. Interestingly, Mawdūdī continued his argument by stressing that this turn to Macchiavellian ethics stood in clear contrast to the religious understanding of man's responsibility towards creation in Judaism and Islam, as well as to the political philosophies of Plato, Aristotle and Roman philosophers. Given however his earlier criticism of Aristotle's ethical thought (see above, Chapter C.3.2.b) and the acceptance that economics played a major role in Aristotle's political thought, this assessment of Mawdūdī's appears somewhat surprising and indicates once again Mawdūdī's difficulties in maintaining consistency within his systematic approach.
394. See Mawdūdī (1969), p. 15.
395. See ibid., pp. 16–26. This view was, of course, not necessarily held by every theorist of liberalism, as for example the fundamental differences between Adam Smith and John Stuart Mill testifies. Compare Smith (1893), pp. 342–59; Mill (1963–91), III: pp. 934–71 (*Principles of Political Economy with some of their Applications to Social Philosophy*; 1848).
396. See Rousseau (1967–71), II: pp. 233f (*Inégalité*); compare, for example, Marx/Engels (1956–90), XXI: pp. 25–173 (Engels: *Der Ursprung der Familie, des Privateigentums und des Staates*; 1884); Rosenberg (1930), pp. 304f; Wieacker (1935), pp. 19f and 49–54; also see Keiser (2005), pp. 37–54.
397. Here belongs already Plato's idea of an egalitarian polity in the prologue of his *Tímaios*, a major characteristic of which is the abandonment of private property (see Plato [1995–6], II: pp. 420f [18St]), but also the political economies of Thomas More (executed 1535), Tommaso Campanella (d. 1639), Claude Henri de Saint-Simon (d. 1825) and others. Compare Mawdūdī (1969), pp. 43f.
398. See ibid., p. 47.
399. Marx/Engels (1956–90), IV: p. 462 (*Manifest* [transl. Samuel Moore]); compare Mawdūdī (1969), pp. 46f.
400. See Marx/Engels (1956–90), XX: pp. 444–55 (Engels: *Der Anteil der Arbeit an der Menschwerdung des Affen*; 1876); compare Mawdūdī (1969), p. 47.
401. Marx/Engels (1956–90), XXIII: p. 789 (*Das Kapital: Kritik der politischen Ökonomie I*; 1867 [transl. Samuel Moore and Edward Aveling], emphasis in the original); also see ibid., pp. 744–61.
402. See Mawdūdī (1969), pp. 48f and 54f.
403. See, for example, Zachariah (2005), pp. 6f and 213f.
404. Marx/Engels (1956–90), XIX: p. 21 (*Kritik des Gothaer Programms*; 1875 [transl. n.n.]).
405. Lenin (1962–70), XXIV: p. 24 (*O zadačax proletariata v dannoj revoljucii*; April 1917); see Marx/Engels (1956–90), IV: pp. 481f (*Manifest*); Boettke (1990), pp. 66–9.

406. See Lenin (1962–70), XXVI: pp. 117f (*Uderžat li bol'ševiki gosudarstvennuju vlast'?*; October 1917).
407. See, for example, Gregory (2004), pp. 26–48.
408. See Mawdūdī (1969), pp. 54f; ibid. (1981), p. 54 (*Insān kā maʿāshī mas'ala awr us kā islāmī ḥall*; 1941); Gregory (2004), pp. 39–44.
409. Lenin (1962–70), XXXI: p. 291; compare Mawdūdī (1969), p. 56 (without him giving an exact reference).
410. See idem (1981), p. 55 (*Insān kā* [...]).
411. See ibid., pp. 61–7; Gregory (2004), pp. 16–18, 126–52 and 186–90.
412. See, for example, Whitman (1991), pp. 757–9 (based on the *Elementi di ordinamento corporativo* [1933] of the two lawyers Rafaello Viglione and Dario Guidi); Schieder (1996), p. 79.
413. See Eatwell (1996), pp. 314–16; Baker (2006), pp. 242f.
414. See Nolte (1960), pp. 258–67 and 270–78; idem (1963), pp. 200–31.
415. See Kühnl (1966), pp. 318, 321f and 324–33; Schieder (1996), pp. 118f; Baker (2006), p. 232.
416. See Kühnl (1966), pp. 321–5; Barkai (1977), pp. 29f, 35f, 82, 177 et passim; Schieder (1996), p. 79; Baker (2006), p. 233.
417. See Turner Jr. (1968), p. 362 et passim; also Barkai (1977), pp. 25f et passim.
418. See ibid., pp. 92–109; Whitman (1991), pp. 760–13; Baker (2006), pp. 234f. In this context, the characterisation of Fascism as the most aggressive form of 'state monopoly capitalism' by the Bulgarian Communist leader Georgi Dimitrov (d. 1949) is significant.
419. For Italy, see, for example, Whitman (1991), pp. 756–63; for Germany see Barkai (1977), pp. 92–109; Schieder (1996), pp. 88–93.
420. See, for example, Baker (2006), pp. 232–6.
421. See Mawdūdī (1969), pp. 70–74.
422. 'In practice, however, the results of this appear to be not much different from those of the Communist theory.' Idem (1981), p. 56 (*Insān kā* [...]).
423. Baker (2006), p. 237. There is, however, a certain awareness of the aggressive potential of National Socialism visible in Mawdūdī's treatment of nationalism. See Mawdūdī (^{4}1994), pp. 127f.
424. See idem (1969), p. 74; compare idem (^{4}1994), pp. 126–32.
425. Idem (1969), p. 75.
426. See ibid., pp. 76f.
427. For India, see Zachariah (2005), pp. 213f, 248 et passim; for the US and Roosevelt's 'New Deal' of the 1930s, see Whitman (1991); for Shōwa Japan, see Lincoln (1990) and the references cited there on p. 207 n. 1.
428. Compare Mawdūdī (1981), p. 55 (*Insān kā* [...]).
429. Rousseau (1967–71), II: p. 279 (*Économie politique* [transl. Cristopher Betts]).
430. Hegel (^{3}1996), VII: p. 398 (*Rechtsphilosophie* [transl. S. W. Dyde]).
431. See den Otter (1996), pp. 152–80; Boucher (1997), pp. xx-xxviii, 130–41 and 173–213.
432. See, for example, McKenzie (1893), pp. 289–95 and 297–308; also den Otter (1996), especially pp. 141f.
433. Compare Hegel (^{3}1996), VII: pp. 102–72 (*Rechtsphilosophie*).
434. Cf. Marx/Engels (1956–90), XIII: pp. 7–11 and 468–77.
435. Additionally and perhaps to support his own interpretations, Mawdūdī had assembled an interesting array of Qur'ānic commentaries which share little, if any commonalities. While his references include the standard *tafāsīr* of Bayḍāwī, Ṭabarī and Ibn Kat͟hīr, they comprise also the *Aḥkām al-qur'ān* of the renowned Ḥanafite scholar Aḥmad ibn ʿAlī al-Jaṣṣāṣ (d. 370/981), the same-titled work by Ibn ʿArabī, the *Kashshāf* of al-Zamak͟hsharī

and al-Ālūsī's *Rūḥ al-maʿānī*. See Mawdūdī (1981), p. 117 (*Qurʾān kī maʿāshī taʿlīmāt*; 1969).
436. See ibid., pp. 69f.
437. See ibid., p. 71; the references used here are Qurʾān 16 (al-Naḥl): 116; al-Bayḍāwī (1330h), III: p. 193, and al-Ālūsī (s.t.), XIV: pp. 246f. Although *ḥalāl* and *ḥarām* are indeed the terms used in the Qurʾānic verse, Mawdūdī's conclusion to restrict acts and relationships generally to these two extreme terms, although consistent with his bipolar worldview, may be interpreted as yet further proof of his rather poor knowledge of Islamic *fiqh*. On the other hand, this view was by no means his alone, for it was a view which became increasingly shared by Muslims worldwide, as the enormous popularity that the book *al-Ḥalāl wa'l-ḥarām fi'l-islām* (1960) of the former Muslim Brother and renowned *faqīh* Yūsuf al-Qaraḍāwī enjoys throughout the Muslim world. See, for example, al-Khateeb (2009), pp. 96f.
438. See Mawdūdī (1981), pp. 72–5 and 229–98 (*Masʾala-yi sūd*; 1948); idem (1949–72), I: pp. 214–17, III: pp. 760 et passim.
439. Ibid., p. 157: *islāmī naẓm-i maʿīshat ke uṣūl awr maqāṣid.*
440. See Barkai (1977), pp. 25–30; compare Hitler (1030), pp. 228f.
441. Qurʾān 2 (al-Baqara): 284.
442. See Mawdūdī (1981), pp. 75f (*Qurʾān kī* [...]).
443. Qurʾān 6 (al-Anʿām): 165.
444. As proof of this, compare the much wider interpretations of the very same verse in al-Bayḍāwī (1330h), II: p. 217; al-Ṭabarī (1322/2001); X: pp. 50f; Ibn Kat͟hīr (1407/1987), II: p. 208.
445. Compare Mawdūdī (1949–72), I: pp. 606f; idem (1981), pp. 78–81 (*Qurʾān kī* [...]).
446. In a lecture delivered in Mecca during his stay on the occasion of the foundation of the *Muslim World League* (*Rābiṭat al-ʿālam al-islāmī*) in May 1962, Mawdūdī defined 'justice' even as an essential goal of Islam. See ibid., p. 379 (*Islām awr ʿadl-i ijtimāʿī*).
447. See idem (1972b), pp. 199–254; idem (1981), pp. 93–6 and 99–107 (*Qurʾān kī* [...]).
448. See idem (1972b), 228f. The Qurʾānic reference 12 (Yūsuf): 37 which Mawdūdī used here to support his argument does not make any sense. What he may have wanted to refer to was 17 (al-Isrāʾ): 11: 'Man asks for the evil [*bi'l-sharr*] as he prays for the good [*bi'l-k͟hayr*], for man is hasty [*wa-kāna al-insān ʿajūlan*]'. Compare Mawdūdī (1949–72), III: p. 159.
449. See idem (1981), p. 83 (*Qurʾān kī* [...]).
450. See ibid., pp. 96f.
451. See ibid., pp. 81–112.
452. Qurʾān 24 (al-Nūr): 55. Also, see above, Chapter C.3.2.a.
453. Qurʾān 24 (al-Nūr): p. 55.
454. See al-Ṭabarī (1322/2001), XVII: pp. 347f; Ibn Kat͟hīr (1407/1987), III: p. 313; also Mawdūdī (1949–72), III: p. 417.
455. It is therefore not surprising that especially the dealing with these two groups received some serious reassessment by Mawdūdī's partisans later on. See below, Chapter E.2.
456. Qurʾān 33 (al-Aḥzāb): 33: *wa-qarna fī buyūtikunna.*
457. However, initial discussion of gender issues by Mawdūdī dates back to his time as editor of *al-Jamʿiyya* and was closely linked to the impact of the *śuddhī*-movement of the *Ārya Samāj* on Muslim women, the possibility of them committing the act of apostasy and the legal consequences this would entail. See, for example, Mawdūdī, 'Musalmān awratoṇ kā irtidād awr uske rokne kī tadābīr', *al-Jamʿiyya*, 4:34 (7 Jumādá al-ūlá 1345/14 November 1926), 2—4:37 (19 Jumādá al-ūlá 1345/26 November 1926), 2; idem, 'Nikāh-i murtadda', *al-Jamʿiyya*, 4:38 (22 Jumādá al-ūlá 1345/29 November 1926), 2 (Mawdūdī's own summary of a series of four articles on the issue by various *ʿulamāʾ*). Also, see above, Chapter B.1.1.

458. See Mawdūdī (1973), pp. 27f. Here, it appears that Mawdūdī had only the Indian situation in view, as he did not consider, for example, the indigenous modernisation efforts in Egypt under Meḥmed of ʿAlī Paşa and in Iran under Naṣīr al-Dīn Shāh Qājār (assassinated 1313/1896). Although the emancipatory ideas of Rifāʿa al-Ṭahṭāwī and Qāsim Amīn were demonstrably influenced by European thought, a Western imposition of their values, mediated by colonialism, can nonetheless been ruled out.
459. See ibid., pp. 18f and 36f.
460. Ibid., p. 37. It is somewhat illuminating of the understanding of the origins of some of Mawdūdī's ideas to see that the last sentence in this quote contains the essence of Chapter IV in John Stuart Mill's treatise *On Liberty* (1859). See Mill (196391), XVIII: pp. 276–91.
461. Mawdūdī (1973), p. 20; see also ibid., pp. 21–4 and 49–53.
462. See ibid., pp. 37–74.
463. See Maus (1962), pp. 16f and 94 (here, however, referring to Bureau's slightly critical stand towards La Play's exclusive acceptance of the *Decalogue* [*Aseret ha-dibberot* or *Dekálogos*] and the doctrines of the Catholic Church for the foundation of society); Clark (1973), pp. 104–11.
464. See Scharlieb (1924), pp. 17–43 and 95–122; also her introduction in Bureau (1925), pp. xi-xvi.
465. Using this term I follow the convincing definition provided by Daechsel (2006), pp. 12–15.
466. See ibid., pp. 106–13. For discussions of the Victorian conception of sexuality, see Stearns/Stearns (1985); Rury (1987), pp. 45–8; Seidman (1990); for the complex issue of the impact of this conception on the military administration of colonial India, see Peers (1998).
467. On Lindsey, see Larsen (1972). Mawdūdī quoted extensively from *The Revolt of Modern Youth*. See Mawdūdī (1973), pp. 76 and 83–5.
468. See Hooker (1921), pp. 13–27. Somewhat revealing is the first sentence in her conclusion: 'From the preceding survey it has been seen (1) that the social evil, comprising prostitution and venereal disease, is a result of the disordered sexual life of the race; (2) that marriage is the expression of a definite racial need, and developed through natural selection as an institution for the preservation of the offspring, and as the vehicle for sexual selection; [...]'. Ibid., p. 349. Mawdūdī's whole exposition of venereal diseases (Mawdūdī [1973], pp. 82f) appears to have been based on Hooker. Compare Hooker (1921), pp. 187–214. On Hooker, see Luker (1998), pp. 620f; Haag (1992), p. 559.
469. See Mawdūdī (1973), p. 81. On Lowry, see Rury (1987), p. 55.
470. See Mawdūdī (1973), p. 86. On Macfadden, see Griffith (2000), pp. 607–13, 619f et passim.
471. See Mawdūdī (1973), pp. 86–8. On Scott, author of thirteen other books mainly on issues of sexuality and corporal punishment, no further biographical information could be retrieved.
472. See ibid., p. 55.
473. See ibid., pp. 89–103.
474. Ibid., p. 101.
475. Compare Aristotle (1984), II: pp. 1988f (1253b [*Politiká*]).
476. See Mawdūdī (1973), pp. 115f.
477. Compare Young (1985), pp. 620–22; Crook (1994), pp. 17f and 33–5.
478. Mawdūdī (1973), p. 115: 'It is the miracle of religion [*madhhab kā muʿjiza*] that it causes man and women both to make sacrifices for the species and civilization [*nawʿ awr tamaddun ke līye*] and become thus ready for the transition from a selfish animal to a human being.'
479. See ibid., p. 159.

480. Compare Qur'ān 51 (al-Dhāriyyāt): 49: 'All things We made in pairs [*zawjayn*]'. Also, see Mawdūdī (1949–72), V: p. 151; idem (1973), p. 161.
481. Ibid., p. 162.
482. The patriarchal reading of this very verse has, just by the way, of course been a major point of recent contestation by feminist Qur'ānic exegetes, like the African-American theologian Amīna Wadūd-Muḥsin (b. 1952), the Pakistani-American theologian Rif'at Ḥasan (b. 1943) and the Lebanese-American jurist and philosopher 'Azīza [bint] Yaḥyá al-Ḥibrī (b. 1943). See Badran (2009), pp. 311–13 and 331f. A comprehensive study of feminist *tafsīr* is still to be written.
483. Mawdūdī (1973), p. 165; also, see idem (1949–72), I: p. 170.
484. See idem (1973), pp. 157f. On Nemilov, see Naiman (1997), pp. 82f, 191–8 and 295–7.
485. See ibid., pp. 195–7.
486. Quoted in Mawdūdī (1973), p. 158.
487. See ibid., pp. 141–4. Apparently, Mawdūdī's shady trick appears to have worked very well, as so far no one has ever questioned the fact that he had indeed read through all these works. Even Irfan Ahmad, otherwise rather critical, has still been duped by this exposition of Mawdūdī's and takes over, among others, even the misspelling of the name 'Woichiechowsky' from the Urdu text. See Ahmad (2008), p. 557 n.16.
488. For Mawdūdī's reference to Emil Novak (here even disguised as a direct quote), compare Nemilov (1932), pp. 116f; for the reference to the Russian neurologist M. N. Lapinski compare ibid., p. 125; for the references to the German sexologist and psychiatrist Richard von Krafft-Ebing (d. 1902) and the American neurologist Max H. Weinberg compare ibid., p. 128; for the Russian neurologist A. Reprev compare ibid., p. 155. Only the references to the British sexologist Havelock Ellis (d. 1939) and the German sexologist Albert Moll (d. 1939) appear not to be based on Nemilov's book, but rather on Ellis' *The Psychic State of Pregnancy* (1914).
489. The dubiousness of the theories and research methods of M. N. Lapinski, for example, then director of the Institute of Neurology at the Russian Academy of Medical Sciences, have most probably been epitomised in the character of Doctor Stravinsky in Mikhail Bulgakov's famous satirical novel *The Master and Margarita* (1929–39). See Natov (1995), p. 184 n.11.
490. Albert Moll (compare Mawdūdī [1973], p. 144), for example, was a close associate of the sexologist and early gay rights advocate Magnus Hirschfeld (d. 1935) who, in turn, was fiercely criticised by Mawdūdī for his advocacy of gay rights. See ibid., p. 54.
491. Ibid., p. 196.
492. Mawdūdī seems to have consciously decided against the use of *qiwām* (*provider*). The Arabic dictionaries give 'commander' (*amīr*) as a synonym to *qawwām*. See Ibn Manẓūr (1300–7h), XV: p. 401; al-Bustānī (1867–70), II: p. 1778. Elsewhere, Mawdūdī himself specified the meaning of *qawwām*, stating that 'this means [he] is the sovereign [*ḥākim*] of the family'. Mawdūdī (1973), p. 176.
493. Ibid., p. 181.
494. See ibid., pp. 184f.
495. See, for example, Metcalf (2000).
496. This term, denoting 'a re-assertion of patriarchy and tradition' has been borrowed from Ahmad (2008), p. 558, who, in turn, has adopted it from Hisham Sharabi's book *Neopatriarchy: A Theory of Distorted Change in Arab Society* (New York: OUP 1988).
497. See Qur'ān 33 (al-Aḥzāb): 33: *wa-qarna fī buyūtikunna*. Also, see Mawdūdī's own rather extensive treatment of this passage in Mawdūdī (1949–72), IV: pp. 90f; idem (1973), pp. 249–51.
498. See Aristotle (1984), II: pp. 1998–2000 (1259b-60b) and 2006 (1264b [*Politiká*]).

499. Qur'ān 9 (al-Tawba): 29: [...] *ṣāghirūn.*
500. See Mawdūdī (1993b). Among the Ḥanafī works Mawdūdī had referred to in his footnotes are found the *Kitāb al-kharāj* of Abū Yūsuf, al-Sarakhsī's *Kitāb al-mabsūṭ* and *Sharḥ al-siyar al-kabīr*, the *Badā'iʿ al-ṣanā'iʿ fī tartīb al-sharā'iʿ* of ʿAlā' al-Dīn al-Kāsānī (d. 587/1189), *ʿInāyat sharḥ al-hidāya* of Akmāl al-Dīn Muḥammad al-Bābartī (d. 786/1384), the *Burhān sharḥ mawāhib al-raḥmān fī madhhab Abī Ḥanīfa al-Nuʿmān* of Ibrāhīm al-Ṭrābulusī (d. 922/1516) and *Durr al-mukhtār* of Muḥammad ʿAlā' al-Dīn al-Ḥaṣkafī (d. 1088/1677).
501. See Fattal (1958), pp. 34–60.
502. See Mawdūdī (1995–6), I: pp. 277f (*Islāmī riyāsat meṇ dhimmī raʿāyā*; 1944); Nasr (1996), p. 100.
503. Hegel (³1996), VII: p. 398 (*Rechtsphilosophie* [transl. S.W. Dyde]).
504. Nasr's stress on Mawdūdī's alleged 'advocacy of *zimmi* [sic]-Muslim separation' (Nasr [1996], p. 102; also see ibid., pp. 100f) seems not entirely correct to me in the light of the Islamic state being a trans-territorial one, constituted alone by the sum of its citizens. Thus, the *ahl al-dhimma* would play only a very marginal role, while Mawdūdī's dichotomy with regard to the citizens of the Islamic state was rather 'Muslim–apostate'.
505. See, for example, Mawdūdī, 'Takfīr bayna 'l-muslimīn awr uske mutaʿalliq-i ʿulamā' kī nakīr', *al-Jamʿiyya*, 4:32 (29 Rabīʿ al-thānī 1345/6 November 1926), p. 1. On the *śuddhī*-movement of the *Ārya Samāj*, see above, Chapter B.1.1.
506. See Nedza (2008), pp. 23–31.
507. See Mawdūdī (1993b), pp. 5–10.
508. Soon, the Qur'ānic injunction 'fight those who believe not in God [..., even if they are] of the People of the Book, until they pay the *jizya* out of hand, being brought low' (9 [al-Tawba]: 29) has been widened for other religious communities then under Muslim rule. See Fattal (1958), pp. 10–14; Friedmann (2003), pp. 59–86; also Mawdūdī (1949–72), IV: p. 188. Later, Mawdūdī did not distinguish any more between *ahl al-kitāb* and followers of other religions. See idem (1993b), pp. 8–26.
509. See idem (²1980), p. 28.
510. See, for example, Hartung (2004b), pp. 143–55.
511. See Mawdūdī (1972b), pp. 30–32.
512. See Metcalf (1993); Sikand (2002a), pp. 65–108; Hartung (2004b), pp. 130–32. It has however to be stressed that the confinement of the focus of the TJ's activities to nominal Muslims appears to be exclusively a South Asian particularity.
513. For the typology of 'guidance-' *versus* 'governance-oriented', see Mukarram (1992), pp. 9–11 et passim; also Hartung (2004b), pp. 124f.
514. al-Bukhārī (1426/2005), p. 1736 (*Kitāb istitābat al-murtaddīn wa'l-muʿānidīn wa-qitālīhim, bāb ḥukm al-murtadd wa'l-murtadda*, Ḥadīth 1, no. 6922); Ibn Māja (1373/1954), II: p. 848 (*Kitāb al-ḥudūd, bāb murtadd ʿan dīnihi*, Ḥadīth 1, no. 2535). Also, see Nedza (2008), pp. 13–23.
515. The two versions of the *ḥadīth* which is usually referred to with regard to the issue of *istitāba* differ significantly in the collections of al-Bukhārī and Abū Dāwūd. See al-Bukhārī (1426/2005), pp. 1736f (*Kitāb istitābat al-murtaddīn wa'l-muʿānidīn wa-qitālīhim, bāb ḥukm al-murtadd wa'l-murtadda*, Ḥadīth 2, no. 6923); contrast Abū Dāwūd (1983), IV: pp. 127f (*Awwal kitāb al-ḥudūd, bāb al-ḥukm fī-man irtadda*, Ḥadīth 6, no. 4356). The matter is even more complicated by a *ḥadīth* in the *Muwaṭṭa* of Mālik ibn Anas (d. 179/796) that provides still further information relating to the dealing with the issue of *istitāba*. See Ibn Anas (1280/1863), pp. 292f (*Kitāb al-aqḍiyya, bāb al-qaḍā' fī-man irtadda ʿan al-islām*, Ḥadīth 2, no. 16).
516. See Friedmann (2003), pp. 130–33 and 142–4; Nedza (2008), pp. 24–30.

517. See Ibn Taymiyya (1413/1993); idem (1420/1999), IV: pp. 257–77; Ibn G͟hannām (²1405/1985); Āl al-Shayk͟h (s.t.); Peskes (1993), pp. 16f; Nedza (2008), pp. 50–62.

518. See Ibn G͟hannām (²1405/1985), pp. 274–88.

519. Mawdūdī (1972b), p. 32.

520. Ibid., p. 76.

521. Ibid., p. 37; compare Ibn G͟hannām (²1405/1985), pp. 405f.

522. See Robespierre's famous speech to the National Convention on 5 February 1794: 'Si le ressort du gouvernement populaire dans la paix est la vertu, le ressort du gouvernement populaire en révolution est à la fois la vertu et la terreur: la vertu, sans laquelle la terreur est funeste; la terreur, sans laquelle la vertu est impuissante. La terreur n'est autre chose que la justice prompte, sévère, inflexible; elle est donc une émanation de la vertu; elle est moins un principe particulier, qu'une conséquence du principe général de la démocratie, appliqué aux plus pressants besoins de la patrie.' (Robespierre [1912–67], X: p. 357 [*Sur les principes de morale politique qui doivent guider la Convention nationale dans l'administration intérieure de la République*].)

523. See Conquest (1990), pp. 4–7, 13 and 16. Although Conquest's book has sparked a hot controversy and has even been declared obsolete by renowned historians like Eric Hobsbawm, the analysis of the ideological justification of the 'Great Purge' is quite convincing to me.

524. See Mawdūdī (²1980), pp. 7–23.

525. See ibid., p. 14.

526. See idem (1993b), pp. 17–20; also Fattal (1958), pp. 159–231.

527. Mawdūdī (²1980), p. 24.

528. Ibid., p. 38.

529. See Fattal (1958), pp. 236–40; also Mawdūdī (1972a), pp. 35f.

530. See Mawdūdī (²1980), p. 30; also Fattal (1958), pp. 240–63.

531. Qur'ān 2 (al-Baqara): 256. On various nuances in the classical understanding of this verse, which serves as a core reference in the discussion of religious tolerance in Islam, see Friedmann (2003), pp. 87–120.

532. Mawdūdī (²1980), p. 39.

533. See ibid., pp. 48f.

534. Ibid., p. 42.

535. See ibid., pp. 42–8 and 51f.

536. Ibid., p. 39.

537. See, for example, Fichte (1845–46), VI: pp. 81–9 and 108–54 (*Französische Revolution*). Especially in the eyes of this perhaps most fervent advocate of freedom as anthropological determinant, a political association has no right to limit the freedom of a person against this person's will. If this nonetheless happens, then the person is permitted to terminate the contract and to leave the association.

538. Mawdūdī referred prominently to the American Civil War of 1861–65 and the Swiss Sonderbund War of 1867 (see Mawdūdī [²1980], pp. 51f). More vaguely, he also discussed the *British Nationality and Status of Aliens Act 1914*, according to which a British citizen 'does not have the right in times of war to renounce British nationality [*briṭānawī qawmiyyat*] and to opt for either becoming a citizen [*wafādārī ikhtiyār kar le*] of a nation or giving allegiance to a state which is at war with the king of England. Such an act according to British law is high treason [*g͟hadr-i kabīr*] and punishable by death.' (Ibid., p. 43).

539. It deems necessary to point out that Islamist theorists and also activists in the wake of Mawdūdī, especially in Egypt, have later developed increasingly concrete but narrow criteria for who could be called a Muslim. See Nedza (2008), pp. 76–97; also below, Chapter E.1.

4. MAKING A SYSTEM HAPPEN

1. This popular saying is commonly attributed to Napoleon Bonaparte, although evidence is lacking.
2. See Koselleck (1989), pp. 70–74.
3. Marx/Engels (1956–90), I: p. 409 (*Kritische Randglossen zu dem Artikel « Der König von Preußen und die Sozialreform. Von einem Preußen »*; 1844 [transl. Richard Dixon], italics in the original).
4. See Plato (1995–6), IV: pp. 222f (51St [*Krítōn*]), V: pp. 637–63 (323–52 St [*Epistoleis*]).
5. See Aristotle (1984), II: pp. 2066–76 (1301a-07b [*Politiká*]).
6. See Lenk ([2]1981), pp. 12f; compare Ibn Manẓūr (1300–7h), II: pp. 176–83 (*q-l-b*), V: pp. 177–81 (*th-w-r*).
7. See Ayalon (1987), pp. 150f; Crone (2004), pp. 23–30.
8. The philosopher al-Fārābī, first main proponent of Islamic Neoplatonism, followed pretty much along the lines of Plato whereby a constitutional change would only be possible by the eventual insight of the philosopher-king alone (see al-Fārābī [[6]1991], pp. 127–30). The unconditional desire for political stability from a more traditionalist perspective, however, is perhaps best expressed in Ibn Taymiyya's well known dictum that 'Sixty years under a tyrannical leader [*imām jāʾir*] are better than a single night without ruler' (Ibn Taymiyya [[3]1408/1988], p. 139). For an early twentieth century perspective on that matter, although much less rigid than Ibn Taymiyya's, see, for example, Riḍā, 'al-Aḥkām al-sharʿiyya al-mutaʿalliqa bi'l-khilāfa al-islāmiyya', *al-Manār*, 24:1 (30 Jumādá al-ūlá 1341/17 January 1923), pp. 36–8.
9. Reichardt (1988a), p. 15 (transl. JPH); also, see Hobsbawm (1992), pp. 73–5; Koselleck (1989), pp. 76–83.
10. Jabārtī (1975), p. 11: 'For when six years ago they distanced themselves from their ruler [*la-mā kharajū ʿalá sulṭānihim*] and killed him [...].' Also, see ibid., p. 46; idem (1389/1969); pp. 31f.
11. See al-Ṭahṭāwī (2002), pp. 219, 224 et passim; Bustānī (1876), VI: p. 337.
12. For India, one may think of Faḍl-i Ḥaqq Khayrābādī's (d. 1278/1861) Arabic account *al-Thawra al-hindiyya* (1860), while Sayyid Aḥmad Khān (d. 1315/1898), in his Urdu analysis of the event from 1859, used the term '[illegitimate] revolt' (*baghāwat*). See Khān ([2]1971). Also the ʿUrābī uprising in Egypt is today known as the 'Urabian Revolution' (*al-thawra al-ʿurābiyya*), while the Mahdist movement in the Sudan became known as 'Mahdist Revolution' (*al-thawra al-mahdiyya*). For the latter, see, for example, Dekmejian (1987).
13. See Horn (1973), pp. 85–91 and 314f; Cole (1999), pp. 133–63 and 234–72; ʿUrābī (1425/2005), I: pp. 368–70.
14. See Ayalon (1987), p. 156.
15. See Algar (1973), pp. 20–53 and 78–100 et passim; Abrahamian (1979), pp. 387–99; Amanat (1993). It appears that only later, in the course of developing an Iranian national historiography, the Constitutional Movement was transformed into a 'revolution' (*inqilāb*). In his programmatic *Tanbīh al-umma wa tanzīh al-milla* (1909), Muḥammad Ḥusayn Nāʾinī (d. 1355/1936), one of the movement's intellectual figureheads, nowhere used the term 'revolution'. See Nāʾinī (1358sh).
16. Especially Twelver Shiite Islam has throughout its history maintained a social-revolutionary potential, which was not least utilised during the Persian Constitutional Movement. See, for example, ibid., pp. 46–50.
17. See Hobbes (1957), pp. 209–18; Locke ([6]1970), pp. 406–28; Lenk ([2]1981), p. 13.
18. The fundamental economic changes in England between 1760 and 1840, and the related social change, significantly contributed to the shaping of the revolutionary situation in

France around 1789. See, for example, Hobsbawm (1992), pp. 77–82. It needs, however, to be emphasised that these economic changes became only later to be known as 'Industrial Revolution' (in 1799 by Napoléon's envoy to England, Louis-Guillaume Otto [d. 1817], and finally, in 1884, in Arnold Toynbee's [d. 1883] *Lectures on the Industrial Revolution in England*).

19. See Mignet (^{6}1836), I: p. 324, II: p. 33; also Reichardt (1988b), pp. 192 and 195.
20. Both political poles, which have been rated differently by the named three thinkers, appear to have found their pendants in later revolutionary movements. While the Jacobins have found their equivalent in the Soviet Russian Bolsheviks and, to an extent, the Fascist movements throughout Europe, the spirit of the Girondins was somehow inherited by the liberalist movements of the nineteenth century. The lines between both poles, however, have then and now often been blurred. See Lenk (^{2}1981), pp. 168f; Mosse (1999), pp. 69–93.
21. See Rousseau (1967–71), II: p. 522 (*Contrat social*).
22. See Robespierre (1912–67), X: pp. 442–65 (*Sur les rapports des idées religieuses et morales avec les principles républicains, et sur les fêtes nationales*; 7 May 1794).
23. See ibid., X: p. 467 (*Société des amis de la liberté et de l'égalité*; 15 May 1794).
24. 'Les rois, les aristocrats, les tyrans quels qu'ils soient, sont des esclaves révoltés contre le souverain de la terre, qui es le *genre humain*, et contre le législateur de l'univers, qui est la *nature*.' Ibid., IX: p. 469 (*Droits de'l homme*; emphases in the original).
25. See ibid., X: pp. 273–83 (*Sur les principes du governement révolutionaire fait au nom du Comité de Salut Public*; 25 December 1793), X: pp. 350–67 (*Sur les principes de morale politique*); Mignet (^{6}1836), I: pp. 322–34, II: pp. 27–145; Aulard (1889–97), V: pp. 64f, 76–185, 208, 235–41 et passim, VI: pp. 1–292.
26. See Fichte (1845–6), I: pp. 302–22 (*GGWL*), VI: pp. 39–41, 48–50 and 148f (*Französische Revolution*).
27. Marx/Engels (1956–90), IV: p. 460.
28. See ibid., XXI: pp. 27f and 165–8 (*Ursprung der Familie*).
29. Marx/Engels (1956–90), XX: p. 262 (*Anti-Dühring*).
30. See Lenin (1962–70), XXV: pp. 395–401 (*Gosudarstvo i revoljucija*).
31. See Marx/Engels (1956–90), XIX: p. 28 (*Gothaer Programm*); Lenin (1962–70), XXV: pp. 397–413 et passim (*Gosudarstvo i revoljucija*), XXVIII: pp. 233–42 et passim (*Proletarskaja revoljucija i renegat' Kautskij*; 1918); Trotsky (1962), pp. 65–81.
32. See Marx/Engels (1956–90), IX: pp. 220–6 (*Ergebnisse* [...] *in Indien*); Lenin (1962–70), XXXI: pp. 240–5 (*Doklat* [...] *po* [...] *kolonial'nomu voprosam*); Zachariah (2005), pp. 162 and 227–9. Also, see above, Chapter B.3.2.a.
33. See Ayalon (1987), pp. 167–72.
34. See, for example, Hobsbawm (1992), pp. 138–63.
35. See Lenin (1962–70), VII: pp. 344 and 381–4 (*Šar vperjod, dva šara nazad*; 1904); IX: pp. 58–60 (*Dve taktiki socialdemokratii v demokratičeskoj revoljucii*; 1905); XXV: pp. 121f (*Možno li zapugat' rabočij klass "jakobistvom"?*; 1917); Mayer (1999), pp. 141–6.
36. See above given quote, Chapter C.4.3.b, n.190, from Robespierre [1912–67], X: p. 357 (*Sur les principes de morale politique*). Interestingly, Trotsky, who, in his autobiography *Moja žizm'* (1929), justified his rigorous measures as Head of the Red Army during the Russia Civil War of 1918–20, which by and large resembled the Jacobin 'Terreur', had earlier dissociated himself explicitly from Lenin's equation of the Bolsheviks with the French Jacobins. See Mayer (1999), p. 145. For the continuance of Jacobinism in various labour movements since the early nineteenth century in general, see Hobsbawm (1992), pp. 256–8.
37. See Hegel (^{3}1996), XII: pp. 524–40 (*Geschichtsphilosophie*); Ritter (1969), pp. 183–255. For Burke's conservative criticism of the French Revolution, see Hobsbawm (1992), pp. 298f; for a comparison of Burke's and Hegel's views, see Suter (1971).

38. See Chamberlain (1916), p. 30; Spengler (1920), p. 98; also Ottmann (1977), I: pp. 155–7.
39. See Farinacci (1937–9), I: pp. 47–66.
40. See Jung (1933), pp. 42–57; Breuer (1993), pp. 180–94.
41. 'Ma non era la rivoluzione sociale; era la rivoluzione russa; era la rivoluzione di un popolo diverso e lontano, per natura, tradizioni, istituti, cultura e stato dalla vita del nostro popolo [...]' (Farinacci [1937–9], I: p. 51). Also, see ibid., III: pp. 263.
42. See ibid., III: pp. 264–6.
43. See Hitler (1930), pp. 13, 15, 434 and 654f; Rosenberg (1930), pp. 485 and 530.
44. See Ottmann (1977), I: pp. 124–81.
45. See Jung (1933), pp. 11f. The leading Right Hegelians in the Third Reich, who emphasised the supremacy of a strong organistic state over the individual wills, were the two jurists Julius Binder (d. 1939) and Karl Larenz (d. 1993). Verhey (2000), pp. 224–7, stresses that prior to and around the time of their seizure of power the National Socialists perceived their 'revolution' as the completion of a revolutionary process that had begun in August 1914: Germany entering the First World War had been religiously elevated and rhetorically depicted as the last moment of the nation appearing unified in their zeal for a common goal. See ibid., pp. 1–11.
46. Jung (1933), p. 14 (transl. JPH).
47. See ibid., pp. 87–94; Breuer (1993), pp. 124–35.
48. See Farinacci (1936–39), I: pp. 124–8, III: pp. 173–8; Hitler (1930), pp. 422–4; Jung (1933), pp. 15–7; Mosse (1999), pp. 137–55.
49. See, for example, Rāy in Adhikari (1971–82), III/C: pp. 680–87 (*The Role of the Proletariat in the National Revolution*; 1928).
50. See Nehru ([14]2001), pp. 361–9 and 591–5.
51. See Daechsel (2006a), pp. 40–56 et passim; Delfs (2008), pp. 44–54.
52. To compare Mawdūdī's understanding of 'revolution' with earlier theorists of whom he was actually aware appears more reasonable than Nasr's reference to the later theories of Hannah Arendt (1965), Samuel P. Huntington (1968) and Charles Tilly (1978). Compare Nasr (1996), pp. 70 and 163 n. 4f. Even for a theoretical introduction to Western theories of 'revolution', this choice of authors was arguably not up-to-date. See, for example, Goldstone (1980), pp. 425–34; Foran (1993), pp. 1–4.
53. See Mawdūdī (1993a), pp. 51–3.
54. See Fichte (1845–6), VI: pp. 86–9 (*Französische Revolution*). Most clearly, Fichte wrote: 'No man can be aligned but by himself: no man can be given a law but by himself. If he permits another will to impose a law on himself then he gives up his humanity and makes an animal of himself which he must not.' (Ibid., pp. 81f [author's translation]).
55. See Hegel ([3]1996), III: pp. 431–41 (*Phänomenologie des Geistes* [*PhdG*]; 1807).
56. See ibid., XII: pp. 524–39 (*Geschichtsphilosophie*).
57. See ibid., III: pp. 441–94 (*PhdG*).
58. Ibid., XII: p. 535 ((*Geschichtsphilosophie* [transl. J. Sibree]).
59. Mawdūdī (1994b), p. 30.
60. Hegel ([3]1996), VII: p. 24 (*Rechtsphilosophie* [transl. S.W. Dyde]).
61. See above, Chapter C.1.2.b.
62. Ibid., XII: p. 32 (*Geschichtsphilosophie* [transl. J. Sibree]). Also, see ibid., pp. 539f.
63. Mawdūdī (1990f), p. 451.
64. See Nietzsche ([2]1988), I: pp. 307–19 (*Unzeitgemässe Betrachtungen II*; 1874). This is, of course, already as far as the commonalities between Mawdūdī and Nietzsche go. The latter's concept of the '*Übermensch*', a later metamorphosis of his '*Freigeist*' (see ibid., II: pp. 193–8 et passim [*Menschliches, Allzumenschliches I*; 1878–80], IV: pp. 8–10 et passim [*Zarathustra*]) presupposes man's absolute freedom and a rejection of his adherence to any kind of val-

ues created by anyone but himself. Muḥammad Iqbāl had however attempted to apply the Nietzsche's concept of the '*Übermensch*' to the Prophet Muḥammad. See Iqbāl (1343sh), pp. 14–21 (*Asrār*); also Schimmel (1963), pp. 323–6.

65. See Mawdūdī (1994b), pp. 17f; compare Hegel ([3]1996), XII: p. 535 (*Geschichtsphilosophie*).
66. See Nasr (1996), p. 71.
67. See, for example, Mawdūdī (1994b), p. 31; idem ([5]1996), pp. 6, 14 and 20f.
68. See Voll (1983), who claims—although a bit too absolutely for my understanding—a synonymy between *tajdīd* and *iṣlāḥ*.
69. For more on Mawdūdī's organicist concept of society, see below, Chapter D.2.
70. Hegel ([3]1996), VII: p. 440 (*Rechtsphilosophie* [transl. S.W. Dyde]).
71. Qur'ān 2 (al-Baqara): p. 143. Also, see Mawdūdī [1949–72], I: pp. 119f; idem ([4]1994), pp. 32–5.
72. Idem [1949–72], I: p. 119.
73. See Qur'ān 3 (Āl ʿImrān): 110. On this normative expectation, see also above, Chapter B.2.1.
74. See, for instance, Voltaire's *L'Education des filles* (1761), Rousseau's *Émile ou d'éducation* (1762) (see idem [196771], III: pp. 242–325), Lessing's *Erziehung des Menschengeschlechts* (1780), the second part of Kant's *Kritik der praktischen Vernunft* (1788) (see idem [1974], VII: pp. 287–99 [A 267–92]), Fichte's *Versuch einer neuen Darstellung der Wissenschaftslehre* (1797–8) (see idem [1845–6], I: pp. 506–15) and Goethe's two education novels *Wilhelm Meisters Lehrjahre* (1795–96) and *Wilhelm Meisters Wanderjahre* (1821–9).
75. Mawdūdī ([10]1992), p. 78 (*Nayā niẓām-i taʿlīm*; 1941).
76. Meanwhile, a vast academic literature exists on the various scholarly movements that emerged around the time of the uprising. To name just a few, see Metcalf (1982); Riexinger (2004); Hartung (2004b), also the works of David Lelyveld (1978) on the Aligarh movement, and Usha Sanyal (1996) on the *Ahl-i sunnat wa jamāʿat*, or *Barelwiyya*.
77. See Mawdūdī ([10]1992), pp. 14f (*Hamāre niẓām-i taʿlīm kā bunyādī naqṣ*; 1935).
78. Idem ([5]1996), pp. 14f.
79. Ibid., p. 18.
80. Idem ([10]1992), pp. 8–12 (*Hamāre niẓām-i taʿlīm* [...]).
81. See ibid., pp. 19f. This, of course, does not acknowledge the complex theological thought behind Sayyid Aḥmad K͟hān's argument for the compatibility of selected fields of Western learning with Islamic contents of education. For a comprehensive analysis of this, see Troll (1978), pp. 144–70. For a good translation of Sayyid Aḥmad's crucial treatise on the matter, *Insān ke k͟hayālāt* (1871), see ibid., pp. 251–7.
82. See Mawdūdī ([10]1992), pp. 20–22.
83. See ibid., p. 23 (*Musalmānoṇ ke li'e jadīd taʿlīmī pālīs awr lā'iḥa-yi ʿamal*; n.d.).
84. Ibid., p. 32.
85. Ibid., p. 36.
86. See ibid., pp. 36f.
87. See ibid., pp. 46 and 48f.
88. Compare, of example, Mill (1963–91), X: pp. 33–74 (*Professor Sedgwick's Discourse—State of Philosophy in England*; 1835); also see Hobsbawm (1992), pp. 233–5. Judging from the fact of his accusing all other Muslim educational institutions of utilitarian orientation, Mawdūdī was apparently not aware that he himself followed the utilitarians almost verbatim. See Mawdūdī ([10]1992), p. 62 (*K͟huṭba-yi taqsīm-i asnād*; n.d.); idem (1994b), p. 19.
89. Compare, for example, Rousseau (1967–71), III: pp. 19–23 (*Émile*); Kant (1974), XII: pp. 697–712 (A 1–34), pp. 746–61 (A 112–46) (*Über Pädagogik*; 1803); den Otter (1996), pp. 47–51; Boucher (1997), pp. xxv-xxviii et passim.
90. Mawdūdī ([10]1992), p. 40 (*Jadīd taʿlīmī pālīs*).
91. See ibid., pp. 40f.
92. See ibid., pp. 48f.

93. Idem (1994b), p. 26; compare and contrast idem (1972a), p. 5 (cited above, Chapter C.2).
94. A prime example for a pre-modern, or at least very early modern Western organicist model would be the political philosophy of Thomas Hobbes, who put forth the allegory of 'the collective body as one person' (Hobbes [1957], p. 119). In the Muslim context the idea of society as an organism can be traced back as far as the political philosophy of al-Fārābī. See al-Fārābī ([6]1991), pp. 118–20. For later examples, see Ibn Khaldūn (1320h), p. 149, and, very much influenced by the former, Iqbāl (1973), p. 13.
95. See, for example, Maurras (1921), pp. 23, 44, 96, 329 and 388; on this also Nolte (1963), p. 147; Hitler (1930), pp. 83, 169, 253f, 430–39 et passim; on this also Nolte (1963), pp. 463 and 492. Nolte has repeatedly emphasised the striking parallels in Maurras's and Hitler's thinking. On the widespread use of the term 'racial corpus' (*Volksgemeinschaft*) throughout the political spectrum in Germany of the 1920s and 1930s, see Verhey (2000), pp. 155, 202f, 213–19 and 236f.
96. This appears obvious already in the writings of Herbert Spencer, such as his *The Man versus the State* (1884), where he spoke of 'society [...] as an organised body' (Spencer [1885], p. 74), thus echoing Thomas Hobbes' mentioned organicist allegory. Also, see den Otter (1996), pp. 156f; Boucher (1997), pp. 3–29 (Henry Jones, *The Social Organism*; 1883). For the appropriation of Spencerian 'organicism' by the ideologues of militant Hindu communalism, see Delfs (2008), pp. 109–14.
97. See, for example, Hitler (1930), passim; compare with above, Chapter A.2.1.
98. Lenin (1962–70), XXII: p. 277 (*Imperializm kak vysšaja stadija kapitalizma*; 1916).
99. Hitler (1930), 334 (transl. JPH). Also, see Nolte (1963), pp. 499, 502f and 509–12.
100. Mawdūdī ([5]1996), p. 49. Also, see Būht'a ([3]1989), pp. 61f.
101. See Mawdūdī ([5]1996), p. 6; Maurras (1909), p. 226.
102. This was for the first time impressively demonstrated in the War of the Sixth Coalition against Napoléon Bonaparte between 1813–15. For its intellectual basis see, for example, Fichte (1845–46), VII: pp. 264–79 (*Reden*).
103. Kant (1974), XI: p. 54 (A 483 [*Was ist Aufklärung?*]; transl. H.B. Nisbet).
104. Ibid.
105. Mawdūdī ([5]1996), p. 5.
106. See Habermas (1990), pp. 178–95.
107. See van Dülmen (1996), pp. 11–17.
108. Habermas (1990), p. 54 (transl. Thomas Burger).
109. See ibid., pp. 81–107; van Dülmen (1996), pp. 18–118.
110. This echoes with Friedrich Engels' apt expression that 'humankind must first of all eat, drink, have shelter and clothing, before it can pursue politics, science, art, religion, etc.'. Marx/Engels (1956–90), XIX: p. 335 (*Das Begräbnis von Karl Marx*; 1883; transl. Mike Lepore). Also, see Hobsbawm (1992), pp. 267f.
111. Habermas (1990), p. 81 (transl. Thomas Burger).
112. See, for example, Robinson (1997); Jalal (2001), pp. 48–58; Stark (2003); Pernau (2008), pp. 117–24.
113. See ibid., p. 117. Both phrases have been borrowed from here.
114. See Reetz (1997) and above, Chapter B.1.1.
115. See Jalal (2001), p. 53; Pernau (2008), pp. 117–20 and 271–8.
116. See above, Chapter B.2.2.
117. Mawdūdī ([5]1996), p. 6.
118. Ibid., p. 5.
119. See ibid., p. 8.
120. See above, Chapter C.3.2.b et passim.
121. See Mawdūdī (1990d), pp. 291f.

122. See ibid., pp. 288–91. Compare, for example, Ibn Hishām ([2]1375/1955), I: pp. 614–7, II: pp. 63–9 and 228–33.
123. Mawdūdī (1990d), p. 292.
124. See al-Bukhārī (1425–6/2005), p. 32 (*Kitāb al-īmān, bāb su'āl Jibrīl al-nabī—ṣallá allāh ʿalayhi wa-salām—ʿan al-īmān wa'l-islām wa'l-iḥsān wa-ʿilm al-sāʿa*, Ḥadīth 1, no. 50); Muslim (1424/2004), pp. 31f (*Kitāb al-īmān, bāb bayān al-īmān wa'l-islām wa'l-iḥsān wa-ʿalāmat al-sāʿa wa-wujūb al-īmān bi-ithbāt qadr allāh subḥānahu wa-taʿālá wa-bayān al-dalīl ʿalá 'l-tibrī mimman lā yu'min bi'l-qadr wa-ighlāẓ al-qawl fī ḥaqqa*, Ḥadīth 2; no. 8m). Also, see Buehler (1998), pp. 4–10.
125. See Mawdūdī (1990d), pp. 293–312.
126. See ibid., pp. 259 and 265–71; also idem ([5]1996), pp. 11–16.
127. Ibid., p. 16.
128. See Nadwī (1982), pp. 42f. The reference in Nasr (1996), p. 154 n.106, could not be verified.
129. For a reproduction of Mawdūdī's article 'Ek ahm dīnī taḥrīk' (*Tarjumān al-qur'ān*, 15:2 [Shaʿbān 1358/October 1939], pp. 59–71) see Nadwī (1982), pp. 100–3. Also, see Mawdūdī (1995–6), IV: pp. 330f (*Tablīghī Jamāʿat ke sāth taʿāwun*; 1958). A good depiction of the religious state in the Mewāt region and the impact of the TJ is shown in Mayaram (1997), pp. 36–52 and 221–54.
130. The reasons for the drifting apart of Mawdūdī and the TJ, which soon became apparent, are indeed manifold and must not be reduced to the one state here. The main point of dissent, however, was their respective views on the role of the state and on religious authority—textually and personally both—which crystallised in a situation of massive competition between various religious and religiously inspired reformist movements over the same clientele. For Mawdūdī's perspective, see Mawdūdī (19956), IV: pp. 331f (*TJ* [...] *taʿāwun*); for that of leading TJ activists, see Zakariyyā ([6]1983); Nadwī ([2]1400/1980); Nuʿmānī (1998), pp. 79–144. Also, see Hartung (2004b), pp. 133–42 and 301f.
131. See Sikand (2002a), pp. 76–80.
132. See, for instance, Marx/Engels (1956–90), XXXIX: pp. 205–7 (*Letter from Engels to Walter Borgius*; 25 January 1894); also Gill (1980), p. 176.
133. Lenin (1962–70), V: p. 440 (*Čto delat'?*; 1902). See also ibid., XXXI: pp. 23–6 (*Detskaja bolezn' «levizny» v kommunizme*; 1920); Voslensky (1984), pp. 18–26; Rigby (1988), p. 526
134. See Voslensky (1984), pp. 261–78; Rigby (1988), pp. 525–7.
135. A clear expression of these powers was the so-called *nomenklatura*-system, the power over all appointments to key positions, which developed under Stalin and ultimately brought about what the Yugoslavian former Communist and author Milovan Djilas (d. 1995) called a 'new aristocracic class' of professional leaders. See Gill (1980), pp. 180–83; Voslensky (1984), pp. 46–52, 62–5 and 68–110; Rigby (1988), 523–5.
136. See, for example, Lenin (1962–70), XXXII: pp. 177f, 241–4 and 260 (*Pervonačal'nyj proekt rezoljuzii X s"ezda RKP o edinstve partii*; 1921).
137. See Gill (1980), pp. 167–71 and 179; Arch Getty (1999), pp. 66–9.
138. See Ray (1985).
139. See Adhikari (1971–82), I: pp. 151–5 and 230–3; III/A: pp. 164–76; III/B: pp. 175f.
140. See ibid., III-B: p. 180.
141. The Central Committee of the CPI with its inherent bodies like a politburo was not formed before autumn 1934. See Joshi/Josh (1992), II: pp. 111 and 135f.
142. See Nolte (1963), pp. 445–85; compare Mawdūdī ([5]1996), p. 31. Although the discrepancies in the understanding of the role of practice in various fascisms, which appear especially striking between the Italian case and others, need to be fully acknowledged, they do nonetheless not make a generic definition of 'Fascism' obsolete. See Nolte (1963), p. 449.
143. See Rosenberg (1930), p. 465, who depicted Fascism as a 'fraternity' (*Männerbund*), simi-

lar to those that were at the foundations of states, peoples, societies and churches. This perception seems to be clearly impacted by the popularity of male youth movements of the first half of the twentieth century, over and above the *Bündische Jugend*, a conservative movement that grew out of various already existing youth associations. See Giesecke (1981), pp. 104–8.

144. See Nolte (1963), pp. 135–8 (*Action française*), 331–4 (*Partito Nazionale Fascista*), 446f, 449f et passim (*NSDAP*); Schieder (1993), pp. 145–7.
145. It has, however, to be acknowledged that at the time of its seizure of power the NSDAP was the numerically largest party in Germany, comprising some 850,000 members. See ibid., p. 150.
146. Nolte (1963), p. 475 (transl. JPH). This image is corroborated by various statements of Gunter d'Alquen (d. 1998), after all a high-ranking member of the SS and editor-in-chief of the organisation's official journal *Das schwarze Korps*. See d'Alquen (1939), pp. 4 and 6f. Also, see Diehl (2005), pp. 151f.
147. See above, Chapters C.2 and D.1.2.
148. See Nolte (1963), pp. 473–5; Kater (^{2}1997), p. 26; Diehl (2005), pp. 159–62.
149. Reichsführer-SS Heinrich Himmler (suicide 1945), cited in: d'Alquen (1939), p. 12 (transl. JPH).
150. Contrary to this, the historicism inherent in the Communist ideology stipulated that in the classless society even the most elitist group within the party would become obsolete.
151. See Diehl (2005), pp. 162–4. Rosenberg, whose own cultural-political ambitions made him soon become one of Himmler's main adversaries (see Kater [^{2}1997], pp. 296–8), remained—perhaps deliberately—rather vague on this point when he wrote that the 'task of this new founder of the state will be to create a fraternity, let us say a German order, which consists of those personalities who have led in the revival of the German people'. (Rosenberg [1930], p. 515 [transl. JPH]).
152. See Kater (^{2}1997), pp. 53–7 et passim.
153. Mawdūdī's early companion Mawlānā Naʿīm Ṣiddīqī (d. 1423/2002) reported in his autobiographically spiced hagiography of Mawdūdī that, in the late 1930s, the latter had lent him his heavily annotated personal copies of al-Mashriqī's two principal works *al-Tadhkira* and *Ishārāt*. See Ṣiddīqī (1983), pp. 38f; also ʿAbd (^{3}1988), p. 141. This suggests that Mawdūdī had indeed been familiar with the *Khāksār*-ideology, which is corroborated by Malik's reference to at least one journal article of Mawdūdī on the *Khāksār*, dating back to the period under review here. See Malik (2000), pp. xv, 42–5 and 163. Mawdūdī's encounter with the *Khāksār* was most likely confined to its Hyderabad branch, then led by the bustling Bahādur Yār Jang (d. 1363/1944). See Pernau (2000), p. 254.
154. For the RSS, see Delfs (2008), pp. 115–31; for al-Mashriqī's explicit reference to the Nazi SA (*ṭūfānī fawj*) and the originally Czech ethnocentric youth sport movement *Sokol*, see his two articles 'Harr Hit'lar kī mashhūr sawāniḥ-i ʿumrī «Māʾī st'ragal», yaʿnī «Merī kashmakash» kā urdū meṇ tarjama awr khulāṣa', *al-Iṣlāḥ*, 2:20 (7 Ṣafar 1354/31 May 1935); 'Sokul taḥrīk: Zechoslowekiyā meṇ ḥurriyat kī ek kāmyāb taḥrīk kī tārīkh', *al-Iṣlāḥ*, 3:4 (1 Dhī 'l-qaʿda 1354/25 January 1936). I am indebted to Markus Daechsel (London) for sharing with me his knowledge on al-Mashriqī and the *Khāksār*, and for providing me with copies of these texts.
155. See Daechsel (2006a), pp. 47f, 85f and 115f. For a comparison with body cult and corporeal self-staging of the SS, see Diehl (2005), 166–220.
156. See Mawdūdī (^{5}1996), 17–21.
157. See Qayyim-i Jamāʿat-i islāmī Pākistān (^{23}1997), pp. 21f.
158. See Mawdūdī (^{2}1997), p. 33.
159. See ibid.

160. See Qur'ān 3 (Āl 'Imrān): 110.
161. While in practice utilitarianism was arguably more widely adhered to, the impact of the sometimes fierce philosophical debates between the protagonists of the two currents demonstrably had an impact on the further development of both.
162. See Boucher (1997), p. xix.
163. See Hegel ([3]1996), VI: pp. 296–301 (*Wissenschaft der Logik II*; 1816). Adherence to Hegelian logic was constitutive for the British idealists of the late nineteenth and early twentieth century in their dissociation from utilitarianism. See den Otter (1996), pp. 52–62.
164. See Hobsbawm (1992), pp. 286f and 302–5.
165. See Mill (1963–91), VII: pp. 57, 70–2 and 388–433 (*A System of Logic, Raciocinative and Inductive*; 1843).
166. See ibid., VIII: 844–78.
167. See ibid., X: pp. 220f and 235–7 (*Utilitarianism*).
168. This has most prominently been advocated by David George Ritchie in his *Principles of State Interference* from 1891. As an idealist, he of course acknowledged the fundamental differences between idealists and utilitarians concerning the basic rationale for an ethics, which was at the core of Bradley's earlier fervent criticism of hedonism as the general principle of utilitarian ethics (see Bradley [1876], pp. 78–127; also Nicholson [1990], pp. 17–28). On the other hand, Ritchie argued for a reformed utilitarianism by allowing utility to play a role in promoting society as a moral organism. See den Otter (1996), pp. 109–11.
169. See ibid., pp. 156–60.
170. See Nicholson (1990), pp. 181–97.
171. See Yack (1986), pp. 185–234 and 365–9.
172. See Norman (1987), pp. 31–4, who, unlike Max Horkheimer (d. 1973) and Theodor W. Adorno (d. 1969) in their *Dialektik der Aufklärung* from 1947, sets out in his critical examination of 'freedom' and its possible instrumentalisation in political ideologies from the two contrasting views of John Stuart Mill and Thomas Hill Green, and situates it thus within the British intellectual tradition.
173. Hence, a notion of 'inequality'—a result of the 'dehumanisation' processes—was introduced by the pioneers of political ideologies which restrict the benefits of 'freedom' to only one group within a given society. An attempt can be made to overcome this inequality by assimilation, as in Communism, or by exclusion, as in Fascism. For the relatedness of 'freedom' and 'equality', see ibid., pp. 107–54.
174. Daechsel (2006a), p. 159.
175. See ibid.; also Gould (2002), pp. 645 and 650f.
176. Daechsel adopts here the classification proposed by the French Marxist sociologist and philosopher Henri Lefebvre (d. 1991) in his *La production de l'espace* from 1974. See ibid., pp. 129f. On the camps in British India, see pp. 155–60.
177. See ibid.; also Malik (2000), sketch-plan of a *Khāksār* camp in Punjabi Gujrāt following p. 180; Delfs (2008), pp. 118f.
178. It appears not merely by accident that this distinction was first introduced into the academic discourse by the German sociologist Ferdinand Tönnies (d. 1936) at a time when almost all so-far accepted values were placed at their disposal. Tönnies' notion of '*Gesellschaft*' and '*Gemeinschaft*' is however quite distinct from Max Weber's later use of the two terms, as the former considered them 'normal types', i.e. empirical entities, while for the latter they constituted only 'ideal types', or theoretical entities.
179. See Rosenthal (1986), pp. 2–14 and 130–60; Giesecke (1981), pp. 12–17 and 84–7; Proctor (2002), pp. 3, 56 et passim.
180. See Giesecke (1981), pp. 88–93.

181. See ibid., pp. 50–59, 87–140 and 180–84; Proctor (2002), pp. 9, 33 and 89f.
182. See, for example, the impact that the Indian variety of the *Boy Scout* movement, combined with proto-fascist organisations, had on the *śākhā*-system of the RSS, in Delfs (2008), pp. 121f. For the outreach of the *Scouts* movement on the colonies especially in the inter-war period, see Proctor (2002), pp. 131–54.
183. See Ibn Hishām (?1375/1955), I: pp. 467–504; al-Ṭabarī (²1426/2005), I: pp. 345–55.
184. In general, see, for example, Qur'ān 4 (al-Nisā'): 97; 29 (al-ʿAnkabūt): 26; for the Prophet and his followers, 8 (alAnfāl): 72–5.
185. The basis for this is Qur'ān 4 (al-Nisā'): 97–100, as well as Prophetic sayings like 'I have nothing to do with Muslims residing amongst the polytheists' (Abū Dāwūd [1983], III: p. 45 [*Kitāb al-jihād, bāb al-nahy ʿan qatl min iʿtiṣām bi'l-sujūd*, Ḥadīth 1, no. 2645]) which, however, is considered abrogated by another Prophetic *ḥadīth*, according to which there would be 'No immigration after the conquest [of Mecca; *lā hijra bāʿd al-fatḥ*]' (al-Bukhārī [1425–6/2005], p. 682 [*Kitāb al-jihād wa'l-siyar, bāb faḍl al-jihād wa'l-siyar*, Ḥadīth 3, no. 2783], also 1049 [*Kitāb al-maghāzī, bāb muqām al-nabī—ṣallá allāh ʿalayhi wa-salām—bi-Makka zamana al-fatḥ 2*, Aḥādīth 6f, nos. 4305f]; Muslim [1424/2004], pp. 947f [*Kitāb al-imāra, bāb al-mubāyaʿa baʿd fatḥ Makka ʿalá al-islām wa'l-jihād wa'l-khayr wa-bayān maʿnan lā hijra bāʿd al-fatḥ*, Ḥadīth 6, no. 4724]; Abū Dāwūd [1983], III: p. 3 [*Kitāb al-jihād, bāb fi'l-hijra hall inqiṭaʿtu*, Ḥadīth 1, no. 2480]; al-Tirmidhī [1938–58], IV: 148f [*Kitāb al-siyar, bāb mā jā' fi'l-hijra*, Ḥadīth 1, no. 1590].
186. See Dihlawī (1321h), I: pp. 30f (*Mas'ala-yi dār al-ḥarb shudan dār al-islām*; 1803); also Qureshi (1999), 174–9.
187. See Minault (1982), pp. 106f; Reetz (1995), pp. 34–9; Qureshi (1999), pp. 183–90 (here with translations of both legal opinions).
188. See Reetz (1995), pp. 77f. In his *fatwá*, first published on 30 July 1920 in the daily *Ahl-i ḥadīth* (Amritsar), Āzād had promised the publication of a *Risālat-i hijra* in which he would provide further elaboration on the matter. This treatise appears to have not been published, nor could I find any reliable indication that it was drafted at all.
189. For this classical etymology see, for instance, Ibn Manẓūr (1300–7h), VII: p. 110.
190. Mawdūdī (1949–72), I: pp. 387f. Interestingly, further down in his commentary on the Qur'ānic verse 4 (al-Nisā'): 100, Mawdūdī rebuffed the opinion widely accepted in classical *fiqh* regarding the above cited *ḥadīth* 'lā hijra bāʿd al-fatḥ'. According to him, this *ḥadīth* did not generally abrogate the duty for *hijra*, which is to be considered a 'permanent injunction' (*dā'imī ḥukm*). This Prophetic saying would in fact relate only to the people of Arabia at that particular time and would therefore 'not at all mean that for all Muslims on the entire earth under all circumstances until Resurrection Day the duty of *hijra* had been abrogated'. Ibid., I: p. 388.
191. See Hartung (2004a), pp. 298–301. To establish *awqāf* as a means of private asset protection had been an especially widespread practice in the Mamluk sultanate of Egypt and Syria between 1250 CE and 1517.
192. See Kozlowski (1985), p. 37.
193. See ibid., pp. 96–155 and 177–91; Hartung (2004a), pp. 305f.
194. See Mawdūdī (²1997), pp. 19f; Nasr (1996), p. 34.
195. See, for example, Mawdūdī, 'Dawlat-i āṣafiyya ke mushkilāt', *al-Jamʿiyya*, 5:30 (3 Dhī 'l-qaʿda 1345/6 May 1927), 2; idem, 'Dawlat-i āṣafiyya ko badnām karne kī koshish', *al-Jamʿiyya*, 7:32 (24 Dhī 'l-qaʿda 1346/14 May 1928), 2; finally Mawdūdī's treatise *Dawlat-i āṣafiyya awr ḥukūmat-i briṭāniyya*, also from 1928.
196. The predominantly hagiographical material tacitly skimmed over the details, mainly in order to construct what became the official narrative of the formative period of the JiI.
197. See Nuʿmānī (1998), p. 27; Gīlānī (1992), p. 95; Nasr (1996), p. 34.

198. For the text of Iqbāl's crucial presidential address to the AIML's session on 29 September 1930 in Allahabad, see Iqbāl (1973), pp. 3–32.
199. See Schimmel (1963), p. 82; Iqbāl (2004), IV: p. 111; also Gīlānī (1992), p. 106. On al-Marāghī, see Hartung (2004b), p. 331.
200. See Gīlānī (1992), pp. 99f; Nasr (1996), p. 35.
201. For the situation in Hyderabad state in the 1920s and 1930s, see Pernau (1999); idem (2000).
202. See, for example, Ṣiddīqī (1983), p. 33; ʿAbd ([3]1988), pp. 123–5; Gīlānī (1992), pp. 84–90. Mawdūdī appears to have worked on the creation of this legend himself. See Mawdūdī ([2]1986), pp. 23f ('Ḥayāt-i Iqbāl kā sabaq', *Jawhar* [Delhi], 1938), 25–8 ('Iqbāl—ʿahd-sāz shakhṣiyyat', *Siyāra* [Lahore], May 1963). Here, Mawdūdī even claimed that 'Iqbāl was my spiritual supporter [*rūḥānī sahārā*]' (25). While earlier scholars like Annemarie Schimmel have fallen prey to Mawdūdī's self-staging (see Schimmel [1963], p. 58), more recent authors have stressed the need for a critical examination of the relationship between Mawdūdī and Iqbāl. See, for example, Nasr (1996), pp. 35–7.
203. For historical examples, see Hartung (2004a), pp. 300f.
204. Although Iqbāl did not explicitly employ the dichotomy of 'dār al-islām' versus 'dār al-ḥarb', his understanding of Indian Muslims as a nation (*qawm*) that deserves a national territory within the Subcontinent may have been fuelled by it nonetheless. Nasr, however, attributes the choice of this name entirely to Mawdūdī. See Nasr (1994), p. 110.
205. Mawdūdī, 'Ishārāt', *Tarjumān al-qurʾān*, 12:5 (Jumādá al-ūlá 1357/July 1938), pp. 3f. I am most grateful to Aysha Shafiq (Islamabad) for providing me with copies of all the earlier and hard-to-get articles from *Tarjumān al-qurʾān* referred to throughout the present work.
206. See Hartung (2011), pp. 295f et passim.
207. It is interesting to note that Iqbāl, too, did not envision a separate Muslim polity in the Subcontinent in strictly legal terms, but rather as a rather vaguely defined cultural entity. See, for example, Iqbāl (1973), pp. 10f.
208. See Mawdūdī (1964), pp. 142–4 (*Shubhāt awr jawābāt*; n.d.).
209. See ibid., p. 143.
210. 'Today, however, we have to say that a state is a human community that (successfully) claims the *monopoly of the legitimate use of physical force* within a given territory.' (Weber [1994], p. 36 [transl. Hans H. Gerth and C. Wright Mills; italics in the original]).
211. Nasr (1996), p. 37 (italics in the original). Besides, his translation of '*umma*' as 'holy community' appears far too colloquial and, therefore, inaccurate. The Qurʾānic usage of the term, apparently revealing its pre-Islamic semantics, denotes a community sharing a common religion and is not confined to the Muslims alone. See, for example, Denny (1975); al-Sayyid (1404/1984), pp. 26–53.
212. Gardet (1965), p. 411.
213. As, for example, in Ibn Taymiyya ([3]1408/1988), pp. 9–25.
214. Gardet (1965), 411. Also, see van Ess (2011), II: pp. 1275–9.
215. See Weber ([5]1972), p. 21 (transl. Talcott Parsons).
216. Ibid.
217. See ibid., p. 19 (italics in the original).
218. See above, Chapter C.2.2.b.
219. Weber ([5]1972), p. 19 (transl. Talcott Parsons). Although Parsons' translation is not very good here, I have to admit that, given the highly abstract and complex style of Weber's writing, I do not have any better alternative at hand.
220. Here, it may help our understanding if we recall that Max Weber stood evidently in the tradition of neo-Kantianism which clearly dominated academic philosophy in Germany in the first half of the twentieth century. See, for example, Schnädelbach (1983), pp. 219–25 and 229–31.

221. See Daechsel (2006a), p. 47.
222. See above, Chapter D.1.2.
223. See Qayyim-i Jamāʿat-i islāmī Pākistān (1989–96), I: pp. 9f.
224. Symptomatic of the level of religious education, Mawdūdī felt the necessity to tour the area and deliver overtly simple lectures on religious basics and in a very plain language. See Mawdūdī (1972b), p. 22.
225. See Nasr (1996), p. 37. On Iqbāl's actual plans, however, I was unable to discover any primary information, so everything regarding his involvement with the *Idāra-yi dār al-islām* should be considered with a certain reservation.
226. See Gīlānī (1992), pp. 100f.
227. See ibid., p. 109; Nuʿmānī (1998), pp. 28–31; Nasr (1996), pp. 37f; Hartung (2004b), pp. 134 and 297–301.
228. See Nadwī (1992), pp. 42f and 97–100; see also above in this Chapter.
229. On the role of *gasht*, derived from *tablīgh* as one of the six main constituents of the activities of the TJ, enshrined in the primer *Chha bātayṇ* (1934) by the movement's founder Muḥammad Ilyās Kāndhalawī, see Bulandshahrī (1998), pp. 34–6; Zakariyyā (2000), pp. 19–32.
230. See Gīlānī (1992), p. 100. One notes the inclusion of physical exercise (*jismānī tarbiyat*) into the activities at *Idāra-yi dār al-islām*, which might serve as a clear indication of the project's camp-character.
231. See Hartung (2004b), pp. 301f.
232. See above, Chapter C.2.1.a.
233. See Gīlānī (1992), pp. 108–10.
234. See ibid., pp. 108f.
235. This they obviously shared with similar Islamist associations. See Badry (1998), pp. 579–86.
236. See Mawdūdī (1964), pp. 33–88 (*Ham kahāṇ khaṛe hayṇ?*; 1935/36); Gīlānī (1992), p. 128.
237. Since I could not find any indication in the existing literature that a formal deed (*waqfiyya*) exists in which purpose, duration and beneficiaries of the *waqf* have been enshrined, the entire nature of the enterprise remains rather doubtful, at least for the time being.
238. See ibid., p. 114; Nasr (1996), p. 39.
239. See Gīlānī (1992), p. 114.
240. Unfortunately, Nasr (1996), pp. 39f, does not give sufficient references to back up his otherwise convincing argument. His notion of 'jamāʿa(t)' as '[political] party' (p. 39), however, appears already too confined to appear entirely satisfying. See my above discussion of this rather complex term.
241. Qayyim-i Jamāʿat-i islāmī Pākistān (1989–96), pp. 7f; Gīlānī (1992), pp. 139–43 and 412–17.

5. THE RECEPTION OF A SYSTEM

1. See Qayyim-i Jamāʿat-i islāmī Pākistān (1989–96), III: pp. 39–43.
2. See above, Chapter B.1.
3. The reputation of the *Nadwat al-ʿulamāʾ* in the Middle East had been so great that, in 1912, the institution was visited by Muḥammad Rashīd Riḍā, the most widely renowned pupil of Muḥammad ʿAbduh and editor of *al-Manār*. See Nadwī (1403/1983), pp. 68f.
4. See Hartung (2004b), pp. 231, 301 and 407.
5. See Qayyim-i Jamāʿat-i islāmī Pākistān (1989–96), III: p. 40, VI: pp. 155–9.
6. See Hartung (2004b), pp. 416–18.
7. See Qayyim-i Jamāʿat-i islāmī Pākistān (1989–96), V: p. 69, VI: p. 155.

8. See ibid., VI: pp. 156f.
9. See Damir-Geilsdorf (2003), p. 86.
10. Here, Damir-Geilsdorf seems to confuse the facts that, first, this work had originally been written in Arabic and was not just a translation from Urdu, and, second, that Quṭb's preface was for the second edition, published in 1952. Compare Hartung (2004b), pp. 309, 329–32 and 409–12.
11. See al-Nadwī (1994), p. 11. Also, see below in this Chapter for a more detailed exposition.
12. See Hartung (2004b), pp. 297f.
13. While, for a long time, the experiences during this journey were considered the trigger for Quṭb's radicalisation, more current studies provide a much more balanced view and stress that these experiences have only reinforced his already prevalent Islamist sentiments. See, for example, Damir-Geilsdorf (2003), pp. 40f, Calvert (2010), pp. 139–55.
14. See Shepard (1996), pp. xviii-liv. For a meticulous and commented list of Sayyid Quṭb's writings, see Damir-Geilsdorf (2003), pp. 376–92.
15. See Quṭb (1962), pp. 83–6 and 110–14; idem ([38]1430/2009), I: p. 440; III: pp. 1443 et passim.
16. Idem ([13]1413/1993), p. 12 (translation follows loosely Shepard [1996], pp. 8f).
17. It has to be acknowledged, however, that the founder of the JIM, Ḥasan al-Bannā, maintained a holistic understanding of Islam, when he said that 'we believe the provisions [*aḥkām*] of Islam and its teachings are all inclusive, encompassing the affairs of man in this world and the Hereafter. [...] Islam is creed and worship, nation and nationality [*waṭan wa-jinsiyya*], religion and state, spirit and deed, text [*muṣḥaf*] and sword.' al-Bannā (1412/1992), p. 119 (*Risālat muʾtamar khāmis*; 1939). However, not until 1942 did al-Bannā employ the term 'niẓām'. See ibid., p. 236 (*Daʿwatunā fī ṭawr jadīd*; 1942).
18. Quṭb ([13]1413/1993), p. 79.
19. See ibid., pp. 79f.
20. Damir-Geilsdorf (2003), p. 62 n. 7, suggests to translate the plural form as 'orders' or 'arrangements', while only the singular form should be translated as 'system'. This appears rather unconvincing to me, especially as, according to standard systems theories of Niklas Luhmann (d. 1998) and others a 'system' always consists of numerous 'sub-systems', which, equally structured as the whole, would be equally self-containing units.
21. Economics, for example, appear to have only been treated in greater detail in *al-ʿAdāla*, even here, however, as 'politics, or management of wealth' (*siyāsat al-māl*). See Quṭb ([13]1413/1993), pp. 84–126.
22. See al-Bannā (21386/1966), pp. 43–5 and 66–70; Mitchell (1969), pp. 4f.
23. See Damir-Geilsdorf (2003), pp. 23–8; Khatab (2006a), pp. 81f; Calvert (2010), pp. 62–98.
24. The most renowned of these appeals is the letter addressed to King Fārūq I (d. 1384/1965) and Prime Minister Muṣṭafá al-Naḥḥās (d. 1385/1965) in 1936. See al-Bannā (1412/1992), pp. 273–94 (*Naḥwa al-nūr*). Here, the date of this letter is given with Rajab 1366 (i.e. June 1947), which, however, appears rather unlikely in view of the events around the end of the Second World War, when the King's power had almost entirely been curtailed by the British.
25. See al-Bannā (21386/1966), pp. 79–83 and 108–16.
26. See Mitchell (1969), pp. 19–104; Damir-Geilsdorf (2003), pp. 28–46. At the time of his accession to the throne, Fārūq I was still under the influence of his mentor, the then *Shaykh al-Azhar* Muḥammad ibn Muṣṭafá al-Marāghī, and displayed a religious attitude, which is why his coronation in 1937 was celebrated by the Fourth General Conference (*muʾtamar rābiʿ*) of the JIM. See Mitchell (1969), pp. 14 and 16.
27. al-Bannā (1412/1992), pp. 108f (*Bayn al-ams wa'l-yawm*; 1943).
28. See Quṭb ([13]1413/1993), pp. 213–16.
29. Already al-Bannā had hinted repeatedly at the need for an Islamic polity, although he had

not really elaborated on its actual organisation. See al-Bannā (1412/1992), pp. 33–55, especially 38, 48f and 52 (*Ilá ayy shay' nadʿu al-nās*; 1934), 229–32 (*Daʿwatunā*) and 95f (*Bayn al-ams*).

30. See Damir-Geilsdorf (2003), pp. 38f.
31. Quṭb ([5]1402/1982), p. 184 (*Yā li-jarāḥāt al-waṭan al-islāmī!*).
32. See, for instance, idem ([13]1413/1993), pp. 19, 51, 149f, 197 and 214f. For a comprehensive treatment of Quṭb's critiques of other prevalent social-political ideologies, see Khatab (2006b), pp. 120–71. Here, however, ideologies, which are somewhat intrinsically linked and would therefore belong together (for example, Socialism and Communism, or Capitalism and Democracy) have oddly all been discussed separately. Anyway, Khatab's differentiation might be following Quṭb's own (compare, for example, Quṭb [[5]1418/1997], p. 170), and would therefore be perfectly justified.
33. Quṭb ([38]1430/2009), pp. 440f.
34. See Damir-Geilsdorf (2003), p. 69.
35. Quṭb ([5]1402/1982), p. 164 (*Mabādi' al-ʿālam al-ḥurr!*). Compare al-Bannā (1412/1992), pp. 277f (*Naḥwa al-nūr*).
36. See Mitchell (1969), pp. 105–62; Damir-Geilsdorf (2003), pp. 43–52; Zollner (2009), pp. 25–37.
37. Female members and sympathisers of the JIM were equally subjected to torture, as the autobiographical account of Zaynab al-Ghazālī al-Jubaylī (d. 1426/2005), founder of the *Jamʿiyyat al-Sayyidāt al-Muslimāt* (JSM) in 1933 on the request of Ḥasan al-Bannā, illustrates vividly. See al-Ghazālī (1420/1999), especially pp. 53–76 and 101–40. On the origins of the JSM, see al-Bannā (21386/1966), p. 98; Mitchell (1969), p. 175.
38. See below, Chapter E.2.
39. Quṭb in al-Nadwī (1994), p. 12.
40. In his article *Daʿwatunā fī ṭawr jadīd* from 1942, for example, Ḥasan al-Bannā referred to the knowledge culture of the pre-Islamic Egyptian society as 'jāhiliyya' and hinted at the absence of Islam as its criterion, although he did not elaborate on it any further. See al-Bannā (1412/1992), p. 230.
41. Khatab (2006a), p. 59, claims that his position in this regard is based on the points raised earlier by Shepard. The latter, however, appears much more considerate in his opinion (See Shepard [2003], pp. 523f and 534). To argue, as Khatab does, that because Shepard 'made it clear that the term *jahiliyyah* was there in the Qur'an and Arabic literature [...] [i]t was then easier for Qutb (who was closely familiar with the Qur'an and its literary structures) to take those concepts from the Qur'an and Arabic literature' (Khatab [2006a], p. 59) seems hardly sustainable as a counter argument.
42. See ibid., pp. 60–78, 85–98 and 109.
43. Although the work had not been published as a monograph of its own before 1944, it had first appeared in 1939 as a two-part article in the renowned Egyptian literary journal *al-Muqtaṭaf*. See Quṭb ([16]1423/2002), pp. 8f; Damir-Geilsdorf (2003), p. 377.
44. Quṭb ([16]1423/2002), p. 225.
45. See Wielandt (2002), pp. 131f. Also, see above, Chapter C.2.2.
46. Khatab (2006a), p. 128, claims the contrary, on the basis that in *al-ʿAdāla* Quṭb had used the term 'jahāla' in conjunction with the 'force of materialism' (*quwwa māddiyya*) (see Quṭb [[13]1413/1993], p. 79). While elsewhere, Khatab argues for a synonymy of 'jahāla' and 'jāhiliyya' (see Khatab [2006a], pp. 59 and 68–72), I do not share his view, as, in my understanding, 'jahāla' denotes a quality, while 'jāhiliyya' is either a temporal or a modal category and indicates more a certain state that is characterised by 'jahāla'.
47. See, for example, Botman (1988), pp. 33–5; Ismael/El-Saʿid (1990), pp. 32f.
48. See Botman (1988), pp. 35–58; Ismael/El-Saʿid (1990), pp. 33–67.
49. See Botman (1988), p. 33; Ismael/El-Saʿid (1990), pp. 4 and 42.

50. See Mitchell (1969), pp. 220–31.
51. See Quṭb ([13]1413/1993), pp. 27, 34, 50f, 54f, 82 and 215f; idem ([10]1408/1987), p. 7; idem ([5]1402/1982), p. 172 (*al-Islām wa'l-isti'mār*; 1952).
52. In fact, it seems as if his critical engagement with liberalism-*cum*-capitalism was only triggered by his study trip to the USA between 1948 and 1951. After his return he wrote his treatise *Ma'rakat al-islām wa'l-ras-māliyya*, which echoed in a theoretical manner his points of criticism of capitalism that had been solidified by his experiences in the USA. See idem ([10]1408/1987), pp. 8–15 et passim.
53. See idem ([13]1413/1993), pp. 190, 214 and 216; idem ([5]1402/1982), p. 172 (*al-Islām wa'l-isti'mār*); Damir-Geilsdorf (2003), pp. 42 and 70.
54. See Hartung (2004b), p. 309.
55. See Damir-Geilsdorf (2003), p. 384; Khatab (2006a), p. 160. On *al-Muslimūn*, see Mitchell (1969), p. 187; Hartung (2004b), pp. 316f.
56. On the history of the redaction and publication of *Fī ẓilāl al-qur'ān*, see al-Khālidī ([2]1414/1994), pp. 544–9; Khatab (2006a), pp. 160f.
57. Quṭb ([38]1430/2009), II: p. 904.
58. See above, Chapter C.1.1.a.
59. Quṭb ([38]1430/2009), V: p. 2861.
60. See ibid., II: 633; III: pp. 1320f and 1444–8.
61. Compare and contrast al-Khālidī ([2]1414/1994), p. 547 and Carré (1984), pp. 26 and 123–42.
62. See Calvert (2010), pp. 209f. Zollner (2009), pp. 52f, on the other hand, tries to put Quṭb's prison writings into the wider context of what she calls 'the discourse of religion and politics' and argues that the uncompromising nature of Quṭb's later writings, besides *Ma'ālim*, should generally be seen as a continuation of 'al-Banna's call to activism and political engagement'.
63. See al-Ghazālī (1420/1999), p. 43; Damir-Geilsdorf (2003), pp. 54 and 389.
64. Quṭb ([18]1405/1985), p. 116.
65. This phrase, which these days is widely associated with the 43rd President of the United States, George W. Bush (b. 1946) who, on 20 September 2001, used it in his address to the US Congress and the Nation to justify the inglorious 'War on Terror', has numerous historic precedents. These range from a similar statement by Jesus in the Gospel of Matthew 12:30, but have gained much momentum in the 'Age of Ideologies'. Thus, both, Lenin and Mussolini are reported to have used this phrase. See Lenin (1962–70), XXXI: p. 366 (*Reč' na Vserossijskom soveščanii politprosvetov rubernskix i uezdnyx otdelov narodnogo obrazovanija*; 1920); for Mussolini's slogan 'O con noi o contro di noi', see Isnenghi (1996), p. 302.
66. See Quṭb ([18]1405/1985), p. 12; also idem ([38]1430/2009), III: pp. 1320f (here Quṭb quoted at length from the Arabic translation of Mawdūdī's *Taḥrīk i islāmī kī akhlāqī bunyāden*). From the preface to *Ma'ālim* it occurs that, given the opportunity, Quṭb would have elaborated further and more systematically on the ideas of 'revolution' and 'vanguard' in subsequent writings. See idem ([18]1405/1985), p. 13.
67. Quṭb ([18]1405/1985), p. 10.
68. See, for example, ibid., p. 5.
69. Ibid., p. 53.
70. See above, Chapter C.1.1.b.
71. See Quṭb ([18]1405/1985), pp. 8 and 34; idem ([10]1408/1987), pp. 55–62.
72. See Mawdūdī (1990b), pp. 123–39; idem ([7]1994), pp. 14–26.
73. See Quṭb ([12]1413/1993), pp. 23f; idem ([13]1413/1993), pp. 80–83.
74. This, of course, has to be regarded as somewhat speculative, as I did not have access to the first edition of *al-'Adāla*, to thoroughly compare the text. However, I follow here Shepard

(1996), pp. xxiv-xxxiv, and Damir-Geilsdorf (2003), p. 80, who both suggest that Quṭb had not developed a stronger notion of *ḥākimiyyat allāh* before the mid-1950s.

75. Mawdūdī ([7]1996), p. 80.
76. Quṭb ([18]1405/1985), p. 53. In a footnote to this passage, Quṭb explicitly referred to the Arabic translation of Mawdūdī's *Risāla-yi dīniyyāt* as *Mabādiʾ al-islām*. Therefore, compare Mawdūdī (1970), pp. 88–91. On the notion of *fiṭra* in Quṭb's thought, see Khatab (2006b), pp. 70–85.
77. Quṭb (1962), p. 66; compare al-Nadwī (1994), p. 93. Quṭb's scepticism regarding the fruitfulness of rational speculation clearly resembled Nadwī's (for a contextualised analysis of the view of the latter, see Hartung [2004b], pp. 47–93). For Quṭb's views on rationality, see Khatab (2006b), pp. 86–92.
78. See, for example, his famous remarks on the matter in his so-called 'Mongol-*fatāwá*': Ibn Taymiyya (1420/1999), IV: pp. 262–6.
79. Quṭb ([15]1422/2001), pp. 17f.
80. On Quṭb's critical notion of rationality (*ʿaql*), and the problematic relationship between man's free will (*irāda*) and his determination by God's *ḥākimiyya*, see Khatab (2006b), pp. 86–99.
81. See above, Chapter C.3.2.
82. Quṭb ([38]1430/2009), I: p. 56.
83. See Mawdūdī (1997b), p. 33; also above, Chapter C.3.2.a.
84. Qurʾān 24 (al-Nūr): 55.
85. See Quṭb ([38]1430/2009), IV: pp. 2528f; idem ([5]1418/1997), pp. 170f.
86. Idem ([38]1430/2009), IV: p. 2529.
87. Ibid., I: p. 57.
88. Ibid., IV: p. 2529.
89. Ibid., I: p. 56; compare, for example, Mawdūdī (1990b), pp. 142–9; also above, Chapters C.1.1.b and C.2.2.
90. See Quṭb ([18]1405/1985), pp. 10f; idem ([15]1422/2001), pp. 89f and 92; idem ([5]1418/1997), passim.
91. See ibid., pp. 171–3; also see Carré (1984), p. 212; Nedza (2008), pp. 8–31.
92. See, for example, Ibn Taymiyya (1420/1999), IV: pp. 273–7; Ibn Ghannām ([2]1405/1985), p. 372.
93. Quṭb ([15]1422/2001), pp. 89f. The passage in quotation marks is Qurʾān 4 (al-Nisāʾ): 76.
94. See idem ([38]1430/2009), III: pp. 1431–44; compare idem ([18]1405/1985), pp. 62–91.
95. Mawdūdī (1972b), p. 329.
96. Ibid., pp. 326f.
97. See Quṭb ([38]1430/2009), III: pp. 1444–52; compare Mawdūdī (1990e).
98. Ibid., p. 384 (italics mine; the passage in quotation marks is from Qurʾān 9 [al-Tawba]: 31); compare Quṭb ([38]1430/2009), III: p. 1450.
99. See al-Jawziyya ([27]1415/1994), III: pp. 158–61; completely quoted in Quṭb ([38]1430/2009), III: pp. 1431f; idem ([18]1405/1985), pp. 62f.
100. *Naskh* refers to the practice of substituting one Qurʾānic ruling by another, usually later one, in order to harmonise the apparent contradictions between them. The justification for this is, among others, given in the verse 2 (al-Baqara): 106: 'Whichever of Our signs We abrogate [*nansakh*] or leave to oblivion, We substitute [them] with something better or similar.'
101. See Quṭb ([38]1430/2009), III: pp. 1432 et passim.
102. al-Jawziyya ([27]1415/1994), III: p. 159; also cited in Quṭb ([38]1430/2009), III: p. 1431; idem ([18]1405/1985), p. 62. The relevant Qurʾānic passages include 9 (al-Tawba): 29: 'Fight [*qātilū*] those who do not believe in God and Judgement Day [*al-yawm al-ākhir*], and who do not

prohibit what God and His Messenger have prohibited, and who do not adhere to the true religion [*dīn al-ḥaqq*]', and 9 (al-Tawba): 36: 'And fight against the unbelievers all together, as they fight you all together.'

103. Quṭb ([18]1405/1985), p. 72. Compare Mawdūdī (1960–1), I: p. 137.
104. Quṭb ([18]1405/1985), pp. 66f.
105. Ibid., p. 68.
106. On Mawdūdī's concept of 'revolution', see above, Chapter D.1.2.
107. Quṭb ([38]1430/2009), III: p. 1446; compare Mawdūdī (1990e), p. 368 (technical terms in square brackets are given for both, the Urdu original and the Arabic translation).
108. Quṭb ([38]1430/2009), III: p. 1508 (italics mine).
109. Here, one is clearly reminded of Rousseau's criticism of man's nature as the root of inequality within human society, as elaborated in his *Discours sur l'origine et fondements de l'inégalité parmi les hommes* from 1755. See, for example, above, C.3.2.a.
110. See above, Chapter C.1.1.b.
111. See Quṭb ([13]1413/1993), pp. 214–17.
112. Mawdūdī (1990e), pp. 375–82 and 388–92, however, appears to have already formed similar ideas, although he did still not confine himself to the use of 'jihād' instead of 'inqilāb', in order to better be able to dissociate himself from Western notions of 'revolution'.
113. See Quṭb ([18]1405/1985), p. 72.
114. *Yā ayyuhā alladhīna amanū qātilū alladhīna yalūnakum min al-kuffār wa'l-yajidū fīkum ghilẓatan.*
115. See Quṭb ([38]1430/2009), III: pp. 1737f.
116. Ibid., III: p. 1739.
117. See ibid., III: pp. 1739–41.
118. See Zollner (2009), pp. 56–63.
119. See Damir-Geilsdorf (2003), pp. 286–99. Since his release from jail in 1972, Muḥammad Quṭb had lived in Saudi Arabia and had been instrumental in editing and publishing his brother's writings.
120. al-Ẓawāhirī ([2]2008), p. 11. The importance of Quṭb is also obvious from the references to *Fī ẓilāl al-qur'ān* in al-Ẓawāhirī's *I'zāz rāyat al-islām* from 2003. See idem (2003), pp. 7, 12f and 59.
121. On the issue of his authorship, see Damir-Geilsdorf (2003), p. 302; Zollner (2009), p. 66.
122. See the valuation of *Du'āt, lā quḍāt* by Ma'mūn al-Huḍaybī (d. 1424/2004), a son of the author and the sixth 'General Guide' (*murshid 'āmm*) of the JIM between 2002 and 2004, in Damir-Geilsdorf (2003), p. 302.
123. See Quṭb ([38]1430/2009), III: pp. 1572–82 and 1610; idem ([18]1405/1985), pp. 62–6; compare al-Jawziyya ([27]1415/1994), III: pp. 158–61.
124. This is one main reason why it remains quite difficult to exactly pinpoint these various groups. This fuzziness extends also to dating their respective origins or establishing their respective memberships, both of which would be necessary to clearly demarcate them from each other. On the other hand, this lack of clarity has also opened the door to the creation of competing narratives. Thus, for example, there exist at least three different versions on the origins and scope of the *Tanẓīm al-jihād al-islāmī*, to which, prominently, the then still relatively unknown al-Ẓawāhirī and Sayyid Imām al-Sharīf belonged.
125. Quṭb ([18]1405/1985), pp. 56f.
126. According to Muṣṭafá himself, the Egyptian authorities confiscated over 4,000 pages of programmatic writings when the group was captured in 1978. See Muṣṭafá (1991a), p. 53. For the time being, however, this statement will be difficult to verify.
127. Also, in the, to date, most comprehensive, although rather normative, presentation of the ideology of the *Jamā'at al-muslimīn* that I know of the term 'jāhiliyya' is hardly ever

mentioned. See Jābir (1407/1987), pp. 10 and 13 (here, the term only appears in the quotations of Qur'ān 5 [al-Mā'ida]: 50).

128. See Muṣṭafá (1991a), pp. 85–7; idem (1991b), pp. 122–7; Damir-Geilsdorf (2003), pp. 250–54.

129. Muṣṭafá (1991a), p. 85. The *ḥadīth* was cited somewhat distorted here. Compare Muslim (1424/2004), pp. 40f (*Kitāb al-īmān, bāb al-amr bi-qitāl al-nās ḥattá yaqūlū lā ilāha illā allāh Muḥammadun rasūl allāh, wa-yuqīmū al-ṣalāt wa-yu'tū al-zakāt wa-yu'minū bi-jamīʿ mā jā' bihi al-nabī—ṣallá allāh ʿalayhi wa-sallam*, Aḥādīth 1–5, nos. 33–7).

130. See Muṣṭafá (1991a), p. 103.

131. See Muslim (1424/2004), p. 930 (*Kitāb al-imāra, bāb faḍīla al-imām al-ʿādil wa-ʿuqūba al-jā'ir wa'l-ḥathth ʿalá al-rifq bi'lraʿiyya wa'l-nahy ʿan idkhāl al-mashaqqa ʿalayhim*, Ḥadīth 4, no. 4617); Abū Dāwūd (1983), III: p. 130 (*Kitāb al-kharāj wa'l-imāra wa'l-fay', bāb mā yulzimu al-imām min ḥaqq al-raʿiyya*, Ḥadīth 1, no. 2928); al-Tirmidhī (1938–58), IV: p. 208 (*Kitāb al-jihād, bāb mā jā' fi'l-imām*, Ḥadīth 1, no. 1705); Ibn Ḥanbal (1413/1993), II: p. 162 (Ḥadīth 6020). Mawdūdī had utilised this *ḥadīth* in the elaboration of his notion of *khilāfa*. See above, Chapter C.3.2.a.

132. The issue of *takfīr al-ḥākim* will be comprehensively discussed in the forthcoming PhD dissertation of Justyna Nedza (Ruhr-University Bochum) on *Die Rolle des* takfīr *im 'ǧihādistischen' Diskurs—Ein Beitrag zur Untersuchung einer Schlüsselkategorie heutigen islamistischen Denkens.*

133. See Qur'ān 4 (al-Nisā'): 60. To use this term as a synonym for an (unjust) ruler or king (*malik*), however, has a tradition that goes well back to the early Islamic period. See Cook (2002), p. 241 n. 32.

134. The so far best and most comprehensive study on the *Ḥizb al-taḥrīr* (HuT) is by Taji-Farouki (1996).

135. See Damir-Geilsdorf (2003), pp. 254f.

136. See al-Ẓawāhirī (2008), p. 13. To what extent Sirriyya's mentioned acquaintance with Zaynab al-Ghazālī, and also Ḥasan al-Huḍaybī, was really true has, for lack of corroborative evidence, to remain an open question.

137. See Taji-Farouki (1996), pp. 37–75.

138. See Sirriyya (1991), pp. 41–4.

139. Ibid., p. 44. Abū Lahab ibn ʿAbd al-Muṭṭalib was one of the main opponents of the Prophet from among the Quraysh in Mecca and was even mentioned in the Qur'ān for his wickedness. See Qur'ān 111 (al-Masad); also Ibn Hishām (²1375/1955), I: pp. 351, 354f, 415f and 423.

140. Ibid., p. 42. For the actual *aḥādīth*, which call upon Muslims not to leave the community in times of battle and hardship, see Muslim (1424/2004), p. 942 (*Kitāb al-imāra, bāb al-amr bi-luzūm al-jamāʿa ʿinda ẓuhūr al-fitan wa-taḥdhīr al-duʿāt ilá al-kufr*, Aḥādīth 5–10, nos. 4681–6). An alternative reading, which refers to the necessity to strictly obey the *amīr* even if in doubt, gives al-Bukhārī (1425–6/2005), p. 1774 (*Kitāb al-fitan, bāb qawl al-nabī—ṣallá allāh ʿalayhi wa-sallam: «satarawan baʿdī umūran tunkirūnahā»*, Aḥādīth 3f, nos. 7053f). Apparently, there exist even sound Twelver Shiite variations, which call upon the acknowledgement of the Hidden Imam as main criterion for sound belief. See, for example, al-Kulaynī (1426/2005), I: p. 194 (*Kitāb al-ḥujja, bāb man māta wa-laysa lahu imām min a'immat al-hudá wa-huwa min al-bāb al-awwal*, Ḥadīth 3, no. 974).

141. See Aḥmad (1988), pp. 65–72.

142. See Gaffney (1994), pp. 82f. A more ideological narrative, which suggests much clearer demarcations between the two, is al-Ẓawāhirī (22008), p. 14.

143. See Gaffney (1994), pp. 90–99; Damir-Geilsdorf (2003), p. 257.

144. See Steinberg (2005), pp. 118–22.

145. See ʿAbd al-Raḥmān (2006), pp. 57–79 and 257–344.

146. See ibid., pp. 664–73.
147. Ibid., p. 664.
148. On this, see the translated mimeographed flyer 'Dirāsāt min Īrān', issued by the *Jamāʿa islāmiyya* of Cairo University and widely circulated throughout Egypt in 1979, in Esposito/Donohue (1982), pp. 246–51; also Gaffney (1993), pp. 83 and 104f.
149. See Faraj (1981), pp. 16–8. In this context, Faraj also vigorously rejected migration (*hijra*) as a possible means to establish an Islamic society: 'And then there are those who say that they will retreat into the mountains, only to return [later] and to encounter the Pharaoh, just like Moses has done, and that God will then sink the Pharaoh and his armies into the ground. All these escapades have no other purpose but to eschew the sound method and only true way [*al-uslūb al-ṣaḥīḥ wa'l-sharʿī al-waḥīd*] for the establishment of the Islamic State.' Ibid., p. 13.
150. The text actually says 'farḍiyya' (i.e. 'possibility'), which appears to be clearly a typo.
151. Ibid., p. 4. The passage in quotation marks is yet another variation of the popular *ḥadīth* that we have already encountered above with Ṣāliḥ Sirriyya.
152. It was this text that the Egyptian Military Court rated as the theoretical justification devised for the assassination of Anwar al-Sādāt, which, in turn, served as grounds for the Court's imposition of the death penalty on Faraj. See Aḥmad (1988), p. 165.
153. See Faraj (1981), pp. 5–10, 14, 21 and 24f.
154. Little biographical information is available on him. See, for example, Aḥmad (1988), who confines himself to an analysis of the various reasons for Islāmbūlī's radicalisation.
155. See ibid., pp. 75, 93–6, 103, 161 et passim; Gaffney (1994), pp. 257–60.
156. See, for example, Ibn ʿAbd al-ʿAzīz (n.d.[a]), pp. 921 and 1064.
157. See Mitchell (1969), pp. 84–6.
158. See ibid., pp. 93 and 160f.
159. On al-Bannā's deep suspicion towards political parties and his Therein rooted refusal to form the JIM into one of them, see, for example, al-Bannā (1412/1992), pp. 165–8 (*Fī muʾtamar ṭalabat al-ikhwān al-muslimīn*; 1928); pp. 214f (*Risālat al-muʾtamar al-sādis*; 1941); pp. 326f (*Niẓām al-ḥukm*; n.d.).
160. al-Huḍaybī (1977), pp. 7f.
161. See Krämer (1999), pp. 192–6 and 227.
162. See Nedza (2008), p. 100.
163. See al-Huḍaybī (1977), pp. 47–107; also Zollner (2008), pp. 71–97.
164. See Damir-Geilsdorf (2003), p. 305; Zollner (2008), p. 165 n.1.
165. See al-Huḍaybī (1977), pp. 16–18.
166. See ibid., pp. 19, 25 and 29f. Interestingly, these passages of al-Huḍaybī's refutation have later been quoted in Abū 'l-Ḥasan ʿAlī Nadwī's own rebuttal of Mawdūdī's and Quṭb's ideological constriction of Islam. See Nadwī ([2]1400/1980), pp. 44–7; al-Nadwī ([2]1400/1980), pp. 47–51.
167. See al-Huḍaybī (1977), pp. 19–31.
168. For the most comprehensive analysis of al-Huḍaybī's *Duʿāt, lā quḍāt* that I am aware of, see Zollner (2008), pp. 71–145.
169. See al-Huḍaybī (1977), pp. 63–94, quoting again from the Arabic translation of Mawdūdī's *Qurʾān kī chār bunyādī iṣṭilāḥeṇ* on pp. 72f.
170. See ibid., pp. 95–7.
171. See ibid., pp. 79–86. To prove his point, al-Huḍaybī referred to the *Jāmiʿ al-aḥkām al-qurʾān* of Abū ʿAbdallāh Muḥammad al-Qurṭubī (d. 671/1273) and to the section on coercion in the *Kitāb al-mullaḥá* of Ibn Ḥazm al-Andalūsī (d. 456/1064).
172. Huḍaybī's references include, besides the Qurʾān and the canonical collections of *ḥadīth*, al-Shāfiʿī's *Kitāb al-umm*, Ibn Khaldūn's *Muqaddima*, Ibn Taymiyya's *Kitāb al-īmān*,

al-Ghazālī's *al-Iqtiṣād wa'l-iʿtiqād*, and the *Kitāb mawāqif fī ʿilm al-kalām* of the Ashʿarite theologian ʿAḍūd al-Dīn al-Ījī (d. 746/1345). The author most frequently and widely referred to, however, is Ibn Ḥazm a-Andalūsī, who is represented here with his *Kitāb al-muḥallá*, *al-Aḥkām fī uṣūl al-aḥkām* and *Jawāmiʿ al-sīra*. See ibid., pp. 129–59.

173. See ibid., pp. 129–32.
174. See ibid., pp. 88–94.
175. See, for example, Qur'ān 2 (al-Baqara): 45 and 153; 3 (Āl ʿImrān): 16, 145, and 199; 46 (al-Aḥqāf): 35. Especially the latter verse '[...] and do not hasten about them [i.e. the unbelievers] [*wa-lā yastaʿjil lahum*]' is relevant in this regard.
176. See al-Huḍaybī (1977), pp. 86–8 and 140–2.
177. See Krämer (1999), pp. 232–47.
178. See Aḥmad (²1423/2003), p. 77.
179. See ibid., pp. 160–63; Ḥāfiẓ/Muḥammad (1420/2004a), pp. 4–6.
180. See Ḥāfiẓ/Muḥammad (1420/2004a), pp. 11–36 and 90–92. On the centrality of *maṣlaḥa* in classical Muslim political thought, see Hartung (2011), pp. 297f.
181. The respective part in the *Jamāʿa islāmiyya*'s revision on *takfīr* (Ḥāfiẓ/Muḥammad [1420/2004b]), does not go as far as explicitly conceding the power of definition to the *fuqahā'*. Their many references to classical legal scholars on this matter, however, would certainly support such a conclusion.
182. See idem (1420/2004c), pp. 103–20.
183. See Faraj (1981), p. 18. Already Ṣāliḥ Sirriyya, the head of the *Shabāb Muḥammad*, had considered armed *jihād* an individual duty. See Sirriyya (1991), p. 42.
184. See Ḥāfiẓ/Muḥammad (1420/2004a), pp. 46–8.
185. See Mawdūdī (1996), p. 7.
186. See ibid., pp. 14–31.
187. Ibid., p. 14.
188. See ibid., pp. 31–7; also Ahmad (2009), p. 79.
189. Jinnāḥ during the First Session of the Constituent Assembly of Pakistan, 11 August 1947, cited in Talbot (1998), p. 136; also Qayyim-i Jamāʿat-i islāmī Pākistān (1989–96), VI: p. 101. On the Constituent Assembly, see Binder (1961), pp. 120–25.
190. See Qayyim-i Jamāʿat-i islāmī Pākistān (1989–96), VI: pp. 103–5.
191. See Nadwī (1990), p. 43; Mūnis (²2001), p. 69; also below, Chapter E.2.2.
192. Mawdūdī's position as ideological point of reference, however, remained almost unchallenged across the subcontinent, even after his death in 1979.
193. See Nasr (1994), pp. 118–23; Qayyim-i Jamāʿat-i islāmī Pākistān (1989–96), VI: pp. 133 and 137–40. For the text of Mawdūdī's speech, which was allegedly the decisive spark for the Government's decision to arrest him, see Mawdūdī (²1997), pp. 72–9.
194. Prime target was the Deobandī scholar Shabbīr Aḥmad ʿUthmānī (d. 1369/1949), founding chief of the *Jamʿiyyat al-ʿulamā'-i islām* and member of the Constituent Assembly, who should bring the demands of the JiI before the congregation. See Binder (1961), pp. 137–42; Nasr (1994), pp. 123f. On ʿUthmānī, see Riḍwī (1992–3), II: pp. 98–102.
195. See Binder (1961), pp. 142–54; Nasr (1994), p. 124; Talbot (1998), pp. 138f. The paragraph in question reads: 'Whereas sovereignty over the entire universe belongs to Allah Almighty alone and the authority which He has delegated to the State of Pakistan, through its people for being exercised within the limits prescribed by Him is a sacred trust.' However, the Objectives Resolution remained outside the eventual Constitution until, in as late as March 1985, the Revival of Constitution of 1973 Order (P.O.No. 14 of 1985) stipulated having it included in the Constitution, Article 2(A).
196. See Gīlānī (1992), pp. 251–8.

197. See Qayyim-i Jamāʿat-i islāmī Pākistān (1989–96), VI: pp. 115–21; ʿAbd ([3]1988), pp. 248–53; Nasr (1994), pp. 28–30 and 127–9.
198. See Binder (1961), pp. 261–96; Friedmann (1989), pp. 38–40; Nasr (1994), pp. 131–6.
199. See, for example, Mawdūdī (1995–6), II: pp. 341–7 (*Khatam-i nubuwwat ke khilāf qādiyānīyoṇ kī ek awr dalīl*; June–July 1952).
200. Idem ([18]1998), p. 17.
201. Ibid., p. 36.
202. See Qayyim-i Jamāʿat-i islāmī Pākistān (1989–96), VII: pp. 75–7; ʿAbd ([3]1988), pp. 258–60; Binder (1961), pp. 302f; Schulze (1990), pp. 362–4; Nasr (1994), pp. 137–41.
203. See ibid., pp. 31–41.
204. This interrelationship of clientelism and 'legal-rational bureaucracy' is, since Shmuel Eisenstadt's *Traditional Patrimonialism and Modern Neopatrimonialism* (London, Beverly Hills, CA: Sage, 1973), discussed under the label 'neopatrimonialism'. For a comprehensive discussion, see Erdmann/Engel (2007).
205. See Nasr (1994), p. 31.
206. See ibid., p. 33. For the 1951 action plan, see Qayyim-i Jamāʿat-i islāmī Pākistān (1989–96), VI: pp. 403–16; also Mawdūdī ([25]2000), pp. 40–44. The four points entailed: (1) the purification and reformation of the individual mind (*taṭhīr-i afkār wa taʿmīr-i afkār*); (2) the organisation and training of virtuous men (*ṣāliḥ afrād kī talāsh, tanẓīm awr tarbiyat*); (3) efforts to better the society (*ijtimāʿī iṣlāḥ kī saʿī*); and, finally, (4) the betterment of the system of governance (*niẓām-i ḥukūmat kī iṣlāḥ*).
207. See idem ([5]1996), p. 19. Notably, despite my best efforts I was unable to locate a copy of the original 1941 statutes of the JiI. It seems that all the copies were called back after the 'Māchhī Got'h-Affair' and were soon after replaced with the amended statutes of 1957. I am most grateful to Jamal Malik (Erfurt) for activating his contacts in Pakistan to find a copy of the 1941 statutes.
208. See Nasr (1994), p. 33.
209. See ʿAbd ([3]1988), p. 273.
210. Interestingly, at the *ijtimāʿ* in November 1955 in Karachi Mawdūdī still publicly declared that constructive criticism was vital for achieving the JiI-P's ultimate goal, that is the establishment of the religion (*iqāmat-i dīn*), and to assume the JiI-P had become a purely political party, was a serious misconception. However, his remark that the JiI-P would not tolerate any subordination foreshadowed also some decisive developments after the 'Māchhī Got'h-Affair'. See Qayyim-i Jamāʿat-i islāmī Pākistān (1989–96), VII: pp. 39–44.
211. See Nuʿmānī (1998), pp. 62–71. It is somewhat telling that the report (*rūdād*) of this meeting had not been included in the published reports of the general meetings of the JiI-P. Also, Sayyid Asʿad Gīlānī (d. 1412/1992), an early activist and between 1969 and 1973 *amīr* of the JiI-P in Western Punjab, conveniently left this episode out of his account of the early history of the JiI.
212. See ʿAbd ([3]1988), pp. 273–5; Nasr (1994), pp. 34–7. Honesty demands acknowledge ment that, in 1942, Mawdūdī did not actually resign, but left it rather as threatening to divide up the JiI and, subsequently, the office of *amīr*. See Nuʿmānī (1998), p. 63. Jackson's uncorroborated statement that Mawdūdī was threatening to dissolve the JiI appears to be rather a little bit off the mark. See Jackson (2011), p. 68.
213. See Nasr (1994), p. 37.
214. See ʿAbd ([3]1988), p. 277; Mawdūdī ([25]2000), p. 154.
215. Ibid., p. 26.
216. For the four time periods that, in Mawdūdī's conception, corresponded to the four strategies outlined in the 1951 action plan, see idem ([25]2000), pp. 58–72.

217. Ibid., p. 33. This line, however, Mawdūdī had quoted from his 1945 speech *Taḥrīk-i islāmī kī akhlāqī bunyāden*. Compare idem (1990d), p. 259.
218. Interesting in this regard are two texts with almost identical titles by Iṣlāḥī and Mawdūdī, respectively, which deal with the concept of the 'purification of the soul' (*tazkiyat al-nafs*). While Iṣlāḥī did not neglect the role that society played for one's own moral reformation, his whole elaboration seems to echo his understanding of the four-point resolution of 1951 and put the emphasis therefore on man's individual relationship with God. See Iṣlāḥī (2002), pp. 314–470. Mawdūdī, on the contrary, made clear that one cannot purify one's soul outside of society—'the social is man's test area [*ijtimāʿiyyat—fard kī imtiḥāngāh*]' (Mawdūdī [[6]1995], p. 6)—and the state, although not explicitly mentioned, would therefore provide the necessary framework conditions.
219. Some fifteen years' later, Mawdūdī went even as far as portraying his adversaries from 1956 as 'a group of *ʿulamāʾ* who had set out to insult and defame me and the *Jamāʿat-i islāmī*'. Idem ([2]1997), p. 61.
220. On this, see above, Chapter D.2.1.
221. See Mawdūdī ([25]2000), p. 112.
222. See ibid., pp. 134–54. Mawdūdī did, of course, not go into even the least detail of how the total rejection of the existing political structures and the resulting 'non-constitutional' (*ghayr-āʾinī*)—violent—means to bring about political change would contradict the *sharīʿa*. See ibid., p. 134.
223. See ibid., pp. 151–3.
224. See Nasr (1994), p. 40.
225. See Mawdūdī ([25]2000), p. 146.
226. See, for example, idem ([2]1997), pp. 14f, 21, 29 and 54.
227. For these developments, see Nasr (1994), pp. 41–3.
228. For collaboration between the JiI-P and Zia ul-Haq, see ibid., pp. 188–95; Malik (1996), pp. 24, 151, 166, 208f and 213–16. For the JiI-P in political opposition, see, for example, Nasr (1994), pp. 147–87; Hartung (2000), pp. 75–8 and 93.
229. See, for example, Nasr (1994), pp. 206–18; von Schwerin (2005).
230. See Nadwī (1990), 43; Mūnis ([2]2001), pp. 69–73.
231. Ibid., p. 69.
232. See Shuʿba-yi tanẓīm-i jamāʿat (1989–2002), I: pp. 5–15; Mūnis ([2]2001), pp. 74f.
233. See Hartung (2004b), pp. 302f.
234. Nadwī (1990), pp. 61f.
235. The Preamble of the 1950 Constitution proclaimed India as a 'sovereign socialist secular democratic republic'.
236. See Shuʿba-yi tanẓīm-i jamāʿat (1998), pp. 45–56; Ahmad (2009), pp. 197f.
237. Nadwī in the JiI-H's paper *al-Inṣāf*, 1 February 1950, cited in Shuʿba-yi tanẓīm-i jamāʿat (1998), p. 59.
238. See Ahmad (2009), pp. 198f.
239. See Nadwī (1960), pp. 19–39.
240. See Shuʿba-yi tanẓīm-i jamāʿat (1989–2002), I: p. 166.
241. See ibid., 190–2; idem (1997), pp. 21f.
242. The official JiI-H literature does not provide any real hint for the reasons behind Abū 'l-Layth Nawdī's replacement as *amīr*. See Ahmad (2009), p. 259 n. 20; also Shuʿba-yi tanẓīm-i jamāʿat (1989–2002), II: pp. 64f.
243. See, although it is slightly erroneous, Schulze (1990), p. 158; Hartung (2004b), pp. 303f, 430 and 433. For a correction of Schulze's possible mistake, see ibid., p. 303 n. 34.
244. See Ahmad (2009), pp. 202f.
245. Shuʿba-yi tanẓīm-i jamāʿat (1989–2002), II: p. 80.

246. See ibid., II: pp. 141–6. Literature on various aspects of the state of emergency in India between 1975 and 1977 is vast. For a concise overview of the reasons and events, see Palmer (1976).
247. See Shuʿba-yi tanẓīm-i jamāʿat (1989–2002), II: pp. 160–76; Ahmad (2009), pp. 203f.
248. Shuʿba-yi tanẓīm-i jamāʿat (1989–2002), II: p. 217.
249. Ibid., II: p. 216.
250. See Agwani (1986), p. 71.
251. In 1974 members of the *Majlis-i shūrá* of the JiI-H requested Mawdūdī's permission to prepare an abridgement of his Qurʾānic commentary, which the latter did not grant until 1978. See Shuʿba-yi tanẓīm-i jamāʿat (1989–2002), II: p. 211.
252. See ibid., II: p. 406. Ahmad (2009), pp. 206–8 claims that by then the ultimate objective of *iqāmat-i dīn* had largely disappeared from what he calls the 'Jamāʿat's discourse', which, as the 1986 strategic plan clearly shows, was certainly not the case. He is, however, correct in stressing that the notion of *ḥukūmat-i ilāhī* had soon been abandoned by the JiI-H. Moreover, on p. 205, Ahmad claims that already in 1984 the *Majlis-i shūrá* had passed, against the strong opposition of Muḥammad Yūsuf, a resolution in which the ban on voting in elections was permanently lifted. I could however not find this one in the officially published collected resolutions and was therefore unable to verify this statement.
253. See ibid., pp. 212–14. Also, see the various resolutions of the *Majlis-i shūrá* on the Bābarī Mosque issue since April 1984 in Shuʿba-yi tanẓīm-i jamāʿat (1997), pp. 301–15. On the history of this issue, see Hartung (2004b), pp. 155–65.
254. I am most indebted to Hanna Thompson (formerly London) for helping me to come to terms with the Bengali texts used here.
255. See Rashiduzzaman (2002), pp. 186–9.
256. See Rahim (2001), p. 237.
257. See ibid., p. 238.
258. See Roy (1983). Although rather critical towards the use of the term 'syncretism' and aware of similar processes throughout the subcontinent, a somewhat similar image of Bengali Muslim religiosity is drawn by Eaton (1993), pp. 268–303. For a timely and critical overall discussion of the issue, see Harder (2008), especially pp. 192–5.
259. See Rahim (2001), p. 240. The published text of Mawdūdī's speech on that occasion, however, appears to have been quickly withdrawn from the market, perhaps to maintain the ideologically fuelled illusion of cultural homogeneity within the JiI-P. On the discrimination of the Bengalis by the Pakistani government prior to 1956, see Lambert (1958), pp. 52–8; Oldenburg (1985), pp. 715–25.
260. See Rahim (2001), p. 237; Kabir (2006), p. 163.
261. See ibid.
262. There seems to be a bit of confusion here in the secondary literature. Kabir claims that the office of *amīr* for the JiI-P of West Pakistan was until 1956 held by Chawdhurī ʿAlī Aḥmad Khān (b. unknown), who actually had been a member of the *Majlis-i shūrá* delegation of 1952. See Kabir (2006), p. 163; Qayyim-i Jamāʿat-i islāmī Pākistān (1989–96), VII: p. 92. While he is correct that Asʿad Gīlānī, the later *amīr* of the JiI-P in Punjab, had served until 1956 as secretary general of the West Pakistan unit (see ibid.), its *amīr* since 1951 had been Abdur Rahīm. See ibid., VII: p. 83.
263. In 1951, the West Pakistani cell of the JiI-P consisted of only twelve members (*arkān*) and about thirty-five sympathisers (*muttafiqūn*), while in 1954 it had grown only to thirty-eight members and eighty sympathisers. See Qayyim-i Jamāʿat-i islāmī Pākistān (1989–96), VI: p. 152; VII: pp. 89 and 92; Rahim (2001), p. 237.
264. See Qayyim-i Jamāʿat-i islāmī Pākistān (1989–96), VII: pp. 91–3; Rahim (2001), p. 238.

Unfortunately, I could not get hold of a copy of the delegation's final report on its visit to West Pakistan.

265. See Mujahid (1971), p. 162; Rahim (2001), p. 238; Kabir (2006), pp. 64f.
266. See Qayyim-i Jamāʿat-i islāmī Pākistān (1989–96), VII: p. 202.
267. For the text of the Six Points, see Rahman (1978), pp. 154f.
268. On this period, see LaPorte Jr. (1972), pp. 98–100; in relation to the JiI-P, see also Nasr (1994), pp. 147–61.
269. See Azam (1968), pp. 25–8 and 75f; Rahim (2001), pp. 243f; Kabir (2006), p. 165.
270. The list proposed by Golām Āzam in 1968 contained fifteen works in Bengali, twelve of them being translations of Mawdūdī's works, while only three had originally been written in Bengali, one of them a hagiography of Mawdūdī by one Khurrām Ālī Khān, and two by Abdur Rahīm (*Īslāmī rajnītir bhumikā* and *Īslāmer arkhanīti*). See Azam (1968), pp. 89–91.
271. See LaPorte Jr. (1972), pp. 100–2; on the October 1970 elections in greater detail, see Mujahid (1971).
272. See Nasr (1994), p. 169; Rahim (2001), p. 245.
273. In an attempt to primarily avoid criticism of its activities in 1971, the ICS was renamed *Islāmī Chātra Śibir* (ICŚ) in 1976. See ibid., p. 261 n. 68.
274. See K͟hālid ([10]1991), pp. 163–6; Rahim (2001), p. 245. The 1952 *Pakistan Army Act* has been published in the official *Gazette of Pakistan*, 1955. In 1965, an amendment was made that included the 'Pakistan Mujahid Force', i.e. noncommissioned officers and combatants under its provision.
275. See Muktijuddha Cetanā Bikāś Kendra ([2]1987), p. 186; Nasr (1994), p. 66. Nizāmī himself, however, appeared to be rather reluctant to reveal the command structures of these paramilitary forces for obvious reasons; hence he did not explicitly confirm his supreme command. See K͟hālid/Muttaqīn al-Raḥmān ([6]1992), II: pp. 234f.
276. See Bose (2005), especially p. 4467. Some justification for these atrocities against intellectuals has come even from Mawdūdī who, in a memorandum to numerous Heads of Muslim majority states, blamed the intellectuals as the force behind the AL and its separatist agenda. See Mawdūdī, 'Mashrīqī Pākistān meṇ afwāj-i Pākistān kī kār-riwāʾī ke k͟hilāf propagend'e kā jawāb', *Tarjumān al-qurʾān*, 75:4 (Rabīʿ al-t͟hānī 1391/June 1971), pp. 9–23.
277. See K͟hālid ([10]1991), pp. 297–330; Kabir (2006), p. 67.
278. Matiur Rahmān Nizāmī is found at the head of a list of seventeen *al-Badr* activists demanded for trial. See Muktijuddha Cetanā Bikāś Kendra ([2]1987), p. 186. Meanwhile, Golām Āzam was implicated as a leading member of the so-called *Kendrīẏa Śānti Kamiṭi*, a body established by the Pakistani army under the pretext of restoring peace and harmony (*śānti*) in East Pakistan, but in fact generating information on the nationalist opposition chiefly by inquisitorial means. See ibid., p. 189. For an apologetic justification of this committee, see K͟hālid ([10]1991), p. 150.
279. See Nasr (1994), pp. 68 and 176. On the origins and structure of the IJT, see ibid., pp. 63–78.
280. See ibid., p. 54; Gīlānī (1992), p. 410. Nasr (1994), p. 53, convincingly argues in this context that 'each transition [of the JiI-P] followed upon the retirement of the amir'.
281. See Rahim (2001), pp. 245f.
282. See Baṁlādeś Jāmāẏāte Islāmī (n.d.), pp. 4 et passim.
283. See, for example, Rahman (1978), pp. 20–33 and 93–109; idem/Hasan (1980). Interestingly, Matiur Rahmān Nizāmī's portrayal of himself, and his lamenting over the AL government of independent Bangladesh, seems to have misled even acknowledged Western academics, like Simon E. Digby (d. 2010), into praising him in back cover quotes as 'Bangladeshi freedom-fighter' and 'sufferer'. See Rahman (1979).

284. On Muḥammad Amīn al-Ḥusaynī and his activities post-1945, see Hartung (2004b), pp. 311–4 and 404f.
285. Khālid ([10]1991), p. 189, cited from the daily *Jasārat* (Karachi), 24 May 1973.
286. Rahim (2001), p. 251; also, see Kabir (2006), pp. 115–18 and 211–16; Codron (2008), pp. 208–12.
287. See, for example, ibid., p. 204.
288. See ibid., pp. 214–24; Riaz (2008), pp. 45 and 125–8.
289. See Islam (1986), pp. 562–7; Rahim (2001), pp. 248f.
290. Formally, the JiI-B was headed by Golām Āzam's associate Ābbās Alī Khān, seconded by Matiur Rahmān Nizāmī as secretary-general (*qayyim*). While Āzam was arguably the top decision maker, he had not been officially elected before 25 December 1991. See Kabir (2006), p. 109.
291. See Rahim (2001), pp. 247–9; Kabir (2006), pp. 68f.
292. See ibid. According to Enayetur Rahim, Abdur Rahīm had left the JiI already in 1977 (see Rahim [2001], p. 247), which appears to be slightly anachronistic and, moreover, is not supported by the reference he gives.
293. See ibid., p. 249; Kabir (2006), p. 69.
294. The Committee was established in 1992 under the aegis of the writer Jāhānārā Imām (d. 1994) as a civic attempt to bring the accused war criminals of 1971 to trial after the long spells of military dictatorship, starting with Golām Āzam. See Khan (1993), pp. 151 and 156; Gosh (1993), pp. 703–6; Kabir (2006), p. 110.
295. Prior to this, however, Āzam was briefly detained for his violation of the *Foreigners Act* of 1946, which was in force in Bangladesh since its inception and which prevented non-citizens from claiming any public office. See ibid., p. 111; Baṁlādeś Jāmāẏāte Islāmī (n.d.), p. 11.
296. See Kabir (2006), pp. 132–86.
297. See Baṁlādeś Jāmāẏāte Islāmī (2008), pp. 11–13.
298. See, for example, Huq (2008), pp. 467, 469f et passim, where the author gives a detailed account of a Qur'ānic study session of a Dhaka unit of the *Baṁlādeś Islāmī Chātrī Saṁsthā* (BICSa), the women's wing of the ICŚ, in 2003.
299. See Shehabuddin (2008), pp. 590–93 and 600f; also Baṁlādeś Jāmāẏāte Islāmī (2008), pp. 40–44.
300. For this, the male preachers refer to popular Prophetic *aḥādīth*, which stress the importance of women as daughters, wives and mothers. See Shehabuddin (2008), pp. 593–6. For one of the frequently quoted *aḥādīth*, see al-Bukhārī (14256/2005), 1516 (*Kitāb al-adab, bāb man aḥaqqu al-nās bi-ḥusn al-ṣuḥba*, Ḥadīth 1, no. 5971).
301. See Baṁlādeś Jāmāẏāte Islāmī (2008), pp. 40f, according to which women are only allowed to form their separate wing within the movement, but kept out of the administration of the JiI-B as a whole.
302. See Behera (2006), pp. 6–16; Khan (2007), pp. 98f.
303. See Behera (2006), pp. 22–9.
304. See ʿAbdallāh (1986), pp. 67–120.
305. See ibid., pp. 375–7; Behera (2006), pp. 106–8. 'Kashmīriyyat' is somewhat epitomised in Shaykh ʿAbdallāh's statement from the early 1950s that 'it was Buddhism that had been watering the noble and sound human magnitude [*sharīf awr ṣāliḥ insānī qadar*] in Kashmir for about a thousand years. Then its buds, which had emerged on the surface of the hearts, opened, and the teachings of our great Rishīs and Elders, such as Lal ʿĀrifa [Lalleśvarī, also known as 'Lal Ded', d. 1392 CE], Shaykh Nūr al-Dīn Nūrānī [commonly known as 'Nand Rishī', d. 842/1440] and other ecstatics, Sufis and Sants [sic] arose from its fading lullabies. Here, Islam was spread by dervishes and Sufis; it was them who

breathed a fresh spirit into the crumbled bones of this culture; Islam was thus the continuation of the Kashmiris' quest for spiritual deliverance [*rūḥānī najāt*].' (ʿAbdallāh [1986], 571f). Also, see the critical analysis by Zutshi (2003), pp. 18–28 and 318–22.

306. See idem (2000), pp. 121–6; Khan (2000).
307. See Ludhiyānawī (1388/1968), pp. 134–6 and 164–73.
308. See Sikand (2002b), pp. 717–23.
309. See ibid.
310. See Mawdūdī ([2]1997), pp. 55f; Nasr (1994), pp. 120f. Representative of the classical legal view on the matter are the statements by the medieval Ḥanbalī jurist Muwaffaq al-Dīn ibn Qudāma al-Maqdisī (d. 620/1223): 'Declaring *jihād* is the responsibility of the ruler [*imām*] and consists of his independent reasoning [*ijtihādihi*]. It is the duty of his people [*al-rāʿiyya*] to obey whatever he considers as appropriate.' (Ibn Qudāma [[3]1417/1997], XIII: p. 16), and by the later Mālikite Abū Barakāt Aḥmad al-Dardīr (d. 1202/1786): 'Proclaiming *jihād* comes through the ruler's assignment of a commander [*amīr*].' (al-Dardīr [1972–4], II: p. 274). Mawdūdī (1995), pp. 238–40, had this legal requirement explicitly discussed, although typically with a reference to two sound *aḥādīth* rather than to any classical legal work.
311. See Shuʿba-yi tanẓīm-i jamāʿat (1989–2002), I: p. 85. According to Sikand (2002b), p. 723, this decision was already made in 1952. I have not found any textual corroboration for this, but have not been able to consult the reports of the annual general conventions where this decision may at least have been premeditated.
312. See Ahmad (1991), p. 506. For the constitutional history of Azad Jammu and Kashmir, see Behera (2006), pp. 172–7.
313. Shuʿba-yi nashr wa ishāʿat ([4]1988), p. 5.
314. See ʿAbdallāh (1986), pp. 237–43.
315. See ibid., pp. 520–52; Behera (2006), pp. 37–9. For extended excerpts from Shaykh ʿAbdallāh's Opening Address to the J&K Constituent Assembly on 5 November 1951, in which he welcomed the *de facto* accession to India, see idem (2000), pp. 315–23.
316. See ibid., pp. 107–57; idem (2006), pp. 39–47.
317. See Sikand (2002b), pp. 732–9.
318. See ibid., p. 748; Behera (2000), pp. 157f; idem (2006), p. 47.
319. See Gīlānī (1995), pp. 25–31.
320. See idem ([2]1993), I: pp. 125–9; Gardīzī (n.d.), pp. 6–8.
321. See Behera (2000), pp. 164–71; idem (2006), pp. 146–8.
322. See Gīlānī ([2]1993), I: p. 154.
323. Ibid.
324. One of those more sympathetic readers of Gīlānī's 'Two-Nation Theory' is Sikand, who emphatically stressed 'that Gilani's understanding of the 'two nation' theory coincides with that of Mawdudi, who differed from the Muslim League's version of the theory which sought to legitimise Indian Muslim nationalism as the basis of a Muslim state.' (Sikand [1998], pp. 248f n.15).
325. See Gīlānī ([2]1993), I: pp. 239f.
326. The Rishī movement originated from the mentioned fifteenth century Shaykh Nūr al-Dīn Nūrānī, more commonly known as 'Nand Rishī'. For a somewhat sympathetic analysis of its origins, see Khan (1994).
327. See Sikand (2002b), pp. 722f and 729f.
328. In an undated pamphlet (*c.* 1995), Gīlānī contrasted, among others, Sufis like Hamadānī, who 'by word and deed live in accordance with the teachings of Qurʾān and Sunna', with 'Sufism or Rishiism' and stressed that 'in the present time where the predominant Muslim majority of Jammu and Kashmir is moaning and sobbing under the evil and ruthless

grip of Indian despotism, attempts are made to breed discord among the common Muslims in the name of 'Sufism', 'Rishiism', 'kashmīriyyat', dogmatism and heterodoxy [*iʿtiqād awr bad-iʿtiqād*] and causing them to deviate from the Straight Path [*ṣirāṭ al-mustaqīm*].' (Gīlānī [n.d.], p. 2).

329. Idem ([2]1993), I: p. 131.
330. See ibid., I: p. 132.
331. For sharing his knowledge on the ḤM with me, I am very much indebted to Paul Rollier (London).
332. See Behera (2000), pp. 180f; idem (2006), p. 52. On the office of *mīr wāʿiẓ* (lit.: head preacher), see Zutshi (2000), pp. 111 and 117f.
333. See Behera (2006), pp. 81–4.
334. See, for example, 'Imtiyāz Aḥmad bhī ḥayāt jāwīdāṇ pā gaʾe', *Jihād-i Kashmīr* 7:4 (16 February 1998), p. 12. The special relationship of the Kashmiri activists with these groups and militant leaders is already hinted at by Gīlānī (1995), pp. 813. The involvement of the JiI-P with the resistance movement in Afghanistan, however, dates back to the Zia ul-Haq era. See Malik (1996), pp. 208f. Amélie Blom even uses the term 'clientelism' to describe the relationship between the ḤM and various Pakistani forces. See Blom (2008), pp. 171–4.
335. Gīlānī ([2]1993), II: p. 103.
336. Idem (1995), p. 67.
337. See idem ([2]1993), II: pp. 102–8.
338. See Gīlānī (1995), pp. 129–43, here especially p. 138.
339. See Behera (2006), p. 161.
340. See Blom (2008), pp. 158f.
341. Sikand (2002b), p. 738, suggests that at least a part of the ḤM cadre had passed though the JiI-J&K educational system. Behera (2000), pp. 177–80, has apparently gained some inside information from interviews with the ḤM commander-in-chief Sayyid Ṣalāḥ al-Dīn, which would, of course, require corroboration. Further snippets are provided by Blom (2008), pp. 16–46.
342. See 'Imtiyāz Aḥmad bhī ḥayāt jāwīdāṇ pā gaʾe', *Jihād-i Kashmīr* 7:4 (16 February 1998), pp. 11–14. On the triangular relationship between JiI-P, *Ḥizb-i islāmī* and the *Ittiḥād al islāmī*, to the latter of which also Usāma ibn Lādin (assassinated 1432/2011) is said to have belonged for a while, see Steinberg (2005), pp. 33–5; to an extent also Blom (2008), p. 156, who included the JiI-AJ&K.
343. See Shuʿba-yi tanẓīm-i jamāʿat (1997), pp. 108–16.
344. This part has to be regarded as tentative at best for two main reasons. First, to my knowledge no academic study on the JiI in Sri Lanka exists, at least in any European language, thus all the following remarks can be considered new ground. Second, my own limitations in terms of language proficiency prevented me from properly using the various primary materials available mostly in Tamil. I am grateful to Dennis McGilvray (Boulder, CO) and Torsten Tschacher (Göttingen) for their kind assistance.
345. See McGilvray (1998), pp. 431f.
346. See ibid., pp. 435–7; Tschacher (2009).
347. See Nuhman (2007), p. 176.
348. See Qayyim-i Jamāʿat-i islāmī Pākistān (1989–96), V: p. 74.
349. See Nuhman (2007), p. 176.
350. See McGilvray (1998), pp. 441–4.
351. See Wilson (2000), pp. 66–81.
352. See McGilvray (1998), pp. 446–54; idem (2011), pp. 51f.
353. See Mahroof (1973), pp. 304–7 et passim; ʿUrābī (1425/2005), III: pp. 1206–36.
354. See Nuhman (2007), p. 176.

355. Compare Mawdūdī ([4]1994), pp. 16f and 33.
356. See McGilvray (2011), pp. 55f.
357. On the 1990 ethnic cleansing, see Singer (1991), p. 142; McGilvray (1998), p. 473; idem (2011), p. 53.
358. See Nuhman (2007), pp. 176f; McGilvray (2011), p. 62 n.6.
359. On the TJ in Sri Lanka, see Ali (1984), pp. 300f; Nuhman (2007), pp. 177 and 179f; McGilvray (2011), p. 54. On the *Tavhīt Jamāt* see Nuhman (2007), pp. 180–83.
360. See ibid., p. 177.
361. See Uyangoda (2010), pp. 204f.
362. See Sri Lanka Democracy Forum (2010), p. 16.
363. While the report from the 1951 *ijtimāʿ* in Karachi referred to a recently established 'Muslim Brotherhood Movement' in Sri Lanka, which had come across some JiI-P treatises and had subsequently requested all of its publications in Arabic and English. See Qayyim-i Jamāʿat-i islāmī Pākistān (1989–96), VI: p. 161. The report of the 1955 congregation did not mention Sri Lanka at all.
364. See Shuʿba-yi tanẓīm-i jamāʿat (1989–2002), I: p. 114 (here the report of the 1956 meeting of the *Majlis-i shūrá*).
365. See ibid., II: pp. 375, 391 and 403f; idem (1997), pp. 402–6.
366. See, for example, www.highbeam.com/doc/1G1–127300323.html, last accessed 24 March 2011.
367. See Reetz (2008).
368. See Nuhman (2007), p. 180.

6. CONCLUSION

1. al-Ẓawāhirī (2003), pp. 18f. It has to be stressed, however, that al-Ẓawāhirī referred in this text explicitly only to Quṭb, not to Mawdūdī. See the almost identical definition of 'jāhiliyya' in Quṭb ([38]1430/2009), II: p. 904; also above, Chapter E.1.1.a.
2. See Hartung (2004b), pp. 307f; Gräf (2009).
3. See al-Qaraḍāwī (1428/2007), pp. 94f and 101f.
4. For the 'invisible hand', see Smith (1893), p. 345; for the use of this metaphor in linguistic theories of language change, see prominently Keller (1990), pp. 60f et passim. For the 'survival of the fittest', a colloquial expression of which would be the proverb 'Eat or be eaten', see Spencer (1898), I: pp. 530f; Darwin ([5]1869), pp. 91f.
5. For the appropriation of the Marxist concept of 'exploitation' by feminism, turning it from a socio-economic term into a socio-cultural one, see Bryson (2004), pp. 16–18, 21f and 25.
6. See Popper (1935), pp. 26–8, 45f and 145–9. The term 'initial condition' follows Popper's own English translation of his 1935 seminal *Logik der Forschung*, prepared in 1959.
7. See ʿAbd al-Raḥmān (2006), pp. 664–73; Ibn ʿAbd al-ʿAzīz (n.d.[a]), pp. 160f (here quoting from Mawdūdī's critical remarks on Western democracy in [[10]1989], pp. 10f, which has been published in Arabic as *al-Islām wa'l-maddaniyya al-ḥadītha*), p. 921 (here a recommendation of Mawdūdī's *Qur'ān kī chār bunyādī iṣṭilāḥeṇ* in Arabic translation), p. 1064 (here a recommendation of the Arabic translation of Mawdūdī's *Islāmī ḥukūmat meṇ ghayr-musalmānoṇ ke ḥuqūq* from 1948); idem (n.d.[b]), pp. 117 and 274 (here references to Mawdūdī's concept of *ḥākimiyya*). I am grateful to Justyna Nedza (Bochum) who has drawn my attention to the latter two of these texts.
8. See Krämer (1999), pp. 88–95 and 258.
9. See ʿAwda (1401/1981), pp. 15–33, 121–33 and 172–228. However, an exception to the rule would certainly be the Sorbonne-educated leader of the Sudanese JIM, Ḥasan al-Turābī (b. 1350/1932), who, despite being considered a Muslim Brother more in the wake of Sayyid

Quṭb, also justified democracy from the premise of man's *khilāfat allāh*. See al-Turābī (1985), pp. 15–22. Also, see Badry (1998), pp. 362–9; Krämer (1999), pp. 102 and 197–206.

10. Sayyid Quṭb, for example, barely went beyond his idea of liberalism and socialism as two (ideological) blocs. Quṭb ([10]1408/1987) is possibly as deep as his analyses of competing ideologies have ever got.
11. Mawdūdī (1994b), pp. 18f.
12. See Krämer (1999), p. 258.

BIBLIOGRAPHY

ʿAbd, Chawdharī ʿAbd al-Raḥmān ([3]1988). *Mufakkir-i islām: Sayyid Abū 'l-Aʿlá Mawdūdī kī sawāniḥ-i ḥayāt, unke afkār awr unkī bar-pā karda taḥrīk-i islāmī kī dāstān*, Lahore: Islāmik pablīkeshanz.

ʿAbdallāh, Shaykh Muḥammad (1986). *Ātish-i chinār. ek āp-bītī*, Lahore: Chawdharī iked'imī.

ʿAbd al-Raḥmān, ʿUmar (s.t.). *Kalimat ḥaqq*, s.l.: Minbar al-tawḥīd wa'l-jihād, www.tawhed.ws/a?a= t44x7zzc, last accessed 28 Apr. 2009.

——— (2006). *Mawqif al-qur'ān min khuṣūmihi*, Cairo: Dār al-maḥrūsa.

Abaelardus, Petrus (1971). *Peter Abelard's Ethics*, ed. and transl. David Edward Luscombe, Oxford: Clarendon.

ʿAbduh, al-Shaykh Muḥammad ([8]1373h). *al-Islām wa'l-naṣrāniyya maʿa al-ʿilm wa'l-maddaniyya*, ed. al-Sayyid Muḥammad Rashīd Riḍā, Cairo: Maktabat wa-maṭbaʿat Muḥammad ʿAlī Ṣubayḥ wa-awlādihi.

Abrahamian, Ervand (1979). 'The Causes of the Constitutional Revolution in Iran', *International Journal of Middle East Studies*, 10:3, pp. 381–414.

Abū Dāwūd, Sulaymān ibn al-Ashʿath al-Sijistānī (1983). *al-Sunan*, al-Ḥamīd, Muḥammad Muḥyī al-Dīn ʿAbd (ed.). 4 vols., Cairo: Dār al-fikr.

Abū Yūsuf, al-Qāḍī (1346h). *Kitāb al-kharāj*, ed. n.n., Cairo: al-Maṭbaʿa al-salafiyya wa-maktabatuhā.

Adhikari, Gangadhar (ed.) (1971–82). *Documents of the History of the Communist Party of India*, 7 vols., New Delhi: People's Publishing House.

al-Afghānī, al-Sayyid Jamāl al-Dīn al-Ḥusaynī and al-Shaykh Muḥammad ʿAbduh ([2]1421h). *al-ʿUrwa al-wuthqá*, ed. Sayyid Hādī Khusrawshāhī, Tehran: al-Majmaʿ al-ʿālamī li'l-taqrīb bayn al-madhāhib al-islāmiyya.

Agwani, M.S. (1986). *Islamic Fundamentalism in India*, Chandigarh: Twenty-First Century Indian Society.

Ahmad, Irfan (2008). 'Cracks in the "Mightiest Fortress": Jamaat-e-Islami's Changing Discourse on Women', *Modern Asian Studies*, 42:2–3, pp. 549–75.

——— (2009). *Islamism and Democracy in India: The Transformation of Jamaat-e-Islami*, Princeton, NJ: PUP.

Aḥmad, Mukarram Muḥammad ([2]1423/2003). *Muʾāmara am murājaʿa? Ḥiwār maʿa qādat al-taṭarruf fī sijn al-ʿAqrab*, Cairo: Dār al-shurūq.

Ahmad, Mumtaz (1991). 'Islamic Fundamentalism in South Asia: The Jamaat-i-Islami and the Tablighi Jamaat of South Asia', in: Marty, Martin E. and R. Scott Appleby (eds). *Fundamentalisms Observed*, Chicago, IL: University of Chicago Press, pp. 457–530.

Aḥmad, Rif'at Sayyid (1988). *al-Islāmbūlī. Ru'ya jadīda li-tanẓīm al-jihād*, Cairo: Maktabat madbūlī.

——— (ed.) (32004). *Rasā'il Juhaymān al-ʿUtaybī, qā'id al-muqtaḥimīn li'l-masjid al-ḥarām bi-Makka: wathā'iq tunsharu li-awwal marra*, Cairo: Maktabat madbūlī.

Ahmed, Nizam and Shahnaz Khan (1995). 'The Development of Parliamentarian Oversight in Bangladesh: A Research Note', *Legislative Studies Quarterly*, 20:4, pp. 573–83.

Āl al-Shaykh, Sulaymān b. ʿAbdallāh (s.t.). *Awthaq ʿará al-īmān*, s.l.: Minbar al-tawḥīd wa'ljihād, www.tawhed.ws/a?a=oxjheqiw, last accessed 3 May 2009.

Algar, Hamid (1973). *Mīrzā Malkum Khān: A Study in the History of Iranian Modernism*, Berkeley, CA et al.: UCP.

——— (2001). 'The Centennial Renewer: Bediüzzaman Said Nursi and the Tradition of *tajdīd*', *Journal of Islamic Studies*, 12:3, pp. 291–311.

Ali, Ameer (1984). 'Islamic Revivalism in Harmony and Conflict: The Experience in Sri Lanka and Malaysia', *Asian Survey*, 24:3, pp. 296–313.

ʿAlī, Mawlawī Raḥmān (1894). *Tadhkira-yi ʿulamā'-i Hind*, Lucknow: Maṭbaʿ Munshī Nawal Kishor.

Ali, Syed Ameer (1928). 'Modern Astronomy and Islam', *Islamic Culture*, 2:2, pp. 237–59.

Allardyce, Gilbert (1979). 'What Fascism is Not: Thoughts on the Deflation of a Concept', *The American Historical Review*, 84:2, pp. 367–88.

al-Ālūsī, Maḥmūd ibn ʿAbdallāh (s.t.). *Rūḥ al-maʿānī fī tafsīr al-qur'ān al-ʿaẓīm wa'l-sabʿ al-mathānī*, al-Ālūsī, Maḥmūd Shukrī (ed.). 30 vols. in 15, Beirut: Dār iḥyā' turāth al-ʿarabī.

Alvi, Sajida S. (1994). 'The *Mujaddid* and *Tajdīd* Traditions in the Indian Subcontinent: An Historical Overview', *Journal of Turkish Studies*, 18, pp. 1–15.

Amanat, Abbas (1993). *s.v.* 'Constitutional Revolution: I. Intellectual Background', in: Yarshater, Ehsan (ed.-in-chief). *Encyclopædia Iranica*, Costa Mesa, CA: Mazda, vol. 6, pp. 163–76.

Anderson, Benedict (1991). *Imagined Communities: Reflections on the Origin and Spread of Nationalism*, London: Verso (revised edition).

Ansari, Humayun Khizar (1990). *The Emergence of Socialist Thought among North Indian Muslims (1917–1947)*, Lahore: Book Traders.

Arch Getty, J. (1999). '*Samokritika* Rituals in the Stalinist Central Committee, 1933–38', *Russian Review*, 58:1, pp. 49–70.

Aristotle (1984). *The Complete Works of Aristotle*, ed. and transl. Jonathan Barnes, 2 vols., Princeton, NJ: PUP.

Arjomand, Said Amir (1988). *Turban for the Crown: The Islamic Revolution in Iran*, Oxford: OUP.

Aschheim, Steven E. (1992). *The Nietzsche Legacy in Germany, 1890–1990*, Berkeley, CA, Los Angeles, CA, Oxford: UCP.

Aulard, F.-A. (1889–97). *La société des Jacobins: Recueil de documents sur l'histoire des club des Jacobins de Paris*, 6 vols., Paris: Maison Quantin.

ʿAwda, al-Shahīd ʿAbd al-Qādir (1401/1981). *al-Islām wa-awḍaʿunā al-siyāsiyya*, Beirut: Mu'assasat al-risāla.

Ayalon, Ami (1987). 'From Fitna to Thawra', *Studia Islamica*, 66, pp. 145–74.

Āzād, Mawlānā Abū 'l-Kalām (1959). *Khuṭbāt-i Āzād*, ed. n.n., Delhi: Urdū kitābghar.

——— (1963). *Mas'ala-yi khilāfat wa jazīra-yi ʿarab*, Lahore: Nāmī press.

Azam, Ghulam (1968). *A Guide to the Islamic Movement*, Dacca: Azami Publ.

Badran, Margot (2009). *Feminism in Islam: Secular and Religious Convergences*, Oxford: Oneworld.

Badry, Roswitha (1998). *Die zeitgenössische Diskussion um den islamischen Beratungsgedanken (šūrā) unter dem besonderen Aspekt ideengeschichtlicher Kontinuitäten und Diskontinuitäten*, Stuttgart: Steiner.

al-Baghdādī [*sic*], Aḥmad Mubārak (2001). *s.v.* 'Consultation', transl. Brannon M. Wheeler, in: McAuliffe, Jane Dammen (ed.-in-chief). *Encyclopaedia of the Qur'ān*, Leiden et al.: Brill, vol. 1, pp. 406–10.

al-Baghdādī, Muḥammad ibn Muḥammad ibn Nuʿmān (1381/1962). *al-Irshād li'l-Shaykh al-Mufīd*, al-Najaf al-ashraf: al-Maṭbaʿa al-ḥaydariyya wa-maktabatuhā.

Baker, David (2006). 'The Political Economy of Fascism: Myth *or* Reality, or Myth *and* Reality?', *New Political Economy*, 11:2, pp. 227–50.

Baljon, J.M.S. (1954). 'A Modern Muslim Decalogue', *Die Welt des Islams*, 3:3–4, pp. 187–200.

——— (1961). *Modern Muslim Koran Interpretation (1880–1960)*, Leiden: Brill.

Ballū, Muḥammad (1951). *Infāq al-maysūr fī ta'rīkh bilād al-takrūr*, Whitting, C.E.J. (ed.), London: Luzac.

Baṁlādeś Jāmāẏāte Islāmī (ed.) (2008). *Gaṭhantantra*, Dhaka: Ālī Āhsān Mohāmmad Mujāhid.

——— (n.d.). *Jāmāẏāt ebaṁ jāmāẏāt netṛtatbar biruddhe yuddhā garadher abhiyog banoẏāṭ mikhyā ṭaddeśya praṇodit*, Dhaka: n.n.

al-Bannā, al-Imām Ḥasan (21386/1966). *Mudhakkirāt al-daʿwa wa'l-dāʿiyya*, Cairo: n.n.

——— (1412/1992). *Majmūʿat rasā'il al-Imām al-Shahīd Ḥasan al-Bannā*, Cairo: Dār al-tawzīʿ wa'l-nashr al-islāmiyya.

Barkai, Avraham (1977). *Das Wirtschaftssystem des Nationalsozialismus: Der historische und ideologische Hintergrund, 1933–1936*, Cologne: Wissenschaft und Politik.

al-Baṣrī, Muḥammad ibn Saʿd (1418/1997). *al-Ṭabaqāt al-kubrá*, 'Aṭā', Muḥammad ʿAbd al-Qādir (ed.). 8 vols., Beirut: Dār al-kutub al-ʿilmiyya.

Bausani, Alessandro (1954). 'The Concept of Time in the Religious Philosophy of Muḥammad Iqbāl', *Die Welt des Islams*, 3:3–4, pp. 158–86.

al-Bayḍāwī, ʿAbdallāh ibn ʿUmar (1330h). *Anwār al-tanzīl wa-asrār al-ta'wīl*, 5 vols., Cairo: Dār al-kutub al-ʿarabiyya al-kubrá.

Behera, Navnita Chadha (2000). *State, Identity and Violence: Jammu, Kashmir, and Ladakh*, New Delhi: Manohar.

——— (2006). *Demystifying Kashmir*, Washington, D.C.: Brookings Institution Press.

Berkes, Niyazi (1954). 'Ziya Gökalp: His Contribution to Turkish Nationalism', *Middle East Journal*, 8:4, pp. 375–90.

Bezikoğlu, Metin (2001). *The Deterioration of Ottoman Administration in the Light of the Ottoman Russian War of 1768–1774*, unpublished MA dissertation, Bilkent Üniversitesi Ankara.

Binder, Leonard (1961). *Religion and Politics in Pakistan*, Berkeley, CA, Los Angeles, CA: UCP.

Bleicken, Jochen (1978). *Prinzipat und Dominat. Gedanken zur Periodisierung der römischen Kaiserzeit*, Wiesbaden: Steiner.

Blom, Amélie (2008). 'Le Hizb-ul-Mujahidin du Cachmire, imaginaires miliciens et clientélisme', in: Gayer, Laurent and Christophe Jaffrelot (eds). *Milices armées d'Asie du Sud*, Paris: Presses de Science Po, pp. 153–77.

Bodin, Jean (1986). *Le six livres de la République*, ed. Frémont, Christiane (ed.). 6 vols., Paris: Fayard.

Boettke, Peter J. (1990). *The Political Economy of Soviet Socialism: The Formative Years, 1918–1928*, Boston, MA, Dordrecht, London: Kluwer.

Bose, Sarmila (2005). 'Anatomy of Violence: Analysis of Civil War in East Pakistan in 1971', *Economic and Political Weekly*, 40:41, pp. 4463–71.

Bose, Subhas Chandra (1998). *The Alternative Leadership. Speeches, Articles, Statements and Letters, June 1939–1941*, Delhi: OUP.

BIBLIOGRAPHY

Bosworth, Edmund C. (1965). *s.v.* 'Djahilliya' [*sic*], in: *The Encyclopaedia of Islam. New Edition*, Leiden et al.: Brill, vol. 2, pp. 383f.

Botman, Selma (1988). *The Rise of Egyptian Communism, 1939–1970*, Syracuse, NY: Syracuse UP.

Boucher, David (ed.) (1997). *The British Idealists*, Cambridge: CUP.

Bourdieu, Pierre (1979). *La distinction: critique sociale de jugement*, Paris: Minuit.

Bradley, F. H. (1876). *Ethical Studies*, London: Henry S. King & Co.

Breuer, Stefan (1993). *Anatomie der konservativen Revolution*, Darmstadt: WUG.

Brown, Daniel (1996). *Rethinking Tradition in Modern Islamic Thought*, Cambridge: CUP.

Brown, Judith M. (2011). 'Gandhi as a Nationalist Leader, 1915–1948', in: idem and Anthony Parel (eds). *The Cambridge Companion to Gandhi*, Cambridge et al.: CUP, pp. 51–68.

Brunschvig, R. (1960). s.v. 'ʿAbd', in: *The Encyclopaedia of Islam. New Edition*, Leiden et al.: Brill, vol. 1, pp. 24f.

Brunt, P.A. (1984). 'The Role of the Senate in the Augustan Regime', *The Classical Quarterly*, 34:2, pp. 423–44.

Bryson, Valerie (2004). 'Marxism and Feminism: Can the "Unhappy Marriage" be Saved?', *Journal of Political Ideologies*, 9:1, pp. 13–30.

Buehler, Arthur F. (1998). *Sufi Heirs of the Prophet. The Indian Naqshbandiyya and the Rise of the Mediating Sufi Shaykh*, Columbia, SC: University of South Carolina Press.

Būht'a, Muḥammad Yūsuf (ed.) ([3]1989). *Mawlānā Mawdūdī apnī awr dusroṇ kī naẓar meṇ*, Lahore: Idāra-yi maʿārif-i islāmī.

al-Bukhārī, Abū ʿAbdallāh Muḥammad (1425–6/2005). *Ṣaḥīḥ al-Bukhārī*, al-ʿAṭṭār, Ṣiddqī Jamīl (ed.), Beirut: Dār al-fikr.

Bulandshahrī, Muḥammad ʿĀshiq-i ilāhī (1998), *Chha bātayṇ*, New Delhi: Idāra-yi ishāʿat-i dīniyyāt.

Bureau, Paul (1925). *Towards Moral Bancruptcy*, transl. Mary Sharlieb, London: Constable.

al-Bustānī, Buṭrus (1867–70). *Muḥīt al-muhīt ayy qāmūs muṭawwal li'l-lugha al-ʿarabiyya*, 2 vols., Beirut: n.n.

——— (1876). *Kitāb dāʾirat al-maʿārif wa-huwa qāmūs ʿāmm li-kull fann wa-maṭlab: Encyclopédie arabe*, 11 vols., Beirut: Maṭbaʿat al-maʿārif.

Büttner, Friedemann (1996). 'Der fundamentalistische Impuls und die Herausforderung der Moderne', *Leviathan*, 4, pp. 469–92.

Calvert, John (2010). *Sayyid Qutb and the Origins of Radical Islamism*, London: Hurst/New York: Columbia UP.

Carré, Olivier (1984). *Mystique et politique. Lecture révolutionnaire du Coran par Sayyid Quṭb, Frère musulman radicale (1906–1966)*, Paris: Cerf.

Chamberlain, Houston Stewart (1916). *Ideal und Macht*, Munich: Bruckmann.

Cicero, M. Tullius (1853). *The Treatises of M.T. Cicero*, transl. and ed. Yonge, C.D., London: H.G. Bohn.

Clarke, P.B. (1980), 'Millenarianism in West Africa: A "Revolutionary" Ideology?', *Religious Studies*, 16:3, pp. 317–39.

Clark, Terry Nicols (1973). *Prophets and Patrons: The French University and the Emergence of the Social Sciences*, Cambridge, MA: Harvard UP.

Codron, Jérémie (2008). 'Les milices islamistes du Bangladesh, symptômes d'un État faible?', in: Gayer, Laurent and Christophe Jaffrelot (eds). *Milices armées d'Asie du Sud*, Paris: Presses de Sciences Po, pp. 201–27.

Cohen, Hermann ([6]1898). 'Einleitung des Herausgebers', in: Lange, Friedrich Albert. *Geschichte des Materialismus und Kritik seiner Bedeutung in der Gegenwart*, 2 vols., Leipzig: Baedeker, vol. 2, pp. xv-lxxvi.

Coker, Francis William (1934). *Recent Political Thought*, New York, London: Appleton-Century Co.

Cole, Juan R.I. (1999). *Colonialism and Revolution in the Middle East: Social and Cultural Origins of Egypt's 'Urabi Movement*, Princeton, NJ: PUP.

Conquest, Robert (1990). *The Great Terror: A Reassessment*, Oxford: OUP.

Cook, David (1997). 'Moral Apocalyptic in Islam', *Studia Islamica*, 86, pp. 37–69.

——— (2002). *Studies in Muslim Apocalyptic*, Princeton, NJ: Darwin Press.

Cook, Michael (2000). *Commanding Right and Forbidding Wrong in Islamic Thought*, Cambridge: CUP.

Corrado, Monica (2011). *Mit Tradition in die Zukunft: Der* tağdīd-*Diskurs in der Azhar und ihrem Umfeld*, Würzburg: Ergon.

Crimmins, James E. (2002). 'Bentham and Hobbes: An Issue of Influence', *Journal of the History of Ideas*, 63:4, pp. 677–96.

Crone, Patricia and Martin Hinds (1986). *God's Caliph: Religious Authority in the First Centuries of Islam*, Cambridge: CUP.

Crone, Patricia (2001). 'Shūrā as an Elective Institution', *Quaderni di Studi Arabi*, 19, pp. 3–39.

——— (2004). *God's Rule. Government and Islam*, New York: Columbia UP.

Crook, Paul (1994). *Darwinism, War and History. The Debate over the Biology of War from the 'Origins of Species' to the First World War*, Cambridge: CUP.

Cuoq, Joseph M. (1975). *Recueil des sources arabes concernant l'Afrique occidentale du VIIIe au XVIe siècle: Bilad al-Sudan*, Paris: Éditions CNRS.

Daechsel, Markus (2006a). *The Politics of Self-Expression. The Urdu-Middle-Class Milieu in Mid-Twentieth Century India and Pakistan*, London, New York: Routledge.

——— (2006b). 'Scienticism and its Discontent: The Indo-Muslim "Fascism" of Inayatullah Khan Mashriqi', *Modern Intellectual History*, 3:3, pp. 443–72.

d'Alquen, Gunter (1939). *Die SS: Geschichte, Aufgabe und Organisation der Schutzstaffel der NSDAP*, Berlin: Junker und Dünnhaupt.

Damir-Geilsdorf, Sabine (2003). *Herrschaft und Gesellschaft: Der islamistische Wegbereiter Sayyid Quṭb und seine Rezeption*, Würzburg: Ergon.

al-Dardīr, al-ʿAllāma Abū Barakāt Aḥmad ibn Muḥammad ibn Aḥmad (1972–74). *al Sharḥ al-ṣaghīr ʿalá aqrab al-masālik ilá madhhab al-Imām Mālik, wa-bi'l-ḥāmish ḥāshiyat al-ʿAllāma al-Shaykh Aḥmad ibn Muḥammad al-Ṣāwī al-Mālikī*, Waṣfī, Dr Muṣṭafá Kamāl (ed.). 4 vols., Cairo: Dār al-maʿārif.

al-Dārimī, Abū Muḥammad ʿAbdallāh (1398/1978). *Sunan al-Dārimī*, 2 vols., Cairo: Dār al-fikr.

Darwin, Charles ([5]1869). *On the Origins of Species by Means of Natural Selection, or the Preservation of Favoured Races in the Struggle for Life*, London: Murray.

——— (1871). *The Descent of Man*, 2 vols., London: Murray.

Dekmejian, R. Hrair (1987). 'Charismatic Leadership in Messianic and Revolutionary Movements', in: Antoun, Richard T. and Mary E. Hegland (eds). *Religious Resurgence: Contemporary Cases in Islam, Christianity, and Judaism*, Syracuse, NY: Syracuse UP, pp. 78–107.

Delfs, Tobias (2008). *Hindu-Nationalismus und europäischer Faschismus. Vergleich, Transfer- und Beziehungsgeschichte*, Schenefeld: EBV.

Denny, Frederick Mathewson (1975). 'The Meaning of *Ummah* in the Qur'ān', *History of Religions*, 15:1, pp. 34–70.

den Otter, Sandra (1996). *British Idealism and Social Explanation. A Study in Late Victorian Thought*, Oxford: Clarendon.

Deringil, Selim (1998). *The Well-Protected Domains: Ideology and the Legitimization of Power in the Ottoman Empire, 1876–1909*, London: I.B. Tauris.

BIBLIOGRAPHY

Diehl, Paula (2005). *Macht—Mythos—Utopie. Die Körperbilder der SS-Männer*, Berlin: Akadamie Verlag.

Dihlawī, Shāh ʿAbd al-ʿAzīz Muḥaddith-i (1321h). *Fatāwá-yi ʿazīzī*, 2 vols., Deoband: Kutubkhāna-yi raḥīmiyya.

Dihlawī, Shāh Walīyallāh Muḥaddith-i (1396/1976). *Izālat al-khafāʾ ʿan khilāfat al-khulafāʾ*, 2 vols., Lahore: Suhayl Akedʿīmī.

——— (1986). *Ḥujjat allāh al-bāligha*, ʿAlī, Wuqār ʿAlī ibn Mukhtār (ed.). 2 vols., Deoband: Maktaba-yi Thānawī.

Dostal, Walter (1991). 'Mecca before the Time of the Prophet—Attempt of an Anthropological Interpretation', *Der Islam*, 68:2, pp. 193–231.

Douglas, Ian Henderson (1988). *Abul Kalam Azad. An Intellectual and Religious Biography*, Minault, Gail and Christian W. Troll (eds), Delhi et al.: OUP.

Doumato, Eleanor Abdella (1995). *s.v.* 'Jāhilīya', in: Esposito, John L. (ed.). *The Oxford Encyclopedia of Islam in the Modern World*, vol. 2, New York et al.: OUP, pp. 344–52.

Dube, Christian (2004). *Religiöse Sprache in Reden Adolf Hitlers. Analysiert an Hand ausgewählter Reden aus den Jahren 1933–1945*, Norderstedt: Books on Demand.

Durkheim, Émile (1897). *Le suicide: étude de sociologie*, Paris: Félix Alcan.

Eaton, Richard Maxwell (1993). *The Rise of Islam and the Bengal Frontier, 1204–1760*, Berkeley, CA, London: UCP.

Eatwell, Roger (1996). 'On Defining the "Fascist Minimum": The Centrality of Ideology', *Journal of Political Ideologies*, 1:3, pp. 303–19.

Erdmann, Gero and Ulf Engel (2007). 'Neopatrimonialism Reconsidered: Critical Review and Elaboration of an Elusive Concept', *Commonwealth & Comparative Politics*, 45:1, pp. 95–119.

Esposito, John L. and John J. Donohue (1982). *Islam in Transition: Muslim Perspectives*, Oxford et al.: OUP.

Fabei, Stefano (2002). *Il fascio, la svastica e la mezzaluna*, Milan: Mursia.

al-Fārābī, Abū Naṣr (⁶1991). *Kitāb ārāʾ ahl al-madīnat al-fāḍila*, Nādir, Albīr Naṣrī (ed.). Beirut: Dār al-mashriq.

Faraj, Muḥammad ʿAbd al-Salām (1981). *al-Jihād. al-farīḍa al-ghāʾiba*, www.e-prism.org/images/ALFAREDA.doc, last accessed 28 Apr. 2009.

Farinacci, Roberto (1937–9). *Storia della rivoluzione fascista*, 3 vols., Cremona: Cremona nuova.

Fattal, Antoine (1958). *Le statut légal des non-musulmans en pays d'Islam*, Beirut: Impr. Catholique.

Fichte, Johann Gottlieb (1845–6). *Johann Gottlieb Fichtes sämmtliche* [sic] *Werke*, Fichte, Immanuel Hermann (ed.). 8 vols., Berlin: Veit.

Fine, Gary Allen and Kent Sandstrom (1993). 'Ideology in Action: A Pragmatic Approach to a Contested Concept', *Sociological Theory*, 11:1, 21–38.

Fischer-Tiné, Harald (1995). *Die* śuddhī*-Bewegung des Ārya Samāj und ihre Rolle bei der Konstituierung einer Hindu Identität*, unpublished MA dissertation, Ruprecht-Karls-Universität Heidelberg.

Flam, Helena (2002). *Soziologie der Emotionen. Eine Einführung*, Konstanz: UVK.

——— and Debra King (eds) (2005). *Emotions and Social Movements*, London, New York: Routledge.

Foran, John (1993). 'Theories of Revolution Revisisted: Towards a Fourth Generation?', *Sociological Theory*, 11:1, pp. 1–20.

Framke, Maria (2007). *Jawaharlal Nehrus Wahrnehmung des Faschismus und seine Auseinandersetzung mit dessen Folgen*, MA dissertation, Humboldt-Universität Berlin, Heidelberg: SavifaDok Publikationsplattform für die Südasienwissenschaften, http://archiv.ub.uni-heidelberg.de/savifadok/volltexte/2007/61/ (stable URL).

Freeden, Michael (1996). 'Editorial', *Journal of Political Ideologies*, 1:1, pp. 5–13.

Friedmann, Yohanan (1971). *Shaykh Aḥmad Sirhindī. An Outline of His Thought and a Study of His Image in the Eyes of Posterity*, Montreal: McGill-Queen's UP.

——— (1989). *Prophecy Continuous: Aspects of Aḥmadī Religious Thought and its Medieval Background*, Berkeley, CA, Los Angeles, CA: UCP.

——— (2003). *Tolerance and Coercion in Islam: Interfaith Relations in the Muslim Tradition*, Cambridge: CUP.

Furnish, Timothy R. (2005). *Holiest Wars: Islamic Mahdis, Their Jihads, and Osama bin Laden*, Westport, CT et al.: Praeger.

Gaffney, Patrick D. (1994). *The Prophet's Pulpit: Islamic Preaching in Contemporary Egypt*, Berkeley, CA, Los Angeles, CA, London: UCP.

Gardet, Louis (1965). *s.v.* 'Djamaʿa', in: *The Encyclopaedia of Islam. New Edition*, Leiden et al.: Brill, vol. 2, p. 411.

Gardīzī, Sayyid Salīm (n.d.). *Āzādī kā qāʾid: Sayyid ʿAlī Gīlānī*, Muzaffarabad: Jamāʿat-i islāmī Āzād Jammūṇ wa Kashmīr.

Gentile, Emilio (1975). *Le origini dell' ideologia fascista (1918–1925)*, Rome, Bari: Laterza.

——— (1996). *The Sacralization of Politics in Fascist Italy*, transl. Keith Botsford, Cambridge, MA, London: Harvard UP.

Ghālib, Asadallāh Khān (1951). *Khuṭūṭ-i Ghālib. Kāmil*, Mihr, Ghulām-i Rasūl (ed.). Lahore et al.: Shaykh Ghulām-i ʿAlī & Sons.

al-Ghazālī, Abū Ḥāmid Muḥammad (1377/1957). *Iḥyāʾ ʿulūm al-dīn*, Ṭabāna, Dr Badawī Aḥmad (ed.), 4 vols., Cairo: Dār iḥyāʾ al-kutub al-ʿarabiyya.

——— ([2]1969). *al-Munqidh min al-ḍalāl wa'l-muwaṣil ilá dhī 'l-ʿizza al-jalāl*, Jabr, Farīd (ed.). Beirut: al-Lajna al-lubnāniyya li-tarjama al-rawāʾiʿ.

al-Ghazālī, Zaynab (1420/1999). *Ayyām min ḥayātī*, Cairo: Dār al-tawzīʿ wa'l-nashr al-islāmiyya.

Giesecke, Hermann (1981). *Vom Wandervogel bis zur Hitlerjugend: Jugenarbeit zwischen Politik und Pädagogik*, Munich: Juventa.

Gīlānī, Sayyid ʿAlī (n.d.). *Ḥaqīqat-i ḥāl*, Srinagar: Polit'īkal Biyūro-yi Jamāʿat-i islāmī Jammūṇ wa Kashmīr.

——— ([2]1993). *Rūdād-i qafas*, 2 vols., Islamabad: Inst'ītyūt' āf pālisī ist'ad'īz.

——— (1995). *Kashmīr: nawā-yi ḥurriyat*, Khālid, Salīm Manṣūr (ed.), Srinagar: Mīzān.

Gīlānī, Sayyid Asʿad (1992). *Jamāʿat-i islāmī 1941ʾ tā 1948ʾ*, Lahore: Fīrūzsanz.

Gill, Graeme (1980). 'The Soviet Leader Cult: Reflections on the Structure of Leadership in the Soviet Union', *British Journal of Political Science*, 10:2, pp. 167–86.

Glaß, Dagmar (2009). 'Reorganising and Disseminating Knowledge during the Nahḍa: Bustānī's *Encyclopédie arabe* Revisited', in: Christmann, Andreas and Jan-Peter Hartung (eds). *Islamica: Studies in Memory of Holger Preißler (1943–2006)*, Oxford: OUP, pp. 101–18.

Goldstone, Jack A. (1980). 'Theories of Revolution: The Third Generation', *World Politics*, 32:3, pp. 425–53.

Goldziher, Ignaz (1961). *Muhammedanische Studien*, Hildesheim et al.: Olms (reprint from 1888–90).

Gosh, Partha (1993). 'Bangladesh at the Crossroads: Religion and Politics', *Asian Survey*, 33:7, pp. 697–710.

Gould, William (2002). 'Congress Radicals and Hindu Militancy: Sampurnanand and Purushottam Das Tandon in the Politics of the United Provinces, 1930–1947', *Modern Asian Studies*, 36:3, pp. 619–55.

Gräf, Bettina (2009). 'The Concept of *waṣatiyya* in the Work of Yūsuf al-Qaraḍāwī', in: idem and Jakob Skovgaard-Petersen (eds). *Global Mufti: The Phenomenon of Yusuf al-Qaradawi*, London: Hurst, pp. 213–38.

Gregory, Paul R. (2004). *The Political Economy of Stalinism: Evidence from the Soviet Secret Archives*, Cambridge: CUP.

Griffith, R. Marie (2000). 'Apostles of Abstinence: Fasting and Masculinity during the Progressive Era', *American Quarterly*, 52:4, pp. 599–638.

Haag, Pamela S. (1992). 'In Search of the "Real Thing": Ideologies of Love, Modern Romance, and Women's Sexual Subjectivity in the United States', *Journal of the History of Sexuality*, 2:4, pp. 547–77.

Haar, J.G.J. ter (1992). *Follower and Heir of the Prophet: Shaykh Aḥmad Sirhindī (1564–1624) and his Followers*, Leiden: Het Oosters Instituut.

Habermas, Jürgen (1990). *Strukturwandel der Öffentlichkeit. Untersuchungen zu einer Kategorie der bürgerlichen Gesellschaft*, Frankfurt/M.: Suhrkamp (revised reprint from 1962).

——— ([11]1994). *Erkenntnis und Interesse*, Frankfurt/M.: Suhrkamp.

——— ([5]1996). *Der philosophische Diskurs der Moderne. Zwölf Vorlesungen*, Frankfurt/M.: Suhrkamp.

Ḥāfiẓ, Usāma Ibrāhim and ʿĀṣim ʿAbd al-Mājid Muḥammad (1420/2004a). *Mubādara waqf al-ʿunf. ruʾyat wāqiʿiyya wa-naẓrat sharʿiyya*, Riyadh, Cairo: Maktabat al-ʿAbīkān.

——— (1420/2004b). *Ḥurmat al-ghuluw fi'l-dīn wa-takfīr al-muslimīn*, Riyadh, Cairo: Maktabat al-ʿAbīkān.

——— (1420/2004c). *Taṣlīṭ al-aḍwāʾ ʿalá mā waqʿ fi'l-jihād min akhṭāʾ*, Riyadh, Cairo: Maktabat al-ʿAbīkān.

Halepota, A.J. (1974a). 'Affinity of Iqbāl with Shāh Walī Allāh', *Iqbal Review*, 15:1, pp. 65–72.

——— (1974b). 'Shah Waliyullah and Iqbal: The Philosophers of the Modern Age', *Islamic Studies*, 13:4, pp. 225–34.

Ḥālī, Alṭāf Ḥusayn (s.t.). *Tarkīb-i band, mawsūm bah shikwa-yi Hind*, Lahore: Mashhūr-i ʿālam press.

——— (1889). *Musaddas-i Ḥālī, musammá bah madd wa jazr-i islām*, Delhi: Maṭbaʿ-i murtaḍawī.

(1958). *Ḥayāt-i jāwīd*, Lahore: Akidimī-yi panjāb.

——— (1971). *Yādgār-i Ghālib*, Rām, Mālik (ed), Delhi: Maktaba-yi jāmiʿa.

Hallaq, Wael (1984). 'Was the Gate of Ijtihad Closed?', *International Journal of Middle East Studies*, 16:1, pp. 3–41.

Halliday, R.J. (1971). 'Social Darwinism: A Definition', *Victorian Studies*, 14:4, pp. 389–405.

Halm, Heinz (1974). *Die Ausbreitung der šāfiʿitischen Rechtsschule von den Anfängen bis zum 8./14. Jahrhundert*, Wiesbaden: Reichert.

Hamza, Feras and Sajjad Rizvi, with Farhana Mayer (eds) (2008). *Understanding the Word of God: An Anthology of Quranic Commentaries*, Oxford: OUP.

Harder, Hans (2008). 'Shrine Veneration *vs.* Reformism, Bengal *vs.* Islam: Some Remarks on Perceptual Difficulties regarding Bengali Islam', in: Lassen, Søren Christian and Hugh van Skyhawk (eds). *Sufi Traditions and New Departures. Recent Scholarship on Continuity and Change in South Asian Sufism*, Islamabad: Taxila Institute of Asian Civilizations, pp. 181–98.

Hardy, Peter (1971). *Partners in Freedom—and True Muslims. The Political Thought of Some Muslim Scholars in British India 1912–1947*, Lund: Studentlitteratur.

Hartung, Jan-Peter (1999). 'A Contribution of Islamic Revivalists to Modernity: The *Ǧamāʿat-i islāmī* as a Practical Approach for the Realization of an Islamic Concept of History', *Folia Orientalia*, 35, pp. 41–54.

——— (2000). 'Gottesstaat versus Kemalismus: Eine islamische Reaktion auf Mušarrafs Putsch in Pakistan', *Religion—Staat—Gesellschaft*, 1:1, pp. 75–94.

——— (2001). 'Affection and Aversion: Ambivalences among Muslim Intellectual Élites in Contemporary South Asia', *South Asia Research*, 21:2, pp. 189–202.

——— (2002). '(Re-)Presenting the Other?—Erkenntniskritische Überlegungen zum Orientalismus', in: Hamann, Christof and Cornelia Siebert (eds). *Räume der Hybridität. Postkoloniale Konzepte in Theorie und Literatur*, Hildesheim, Zurich, New York: Olms, pp. 135–50.

——— (2004a) 'Die fromme Stiftung (*waqf*): Eine islamische Analogie zur Körperschaft?', in: Kippenberg, Hans-G. and Gunnar Folke Schuppert (eds). *Die verrechtlichte Religion. Der Öffentlichkeitsstatus von Religionsgemeinschaften*, Tübingen: Mohr-Siebeck, pp. 287–314.

——— (2004b). *Viele Wege und ein Ziel. Leben und Werk von Sayyid Abū l-Ḥasan ʿAlī al-Ḥasanī Nadwī (1914–1999)*, Würzburg: Ergon.

——— (2008). 'Wahhābīs and Anti-Wahhābīs: The Learned Discourse on Sufism in Contemporary South Asia', in: Lassen, Søren Christian and Hugh van Skyhawk (eds). *Sufi Traditions and New Departures. Recent Scholarship on Continuity and Change in South Asian Sufism*, Islamabad: Taxila Institute of Asian Civilizations, pp. 82–110.

——— (2009). 'Religious Education in Transition: The Moral and Academic Training of Mawlānā Sayyid Abū 'l-Ḥasan ʿAlī Nadwī', in: idem and Andreas Christmann (eds). *Islamica. Studies in Memory of Holger Preißler (1943–2006)*, Oxford: OUP, pp. 231–55.

——— (2011). 'Enacting the Rule of Islam: On Courtly Patronage of Religious Scholars', in: idem and Albrecht Fuess (eds). *Court Culture in the Muslim World. Seventh to Nineteenth Centuries*, London, New York: Routledge, pp. 295–325.

——— (forthcoming). 'Islamische Philosophie in Südasien: Das 20. Jahrhundert', in: Rudolph, Ulrich (ed.-in-chief). *Grundriss der Geschichte der Philosophie, begründet von Friedrich Ueberweg: Philosophie in der Islamischen Welt*, vol. 4, Basel: Schwabe.

Hasan, Mushirul (1987). *A Nationalist Conscience: M.A. Ansari, the Congress and the Raj*, New Delhi: Manohar.

——— (1992). 'Secular and Communitarian Representations of Indian Nationalism: Ideology and Praxis of Azad and Mohamed Ali [*sic*]', in: idem (ed.). *Islam and Indian Nationalism: Reflections on Abul Kalam Azad*, New Delhi: Manohar, pp. 77–99.

Hassan, Mona F. (2008). *Loss of Caliphate: The Trauma and Aftermath of 1258 and 1924*, unpublished Ph.D. dissertation, Princeton University.

Hegel, Georg Wilhelm Friedrich ([3]1996). *Werke*, Moldenhauer, Eva and Karl Markus Michel (eds). 20 vols., Frankfurt/M.: Suhrkamp.

Hegghammer, Thomas and Stéphane Lacroix (2007). 'Rejectionist Islamism in Saudi Arabia: The Story of Juhayman al-ʿUtaybi Revisited', *International Journal of Middle East Studies*, 39:1, pp. 103–22.

Hildebrandt, Thomas (2002). 'Waren Ǧamāl ad-Dīn al-Afġānī und Muḥammad ʿAbduh Neo-Muʿtaziliten?', *Die Welt des Islams*, 42:2, pp. 207–62.

——— (2007). *Neo-Muʿtazilismus? Intention und Kontext im modernen arabischen Umgang mit dem rationalistischen Erbe des Islam*, Leiden, Boston, MA, Cologne: Brill.

——— (transl.) (2008). *Nasr Hamid Abu Zaid: Gottes Menschenwort. Für ein humanistisches Verständnis des Koran*, Freiburg i.B.: Herder.

Hitler, Adolf (1930). *Mein Kampf. Zwei Bände in einem Band*, Munich: F. Eher.

Hobbes, Thomas (1957). *Leviathan, ore The Matter, Forme & Power of a Common-Wealth Ecclesiasticall and Civill*, Oakeshott, Michael (ed.), Oxford: Blackwell.

Hobsbawm, Eric (1975). *The Age of Capital: 1848–1875*, London: Weidenfeld & Nicolson.

——— (1992). *The Age of Revolution. Europe 1789–1848*, London: Abacus (reprint from 1962).

——— (1994). *The Age of Empire: 1875–1914*, London: Abacus (reprint from 1987).

Hooker, Edith Houghton (1921). *The Laws of Sex*, Boston, MA: Richard G. Badger.

Horn, Michael Serge (1973). *The ʿUrabi Revolution: Convergent Crises in Nineteenth-Century Egypt*, unpublished PhD dissertation, Harvard University.

Hourani, Albert (1983). *Arabic Thought in the Liberal Age, 1798–1939*, Cambridge: CUP (reissued).

al-Huḍaybī, Ḥasan Ismāʿīl (1977). *Duʿāt, lā quḍāt: abḥāth fi'l-ʿaqīda al-islāmiyya wa-manhaj al-daʿwa ilá allāh*, Cairo: Dār al-ṭibāʿa wa'l-nashr al-islāmiyya.

Hunt, Alan (1999). 'Anxiety and Social Explanation', *Journal of Social History*, 32:3, pp. 509–28.

Huq, Maimuna (2008). 'Reading the Qur'an in Bangladesh: The Politics of "Belief" among Islamist Women', *Modern Asian Studies*, 42:2–3, pp. 457–88.

Ibn ʿAbd al-ʿAzīz, ʿAbd al-Qādir (n.d.[a]). *al-Jāmiʿ fī ṭalab al-ʿilm al-sharīf*, s.l.: Minbar al-tawḥīd wa'l-jihād, www.tawhed.ws/a?a=85ud42ss, last accessed 27 Apr. 2011.

——— (n.d.[b]). *Risālat al-ʿumda fī iʿdād al-ʿudda li'l-jihād fī sabīl allāh taʿālá*, s.l.: Minbar al-tawḥīd wa'l-jihād, www.tawhed.ws/a?a=85ud42ss, last accessed 27 Apr. 2011.

Ibn Abī Ṭālib, ʿAlī (1410/1990). *Nahj al-balāgha wa-huwa majmūʿ mā akhtār al-Sharīf al-Rāḍī min kalām al-imām amīr al-mu'minīn ʿAlī ibn Abī Ṭālib*, Beirut: Dār al-taʿāruf li'l-maṭbūʿāt.

Ibn Anas, Mālik (1280/1863). *al-Muwaṭṭa'*, ed. n.n., Tunis: n.n.

Ibn Fūdī, Shaykh ʿUthmān (1985). *Die Lampe der Brüder (Sirāǧ al-iḫwān) von ʿUṯmān b. Fūdī. Reform und Ǧihād im Sūdān*, ed. and transl. Rebstock, Ulrich, Walldorf-Hessen: VfO.

Ibn Ghannām, al-Shaykh al-Imām Ḥusayn ([2]1405/1985). *Ta'rīkh Najd*, al-Asad, Dr Nāṣir al-Dīn (ed.), Beirut: Dār al-shurūq.

Ibn Ḥanbal, Aḥmad b. Muḥammad (1413/1993). *Musnad al-Imām Aḥmad ibn Ḥanbal*, al-Majdhūb, Dr Samīr Ṭāhā (ed.). 8 vols., Beirut, Damascus, Amman: al-Maktab al-islāmī.

Ibn Hishām, ʿAbd al-Malik ([2]1375/1955). *al-Sīra al-nabawiyya*, al-Saqqā, Muṣṭafá et al. (ed.). 4 vols. in two, Cairo: Muṣṭafá al-Bābī al-Ḥalabī.

Ibn al-Jawzī, al-Imām Abū 'l-Faraj ʿAbd al-Raḥmān (1417/1996). *Sīrat wa-manāqib ʿUmar ibn ʿAbd al-ʿAzīz*, Saʿd, Ṭāhā ʿAbd al-Ra'ūf (ed.), Alexandria: Dār Ibn Khaldūn.

Ibn Kathīr, Ismāʿīl ibn ʿUmar (1407/1987). *Tafsīr al-qur'ān al-ʿaẓīm*, al-Marʿāshī, Yūsuf ʿAbd al-Raḥmān (ed.). 4 vols., Beirut: Dār al-maʿrifa.

Ibn Khaldūn, ʿAbd al-Raḥmān (1320h). *al-Muqaddima li'l-ʿAllāma Ibn Khaldūn*, al-Fāsī, Aḥmad ibn Saʿīd (ed.), Cairo: al-Bulāq.

Ibn Māja, al-Ḥāfiẓ Abī ʿAbdallāh Muḥammad (1373/1954). *Sunan*, ʿAbd al-Bāqī, Fu'ād (ed.). 2 vols., Cairo: Dār iḥyā' al-kutub al-ʿarabiyya.

Ibn Manẓūr, Abū 'l-Faḍl (1300–7h), *Lisān al-ʿarab*, 20 vols., Cairo: al-Maṭbaʿa al-kubrá al-mīriyya.

Ibn Qudāma, Abū Muḥammad ʿAbdallāh ([3]1417/1997). *al-Mughnī*, al-Turkī, ʿAbdallāh ibn ʿAbd al-Muḥsin and ʿAbd al-Fatāḥ Muḥammad al-Ḥulw (eds). 15 vols., Riyadh: Dār ʿālam al-kutub.

Ibn Taymiyya, al-Imām Shaykh al-islām Taqī al-Dīn Abū ʿAbbās Aḥmad (1396/1976). *al-ʿUbūdiyya*, al-Salafī, Ghaḍanfar, Maḥmūd Aḥmad (ed.), Lahore: Ibn Taymiyya Akīdīmī.

——— (1403/1983). *al-Ḥisba fi'l-islām*, Saʿda, Sayyid ibn Muḥammad ibn Abī (ed.). Kuwait: Dār al-arqam.

——— ([3]1408/1988). *Kitāb al-siyāsa al-sharʿiyya fī iṣlāḥ al-raʿī wa'l-raʿiyya*, Lajnat iḥyā' al-turāth al-ʿarabī fī dār al-āfāq al-jadīda (ed.), Beirut: Dār al-jīl.

——— (1413/1993). *Iqtiḍā' al-ṣirāṭ al-mustaqīm mukhālifa aṣḥāb al-jāhīm*, al-Ḥaristānī, ʿIṣām Fāris and Muḥammad Ibrāhīm al-Zaghlī (eds), Beirut: Dār al-jīl.

——— (1420/1999). *al-Fatāwá al-kubrá: Majmūʿat fatāwá*, Lanʿān, Aḥmad (ed.) 5 vols., Beirut: Dār al-arqam.

Idris, Jaafar Sheikh (1990). 'Is Man the Viceregent of God?', *Journal of Islamic Studies*, 1, pp. 99–110.

Iqbāl, Dr Jāwīd (2004). *Zinda rūd: ʿAllāma Iqbāl kī mukammal sawāniḥ-i ḥayāt*, 4 vols., Lahore: n.n.

Iqbāl, Muḥammad ([2]1926). *Bang-i darā: majmūʿa-yi kalām-i urdū-yi murattaba-yi muṣannif*, Lucknow: al-Nāẓir buk ejansī.

——— (1934). *The Reconstruction of Religious Thought in Islam*, Oxford: OUP.

——— (1935). *Bāl-i jibrīl*, Lahore: Tāj kampanī.

——— (1343sh). *Kulliyāt-i ashʿār-i fārsī-i Mawlānā Iqbāl-i Lāhawrī. shāmil majallāt*, Surūsh, Aḥmad (ed.), Tehran: Kitābkhāna-yi sināʾī.

——— (1999). *Ḍarb-i kalīm*, Aligarh: Ejūkeshnal buk hāʾus.

——— (1973). *Speeches and Statements of Iqbal*, Tariq, A. R. (ed.), Lahore: Sh. Ghulam Ali & Sons.

Iṣlāḥī, Amīn Aḥsan (2002). *Tazkiyat-i nafs. mukammal*, Delhi: Markazī maktaba-yi islāmī.

Islam, Syed Sirajul (1984). 'The State in Bangladesh under Zia (1975–81)', *Asian Survey*, 24:5, pp. 556–73.

Ismael, Tareq Y. and Rifaʿat El-Saʿid (1990). *The Communist Movement in Egypt, 1920–1988*, Syracuse, NY: Syracuse UP.

Isnenghi, Mario (1996). *L'Italia del fascio*, Florence: Giunti.

Jabārtī, ʿAbd al-Raḥmān (1389/1969). *Maẓhar al-taqdīs bi-dhahāb dawlat al-faransīs*, Jawhar, Ḥasan Muḥammad and ʿUmar al-Dasūqī (eds), Cairo: Lajnat al-bayān al-ʿarabī.

——— (1975). *al-Jabarti's Chronicle of the First Seven Months of the French Occupation of Egypt: Muḥarram-Rajab 1213, 15 June–December 1798 = Taʾrīkh muddat al-faransīs bi-Miṣr*, ed. and transl. Moreh, Shmuel, Leiden: Brill.

——— (1998). *Ajāʾib al-āthār fī'l-tarājim wa'l-akhbār*, 4 vols., ʿAbd al-Raḥīm, ʿAbd al-Raḥīm ibn ʿAbd al-Raḥmān (ed), Cairo: Maṭbaʿat dār al-kutub al-miṣriyya.

Jābir, Ḥusayn ibn Muḥammad ibn ʿAlī (1407/1987). *al-Ṭarīq ilá jamāʿat al-muslimīn*, Cairo: Dār al-wafāʾ.

Jackson, Roy (2011). *Mawlana Mawdudi and Political Islam*, London, New York: Routledge.

Jalal, Ayesha (2001). *Self and Sovereignty: Individual and Community in South Asian Islam since 1850*, New Delhi et al.: OUP.

Jasper, James M. (1998). 'The Emotions of Protest: Affective and Reactive Emotions in and around Social Movements', *Sociological Forum*, 13:3, pp. 397–424.

al-Jawziyya, Ibn Qayyim ([27]1415/1994). *Zād al-maʿād fī hadī khayr al-ʿibād*, 6 vols., al-Arnaʾūṭ, Shuʿayb and ʿAbd al-Qādir al-Arnaʾūṭ (eds), Beirut: Muʾassasat al-risāla/Kuwait: al-Maktaba al-manār al-islāmiyya.

Jelumī, Faqīr Muḥammad (1324/1906). *Ḥadāʾiq al-ḥanafiyya*, Lucknow: Maṭbaʿ Munshī Nawal Kishor.

Johansen, Baber (1999). 'The Muslim *Fiqh* as a Sacred Law. Religion, Law and Ethics in a Normative System', in: idem *Contingency in a Sacred Law. Legal and Ethical Norms in the Muslim* Fiqh, Leiden, Boston, MA, Cologne: Brill, pp. 1–76.

Joshi, Shashi and Bhagwan Josh (1992). *Struggle for Hegemony in India, 1920–47: The Colonial State, the Left and the National Movement*, 3 vols., New Delhi, Thousand Oaks, CA, London: Sage.

Jūmī, Abū Bakr Maḥmūd (1392/1972). *al-ʿAqīda al-ṣaḥīḥa bi-mawāfiqat al-sharīʿa*, Beirut: Dār al-ʿarabiyya.

Jung, Edgar J. (1933). *Sinndeutung der deutschen Revolution*, Oldenburg: Gerhard Stalling.

Kabir, Bhuian Md. Monoar (2006). *Politics and Development of the Jamaat-e-Islami, Bangladesh*, Dhaka: A.H. Development Pub. House.

Kant, Immanuel (1974). *Werke*, Weischedel, Wilhelm (ed.). 12 vols., Frankfurt/M.: Suhrkamp.

Kater, Michael H. ([2]1997). *Das "Ahnenerbe" der SS, 1935–1945: Ein Beitrag zur Kulturpolik des Dritten Reiches*, Munich: Oldenbourg.

Keddie, Nikki R. (1968). *An Islamic Response to Imperialism: Political and Religious Writings of Sayyid Jamāl al-Dīn "al-Afghānī"*, Berkeley, CA, Los Angeles, CA, London: UCP.

——— (1972). *Sayyid Jamāl al-Dīn "al-Afghānī": A Political Biography*, Berkeley, CA, Los Angeles, CA, London: UCP.

Keiser, Thorsten (2005). *Eigentumsrecht in Nationalsozialismus und Fascismo*, Tübingen: Mohr-Siebeck.

Keller, Rudi (1990). *Sprachwandel: Von der unsichtbaren Hand in der Sprache*, Tübingen: Francke.

Khālid, Salīm Manṣūr ([10]1991). *al-Badr*, Lahore: Idāra-yi maṭbūʿāt-i ṭalaba.

——— and Sayyid Muttaqīn al-Raḥmān ([6]1992). *Jab wah nāẓim-i aʿlá the! Islāmī Jamāʿat-i Ṭalaba-yi Pākistān ke pahle āt'h nāẓimīn-i aʿlá ke intarwiyūz*, 2 vols., Lahore: Idāra-yi maṭbūʿāt-i ṭalaba.

al-Khālidī, Dr Ṣalāḥ ʿAbd al-Fatāḥ ([2]1414/1994). *Sayyid Quṭb min milād ilá istishhād*, Damascus: Dār al-qalam/Beirut: al-Dār al-shāmiyya.

Khan, Bashir Ahmad (2000). 'The Ahl-i Ḥadīth: A Socio-Religious Reform Movement in Kashmir', *The Muslim World*, 90:1–2, pp. 133–57.

Khan, Muhammad Ishaq (1994). *Kashmir's Transition to Islam: The Role of Muslim Rishis (Fifteenth to Eighteenth Century)*, New Delhi: Manohar.

Khān, Muḥammad Sarfarāz (1416/1995). 'ʿAllāma Mashriqī kī sawāniḥ-i ḥayāt', in: Mashriqī, ʿInāyatallāh. *Khuṭbāt wa maqālāt*, Khʷāja, Ghulām-i Qadīr (ed.), Lahore: Fayṣal, pp. 20–32.

Khān, Sayyid Aḥmad (1872). *Review on Dr. Hunter's Indian Musalmans: Are they Bound to Rebel against the Queen?*, Benares: Medical Hall Press.

——— ([2]1916). *The Truth About the Khilafat*, Ahmed, Kazi Siraj-ud-din (ed.), Lahore: Ripon Press.

——— ([2]1971). *Asbāb-i baghāwat-i Hind*, Delhi: Kitābkhāna-yi anjumān-i taraqqī-yi urdū.

Khan, Yasmin (2007). *The Great Partition: The Making of India and Pakistan*, New Haven, CT: Yale UP.

Khan, Zillur R. (1993). 'Bangladesh in 1992: Dilemmas of Democratization', *Asian Survey*, 33:2, pp. 150–56.

Khatab, Sayed (2006a). *The Political Thought of Sayyid Qutb: The Theory of* jahiliyyah, London, New York: Routledge.

——— (2006b). *The Power of Sovereignty. The Political and Ideological Philosophy of Sayyid Qutb*, London, New York: Routledge.

al-Khateeb, Motaz (2009). 'Yūsuf al-Qaraḍāwī as an Authoritative Reference (*marjiʿiyya*)', in: Gräf, Bettina and Jakob Skovgaard-Petersen (eds). *Global Mufti: The Phenomenon of Yusuf al-Qaradawi*, London: Hurst, pp. 85–108.

al-Khaṭīb al-Baghdādī, Abū Bakr (1931). *Taʾrīkh Baghdād aw Madīnat al-salām*, al-Khānjī, Muḥammad Amīn (ed.). 14 vols., Cairo: n.n.

Khir, Bustami M. (1996). *The Concept of Sovereignty in Modern Islamic Political Thought*, Leeds: Leeds Institute for Middle Eastern Studies.

——— (2006). *s.v.* 'Sovereignty', in: McAuliffe, Jane Dammen (ed.-in-chief). *Encyclopaedia of the Qurʾān*, Leiden et al.: Brill, vol. 5, p. 102.

Khumaynī, al-Imām (s.t.). *Ḥukūmat-i islāmī yā wilāyat-i faqīh. Majmūʿa-yi dars'hā-yi Ḥaḍrat Āyatallāh al-ʿuẓmá al-imām al-Khumaynī—mattaʿ allāh al-muslimīn bi-ṭawl baqāʾihi al-sharīf—ki dar mawḍūʿ-i wilāyat-i faqīh takht-i ʿanwān-i ḥukūmat-i islāmī, dar Najaf-i ashraf īrād farmūdand*, 6 vols., Najaf: Chāpkhāna-yi ādāb.

Kister, M. J. (1964). 'Notes on an Account of the Shura appointed by ʿUmar b. al-Khattab', *Journal of Semitic Studies*, 9:2, pp. 320–26.

——— (1990). *Society and Religion from Jāhiliyya to Islam*, Aldershot: Variorum.

Kolakowski, Leszek (1985). *Bergson*, Oxford: OUP.

Koselleck, Reinhard (1989). *Vergangene Zukunft. Zur Semantik geschichtlicher Zeiten*, Frankfurt/M.: Suhrkamp.

Kozlowski, Gregory C. (1985). *Muslim Endowments and Society in British India*, Cambridge: CUP.

Krämer, Gudrun (1999). *Gottes Staat als Republik: Reflexionen zeitgenössischer Muslime zu Islam, Menschenrechten und Demokratie*, Baden-Baden: Nomos.

Kramer, Martin (1986). *Islam Assembled. The Advent of the Muslim Congresses*, New York: Columbia UP.

Kroeber, Clifton B. (1996). 'Theory and History of Revolution', *Journal of World History*, 7:1, pp. 21–40.

Kühnl, Reinhard (1966). 'Zur Programmatik der nationalsozialistischen Linken: Das Strasser–Programm von 1926/26', *Vierteljahreshefte für Zeitgeschichte*, 14:3, pp. 317–33.

al-Kulaynī, Abū Jaʿfar Muḥammad ibn Yaʿqūb (1426/2005). *al-Kāfī min al-uṣūl*, al-Ghaffārī, ʿAlī Akbar (ed.). 3 vols., Qom: al-Anṣāriyān.

Lambert, Richard D. (1959). 'Factors in Bengali Regionalism in Pakistan', *Far Eastern Survey*, 28:4, pp. 49–58.

Lambton, Ann K. (1965). 'The Tobacco Regie: Prelude to Revolution', *Studia Islamica*, 22, pp. 119–57 (Part I); 23, pp. 71–90 (Part II).

Landau-Tasseron, Ella (1989). 'The "Cyclical Reform": A Study of the Mujaddid Tradition', *Studia Islamica*, 70, pp. 79–118.

LaPorte Jr., Robert (1972). 'Pakistan in 1971: The Disintegration of a Nation', *Asian Survey*, 12:2, pp. 97–108.

Larsen, Charles E. (1972). *The Good Fight: The Life and Times of Ben B. Lindsey*, Chicago, IL: Quadrangle Books.

Lazarus-Yafeh, Hava (1986). 'Tajdīd al-Dīn: A Reconsideration of its Meaning, Roots and Influence in Islam', in: Brinner, William M. and Stephen D. Ricks (eds). *Studies in Islamic and Judaic Traditions. Papers Presented at the Institute for Islamic Judaic Studies*, Atlanta, GA: Scholars Press, pp. 99–108.

Leighton, Joseph Alexander (1937). *Social Philosophies in Conflict: Fascism & Nazism, Communism, Liberal Democracy*, New York, London: Appleton-Century Co.

Lelyveld, David (1978). *Aligarh's First Generation: Muslim Solidarity in British India*, Princeton, NJ: PUP.

——— (1993). '*Zuban-e Urdu-e Muʿalla* and the Idol of Linguistic Origins', *The Annual of Urdu Studies*, 8, pp. 57–67.

Lenin, Vladimir I. (1962–70). *Collected Works*, 45 vols., Moscow: Progress Publications.

Lenk, Kurt (²1981). *Theorien der Revolution*, Munich: Fink.

Levtzion, Nehemia (1986). 'Eighteenth-Century Renewal and Reform Movements in Islam', *Ha-mizra he-hadash*, 31, pp. 48–70.

Liebmann, Otto (1865). *Kant und die Epigonen: Eine kritische Abhandlung*, Stuttgart: Schober.

Lincoln, Edward J. (1990). 'The Showa Economic Experience', *Dædalus*, 119:3, pp. 191–208.

Locke, John (⁶1970). *John Locke's Two Treatises of Government*, Laslett, Peter (ed.), Cambridge: CUP.

Loimeier, Roman (1993). *Islamische Erneuerung und politischer Wandel in Nordnigeria. Die Auseinandersetzungen zwischen den Sufi-Bruderschaften und ihren Gegnern seit Ende der 50er Jahre*, Münster, Hamburg: LIT.

Ludhiyānawī, Tāj al-Dīn (1388/1968). *Taḥrīk-i Kashmīr awr Aḥrār*, Lahore, Multān: Markazī maktaba-yi majlis-i aḥrār-i islām Pākistān.

Luker, Kristin (1998). 'Social Hygiene and the State: The Double-Edged Sword of Social Reform', *Theory and Society*, 27:5, pp. 601–34.

Luther, Martin (1995). *Ausgewählte Schriften*, 6 vols., Frankfurt/M., Leipzig: Insel.

Machiavelli, Nicolò (1979). *Il Principe (De principatibus)*, Richardson, Brian (ed.), Manchester: MUB.

Madelung, Wilferd (1997). *The Succession to Muḥammad. A Study of the Early Caliphate*, Cambridge: CUP.

Mahroof, M.M.M. (1973). 'Muslim Education in Ceylon (Sri Lanka) 1881–1901', *Islamic Culture*, 47:4, pp. 301–25.
Majeed, Javed (1993). 'Putting God in His Place: Bradley, McTaggart, and Muhammad Iqbal', *Journal of Islamic Studies*, 4:2, pp. 208–36.
Makdisi, George (1974). 'Ibn Taimiya: A Sufi of the Qadiriya Order', *American Journal of Arabic Studies*, 1, pp. 118–29.
Malik, Jamal (1996). *Colonialization of Islam: Dissolution of Traditional Institutions in Pakistan*, New Delhi: Manohar/Lahore: Vanguard.
Malik, Muhammad Aslam (2000). *Allama Inayatullah Mashraqi* [sic]*: A Political Biography*, Karachi: OUP.
Marx, Karl and Friedrich Engels (1956–90). *Werke*, Institut für Marxismus-Leninismus des ZK der SED et al. (eds). 43 vols., Berlin: Dietz.
al-Mashriqī, ʿAllāma Muḥammad ʿInāyatallāh (1976). *Qur'ān-i ḥakīm kī taʿlīmī khulāṣa*, Khān, Muḥammad Ayyūb (ed.), Lahore: Idāra-yi taʿlīmāt-i Mashriqī.
——— (1416/1995). *Khuṭbāt wa maqālāt*, Khwāja, Ghulām-i Qadīr (ed.). Lahore: Fayṣal.
Maudoodi, Abul Ala (1963). 'Economic and Political Teachings of the Qur'ān', in: Sharif, M.M. (ed.). *A History of Muslim Philosophy*, vol. 1, Wiesbaden: Harrassowitz, pp. 178–98.
Maurras, Charles (1909). *Enquête sur la monarchie, 1900–1909*, Paris: Nouvelle libraire nationale.
——— (1921). *La démocratie religieuse*, 2 vols., Paris: Nouvelle libraire nationale.
Maus, Heinz (1962). *A Short History of Sociology*, London: Routledge.
Mawdūdī, Sayyid Abū 'l-Aʿlá (⁶1947–55). *Musalmān awr mawjūda siyāsī kashmakash*, 3 vols., Dār al-islām [Paṭ'hānkoṭ']: Maktaba-yi Jamāʿat-i islāmī.
——— (1949–72). *Tafhīm al-qur'ān*, 4 vols., Lahore: Idāra-yi tarjumān al-qur'ān.
——— (1960–61). *Tafhīmāt*, 3 vols., Delhi: Markazī-yi maktaba-yi Jamāʿat-i islāmī Hind.
——— (1964). *Taḥrīk-i āzādī-yi Hind awr musalmān*, Aḥmad, Khurshīd (ed.), Lahore: Islāmik pablīkeshanz.
——— (1969). *Islām awr jadīd maʿāshī naẓariyyāt*, Delhi: Markazī maktaba-yi islāmī.
——— (1970). *Dīniyyāt*, Delhi: Markazī maktaba-yi islāmī.
——— (1972a). *Islām kā naẓariyya-yi siyāsī*, Delhi: Markazī maktaba-yi islāmī.
——— (1972b). *Khuṭbāt. Islām ke bunyādī arkān kī ahmiyyat wa ḍarūrat par dil-nashīn awr āsān-andāz meṇ yaqīn āfreṇ dalā'il*, Delhi: Markazī maktaba-yi islāmī.
——— (1973). *Parda*, Delhi: Markazī maktaba-yi islāmī.
——— (²1980). *Murtadd kī sazā islāmī qānūn meṇ*, Delhi: Markazī maktaba-yi islāmī.
——— (1981). *Maʿāshiyyāt-i islām*, Aḥmad, Khurshīd (ed.), Delhi: Markazī maktaba-yi islāmī.
——— (²1986). *Iqbāliyyāt*, Samīʿallāh and Khālid Humāyūn (eds), Delhi: Markazī maktaba-yi islāmī.
——— (¹⁰1989). *Jamāʿat-i islāmī kī daʿwat*, Delhi: Markazī maktaba-yi islāmī.
——— (1990a). 'Salāmatī kā rāsta', in: idem. *Islāmī niẓām-i zindagī awr uske bunyādī taṣawwurāt*, Delhi: Markazī maktaba-yi islāmī, pp. 73–112.
——— (1990b). 'Islām awr jāhiliyyat', in: idem. *Islāmī niẓām-i zindagī awr uske bunyādī taṣawwurāt*, Delhi: Markazī maktaba-yi islāmī, pp. 115–59.
——— (1990c). 'Dīn-i ḥaqq', in: idem. *Islāmī niẓām-i zindagī awr uske bunyādī taṣawwurāt*, Delhi: Markazī maktaba-yi islāmī, pp. 163–207.
——— (1990d). 'Taḥrīk-i islāmī kī akhlāqī bunyādeṇ', in: idem. *Islāmī niẓām-i zindagī awr uske bunyādī taṣawwurāt*, Delhi: Markazī maktaba-yi islāmī, pp. 259–320.
——— (1990e). 'Jihād fī sabīl allāh', in: idem. *Islāmī niẓām-i zindagī awr uske bunyādī taṣawwurāt*, Delhi: Markazī maktaba-yi islāmī, pp. 363–99.
——— (1990f). 'Musalmānoṇ kā māḍī ḥāl awr mustaqbal', in: idem. *Islāmī niẓām-i zindagī awr uske bunyādī taṣawwurāt*, Delhi: Markazī maktaba-yi islāmī, pp. 426–501.

——— (1990g). *Islāmī taḥrīk kā makhṣūṣ ṭarīq-i kār*, Delhi: Markazī maktaba-yi islāmī.

——— (^{2}1990). *Taṣawwuf awr taʿmīr-i sīrat Mawlānā Mawdūdī kī taḥrīroṇ kī rawshanī meṇ*, Nuʿmānī, ʿĀṣim (ed.), Delhi: Markazī maktaba-yi islāmī.

——— (^{10}1992). *Taʿlīmāt*, Lahore: Islāmik pablīkeshanz.

——— (1993a). *Akhlāqiyyāt-i ijtimāʿiyya awr uskā falsafa*, Delhi: Markazī maktaba-yi islāmī.

——— (1993b). *Islāmī ḥukūmat meṇ ghayr-musalmānoṇ ke ḥuqūq*, Delhi: Markazī maktaba-yi islāmī.

——— (1994a). *Amīr wa mamūr*, Delhi: Markazī maktaba-yi islāmī.

——— (1994b). *Islāmī ḥukūmat kis ṭaraḥ qāʾim hotī he?*, Delhi: Markazī maktaba-yi islāmī.

——— (^{4}1994). *Masʾala-yi qawmiyyat*, Delhi: Markazī maktaba-yi islāmī.

——— (^{7}1994). *Tajdīd wa iḥyāʾ-i dīn*, Delhi: Markazī maktaba-yi islāmī.

——— (1995). *al-Jihād fiʾl-islām*, Delhi: Markazī maktaba-yi islāmī.

——— (^{6}1995). *Islāmī tazkiyat-i nafs*, Delhi: Markazī maktaba-yi islāmī.

——— (1995–6). *Rasāʾil wa masāʾil*, 5 vols., Delhi: Markazī maktaba-yi islāmī (reprint from 1993).

——— (1996). *Khuṭba-yi Madrās*, Delhi: Markazī maktaba-yi islāmī (reprint from 1992–93).

——— (^{5}1996). *Taḥrīk-i islāmī kāmyābī ke sharāʾiṭ*, Delhi: Markazī maktaba-yi islāmī.

——— (^{7}1996). *Qurʾān kī chār bunyādī iṣṭilāḥeṇ*, Delhi: Markazī maktaba-yi islāmī.

——— (^{28}1996). *Jamāʿat-i islāmī kā maqṣad, tārīkh awr lāʾiḥa-yi ʿamal*, Lahore: Shuʿba-yi nashr wa ishāʿat-i Jamāʿat-i islāmī Pākistān.

——— (1997). *Khilāfat wa mulūkiyyat*, Delhi: Markazī maktaba-yi islāmī.

——— (^{2}1997). *Jamāʿat-i islāmī ke untīs sāl*, Lahore: Islāmik pablīkeshanz.

——— (^{18}1998). *Qādiyānī masʾala*, Lahore: Islāmik pablīkeshanz.

——— (^{25}2000). *Taḥrīk-i islāmī kā āʾinda lāʾiḥa-yi ʿamal*, Lahore: Islāmik pablīkeshanz.

Mayaram, Shail (1997). *Resisting Regimes: Myth, Memory and the Shaping of a Muslim Identity*, New Delhi: OUP.

Mayer, Robert (1999). 'Lenin and the Jacobin Identity in Russia', *Studies in East European Thought*, 51:2, pp. 127–54.

McCutcheon, Russell T. (ed.) (1999). *The Insider/Outsider Problem in the Study of Religion. A Reader*, London, New York: Cassell.

McGilvray, Dennis B. (1998). 'Arabs, Moors and Muslims: Sri Lankan Muslim Ethnicity in Regional Perspective', *Contributions to Indian Sociology*, 32:2, pp. 431–83.

——— (2011). 'Sri Lankan Muslims: Between Ethno-Nationalism and the Global *Umma*', *Nations and Nationalism*, 17:1, pp. 45–64.

McKenzie, John Stuart (1893). 'The Relation between Ethics and Economics', *The International Journal of Ethics*, 3:3, pp. 281–308.

McTaggart, J. McT. Ellis (1996). *Philosophical Studies*, Keeling, S. V. (ed.), Bristol: Thoemmes (reprint from 1934).

Metcalf, Barbara Daly (1982). *Islamic Revival in British India: Deoband, 1860–1900*, Princeton, NJ: PUP.

——— (1993). 'Living Ḥadīth in the Tablīghī Jamaʿāt [*sic*]', *Journal of Asian Studies*, 52:3, pp. 584–608.

——— (2000). 'Tablīghī Jamāʿat and Women', in: Masud, Muhammad Khalid (ed.). *Travellers in Faith: Studies of the Tablīghī Jamāʿat as a Transnational Movement for Faith Renewal*, Leiden, Boston, MA, Cologne: Brill, pp. 44–58.

——— (2007). 'Observant Muslims, Secular Indians: The Political Vision of Maulana Husain Ahmad Madani, 1938–1957', in: Chakrabarty, Dipesh and Rochona Majumdar (eds). *From the Colonial to the Postcolonial: India and Pakistan in Transition*, Oxford et al.: OUP, pp. 96–118.

Mignet, François-Auguste ([6]1836). *Histoire de la Révolution française: depuis 1789 jusqu'en 1814*, 2 vols., Paris: Firmin Didot Frères.

Mill, John Stuart (1963–91). *The Collected Works of John Stuart Mill*, Robson, John M. et al. (eds). 33 vols., London: Routledge & Kegan Paul.

Minault, Gail (1974). 'Urdu Political Poetry during the Khilafat Movement', *Modern Asian Studies*, 8:4, pp. 459–71.

——— (1982). *The Khilafat Movement: Religious Symbolism and Political Mobilization in India*, New York: Columbia UP.

——— (1999). 'Delhi College and Urdu', *The Annual of Urdu Studies*, 14, pp. 119–34.

Mitchell, Richard P. (1969). *The Society of the Muslim Brothers*, Oxford et al.: OUP.

Moaddel, Mansoor (1992). 'Shi'i Political Discourse and Class Mobilization in the Tobacco Movement of 1890–1892', *Sociological Review*, 7:3, pp. 447–68.

Moïsi, Dominique (2010). *La géopolitique de l'émotion*, Paris: Flammarion (reprint from 2008).

Mosse, George L. (1999). *The Fascist Revolution: Towards a General Theory of Fascism*, New York: Howard Fertig.

Mujahid, Sharif al [*sic*] (1971). 'Pakistan: First General Elections', *Asian Survey*, 11:2, pp. 159–71.

Mukarram, Ahmed (1992). *Some Aspects of Contemporary Islamic Thought; Guidance and Governance in the Work of Mawlana Abul Hasan Ali Nadwi and Mawlana Abul Aala Mawdudi* [sic], unpublished PhD dissertation, University of Oxford.

Muktijuddha Cetanā Bikāś Kendra (ed.) ([2]1987). *Ekāttarer ghātak o dālālerā ke kothāẏ?*, Dhaka: Muktijuddha cetanā bikāś kendra.

Mūnis, Muḥammad Shāfiʿ ([2]2001). *Mukhtaṣar-i tārīkh-i Jamāʿat-i islāmī Hind*, New Delhi: Markazī maktaba-yi islāmī.

Muslim, Abū Ḥusayn (1424/2004). *Ṣaḥīḥ Muslim*, al-ʿAṭṭār, Ṣidqī Jamīl (ed.), Beirut: Dār al-fikr.

Mussolini, Benito (1951–62). *Opera omnia*, Edoardo and Duilio Susmel (eds), 35 vols., Florence: La Fenice.

Muṣṭafá, Shukrī Aḥmad (1991a). 'Naṣṣ al-kāmil li-aqwāl wa-iʿtirāfāt Shukrī Aḥmad Muṣṭafá, 'Amīr Jamāʿat al-muslimīn' (al-Takfīr wa'l-hijra) imām muḥakma aman al-dawla al-ʿaskariyya al-ʿaliyā (1977m)', in: Aḥmad, Rifʿat Sayyid (ed.). *al-Nabī al-musallaḥ*, 2 vols., London: Riad El-Rayyes Books, vol. 1, pp. 53–109.

——— (1991b). 'Wathīqat al-khilāfa', in: Aḥmad, Rifʿat Sayyid (ed.). *al-Nabī al-musallaḥ*, 2 vols., London: Riad El-Rayyes Books, vol. 2, pp. 115–60.

al-Nadwī, Abū 'l-Ḥasan ([2]1400/1980). *al-Tafsīr al-siyāsī li'l-islām fī mir'āt kitābāt al-ustādh Abī 'l-Aʿlā Mawdūdī wa'l-shahīd Sayyid Quṭb*, Cairo: Dār āfāq al-ghadd.

——— (1994). *Mā-dhā khasira al-ʿālam bi-inḥiṭāṭ al-muslimīn?*, Cairo: Maktabat fayyāḍ.

Nadwī, Abū 'l-Ḥasan ʿAlī (1400/1980). *Madhhab wa tamaddun*, Lucknow: Majlis-i taḥqīqāt wa nashriyyāt-i islām.

——— ([2]1400/1980). *ʿAṣr-i ḥāḍir meṇ dīn kī tafhīm wa tashrīḥ*, Lucknow: Majlis-i taḥqīqāt wa nashriyyāt-i islām.

——— ([7]1406/1986). *Sīrat-i Sayyid Aḥmad-i Shahīd*, 2 vols., Lucknow: Majlis-i taḥqīqāt wa nashriyyāt-i islām.

——— ([4]1418/1997). *Manṣib-i nubuwwat awr uske ʿālá maqām-i ḥāmilīn*, Lucknow: Majlis-i taḥqīqāt wa nashriyyāt-i islām.

Nadwī, Abū 'l-Layth Iṣlāḥī (1960). *Khuṭba-yi ṣadārat-i Āl Ind'iyā ijtimāʿ-i Jamāʿat-i islāmī Hind, munʿaqada Dihlī mu'arrakha 11 tā 14 Novimbar sana-yi 1960'*, Delhi: Kūh-i nūr print'ing press.

——— (1990). *Tashkīl-i Jamāʿat-i islāmī Hind—kyoṇ awr kayse*, Delhi: Markazī maktaba-yi islāmī.

Nadwī, Iqbāl Aḥmad (1992). *Mawlānā Mawdūdī awr ʿulamāʾ-i kirām. ek tajziyya*, Lahore: Islāmik pablīkeshanz.

Nadwī, Muḥammad Isḥāq Jalīs (1403/1983). *Tārīkh-i Nadwat al-ʿulamāʾ*, vol. 1, Lucknow: Daftar-i niẓāmat-i Nadwat al-ʿulamāʾ.

Naiman, Eric (1997). *Sex in Public: The Incarnation of Early Soviet Ideology*, Princeton, NJ: PUP.

Nāʾinī, Āqā Shaykh Muḥammad Ḥusayn ([5]1358sh). *Tanbīh al-umma wa tanzīl al-milla yā ḥukūmat az naẓr-i islām*, Tehran: Shirkat-i sahāmī-yi intishār.

Nallino, Carlo Alfonso (1917). *Appunti sulla natura del «Califfato» in genere e sul presunto «Califfato ottomano»*, Rome: Tipografia del ministero degli affari esteri.

Nasr, Seyyed Vali Reza (1994). *The Vanguard of the Islamic Revolution. The* Jamaʿat-i Islami *of Pakistan*, Berkeley, CA et al.: UCP.

——— (1996). *Mawdudi and the Making of Islamic Revivalism*, New York et al.: OUP.

Natov, Nadine (1995). 'The Meaning of Music and Musical Images in the Works of Mikhail Bulgakov', in: Milne, Leslie (ed.). *Bulgakov: The Novelist—Playwright*, Amsterdam: Harwood Academic Publ., pp. 171–86.

Nedza, Justyna (2008). *Das* takfīr*-Konzept im Wandel? Erklärungsversuch zu einer Kategorie heutigen islamistischen Denkens*, unpublished MA dissertation, Ruhr-Universität Bochum.

Nehru, Jawaharlal ([14]2001). *An Autobiography*, New Delhi et al.: OUP.

Nemilov, Anton (1932). *The Biological Tragedy of Women*, transl. Stephanie Offental, London: Allen & Unwin.

Nicholson, Peter P. (1990). *The Political Philosophy of the British Idealists. Selected Studies*, Cambridge: CUP.

Nietzsche, Friedrich ([2]1988). *Sämtliche Werke. Kritische Studienausgabe*, Colli, Giorgio and Mazzino Montinari (eds). 15 vols., Munich, Berlin, New York: dtv/de Gruyter.

Nolte, Ernst (1960). 'Marx und Nietzsche im Sozialismus des jungen Mussolini', *Historische Zeitschrift*, 191:2, pp. 249–335.

——— (1963). *Der Faschismus in seiner Epoche: Action Française—Italienischer Faschismus—Nationalsozialismus*, Munich: Pieper & Co.

Norman, Richard (1987). *Free and Equal. A Philosophical Examination of Political Values*, New York: OUP.

Noth, Albrecht (1998). 'Von der medinensischen "Umma" zu einer muslimischen Ökumene', in: idem and Jürgen Paul (eds). *Der islamische Orient. Grundzüge seiner Geschichte*, Würzburg: Ergon, pp. 81–132.

Nuhman, M.A. (2007). *Sri Lankan Muslims: Ethnic Identity within Cultural Diversity*, Colombo: International Centre for Ethnic Studies.

Nuʿmānī, Muḥammad Manẓūr (1998). *Mawlānā Mawdūdī ke sāth merī rafāqat kī sar-guzasht awr ab merā mawqif!*, Lucknow: al-Furqān Bukd'ipo.

Nuʿmānī, Shiblī (1999). *Safarnāma-yi Rūm wa Miṣr wa Shām*, Aʿzamgaṛh: Dār al-muṣannifīn (reprint).

Oldenburg, Philip (1985). '"A Place Insufficiently Imagined": Language, Belief, and the Pakistan Crisis of 1971', *Journal of Asian Studies*, 44:4, pp. 711–33.

Osterhammel, Jürgen (1998). *Die Entzauberung Asiens: Europa und die asiatischen Reiche im 18. Jahrhundert*, Munich: C.H. Beck.

Ottmann, Henning (1977). *Individuum und Gemeinschaft bei Hegel*, 2 vols., Berlin, New York: de Gruyter.

Özcan, Azmi (1997). *Pan-Islamism: Indian Muslims, The Ottomans and Britain, 1877–1924*, Leiden, New York, Cologne: Brill.

Palmer, H.R. (1914–5). 'An Early Fulani Conception of Islam', *Journal of the African Society*, 13:52, pp. 407–414 (part 1); 14:53, pp. 53–59 (part 2); 14:54, pp. 185–92 (part 3).

Palmer, Norman D. (1976). 'India in 1975: Democracy in Eclipse', *Asian Survey*, 16:2, pp. 95–110.

Panesar, Rita (2006). *Medien religiöser Sinnstiftung: Der ›Volkserzieher‹, die Zeitschriften des ›Deutschen Monistenbundes‹ und die ›Neue Metaphysische Rundschau‹, 1897–1936*, Stuttgart: Kohlhammer.

Peers, Douglas M. (1998). 'Privates off Parade: Regimenting Sexuality in the Nineteenth-Century Indian Empire', *The International History Review*, 20:4, pp. 823–54.

Pernau, Margrit (1999). 'Reaping the Whirlwind: Nizam and the Khilafat Movement', *Economic and Political Weekly*, 34:38, pp. 2745–51.

——— (2000). *The Passing of Patrimonialism: Politics and Political Culture in Hyderabad, 1911–1948*, New Delhi: Manohar.

——— (ed.) (2006). *The Delhi College. Traditional Elites, the Colonial State, and Education Before 1857*, New Delhi et al.: OUP.

——— (2008). *Bürger mit Turban. Muslime in Delhi im 19. Jahrhundert*, Göttingen: Vandenhoeck & Ruprecht.

Peskes, Esther (1993). *Muḥammad b. ʿAbdalwahhāb (1703–92) im Widerstreit. Untersuchungen zur Rekonstruktion der Frühgeschichte der Wahhābīya*, Beirut: Steiner.

Pettenkofer, Andreas (2006). 'Die Euphorie des Protestes: Starke Emotionen in sozialen Bewegungen', in: Schützeichel, Rainer (ed.). *Emotionen und Sozialtheorie. Disziplinäre Ansätze*, Frankfurt/M.: Campus, pp. 256–85.

Pitts, Jennifer (2003). 'Legislator of the World? A Rereading of Bentham on Colonies', *Political Theory*, 31:2, pp. 200–34.

Plamper, Jan (2010). 'The History of Emotions: An Interview with William Reddy, Barbara Rosenwein, and Peter Stearns', *History and Theory*, 49:2, pp. 237–65.

Plato (1995–6). *The Works of Plato*, transl. and ed. Thomas Taylor and Floyer Sydenham, 5 vols., Somerset: The Prometheus Trust.

Popper, Karl R. (1935). *Logik der Forschung: Zur Erkenntnistheorie der modernen Naturwissenschaften*, Vienna: Julius Springer.

Powell, Avril A. (1993). *Muslims and Missionaries in Pre-Mutiny India*, Richmond: Curzon.

Preckel, Claudia (2005). *Islamische Bildungsnetzwerke und Gelehrtenkultur im Indien des 19. Jahrhunderts: Muḥammad Ṣiddīq Ḥasan Ḫān (st. 1890) und die Entstehung der Ahl-e ḥadīth-Bewegung in Bhopal*, PhD dissertation Ruhr-Universität Bochum, www-brs.ub.ruhr-uni-bochum.de/netahtml/HSS/Diss/PreckelClaudia/diss.pdf/ (stable URL).

Pritchett, Frances W. (1994). *Nets of Awareness. Urdu Poetry and Its Critics*, Berkeley, CA, Los Angeles, CA, London: UCP.

Proctor, Tammy M. (2002). 'On my Honour: Guides and Scouts in Interwar Britain', *Transactions of the American Philosophical Society*, 92:2.

al-Qaraḍāwī, Yūsuf (1428/2007). *al-Dīn wa'l-siyāsa: taṣīl wa-radd shubuhāt*, Cairo: Dār al-shurūq.

Qayyim-i Jamāʿat-i islāmī Pākistān (ed.) (1989–96). *Rūdād-i Jamāʿat-i islāmī*, 7 vols., Lahore: Shuʿba-yi nashr wa ishāʿat-i Jamāʿat-i islāmī Pākistān.

——— ([23]1997). *Dastūr-i Jamāʿat-i islāmī Pākistān, manẓūr karda Markazī majlis-i shūrá-i Jamāʿat-i islāmī dar ijlās munʿaqida 19 tā 26 Maī 1957 bi-maqām-i Kot' Shīr Singh, ḍilaʿ Lāhawr*, Lahore: Jamāʿat-i islāmī Pākistān.

Qureshi, M. Naeem (1999). *Pan-Islam in British Indian Politics: A Study of the Khilafat Movement, 1918–1924*, Leiden, Boston, Cologne: Brill.

Quṭb, Sayyid (1962). *Khaṣāʾiṣ al-taṣawwur al-islāmī wa-muqawwimātuhu*, Cairo: ʿĪsá al-Bābī al-Ḥalabī.

——— ([5]1402/1982). *Dirāsāt islāmiyya*, Cairo, Beirut: Dār al-shurūq.

——— ([18]1405/1985). *Maʿālim fi'l-ṭarīq*, Beirut: Dār al-shurūq.

——— ([10]1408/1987). *Maʿrakat al-islām wa'l-ras-māliyya*, Cairo, Beirut: Dār al-shurūq.
——— ([12]1413/1993). *al-Salām al-ʿālamī wa'l-islām*, Cairo, Beirut: Dār al-shurūq.
——— ([13]1413/1993). *al-ʿAdāla al-ijtimāʿiyya fi'l-islām*, Cairo, Beirut: Dār al-shurūq.
——— ([5]1418/1997). *Muqawwimāt al-taṣawwur al-islāmī*, Cairo, Beirut: Dār al-shurūq.
——— ([15]1422/2001). *Hādhā al-dīn*, Cairo: Dār al-shurūq.
——— ([16]1423/2002). *al-Taṣwīr al-fannī fi'l-qur'ān*, Cairo: Dār al-shurūq.
——— ([38]1430/2009). *Fī ẓilāl al-qur'ān*, 6 vols., Cairo, Beirut: Dār al-shurūq.
Rahim, Enayetur (2001). 'Bengali Muslims and Islamic Fundamentalism: The Jama't-i-Islami [sic] in Bangladesh', in: Ahmed, Rafiuddin (ed.). *Understanding the Bengal Muslims. Interpretative Essays*, New Delhi et al.: OUP, pp. 236–61.
Rahman, Matiur (1978). *Bangladesh Today: An Indictment and a Lament*, London: News and Media Ltd.
——— (1979). *Second Thoughts on Bangladesh*, London: News and Media Ltd.
——— and Naeem Hasan (1980). *Iron Bars of Freedom*, London: News and Media Ltd.
Rahman, Munibur (1983). 'The Musha'irah', *Annual of Urdu Studies*, 3, pp. 75–84.
Rashiduzzaman, M. (2002). 'Bangladesh in 2001: The Elections and a New Political Reality?', *Asian Survey*, 42:1, pp. 183–91.
Ray, Rajat K. (1985). 'Revolutionaries, Pan-Islamists and Bolsheviks: Maulana Abul Kalam Azad and the Political Underworld in Calcutta, 1905–1925', in: Hasan, Mushirul (ed.). *Communal and Pan-Islamic Trends in Colonial India*, New Delhi: Manohar, pp. 101–24.
Reichardt, Rolf (1988a). 'Zur Einführung', in: idem and Reinhart Koselleck (eds). *Die Französische Revolution als Bruch des gesellschaftlichen Bewußtseins*, Munich: Oldenbourg, pp. 15–22.
——— (1988b). 'Revolutionäre Mentalitäten und Netze politischer Grundbegriffe in Frankreich, 17891795', in: idem and Reinhart Koselleck (eds). *Die Französische Revolution als Bruch des gesellschaftlichen Bewußtseins*, Munich: Oldenbourg, pp. 185–215.
Rebstock, Ulrich (1978). 'Ein magribinischer Gelehrter im Sudan: Muḥammad b. ʿAbdalkarīm al-Maġīlī at-Tilimsānī', *Boletín de la Asciación Española de Orientalistas*, 14, pp. 111–18.
Reetz, Dietrich (1995). *Hijrat: The Flight of the Faithful. A British File on the Exodus of Muslim Peasants from North India to Afghanistan in 1920*, Berlin: Das Arabische Buch.
——— (1997). 'Akteure des Wandels und die Globalisierung. Zur Einführung', in: idem and Heike Liebau (eds). *Globale Prozesse und "Akteure des Wandels". Quellen und Methoden ihrer Untersuchung*, Berlin: Das Arabische Buch, pp. 5–17.
——— (2008). 'The "Faith Bureacracy" of the Tablighi Jamaʿat: An Insight into their System of SelfOrganization (*Intizam*)', in: Beckerlegge, Gwilym (ed.). *Colonialism, Modernity, and Religious Identities: Religious Reform Movements in South Asia*, New Delhi et al.: OUP, pp. 98–124.
Riaz, Ali (2008). *Islamist Militancy in Bangladesh: A Complex Web*, London, New York: Routledge.
Riḍā, al-Sayyid al-Imām Muḥammad Rashīd (1420/1999). *Tafsīr al-qur'ān al-ḥakīm al-mashhūr bi-Tafsīr al-manār*, Shams al-Dīn, Ibrāhīm (ed.). 12 vols., Beirut: Dār al-kutub al-ʿilmiyya.
Riḍwī, Sayyid Maḥbūb (1992–3). *Tārīkh-i Dār al-ʿulūm Deoband*, 2 vols., Deoband: Idāra-yi ihtimām-i Dār al-ʿulūm.
Riesebrodt, Martin (2001). *Die Rückkehr der Religionen. Fundamentalismus und der «Kampf der Kulturen»*, Munich: Beck.
Riexinger, Martin (2004). *Sanā'ullāh Amritsarī (1868–1948) und die Ahl-i-Ḥadīs* [sic] *im Punjab unter britischer Herrschaft*, Würzburg: Ergon.
Rigby, T.H. (1988). 'Staffing USSR Incorporated: The Origins of the Nomenklatura System', *Soviet Studies*, 40:4, pp. 523–37.

Ritter, Joachim (1969). *Metaphysik und Politik: Studien zu Aristoteles und Hegel*, Frankfurt/M.: Suhrkamp.

Roberts, David D. (2000). 'How not to Think About Fascism and Ideology, Intellectual Antecedents and Historical Meaning', *Journal of Contemporary History*, 35:2, pp. 185–211.

Robespierre, Maximilien de (1912–67). *Œuvres de Maximilien Robespierre*, Boloiseau, Marc and Albert Soboul (eds-in-chief). 10 vols., Paris: Presses universitaires de France.

Robinson, Francis (1997). 'Islam and the Impact of Print in South Asia', in: Crook, Nigel (ed.). *Transmission of Knowledge in South Asia: Essays on Education, Religion, History and Politics*, New Delhi et al.: OUP, pp. 62–97.

——— (2001). ''Abd al-Bari and the Events of January 1926', in: idem. *The 'Ulama of Farangi Mahall and Islamic Culture in South Asia*, New Delhi: Permanent Black, pp. 145–76.

Rochelle, Gerald (1996). 'Introduction', in: McTaggart, J. McT. Ellis. *Philosophical Studies*, Keeling, S.V. (ed.), Bristol: Thoemmes, pp. v-xxii.

Rosenberg, Alfred (1930). *Der Mythus des 20. Jahrhunderts: Eine Wertung der seelisch-geistigen Gestaltenkämpfe unserer Zeit*, Munich: Hoheneichen-Verlag.

Rosenthal, Franz (1983). *"Sweeter than Hope": Complaint and Hope in Medieval Islam*, Leiden: Brill.

Rosenthal, Michael (1986). *The Character Factory: Baden-Powell and the Origins of the Boy Scouts*, New York: Pantheon.

Rosenwein, Barbara H. (2002). 'Worrying about Emotions in History', *The American History Review*, 107:3, pp. 821–45.

——— (2006). *Emotional Communities in the Early Middle Ages*, Ithaca, NY: Cornell UP.

Rothermund, Dietmar (1996). *The Global Impact of the Great Depression, 1929–1939*, London, New York: Routledge.

Rousseau, Jean Jacques (1967–71). *Œuvres complètes*, Launay, Michel (ed.). 3 vols., Paris: Seuil.

Roy, Asim (1983). *Islamic Syncretistic Tradition in Bengal*, Princeton, NJ: PUP.

Roy, M. N. (1964). *M.N. Roy's Memoirs*, Bombay et al.: Allied Publishers.

Roy, Samaren (1997). *M.N. Roy: A Political Biography*, New Delhi: Orient Longman.

Rugh, Andrea B. (1984). *Family in Contemporary Egypt*, Syracuse, NY: Syracuse UP.

Rury, John L. (1987). '«We Teach the Girls Repression, the Boys Expression»: Sexuality, Sex Equity and Education in Historical Perspective', *Peabody Journal of Education*, 64:4, pp. 44–58.

Ruthven, Malise (2004). *Fundamentalism: The Search for Meaning*, Oxford: OUP.

al-Ṣaʿīdī, ʿAbd al-Mutaʿāl (1416/1996). *al-Mujaddidūn fi'l-islām min qarn al-awwal ilá al-rābiʿ ashar (100h-1370h)*, Cairo: Maktabat al-ādāb.

Samiuddin, Abida (2007). *Encyclopaedic Dictionary of Urdu Literature*, 2 vols., New Delhi: Global Vision Publ.

Sanyal, Usha (1996). *Devotional Islam and Politics in British India: Ahmad Riza Khan Barelwi and his Movement, 1870–1920*, New Delhi et al.: OUP.

Sareen, T.R. (1996). *Subhas Chandra Bose and Nazi Germany*, New Delhi: Mounto Publ. House.

al-Sayyid, Riḍwān (1404/1984). *al-Umma wa'l-jamāʿa wa'l-sulṭa: dirāsāt fi'l-fikr al-siyāsī al-ʿarabī al-islāmī*, Beirut: Dār Iqrāʾ.

Scharlieb, Mary (1924). *Reminiscences*, London: Williams and Norgate.

Schieder, Wolfgang (1993). 'Die NSDAP vor 1933. Profil einer faschistischen Partei', *Geschichte und Gesellschaft*, 19:2, pp. 141–54.

——— (1996). 'Das italienische Experiment: Der Faschismus als Vorbild in der Krise der Weimarer Republik', *Historische Zeitschrift*, 262, pp. 73–125.

Schimmel, Annemarie (1963). *Gabriel's Wing: A Study into the Religious Ideas of Sir Muhammad Iqbal*, Leiden: Brill.

——— (1975). *Mystical Dimensions of Islam*, Chapel Hill, NC: Univ. of North Carolina Press.

Schnädelbach, Herbert (1983). *Philosophie in Deutschland, 1831–1933*, Frankfurt/M.: Suhrkamp.

Schölch, Alexander (1972). *Ägypten den Ägyptern. Die politische und gesellschaftliche Krise der Jahre 1878–1882 in Ägypten*, Zurich et al.: Atlantis.

Schulze, Reinhard (1990). *Islamischer Internationalismus im 20. Jahrhundert: Untersuchungen zur Geschichte der Islamischen Weltliga*, Leiden et al.: Brill.

——— (2000). *A Modern History of the Islamic World*, London: I.B. Tauris.

Schweber, Silvan S. (1980). 'Darwin and the Political Economists: Divergence of Character', *Journal of the History of Biology*, 13:2, pp. 195–289.

Seidman, Steven (1990). 'The Power of Desire and the Dangers of Pleasure: Victorian Sexuality Reconsidered', *Journal of Social History*, 24:1, pp. 47–67.

Serjeant, R. B. (1978). 'The *Sunnah Jāmiʿah*, Pacts with the Yat͟hrib Jews, and the *Tahrīm* of Yat͟hrib: Analysis and Translation of the Documents Comprised in the so-called «Constitution of Medina»', *Bulletin of the School of Oriental and African Studies*, 41:1, pp. 1–42.

al-Shāfiʿī, Muḥammad ibn Idrīs (s.t.). *al-Risāla*, Shākir, Aḥmad Muḥammad (ed.). Beirut: Dār al-kutub al-ʿilmiyya (Reprint of the edition Cairo 1358/1939).

Shaikh, Farzana (1992). 'Azad and Iqbal: The Quest for the Islamic «Good»', in: Hasan, Mushirul (ed.). *Islam and Indian Nationalism: Reflections on Abul Kalam Azad*, New Delhi: Manohar, pp. 59–76.

al-Shāṭibī, Ibrāhīm ibn Mūsá (s.t.). *al-Muwāfaqāt fī uṣūl al-sharīʿa*, 4 vols., Cairo: al-Maktaba al-tijāriyya al-kubrá.

Shehabuddin, Elora (2008). 'Jamaat-i Islami in Bangladesh: Women, Democracy and the Transformation of Islamist Politics', *Modern Asian Studies*. 42:2–3, pp. 577–603.

Shepard, William E. (1996). *Sayyid Qutb and Islamic Activism: A Translation and Critical Analysis of Social Justice in Islam*, Leiden, New York, Cologne: Brill.

——— (2001). *s.v.* 'Age of Ignorance', in: McAuliffe, Jane Dammen (ed.-in-chief). *Encyclopaedia of the Qurʾān*, Leiden et al.: Brill, vol. 1, pp. 37–40.

——— (2003). 'Sayyid Qutb's [*sic*] Doctrine of *Jāhiliyya*', *International Journal of Middle East Studies*, 35:4, pp. 521–45.

Shinar, P. and Werner Ende (1995), *s.v.* 'Salafiyya', in: *The Encyclopaedia of Islam. New Edition*, Leiden et al.: Brill, vol. 8, pp. 900–9.

Shuʿba-yi nashr wa ishāʿat ([4]1988). *Dastūr-i Jamāʿat-i islāmī Āzād Jammūṇ wa Kashmīr*, Muzaffarabad: ʿAbd al-Rashīd Turābī.

Shuʿba-yi tanẓīm-i jamāʿat (1989–2002). *Rudād-i majlis-i shūrá-i Jamāʿat-i islāmī-i Hind*, vols. 1 and 2, Delhi: Markazī maktaba-yi islāmī.

——— (1997). *Markazī majlis-i shūrá-i Jamāʿat-i islāmī-i Hind kī qarārdādeṇ: 15 Jūlāʾī 1961 tā 7 Jūlāʾī 1997*, Delhi: Markazī maktaba-yi islāmī.

——— (1998). *Rudād-i ijtimāʿ-i Rāmpūr-i Jamāʿat-i islāmī-i Hind*, Delhi: Markazī maktaba-yi islāmī (Reprint from 1951).

Siddiqi, Muhammad Nejatullah (1979). '*Tawḥīd*: The Concept and the Process', in: Ahmad, Khurshid and Zafar Ishaq Ansari (eds). *Islamic Perspectives. Studies in Honour of Sayyid Abul Aʿla Mawdudi*, Leicester: The Islamic Foundation, pp. 17–33.

Ṣiddīqī, Naʿīm (1983). *al-Mawdūdī*, Lahore: Idāra-yi maʿārif-i islāmī.

Ṣiddīqī, Ẓafar ʿAlī (1998). *Mawlānā Muḥammad ʿAlī awr jang-i āzādī*, Rampur: Rāmpūr Riḍā Lāʾibrirī.

Sikand, Yoginder (1998). 'For Islam and Kashmir: The Prison Diaries of Sayyed Ali Gilani of the *Jamaʿat-i-Islami* [sic] of Jammu and Kashmir', *Journal of Muslim Minority Affairs*, 18:2, pp. 241–9.

——— (2002a). *The Origins and Development of the Tablighi-Jamaʿat (1920–2000): A Cross-Country Comparative Study*, New Delhi: Orient Longman.

——— (2002b). 'The Emergence and Development of the Jamaʿat-i-Islami of Jammu and Kashmir (1940s–1990)', *Modern Asian Studies*, 36:3, pp. 705–51.

Singer, Marshall R. (1991). 'Sri Lanka in 1990: The Ethnic Strife Continues', *Asian Survey*, 31:2, pp. 140–45.

Sirriyya, Ṣāliḥ (1991). 'Risālat al-īmān', in: Aḥmad, Rifʿat Sayyid (ed.). *al-Nabī al-musallaḥ*, 2 vols., London: Riad El-Rayyes Books, vol. 1, pp. 31–52.

Smith, Adam (1893). *An Inquiry into the Nature and Causes of the Wealth of Nations*, London: Routledge/New York: Dutton & Co.

Spencer, Herbert (1885). *The Man versus the State*, London, Edinburgh: Williams and Norgate.

——— (1898). *The Principles of Biology*, 2 vols., rev. and enlarged ed., New York: D. Appleton & Co.

Spengler, Oswald (1920). *Preußentum und Sozialismus*, Munich: C.H. Beck.

——— (^{42}1922–^{47}3). *Der Untergang des Abendlandes. Umrisse einer Morphologie der Weltgeschichte*, 2 vols., Munich: C.H. Beck.

Sri Lanka Democracy Forum (2010). 'Tamil-Muslim Relations: Remembering the Eviction of Northern Muslims', *Dissenting Dialogues* 1, pp. 16f.

Stark, Rodney and William Sims Bainbridge (1987). *A Theory of Religion*, New Brunswick, NJ: Rutgers UP.

Stark, Ulrike (2003). 'Politics, Public Issues and the Promotion of Urdu Literature: *Avadh Akhbar*, the First Urdu Daily in Northern India', *The Annual of Urdu Studies*, 18, pp. 66–94.

Stearns, Peter N. and Carol Zisowitz Stearns (1985). 'Victorian Sexuality: Can Historians Do It Better?', *Journal of Social History*, 18:4, pp. 625–34.

Stegmüller, Wolfgang (^{4}1969–75). *Hauptströmungen der Gegenwartsphilosophie. Eine kritische Einführung*, 2 vols., Stuttgart: Kröner.

Steinberg, Guido (2002). *Religion und Staat in Saudi-Arabien. Die wahhabitischen Gelehrten 1902–1953*, Würzburg: Ergon.

——— (2005). *Der nahe und der ferne Feind: Die Netzwerke des islamistischen Terrorismus*, Munich: Beck.

Sternhell, Zeev, Mario Sznajder and Maia Ashéri (1989). *Naissance de l'idéologie fasciste*, Paris: Fayard.

Suter, Jean-François (1971). 'Burke, Hegel, and the French Revolution', in: Pełczyński, Zbigniew Andrzej (ed.). *Hegel's Political Philosophy: Problems and Perspectives*, Cambridge: CUP, pp. 52–72.

al-Ṭabarī, Muḥammad ibn Jarīr (1322/2001). *Tafsīr al-Ṭabarī: jāmiʿ al-bayān ʿan taʾwīl āyat al-qurʾān*, al-Turkī, ʿAbdallāh ibn ʿAbd al-Muḥsin (ed.). 26 vols., Cairo et al.: Dār Hajar.

——— (^{2}1426/2005). *Taʾrīkh al-Ṭabarī: tarīkh al-umam wa'l-mulūk*, al-Jarrāḥ, Nawāf (ed.). 6 vols., Beirut: Dār Ṣādir.

al-Ṭahṭāwī, Rifāʿa Rāfiʿ (2002). *al-Dīwān al-nafīs fī īwān Bārīs, aw takhlīs al-ibrīs fī talkhīṣ Bārīs*, Kanʿān, ʿAlī Aḥmad (ed.), Abu Dhabi: Dār al-suwaydī li'l-nashr wa'l-tawzīʿ/Beirut: al-Muʾassasa al-ʿarabiyya li'l-dirāsāt wa'l-nashr.

Taji-Farouki, Suha (1996). *A Fundamental Quest:* Hizb al-Tahrir *and the Search for the Islamic Caliphate*, London: Grey Seal.

Talbot, Ian (1998). *Pakistan: A Modern History*, New York: St. Martin's Press.

Temin, Peter (1991). 'Soviet and Nazi Economic Planning in the 1930s', *Economic History Review*, 44:4, pp. 573–93.

Thielmann, Jörn (2003). *Naṣr Ḥāmid Abū Zaid und die wiedererfundene* ḥisba. Šarīʿa *und* Qānūn *im heutigen Ägypten*, Würzburg: Ergon.

al-Tirmidhī, Muḥammad ibn ʿĪsá (1938–58). *al-Jāmiʿ al-ṣaḥīḥ wa-huwa sunan al-Tirmidhī*, al-Bāqī, Muḥammad Fuʾād ʿAbd (ed.). 5 vols., Cairo: Muṣṭafá al-Bābī al-Ḥalabī.

Troll, Christian W. (1978). *Sayyid Ahmad Khan. A Reinterpretation of Muslim Theology*, New Delhi et al.: Vikas.

Trotsky, Leon (1962). *The Permanent Revolution/Results and Prospects*, transl. John G. Wright and Brian Pearce, London: New Park.

Tschacher, Torsten (2009). 'Circulating Islam: Understanding Convergence and Divergence in the Islamic Traditions of Ma'bar and Nusantra', in: Feener, R. Michael and Terenjit Sevea (eds). *Islamic Connections: Studies of South and Southeast Asia*, Singapore: Institute of Southeast Asian Studies, pp. 48–67.

al-Turābī, Ḥasan (1985). 'al-Shūrá wa'l-dimūqrāṭiyya: ishkālāt al-muṣṭalaḥ wa'l-mafhūm', *al-Mustaqbal al-ʿarabī* 75, pp. 4–22.

Turner Jr., Henry Ashby (1968). 'Hitler's Secret Pamphlet for Industrialists, 1927', *The Journal of Modern History*, 40:3, 348–74.

ʿUrābī, Aḥmad (1425/2005). *Mudhakkirāt al-zaʿīm Aḥmad ʿUrābī: kashf al-sitār ʿan sirr al-asrār fi'l-nahḍa al-miṣriyya al-mashhūra bi'l-thawra al-ʿurābiyya*, al-Jumayʿī, ʿAbd al-Munʿīm Ibrāhīm (ed.). 3 vols., Cairo: Maṭbaʿat dār al-kutub wa'l-wathāʾiq al-qawmiyya bi'l-Qāhira.

Uyangoda, Jayadeva (2010). 'Sri Lanka in 2009: From Civil War to Political Uncertainties', *Asian Survey*, 50:1, pp. 104–11.

van den Beld, Ton (2001). 'The Morality System with and without God', *Ethical Theory and Moral Practice*, 4:4, pp. 383–99.

van Dülmen, Richard (1996). *Die Gesellschaft der Aufklärer. Zur bürgerlichen Emanzipation und aufklärerischen Kulture in Deutschland*, Frankfurt/M.: Fischer.

van Ess, Josef (1991–7). *Theologie und Gesellschaft im 2. und 3. Jahrhundert Hidschra. Eine Geschichte des religiösen Denkens im frühen Islam*, 6 vols., Berlin—New York: de Gruyter.

——— (2011). *Der Eine und das Andere. Beobachtungen an häresiographischen Texten*, 2 vols., Berlin, New York: de Gruyter.

Verhey, Jeffrey (2000). *The Spirit of 1914: Militarism, Myth, and Mobilization in Germany*, Cambridge: CUP.

Voslensky, Michael (1984). *Nomenklatura. Anatomy of the Soviet Ruling Class*, transl. Eric Mosbacher, London, Sydney, Toronto: The Bodley Head.

Voll, John O. (1983). 'Renewal and Reform in Islamic History: *Tajdid* and *Islah*', in: Esposito, J. (ed.). *Voices of Resurgent Islam*, New York, Oxford: OUP, pp. 32–47.

von Schwerin, Ulrich (2005). 'Die Muttahida Majlis-e Amal—Ursachen des Wahlerfolges der Islamisten bei den pakistanischen Wahlen im Oktober 2002', *Asien*, 97, pp. 76–83.

Vossler, Otto (1963). *Rousseaus Freiheitslehre*, Göttingen: Vandenhoeck & Ruprecht.

Wallis, Roy and Steve Bruce (1984). 'The Stark-Bainbridge Theory of Religion: A Critical Analysis and Counter Proposals', *Sociological Analysis*, 45:1, pp. 11–27.

Weber, Max ([5]1972). *Wirtschaft und Gesellschaft. Grundriß der verstehenden Soziologie*, Winckelmann, Johannes (ed.), Tübingen: Mohr.

——— ([9]1988). *Gesammelte Aufsätze zur Religionssoziologie*, vol. 1, Tübingen: Mohr (reprint from 1920).

——— (1994). *Wissenschaft als Beruf/Politik als Beruf. Studienausgabe*, Mommsen, Wolfgang J. and Wolfgang Schluchter (eds), Tübingen: Mohr.

White, Geoffrey M. (1990). 'Moral Discourse and the Rhetoric of Emotions', in: Lutz, Chatherine A. and Lila Abu-Lughod (eds). *Language and the Politics of Emotion*, Cambridge: CUP, pp. 46–68.

Whitman, James Q. (1991). 'Of Corporatism, Fascism, and the First New Deal', *The American Journal of Comparative Law*, 39:4, pp. 747–78.

Wieacker, Franz (1935). *Wandlungen der Eigentumsverfassung*, Hamburg: Hanseatische Verlagsanstalt.

Wielandt, Rotraud (2002). *s.v.* 'Exegesis of the Qur'ān: Early Modern and Contemporary', in: McAuliffe, Jane D. (ed.-in-chief). *Encyclopeadia of the Qurʾān*, vol. 2, Leiden et al.: Brill, pp. 124–42.

Willis, Kirk (1988). 'The Introduction and Critical Reception of Hegelian Thought in Britain, 1830–1900', *Victorian Studies*, 32:1, pp. 85–111.

Wilson, A. Jeyaratnam (2000). *Sri Lankan Tamil Nationalism: Its Origins and Development in the Nineteenth and Twentieth Centuries*, London: Hurst.

Wright Jr., Theodore P. (1999). 'The Changing Role of the *Sādāt* in India and Pakistan', *Oriente Moderno*, 18 (79):2, pp. 649–59.

Yack, Bernard (1986). *The Longing for Total Revolution. Philosophical Sources of Social Discontent from Rousseau to Marx and Nietzsche*, Princeton, NJ: PUP.

Young, Robert M. (1985). 'Darwinism *is* Social', in: Kohn, David (ed.). *The Darwinian Heritage*, Princeton, NJ, Guildford: PUP, pp. 609–38.

al-Zabīdī, al-ʿAllāma al-Sayyid Muḥammad ibn Muḥammad al-Ḥusaynī (1414/1994). *Itḥāf al-sāda almuttaqīn bi-sharḥ iḥyāʾ ʿulūm al-dīn*, al-ʿAydarūs, ʿAbd al-Qādir ibn ʿAbdallāh (ed.). 10 vols., Beirut: Muʾassasat al-taʾrīkh al-ʿarabī (reprint of ed. Cairo 1311/1894).

Zachariah, Benjamin (2004). *Nehru*, London, New York: Routledge.

——— (2005). *Developing India: A Social and Intellectual History, c. 1930–1950*, Delhi et al.: OUP.

Zaidi, A. Moin (ed.). (1976–85). *The Encyclopedia of the Indian National Congress*, 26 vols., New Delhi: S. Chand.

Zakariyyā, Muḥammad (⁶1983). *Fitna-yi mawdūdiyyat yā jamāʿat-i islāmī ek lamḥa-yi fikriyya*, Sahāranpūr: Kutubkhāna-yi ishāʿat al-ʿulūm.

——— (2000). *Faḍāʾil-i tablīgh: jis meṇ tablīgh kī ahmiyyat awr uske ādāb nīz muballighīn awr ʿāmm logoṇ ke farāʾiḍ*, New Delhi: Idāra-yi ishāʿat-i dīniyyāt.

al-Ẓawāhirī, Ayman (2003). *Iʿzāz rāyat al-islām: risāla fī takīd talāzim al-ḥākimiyya wa'l-tawḥīd*, s.l.: al-Saḥāb.

——— (22008). *Fursān taḥta rāyat al-nabī—ṣallá allāh ʿalayhi wa-sallam. al-juzʾ al-awwal*, s.l.: al-Saḥāb.

Zimmermann, Clemens (2006). 'Die Zeitschrift–Medium der Moderne. Publikumszeitschriften im 20. Jahrhundert', in: idem and Manfred Schmeling (eds) (2006). *Die Zeitschrift–Medium der Moderne/La presse magazine–un média de l'époque moderne: Deutschland und Frankreich im Vergleich*, Bielefeld: transcript, pp. 15–42.

Zollner, Barbara H.E. (2009). *The Muslim Brotherhood: Hasan al-Hudaybi and Ideology*, London, New York: Routledge.

Zöllner, Hans-Bernd (2000). *Der Feind meines Feindes ist mein Freund: Subhas Chandra Bose und das zeitgenössische Deutschland unter dem Nationalsozialismus, 1933–1943*, Hamburg: LIT.

Zutshi, Chitralekha (2000). 'Religion, State, and Community: Contested Identities in the Kashmir Valley, c. 1880–1920', *South Asia*, 23:1, pp. 109–28.

——— (2003). *Languages of Belonging: Islam, Regional Identity, and the Making of Kashmir*, New Delhi: Permanent Black/London: Hurst.

Zwanzig, Rebekah (2008). *An Analysis of Ibn al-ʿArabi's al-Insan al-Kamil, the Perfect Individual, with a Brief Comparison to the Thought of Sir Muhammad Iqbal*, unpublished MA dissertation, Brock University, Ontario.

Journals

al-Hilāl (Calcutta)

al-Iṣlāḥ (Lahore)

al-Jamʿiyya (Delhi)

Jihād-i Kashmīr (Muzaffarabad, Rawalpindi)

al-Manār (Cairo)

Tarjumān al-qurʾān (Hyderabad, Lahore et al.)

INDEX

Ashhar, Sayyid Manẓar ʿAlī: *Manẓar al-kirām: Ḥaydarābād-i Dakkan ke mashāhīr kā tadhkira*, 11
Ashʿarism: 75–6
'Augustus', Gaius Julius Octavius: 127
Awami League (AL): 241; electoral performance of (1970), 238; Six Point Programme, 237
'Āzād', Abū 'l-Kalām: 29, 32, 34, 37; background of, 32–3; *al-Hilāl*, 29–30; influence on Indian Caliphate Movement, 32; speech to All-India Khilafāt Conference (1921), 33
Āzam, Golām: 238, 240; return of (1978), 240
al-ʿAzīz, Shāh ʿAbd: family of, 185

Baʿathism: 217
Baladhūrī, Aḥmad ibn Yaḥyá: *Futūḥ al-buldān*, 149
Bāṃglādeś Jāmāyāte Islāmī (JiI-B): 236, 239–41; languages used by, 252; members of, 238–9, 241
Bangladesh: 239, 241, 248; Dacca, 237; Liberation War (1971), 238–9, 241
Bangladesh Nationalist Party (BJD): 238, 240–1; members of, 236
al-Bannā, Ḥasan: 199–200; assassination of, 197–8; founder of JIM, 197, 221
Barakatallāh, Mawlānā Muḥammad: delegation to Moscow led by (1919), 47
Barelwī, Sayyid Aḥmad: 79
al-Bayḍāwī, ʿAbdallāh ibn ʿUmar: 71; view of *jāhiliyya*, 64
Bengal: 236; Muslim population of, 236
Bengali (language): 237–8
Bentham, Jeremy: 40, 171
Bergson, Henri: 41–2; influence of, 53, 55
Bhāratīya Hindū Śuddhī Sabhā: members of, 17
Bhāratīya Janatā Party (BJP): 236
Bhat', Maqbūl: co-founder of JKLF, 245
Bhutto, Zulfikar Ali: administration of, 239
Bodin, Jean: theories of, 101
Bolsheviks: 45–7, 54, 161, 166
Bonaparte, Napoléon: Egyptian expedition of (1798–1801), 23
Borodin, Mikhail M.: influence of, 46
Bos (Bose), Subhāṣ Chandra: 58; founder of All India Forward Bloc, 56; relationship with fascist governments, 56
Bosanquet, Bernard: 41, 139
Bradley, Francis Herbert: 41, 139
Brahmo Samāj: affiliates of, 43
British East India Company: 22
Brown, Daniel W.: concept of 'Prism of Modernity', 6–7
Buddhism: 242
Bukharin, Nikolai I.: 46
Bureau, Paul: 146; *D'Indiscipline des mœrs* (1921), 145
Burke, Edmund: 161, 163

Caliphate Movement: 17
Camp David Accords (1978): 2, 219
capitalism: 45, 68, 140, 202; roots in feudalism, 66, 133–4
Cassirer, Ernst: 101–2
Cāypu, Jeylānī: founder of JiI-SL, 249; journals edited by, 250
Chamberlain, Houston Steward: 52–3
Christianity: 51, 118–19, 219; Bible, 87, 107, 120; conception of God, 119
colonialism: 157; European, 144; Western, 38, 64
communism: 39, 44–6, 48, 50, 55, 66, 97, 112, 121, 133, 137–8, 140, 143, 162, 178–9, 183, 199, 201, 204–5, 213, 217, 231, 257–8; historical materialism, 104; state theory of, 134–5
Communist Party of India (CPI): establishment of (1920), 46; members of, 179
Communist Party of the Soviet Union (CPSU): Politburo of the Central

Nizāmī, Matiur Rahmān: *amīr* of JiI-B, 241
Noah: as part of line of prophets, 62
Nolte, Ernst: 50, 53–4
Nuʿmānī, Muḥammad Manẓūr: 231
Nuʿmānī, Muḥammad Shiblī: 26, 191

occidentalism: 43
orientalism: 4, 26; 'oriental despotism', 125
Ottoman Empire: 15, 28, 30, 46; abolition of (1924), 35–6, 116; Sublime Porte, 29; *tanẓīmāt* reforms, 29; territory of, 29, 158

Pahlawī, Muḥammad Riḍā Shāh: White Revolution, 2
Pakistan: 17, 187, 221, 226–8, 239–40, 245, 248, 252, 257; anti-Aḥmadiyya agitation (1953–4), 228–9; Constitution of, 227, 247; government of, 227–8, 237; Independence of (1947), 132, 225, 242–4; Inter-Service Intelligence (ISI), 246–7; Karachi, 194, 237; Lahore, 30, 49, 110, 192, 210, 227; North-West Frontier Province, 247; Pakistan Army Act (1952), 238; Peshawar, 65; Punjab, 228
Pakistan Muslim League (PML): members of, 233
Partito Nazionale Fascista (PNF): members of, 162, 232
Paşa, Ismāʿīl: Khedive of Egypt and Sudan, 23
Paşa, Meḥmed ʿAlī: Viceroy of Ottoman Empire, 23
Paşa 'Atatürk', Muṣṭafá Kemal: 36; supporters of, 35
Pāshā, Aḥmad ʿUrābī: 158
Pashtun: territory inhabited by, 243
Paul, Apostle: Epistles to the Romans, 4
Payk-i islām: editorial staff of, 29
periodic religious renewal (*tajdīd al-dīn*): 74, 166; concept of, 72; 'Establishment of the Religion' (*iqāmat al-dīn*), 75; 'Reform' (*iṣlāḥ*), 75, 166; traditions of, 77; use of, 74, 80–1
Persian Constitutional Movement: 159
Peshawarī, ʿAbd al-Rabb: 48; role in establishment of InRA, 47
positivism: 119
Plato: 117, 119, 158–9; *Politeía*, 118; students of, 116

al-Qahṭānī, Muḥammad ʿAbdallāh: 3
al-Qāʿida: role in 9/11 Attacks, 255
Qamaruzzamān, Abul Hasnat Muhāmmad: Bangladeshi Home Minister, 238
al-Qaraḍāwī, Yūsuf: writings of, 256
Qatar: 256
Quraysh: 77; prominent members of, 125
Quṭb, Sayyid: 8, 205–10, 216, 218, 221–3, 225, 255–6; *al-ʿAdāla al-ijtimāʿiyya fi'l-islām* (1964), 195, 198–202, 205, 212; background of, 197; conception of *jāhiliyya*, 196, 200, 202–5, 208, 217, 224; conception of *jihād*, 211–15, 217, 219, 224; conception of *takfīr*, 224; conception of *ṭāghūt*, 209; criticisms of communism, 204–5; death of (1966), 195, 199, 215; *Fī ẓilāl al-qur'ān* (1951), 195, 202, 210; *Hādhā al-dīn*, 206, 208–9; imprisonment of, 195; *Khaṣā'iṣ al-taṣawwur al-islāmī wa-muqawwimātuhu*, 206; *Maʿālim fi'l-ṭarīq* (1962), 195, 200, 204–5, 210; *Muqawwimāt al-taṣawwur al-islāmī*, 209; *al-Salām al-ʿālamī wa'l-islām* (1951), 205; *al-Taṣwīr al-fannī fi'l-qur'ān*, 201, 203; view of *dīn*, 196; visit to USA, 195, 198, 202

rabb: 91–4, 96, 99; concept of, 91, 93, 101
Rahīm, Abdur: 237; *amīr* of JiI, 240; founder of IAJ, 240

al-Sharīf, Sayyid Imām: 220, 257; leader of *Tanẓīm jamā'at al-jihād*, 214
al-Shawkānī, Muḥammad ibn ʿAlī: *Fatḥ al-qadīr*, 149
Shiism: 67, 170
shūrá: 125; *ahl al-shūrá*, 130; *Majlis-i shūrá*, 127–31, 191, 229–31, 233–5, 237, 243, 252; use as electoral tool, 126
al-Ṣiddīq, Abū Bakr: election of, 127
Siṃgh, Hari: 242
Sindhi (language): 193
Sindhī, ʿUbaydallāh: 113
Sirhindī, Aḥmad Fārūqī: 76–7, 79
Sirriyya, Ṣāliḥ: head of *Munaẓẓamat al-fanniyya al-ʿaskariyya*, 217–18
Smith, Adam: 256; *Inquiry into the Nature and Causes of the Wealth of Nations* (1776), 132
Socialism: 42, 54, 211, 217; Muslim, 114
Soviet Union (USSR): 43, 152, 166, 201; All Russian Central Executive Commission, 47; economy of, 135, 138; Invasion of Afghanistan (1979–89), 3–4, 247; Moscow, 46–7; regional influence of, 2, 163
Spain: 50
Spencer, Herbert: 146, 256; influence of, 118
Spengler, Oswald: 41, 53; *Der Untergang des Abendlandes*, 43; influence of, 42
Sri Lanka: Central Province, 248; Civil War (1983–2009), 248–51; Colombo, 248, 251; Independence of (1948), 249; Muslim population of, 249–50, 252
Stalin, Josef: 152, 178, 257; establishment of *nomenklatura*, 179; Great Purges (1936–8), 46, 232; theory of societal progress, 43
Sēnānāyakā, Ḍon Stēpan: Sri Lankan Prime Minister, 249
Sternhell, Ze'ev: 50
Stoicism: 118; conception of God, 119
Strasser, Gregor: head of NSDAP, 136
Strasser, Otto: head of NSDAP, 136
Sudan: Mahdī movement (1881–99), 158
Sufism: 67, 75, 95, 100, 177, 236, 246, 253; ascetic, 68; Chishti order, 12; criticisms of, 14, 68–9; Naqshbandī, 76–7; Rishīs, 246
Sunnism: 170
al-Suyūṭī, Jalāl al-Dīn: 74, 76–7
Sweden: Stockholm, 47
Switzerland: 55, 154
Syria: 29, 217

al-Ṭabarī, Muḥammad ibn Jarīr: 106
Tablīghī Jamāʿat (TJ): 68, 177–8, 191, 253; ideology of, 150–1, 231
al-Ṭahṭāwī, Rifāʿa Rāfiʿ: writings of, 23
takfīr: 225, 257; conceptions of, 224; *takfīr al-ḥākim*, 217
Tamil (language): 193, 249–51
Tanẓīm jamāʿat al-jihād: members of, 214
Tanẓīm al-jihād al-islāmī: members of, 220; origins of, 218
Taplīk Jamāt (TJ): 251
Tarabālī, Saʿd al-Dīn: 242–3; *amīr* of JiI-J&K, 246
Tavhīt Jamāt (*Jamāʿat al-Tawḥīd*): establishment of (1947), 251
tawḥīd: 91–2, 94
theo-democracy: 124; concept of, 109
Third International (Comintern) (1919–43): 48, 161; aims of, 45; First Congress (1919), 46; Second Congress (1920), 48
Third Reich (1933–45): 50, 53–5, 58, 137–8, 162, 179; Final Solution, 54; Night of the Long Knives (1934), 232; Nuremburg Rally (1933), 180; *Schutzstaffel* (SS), 179–80; *Sturmabteilung* (SA), 180
Third Zimmerwald Conference (1917): attendees of, 47
Tilak, Bāl Gaṁgadhar: 163

al-Tilimsānī, Muḥammad ʿAbd al-Karīm al-Maghīlī: 76–7
Trotsky, Lev D.: 46, 160; 'law of uneven development', 48
Turkey: 30, 116; Grand National Assembly, 35; Istanbul, 47; Smyrna (İzmir), 16

ʿulamāʾ: 14, 87, 95, 130, 191, 223, 227, 229–30; Deobandc, 113; factions within, 32; influence of, 88; manipulation of, 103; prominent members of, 32, 231
Umayyad Caliphate: 74; use of *shūrá* as electoral tool by, 126
umma: 72–3, 105, 127, 173, 189; schism in, 158
United Kingdom (UK): 146, 154; Cambridge University, 43; Civil War (1642–9), 159; Glorious Revolution (1688), 159; government of, 22; London, 55; Oxford University, 41
United Nations (UN): Resolution 47, 244; Security Council, 244
United States of America (USA): 145, 154, 195, 198, 202; 9/11 Attacks, 3, 255; Pentagon, 255; Washington DC, 255; World Trade Center bombing (1993), 224
Urdu (language): 15–16, 30, 172, 175, 193, 237, 249; promotion of, 22, 27–8
al-ʿUtaybī, Juhaymān ibn Muḥammad: role in Grand Mosque Seizure (1979), 3
utilitarianism: 119, 121, 171, 182
Uẏājed, Śekh Hāsinā: family of, 241; head of AL, 241
Uzbekistan: Tashkent, 46–7

Voltaire: 159

Wahhābiyya: 2, 20–1, 151; influence of, 235; origins of, 20; *ʿulamāʾ* of, 20–1
waqf: 192; concept of, 185; examples of, 186–7
Weber, Max: 95; view of religion, 189–90
Weimar Republic (1919–33): 183
women: 144–8, 154–5; gender equality, 147–8; sexual morality issues, 145–6

al-Ẓawāhirī, Ayman: 215, 220; *Fursān taḥta rāyat al-nabī*, 214; Iʿzāz rāyat al-islām, 255; leader of *Tanẓīm jamāʿat al-jihād*, 214
Zédōng, Máo: 257
Ziẏā, Khāledā: 240; administration of, 241; leader of BJD, 236, 238
Zuhdī, Karam Muḥammad: 220, 224–5